"A fascinating biography ... doub[...]
driven irresistibly by the tension b[...]
energy and the hollowness that w[...]
—Christopher Leh[...] *New York Times*

"That inner man is probably brought as far out of his shell by James Park Sloan as he is ever likely to come. Sloan has weighed the testimony with judiciousness and sympathy ... his judgment is acute." —Jonathan Yardley, *Washington Post Book World*

"Mesmerizing ... unmasks one of the most complex and tragic figures of our literary era ... a riveting historical detective story, a political and philosophical exploration, and an acute literary analysis." —Thomas Fleming

"Truly excellent.... In his meticulous, even dogged, research Sloan is a paragon of fairness." —*Boston Sunday Globe*

"Fascinating ... James Park Sloan has applied his tremendous intelligence to the tremendous puzzle of the lives and lies of one Jerzy Kosinski." —Lore Segal

"Insightful ... traces Kosinski's trials with empathy tempered by a quest for objectivity." —*Seattle Times*

"Compelling and definitive ... justifies its subject and resolves the paradoxes of a haunted, self-promoting, but powerful storyteller." —*Library Journal*

"Insightful and eloquent ... fills in the blanks of Kosinski's purposefully obscured life, and with deep sensitivity, decodes his convoluted personality." —*Booklist*

"Compelling ... a life of sex clubs, infidelity and an unquenchable passion for something new, always something new." —*Jewish News*

JAMES PARK SLOAN was a National Book Award finalist for *The Case History of Comrade V.* A frequent reviewer for the *Chicago Tribune Book World* and the *New York Times Book Review*, he is a professor of English at the University of Illinois. He lives in Chicago.

JERZY KOSINSKI

A BIOGRAPHY

James Park Sloan

A PLUME BOOK

To Sally Ruth

PLUME
Published by the Penguin Group
Penguin Books USA Inc., 375 Hudson Street, New York, New York 10014, U.S.A.
Penguin Books Ltd, 27 Wrights Lane, London W8 5TZ, England
Penguin Books Australia Ltd, Ringwood, Victoria, Australia
Penguin Books Canada Ltd, 10 Alcorn Avenue, Toronto, Ontario, Canada M4V 3B2
Penguin Books (N.Z.) Ltd, 182–190 Wairau Road, Auckland 10, New Zealand

Penguin Books Ltd, Registered Offices:
Harmondsworth, Middlesex, England

Published by Plume, an imprint of Dutton Signet, a division of Penguin Books USA Inc.
Previously published in a Dutton edition.

First Plume Printing, March, 1997
10 9 8 7 6 5 4 3 2 1

® REGISTERED TRADEMARK—MARCA REGISTRADA

The Library of Congress has catalogued the Dutton edition as follows:

Sloan, James Park.
Jerzy Kosinski: a biography/James Park Sloan.
p. cm.
ISBN 0-452-27167-3 (pbk.) 0-525-93784-6 (hc.)
1. Kosinski, Jerzy N., 1993–1991—Biography. 2. Novelists, American—20th century—
Biography. 3. World War, 1939–1945—Poland—Biography. 4. Jews—United States—
Biography. 5. Polish Americans—Biography. I. Title.
PS3561.O8Z875 1996

813'.54—dc20   95-34848
[B]
                                                                 CIP

Printed in the United States of America
Original hardcover design by Leonard Telesca

BOOKS ARE AVAILABLE AT QUANTITY DISCOUNTS WHEN USED TO PROMOTE PRODUCTS OR
SERVICES. FOR INFORMATION PLEASE WRITE TO PREMIUM MARKETING DIVISION, PENGUIN
BOOKS USA INC., 375 HUDSON STREET, NEW YORK, NY 10014.

CONTENTS

PROLOGUE

MAY 2, 1991

Early in the evening of Thursday, May 2, 1991, Jerzy Kosinski attended a cocktail party at the apartment of Gay and Nan Talese. The guest of honor was U.S. Senator William Cohen, whose novel *One-Eyed Kings* had just been brought out by Doubleday, with Nan Talese as its editor, and the guest list commingled the literary elite with heavyweights from politics and the media—the overlapping circles in which Kosinski had moved for much of the last twenty years of his life. Dan Rather and Arthur Liman were there as the party's cosponsors—in fact, Liman, former chief counsel to the Senate Irangate Committee, was to have been the host, until a doormen's strike at his apartment building led Nan Talese to offer her home as a substitute.

Kosinski disliked cocktail parties, and he often complained about them to his wife, Kiki. They were a frivolous waste of time and energy. No serious conversation was possible, and they cost at least two days of work—the day of the party itself and the day after, which was the absolute minimum required to get back into the flow of a project. And beyond the disruption to a writer's schedule, parties were inherently an encroachment upon the self. Parties demanded that one compose a face and present it to the world. They thereby imperiled that most precious sanctuary where one lived at uneasy peace with his inner being.

Few writers had given more thought to the problems of the

self—its boundaries, its divisions, its enemies, its very essence. What, after all, was the self? How did one manage to protect and defend it? "Hell is other people," Kosinski liked to quote Sartre. Other people had the power to challenge the self—to tell you that you were not the person you knew yourself to be. To move among other people required constant readiness to guard the boundaries of that fragile innermost repository. It took great energy and vigilance to defend the inner self in public. Yet venturing into the world was unavoidable. The alternative was solitude, which had its own kind of peril. If others judged you, how much more severe were the judgments your self imposed upon you? In the absence of support from others, such judgments could be overwhelming.

That evening Kosinski appeared to circulate comfortably among the other guests. From a host's point of view, Kosinski was an ideal guest. He was never drunk or contentious, like so many writers, and he was always full of charming and outrageous stories. And whatever his private opinion of parties, he attended a great many of them; he could be depended upon. Gay Talese clapped a hand on his back for a brief exchange. Spying the guest of honor, Kosinski presented Senator Cohen with his card and held out a copy of *One-Eyed Kings* for the senator to autograph. Cohen returned the book inscribed, misspelling Kosinski's name exactly as Houghton Mifflin, publisher of *The Painted Bird*, had done in the first ads: For Jerzy Kosinsky, With Best Wishes, To a Truly gifted writer—With Admiration, Bill Cohen.

Leaving the Talese party at 7:30, Jerzy suggested to Kiki that they have dinner at Wolf's Delicatessen, across the street from their Hemisphere House apartment. Wolf's was their favorite place, so much so that the Kosinskis maintained an account there. But tonight, Kiki reminded him, they needed to pack. They were scheduled to leave for Poland on May 5, to preside at the opening of AmerBank, the Polish-American bank that Jerzy had been instrumental in organizing. In their apartment, however, there was a message on their machine from Ula Dudziak, asking if they were busy. Jerzy called her and suggested meeting at Wolf's. Kiki, adamant, stayed home.

While Kiki packed alone, Jerzy and Ula dined at Wolf's, then decided to take in a movie. Peter Greenaway's *Drowning by Numbers* was playing at the nearby Loews Festival Theater, and they made the 9:25 showing. It was a typically surreal Greenaway film, full of self-conscious artifice presented in dazzling colors. The rather rarefied plot involved three women who murder their husbands by drowning them—the first holding down her besotted mate in a bathtub while his lover lolls unconscious a few feet away. In the final scene, the three wives collaborate to drown the coroner who had helped cover up their crimes, leaving him, a non-swimmer, in a slowly sinking boat. One can imagine the impact of this scene on Jerzy who, since a boyhood incident, had a terror of being pushed under water.

After the movie, Jerzy and Ula had tea at the Parker Meridien bar, leaving after midnight. "You looked lovely tonight, Ulenka," he told her, and they made a date to meet the following day for a walk in Central Park. When Jerzy got home, Kiki was asleep in the outer room of their two-room apartment, behind a curtain which marked off her sleeping space. He was alone with his thoughts.

Suicide had been a recurrent, though not predominant, motif in his work. His most recent novel, *The Hermit of 69th Street*, had dwelled on the subject more than most, detailing the deaths of Arthur and Cynthia Koestler by means of alcohol, barbiturates, and plastic bag—the method recommended by the Hemlock Society, a New Orleans group that helps people suffering from lingering diseases. In his 1991 book *Final Exit*, Hemlock Society founder Derek Humphrey had commended as painless and certain the combination of barbiturates and plastic bag. The redundancy was important; it assured that one did not accidentally survive in some damaged state. The inhalation of one's own carbon dioxide had the effect of a slow dozing off.

Some time after 1:00 A.M., Kosinski apparently reached his decision. A methodical man, he followed the Hemlock Society method to the last detail. To the alcohol he had already consumed—enough to make him legally drunk—he added a lethal dose of barbiturates. He then entered the bathroom which adjoined his combination bedroom-study and lowered himself into the tub. He had always had an unusual interest in bathtubs. He had been one of the first to have his own Jacuzzi, at least among the intellectual set at Yale, and he sometimes took friends along when buying bathtub accessories. Now settled into a comfortable posture in the water he both loved and feared, he pulled a plastic bag over his head and gave it a twist.

Literary suicides have attained, in the twentieth century, the status of a virtual art form. Kosinski joined the ranks of Hemingway, Primo Levi, Tadeusz Borowski, Sylvia Plath, Anne Sexton, and John Berryman (with whom he shared the winners' table at the 1969 National Book Awards) as a writer whose departure from the world was in a manner, and at a time, of his own choosing. In such cases, one is inclined to seek, within the mystery of private motive, a conscious or unconscious public statement. If writers tend to leave behind a personal myth, then suicide becomes the final act of that myth. It may either confirm the direction of a life and work—stand, in effect, as a validation of the writer's absolute good faith—or, conversely, call everything the writer stood for into question. Hemingway is the premier case of a suicide open to two interpretations—as an affirmation of his fearless personal code or as a cowardly escape from a sea of trouble and pain.

Few writers cultivated a personal myth as assiduously as Jerzy Kosinski. From the publication of his celebrated first novel, *The Painted Bird*, he had been marked as a writer who probed the limits of human experience—and whose life engaged the same issues as his art. His interactions with others often took the shape of small experiments in human behavior. He delighted in setting up miniature psychodramas to see what they would produce. There were dozens, hundreds even, of Kosinski stories: the huge chocolate cake he sent to the fat man at the next table, the Satanists and the phony tap dancers he brought into his classroom at Yale. Then there was Kosinski himself living on the edge, obsessively visiting the sex clubs, wandering in the dead of night through neighborhoods where no sane man would stray. More than one friend had worried for his safety. Was the way in which his life ended one more self-invented drama of living at the edge?

Some thought so. There were those among Kosinski's close friends who professed to be utterly shocked by his death, insisting that he had been his usual outgoing and vital self until the end. Others observed that he had seemed depressed. Ultimately, the questions posed by Kosinski's death could be answered only by addressing the questions posed by Kosinski's life.

Each human existence is an experiment—an answer posited to the question of what to do with a single life. Jerzy Kosinski's answer was one of the more interesting, both in the range of possibilities he saw and in the range of events and historical movements that bore upon and influenced his choices. He was born in pre–World War II Poland, a Jew in an anti-Semitic country, amidst the gathering clouds of the great Nazi pogrom. He spent his most formative years in hiding under Nazi occupation, and his adolescence and early manhood as a privileged, but marked, individual under Stalinist tyranny. Emigrating to the West, he reached the pinnacle of literary success and parlayed that success into a more general celebrity, appearing frequently on television, acting in Warren Beatty's film *Reds*, and skiing or playing polo with the rich and celebrated.

He made a brilliant beginning as a writer. *The Painted Bird* was translated into most major languages and many minor ones, became a bestseller in Europe and an instant cult classic on American campuses, and won the French Prix du Meilleur Livre Étranger. Subsequent books never received quite the same acclaim, although his second novel, *Steps*, won the National Book Award, and all except the last sold reasonably well for works of serious literary intent. He served two terms as president of PEN, the most important writers' organization, and was generally thought to have done a good job, especially in the twin causes of free speech and human rights. Then at the height of his success a scandal tarnished his carefully cultivated myth.

On June 22, 1982, two journalists writing in the *Village Voice* challenged the veracity of Kosinski's basic account of himself. They challenged his extensive use of private editors in the production of his novels and insinuated that *The Painted Bird*, his masterpiece, and *Being There*, which had been made into a hit movie, had been plagiarized from other sources. Underlying the uncertainties raised by the *Village Voice* exposé lurked a core question: was Kosinski of interest only as a phenomenon—an exemplar and symptom of the times—or was he, in spite of all, a serious writer whose work deserved careful and thoughtful examination? A notion of Kosinski as some sort of literary Great Pretender—a latter-day Baron Corvo—had gained currency in many quarters. Was this view accurate and fair, or was he, as many critics would have argued before the scandal, an eccentric but important writer-thinker in the existentialist mode of Sartre and Camus?

The *Village Voice* allegations not only had a devastating effect on his career but caused him tremendous personal pain. This he publicly concealed, but being Jerzy Kosinski was suddenly not the purely exhilarating experience it had once appeared to be. The feelings of emptiness and worthlessness that pursue Holocaust survivors are well documented, and were factors in such notable literary suicides as Levi's and Borowski's. Had the attack on his work struck a hollow man, or a man sensitized by earlier pain? If the *Village Voice* had shattered his life, perhaps precipitating a delayed-reaction suicide, was there additionally some dark secret—some hidden flaw—which left him vulnerable to destruction?

One can find no good answer to these questions without examining the totality of his life, and few lives are more resistant to easy summation. Many people counted themselves his friends, but each seems to have known him as the blind men knew the elephant—by parts only, and, in this case, by the parts the elephant chose to display. Kosinski's was an exemplary twentieth-century life—a life entwined with both Hitler's and Stalin's; with the great totalitarianisms and American materialism; with sexuality unbounded and violence unrestrained; with instant celebrity and the life of the very rich; with extraordinary falseness and extraordinary authenticity. He was, if nothing else, a literary creator who probed the rules and the boundaries of literary creation, whose first and greatest creation was himself.

I

MOSES' SON

1.

In the first weeks of World War II, in the fall of 1939, a six-year-old boy from a large city in Eastern Europe was sent by his parents, like thousands of other children, to the shelter of a distant village. Thus began *The Painted Bird,* which chronicled the wanderings of that boy somewhere in the primitive borderlands of Eastern Europe during the German occupation. Separated from his parents, the boy is compelled to live by his wits amidst brutal and illiterate peasants who demonstrate an exceptional predilection for incest, sodomy, and meaningless violence. A gang of toughs pushes the boy, a presumed Gypsy or Jew, below the ice of a frozen pond. A farmer forces him to hang by his hands from a rafter, just out of reach of a vicious dog. In the culminating incident of the book, the boy drops a missal while helping to serve Mass and is flung by angry parishioners into a pit of manure. Emerging from the pit, he realizes that he has lost the power of speech. The book's title—and governing metaphor—derives from a feebleminded character named Lekh who amuses himself by capturing wild birds, painting their feathers in brilliant colors, and releasing them to be pecked from the sky by their own kind.

Many saw the book, which was published in 1965 and made Kosinski's reputation, as a thinly disguised autobiographical account. The boy's story was, quite simply, Kosinski's story, with a few details changed either from poetic license or for legal reasons.

Later, questions concerning *The Painted Bird*'s facticity gave rise to a series of controversies. Did it actually portray Kosinski's personal experiences, or someone else's? Did it matter? Was facticity the same thing as authenticity? If *The Painted Bird* was less factual than supposed, was it therefore a lesser book? And if it was to some degree based on actual experience, where did the factual truth leave off and the imagination begin? Some of the answers, though not all, lie in the extraordinary facts of Kosinski's actual childhood.

2.

In January 1933 Adolf Hitler was summoned by President Hindenburg to become chancellor of Germany. Having already reinvented himself, this World War I corporal and son of a minor Austrian bureaucrat now set out to realize the grandiose dream of reinventing first Germany, then the whole of Europe. In February a Nazi provocateur set fire to the Reichstag, a deed that would be written into the legal and historical record as the act of Hitler's invented villains, the Jews. In April, amidst the upsurge of nationalist feeling that followed the Reichstag burning, the Nazis won their first plurality in a nationwide vote, and Hitler tightened his grip on power. On June 14 of that same year, Jerzy Nikodem Kosinski was born in Lodz, Poland.

The family name was, in fact, Lewinkopf. In a perverse parallel with Hitler's father, who had abandoned his mother's name (Schicklgruber) for a variant of his stepfather's (Hiedler), the father of young Jerzy was to transform Lewinkopf into Kosinski, a name so common in Poland as to be the equivalent of Smith. "Live your life unnoticed" was one of the maxims he would hand down to his son, and escaping notice would, at a critical juncture, require getting rid of a foreign and Jewish-sounding name. He had been born Mojzesz (Moses) Lewinkopf in Zamosc. Described by his son as having been "born in Russia," and having seen the Revolution of 1905, Moses Lewinkopf had firsthand experience of the dangers of visibility.

Lodz—the Polish common noun means "boat"—is an undistinguished manufacturing town in the geographic center of Poland. Lacking in architectural grace or historical importance, it is best known for its textile industry, and is often referred to as "the Polish Manchester." In Lodz, Moses Lewinkopf had found a perfect setting for Maxim Number One, a place in which to live out an obscure life in nondescript surroundings. A quiet and scholarly man, comfortable in the universe of his own thoughts, he did not miss the stimulation of physical beauty or brilliant society.

For his wife, Elzbieta Liniecka Lewinkopf, living in Lodz was less of a choice and not so congenial. Although her family was said to have come from Vilnius, she was born Elzbieta Wanda Weinreich in Lodz, on January 6, 1899, the only daughter of Meyer and Sura Weinreich. She was often described by her son as a "concert pianist" who seldom performed in public. Public performance, it was said, displeased her husband—the given reason, perhaps a jest, being that her outsize breasts made public performance awkward.

The Lodz in which the Lewinkopfs lived was known as a three-nation city, almost equally divided among citizens of Jewish, German and Polish descent. Jewish Lodz of the period before World War I is richly described in I. J. Singer's *The Brothers Ashkenazy*, which gives thinly veiled histories of the great Jewish families of the city—the Kohns, Ejtingons, Zylbersztajns, Rozenblatts, and, especially, the Poznanskis, the richest of all, who had literally begun their rise as ragpickers. Along with wealth came intellectual and artistic accomplishment, much of it tied to the Jewish third of the city.

Lodz might be physically drab, but it had Poland's best symphony orchestra, a largely Jewish enterprise, as well as a thriving theatre. Julian Tuwim (1894–1953) drew his poems of the emptiness of urban life from his home city of Lodz. The center of intellectual life, however, was the so-called "working intelligentsia," made up of doctors, lawyers, engineers, and other professionals with strong side interests in the world of arts and letters.

There were sixty-six Lewinkopfs and Weinreichs living in Lodz at the outset of World War II. The great majority of them were Weinreichs, as Moses Lewinkopf had not arrived until the 1920s. Because Weinreich is a name of unambiguously German origin, it is tempting to question the tradition that the Weinreichs came from Vilnius, especially as some sources give Latvia, not Lithuania, as the family's country of origin. Lodz lies to the west of Warsaw, where German and Polish cultures intermingle. German claims on Polish territory have frequently included Lodz—a fact that was to play a role in the Lewinkopf family odyssey—and to this day many names in Lodz are of German origin, a fact its current citizens acknowledge with reluctance. In any case, the Weinreichs would seem to have been well settled in Lodz, where they were engaged in the manufacture of leather goods.

The description of Moses Lewinkopf as "a Russian Jew" is an approximation requiring clarification. He was born in Zamosc, on October 18, 1891, the son of Nusyn and Basia Lewinkopf. Zamosc today falls within the borders of eastern Poland, not far from the Ukrainian border. In 1891, however, it was under Russian control, as it had been for the better part of the two centuries of Partition. Moses Lewinkopf was therefore born in a historically Polish town, but one under Russian administration, where the Russian language reigned in business matters. Also the birthplace of Rosa Luxemburg, Zamosc was 45 percent Jewish on the eve of World War II. Zamosc was also a center of the Haskalah movement which turned away from the Hasidic Revival, so popular in the area, to more secular and assimilationist values.

This geographic accident—that Moses Lewinkopf was born into a small island of secularism amidst a sea of Hasidic fervor—was to have decisive importance later, when he came to frame a strategy for surviving the German occupation. It was also an important legacy which he passed to his son. Late in life, when Jerzy Kosinski created the Jewish Presence Foundation to balance the horrors of the Holocaust with celebration of Jewish accomplishment, those accomplishments—in science, scholarship, and the arts—were in many ways a reflection of the secular "enlightenment" values of the Haskalah movement.

Lacking deep religious roots, the Lewinkopfs also seem to have been only weakly bound by a sense of place. Moses Lewinkopf had a single brother, Paul, who spelled the family name Lewinkoff (whereas later documents, prepared by the son, often used the German Löwenkopf, or "lion head"). Paul Lewinkoff left Poland entirely to become an American merchant seaman. The departure of Moses Lewinkopf from Zamosc to Lodz quite likely was prompted by the Bolshevik Revolution, although whether out of ideological distaste or merely to escape a chaos which hindered business it is impossible to say.

Moses Lewinkopf was often described by his son as a linguistics scholar, and sometimes as a professor of linguistics—a story that included the odd modification that he did not give public lectures. This reticence was attributed to his principle of "living life unnoticed." While a preference for obscurity was certainly a part of his character, the assertion that Moses Lewinkopf was a linguistics scholar *by profession* does not bear close scrutiny. In the Lodz of the 1930s there was no professional position for a professor of linguistics. Quite simply, he couldn't have made a living at it. It certainly would not have supported the way of life enjoyed by the Lewinkopf household, nor could it have generated the resources that would facilitate their survival during the war.

Moses Lewinkopf was, rather, one of the "working intelligentsia." The business of Moses Lewinkopf was textiles, which was also the primary commercial activity in Lodz. He is described by some as a shareholder and by others as a manager skilled in quality measurements and chemical processes. Quite likely, he was both. He would later show evidence of both financial resource and hands-on knowledge. In one way, however, his son's description does not miss the mark. He was, with certainty, a man of parts, exceptionally well informed about political developments and keenly interested in such subjects as mathematics and chess. Such interests were not uncommon among Jewish businessmen of that era in central Europe, and they would have been consistent with the values of the Haskalah movement, which turned from Talmudic studies to the general questions and interests of Western culture.

Fluent in Russian from childhood, Moses also knew German and English and had likely studied Latin and Hebrew. Growing up in Zamosc, he would be expected to be familiar with Yiddish. It is not impossible that, as his son would claim, he had pursued an interest in Sanskrit and Esperanto as well. Nevertheless, his interest in languages was in the nature of a sideline. A broad interest in secular learning clearly marked his character, part of the same cast of mind that would later enable him to exhibit a pragmatic flexibility about his Jewish identity.

The first six years in the life of Jerzy Lewinkopf are obscured by more than the usual mists of childhood. The German occupation of Poland left a human and administrative desert, forever destroying many means of verification, while the Cold War placed a physical and psychological barrier down the center of Europe during the years when reconstruction of the prewar past might have readily been accomplished. What can be known with certainty is restricted to the address, 74 Gdanska Street in Lodz, which appears on several wartime documents. Even his official birth certificate, which dates from the restoration of records in 1950, gives the name as Jerzy Nikodem Kosinski.

In *The Hermit of 69th Street*, Kosinski provides a series of snapshots—"memory slides," as they are called in the book—that represent a family very like his own. The father in the novel is Israel Kosky, a name that preserves the Biblical connotation of Moses Lewinkopf, while the mother is Elisabeth Weinreich, which is simply Elzbieta Weinreich anglicized. The speeches of both parents are boldfaced (a device used in the novel to set apart attributed factual quotation), and sprinkled throughout the novel are a series of brief scenes that probably present a limited and tinted window upon the Lewinkopf/Kosinski household before the war.

Is it legitimate to think of these scenes as factually accurate? Absolutely not. Many accounts that Kosinski gave of his early life, including comments made in interviews and published essays, are demonstrably untrue. Unless supported by separate corroboration, the details and scenes in *Hermit* must therefore be subjected to careful cross-examination. The suggestion, for example, that Elzbieta Weinreich had an aborted career as a concert pianist, like Moses Lewinkopf's career as a linguistics scholar, does not stand up to close examination. Put forward in lectures and interviews, as well as in *Hermit* and *Blind Date*, and suggested further by the naming of a piano prize in *Passion Play*, the aborted concert career of Elzbieta Lewinkopf would nevertheless appear to be as mythical as its later fictive contexts. By happenstance, a close adolescent friend who spent many hours in the postwar Kosinski home, Zygmunt Krauze, grew up to be a composer and conductor. If, as he puts it, she had been a concert-level musician, he would certainly not have been unaware of it.

Yet if the details given in *Hermit* are not factually reliable, they provide important insight as an expression of personal myth, and, in some cases, a bit more. In this light, the mother's aborted concert career amounts to the fabrication of properly pedigreed ancestry for a person who intended to define himself as an artist and impose that construction of himself upon the world. It was important to the adult writer to have a mother who was not only spontaneous, creative, and full of life, but who was also more than just a housewife. It served similarly to have a father whose primary skill, though more pedestrian than that of his son, lay with words, and in particular with foreign languages. And in a deeper sense, both these characterizations contain more than a kernel of truth.

Overall, the father in *Hermit* is a forbidding figure. An intellectual rather than an artist, he is depicted as cool, distant, and censorious. Later, the adult Kosinski would attempt to produce the kind of intellectual achievements with which he credited his father, but in the end he would give them up. They were, simply, not his game. He did not have the patience for the slow uncovering of fact, and ultimately he did not believe in it. It is nevertheless revealing that the son, early on, sought his destiny in the field of sociology, a less abstract discipline than linguistics, but a discipline nonetheless. The father who comes through between the lines of *Hermit* and several other books is a father the son wished desperately not to become, but who was still a formidable model and judging presence. Jerzy's later efforts to please that father call to mind the unhappy experiences of Kafka and Mann.

The mother is depicted in *Hermit*, and elsewhere, as sensitive, sensuous, and artistic. There are hints that she herself is dissatisfied, perhaps with her husband and certainly with the terms of her life in the colorless factory town of Lodz. In this she resembles such other prominent literary matriarchs as the mothers of Mann and Hemingway, while the devotion she inspired, though eventually expressed at a considerable distance, recalls Faulkner's lifelong daily visits to his mother. There is even, in several of the novels, a suggestion that she has turned from her imperfectly satisfying husband to create an unusually close bond with her son.

In *Hermit*, the protagonist's earliest recollections include his mother seated at the piano in their home, "a piano player too bosomy to play a piano," as her husband said. Both her musical aspirations and her physiognomy leave a lasting impression on the young child, as does the life-embracing spontaneity that prompts her to ask her three-or-four-year-old son, "Don't I look like a Gypsy?" In contrast to her husband, she seems to be suggesting that somewhere *out there*, beyond the constraints of Lodz, there is *more*, and that those with imagination may *get there* and choose what they are to be.

Such a family constellation is not unusual in the background of individuals who grow up to be artists or writers, but the depiction of young "Norbert Kosky" as his mother's adored favorite and confidant sometimes exceeds the ordinarily accepted boundaries. "Breast Symphony is what your father likes me to play for him most"—thus the Elisabeth Weinreich of the novel unburdens herself to her five-year-old son and "suitor." That a mother would speak so frankly implies a bond that defies convention. The conspiratorial closeness of this bond, in the son's eyes, is undeniable, even if one chooses to look with Freudian skepticism on the literal quote—and on the later scene in which the mother drops the top of her bathing suit to bare her breasts for her son's inspection.

A picture from before the war shows the Lewinkopfs, mother and son, on the beach at the Baltic resort of Sopot, her hands gently enveloping the delighted toddler as one might touch either a highly favored child or a lover. There is languorous sensuality in the mother's posture and an inward-turning opacity in her eyes. The son, secure in his mother's affection, turns his own eyes outward to the camera and the world. The resemblance in the two darkly Semitic faces is striking.

The son's identification of creative pursuits with his mother's side is further suggested in *Hermit* by his citing her father—called Maximilian Weinreich—as "the famous chess player born in Lodz." As with his mother's concert career, there is no evidence that this assertion of a great chess talent is factual. Chess histories contain no mention of any Meyer Weinreich, his actual name. More likely, this invention stemmed from the period in which Kosinski accompanied Gary Kasparov on a tour of New York.

It was, in fact, Moses Lewinkopf who played chess. He played it casually and no doubt competently, but by no means famously. As with scholarly discipline, chess was a pursuit of the father's that the son watched from a distance and did not fully grasp. Chess is a game of patient analysis and ruthless cunning, closer in spirit to the discipline of mathematics than to the flamboyance of literary creation. It is a game of quiet concentration, consistent with the high valuation of interior life reflected in Israel Kosky's warning to his son: "Don't ever let the waves of the mundane flood you from within." The events of the times, however, were drawing the reflections of Israel Kosky's real-life counterpart outward toward the rough-and-tumble game of geopolitics.

By the late 1930s, it must have been evident to Moses Lewinkopf that forces of surreal horror were loose in the world. In March of 1936 Hitler was confident enough of his reshaping of Germany to remilitarize the Rhineland. When this was achieved without resistance, he followed up a year later with the Anschluss, occupying Austria and assimilating it into the German Reich. In September of 1938 he bluffed the British and French leaders into a dismemberment of Czechoslovakia, by which Sudeten Germans were pulled back into Greater Germany. With the ink on the agreement hardly dry, he marched into what remained of Czechoslovakia. On November 9 the Nazi doctrine of racial hatred was given a concrete life in Kristallnacht. Nominally in response to the assassination of a German diplomat in Paris, the windows of Jewish shops were smashed, hundreds of synagogues were defaced, and Jewish citizens were beaten on streets throughout the Reich. Ninety-one Jews were killed, in what was a first foreshadowing of the coming Holocaust.

Moses Lewinkopf was a man who could read the signs of disaster in several languages, and he was also a man who could read a map. The immediate problem lay to the northwest in the so-called Polish Corridor, the section of East Prussia that had been awarded to Poland at the end of World War I to provide an outlet to the Baltic Sea. The trouble centered on Danzig (now Gdansk), which had been declared a free city, although its population was predominantly German. For Hitler, the Volksdeutsche population of Danzig could be depicted as an oppressed minority, much as he had depicted the Sudeten Germans in Czechoslovakia. By 1939 only Stalin's opposition stayed his hand. Then in August, Ribbentrop and Molotov, the foreign ministers of Germany and the Soviet Union, signed a nonaggression pact that implicitly cleared the way for dismemberment and division of Poland. On September 1, German forces crossed the border into Poland.

Up to this point, Moses Lewinkopf responded to events with the cool appraisal of a businessman. The events of September 1939 called for more. A man accustomed to looking several chess moves ahead, he could see that Polish resistance was crumbling. The Germans were going to win, and win quickly. He knew very well the consequences a German victory entailed. There would be an occupation, and that occupation would last until the end of the war. Who could say how long that might be? And what of the Jews? Hitler had made his intentions plain to anyone capable of clear-sighted analysis. In this increasingly desperate state of affairs, many responded with horror and paralysis. Moses Lewinkopf had already begun making preparations. There was no use in denial. What would come, would come. The thing was to bend one's every resource to survival.

And to survive would require more than a talent for quiet analysis. It would require cunning. It would compel one to call upon the skills acquired over a lifetime, and to offer up a lifetime's wealth as well. It was very well to have vision, but a prophet who wished to lead those in his care through a wilderness, surrounded by pestilence and death, would be called upon to display ruthlessness—a ruthlessness Moses Lewinkopf justified to his son by a quotation from the Talmud: "Your life is more important than your neighbor's."

In the event, Moses was aptly named.

3.

When Moses Lewinkopf looked out on the shambles being made
of Poland in September 1939, two thoughts must have been up-
permost in his mind. One was that Lodz, which lay in long-
disputed territory, would shortly be "incorporated" into the
German Reich. As part of Germany proper, Lodz was likely to be
far more tightly administered than portions of the country that
were merely under occupation. And where could a person hide in
Lodz anyway? The Lewinkopfs were known in Lodz. Even if they
found an attic or a cellar, they would be in peril if they ventured
out. And attics and cellars were not the Lewinkopf way.

His second thought must have concerned the prospects for
Jews within territory under German control. With hindsight, it is
easy to predict the outcome, but the initial attitude of many Polish Jews was denial. Could Moses Lewinkopf discern, even then,
the contours of the coming Holocaust? If not, he at least grasped
fully that the key to survival was camouflage, and that the first
step in this camouflage was to get rid of one's Jewish identity.
Only with a Polish identity was it possible to become invisible by
blending in with the larger population.

To appreciate the clearsightedness of Moses Lewinkopf, one
must remember that the Holocaust lay in the future. There were
Jewish forced-labor camps in Poland by the end of 1939, and a
ghetto was established at Piotrkow in October, but the first German atrocities were committed primarily against Poles. On December 7 there were mass executions in the Kampinos Forest,
near Palmiry. When word got around that Germans were executing Polish Catholics, Jews were reassured that they were not
threatened with genocide, a view that German propaganda was
at pains to reinforce.

Both German and Soviet occupiers exploited divisions between
Jewish and Catholic Poles, and in the eastern area some Polish
Jews greeted the Soviet army with gifts of bread and salt. Incredible as it may seem, parts of the western Jewish population
greeted the Germans similarly—as deliverers from the Polish
Catholic majority. Moses Lewinkopf apparently was not moved
by either of these self-deceptions.

Sometime in those first weeks a plan must have taken shape in his mind, a plan that built upon his adaptability and resourcefulness, and that drew upon his knowledge of the region in which he was born. He and his family would head toward the eastern borderland, the very area marked off on the maps of the Molotov-Ribbentrop agreement. There they would hide by blending into the local populace at the point where both German and Russian power were most extended.

Swarms of refugees had a similar idea, filling the roads to the east. But Moses Lewinkopf had in his possession something that few of the refugees possessed—papers for his entire family in a Gentile name, showing them to be not Lewinkopfs but Kosinskis. He also had a destination—Sandomierz. Set on a hill above a curve in the Vistula, it was less than a hundred kilometers from Zamosc, thus familiar terrain. As part of a bulge in the Molotov-Ribbentrop line, it stood only 120 kilometers from the new Soviet border, at the boundary of German and Soviet influence, where each power was likely to be weakest. During the first months, as it turned out, many smaller villages in the area had no German garrison, while some of the smallest never even saw a German. Moreover, the Salamonowiczes, friends from Lodz, had relatives there, and were on their way as well. Sandomierz had a large Jewish community, where a new arrival might not be too noticeable. It would be possible to blend in at first, then quietly slip away, changing at the appropriate time to their Gentile identity as Kosinskis.

The Lewinkopfs arrived in Sandomierz sometime between the outbreak of the war on September 1 and the turn of the year. Their escape came none too soon. Beginning on October 30, 1939, at the order of SS-Reichsführer Heinrich Himmler, the Germans began the systematic deportation of Jews from "annexed" provinces into the "General Government" formed in central Poland. The single exception was Lodz, which the Germans renamed Litzmannstadt. In February of 1940 the Germans began to form the Jews of Lodz into the Litzmannstadt Ghetto. By the end of April, 165,000 Jews—the second-largest Jewish community in Poland—were sealed into a space of only four square kilometers. Those who had not escaped by April 1940 were doomed, after a long agony of humiliating negotiation, to be transported to Auschwitz.

On January 8, 1940, the Lewinkopfs—father, mother and son—registered as residents at 8 Zamkowa Street in Sandomierz, a short way down a sloping street from the main square, at a rooming house belonging to a Polish Gentile named Jan Lipinski. Lipinski had purchased the row house in 1928 from a Jew named Werner, and the tenants were largely Jewish, a highly desirable clientele regular in their payments and not given to drunken and disorderly behavior. Lipinski seems to have been fascinated with his Jewish renters, and impressed with their skills at business; he even spoke with them in Yiddish.

The Lewinkopfs arrived with a few suitcases, but with something far more valuable than incidental possessions—American dollars. This piece of foresight must have further expanded Jan Lipinski's regard for Jewish financial acumen.

Although they had no apartment available at the time, the Lipinskis rented the Lewinkopfs the largest room in their own family space. Unlike the other tenants, who were local in origin, the Lewinkopfs did not work. They rose late, read the newspapers, and were served breakfast by Jan Lipinski's wife, who balanced the roles of household servant and landlady.

To the Lipinskis, the Lewinkopfs were people of refinement, polite, soft-spoken, and charming—a cut above the tenants they were used to, and several cuts above their neighbors. Moses Lewinkopf knew how to play upon the appeal of affluence and higher social status, binding the Lipinskis in the ambiguous position of servant-landlord-protector, and making them feel privileged to have the opportunity. Meanwhile, his friendly interrogations about the word from the marketplace turned Lipinski into a source of political intelligence. Thus the Lewinkopfs learned about the gradual deterioration of Jewish life in Sandomierz.

The Lipinskis seem never to have been troubled by the notion that this polite, charming man was thinking circles around them. He had an invariably helpful spirit. Once when the Lipinskis could not obtain soap, he offered to make it for them himself, from fat. And he *knew how*. Skills like the ability to make soap, which he ascribed to work he had done in a factory before the war, went a long way with a small-town craftsman who might otherwise have eventually been put off by wealth and fine manners.

There is evidence that their protectors found Elzbieta Lewinkopf less ingratiating. She had airs, and it was difficult for her to recognize the situation and put them aside. She was always perfumed. Her nails were always done. She had a habit of giving commands. It is worth noting that these details, especially the painted nails, matched exactly the stereotype of Jewish women held among rural Poles. With the Lipinskis, at least, she won grudging recognition as a woman who kept herself up under trying circumstances, even though her emphasis on her superficial presentation was resented.

Up to this point the status of the Lewinkopfs was perfectly legal. They were still known as Lewinkopf. Their presence was recorded in the comprehensive document drawn up for the Germans by the Judenrat, where they were listed as Household Number 96, Lewinkop [sic], Mojzesz, with wife Elzbieta and son Jerzy, cross-referenced with the Blusztajn family, who were also tenants at 8 Zamkowa.

Yet the Lewinkopfs stood apart from the other Jewish families at 8 Zamkowa. Although there were a number of children who played together inside the house and out, Jerzy Lewinkopf did not join in their games. He was invited but refused, giving as the reason that he was a Pole and did not play with Jews. He wore a religious medal around his neck, which he would show as proof, and he knew how to recite the Lord's Prayer and other prayers in flawless Polish. It was then that young Jerzy made a strange and incomprehensible assertion. His name, he said, was not Jerzy Lewinkopf; it was Jurek Kosinski (Jurek being the common diminutive of Jerzy).

Hearing this astonishing falsehood, the other children naturally mocked him, calling him "Josek." Closely resembling his mother, whose darkly Semitic looks he shared, he was quickly typed as a withdrawn, standoffish mother's boy. Taunted as "Josek," he struck back at the smaller and weaker children of the Lewinkopfs' fellow Jewish tenants. He whacked one younger boy and spat on little Rebeka Blusztajn, calling her "a dirty Jew."

The episode provides evidence that Moses Lewinkopf had already begun to drill his son in the new family identity. One can only imagine the technique of indoctrination, perhaps a sort of game, perhaps stern admonition, perhaps more. Many factors in Kosinski's later life point to the possibility of an undocumented incident of sharp and traumatic abuse in early childhood, and it is tempting to think that the incident may have taken place during this indoctrination. While many harrowing episodes of *The Painted Bird* did not happen literally as Kosinski would write and speak of them, the intensity of his inner response to several later events makes sense if one views these as reverberative of an earlier ordeal. At least one medical professional was persuaded that Kosinski's anatomy revealed a physically traumatic event in which his shoulder sockets were damaged. It is highly unlikely that such an event occurred where he placed it in his own accounts, but ensuing episodes of hostility and physical violence directed toward his father suggest that something may have taken place at this point which, at least within the frame of a young child's world, had the effect of a major trauma.

Speculation aside, all that we know of the matter was observed from a distance and then remembered after many years by individuals who were themselves children at the time. What they saw was the training of a seven-year-old undercover agent. "Watch your accent," his mother sometimes said, enjoining him not to play with the other Jewish children lest he pick up their telltale patterns of speech. So he *was* Jerzy Kosinski, but not quite yet. The "cover story" was planted so firmly that it slipped out prematurely.

4.

By the beginning of 1941, the tone of the German occupation had begun to move into a new phase. When the Lewinkopfs first arrived in Sandomierz, there were few signs of the coming Holocaust, and members of the local Judenrat actually served as interpreters for the Gestapo. Why not? Did they not, in a sense,

share more with their conquerors than with their Polish neighbors, whose casual anti-Semitism was historical and well known?

But now all this was beginning to change. The roundup of
Jews had reached eastern Poland, and so had edicts requiring
Jews to wear the Star of David. Moses Lewinkopf did not miss
the signs. The house at 8 Zamkowa opened onto a street that ran
up to the marketplace, but a rear balcony to the Lipinskis'
second-story apartment provided a view over a sloping ravine to
the banks of the Vistula, and farther. Just outside Sandomierz the
Vistula divided in two. The larger branch, the Vistula itself,
curved back toward Cracow, while the smaller branch, the San,
bent eastward toward the Ukrainian border. On a clear day you
could see from the Lipinski balcony upwards of ten kilometers.
Beyond the far bank of the Vistula lay rocky farmland, bracketed
by the Janow and Solska forests. It was, in a sense, a wilderness.
To Moses Lewinkopf it offered the promise of deliverance.

He made his first effort at escaping into the wilderness before
leaving the Lipinskis', an approach to the Lipinskis' eldest daughter, whose husband ran a country estate at Miedzygorze. This attempt failed when the Lipinski son-in-law declined to involve his
employers by hiding a Jewish family; as he pointed out, the estate
employed a large number of resident workers who posed a risk
as potential informers.

In March of 1941 the Lewinkopfs settled for a stopgap measure. They took their leave of the Lipinskis with warm goodbyes
but without mentioning their destination. Their new location was
the second-story attic of a house at 3 Golebicka Street, an entirely
Catholic neighborhood on the outskirts of town. The landlord,
who lived downstairs, was a wagoner named Waclaw Skobel
who had been found for them by a servant of their friends the
Salamonowiczes. The relocation was timely. The houses on
Zamkowa Street, historically Jewish, were eventually incorporated into the Sandomierz Ghetto. The Lipinskis were dispos-
sessed and forced to live by their wits, while all of the Jewish
tenants still living at 8 Zamkowa perished.

Through much of 1941 little Jerzy Lewinkopf continued to enjoy a few remnants of normal childhood. He was allowed to play

with Stefan Salamonowicz, who was the same age, and with the children of the Salamonowiczes' Gentile friends, the Justynskis. There were five children in the Justynski family, several close enough in age to be playmates, and the two boys from wealthy and cosmopolitan Jewish families went through a cultural reversal, finding the simple potato soup and other ordinary dishes they were offered in the Justynski household wonderful and exotic. With two of the Justynski brothers, they played "horses and coachmen," taking turns in the roles of beast and master with whip. While the two Jewish boys were playing the beasts, Stefan's grandfather happened upon the game and insisted they switch to roles more accurately reflecting their relative social status.

The Justynskis were prepared to accept this from the most important Jewish family in town, which had the accumulated credits of a lifetime and owned most of the buildings in the main square. The Lewinkopfs were upstarts in Sandomierz, however, and a haughtiness of attitude was remarked in both mother and son. Mrs. Lewinkopf had a way of giving orders to people, setting limits on what could be touched. Had she grown up with the Justynskis, as Hanka Salamonowicz had, she would not have addressed them in this way, or at least she would have couched her prohibitions in more polite language. As for her son, he was a smart boy, but already something of a dandy. Better dressed than the other children, he didn't like to get his clothes soiled. He avoided rough games, and if he fell, he immediately brushed the dirt off his suit.

Even his mother was forced to acknowledge that little Jerzy was developing behavioral problems. The strain of their unusual circumstances was taking its toll. Unable to handle his unruly conduct, especially when they were cooped up together for days at a time, she frequently put him in the hands of Celina Skazowska, who worked for a local social self-help agency. Skazowska, whose mother had begun helping the Kosinskis in 1940, also brought them gifts of flour and fat. She quickly discovered the young Kosinski's precocious facility for language, but also frequently witnessed his unbridled outbursts.

Occasionally his bottled-up anger and frustration erupted in behavior that was downright dangerous. One day he and Stefan Salamonowicz put little Maria Justynska, a mere toddler, into a baby carriage and pushed her down one of the steep Sandomierz hills. Baby Maria could easily have been seriously injured, even killed. In the investigation that followed, Stefan Salamonowicz took the blame as the primary culprit, although it was not clear who actually had the idea. In any case, Stefan wept with remorse; little Jurek Kosinski, on the other hand, had observed the wild ride coolly, and laughed.

The Skobels' attic room was the last place the Lewinkopfs stayed legally, under their real names. Their next brief sojourn, with Celina Skazowska's parents, the Margens, was not reported on any official rosters. By then the situation in Sandomierz was changing rapidly. On June 28, 1941, German columns stepped off for the invasion of the Soviet Union, and while this new front might offer hope of eventual salvation, the initial news was not encouraging. In the meantime, the German policy of a grand pogrom was becoming increasingly clear. In January of 1942 the Wannsee Conference spelled out that policy as extermination of the Jews of Europe—the "final solution."

The effects of the Wannsee Protocol were quickly felt in Sandomierz. Early in 1942 a ghetto was established in the center, incorporating the old Zamkowa Street house, and Jews were brought in from smaller towns of the area. The ghetto was closed in August. By late October, after the Judenrat had put off the Germans with bribes as long as they could, the SS began transporting the citizens of the Sandomierz Ghetto to Auschwitz. November 29, 1942, was the end of Jewish Sandomierz.

According to a document in the Sandomierz State Archive, the Lewinkopfs registered on August 16 as residents of 4 Za Bramka Street. The address, on a street one level below the Lipinski house at 8 Zamkowa, is imaginary. To get to the empty lot, one descends through the Ucho Igielne, or "needle's eye"—a slender hole in the old city wall. The use of a fictitious address seems to have been a deception by Moses Lewinkopf to put bounty hunters off his trail, and perhaps also to protect his Gentile protectors. Looking out the back window of his first landlords, the Lipinskis, one might have noticed the tip of a thatched roof peeking above the top of the ravine. Continuing the line of march down a narrow path through a thickly grown ravine, one would have come to a small cottage set in the middle of a meadow, in splendid isolation, with a clear view to the Vistula. That cottage—in a separately administered district known as Rokitnik—was to be the next stopgap residence.

The cottage belonged to Marianna Pasiowa, the Justynskis' aunt, a poor peasant woman and a hunchback. The arrival at Pasiowa's cottage evidently marked an important moment in the consciousness of little Jerzy, for he makes it the stepping-off point of the boy's journey in *The Painted Bird*. Describing Marta, the character based upon Pasiowa, he wrote: "She was old and always bent over, as though she wanted to break herself in half but could not. Her long hair, never combed, had knotted itself into innumerable thick braids impossible to unravel. These she called elflocks. . . . She hobbled around, leaning on a gnarled stick, muttering to herself in a language I could not quite understand. Her small withered face was covered with a net of wrinkles, and her skin was reddish brown like that of an overbaked apple."

The passage goes on to describe her constant trembling, bony hands, scraggy neck, coursing tears, and the "glutinous threads hanging from her nose and the bubbly saliva dripping from her lips"—an extended piece of extraordinarily close observation. An exquisite awareness of his surroundings seems suddenly to have come together in the nine-year-old Jerzy/Jurek. There is a special feeling to the meadow that surrounded Pasiowa's cottage and to the surrounding woods, a feeling that can best be described as a kind of dark enchantment. It is the Everyplace and Noplace of the forests from the Brothers Grimm, almost perfectly matched to a child's inner landscape of menacing forces, inarticulable fears, and the faint hope of magical deliverance—a place where the secret passions and fears of the human heart may assume the shapes of unimaginable beasts. In the vision he later rendered, Jerzy Kosinski captured that meadow and wood with the preternatural clarity of a dream recalled.

The real-life Marianna Pasiowa was a simple, goodhearted old woman who was part of an underground railroad helping Jews escape from Sandomierz. There is still a hole on the side of a hill, some fifty meters away, where she hid a Jewish infant during the closing of the ghetto. The infant's mother came at night when she could get out, and when she couldn't, Pasiowa fed the child with cow's milk. Another Jewish family she helped made her the odd gift of a small piece of glass, which family members later decided must have been a diamond.

Relations between Jews and Polish Catholics in divided towns like Sandomierz were undeniably complex. The local cathedral contains a fresco depicting the ritual murder of a Christian child by a congregation of rapacious and stereotypic Jews; in that same church, however, Jews were hidden in the presbytery with the knowledge and aid of the parishioners.

In this environment, it is not surprising that the attitude of the Pas family should reflect a certain ambiguity. While never exactly anti-Semites, the men of Pasiowa's family seem to have felt that Jews, with their odd habits, were fair game for pranks. Before the war, both Marianna Pasiowa's husband and her son had partici- pated in the sport of waiting outside the Jewish baths to touch women after they bathed, compelling them to return for re- purification. Another favorite stemmed from the employment of Polish Catholics to perform menial household tasks on the Sab- bath. Gathering wood in the course of doing odd jobs, the Pas men would place a small explosive in the fireplace and giggle about the ruckus that must have been created when it went off. One may take various views of such "harmless" pranks, but it is clear that in the crisis all members of the Pas family came through with indispensable help.

For the Lewinkopfs, the advantages of staying with Pasiowa included the availability of fresh bread, as her son worked in the local bakery and could sometimes bring home flour. When they stole back to the town center to confer with the Salamonowiczes, they could leave young Jerzy in her care. In an important sense, the Pasiowa cottage marked the transition in the family odyssey from the town, where the trappings of life bore at least some re- semblance to their earlier life in Lodz, to the primitive conditions of the countryside. They entered it as Lewinkopfs, an urban, and urbane, Jewish family, but emerged from it as Kosinskis, Polish Gentiles in name, into a world that bore little resemblance to anything they had known before.

5.

One night in the fall of 1942, Waclaw Skobel loaded the Lewinkopf family into his cart and drove them across the Vistula through the delta where the rivers forked to the smaller town of Radomysl-on-San. With them they had a new family member— Henryk, or "Henio" as he was called, a toddler who was accompanied by an elderly Polish caretaker named Katarzyna.

Who was Henryk? The reasonable supposition is that he was the child of Jewish parents in Sandomierz who were not themselves able to escape. In the summer of 1942, as the Sandomierz Ghetto was being closed, they would have prevailed upon the Lewinkopfs/Kosinskis, who had papers and a chance for survival, to take their son.

Why did Moses Lewinkopf, already burdened with wife and child, accept two additional wards, one almost an infant and the other already old? Perhaps the parents were able to appeal to his sense of himself as a deliverer. Perhaps they were able to contribute what remained of their own resources. Documents composed years after the fact give the birthplace of Henryk Kosinski as Sandomierz, and the date as 1940. The name of his parents was remembered as having been Chustecki, or perhaps Chrustecki, which is more common in the area.

There is irony in the arrival of Henryk Kosinski. Like the boy of whom Jerzy would write in *The Painted Bird*, he was newly separated from his parents and entrusted to the care of strangers. Unlike the boy, however, he was blue-eyed and fair and had straight hair. He could pass for a Pole, and some people even felt he bore a resemblance to Moses Lewinkopf. He might be excess baggage, but he certainly contributed to the family's camouflage.

At Radomysl, Skobel passed the Kosinski group, now five in number, into the hands of the local priest, one Eugeniusz Okon.

"The priest took me away in a borrowed cart," Kosinski wrote in *The Painted Bird*. "He said that he would find someone in a nearby village to take care of me until the end of the war. Before reaching the village we stopped at the local church. The priest left me in the cart and went alone to the vicarage, where I saw him arguing with the vicar."

This Okon was constantly in trouble with his superiors. Like the defrocked priest of Graham Greene's *The Power and the Glory*, he liked whiskey and had a mistress who bore him children. He also had an affinity for radical politics. He gave spellbinding fire-and-brimstone sermons, which he dramatized by lying on the church floor, arms outstretched in the extreme devotional posture of the cross. He also helped Jews, in the early days of the war arranging visas for some to emigrate to the United States and later managing to place Jewish families with false documents in out-of-the-way villages.

Father Okon had arranged for the Kosinskis—for that was now their name—to come to the small village of Dabrowa Rzeczycka, located just west of the San River. Using his ecclesiastical authority, he had enlisted the help of Jozef Stepak, the administrator of Dabrowa and nearby Kepa; the two men acting together were then able to enlist the villagers in a conspiracy of silence. The home Okon found for the Kosinskis was in a semidetached apartment owned by a Polish Catholic farmer, Andrzej Warchol.

In *The Painted Bird*, the priest has difficulty persuading a farmer to accept the boy. The farmer, called Garbos, argues that keeping the boy will expose him to great danger, as Germans often visit the village. The priest finally takes the man by the arm and whispers into his ear, whereupon the peasant "became subdued and, cursing, told me to follow him into the hut."

In the beginning, there was also argument in the Warchol household about the Kosinskis. Maria Warchol questioned her husband's judgment in accepting a family of Jewish tenants, pointing out the risks to her own children—Edward, who was fifteen when the Kosinskis arrived, and Stefania, who was three—and to the entire village. The previous residents, also Jews, had only recently been shot dead, and their son still roamed the nearby woods.

Andrzej Warchol countered by restating the priest's arguments. There was also the matter of rent, from a tenant whose dependability was assured.

Once the Kosinskis were installed, the argument seems to have ceased. "How can we ever repay you?" Elzbieta Kosinska asked repeatedly.

"Let us all survive, this is most important," Maria Warchol would reply.

While small, the Kosinskis' apartment was reasonably comfortable, containing furniture left by the previous owners, the Liebeskinds. Liebeskind had operated the local sawmill, which was part of the large Lubomirski estate. Responding to the summons for Jews to gather in the square of nearby Zaklikow, both husband and wife had been shot down on the spot. Their teenage son, Karol, fled to the wood and led a hand-to-mouth existence with occasional help from local farmers, while their daughter escaped the country. Karol Liebeskind survived until near the end of the war, when he was discovered by the Germans and killed; his ghostly presence is the genesis of references in *The Painted Bird* to a Jew who lived in the nearby woods.

The Kosinskis slept in twin beds, together with Jurek, while the elderly Katarzyna and little Henio slept on a bed of boards in the kitchen. Early in their stay, Elzbieta Kosinska inquired whether Maria Warchol would care to earn extra money by serving as her maid—the same arrangement she had managed to work out with Jan Lipinski's wife—but Mrs. Warchol refused. Not only did she have her hands full with the house and a young child, but such work was beneath her dignity. Mrs. Warchol's peasant pride, so different from the attitude of the town-dwelling poor, took Elzbieta by surprise, but the two women patched it up, and Mrs. Warchol helped in the search for a "suitable" maid, trying first two neighbor women and then a local widow named Stefania Labina who desperately needed money.

Labina came to the Kosinskis' apartment daily, scrubbing floors, grinding grain, baking bread, and doing the wash on a wooden washboard. Labina is memorialized in *The Painted Bird* by a character of the same name with whom the boy has a brief sojourn. A woman of loose morals, she is the widow of Laba the Handsome (Labina being the feminine form of Laba) who committed suicide when someone stole his stash of fine clothes.

During the first months the Kosinskis spent in Dabrowa, Father Okon periodically bicycled from Radomysl to inquire about them. He asked the Warchols about their acceptance by the other villagers. To reinforce the conspiracy of silence, he was prepared to invoke the authority of the Church—delivering privately, if necessary, one of his sermons about the grim future that awaited sinners in Hell. But within a few months Okon stopped coming, having himself become a fugitive from the Gestapo. (He would survive the war and live to see his good works recognized in a biography.)

The Kosinskis settled in cautiously. At first, Mieczyslaw Kosinski—the name by which Moses Lewinkopf would henceforth be known—ventured out in public only when absolutely necessary, and with his collar turned up. Never speaking to passersby, he made the short walk to nearby Kepa to buy food. Slowly he probed for the response of the villagers.

Gradually a way of life began to take shape. Elzbieta Kosinska, who had the "worst"—the most Jewish—looks, stayed inside the apartment. Katarzyna, Henio's elderly caretaker and a Polish Catholic, busied herself in the yard. There she kept a close eye on young Henio, who had light hair and passable features but wore three layers of trousers as a safeguard against revealing his circumcised penis. Young Jerzy/Jurek also played in the yard, his dark hair cropped short; the distinctively beaky nose was not to develop until he was a teenager.

Little by little, Mieczyslaw Kosinski began to go out among the villagers. Isolation, he seemed to realize, was as risky as mingling with the locals. He had to go out, in any case, to buy food—and by going out regularly he could acquire that most precious commodity—information. The secret to survival, after all, was to blend in and become a part of things. He began giving lessons to children who wished to go beyond the level of the local four-year school; he was qualified to teach all the high-school subjects. The villagers took to calling him "professor" and referring to Elzbieta as "the professor's wife."

It was not, therefore, an entire fabrication when his son, years later, presented his father's occupation as "professor." He was, to the simple villagers of Dabrowa, "the professor," and it was in that guise that his nine-year-old son would have seen him. As he had with the Lipinskis in Sandomierz, the elder Kosinski knew how to use his knowledge and manner to position himself among the villagers. The honorific encapsulated their sense of him as a man of refinement, but a man whose attainments they did not resent. They took pride in their role in saving such a man. At the market in Kepa, some of the vendors reduced their prices in deference to a man of standing. To the peasants, the Kosinskis offered a connection to the great world outside the village. On at least one occasion he was approached by a peasant with a desperately ill child, seeking a letter of introduction to a doctor in Radomysl who was of Jewish origin. Apparently at least familiar with the doctor, Elzbieta provided the letter, and the child was given treatment.

6.

By the time the Kosinskis arrived in Dabrowa Rzeczycka, the tide of war had begun to turn against the Germans. In October of 1942 the German conquests in North Africa had reached their limits, and Rommel had suffered a disastrous defeat at El Alamein. The Americans had entered the war the previous December, and would make their presence felt in the Atlantic Theater in November of 1942, invading North Africa. Both these events, however, were far from eastern Poland, and had limited relevance to the situation in Dabrowa. The events of December 1942 and January 1943 were directly relevant, however. The German 6th Army, under General von Paulus, captured three-quarters of Stalingrad but could advance no farther; caught in a pincer of Russian reinforcements, virtually the entire German force was destroyed or captured. From that time on, an informed individual—an individual like Mieczyslaw Kosinski—could plot the inexorable daily ad-

vance of the Red Army as it moved toward the liberation of
Poland.

While the Battle of Stalingrad raged, the Kosinskis were invited to celebrate Christmas in Dabrowa—a celebration new to
their experience and deeply ironic, but useful. Their hosts were
the Migdaleks, who lived in a frame house across a small yard,
with a permanently open gate. Although not Jewish, they had
fled Silesia during the German onslaught in 1939, settling in
Dabrowa, where they had relatives. Mr. Migdalek taught in the
local elementary school. There were two Migdalek children—
Ewka, who was a year older than Jurek Kosinski, and Andrzej,
nicknamed "Bumek," who was a year younger.

Mrs. Migdalek's invitation was a statement at several levels.
More than a neighborly gesture, it was a way of saying to the rest
of the village that the Migdaleks—who would themselves later
take in two Jewish children related by marriage—were unafraid
of associating with a family known to be Jewish. And at another
level, there was the matter of class; the Migdaleks thought of
themselves as educated people like the Kosinskis, people who
stood apart from the ordinary citizenry of places like Dabrowa.

It was a meager Christmas Eve dinner when compared with
normal times. There was only bread, and a sour soup with potatoes. The occupying Germans imposed steep levies on foodstuffs,
and the soil of Dabrowa was sandier than that of surrounding villages. Daily fare during the war years included pigweed, of
which a soup could be made, potatoes, and beetroot, which was
used in soup and to make marmalade. Later in life, Kosinski
would surprise hosts and annoy restaurants by asking for plates
of raw onions; root crops also remained as an adult taste. Such
preferences, which left him chronically underweight, reflected the
eating habits formed in Dabrowa during the war.

The Migdalek children were young Jurek Kosinski's constant
playmates. There were really no alternatives. Edek Warchol was
already a teenager, and Stefania Warchol was still a baby. The
Warchol apartments and the Migdalek house stood a bit apart
from the rest of the village, and even if they hadn't, there was a
strong prohibition against mixing with the village children, who
pointed at little Jurek and Henio and shouted, *"Zydy, Zydki."* A

retarded boy, Jas Cholody, shouted, _"Jude, 'raus!"_ each time he passed the Warchol apartments. Children were, in a way, the greatest danger. Mieczyslaw Kosinski could change his name and hide his wife; he could win over the adult villagers and train his own child to conceal the marks of his identity. But the children of the village were beyond his control. They could blurt out the truth at any moment, no matter who happened to be listening.

Perhaps it was no real solution to keep young Jurek away from other children, but prudence dictated such caution. And whether by nature or because he had been so strongly indoctrinated, he was a child of incredible discipline. He didn't run off without permission. He didn't even have to be tended. He was careful never to urinate in public like the other boys, but always to seek concealment. When the Migdalek children were unavailable, he spent his days with his elbows propped on the fence, watching the other children at play.

Witnesses differ as to the frequency with which Jurek Kosinski left his yard, but several occasions remain clear in the memory of more than one observer. On the first, the whole village was summoned to the banks of the San to see an enormous catfish a village boy had caught. The stir caused by the fish is a telling indication of the slow pace of life in the village, and it must have made a strong impression on young Kosinski, who later described it in _The Painted Bird_ as "a huge catfish with long whiskers stiffly sprouting from its snout.... a powerful-looking, monstrous fish" with an air bladder large enough to support the boy as he floats downstream.

His companion on the trip to see the catfish was Andrzej Migdalek, and it was Andrzej Migdalek who accompanied him on a second trip as well, along with little Henio. Their destination was a small stream where village boys bathed and swam. Andrzej Migdalek joined in with the others, but the two Kosinskis merely stood and watched, refusing to undress. When they returned to the apartment, they were spanked severely. If they ever left again without permission, there are no accounts of it.

Another foray was undertaken with maternal sanction. The neighborhood children often skated on a nearby pond, using ice skates made of pieces of wood nailed with a sickle, which could be tied to the bottoms of their boots. Jurek Kosinski had gotten a pair of skates, and received permission to go out with Andrzej Migdalek. On his first visit, older children skated past threateningly, shouting, "*Zydek, Zydziok*," and the boys went home. They overcame their fear, however, and went a second time. This time the older boys shouted at Jurek to lower his pants and show them his penis. The ringleader was a boy named Swietlik, himself of a family of converted Jews, and Andrzej Migdalek shouted for him to show his own. Swietlik then knocked little Jurek to the ice and began pulling down his pants, while Jurek fought back and shouted, "*Mame, mame.*" Hearing his cries, Edek Warchol, the landlord's son, skated up and scattered the assailants.

Part of the Kosinski/Lewinkopf strategy was camouflage, and simply living in the village was not enough. A part of the life of a secret agent is to "live his cover," and despite the discrepancies in looks, wealth, and education, the Kosinskis lived their cover in one remarkable way. Their apartment was decorated with crucifixes and images of the Virgin—too many, some of the locals thought. Attentive to detail, they let the religious images collect dust and cobwebs, so that they would not appear as recent additions. And they attended church fairly regularly at nearby Wola Rzeczycka, or at least the father and son did, with the mother attending more occasionally. They sat in the back corners, half hidden but determined to demonstrate their presence, at the same masses attended by soldiers from the German garrison.

But one more step was necessary. During the winter of 1943 little Jurek began confirmation classes along with Andrzej Migdalek and other boys his age. The parish priest, Father Sebastianski, had been briefed by Father Okon and was sympathetic. After the religious classes, the boys walked home to Dabrowa, playing war games by throwing stones at each other. Jurek Kosinski refused to participate and was ridiculed as a mother's boy, at times even by his friends. But he was under firm instructions to return alone and not to play with the other children.

Jurek and Andrzej did well in the confirmation classes, and as a result they were selected to serve as altar boys during evening masses. At one of those masses, with the older boys laughing and poking—perhaps at the spectacle of a Jewish altar boy—Jurek Kosinski dropped the missal he was passing to the priest. He picked it up immediately, handed it to Father Sebastianski, and was not disciplined. In his inner life, however, the dropping of the missal was clearly a devastating and pivotal event, albeit unremarked by the outside world. Cast in the role of preadolescent anthropologist, he was forced to figure out an alien culture and pass a test upon which his survival, and the survival of his family, might depend. When the missal dropped from his hands, it seemed to him that he had failed that test. Over the years the dropping of the missal would grow into a major episode of *The Painted Bird* in which the boy is expelled from the community— literally flung into a pit.

The culmination of this religious training took place in May of 1943 when Jurek Kosinski, along with Andrzej Migdalek and the other local boys of his age, received Holy Communion for the first time. To celebrate the occasion the Kosinskis gave a party, not only for Jurek but for all the children taking First Communion. It must have been a difficult decision. Weighing on the one side was the risk of a public mingling in which Elzbieta Kosinska, with her Jewish "look," would have to take part; on the other was the risk of standing apart from the community—and, conversely, the benefit from placing themselves at the center of Dabrowa life. The right choice was clearly to stick to the difficult strategy of blending in.

The party was held in the churchyard at Wola Rzeczycka, and benches were set out for the children with cookies and cups of hot cocoa—an unheard-of luxury. Fifty years later villagers would remember the impression made by the sudden appearance of cocoa—where could it have come from?—and by the rare appearance of Elzbieta Kosinska. They noted her smart dress, her makeup, and her plucked eyebrows. It was known that while maids cleaned her house, she sat at the table and drew designs for her own dresses, often with high necks to conceal her enlarged thyroid. For her son's First Communion, she finally came outside—and she was wearing, scandalously, nail polish!

7.

The stress of this secret life began to take its toll on Jurek Kosinski. It wasn't natural for a ten-year-old to constantly pretend and bottle up the truth, nor was it normal to stand and watch all day as life passed by on the far side of the fence. One day, alone with Ewka Migdalek, young Jurek informed her that he was not Jurek Kosinski but Jerzy Lewinkopf; he was a Jew, and came from Lodz; his mother was from a wealthy family, in leather goods, and always had beautiful gloves; he was circumcised, and for that reason was not allowed to go out and play.

Ewka relayed this information to her parents, who immediately told the Kosinskis. Mieczyslaw Kosinski confronted his son, who denied having told anything. He swore Ewka had made the story up. To resolve the matter, the elder Kosinski settled on the version that Jurek had a crush on Ewka and had made up wild stories to get her attention. In his humiliation, Jurek was presented with an unpalatable commentary on the nature of truth and the nature of lies. It was the mirror image of the slip he had made at 8 Zamkowa among the Jews who rented from the Lipinskis. There he had said he was not a Jew but a Gentile, Jurek Kosinski; in Dabrowa, among Gentiles, he admitted that he was a Jew, Jerzy Lewinkopf. A large and seamless lie, the lie that enabled his family to survive, had become the truth—whereas the truth, which he told, had become officially rejected by all responsible adults as a lie.

The episode with Ewka marks a further stop on the journey begun at the cottage of Marianna Pasiowa, in which a world of primal immediacy impinges on the inner life of an indulged child. He would draw upon Ewka in two of his novels, presenting her each time in eroticized terms. She appears in *The Painted Bird* under her own name as Ewka, who has sexual relations with both her father and her brother and is given by her father in sexual congress with a goat; in *Hermit*, she is the prototype for both Ewunia, who has a sexual relationship with her brother, and Bozena, who has an abortive tryst with the character based upon the young Kosinski. Approaching adolescence while living in cramped quarters with his parents, he was beginning to suffer the

effects of lack of privacy and the absence of normal boundaries—
even, and perhaps especially, in the family sleeping arrangements. His later writings suggest that this period marked the
beginning of powerful erotic fantasies, and that those fantasies
were shaped in some measure by his peculiar surroundings.

He was not personally responsible for the care of animals, but
living only a few meters away from a barn (which still stands), he
was thrown into close proximity to them: to goats, rabbits, and
dogs, whose unaccountable rudenesses of behavior and uncon-
strained sexual expression must have come as a shock.

By the standards of young Jurek, the Migdaleks and the
Warchols would have seemed almost as primitive as the animals
themselves. Dependent on such people on a daily basis, he would
certainly have resented that dependency, and have directed the
resentment at his saviors. The two aspects of his situation seem to
have come together into what became a lifelong pattern: the
eroticization of pain, anger, guilt, and loss, in which the intensity
of his pain is expressed through erotic cues.

Along with questions of dependency and awakening sexuality
was the core question of identity. The others in his experience
were either Jews or Gentiles. If not a Jew and not a Gentile, what
was he? *Who* was he? If identities could be given and taken away
so easily, what part of himself could a person claim? And the
question was not posed abstractly. Its context might be cultural,
but its chief focus was physical, and local. With his hair cut short
and the beaky nose yet to develop, he might pass at a glance
as one of the village boys. But in one place, his difference was
undeniable.

The need to conceal his penis, countering the drive of the other
children to uncover it, was a central fact of his childhood. To the
other children, it might be a game undertaken in good fun, out of
childish curiosity; to him, it was a matter of life and death. And
it led to fundamental questions of boundary and identity. Where
did he leave off and the rest of the world begin? Was the self centered in the body? Or was it, perhaps, centered in some *part* of the
body? "I *have* my body but I also *am* my body," he would write
in his final novel, quoting Helmuth Plessner, and at another point
he would discuss his body as republic, of which he resided at the

center as president-for-life. At one level, such a description amounts to deep philosophical exploration, while at another it suggests the self-alienated view of the schizophrenic.

Whatever way he looked at things, one fact was obvious: he did not draw his identity from any group. The clearest identification of self was that inner executive—the president-for-life directing his external actions—which was invisible to the other children, and to most adults as well. Behind the mask of invisibility it could observe them secretly, while thinking circles around their motives and behavior—a talent he shared with his father. This elusive self, the "I" that seemed to disappear when one reached out to touch it, was balanced by that other tangible element, the thing that made him one with all other males but, in his case, was so perilously different—his circumcised penis.

Not Pole nor Jew, neither fish nor fowl, he was a pariah, yet an adored pariah. His solace and his curse resided in his extraordinary repertoire of secret thoughts. Placed by circumstance and preference in the confined space of his parents' marital bed, those secret thoughts must have traveled to that locus of identity which was the object of the world's fascination, his vehicle of magical power and the potential source of his downfall, a secret treasure he must forever protect.

Trapped behind the Warchol fence, he continued in the two activities his circumstances permitted: watching and fantasizing. Across the street from the Warchol apartments, less than fifty meters down a narrow lane, was the cottage of the Tracz family, whose teenage son had suffered brain damage from encephalitis—"brain fever," as it was called by the villagers. Mrs. Tracz had worked briefly as a maid for the Kosinskis before the coming of Labina. From his favorite post at the front fence, he could see the comings and goings of the Tracz son, Aleksander, who despite his affliction was clever with his hands and comfortable in the nearby woods. Lech, as the boy was called for short, was skilled at trapping birds, especially crows, which he kept in handmade wooden cages. Sometimes he painted those captured birds with lime wash and turned them loose to see what would happen.

The painting of birds was long known in the region, being

mentioned in medieval texts. When released, the bird would fly back to rejoin its kind, who—at least in folklore—would attack the painted bird and kill it. It is not certain whether young Jurek Kosinski ever actually saw Lech Tracz release one of his painted birds. Yet Tracz was something of a local legend. He held the fascination of a simpleminded, thus unknowable, individual who had a single exceptional skill. He was gentle and harmless, yet in his simplicity lived close to nature, where unconscious cruelty seemed ever present. A local oddity who had become an accepted part of the Dabrowa landscape, he left an indelible impression on Jurek Kosinski. From a tiny speck on the periphery of a child's vision, his painted birds would grow over twenty years into a metaphor for all human society.

8.

During May of 1943, the month when Jurek Kosinski celebrated his First Communion, the German army was completing its reduction of the Warsaw Ghetto. The final liquidation had begun on April 19, setting off an armed rebellion involving extraordinary displays of personal heroism. Operating out of an improvised command bunker at 18 Mila Street, Jewish resistance fighters led by the legendary Mordecai Anielewicz fought German regulars to a standstill. Using tanks and armored cars, the Germans overcame all significant resistance by May 8, with sporadic fighting continuing for a few more days. Anielewicz and his entire staff committed suicide in the command bunker rather than surrender. Seven thousand Jews were killed in the military side of the operation, and another six thousand were burned alive in the buildings. The entire population of the ghetto perished.

The Holocaust as it is known in history had then been going on for a little over a year—since the Wannsee Conference in January of 1942. Before that there had been mass executions as well as more or less intentional massacres by overwork and poor conditions in the camps, but they were sporadic by comparison with what followed. Ironically, the largest part of the crime of genocide was carried out while German armies were in full retreat on every front. After El Alamein and Stalingrad, the German cause was militarily hopeless, and deliverance was only a matter of time. Yet during this period the Jewish population of Europe was very nearly wiped out.

In the region around Dabrowa, the rounding up of Jews was intermittent, and the policies of the Reich were carried out unevenly. *Private War*, a memoir by Dr. Eugene Lazowski, who saved many candidates for deportation by giving them injections that caused symptoms resembling typhus, described the conditions in the area centered in Rozwadow, only a few kilometers from Dabrowa. German policy was to use the area of Poland under the General Government to feed the Reich and its armies, while gradually starving the indigenous population. To this end, the Polish estates were placed in the hands of the German military under the Liegenschaft, and the best of the produce was administered through agricultural cooperatives under German control.

In the Rozwadow area, the estate belonging to Prince Jerzy Lubomirski was placed under the control of Oberleiter Martin Fuldner. A tall and imposing man, Fuldner with his wife and his son Horst moved into the Lubomirski "palace" in Charzewice and began replacing local stewards with reliable Volksdeutsche collaborators. Among the properties included in the Lubomirski estate was a sawmill, which had been operated before the war by a Mr. Liebeskind—the man whose apartment the Kosinskis now occupied. The apartments owned by Warchol and the similar building which housed the Migdaleks were known as the "sawmill houses."

While the overall policy of the Reich was to feed Germans and starve the Polish and Jewish "half-humans," there was also in this arrangement an element of profiteering and political reward. Fuldner was a committed Nazi—his family observed the ritual saluting of Hitler, and he replaced the portrait of a Lubomirski ancestor with a huge portrait of Hitler—but he also saw the governorship of the Rozwadow area as the route to his personal fortune.

Early in 1943, Mieczyslaw Kosinski began working on the staff of the center for agricultural levies in Dabrowa. His supervisor was one A. Treczko, another elegantly dressed and educated out-sider who had come to Dabrowa from Gdynia. Treczko talked Kosinski into going to work for him, or so the story went, and the two men were often seen discussing politics. The new employee was splendid help. He could do sums with astonishing speed, and without ever making a mistake. There was a combination of facility and reliability, to say nothing of managerial skill, with which the village was unacquainted.

To the villagers, the elder Kosinski's decision to go to work at the center was hard to understand. The pay was poor. The risks, or so it seemed to them, were great. By working there, he endangered the whole village. If he was found out, inquiries would be made, and Dabrowa might well be burned to the ground like Rzeczycka Dluga. They were quite conscious of his vulnerability. Short, bespectacled, subtly different from the natives, he fit too well one of the Nazi stereotypes for a Jew, albeit different from the stereotype embodied in his wife and son. Was it worthwhile to risk showing himself in public in order to take home pilfered potatoes and pockets full of wheat and rye?

To Mieczyslaw Kosinski—the same Moses Lewinkopf who had thought through the implications of the coming German occupa-tion in 1939—the risks would have looked very different. Having tested the waters during his first weeks in Dabrowa, he must have decided that the better odds—for himself, if not for his wife and son—lay in venturing out into the world. The trick was to be-come a part of the world's clutter—to hide himself and his family like Sherlock Holmes's famous Naval Treaty, right out in the open. After the initial roundups, like the one in Zaklikow in which the Liebeskinds died, seeking out of Jews was somewhat random. Besides, the center for agricultural levies was also the premier location in the region for receiving information, and in-formation was not only his chief tool for survival but, of course, his chief source of entertainment.

And there was one other factor that may have occurred to him. The German proclamation on the penalty for failing to report Jews had an ironic corollary. While it made the early days danger-ous in any new locale, it had the effect of binding into secrecy all those who knew of his presence for any period of time. For why hadn't they reported him immediately? In a sense, then, a large circle of contacts was a safeguard. If everyone in the village knew about him, the village itself had an interest in maintaining the secret. Only a man who thought the world through, upside down and inside out, could have used such logic; to reason thus, it was necessary to put oneself into the place of the peasants, to see the world as the peasants would see it. To employ such a strategy was to demonstrate extraordinary confidence in the power of one's own insights.

As a whole, the strategy worked wonderfully. It allied him with the powers that governed the area. A young coworker with a high-school education, Stefan Kochan, came home with him on occasion for a game of chess—the only game of chess he was likely to find in the area. The information-gathering purpose was also served admirably. Possession of a radio or underground newspaper—the only reliable news sources—was punishable by death. Yet Kochan watched on several occasions as the older Kosinski took out and unfolded a map, pointing with a long stick to explain the advance of the Soviet army. Once again he was readying himself to use information to stay a step ahead of the unfolding of events.

The nearest significant German garrisons were located in Rozwadow and Zaklikow, each about ten kilometers away, but in the normal course of events they had little reason to come to Dabrowa. There were Germans at the nearby railroad station and two guards at the railroad bridge across the San, but they were generally engaged in their specific tasks. Mieczyslaw Kosinski was hiding, in essence, under the curve of probability. Twice it seemed to have caught up with him.

On the first occasion, a group of Germans arrived to inquire about a warehouse that had burned. Although they were talking primarily to Treczko, a question was addressed to Kosinski, who answered in such beautiful German that the soldiers were startled. They began asking questions about his background, and he mumbled an answer. With other things on their minds, they let his answer pass.

The second time, a soldier with a large German shepherd walked straight up to him and began to interrogate him in a rough voice. This time he did not answer, but slumped down in his chair. The German had his hand on his holster. Suddenly, he turned and left. A moment later Mieczyslaw Kosinski also bolted. The following day, however, he was back at his desk.

One of the powerful associations Mieczyslaw Kosinski gained through work at the center was with Jozef Stepak, the administrator of Dabrowa and Kepa. He was able to help Stepak with the business aspects of his job, as well as with German documents. In return, Mrs. Stepak frequently sent him home with extra foodstuffs.

Three times in Stepak's company, there were close brushes with Germans. Once, visiting the Stepak family on the way home from church, the entire Kosinski family was trapped in the Stepak kitchen when Germans arrived to ask him a question. The Kosinskis froze. The Germans asked their question without so much as a look at the Kosinskis, then left. The context, sitting in the presence of the local administrator on a Sunday afternoon, had been enough.

The second occasion was a closer call. Kosinski was walking in Kepa with Stepak and Andrzej Warchol, his landlord, when a chaise drove past bearing Martin Fuldner himself. Fuldner jumped down from the chaise and asked the men where they were going.

Warchol, in halting German, explained truthfully that he had just bought some oats and was going home.

Fuldner then turned his attention to Kosinski, saying, *"Jude, Jude."* He pulled his pistol and trained it on Kosinski.

Warchol spoke up to say that Kosinski was not a Jew but the local teacher. Stepak confirmed the story.

"Then why isn't he at school?" Fuldner wanted to know.

There was a tense moment, but then Fuldner holstered the pistol. He got in the chaise and left.

Finally, in the summer of 1943, the Germans came to Dabrowa on a sweep for guerrillas. While other villagers hid in the nearby forest, the Kosinskis threw themselves on the mercy of the Stepaks. They were shown to the hayloft, but when Mieczyslaw Kosinski proved to be allergic to the hay, he was moved to the garden. Stepak met the Germans as the administrator, serving them soup and vodka. When two of the Germans stepped outside to urinate, the elder Kosinski, hiding behind a bush, had to control a powerful impulse to leap up and run. Trembling, he waited as they urinated only a few feet away.

At about the same time, on June 24, 1943, there occurred a German atrocity that stands out to this day in the history of the region—perhaps because it was committed against Polish Catholics and members of the lesser nobility. Invading the estate of Zbigniew Horodynski at Zbydniow on the evening following a wedding, an SS unit massacred the Horodynski family, the servants, and a number of wedding guests—twenty-one people in all.

The massacre was Fuldner's doing. By that time he had gained control of all the major Lubomirski properties on the pretext that they were not meeting production quotas. The Horodynskis, however, managed their estate efficiently and met their quotas; Zbydniow remained in their hands. A few days before the massacre a company of SS troopers had arrived at Fuldner's headquarters on rotation from the Russian front. At a dinner for the SS officers, a lavish affair at which drink flowed freely, Fuldner explained his difficulty in getting control of the estate of Zbydniow.

"Don't worry, Martin," the SS chief assured him, "it can be taken care of."

Coming upon the scene shortly after the massacre, an observer saw Fuldner himself holstering his pistol. Some time later, the conversation at Fuldner's dinner table, including the remark of the SS chief, was reported to agents of the Home Army by a Polish chambermaid who had concealed the fact that she understood German.

On October 13, 1943, while Mrs. Fuldner was out shopping, Home Army soldiers dressed in German uniforms arrived at the residence Fuldner had appropriated from the Lubomirskis. The Fuldners were serving as hosts to Fuldner's boss, Herr Weber, from Cracow. The Home Army soldiers gathered Fuldner, his son Horst, Weber, and the chambermaid into the living room. When they said, "Hands high," Weber thought it was a prank, but they soon conveyed their serious intent and ordered everyone to lie on the floor. The phone lines had been cut, and Home Army guerrillas controlled the front gate and grounds.

The partisans explained that they were present not merely to kill Germans but to carry out a sentence of the Polish Underground Court. Herr Weber, they said, would be their witness. They then read the sentence in Polish and German: Martin Fuldner, his wife, and his son were condemned to death. Fuldner and his son were shot on the spot. Mrs. Fuldner returned shortly in her carriage and was shot against the wall of the Lubomirski palace. Thus ended the career of the man who had trained his pistol on Mieczyslaw Kosinski.

The chambermaid and Herr Weber had been instructed to wait one hour before calling the Gestapo. Later, she reported her observations to her underground contact in full detail. She said that when she informed Weber the hour was up, he looked at his watch. "You are wrong," the terrified German cautioned her. "We have six more minutes to wait."

9.

The sort of exceptional good luck enjoyed by Mieczyslaw Kosinski would give rise, in later years, to speculation that he was somehow wired into the German occupiers. There were similar insinuations about his colleague Treczko, who was deemed too well dressed and educated for the region, and whose sudden appearance in Dabrowa was hard to explain. The speculation may have been connected to the practice by Fuldner of bringing in Volksdeutsche administrators from other parts of Poland. Evidence is lacking, however, and the character of Martin Fuldner does not make such insinuation very credible. He was an unscrupulous profiteer, certainly, but he was also a committed Nazi ideologue and unlikely to be party to a bargain with a Jew from Lodz.

The assassination of Martin Fuldner coincided with a new phase of the occupation. It was clear to everyone, occupier and occupied, that the final defeat of Germany was only a matter of time. The local German garrisons hunkered down in defensive posture, from which they constituted less of a threat, while the level of guerrilla activity steadily increased. At the same time, the tentative unity which had bound guerrillas of the Left and Right—and not a few bands of opportunistic thugs—now began to break down into a factional struggle for power in the postwar world.

As one of the poorest parts of Poland, the area surrounding Dabrowa had been marked before the war by its leftist sympathies. In nearby Wola, May Day was celebrated with parades and the display of red banners and the singing of the "Internationale." The sawmill of the Lubomirski estate, managed by the Liebeskind whose apartment the Kosinskis inherited, was bankrupted by recurring strikes. It is not surprising that the "red" guerrillas found the area fertile ground for recruitment.

Supporters of the red guerrillas were organized as the Polish Workers' Party (PPR), the name given to a combination of the old Polish Communist Party with the Union of Polish Patriots, a puppet organization of Polish exiles and Russians with polonized names set up by Stalin. The anticommunist "white" guerrillas generally belonged to the Home Army, a strongly nationalist group and also a formidable force, as evidenced by its successful raid taking vengeance for Zbydniow. By the spring of 1944, action against the Germans was becoming secondary as the two factions struggled for control of southeastern Poland. In that struggle, the previously soft-spoken Mieczyslaw Kosinski, who had always advocated the obscure unnoticed life, suddenly emerged as a man with strong views.

His sympathies were with the Left. This should not, perhaps, come as a surprise, as it reflected a pattern among Jewish Poles who had survived the occupation in the country. Most had done so by taking Gentile names and identities, which they kept at the end of the war. Along with the Gentile name came a shift from religious identity to identification with an ideal—supposedly standing outside of race and nationality—which promised to banish forever the sort of experience through which they had just passed. Many Jewish survivors, inspired by this ideal, participated in the two-year postwar struggle on the side of the Left and rose to prominent positions in the Communist Party, including the administration of the state security apparatus.

Whether the Marxist ideal was a significant motive for Mieczyslaw Kosinski is difficult to say. His son later gave two seemingly opposing versions of his father's politics: as a Jew "born in Russia" who had "escaped the Bolshevik Revolution" and as a professor with prewar socialist sympathies who knew early on that he would be a target of the Nazis. It is not impossible that both claims contain elements of the truth. Spotters for the Polish Workers' Party dispatched Michal Pawelec to recruit Kosinski, whom they described as "a leftist professor from Lodz." While he had hardly been a "leftist professor," he might well have combined his status as urbane businessman and "working intellectual" with socialist political sympathies. In any case, he joined the Party, which was to be the local vanguard for Polish Communism. His formal recruitment took place over a game of chess with one Stash Kolodziej, member of a well-off peasant family from nearby Wola.

As a newly recruited member of the PPR, Mieczyslaw Kosinski was given duties that included conducting lectures on the basic principles of Marxism for the barely literate foot soldiers of the party, as well as a special course to prepare them for the examination for the General Certificate of Secondary Education. Another task involved preparing a detailed plan for the breakup of the Charzewice agricultural estate. Although the actual breakup took place after the arrival of the Soviet army, his work in agrarian reform, as well as his work as teacher, was well received. In return he began to receive special protection from the PPR, which dispatched a courier to warn him when Germans were coming and added its own powers of intimidation to assure that none of the locals reported the presence of the Kosinskis.

The new leftist connection soon produced an alteration in the relationship between the Kosinskis and their neighbors, and with Andrzej Warchol, who had Home Army sympathies, in particular. The two men began with a more or less amiable exchange of propaganda leaflets for their respective parties. Soon, however, relations grew strained, resulting in accusations and counteraccusations, even threats. The Kosinskis no longer paid the rent,

Warchol accused, and he had caught Kosinski chopping up a portion of his fence for firewood. The disagreement finally erupted into a drunken shouting match, this time over some wood that Warchol had cut down and Kosinski had transported and sold. The quarrel ended with Warchol calling Kosinski a Jew and ordering him out of the apartment. Kosinski responded with threats of his own. Although the Kosinskis were not, in the end, forced to leave, the two men stopped speaking.

With others Kosinski argued in ways suggestive of his deeper motives for joining the PPR. The Home Army, he told the son of a Home Army officer on furlough, was pointless. It was swimming against the tide of history. The Russians were on their way, and it was Poland's fate to be under Soviet domination, whatever one's views. To Jan Pamula, whose father supported the Home Army and whose mother's strong Catholic beliefs were put on public display, he urged caution. In every argument, he argued against opposing the inevitable. The most important ideology was the pragmatic one: survival.

By this time the Soviet army was approaching Dabrowa. The Germans began to pull out, leaving the area to a division of Kalmuk cavalry. The Kalmuks were a pure Mongol race of nomads who had settled in Russia in the thirteenth century. Persecuted by Stalin because of their opposition to Communist authority, they had volunteered in large numbers for the army of the invading Germans. Even the Germans, however, blanched at the brutal scorched-earth tactics of the Kalmuk light horsemen, in particular their custom of killing prisoners. Now, with the German defeat, the Kalmuks were caught in a historical whipsaw, with no place to go.

In July of 1944 the retreating Kalmuks stopped over in the region, raping and pillaging in Rzeczycka Okragla and burning most of Rzeczycka Dluga. In Dabrowa, however, everyone fled to the nearby forest and remained there for several days, the Kosinskis among them. Although they stole food, the Kalmuks did not rape or burn in Dabrowa, and no one was killed. Young Jurek Kosinski did not witness personally the Kalmuk rampage, which he later described in *The Painted Bird*, although it is likely

that he saw individual Kalmuk cavalrymen, who had been operating in the general area under German regular army supervision
for some months.

On July 28, close on the heels of the retreating Kalmuks, the
Red Army entered Dabrowa. While much of the village again retreated to the woods, Mieczyslaw Kosinski and his family stayed,
along with the red partisans, to greet the Russians. They bore
welcoming red banners and hammer-and-sickle emblems—and
Henryk Kosinski, now all of four years old, wore a Red Army
uniform complete to field cap with red star and an automatic pistol carved out of wood. Once again it is little Henio, the younger
adoptive brother, whose experience parallels that of the boy in
The Painted Bird. Separated from his parents at the place of the
novel's beginning, he has now become, like the boy of the story,
the mascot of the Soviet regiment.

In the Kosinski household life took a marked turn for the better. The NKVD officers traveling with the front-line unit—better
educated, as members of the state security apparatus were prone
to be—were aware of Mieczyslaw Kosinski's sympathies, and
made use of him as a translator. Settling into the main Warchol
house, they shared food with the Kosinskis and drank into the
evenings with Mieczyslaw. When it came to organizing a civic administration under Soviet rule, it was natural that they should
turn to this established PPR member whose Russian was as flawless as their own. His influence in the new order is clear from instances when he was called to adjudicate, in one case vouching
for a harmless teenager who had hidden an illegal weapon.

With the arrival of the Red Army, the wartime ordeal of the
Kosinski family was drawing to a close. Ironically, their deliverance coincided almost exactly with the final destruction of the
Lodz (or Litzmannstadt) Ghetto. The Jews of Lodz had responded
to the German occupation in a unique and controversial way.
Chaim Rumkowski, who was given absolute power as Jewish "elder" by the Germans, had implemented a policy of survival by
collaboration, meeting German quotas for deportation by offering
up first the elderly and ill, and then children. As a result, it was
the last major group of Polish Jews not yet sent to death camps,

and a significant number might have survived had not the Red Army paused in its advance to allow the destruction of Warsaw.

In the summer of 1944 the highest levels of the Nazi administration decided to liquidate the ghetto. Despite the opposition of Albert Speer, who argued that the ghetto should be preserved because of its continuing contribution to the German war effort, the final 80,000 Jews of Lodz were deported to Auschwitz in August. About a thousand remained to dismantle the plants and machinery where they had worked, and were saved by the arrival of the Red Army. With one exception, a cousin who emigrated to Israel, every member of the extensive Lewinkopf-Weinreich family—more than sixty at their last family reunion in 1938—had perished.

10.

Jerzy Nikodem Kosinski—the name by which he would henceforth be known—had survived the war. Up to this point, his experience was that of a small bit of human flotsam on the vast tides of history. In the face of great geopolitical forces, even strong and resourceful adults had discovered the limitations of human power to influence events. To a sensitive child, capable of grasping, intuitively if not always intellectually, the extreme weakness of his position, this situation might have carried powerful imperatives.

Of the violent scenes that conclude *The Painted Bird*, there is no evidence that either of the revenge episodes carried out by others—the slaughter of the Kalmuks or the vengeance of the Russian sniper upon the villagers—actually took place. Nor is there any factual account of a train wreck like that attributed to "the Silent One." Yet Kosinski's fictional accounts attest to his pent-up anger and sense of powerlessness.

At the same time, a new theme was emerging in his life. Among the Soviet liberators, two soldiers took an interest in young Kosinski—an enlisted man named Mitka, who represented anarchic individualism combined with the high technical skill of a sniper, and a senior political officer named Gavrila. With these two, Kosinski seems to have begun the young man's process of sorting through father figures—seeking mentors whose values and attributes improve upon the original.

In *The Painted Bird* the character named Gavrila, drawn from his real-life namesake, explains Marxist doctrine to the boy. From him the boy learns that God does not exist but is a fabrication of the priests to control the superstitious peasants. Men control their own lives, and their actions add up to a pattern that can be discerned only by those at the summit of society. Occasionally, however, a wise and great man assumes a leadership position. The model for such a man is Stalin, who in portraits and photographs has "a kind face and compassionate eyes." Looking at the pictures of Stalin, the boy sees his own "very black, bushy hair, dark eyes, heavy eyebrows, and later even a black mustache. He looked more of a Gypsy than I did, more Jewish than the Jew killed by the German officer in the black uniform, more Jewish than the boy found by the peasants on the railroad tracks." Thus in Gavrila—and especially in Gavrila's own hero, Stalin—the preadolescent Jurek Kosinski found the image of a father who not only seemed to embody the best values, but in whom he could recognize superficial aspects of himself.

It is perhaps not surprising that an eleven-year-old boy might prefer to attach his power fantasies to an officer of the conquering Red Army. Later he told the story that Gavrila wished to adopt him and had given him up only reluctantly, in accordance with strict army policy. The story, which is tied to a broader fictionalization of that period in his life, is almost certainly apocryphal, but at a psychological level it is both moving and revealing. As a fantasy father, Gavrila fit perfectly with a young boy's desperate need to triumph—to reverse his status as everyone's victim—a need that would become the major revenge motif in his writing. Ironically, of course, the practical role model for an applied version of those fantasies was present all the time, never more than a short distance away, often in the same bedroom. The helplessness of childhood does not lend itself to full appreciation of the qualities or accomplishments of one's parents. While the young Jerzy Kosinski watched helplessly, Moses Lewinkopf expressed himself in immediate and effective actions, not always in ways that a small boy could admire or even understand, but with resolve, cunning and toughmindedness that he could hardly miss. For the ability to make an extreme response to an extreme situation, Kosinski needed to look no farther than his own father, who had, in a real sense, triumphed over his personal pharaoh.

In incalculable ways, his father would always be a primary and troubling model in his life. It would be a mistake, however, to underestimate the importance of the two other distant but powerful male figures of his childhood and youth. Identification with one's victimizer is a well-established pattern observed in survivors. Both happened to be creators, artists who painted upon a canvas of human misery. The painter of birds is a metaphor for that artist, whose handiwork is to project his own sadness and insufficiency onto others. His immediate prototype was the feebleminded birdcatcher Lech Tracz, but the true creative reshaper of Kosinski's personal experience, who stood in relation to villagers and soldiers as Lech to the flock of birds, was Adolf Hitler.

Set in opposition to Hitler was Stalin, whose true colors, in 1944, had not yet become clear. While Kosinski's everyday life for twenty years involved a struggle against first one and then the other, their methods and values quietly imprinted themselves on his psyche. Both were self-invented, renamed men. Both were ruthless in their pursuit of personal destiny. Both were powerful reshapers of the world around them, however ill-conceived their plots. And both saw the truth as malleable. Truth was not an absolute entity, but whatever version they could make stick. Truth was whatever worked for them—the reality that served their goals and their myths. They were both, in that sense, born storytellers.

Though their war ended with liberation by the Red Army in July of 1944, the Kosinskis were not yet quite out of the woods. In the immediate aftermath of World War II the situation in many parts of rural Poland was extremely fluid. The ultimate triumph of the Communists may appear in hindsight a foregone conclusion—with the victorious Red Army in place to enforce Stalin's

will upon a defeated and newly liberated populace—but at
ground level the outcome seemed, to many Poles, very much in
doubt. As the Polish Workers' Party, under the leadership of
Wladyslaw Gomulka, moved to consolidate power, the situation
in parts of the countryside approached a state of civil war.

At the outset this made Mieczyslaw Kosinski a more important
figure in Dabrowa, and Jerzy Kosinski again found himself a
child of privilege. The PPR, gaining the upper hand under the
umbrella of the Red Army, began carrying out reprisals against
the Home Army, while the Soviet political officers undertook the
task of rooting out future opponents of the regime. Among those
targeted were Andrzej Warchol, the Kosinskis' landlord, and Jozef
Stepak, the administrator from Kepa who had faced down
Fuldner and hidden the Kosinskis in his hayloft.

Both Warchol and Stepak were associated with the wealthier,
and therefore more recalcitrant, class of peasants. Warchol was
beaten by leftist guerrillas, grazed by a bullet, and left in a
creekbed for dead. Official arrests soon followed, on charges of
collaboration or hoarding, with the Home Army partisans as primary targets. As a man whose work had given him detailed
knowledge of commerce in the village, yet an outsider without
long-standing personal axes to grind, Mieczyslaw Kosinski was a
central informant in the Soviet "cleansing." He apparently tried
to warn Warchol of coming arrest, to no avail.

Stepak was arrested, sentenced, and sent to Siberia, where he
died in a prison camp. Warchol was arrested and held locally for
a year and a half awaiting trial, then acquitted and released. The
weight of the evidence is that Mieczyslaw played a constructive
role in Warchol's case, although it is impossible to be certain. In
any case, Mieczyslaw Kosinski had once again become a marked
man. He was put under sentence of death by the nationalist guerrillas, and an assassin was dispatched to Dabrowa.

On the night of April 28, 1945, a group of armed men smashed
in the door of the Kosinskis' apartment, rousting the children,
Elzbieta, and the nanny Katarzyna from bed. They searched, but
failed to find the elder Kosinski, who had left for a few days to
perform a reconnaissance of Lodz. The next morning Elzbieta

Kosinska met her husband at the train station in Kepa and explained what had happened. Sending her home to pack, he rushed to borrow a horse and cart from a neighbor. Quickly gathering their worldly possessions into suitcases and bundles, the Kosinskis drove the cart to Rozwadow. The next day, they took the train for Lodz.

II

ASPIRANT

1.

It was a grim homecoming. The Lodz that the Kosinskis had known—a center for Jewish writers, artists, and "working intelligentsia"—was gone forever. Moreover, they were still at risk. Mieczyslaw Kosinski was known as a "leftist professor from Lodz," and it was not so far from Dabrowa to Lodz that he could not be tracked down, if anyone really wished to do so. One day at the railroad station he bumped into Rysiek Bogucki, from Rzeczycka Okragla, whom he had met when working at the marketplace in Kepa. Was it an accident, or had Bogucki been dispatched to hunt him down?

It was clear that Lodz in 1945 was too hot for a family associated with pro-Soviet partisans. At the same time, a solution beckoned. In redrawing the map at the conclusion of the war, the victorious Allies shifted the borders of Poland westward: the Soviet Union appropriated much of the territory lying to the east of Lublin, while the Poles were compensated at the expense of Germany with the portion of prewar Germany that lay east of the Oder and Neisse rivers, including Silesia. In these "new territories," property formerly held by German nationals was forfeit, and the new Polish government set out to resettle the area with ethnic Poles. Much of the population of Lvov, which was annexed by the Soviets, was moved some three hundred miles west to

Wroclaw (formerly Breslau), while the German population was pushed into Germany.

The resettlement of the population of Lvov was forced, but for persons who stood well with the new powers in Warsaw, the area around Wroclaw was a land of opportunity not unlike the American frontier—a land of abundant resources seemingly open for the taking—with the added inducement that decent housing and fully equipped factories were, to a degree, already in place. In Jelenia Gora, fifteen miles west of Wroclaw and near both the Czech and German borders, the Kosinskis were given a well-appointed house, while Mieczyslaw Kosinski was assigned to be transitional manager of a local company.

Jerzy Kosinski drew upon this experience in *Cockpit*, his fifth novel. "When I was twelve," he wrote, "the new government uprooted hundreds of thousands of families, my own included, and resettled them in recently annexed territories along the new border. None of the resettled families was allowed to take anything except minimal personal belongings; they had to leave behind homes full of furniture and objects collected over the years, and move across the country into households furnished with objects that others had been forced to abandon." The anecdote develops into a revenge drama as the young protagonist, upset at the forced move (based on the Kosinskis' subsequent move back to Lodz) and his father's acquiescence, impersonates an official and sends unsuspecting residents on pointless expeditions to Warsaw for nonexistent resettlement documents.

The account of resettlement was grounded in historical fact, but it hardly described the situation of the Kosinskis, for whom relocation in Jelenia Gora was both a matter of choice and the closest thing possible under postwar conditions to a restoration of their status before the war.

The image of leaving behind "homes full of furniture and objects collected over the years" is an interesting one. It seems unlikely that, after five years of German and then Soviet occupation, the house on Gdanska Street in Lodz would have contained much in the way of family treasures. The abandoned property collected over the years had been irretrievably lost in 1939, although to a child's mind it may have been the move to Jelenia Gora in February 1946 that sealed forever the loss of an Edenic past. What was lost to the Germans was more than a collection of familiar household objects, it was childhood itself, as exemplified by family days in 1939 on the beach at Sopot. The physical removal to yet another unfamiliar setting confirmed the wistful lament of Thomas Wolfe, in this case politically and historically buttressed, that you can't go home again.

Not that life in Jelenia Gora was without its inducements. Mieczyslaw Kosinski was now an honored apparatchik—a member of what Milovan Djilas was to label "the new class"—and he was awarded such perks as a car and driver. As a son of the managerial class, thirteen-year-old Jurek was given skiing lessons in the nearby Karkonosze Mountains—the beginning of a lifelong passion. After a period of private tutoring, he was enrolled in the local gymnasium, his first formal schooling worthy of the name. Suddenly he found himself thrust into a simulacrum of normal early adolescence.

Life was not, however, so easily made normal. Later Kosinski claimed that he had spent part of the immediate postwar years in a hospital; in other versions, it was not a hospital, but a reform school, a special school for the handicapped, or a school for the deaf. The public record says otherwise, but these melodramatic claims no doubt embody an inner truth. He frequently had nightmares and woke up screaming, the nightmares persisting, according to friends with whom he spent ski outings, all the way into the 1950s.

The Painted Bird, among other sources, gives an account of behavior which was antisocial and sometimes bordered on the sociopathic. It describes, for example, his sneaking out at night to wander the streets—the beginning of a lifelong predilection. Though the novel places these night wanderings in the early days after liberation, they actually began in Jelenia Gora, where they are accurately placed by oblique reference in his later novel *Blind Date*. Nor can these night excursions have been, as *The Painted Bird* suggests, a continuation of the wild freedom of his war years; they must have been rather a desperate response to years of being cooped up.

Jerzy Kosinski had been, from an early age, a difficult child, from whom his mother had difficulty in compelling obedience; this accounted for her determination to farm him out to teachers and nannies, even under the straitened conditions of the occupation. At home, under an ordinary domestic regime, he continued to be difficult. There was additionally, in Jelenia Gora, a growing conflict with his father, whose nuggets of worldly wisdom and advice were increasingly unwelcome. There is a thin line between a wise aphoristic consigliere and a meddlesome platitudinous Polonius. Mieczyslaw Kosinski seemed more and more often to have crossed that line, at least in the eyes of his son, who responded with predictable surliness. In the eyes of the adults who knew him, the boy simply had a mean streak. The next-to-last chapter of *The Painted Bird* recounts an episode in which the boy, reunited with his family, breaks the arm of his new brother. Henryk Kosinski denies that his older brother actually broke his arm, but others recall that one of the purposes in hiring a live-in nanny, Anna Grzelak, who was to take care of both boys throughout their childhoods, was to prevent him from doing harm to Henryk. A witness to so much violence, while he himself was compelled to self-restraint, Kosinski now bore within him the seeds of the imaginative revenge dramas he would one day create.

Among the friends Kosinski made in Jelenia Gora was Jerzy Urban, whose family had had a similar wartime history. The Urbans were also Jews from Lodz, and like the Kosinskis they had gone to ground in the countryside and managed to survive the Nazi occupation. The elder Urban had been a political leftist even before the war and, like the elder Kosinski, emerged from the war as a trusted Communist functionary. Sharing so much, the two fathers became close friends.

The young Urban was short, round-faced, and chubby—in every way the antithesis of Jurek Kosinski, who was by then beginning to develop the distinctive gaunt and beaky look that captivated American television audiences. Urban's most distinctive feature—the counterpart of Kosinski's extraordinary nose—was a pair of ears that made him, as an adult, resemble a well-fed leprechaun. Yet Urban's clownlike exterior masked exceptional shrewdness. He would have three separate, if related, careers:

first as one of the most respected journalists in Marxist Poland, then as the hated spokesman and symbol for General Jaruzelski's martial-law regime, and finally as founder and publisher of *NIE!*, a spectacularly successful weekly tabloid which became required reading for the hip and well informed of the new capitalist Poland. Although he chose to remain in Poland, Urban's ideological flexibility and his propensity for landing on his feet match in some measure the more flamboyant career turns of his friend Kosinski. The contacts between the two boys were not close enough for a deep friendship to form—they were slightly different in age, and would see each other only occasionally later in Lodz—but a couple of incidents suggest the nature of the bond that would enable them to meet as friends, forty years later, though on different sides of an important ideological divide.

The first occurred when Urban ran away from a ski camp to which his parents had sent him in the Tatras at the age of twelve. Urban made his way to the Kosinskis' house at 9 Wyspianskiego in Jelenia Gora and settled in with them for two weeks to hide while his parents looked for him. It is not known how soon the Kosinskis notified the Urbans, but their handling of the situation seems to have provoked no enduring ill will. Later, when both families had moved back to Lodz, the two mothers became close friends; it was, in fact, Mrs. Urban who, in 1972, performed the burial preparations for Elzbieta Kosinska.

The second incident took place on a car trip from Jelenia Gora to Warsaw. The two men, Kosinski and Urban, both had business there, and they had taken the boys along to see the capital. Somewhere on the road they were stopped by "white" guerrillas, probably a vestigial unit of the Home Army, who were making a final thrust of counterrevolutionary terrorism against the victorious Communists. Fathers and sons alike sat in the car and trembled as the guerrillas looked over their documents. Finally the guerrilla leader returned the documents and waved them on. Perhaps they were looking for someone else, someone specific. Nevertheless, had they realized the position of the men in the car, the senior Kosinski and Urban would almost certainly have been shot on the spot.

The elections of 1947 brought an effective end to this sort of guerrilla activity. The "Democratic Bloc"—an alliance of Communists and socialists—won a decisive victory, and Poland was locked firmly into the new Stalinist Eastern Europe. The pressures of the emerging Cold War would seal that position for two generations. With the end of the transitional period, the Kosinski family made the decision to return to Lodz. There was no longer anything to fear from organized rightist assassins. Moreover, weakened by wartime stress and privation, Mieczyslaw Kosinski, now a man of fifty-six, had suffered the first of a number of heart attacks. The return to Lodz meant his effective retirement, and he was ready for it.

The terms of this second resettlement are recapitulated in the episode from *Cockpit*. For agreeing to give up all claims to their prewar house, the Kosinskis received a new residence, complete with someone else's furnishings. In the episode, it is the son who receives the news by telephone and informs his father: "I gave my father the message after he returned from work. I expected him to be unhappy. The government was forcing him to abandon all hope of going back to the place where he had lived all his life. But he was delighted we would not have to resettle again. He no longer seemed to mind living among unfamiliar paintings, ugly, heavy furniture, and some stranger's bric-a-brac, using silverware with strange monograms. Only a few months earlier, he had labeled the leader of the new government a Party puppet, accusing him of condoning the deaths of countless people, including my aunts and uncles. Now, he spoke impassively of the dead as victims of impersonal Party bureaucracy. My mother remarked that the most important thing was once again having a home where she and my father could raise me as a civilized human being."

Civilizing him was not to be so easy. Out of the cage at last, he had gotten a whiff of freedom and possibility, and his experiences had provided more than a whiff of unusual pleasures. He had, after all, firsthand experience of human cruelty.

His old playmates Ewka and Andrezj ("Bumek") Migdalek— the next-door neighbors' children during the Kosinskis' stay at the Warchols'—had left Dabrowa for Rzeszow, then returned to live successively in the small villages of Szeroka and Jastrzebie. One day, to their astonishment, a letter arrived addressed to the "own hands of Bumek and Ewa." It called them a series of dirty names—wicked, sexual, suggestive names—and warned them that they should toe the line or be turned over to the UB, the Polish secret police. It boasted of knowledge of secret things, as if the writer had high Party connections. The letter was several pages long, but sparse in a way, with big spaces between words, and written in flawless adult language. Its author was Jerzy Kosinski.

2.

Upon their return to Lodz in May 1947, the Kosinskis settled into a villa with a garden at 4 Strzelczyka (also called Senatorska) Street. By the terms under which they held the villa, there were other tenants at times, in sections with separate access, but by the standards of the time it afforded a considerable amount of privacy. Spacious and comfortable, their new house had been before the war the home of an industrial manager, and it stood among rather palatial houses formerly occupied by important factory owners, though the typically mixed Lodz neighborhood also contained worker housing and factories themselves. (Today it houses a government social service agency.)

Through their years at 4 Strzelczyka, the Kosinskis had a live-in servant and enjoyed a comfortable lifestyle, thanks in part to the fact that Mieczyslaw Kosinski's income as a pensioner was supplemented by his wife's new job. Elzbieta Kosinska had found work as a clerk in the prosecutor's office, a position that capitalized on, and could only solidify, the family's Party connection. Jurek Kosinski, now a teenager, attended School #3 of the Association of Friends of the Children, a combination gymnasium and lycée of the European type, combining the upper level of grade school with high school. The high school was named in honor of Stefan Zeromski (1864–1925), the nationalist Polish novelist who spent much of his life in exile. At Stefan Zeromski, Kosinski passed three relatively normal high-school years punctuated by a few isolated episodes that suggested the controversial life to come.

One of these had to do with ZMP, the Union of Youth of Poland (the youth organization of the Party), from which Kosinski was expelled on June 24, 1949. The official record states that "in the presence of fifty-seven members colleague Kosinski was removed from the group for having taken a political attitude which is adverse to our organization." It was his first brush with state authority in the form of its youth organ, but not the last, and as in each subsequent case, the cause of the conflict is a subject of debate.

The charges against Kosinski included claims that he aspired to "an imperialist American lifestyle" and "was hostile toward the socialist reality and questioned the authority of our political leaders." Some attribute the expulsion to an insert he edited, entitled *This and That Among the Humanists,* for a school paper called *The World Is Moving Forward.* One may well imagine its content. To an exceptionally egocentric and individualistic teenager who had spent his preteen years in a virtual cage, both the ideal and the reality of Marxism must certainly have seemed a world moving backward.

Yet others who knew him at the time saw his expulsion from the ZMP as a matter not so much of content as of style. Each member of the ZMP was required to wear a white shirt and red tie, signifying submission and loyalty to the ideal. It happened that Kosinski, who was chicken-breasted, was issued too wide a shirt, and rather than be mocked passively, he exacerbated its ridiculous fit, walking bent over like an ape. Still others remember that he flouted the dress code at the margins, wearing multicolored socks with a pattern. Although the design of one's socks was not specifically prescribed, it was seen as an expression of individuality—a political statement—to stand out in this way.

Perhaps Kosinski's expulsion from the ZMP resulted from an accumulation of transgressions, both intellectual and cultural. It was, in any case, no light matter. Approval from the ZMP was one of the necessary conditions for admission to university, and Kosinski had created a hurdle for himself by the end of his junior year in high school. His anger and frustration amidst the enforced conformity of newly Marxist Poland would be expressed later in several of his novels, most notably in *Steps,* as well as in the two nonfiction books on collective behavior published under the nom de plume of Joseph Novak. Its fullest expression, however, may have been the overall strategy he developed for living his life.

Yet Kosinski's life at Stefan Zeromski High School was not constituted wholly of revolt against collective society. Political struggle was only a part of his high-school experience, and a minor part at that. His closest friend was Stanislaw Pomorski, who prefigured Kosinski's tendency over the years to have always in his life one or two associates who were without artistic or intellectual bent. He and Stash sat generally in adjacent desks in the second row, behind the teacher's pets but far in front of the back-row hooligans and incorrigibles. It was with Pomorski that Kosinski, a camera around his neck, took daily after-school strolls down the "promenade," the section of the city's main street that was the center of social life for the young, and it was to Stash Pomorski that Kosinski gave occasional glimpses of his more private character and his dreams for the future.

Poland was afflicted in that period by an epidemic of petty thuggery, which authorities at once denied and attempted to eradicate. Street gangs virtually reigned in whole sections of the major cities, as chronicled by Leopold Tyrmand in *Zly* (The Bad One; 1954). One of their shakedown techniques was to send out a child of seven or so to give their victim a kick in the shins; when the victim turned on the child, the gang members would emerge to rob him and deliver a terrific beating. Every teenager was victimized in this way over and over with the exception of Kosinski, who, as Pomorski recalls, could talk his way out of even the most dire situation. His honey-tongued performances saved him in every instance but one, when the beating was administered before Kosinski had a chance to open his mouth.

In fact, Kosinski seemed to have an almost preternatural sense of danger—the same sense, perhaps, that would in later years get him through night-crawling in New York neighborhoods in which friends feared for his life. The two boys vacationed together regularly in Jelenia Gora, with its ready access to mountains, and on one mountaineering occasion Pomorski suggested they explore a mineshaft that appeared to hold interesting artifacts. Kosinski said a firm "no," and their landlady told them on their return that the mineshaft contained uranium, and a visit there would have bought a quick ticket to Siberia.

On another trek in the Tatras, Pomorski became separated from Kosinski and strayed across the Czech border. Being without documents, he was arrested immediately, even though he had violated the border by only a few meters, and he fully expected to spend a long period in a Czech jail. The next day, however, Kosinski arrived with the papers necessary for his release. For the rest of their years together, Pomorski would wonder how Kosinski came to know the situation and the place where he was held. Kosinski himself never explained.

It was also while he was best friends with Pomorski that Kosinski began his lifelong pursuit of women. Pomorski envied the hypnotic impact Kosinski could have on people, women especially, just by talking. After fifteen minutes with him, people felt they had known him all their lives. Girls would pour out their hearts, tell him their intimate secrets, share with him their most treasured selves. Why? Kosinski hadn't the slightest trouble talking girls into bed, often using the device of taking photographs as part of his modus operandi. What was the trick of this thin, physically unimposing man? Was that how he had gotten through the experiences he described from the war?

To Pomorski, a clue lay in Kosinski's preoccupation with another young man, a hairdresser only five feet tall but, according to the story, with a penis that, in Pomorski's hyperbolic language, hung to his knees, and consequently in great demand among women. Kosinski often referred to this hairdresser, concerned that his own more modest manhood was not competitive. To overcome this handicap, he studied to make the most of what he had. He explained his technique. A diligent student, he worked tirelessly to perfect his English. In bed with one of his conquests, he would repeat English words he was adding to his vocabulary.

Whatever his talents as a lover, Kosinski soon displayed extraordinary gifts as a *seducer*. Pomorski marveled at the rapidity with which his friend could talk the young high-school girls out of their clothes. And he had already learned some of the uses to which such a skill could be put. Once before leaving for two weeks in Warsaw, he bet Pomorski that he could manage to meet a number of top officials of the Party. Pomorski took the bet, believing such an accomplishment to be impossible. But Kosinski managed it, and he returned with proof—photos showing himself with Cyrankiewicz and even Marshal Rokossowski. He explained to Pomorski that his technique was very simple: meet the official's secretary, send her flowers, and visit her flat. The rest was easily arranged. Possibly the meetings had been helped along by his father's friends in the Party, but Pomorski, at least, was mightily impressed by his stories.

About his war experiences Kosinski had a tendency to be vague, as well as a propensity for mixing up things that happened to others with things that happened to him. This much, however, was well known to everyone of his acquaintance: he didn't like water and he didn't like dogs, especially German shepherds. He gave large dogs a wide berth but abused small ones, including Pomorski's, which he pinched around the eyes whenever he saw it. In Pomorski's view, those pinches were the reason the dog eventually got cancer.

One day Kosinski came running up to Pomorski with a book in his hand. It was, he told Pomorski, his favorite book, "one of the best books ever written." He insisted that Pomorski read it and share in his enthusiasm. Pomorski had never seen his friend so excited, although the book itself was neither a grand work of literature nor an obscure work just discovered. It was, in fact, a prewar bestseller—a *brukowiec,* in the Polish expression, meaning a first-rate second-class book. It was a novel by Tadeusz Dolega-Mostowicz entitled *The Career of Nikodem Dyzma.*

A down-on-his-luck small-town postal clerk, Nikodem Dyzma, comes to Warsaw seeking his fortune. Unable to get a job as a dancer in a club, he stumbles upon a lost letter with an invitation to a reception at the Europejski, and, assured that no one checks the guests as they arrive, he dons his performer's tux and joins the crowd. He is, after all, half starved, and there will be an unlimited supply of free food. At every stage he is ridden with tension, but as no one seems to notice him, he goes ahead. He fills his plate and takes it to a quiet place to eat, but someone bumps him, making him spill the food. Outraged and still hungry,

Dyzma loudly reprimands the man—who turns out to be an important, but boorish, official who is universally feared and hated.

Suddenly Dyzma is the hero of the occasion. As people congratulate him on his courage, he makes simpleminded responses, which are taken as ironic wisdom and brilliant jokes. An old man who has watched everything approaches him. Dyzma is at first terrified that he has been found out, but the old man, a businessman in the railroad-tie trade, only wants an introduction to an official who has just spoken with Dyzma. He offers Dyzma a bribe. Dyzma insists that he cannot make the introduction, but no sooner are the words out of his mouth than the official walks past and the introduction is routinely effected.

With the sponsorship of the old man and his young wife, Dyzma's career rapidly takes off. He moves in with the old man, takes over the young wife, and upon the old man's death rises in such influence and eminence that he is the chief candidate for prime minister.

The Career of Nikodem Dyzma is a playful turn on a very basic plot: a young man from the provinces, of no particular background, makes it to the top with the help of sympathetic women. A far smaller figure than Julien Sorel, he nevertheless exemplifies the giddy sense of fraudulence that often accompanies the ascent of self-made men. To Kosinski, however, the book was far more than a work of literature. It was more on the order of a blueprint, a plan of action for life. He assured Stash Pomorski of his intention to follow in the footsteps of Nikodem Dyzma, who bore, after all, his own uncommon middle name.

How, Pomorski wondered, was he going to pull it off?

He would marry a rich Swedish woman, Kosinski replied.

And how would he manage that?

Kosinski said he would accomplish something that would impress such a woman.

Thus the accusation, years later, that Kosinski's *Being There* had plagiarized *Nikodem Dyzma* missed a complicating intermediate step. It was one of those instances that demonstrate how intricately entangled are art and life, especially when the artist is Jerzy Kosinski; not only does art imitate art, but art and life imitate each other. By the time he came to write *Being There*, Kosinski was, in a sense, drawing upon his own experience, an altogether legitimate enterprise.

In *The Career of Nikodem Dyzma*, Dolega-Mostowicz had given young Jerzy Kosinski a model and a strategy for getting along and getting ahead in the world. He would pursue that strategy on two parallel tracks, the one scholarly, the other creative.

3.

Lodz, in the year 1950, was indisputably the most exciting place in Poland for an individual of creative bent. If it was no longer a city of theater, the symphony, and a "working intelligentsia"—these being the product of a Jewish population that had largely been destroyed—it was something quite as good, and perhaps better, though in a very different way.

Creative and bohemian life in postwar Lodz had two overlapping centers, cafe society and the film school. As a high-school student, Kosinski with his crowd of friends frequented the various cafes on or near the "promenade"—the Egzotyczna, the Grandka, which was the coffeeshop of the Grand Hotel, and even the "fireplace room" of the local YMCA, where one could play Western jazz records. Indeed, jazz—the "forbidden music"—served Polish youth of 1950 much as it had served its black American creators: as both a personal diversion and a form of subterranean cultural protest against what they saw as a stultifying official culture. Some clubs featured live jazz performances, and their smoky, sexual atmosphere carried a message for which the puritanical values and monumental art of Marxist officialdom were an ideal foil.

And Marxist officialdom was not the only authority to which jazz served as protest. Mieczyslaw Kosinski, with his roots in the old Lodz of elite culture and "working intelligentsia," did not see the virtues of the new cultural era. One night as Jerzy was leaving, he asked where his son was going.

"Honoratka," was the answer.

To which the elder Kosinski responded: "Nothing clever was ever said in a cafe."

It was the classic parental response to the cultural revolt of youth and, naturally, it made cafe life all the more attractive. By then, the uneasy rivalry between the two Kosinski males periodically broke into open conflict, with shouting tirades that sometimes led to actual shoving and wrestling matches. Mieczyslaw Kosinski had a temper, and had once in a rage slashed some of his wife's dresses as they hung in the closet; yet on occasion, the elder Kosinski hid in that same closet from his angry son.

By and large, the father's view seems to have been that his son was too flamboyant, that he lacked discipline and sustained application to intellectual tasks. He may have had trouble, too, with the constant parade of girlfriends. There is a poignant scene in *Passion Play* in which the teenage son, in an apartment that closely resembles the Kosinskis' living arrangements at 4 Senatorska, makes his way back to his room one morning from a tryst with the simple factory girl who has taken the apartment across the hall. He is barefoot, and naked beneath his raincoat. The father looks at his son anxiously, pulls him close enough that the boy can feel the stubble of his father's cheek, and pats his head to see if it is wet. "Thank God it isn't raining," he says. "On a night like this, you went out only in a raincoat? Not even a hat and scarf?"

"All my father saw was what he wanted to see," the boy, grown up, tells a woman friend. In the larger sense it was a testament to the determination of both father and son to manage their private detente—a "peaceful coexistence" within the household—despite a vast temperamental difference. The son's preferences, however, were not to be discouraged.

"There is nothing wrong with cafes," Kosinski would continue the argument almost forty years later. Citing Poland as the location of the "most enjoyable cafes full of life," he added, "Such cafes are not to be found anywhere else in the world. I speak from experience; after all, I am a cafe person. The cafe is a very important element of culture."

Honoratka, the cafe which both incited father-son conflict and inspired Kosinski's retrospective paean, was founded in 1950 by a couple remembered only as Boleslaw and Stefania, and quickly surpassed all rivals as the place for Lodz bohemians to assemble. Without alcohol or music, it served coffee, cranberry juice, and Stefania's apple pie and cheesecake. But it was somehow *the* place to go, especially for students and masters at the newly important film school. The great Wajda held court there. Other regulars included Jerzy Grohman, Andrzej Kern, Jerzy Passendorfer, Wojtek Frykowski and his future wife Ewa, the trumpeter and novelist-to-be Andrzej Mackowiecki, and an aspiring young film student named Romek Polanski.

The national film school had been instituted by the authorities at the end of the war because of the importance Leninist doctrine placed upon film, and its great influence was the Russian realism of Eisenstein. It owed its location in Lodz to the virtual destruction of Warsaw by the Germans, and by the early 1950s film had replaced textile manufacture as the signatory industry of the city. In a society where the national academy and the center of action—theory and practice—were one, it was a magnet for the nation's best, who came also spurred by the possibility of seeing forbidden Western films, and for free.

Kosinski and Polanski knew each other slightly in their Honoratka days, although their meeting, which occurred when Polanski came to take the examinations for admission to the film school in 1950, tells something of the character of both young men. Kosinski never wore slacks with a simple sweater or jacket, believing that his high waist was an unattractive feature. Always meticulous about his appearance, he instead affected full suits. Spotting him across the room, Polanski walked over and threw a full cup of tea on Kosinski's suit.

"Why did you do that?" Kosinski asked.

"Because I wanted to figure out how someone as well organized as you would react," Polanski replied.

It would make for a more charming story if the encounter had turned out to be the beginning of a deep friendship, but in reality Kosinski and Polanski were men whose lives would cross briefly and occasionally—and on occasion narrowly fail to cross—until the joint status of hometown-boys-made-good brought them into slightly more frequent contact. In the early Honoratka days, both were outsiders looking in, but with a difference. Polanski was already edging his way to the center as one of the original minds among Polish filmmakers. Kosinski, to his chagrin, remained outside the circle, a hanger-on with a camera strung around his neck, still looking for his opening.

An opening of sorts came in his association with Jerzy Neugebauer, another young still-photographer from his set in Lodz. They met at a showing of Neugebauer's work in the gallery of the Photographic Society of Lodz. After the lecture, Kosinski approached Neugebauer and introduced himself. He explained that he, too, was interested in photography. They made an appointment to meet, and Kosinski showed Neugebauer his own pictures.

In Neugebauer's view, the pictures were amateurish, but there was something appealing about Kosinski himself. He had energy, and he was full of ideas. The two young men began working together, putting in long hours in the badly ventilated darkroom, once even coming down with chemical poisoning. Kosinski made astonishing progress. It helped that his uncle, Paul Lewinkoff, the intellectual merchant seaman, mailed them the latest Western photographic journals from New York. Soon they were entering shows all over the world with photographs labeled Kosinski and Neugebauer, and before long they began to win medals.

Unfortunately, the prizes carried no cash awards. Neugebauer had a job at the time with the Polish Film Studio, but Kosinski was still living with his parents and depending upon them for pocket money, and with only his mother working, their financial circumstances were straitened. He and Neugebauer struggled to pay for chemicals, but a true crisis came when they were invited to join the Royal Photographic Society of Great Britain. For two unknown Poles, it was a great accomplishment, but it carried with it a membership fee of nineteen pounds—an almost unimaginable sum. Kosinski finally managed to scrape up the money. Years later, after great success as a writer, Kosinski still listed the Royal Photographic Society whenever asked to list memberships, affiliations, or achievements.

Neugebauer was primarily a portraitist and later earned his

living by making official photographs for state-sponsored dance troupes and the like. He was often put off by Kosinski's blithe dismissal of technical skill. Kosinski once rebuked him in turn: "You aren't a navvy. You have to have an idea and release the shutter. They'll do the technical work for you at the lab." He cared as little for the rules of composition as for the details of photochemistry—an attitude that freed him to experiment, using wide-angle lenses, for example, to produce sometimes grotesque and almost unidentifiable images of the human face and figure.

Ironically, it was the chemical and technical side of photography of which he would later talk, as if, after leaving Lodz, he had somehow absorbed Neugebauer's persona. The very junior Kosinski may well have deserved his billing as co-author. The two men did make a successful team. Kosinski had the idea, while Neugebauer carried out the details. When it came to exhibitions, Kosinski made the speeches.

In the beginning a favorite Kosinski-Neugebauer theme was old age. One day they found a wonderful bearded old man with a cane begging on the street, and took him to their studio in a taxi. After the first shot the old man collapsed. Both young men froze in horror, but a moment later the old man got up smiling at his joke. The picture, which beautifully displays the old man's beard, is an exquisite example of portraiture in the Avedon/ Arbus mode depicting magnetic ugliness incongruously framed. Kosinski would later make use of just such a juxtaposition in the interplay between tone and content in his novels.

Another of Kosinski's ideas was an expedition to the home for the aged on Wroblewskiego Street, where a nurse led them around, an experience he recorded in *Steps*. "I was surrounded, pushed, pulled, spat on and cursed by some of these old people, and, on occasion, physically soiled. . . . There was an oppressive stench of sweat and urine, against which no disinfectant could make headway." So speaks the nameless protagonist, who has been dispatched to depict the serenity and peace of old age. "Some of the patients I selected refused to pose, claiming they were blinded by the spotlights; others, shaking and spitting, crowded in front of my camera to flaunt their wrinkled, flabby bodies, pulling back their lips and drooling through shrunken and toothless gums."

The hypnotic images of the old people both repel and attract, punishing the viewer who at the same time cannot turn away from their vividness. It is a response to the grotesque that continued to inform both Kosinski's life and his art. Central to the episode is the primacy of physical need, including the sexual need of the drooling and wretched inmates, which is echoed in the sexual liaison the nurse is found to be conducting with a half-human misfit. Yet even more crushing is the protagonist's identification with the inmates, as his feelings for the nurse lead him to "the realization that one day I would become what they were now," a remark that both recalls the gatekeepers of Camus and Kafka and resonates a more private pain.

The inability to look away, followed by fascination, then identification, was a harbinger of Kosinski's future response to the grotesque. Neugebauer, by contrast, could look away. Returning from the home, he vowed never again to shoot pictures of people who were old and unhappy. Kosinski acquiesced without a recorded dissent. From the beginning, his favorite subject had been the female nude. Now he and Neugebauer set out in earnest—so many potential female nudes, so little time—to explore this more appealing subject matter.

Soon the Kosinski-Neugebauer partnership took the cast of a series of farcical misadventures, as Kosinski showed his friend the double use to which one could put their art. Neugebauer learned that his friend had a capacity for engendering unexpected consequences only to disappear conveniently at the moment of crisis. Neugebauer's life began to be filled with encounters with angry boyfriends, fathers, and husbands. Once Kosinski had a truly narrow escape. He had photographed and seduced a woman who turned out to be the wife of a policeman. When the policeman appeared suddenly with a gun drawn, Kosinski disappeared out the window with the photographs in his hand. He arrived shortly after at the home of his other friend, Stash Pomorski, and was shown to the bathroom to clean himself, having lost control of his bowels.

The most memorable episode from this period occurred when

Kosinski undertook to advertise in the newspaper that the Film Studio needed young, beautiful girls to try out as actresses: "Young girls wanted by Film Polski. . . ." The future film stars were invited to apply at his home address at 4 Senatorska Street. The following morning Neugebauer received a telephone call from a badly shaken Kosinski. Walking past to observe for himself, he saw a large crowd of women, of all ages from fourteen to forty, milling around in the street in front of the Kosinskis' house.

The partnership of Kosinski and Neugebauer reached its high point in Poland when Krzywe Kolo, an art gallery in Warsaw's Old Town, held an exhibit of their photographs. Characteristically, Kosinski found a way to build upon the relationship established with the gallery. Learning that he had good speaking and reading knowledge of Russian, the gallery employed him periodically as a translator. Because his family's Party affiliation enabled him to leave the country with minimal difficulty, he was able to enjoy a perk of this translating job—two brief trips to Moscow.

These were not his first visits to the Soviet capital—he had gone there briefly on a student exchange in 1951—but they increased his fascination with things Russian, which for a time in the 1950s equaled, or even exceeded, his fascination with America. Later, after he came to the United States, those early trips to the USSR would spur rumblings, especially among the community of Polish émigrés, that he had some sort of connection with the KGB, or other Eastern Intelligence agencies. How did he manage to wangle trips to Moscow in those days?

In fact, travel to Moscow was not so heavily in demand as to be difficult, especially for the son of a Party member in good standing. Sometimes student exchange programs had trouble filling their quotas. And Kosinski himself may have contributed to the myth of Kosinski the Teenage Spook. Later he explained that his Russian hosts sometimes suspected that a young Pole on the loose must be on an intelligence mission, while naive members of his circle in Warsaw thought the same. Kosinski did nothing to discourage these rumors, which added glamour and the suggestion of power, although, to a rational and informed observer, it would appear hard to conceive what intelligence task he might have performed for the Soviets.

But perhaps this position is slightly too dismissive. While in Moscow, Kosinski did—by his own account—look up Gavrila, the political officer in the liberating unit of the Red Army who had befriended both Kosinski and his father in Dabrowa in 1944. Kosinski's accounts of seeing Gavrila in Moscow, unfortunately, are not verifiable after the passage of more than forty years. If influence eased the way for his travel to Moscow, however, it is not altogether unlikely that this influence was exerted by Gavrila, who would have remembered his young friend and the cooperation of that young friend's father. The trips, in any case, served Kosinski usefully a decade later, when he came to write his first American book, an account of travels in Russia, published under the pen name Joseph Novak as *The Future Is Ours, Comrade*.

Meanwhile, the relationship between Kosinski and Neugebauer suffered occasional strains, usually as a result of Kosinski's more aggressive and ambitious personality, but never more so than when Neugebauer's girlfriend informed him that Kosinski had propositioned her. Confronted by his friend, Kosinski sank to his knees and pleaded, "You don't believe me? Then cut off this finger." After a moment's hesitation, he offered the other hand. "No, not the right-hand one, cut the one on the left!" The performance was irresistible, and the two men were reconciled.

Then there were the episodes in which Neugebauer found himself drawn into Kosinski's ideological dramas. Kosinski insisted that they apply for membership in the ZPAF—the Union of Polish Art Photographers—which was the only vehicle by which one could work as a photographer in the Poland of the 1950s. Neugebauer argued that they weren't yet good enough, that the officials were not well disposed toward them, that there were difficult examinations in practice and theory, to which Kosinski replied: nonsense. They applied, and Neugebauer was accepted on a probationary basis, while Kosinski was turned down.

Kosinski was furious because in the union examination he had been failed in the history of art, a subject in which he got high marks in school. He insisted upon appealing the decision, compelling Neugebauer, himself not yet a full member, to stand up and accuse the president of the ZPAF of abusing his authority. Failing to get satisfaction, he then managed to get a note placed in the *Zycie Warszawy*, a Warsaw daily, saying that "two exceptionally talented Polish photographers, members of the Royal Photographic Society of Great Britain, cannot join the exclusive Union of Polish Art Photographers." The case eventually made its way all the way to the Central Committee of the Communist Party.

It is not unlikely that prejudice, accompanied by abuse of power, played a role in Kosinski's exclusion from the ZPAF. Institutionalized arbiters in the creative world, wherever they hold sway, do not take kindly to upstarts who seek to take shortcuts and avoid rites of initiation; this is true regardless of the perceived merit of the work.

Still, Kosinski's protest would provide a lifelong paradigm for response under attack. It involved not mere assertion of the merits of the case but the invocation of outside authority and the manipulation of the fears, sympathies, and aspirations of his audience, and it brought into the fray a friend who was expected to toe the personal party line. Acceptance by the Royal Society may or may not have involved criteria meaningful to the Polish Union, but it was certainly calculated to strike at their hidden sense of inferiority to the materially—and creatively—powerful West. To the elevated politicos of the Central Committee, it resonated similarly, holding the local authorities up to ridicule.

The appeal succeeded, and the local officials were forced to yield, granting Kosinski status as candidate member of the Art Photographers Union. Within a year of the final decision, Kosinski was to leave Poland, while Neugebauer, who would never leave, bore the stigma of the dispute through the remainder of his professional life. The success confirmed Kosinski in his method of dealing with artistic disputes—to get outside the terms in which a problem is framed, invoking authorities and issues that shift the frame of the discussion—a method that would serve him unevenly over the years.

The Kosinski-Neugebauer partnership lasted, at least to some degree, until Kosinski left Poland. Two events reveal the direction his thoughts were beginning to take. In one of them, he had organized the first exhibition of American photography to be shown in Lodz after the war. As the opening approached, with everything in readiness, Kosinski produced an American flag, which hung at the Photographic Society of Lodz on the promenade for two days before taken down.

The other event was the acceptance of Kosinski and Neugebauer to study at the American School of Photographers in Santa Barbara. Kosinski wanted to go. Neugebauer was tempted, but by then he had a wife, a house, a stake in his work at the Film Studio. Kosinski decided not to go alone, perhaps aware that Neugebauer's contribution to the partnership was essential. Or perhaps at some deeper level he knew that, while he was a good enough photographer, photography was not to be the vehicle by which he would, like Nikodem Dyzma, ascend to the heights. He would eventually find another way. Many years later, however, he told interviewers in America, as one variant to the story of his departure from Poland, that he had come as a result of winning a photography contest. The stipend had been small, he said, but he had persuaded the relevant authorities to let him go by adding three zeros to the number.

4.

As with his photographic work, the academic and scholarly side of Kosinski's life in Poland was strewn with obstacles. At the time of his graduation from Stefan Zeromski High School, in June of 1950, there was still the problem of his dismissal from the ZMP. In order to enter university, one needed not only adequate academic marks but a summary statement from the local ZMP chapter. The statement on Kosinski was, to say the least, devastating.

Kosinski set out to solve the problem with characteristic vigor. Although officially blacklisted, he applied to the local University of Lodz, a regional institution then energetically on the make, with particular emphasis in the areas of sociology and Marxist theory. Kosinski went straight to an officer of the admissions department and showed the man his diploma, displaying his high marks in academic subjects. The admissions officer passed

Kosinski along to Professor Jozef Chalasinski, the head of the Social Science Institute, who at that time was also rector of the university. Kosinski made a positive impression on Chalasinski, who
expressed surprise that such a brilliant young man should have
acquired such a bad reputation.

At Chalasinski's insistence, Kosinski was accepted into the university in the area of social science. As the university operated on
the European system, he would be a candidate for the degree of
Master of Social Sciences, which is equivalent in some respects to
the American B.A., though with the level of specialization required for the M.A. For the next six years Chalasinski would be
Kosinski's mentor and protector, seeing his young protégé
through a number of scrapes and opening doors that only a powerful and respected sponsor could open.

There is a certain logic in the fact that his creative activity,
photography, was involved significantly with women, while his
activity in the world of scholarship—his father's temperamental
and elective interest—involved primarily men, and among them
a powerful father figure. Chalasinski served grandly as a surrogate father. He was everything a father *ought* to be: a strong and
principled man, a brilliant and acclaimed man whose image one
could bear with pride, a figure of authority who was yet permissive and unquestioning about one's minor scrapes. For the
seventeen-year-old Kosinski, he became a compelling role model.

In practical terms, to have Jozef Chalasinski as mentor and
sponsor was no small thing. An authentic peasant by origin,
Chalasinski was universally respected for keen intellect, which
was leavened by a down-to-earth bluntness of speech uncommon
in the early days of Polish Communism. The Department of Philosophy and History at Lodz ("philosophy" in the Eastern European sense encompassing the social sciences) was a center of
subtle dissent to Marxist orthodoxy, with faculty who saw themselves as bearing responsibility to the truth—often defined as a
more "humane" Marxism—while hanging on, often tenuously, to
their official positions. Among them were Professor Henry Katz,
whose works included articles with such titles as "To Forbid
Marxism to Lie," and Professor Jan Szczepanski, himself later rector at Lodz and president of the International Sociological Asso-

ciation. Many of them published in the journal *Po Prostu* (Simply), which walked a thin line at the edge of outright dissent; dependent on state sponsorship like all Polish publications, *Po Prostu* often faced not only frowns directed at its content but unexplained bottlenecks in its allocation of paper.

Of this group Chalasinski was both a leader and a somewhat idiosyncratic trailbreaker, and in 1953 he published an article that was to have astonishing consequences. Framed as a review of a book entitled *Literary Periodicals in the Kingdom of Poland in the Years 1832–48* and published in a typically obscure and esoteric journal, Chalasinski's article challenged a number of basic tenets of Marxism. Chalasinski argued that classic Marxist theory must be modified by "supplementary principles" deriving from the overall intent of Marxism, and that it should draw on values from outside the Marxist-Leninist canon. Just in case anyone had missed his point, he went on to argue that Marxist humanism was in decline because of its "scholarly incompetence, a lack of understanding of relevant issues, or the downright falsification of the true picture of bourgeois learning."

Here, indeed, was a spiritual father for Kosinski. In the intellectual climate of the 1950s, Chalasinski's article provoked an instant furor. The Department of Social Sciences of the Polish Academy in Warsaw called a conference in Zakopane in February 1955, with the express purpose of repudiating and humiliating Chalasinski. But a strange and completely unexpected thing happened: the conference at Zakopane failed. More orthodox Marxists then published counterarguments, calling Chalasinski's review a political attack on the very basis of Marxist society. One of the Marxist conservatives concluded his article by saying, "I regret if I have been unable to convince you. I recognize that I am sometimes short of arguments. This does not mean, however, that I intend to give way." Efforts such as these seemed to reinforce Chalasinski's point, and had the effect of rallying moderates to support him.

The "Chalasinski affair" found its way to the Central Committee of the Communist Party, which itself split down the middle. Chalasinski's dissent became the basis for the assertion of a "Polish" version of Marxism. This movement would gain momentum when reports of Khrushchev's "secret speech" denouncing Stalin, in February 1956, began to reach Poland, and it became irresistible when workers in Poznan rioted in the early summer. Wladislaw Gomulka, the postwar leader, was recalled from prison to assume power. The result was the "thaw" of 1956–57, the first serious Eastern European modification of Stalinism, although Chalasinski would eventually pay a heavy price when resurgent Marxist intellectuals closed down his institute.

To Jerzy Kosinski, the Chalasinski affair reinforced the notion that intellectual matters are always, in some sense, political—and that the way to contest them is on political grounds. It further reinforced the notion that one's best asset may sometimes be one's very enemies, whose intemperance and stupidity can be put to good use. As with the Lodz chapter of the Art Photographers Union, so it was with the body of mainstream Marxist intellectuals. The tactic was to divert attention to the tendentious and flawed position of one's adversaries. What he missed was that Chalasinski had not planned it that way. Chalasinski had taken a principled position, and while others venally defended their turf, he had stood his ground in a way that rallied principled, if less courageous, men to his side.

Coincidentally, Chalasinski had been rallying to Kosinski's side at almost exactly the moment that he was preparing his controversial review. As in high school, Kosinski had run afoul of the student organization—this time the ZSP, the Party-sponsored organization of university students. In June 1953 he was expelled from the ZSP, which carried a number of serious consequences—among them the economic hardship of expulsion from the student dining facility, as well as the threat of expulsion from the university and denial of his pending degree. The immediate cause of Kosinski's expulsion was his refusal to speak on the subject of the Korean War unless permitted to present both sides of the issue; the underlying cause was undoubtedly his consistent assertion of his profoundly unorganizable character.

Chalasinski came forcefully to Kosinski's defense. If students could expel one of their own for such a flimsy cause, he argued, what would prevent them, at some future time, from expelling *him*? He even threatened to resign as rector. The ZSP backed down, restoring Kosinski's access to the dining facility, and on June 24, 1953, he received his degree as Master of Social Sciences. In September he was readmitted to the university as a candidate for Master of History. He was never readmitted to the ZSP.

During the fall of 1953 Kosinski took the seminar "History of Modern Social Thought and Sociology" taught by Professors Chalasinski, Jan Szczepanski, and Jan Lutynski—the big three of Polish sociology. He received a mark of *bardzo dobrze* (very good) in the seminar, as he did in the history and structure of the Russian language and in statistics. His grade in English was merely *dobrze* (good), one of the few less-than-perfect marks in his Polish academic record.

His preoccupation at that time lay not to the west but to the east. Funded by an Achievement Scholarship, which included a research trip to Moscow's Lomonosov University, he prepared two monographs, both of which were published in the *Review of Historical and Social Sciences* and subsequently issued as separate booklets.

The first of these monographs, translated as "Documents Concerning the Struggle of Man," examined the views of political prisoners in nineteenth-century Russia, drawing upon court records and prisoners' correspondence. Nominally a work of history, it was actually a metaphor for opposition to police-state authority from within. Similarly, the second monograph, translated as "The Program of the Social Revolution of Jakub Jaworski," purported to be a gloss on the social program of a Ukrainian reformer, based upon the single surviving copy of a manuscript confiscated by Czarist police at the Russian border in 1846 or 1847. In reality, it was an expression of an alternative vision for a more humane socialism.

The two monographs, while examples of ordinarily solid graduate-student work, reveal the profound influence of Chalasinski upon Kosinski's thinking in this period. Both echo the form and substance of Chalasinski's article, deriving from subject matter pious enough (having to do with early reform) and far enough removed from the present (the mid-nineteenth century) to be

seemingly "safe"—yet containing, from within the system, a metaphoric critique calculated to pull the system down.

Beyond the structural similarities, Kosinski owed to Chalasinski a heightened appreciation of the delicate art of having one
foot in both camps, of standing both within the system and outside it. This was the situation, perforce, of serious Polish intellectuals in the 1950s. As for Kosinski, it resonated and extended his
experience during the war—of being a part, and yet not truly a
part, of his environment. Both experiences accustomed him to being part of a social universe while, at the same time, holding a
part of himself outside of it as critic—a posture he would often
adopt in later life when the issues and the stakes were altogether
different.

Not all of Kosinski's university years in Lodz were spent in
scholarly drudgery or esoteric disputation. Not only was there his
career as a photographer—which took place simultaneously with
his career as a student—but there were annual student vacations,
first to Zakopane and then to Miedzyzdroje. There are surviving
pictures of Kosinski-as-skier at Zakopane, often with attractive
women at his side. He later claimed to have been a ski instructor
there, although others who knew him at the time, and some who
skied with him later in Switzerland, cast doubt upon those
claims. Perhaps he was an official instructor, or perhaps his memory built upon recollections of moments on ski outings when he
rendered assistance to beginners—perhaps the young women
with whom he is pictured.

His status at Miedzyzdroje, on the other hand, was indisputably of an official nature. Under a "Fund for Workers' Holidays,"
the Party had instituted a program sending peasants and workers
for two or three weeks of free vacation to the sea shore, where
they received, in addition to a vacation, daily units of cultural
instruction. The instructors were social-science students from the
universities, an elite chosen to explain Marxist doctrine to the uneducated workers. As a scholar with a near-perfect record,
Kosinski was selected yearly beginning in 1951, his first year.

Always skilled at making his experiences serve multiple purposes, Kosinski turned his observations in Miedzyzdroje into a

research contribution to a project of Chalasinski's Polish Social Science Institute entitled "Orientation of Workers and Intelligentsia: Study on Leisure Time and Vacations Paid by the Government."

Kosinski also drew upon the vacations at Zakopane for an episode in *Blind Date*, somewhat rearranging the relationships among workers, ski instructors, and cultural instructors. In the fictional version, the protagonist is a "university-educated ski instructor," one of whose tasks is to "indoctrinate the local ski teachers." The point of contention is the ski instructors' semiannual competition, held in December and March, which includes a long-distance cross-country race. Humiliated by finishing last, far behind the other instructors, the protagonist asserts his power in the cultural lessons, asking the yokels such questions as "What, according to Comrade Stalin, are the five factors that determine victory in war?"

Knowledge, to the protagonist, is power, particularly knowledge that is wired into a dominant ideology. The life of the intellect is seen as something like an athletic contest, possessing the power, in fact, to overturn the results achieved by actual physical prowess.

Another episode from Miedzyzdroje illustrates Kosinski's sensitivity to the nuances of ideological power. As he later told the story, the incident began when he reported a minor party official for the illegal sale of food. Understanding that the best defense is an attack, the official then turned Kosinski in for having led a lascivious life during the vacations. Specifically, he was accused of taking nude photographs of a female factory worker from Lodz, who was not aware that the photographs were being made. The factory worker herself was obliged to go along with the story, at least in Kosinski's version, because allowing herself to be photographed *willingly* would have been an illegal act. Thus the web of an ideologically mandated and nuanced (and highly puritanical) society.

The Party Disciplinary Committee in Lodz, as Kosinski told it, sought his expulsion from the university. He was saved, he said, by an older woman, a Party activist who came to the university by Party assignment. At the meeting debating his expulsion, this older woman stood up and said that for three years, during the times when Kosinski was accused of being with various women, he had in fact been tutoring her almost every evening. Her motive appears to have been personal malice—anger at Kosinski's fellow students, who had mocked her lack of intellectual polish.

It makes yet another strongly illustrative revenge story, and may have been at least partially apocryphal. Kosinski's close associate at Miedzyzdroje was Janusz Kuczynski, then head of the Scientific Circles, the organization of prospective scholars in the social sciences, and the future head of the Philosophy Department of the University of Warsaw. Kuczynski does not remember the incident of the food profiteer, or the episode of Kosinski being called on the carpet by the Disciplinary Committee.

He does remember, from Miedzyzdroje days, Kosinski's interest in women, which was quite extraordinary. Women were never far from Kosinski's thoughts, no matter what the time and place. And with his camera as a prop, he had considerable success with them. Even without the use of a camera, his powers of persuasion were formidable. Once, a short time before departure, he recalls Kosinski proposing to a woman with whom he had no previous connection: "We still have two hours. Why not go to bed together?"

5.

Upon completion of his second Master's, in history, which he received on June 26, 1955, Kosinski was enrolled as a doctoral student in the Institute of History of Culture of the Polish Academy of Sciences in Warsaw. His academic title was *aspirant*. Later in America, he represented this position as having been the equivalent of an American assistant, or sometimes even an associate, professor; in actuality it meant an "assistant-researcher" on the Russian model, a position that finds its closest equivalent in American universities in the much lower rank of graduate teaching assistant. To American audiences, it was a minor, and seemingly safe, misrepresentation—and one that has been made by more than one American teaching assistant—although it conveyed an image of rather remarkable precocity which might have raised eyebrows among those familiar with the academic sense of hierarchy.

With his acceptance at the Polish Academy, the primary locus of Kosinski's life shifted from Lodz to Warsaw. One of the high moments of that period was the World Gathering of Youth, held in 1955 in Warsaw. Designed to showcase the new socialist utopia to students from the rest of the world, it had rather the opposite effect, bringing in Western and Third World young people who opened the eyes of the Polish and Eastern Bloc students to the pleasures of free expression. In the process, the costs of showing off socialism got seriously out of hand, straining the national budget. All of this was a pure delight to Kosinski, who played a role in discussion groups studying the first half of the nineteenth century—a safe enough area inasmuch as Marx's writings in the period were still dominated by his discipleship to Hegel, while Eastern Europe was safely frozen under Prussian, Austrian, and Czarist Russian oppression.

Less pleasant was his service in the Polish Army Reserve. The requirement for student reservists was six hours of service every two weeks with three months of active duty in the summer. Kosinski served his three months in the summer of 1955. One can scarcely conceive a more unlikely soldier. Kosinski looked upon the intrusion of his military obligation with the distaste and resentment shared by bohemians and individualists the world over. Every aspect of military service was calculated to annoy him—the regimentation and emphasis on conformity, the instruction in pointless skills, the unsatisfactory living arrangements, the enforced company of dullards, and the absence of agreeable women. The petty constraints and violations imposed upon his most precious possession—his self—filled him with rage. Kosinski's experience of the military involved the usual scrapes which individuals of his type were prone to get into, and he recounted them later, in interviews and private conversations, and finally in his books, with the usual embellishments. One of the stories he told his friends in Warsaw was of taking off his uniform and hiding naked in the woods during a regimental review. In the version of this anecdote he later told in *Steps*, the young soldier leaps to his feet upon being discovered only to realize that he has an erection. This full-body version of giving, literally, "the bird" may be the most eloquent expression of what Kosinski thought of military life.

Assigned as a clerk, he worked at the preparation of training schedules, a task which put him in daily contact with the few actual veterans present among the summer reservists. No longer were veterans of the Great Patriotic War seen, like Mitka and Gavrila, as demigods. Rather, the proximity to seasoned and committed soldiers seems to have produced the major conflicts of his military experience. Among his bohemian friends in Warsaw, he told tales of revenge he took upon veterans who had objected to his shirking. One officer in particular, a hero of the war, had first befriended Kosinski, relying upon his organizational skills, then determined to make an example of him for poor attitude by means of a public humiliation. In return, Kosinski capitalized upon the officer's character flaw—drunkenness—to implicate the man in a serious breach of security.

All things considered, it seems the kind of exploit young individualists in the military boast about but rarely accomplish, although Kosinski used a variant of the anecdote in two novels, *Steps* and *Blind Date*. In the *Steps* version, the adversary is an enemy from the university who is involved in "the para-military student defense corps"; the protagonist gives a false order over the telephone, prompting the man to lead his army against the local arsenal, triggering a full alert.

The *Blind Date* version more closely tracks the story he told in Warsaw. The hero's antagonist is Captain Barbatov, a half-literate peasant and alcoholic, but a genuine hero. At first, the protagonist is his favored assistant. Barbatov's decision to make an example of him, followed by the protagonist's revenge, stems from a single conversation.

"You think I'm an alcoholic numskull, don't you?" Barbatov asks in a drunken stupor.

"I think about my work," the young man answers.

"To you I am an uneducated peasant, stupid enough to get himself wounded fighting the Nazis, while you, the intellectual, slept at home."

"During the war I was too young to fight the Nazis," the young man answers. "The only reason I'm alive today is that I kept running away from them."

"Running away, running away!" Barbatov shouts. "That's all you Jews did for centuries. Even when the Jews in the ghettos finally rebelled and fought the Nazis, they knew they couldn't win. They fought to bargain. You hear? Always to bargain."

The dialogue may or may not have been true to life. What it has is the tone of an inner debate, which the outer experience of military life, and particularly encounters with seasoned war veterans, had the power to incite. It reveals the extent to which, in the mid-1950s, Kosinski held submerged resentment toward figures suggestive of his "peasant saviors"—despite, or rather *because of*, the fact that they had saved him.

In his life as a graduate student in Warsaw, Kosinski became close to Tadeusz Krauze, a fellow student of sociology who was also from Lodz, though of a different circle. The two young men shared access to an apartment belonging to a worker in a vodka factory. In his absence, they could use the apartment for sleep or study, and most importantly for trysts. Like each of his close friends, Krauze was immediately and greatly impressed by Kosinski's talent for seduction. Indeed, seduction, as Kosinski practiced it, was a veritable art form; Krauze is not the only acquaintance of that period who remembers Kosinski as having the ability to pick up a woman "between tram stops." Once as they were walking together in Warsaw, Krauze noticed an attractive woman accompanied by a man and commented that she had "a nice ass."

"I'm going to fuck her," Kosinski said flatly.

As the woman was accompanied by a man, Krauze replied that he didn't see quite how that could be arranged, but Kosinski was undeterred. To Krauze's astonishment, he found a pretext for introducing himself to the couple. "I would like to make your portraits," he said, addressing the man rather than the woman. He introduced Krauze, and a short conversation ensued, at the end of which Kosinski gave the man his card. The arrangements were made, and Kosinski shortly made good on his boast.

On another occasion Krauze had met and become infatuated with a young woman named Anna, who was already engaged. He explained to Kosinski that he couldn't manage to get a date with her. This was not a problem, Kosinski responded. He asked for her phone number and invited the couple over for a visit, the woman along with her fiancé. They went together to a nightclub. In the course of the evening, Kosinski managed to create a social situation that made the fiancé uncomfortable, and the man left. Kosinski then suggested that the three of them go to bed together, but Krauze protested, "I found Anna"—a point which Kosinski conceded, allowing the two of them to go off alone.

The two men did have a number of women together, which gave Krauze an opportunity to observe certain unusual features of Kosinski's sexual performance. He boasted that he often busied himself preparing lectures in his head while making love, and Krauze did not doubt him. He was stunned by Kosinski's capacity to produce instant erections upon demand, and to sustain an erection beyond all imaginable human limits. Once he read a book while making love, which deeply offended the woman involved. On another occasion he answered the telephone and conducted a conversation without interrupting his lovemaking, an experience preserved in an episode of *Steps*.

Kosinski's sexual appetite seemed limitless, as did his openness to experimentation and desire to test boundaries. Once he suggested to Krauze that they should have sex with each other, as an *experiment*. He vigorously denied that he was homosexual. It was rather a matter of not leaving any form of sexual experience unexplored. In this case, Krauze demurred. They attempted, however, most of the permutations that could be done with women, including watching. Of everything they did, however, the thing that astonished Krauze most was a demonstration Kosinski performed with his amazing penis. Commanding an instant erection, he produced a toothbrush and rubbed it up and down the sides and over the tip, displaying its incredible resistance to pain.

Krauze and his younger brother Zygmunt also witnessed displays of the power Kosinski's seductions could wield, two of them having to do with telephones. He seduced a secretary at *Trybuna Ludu*, the Communist Party daily, in order to have access to her official telephone. To be able to say, "I'm Jerzy Kosinski, and I'm calling from *Trybuna Ludu*"—that had a certain ring to it. On a second occasion he had applied for his own telephone, but in those days telephone service was hard to get and could take months. Letters from the Polish Academy had been unavailing, and Kosinski's father, now an ailing pensioner, could wield no effective influence. Losing patience, Kosinski went straight to the source, seducing a secretary in the appropriate office, and the telephone was installed within three days. Some years later, when she took an apartment in Warsaw, his mother became the heir of that telephone number, keeping it until her death almost twenty years later.

Krauze's father was a successful businessman involved in publishing, and under the new socialist regime, he operated at the borderline of the legal and permissible, and sometimes just over it, being arrested and jailed for a period in 1949. Although the two families knew each other only by name, the sons became frequent guests in each other's homes back in Lodz. Not only did the young men study and socialize together, they entered into a business arrangement, bringing in Krauze's father. It was Jerzy's idea, and in a way it prefigured the business ventures he would enter into more than thirty years later, near the end of his life. This time, however, the stakes were smaller. It was not so much a business deal as a hustle. They would buy up some foreign encyclopedias which were available at the Palace of Science and Culture for a nominal amount and resell them at the retail price. It looked like an easy killing, and Alfons Krauze put up the money. Alas, their market research was faulty. Years later the Krauze family was still offering those books to anyone who might be interested.

At least there seem to have been no hard feelings among the business partners. A couple of years later, when Kosinski left for the United States, it was Alfons Krauze who advanced him the money.

6.

Few events in Kosinski's life generated more enduring controversy than the manner of his departure from Poland. Besides the apocryphal story of adding zeros to a prize he won in a photography contest, Kosinski told a number of versions over the years. In his *Paris Review* interview with Rocco Landesman in 1972, he claimed that the United States had not even been his first choice, that he had "three priorities on my list, in alphabetical order: Argentina, Brazil, and the United States, all large multiethnic societies where I could find anonymity. I remember that first I carefully began collecting Spanish and Portuguese dictionaries. Only later, English and American ones. I knew a bit of French and Latin and Esperanto in addition to Russian. I assumed it would have been easier for me to pick up Spanish or Portuguese. But I was turned down by both Argentina and Brazil. They wouldn't accept me because I had a 'Marxist' background."

Perhaps. There is, however, no surviving paper trail indicating that Kosinski ever had applied to visit Argentina or Brazil, nor is it easy to understand what sort of arrangements he might have had in mind, and when it came to actual departure, his arrangements were meticulous and thorough. There is a whimsical element to this story—in another interview he said that he began with countries at the beginning of the alphabet, and, failing there, flipped to countries at the end—but the effect of the whimsical tone is to emphasize his most imperative motivation, to *get out*, no matter how or where.

"You must get out of here. Get out the first chance you get!" Israel Kosky instructs his son in *Hermit*.

"When do you want me to go?" the son responds, taking the advice at the emotional level as a pushing away, pained that his father would send him out into the unknown.

"Go the minute your English is good enough . . ." the father replies.

The fictional conversation takes place in 1946. A decade later, both Mieczyslaw Kosinski and his son could only have been more embittered about the restrictions upon personal freedom imposed by the great ideal, and more pessimistic about the opportunities to realize one's full potential within Marxist Poland. Under the circumstances, for a man clearheaded enough to hold dollar assets in 1939, the logical place was America, and English was the language to acquire. And Kosinski had been busy acquiring it. Not only did he review English words while making love, but friends remember his withdrawing to closets or toilets to study in the middle of a party if he had not yet learned his daily quota of words. For years before his departure English was the single absolute priority of his life, the one thing that could even take precedence over manipulation and mischief.

If Kosinski had a serious alternative to the United States, it would almost certainly have been the Soviet Union, which he visited for the last time in 1957. Russian he already knew from the Kosinski household, with sufficient skill both to speak and to translate written material. And in 1957 the Soviet Union seemed the other great center of energy. Two Sputniks went up that year, and Khrushchev seemed to be dismantling the legacy of Stalin. It was the country of Gavrila, his old friend and mentor from liberation days, and it was the heart of the ideal under which he had grown up. And what if, in the boast embodied in the title of his first book, the future was theirs?

There is fragmentary evidence that for a time in 1957 Kosinski took the Russian alternative very seriously indeed. Later, as he moved farther away in time, geography, and the state of his career, he would push his "defection" from the East back in time, describing himself as an "inner émigré" beginning at ever earlier points. Among the hints to the contrary, however, is a passage in *No Third Path*, his second nonfiction book, in which Gavrila urges him to get off the fence between Western individualism and real commitment to the socialist collective. Their conversation, at least as represented in the book, took place in 1957.

During his stay that year in Moscow, Kosinski was housed at Lomonosov University, a premier Russian research institution. His primary task, as a visiting graduate student there, was to extend the research he was doing under Chalasinski on the subject of "family life in the new housing system." The product of that research would eventually become the first chapter of *The Future Is Ours, Comrade*. With introductions from Gavrila, however, he also traveled to Odessa and Leningrad, and the range of his interviews, later used as the basis of the Joseph Novak book, greatly exceeded his narrow academic target. In fact, he seems to have taken notes on even the most casual interactions, as though his whole life in Russia were part of a massive research project. Even then he may have had future writing in mind, although his inquiry into Soviet society is also suggestive of a young man trying to reach a personal decision.

Was the USSR for him? It's hard to see how the young man who couldn't stay out of trouble in relatively liberal Poland could have prospered there. Kosinski eventually came to the same conclusion. During this last trip to Moscow, an incident took place which put any doubts he might have had into focus. While he was photographing landscapes on the outskirts of Moscow, a militia officer approached, demanded his papers, and made him expose his film. As he later told the story in *Blind Date*, Kosinski asked the officer to look through the camera at what he was shooting, a field with "the fence that crosses it, and an old man who walked past."

The officer replied: "You are here, on one of the coldest days of the year, in the middle of a storm, just to take pictures of an empty field, a broken fence, and some old man passing by." Pointing out that such a field might be a landing site for invading paratroopers, the officer insisted that the film be exposed. (In the fictional version the student returned the next day and reshot the scene.)

As Kosinski continued to poke around in his assigned research task, he must have seen clearly that while Moscow was an interesting place to visit, of all the world's capitals it was the least likely to be hospitable to a person of his flamboyant temperament. As he would describe in *The Future Is Ours, Comrade*, it was a society without privacy or boundaries, where anyone could be called on a whim to give an account of himself. If this was the future, they could have it.

An episode in *Steps*, in which the protagonist pins condoms on the chests of high officials at a diplomatic reception, neatly summarizes the insouciant attitude Kosinski eventually took. In casual tellings, he described the gathering as part of the Moscow

Festival of Youth in 1957, describing the golden prophylactics as Argentinian in origin. He pinned them on officials on a bet, he said. However, as he tended to embellish both his stories and his role at the Youth Festival, the actual origins of this episode remain shadowy. Such an action would have carried significant risks for a visitor to the Soviet Union in 1957, and Kosinski generally avoided tempting the gods. It is not impossible that the anecdote was invented—as something he would have liked to have done—or, alternatively, that a somewhat scaled-down version actually took place at the Warsaw Youth Gathering of 1955.

Returning from Moscow, he knew that his destination was the United States, and that he needed to get there soon. The "thaw" of 1956—the liberalization of the Polish regime engendered in part by his mentor Chalasinski—was in full flow, but who knew how long it would last? In fact, within less than a year the tide would begin to turn back toward neo-Stalinist repression. For a young man determined to get out, the year 1957 was a window of opportunity. But how?

For years Kosinski told the story of the imaginary grant and the four (sometimes three) academicians he invented to write his recommendations. It incorporated his knowledge of the Palace of Science and Culture—an ornate high-rise located in the center of a barren Warsaw square called the "Tundra" and contemptuously known to locals as the "Russian Cake"—as well as elements of the myth he had spread concerning his travels to the Soviet Union. As a story about Marxist bureaucracy, about bureaucracy *period*, it was worthy of Kafka. Complications multiplied, and the story grew with each telling, reaching its fullest (and somewhat overblown) version in his fifth novel, *Cockpit*.

"To leave the country legally I needed a passport," he wrote. "I knew it would be impossible to get an official Academy one, so I decided to apply for a short-term tourist passport. Before the Internal Security Police would issue me one, I had to present them with an authorized application specifying the State's reason for sending me abroad, my itinerary and my foreign sources of maintenance."

Thus the problem. To solve it, the protagonist, Tarden, invents four professors, orders stationery and stamps in their names, and has them write letters on his behalf, one of them sufficiently neg-ative that his file will not look *too* good. As part of his bureau-cratic game, he suggests to one official that he doesn't want to go after all, because of a new love affair, and hints that he is on a se-cret assignment; naturally the official expedites his request. To top it off, he includes the detail of a cyanide pellet kept in his pocket in case his plan should fail. It was a marvelous story, and—aside from his intimate knowledge of the Palace of Science and Culture, where he had recently acquired the encyclopedias, and certain details of his life in academe—entirely the product of Kosinski's imagination.

The real story of Kosinski's departure was both simpler and more convoluted. In August of 1957, the Ford Foundation gave fi-nal approval to the Institute of International Education for a $200,000 grant in support of a program for the exchange of stu-dents, professors, and specialists between the United States and Poland. In anticipation of this grant, Shepard Stone, the originator and overall administrator of the program, who had previously worked on the U.S. High Commission for Germany under John J. McCloy, had already made a recruiting tour in May, contacting potential Polish exchange students, many of them graduate stu-dents in the social sciences. On the Polish end, Kosinski's old sponsors and mentors—Jozef Chalasinski, Jan Szczepanski, and Jan Lutynski—had been involved in the selection process. A number of Kosinski's fellow graduate students had applied for the fellowships, and nineteen successful fellows had been se-lected from the applicant pool.

Kosinski did not apply. The reasons are unclear. Perhaps he simply missed the deadline. In May, when the visiting American team was conducting interviews in Warsaw, he was still in the So-viet Union. By the time he returned to Warsaw, after the Moscow Festival of Youth in August, the list may already have been final-ized. On the other hand, he may have been apprehensive that he would be blackballed on the Polish side of the selection process because of his reputation. And simple fear of rejection may have come into play. In the early rounds of application very able can-didates, Leopold Tyrmand among them, were rejected because they did not fit perfectly with the program's charter. Later, when he approached the I.I.E. through a side door, its Polish coordinator said that Kosinski would have been at the top of the list, had he applied. But for all his brashness, Kosinski's ego did not stand up well to the risk of public failure. Then again, possibly the best explanation lay in his need to do as little as possible in the obvious way; how much better to avoid the group process and achieve one's goals by a circuitous path.

Whatever the reason, by September of 1957 Kosinski found himself in the position of seeing the best of his peers on their way to accomplishing the thing he most desired, leaving Poland for America—and with a free ride as the pilot group of a prestigious new program. Kosinski desperately cast about for a solution. When it came, it was, as usual, through Chalasinski. He would go, if necessary, as a freelance researcher. Chalasinski provided a generous letter of introduction. Kosinski would find the money himself.

The obstacle to this course of action lay not with the Polish authorities—in late 1957 the Central Committee was involved with more fundamental issues than whether young people might leave the country to study—but with the American Embassy. What the *Americans* required, to issue a visa, were exactly the things mentioned in *Cockpit* as the requirements of the "Internal Security Police": an Affidavit of Support and a reason for his visit, which is to say, a Form I-20 Certificate of Eligibility for "F" Nonimmigrant Student Status. The Affidavit of Support was the easy part. He got that from his father's brother, whom he had never seen; Paul Lewinkoff, the retired merchant seaman, an American citizen since 1928 and now living in New York City, placed the required sum of five hundred dollars in a special account for his nephew in the Manhattan Bank.

In hopes of meeting the second requirement, Paul Lewinkoff called the admissions office at Columbia University and asked them to send an application packet to his nephew in Lodz. The packet was mailed on September 19. By then Kosinski had his passport in hand, and permission to leave Poland as soon as he met the American requirements. Unfortunately, the Columbia letter of September 19 was written in American bureaucratese.

There were requirements that might not be met by the November 1 deadline, and even if he were successful, the outcome would not be known promptly enough to get the necessary paperwork through the American Embassy. The Columbia solution wouldn't work.

Once again it was Chalasinski who came up with a solution. He happened to know an American sociologist, Jiri Kolaja, at Talladega College in Alabama, who might be willing to do him a favor. At Chalasinski's suggestion, on September 25 Kosinski wrote Kolaja, explaining his problem. He mentioned Chalasinski, gave his brief list of credentials, and expressed an interest in working in the area of "Contemporary Family Research in the USA." He wondered about the possibility of simply working on his thesis at an American sociological institute, rather than repeating, in effect, his Polish M.A. and doctoral course work. As a footnote, he asked about the possibility of a scholarship or grant, saying that he could not expect support from his uncle, who was blind. He mentioned that he was qualified to work in a photographic lab.

Kolaja responded that he would like to help, but that Talladega College had no suitable institute. Instead, he contacted Professor Paul B. Foreman, chairman of the sociology department of the University of Alabama, which had an M.A. program, and asked for Foreman's assistance. Foreman replied that he would be delighted to have Mr. Kosinski if Mr. Kosinski could handle oral English well enough to benefit from class work and if he thought a semester of informal study might help him before plunging into doctoral work. Foreman requested, and received, a letter of recommendation from Kolaja, whose experience of Kosinski was limited to one letter containing grammatical errors ("Professor Chalasinski with whom I spoke yesterday in the Academy in Warsaw told me my applying to you in the above matter would do [sic] advisable") and one cable. Such was the influence of Chalasinski.

Meanwhile letters from three quite real Polish academicians were added to the Kosinski files at Alabama and Columbia, and eventually at the Institute for International Education and the Ford Foundation. The academicians who wrote glowing letters praising Kosinski's intellect, his work habits, and his popularity among his peers were again the big three of Polish sociology: Professors Lutynski, Szczepanski, and Chalasinski.

On November 21 a letter was sent by A. B. Moore, Dean of the Graduate School, admitting him to graduate study at the University of Alabama for the term beginning January 31, 1958. Accompanying the letter was a Form I-20, attesting to his "student status" for the satisfaction of the American Embassy. The letter requested, as an afterthought, that he have the proper authority at the University of Lodz mail a record of his work at that institution. Kosinski promptly received his visa, and prepared to leave Poland to become a graduate student at the University of Alabama.

His departure was set for December 20. Alfons Krauze had advanced him a little more than a thousand dollars for the air ticket and expenses, with the understanding that it would be paid back as soon as Kosinski had the means. In Lodz, Kosinski gave a farewell party for his high-school and university friends at the Malinowa, the dining room of the Grand Hotel. Turning to Jerzy Neugebauer, he delivered a piece of advice: "Take whatever you can from others, and when there is nothing left, forget about them." Neugebauer accepted this pronouncement, as he had others of the kind, as the brash heartlessness affected by a troubled young man. To Tadeusz Krauze, he left instructions to throw a party in Warsaw and invite some twenty women with whom Jerzy had had affairs. At the airport, Krauze removed the cardigan he was wearing and gave it to Kosinski.

In later years Kosinski spoke generously of Chalasinski in interviews and private conversation, recognizing the important roles this mentor, sponsor, and surrogate father had played in his life. When Chalasinski was dismissed from the university and his institute closed down by neo-Stalinists on November 27, 1959, Kosinski expressed his sincere regret. He was delighted when Chalasinski himself received an exchange professorship under the I.I.E. to Berkeley. As a father figure supreme, however, he could not be left without a revision. In the conclusion of the episode of the "academicians" in Cockpit, the protagonist, who has secretly solicited actual opinions from teachers and colleagues, confronts an elderly professor, now in the States and filled with self-pity because of his dismissal. He taunts the professor for anti-Semitic attitudes expressed in an early monograph and catches him in a lie about the tone of the recommendation he wrote. Unidentifiable except to a handful of readers with a key, the professor, who has been fired for a "monograph on the plight of the nineteenth-century revolutionaries," bears close resemblance to Jozef Chalasinski.

III

GETTING THERE

1.

On December 20, 1957, Kosinski took off from Warsaw on SAS flight 911 bound for Idlewild with a stop in Copenhagen. *Steps* contains an extended and moving description of the suspended moment aboard that plane, as the protagonist sits and reflects, uneasy that he has "done nothing . . . to make my imminent arrival in another continent more real." Wistfully, he expresses the desire that the plane might be fixed permanently in the sky, and that he himself remain there "timeless, unmeasured, unjudged, bothering no one, suspended forever between my past and my future." It was the second great punctuation mark in his life (the first was the liberation of Dabrowa), and a suitable moment for meditation.

The plane landed at Idlewild in a driving rainstorm, and Kosinski had to make his way across a stretch of concrete from the old-fashioned ramp to the wing housing Immigration. He had dressed for the trip in what seemed to him Eastern European elegance, with a heavy Russian muskrat topcoat. He had the most stylish Polish-made luggage, which, however, was fabricated from textured cardboard. Soaked with rain, the suitcase warped and virtually melted. Meanwhile, the coat became heavy on his back; later he would discover how severely it had been damaged, shrinking and shriveling away, with a loosened sleeve. Thus he appeared at Customs in the condition of a bedraggled rat.

Despite such typical immigrant misadventures, he hit the ground running. By the time he left Poland, he had been accepted into the doctoral program in sociology at Columbia University. He set out immediately to unwind the short-term arrangement he had made with Alabama, acquiring a Certificate of Eligibility for "F" Nonimmigrant Student Status from Columbia on December 30. On December 31 he petitioned the district director of the Immigration and Naturalization Service in Atlanta for permission to transfer from Alabama to Columbia. The petition was routinely approved.

With that detail taken care of, Kosinski set out to arrange the rest of his life. For his first few weeks in the United States, he stayed at the YMCA at Ninth Avenue and Thirty-fourth Street. It was the logical choice for a rank greenhorn. He undoubtedly felt that it offered more privacy and space for maneuver than a stop-over with his aged, blind uncle, and it had a familiar point of reference—the old "Y" in Lodz, where he and his teenage friends played jazz records. Within a month he moved out, and into the International House for Students at 500 Riverside Drive.

The next important issue was money. By the account he later told, he had arrived in America with exactly $2.80 in his pocket. It may be the literal truth, although the funds at his disposal included both the $500.00 account set up by Paul Lewinkoff and what was left of the Krauze loan. He was not quite destitute. Yet the $2.80 may be quite accurate as metaphor. He had no source of income, and he needed to move immediately to solve the money problem if he was to have any chance of carrying out a sustained course of study. A possible solution lay in the Institute of International Education, to which he had failed to apply in May while he was still in Poland. Now established in America and accepted as a graduate student at Columbia, he wrote an energetic letter to Shepard Stone, the man who could make things happen at the Institute. He recapitulated his academic history and took the liberty of enclosing excerpts of the letters from his three professors—Lutynski, Szczepanski, and Chalasinski—mentioning the fact that another superior and "colleague," Professor Novakowski, had just come to the University of Chicago. He also enclosed two posters from a public exhibition in Warsaw of his work on "Polish perspectives on American family life."

Shepard Stone was suitably impressed. It was neither the first nor the last time that Kosinski would play an intercultural game to advantage. The posters were emblematic of an unfolding career strategy: to stand a bit apart from his Polish peers by focusing on Americans, then sell the Americans the frame of his outside point of view. Here, it must have struck him, was an ever repeatable device, the blueprint for an intercultural Nikodem Dyzma. It was a little like pretending to be a Polish spy among the Russians and a Russian spy among the Poles—a neat trick until it turned around and bit you.

If Stone was impressed by the letter, he was even more impressed by the reports from followup interviews. Kosinski briefed his interviewers in detail on the situation at the Polish Academy of Sciences, particularly on developments around Chalasinski and his institute. His American interlocutors listened with rapt attention and praised his organization and fluent manner. An interviewer of Polish background threw in the fact that he came from a good family—"intelligentsia" class. The decision was made in principle to accept Kosinski into the program, so long as there were no objections on the Polish end.

Inquiries were undertaken in Poland, and Dr. Ludwik Leszczynski responded on behalf of the Polish Academy. Not only was Kosinski acceptable, but his name was at the head of the original list submitted by the Polish Academy, which, he affirmed, meant the top priority. By March 21 it was a done deal, and Kosinski was awarded a Ford Foundation Fellowship, through the Institute of International Education, covering all tuition and fees at Columbia, a $200 book allowance, a $100 travel budget, and a stipend of $230 dollars a month. The confirming letter to the vice president of the I.I.E. included the minor caveat that Mr. Stone "feels that it might be preferable not to include Mr. Kosinski's name in reports you send to Mr. Leszczynski."

Such convoluted goings-on later gave support to the rumors that Kosinski had come to the United States under irregular circumstances of one sort or another: that he was some sort of intelligence operative, for the CIA, or, in a more far-fetched version,

for Polish intelligence. The most popular version had it that the
I.I.E. was a CIA front organization, funded through its Establishment connections at the Ford Foundation; revelations in the late
1960s about CIA funding of the National Student Association and
other student groups, and its use of the Ford Foundation to fund
the literary quarterly *Encounter*, added credibility to such rumors.

The question about the Institute of International Education is
worth a brief examination. Considering Shepard Stone's background with the U.S. High Commission, and the informal inter-
locking directorate of policymakers that tied the Ford Foundation
to American foreign policy, it would be naive to think that the
Polish exchange program was altogether without Cold War implications. The main purpose of such programs, aside from helping
worthy individuals and fostering general "international understanding," was to give promising young Eastern European intellectuals a look at the better side of the United States, an
eye-opening that was certain to put some heat on their local regimes in the long run. It would not be astonishing to learn that
some among the Fellows received approaches from American intelligence agencies. Yet to view the program as a CIA recruiting
operation is simply a mistake; it was exactly what it said it was,
an international student exchange. By 1964 it had run into difficulty, not because of any monkey business on the part of the CIA,
but because the Polish neo-Stalinists, now back in power, wished
to control the selection of appointees, choosing according to criteria other than academic promise. As a result, the program was
discontinued.

Stone's caution not to include Kosinski on lists sent back to Poland was an anticipation of exactly the sort of problem the program eventually encountered. At stake was neither espionage nor
ideology, but turf. The clearing of his appointment with Dr.
Leszczynski was done as a courtesy, so as not to appear to be
shoving an American choice down the throats of the Polish selection committee. The upshot was that Kosinski received exactly
the same appointment with exactly the same terms as the nineteen students who had been selected from the group interviewed
in Poland the previous May. Unlike the others, he had paid his

own air fare. He also held the unique designation of "Special Scholar," a designation he would strive mightily to live up to.

The tidying up of Kosinski's academic status was timely. On April 22, 1958, he applied to the Immigration and Naturalization Service for the first of several extensions of his initial short-term visa. The application was approved routinely, and Kosinski's stay extended until May 11, 1959. With his presence legitimized and his institutional affiliation established, Kosinski could turn his attention to substantive matters. He enrolled in summer school at Columbia, which would give him a running start in the program and also a chance to test his ability to accomplish doctoral work in English. It was a point on which he could by no means have been sure, despite his forceful presentations in several interviews. Documents from that period, including various application forms, reveal his tenuous hold on the language. French, in fact, seems to have been more comfortable for him; in several written documents, he refers to Paul Lewinkoff as his "oncle," and similarly writes the month as "mai."

Beyond the literal elements of English, there was the larger question of the vocabulary of American culture. Asked his occupation, he wrote on one of the Immigration Service documents "scientific worker (student)." Nothing could better encapsulate the distance between the United States and Poland. In Poland "science" encompassed the "social" as well as the "natural" sciences and the culture was at pains not to say, simply, "scientist" or "sociologist," which might imply superior *rank*, but to enforce linguistically the democratic pretense that intellectuals were merely "workers," like employees in a factory. Later, such turns of language would be charming. Kosinski would learn to make good use of stilted speech and cultural difference; in conversation, it would inflect the punch lines of his anecdotes, while in his books it would provide a built-in eccentricity of style and tone. In his first months in America, however, such failures of idiom were an embarrassment and, in his work at the university, a very real threat. His study of English was now reinforced by the total-immersion course of daily life, with a new wrinkle that would later become part of his intercultural myth: whenever unsure of an idiom, he would pick up the telephone and run it by the operator. One wonders, in the New York of the 1950s, what responses he must have sometimes received.

By April, Kosinski was beginning to move forward in his career of interpreting Marxist society to Americans, accepting an invitation to speak to Professor Nathan Reich's economics class at Hunter College. This sort of presentation would expand in the next few years and provide the model for his first literary success. Meanwhile, however, there was still the question of money. His need for it was immediate, and unrelenting. His Ford Foundation stipends did not begin until July. Even if his initial resources were significantly greater than the stated $2.80, they were going to be seriously depleted long before then. He would not feel able to apply for permission to accept legal employment until February of 1959, so his options were limited to the kinds of work for which one did not have to have documents. Many of the jobs he did take would eventually be dramatized in *Steps*, among them parking cars, driving a truck, cleaning apartments, serving as handyman at a restaurant, scraping paint and rust from ships, and serving as chauffeur for a black drug lord in Harlem. Kosinski later insisted that each of these was an actual job at which he had worked, although only his experience as a car parker, which is documented by a photograph taken at a Kinney lot with Kosinski in his Kinney uniform, and his experience as a paint scraper, which is recalled by a friend, can be objectively verified.

The story of chauffeuring, which he sometimes boasted "broke the color barrier in Harlem," was the source of more than one incident in *Steps*. Given the chance to operate a powerful car, the protagonist is instructed by his employer to "drive it at high speed and keep it very close to the other cars, giving his associates the impression that a collision was imminent. This, he hoped, would frighten them into paying far less attention to him than usual. It was certain, he argued, that their pride would not allow them to show their fear to a white man." The protagonist becomes so skillful at his "passing maneuver" that his employer backs him in games of "book-knock-off," competitions on city streets in which the driver is scored for knocking off books taped to parked cars while driving at high speeds. Both stories have a distinctly apocryphal ring, and would be readily dismissible as pure fiction had not Kosinski, in the presence of reliable observers, performed driving demonstrations which lent them, at least from the standpoint of his driving skills, a certain plausibility.

In the job chipping paint and rust from ships, Kosinski ran afoul of the closed circle of Greek immigrants who controlled this particular area. They roughed him up a bit and managed to get him dismissed. A version of the story is told in *Steps*, with its focus shifted artfully to his already damaged muskrat coat. In the process of roughing up the young protagonist, his fellow workers (whose ethnic identity is not specified) destroy the wonderful protective fur coat the young man has brought with him to his new country. The destruction of the coat resonates powerfully with both past and future experiences, and with their future representation in Kosinski's novels. The coat that is attacked, battered, and finally destroyed by uncomprehending adversaries is Kosinski's symbolic skin—his "hide," as it were. It is one of the many layers underneath which resides his true self, a thing encased deep within social and physical protections; when the coat is gone, the outside world is one step closer to getting at *him*. The coat, like the Warchols' fence, like the protective barrier of alien language and culture, like his very body—which he saw sometimes as "himself" and sometimes as a mechanical device in which his "self" resided—is one more element of the "sacred armor" within which each individual takes refuge from a hostile world.

The need for money would continue to be pressing over the next several years, and Kosinski would frequently invoke the assistance of friends, many of them from the community of his fellow Polish émigrés. In between times he sometimes stole food from supermarkets. Typically, according to the version he told in *Steps*, he stole the food highest in caloric value—black caviar.

2.

On the day after his arrival Kosinski called Mira Michalowska, a journalist and the wife of Jerzy Michalowski, the Polish delegate to the United Nations. He introduced himself as a reader of her column, and Michalowska responded warmly to this new émigré from her home country. She immediately invited him to her home for tea. There was a pause as Kosinski considered.

"Have you children?" he asked.

Michalowska replied that she had two small boys.

"Have you got a dog?"

Yes, she said, she had a black poodle.

"In that case," he said, "would you mind if we meet somewhere other than your house?"

They met for lunch at Schrafft's, where Kosinski began by apologizing for his rudeness about the children and dog. He explained that he had had terrible experiences during the occupation, and that children and dogs had been a major part of it. Michalowska listened with interest. As it happened, there was a party coming up for delegates to the UN General Assembly. "Come to the party," she told him. "There are no children and no dogs, and you are going to meet a lot of people."

Kosinski came to the party and charmed both Michalowska and the other guests. Most people who met Kosinski in those first days were instantly impressed. There was a quality about him that brought out a fatherly instinct in men, and in women the corresponding motherly instinct, and often more. Witty, accomplished, elegant in a modest student way, and, of course, exotically handsome, he seemed at the same time a young man badly in need of looking after. Michalowska cheerfully took on her share of the task. They began meeting every Wednesday at Schrafft's, for lunches lasting an hour and a half, in which Kosinski did most of the talking, regaling her with stories of his latest adventures at the university. He was never dull.

One of the stories concerned his roommate, Robert, whom he had met when he moved to International House. They hit it off splendidly, and Robert suggested that Kosinski move into the spare bedroom in his eighth-story apartment at 110 Morningside Drive, a building owned by the university. Robert was presently sharing the space with his girlfriend. The girlfriend left to spend the summer with her family in Germany, and Kosinski moved in in July. It was a step up from his cramped non-air-conditioned room to a suite, where from the living room windows he could watch ships making their way up the river and see the skyscrapers of the financial district and even the silhouette of the Statue of Liberty.

The arrangement worked well in other ways, too. Kosinski retold the story literally in *Cockpit*, according to Michalowska (who thirty years later, by the kind of coincidence that occurs in the small world of Polish intellectuals, was to be the novel's Polish translator). Robert showered Kosinski with small kindnesses. He reminded Kosinski—by then overwhelmed with class work—that he had to make time to eat, and he took him to the university swimming pool for exercise. He corrected Kosinski's unidiomatic and often halting speech and went over his term papers for grammatical mistakes. He even guided Kosinski in the purchase of a lightweight summer suit, and, as Kosinski later discovered, managed surreptitiously to pay half the cost. But the crowning kindness came in the form of letters written by Robert to his parents back in Poland, assuring them that their son was well and well cared-for, and brimming over with appreciations of Kosinski.

One morning Michalowska received a telephone call from a badly shaken Kosinski. "I had a terrible night," he began, and explained that Robert had tried to kill him with a knife; the police came, and Robert had been taken away. Kosinski filled in the details later at Schrafft's. Once before, he had awakened with a flashlight in his face and knocked down the intruder, who proved to be Robert. This time he had come home to find Robert sitting in a near-catatonic state, his eyes vacant. Trying to get a response, he had splashed cold water in Robert's face, whereupon Robert had dashed to the kitchen, seized a long carving knife, and proceeded to chase Kosinski around the apartment. After the police subdued him, Robert was sedated and placed in a psychiatric ward. Robert's father flew in the next day and explained that Robert had a long history of hospitalization for mental illness. One detail must certainly have struck Kosinski with particular force: Robert had killed his pet dog, cutting off its head.

Michalowska quickly grasped that Kosinski was a young man with an unusual affinity for borderline experiences. Along with the stories of his daily doings at Columbia, he had begun telling her stories fleshing out his "terrible experiences during the occupation." She listened intently as he described Polish villages and peasant rituals that were as alien to her—the daughter of a cosmopolitan family who had spent much of her childhood abroad—as they had once been to him, and would eventually be to readers the world over. In the stories he told, familiar figures from his wartime began to resurface. There was the old woman Pasiowa, who lived in a hut, and Warchol the peasant farmer. There were local children and the village toughs who attacked him on the icy pond. There was Mitka the rifleman and Gavrila the Soviet officer.

But at the same time, new elements were beginning to appear in the version of his life he presented to Mira Michalowska. The central one was that he had been separated from his parents. They had sent him away with a man who abandoned him, and he had wandered on his own for six years, from 1939 to 1945, being reunited with his parents only by accident. He had been seen by a friend of his mother's, who noted the family resemblance. Unable to identify him with certainty, his mother had verified that he was her child by examining the birthmark on his rib cage. Throughout that period he had undergone a series of brutal and fearsome experiences *entirely on his own*. It was not an assertion that Michalowska was prepared to challenge. Many children must, surely, have been separated from their parents in the chaos of 1939, and there was no reason to disbelieve that Kosinski had been one of them.

Michalowska was stunned by certain of the episodes he recounted. A particularly graphic episode had to do with the peasant—the image of Andrzej Warchol—who had hung Kosinski up by his hands with leather straps whenever he went out. That was one of the sources of Kosinski's fear of dogs. The peasant had a large, vicious dog, and while little Kosinski was hanging by his hands, the dog leaped at his feet, just out of reach. Another episode of surreal horror was his dropping of a missal at a Catholic mass, after which the parishioners beat him brutally and flung him into a pit of ordure. And here another new biographical element entered: when little Jurek Kosinski emerged from the pit, he realized that he had lost the power of speech. As Michalowska listened sympathetically, he filled in details. He had been mute for almost six years, from, say, some time in 1942 until 1948. He had regained his speech after being knocked unconscious in a skiing accident near Jelenia Gora.

Kosinski's stories were at once entertaining, appalling, and totally persuasive. After a few weeks of listening, having no reason to doubt that she was hearing a literal account of his life, she said to him, "Now, listen! You better go see a psychiatrist, psychologist. Somebody who's been through all this, you've got to do something. It's a terrible burden to carry."

"Mira," he replied, "I really know very well the difference between neurosis and psychosis. I might be neurotic, but I'm not psychotic. And I cope very well. I get up in the morning. I take a bath. I dress. I go to the university. There's no reason for me to go see a psychiatrist."

Michalowska could see that he was quite upset.

"In that case," she said, "*write a book*. You've got to get it out of you—out of your system."

Six years later Kosinski would take her advice. The ideas for *The Painted Bird* were already present—including the central one: turning his wartime experiences into a solitary child's journey—but before he could write them, he needed to allow them a further period of fermentation. There were also formal questions to be answered: whether to write in Polish or English, for one. For the time being, it was enough to live the story—to give various versions a tryout while monitoring the responses of his audiences. As to his response to the suggestion that he see a psychiatrist, it raises a core question about Kosinski's subsequent public career. There is a moment in *Don Quixote* in which friends of the old country gentleman seek to probe whether he has gone mad; the Knight replies simply and ambiguously: "I know who I am."

Did Kosinski know the truth and consciously embellish it, or had he lost the ability to distinguish between the real and the products of his imagination? Or is there some intermediate state which best describes the presentations he made to Mira Michalowska? A thorough pursuit of the answer must include a careful examination of the concept of truth. Kosinski often remarked upon the fallibility of memory, which makes every life a fiction created by its own author. If his personal view of truth, framed in the definition embraced by both Hitler and Stalin, was whatever one can persuade others to believe, was it necessary, first, to persuade himself?

An event that took place that fall serves to underscore the protean nature of truth in all matters having to do with Kosinski. One night Mira Michalowska received a call from Kosinski, who had been ill for several days and was running a high fever. She sent her personal physician, a Dr. Stein. He called shortly to reassure her; the young man had a simple case of the flu and would soon recover. A few weeks later Stein came to dinner with Michalowska. At dinner he told Michalowska that he had had a most interesting time chatting with the engaging young man, who had given an account of some extraordinary wartime experiences. And, oh yes, there was one anatomical peculiarity. Very strange. The young man's shoulder joints were *turned*, as if he had spent time hanging by his hands from the ceiling. The young man told him that a sadistic teacher had left him to hang just out of reach of a dog.

3.

That summer, as he met with Mira Michalowska and coped with the daily details of life in a new country, Kosinski was learning just how difficult doctoral work in an alien language was going to be. It began easily enough, with a social event at which Kosinski took pictures of the guests, sending prints to the flattered and appreciative I.I.E. program specialist Jane Addams; taking pictures at parties and sending prints to key attendees would become over the years a Kosinski trademark. In July he reported to his advisor, Professor Paul Lazarsfeld, a sociologist of wide renown who was known as an exacting taskmaster. Lazarsfeld expected his students to have a solid command of the fundamental methodologies, and while Kosinski was a young man of many talents, a friendly relationship with numbers was not among them. In a sense, then, he found himself faced with the necessity of acquiring two notably difficult languages, English and mathematics. He also found himself in the hands of a mentor and father substitute who, in his preference for quiet and thorough performance, too closely resembled the original.

Kosinski struggled with his course work. In part it was a matter of English. He did passably in "History of Functional Theory in Sociology," finally earning a B, but received a C, unsatisfactory at the graduate level, in "The Study of Small Groups," which was, ironically, the area in which he promptly stated the intention to do his dissertation. His best mark, a B+, came in "Social Stratification"; his fascination with varying social strata would be more fully revealed over time.

Yet with all the difficulties—with money problems and Lazarsfeld and the maniacal Robert and his course work—he managed to survive the summer as a graduate student in good standing, and, astonishingly, he had a contract with Doubleday to produce *a book*. It was not the book Mira had suggested that he write, but a book drawing upon his travels in Russia and the sociological research he had been doing for Chalasinski. In the first version of the contract, dated August 4, 1958, the work is described simply as "book on Russia, by a presently unnamed author." Penciled in sometime between August 4 and August 18 is the title *At Home with the Russians*, and the name of the author: Joseph Novak. *At Home with the Russians* is lined through, to be replaced by the title written above it, the title eventually used: *The Future Is Ours, Comrade*. How Kosinski came to hold that contract, less than eight months after his arrival in the United States and while a struggling graduate student with imperfect command of English, is one of the imperfectly illuminated mysteries of Kosinski's life.

The story Kosinski told was that "Roger Shaw," a student at Columbia's Russian Institute, had heard some of his stories about Russia and decided that they would make a fine book; Shaw was well placed to move the process along because he had connections at Doubleday, by one account as a junior, or summer, employee. It is not inconceivable that a Roger Shaw played some role in the process that followed, but acquisition of literary properties by unknown authors is not among the routine responsibilities of summer help at major publishing houses. A teasing possibility is suggested by the fact that Kosinski once mistakenly referred to Roger Shaw as "Robert." The Robert of the knife story is depicted as a fellow university student; whereas the protagonist of *Cockpit* is in need of help with his English, "Robert" is in need of help with his rudimentary "Ruthenian," the Eastern European dialect Kosinski used in the book in place of Polish or Russian. Was "Robert" actually Roger Shaw? Was a Roger Shaw involved at all?

Doubleday's personnel files show no record whatever of a Roger or Robert Shaw. Adam Yarmolinsky, Doubleday's public affairs editor at that time and editor of the first Novak book, did not meet the author, and states to this day that he has "no reason to think that the author was Kosinski." He was, in fact, unaware that any royalty account had been set up for the book. His sole connection with the book's origin was Frank Gibney, then a correspondent for *Life* magazine. When Gibney brought him the manuscript, Yarmolinsky circulated it among friends at the CIA, asking their opinion on its authenticity. They responded that it appeared to be authentic.

At *Life* Frank Gibney's beat included Eastern Europe, and especially Eastern European defectors, so he had excellent access and contacts at the CIA. When they had a defector they wished to publicize, the CIA contacted Gibney's boss, C. D. Jackson, or sometimes Gibney himself, and Gibney generally wrote the story. He had been allowed unusual access to CIA archives as editor of *The Penkovsky Papers*, the (supposed) papers of an American agent in the Soviet Union. In 1958 he was working on a book entitled *The Secret World* about Soviet defector Peter Deriabin, with Doubleday as his publisher; thus he had a good connection with Doubleday. At the same time he was completing a book entitled *The Frozen Revolution* dealing with the "thaw" in Poland and dissident Polish intellectuals. Aiding him in that research was a Polish émigré named Tony Czartoryski.

Czartoryski was a member of the renowned, noble Czartoryski family from Cracow, whose palace would eventually become a museum housing the family's art collection, including Leonardo da Vinci's *Lady in Ermine*. As an émigré in America, he worked in the library of the Polish Institute of Arts and Sciences and also as a contract worker for Radio Free Europe, which made him, at least indirectly, an employee of the CIA. At that time, the CIA was interested in supporting anticommunist books, using financial subsidies to authors or publishers. Such "intermediated" books were part of a program begun in 1956 and administered through the United States Information Agency under the rubric of "book development" in which at least 104 titles with messages supportive of the American point of view were published with either direct assistance to the author or purchase guarantees to the publisher. In some cases, the author may not have been aware of participation in the USIA program, behind which the CIA was responsible for many of the selections.

Between Kosinski's penchant for telling more than the truth and the CIA's adamant insistence on telling as little as possible, the specific financial arrangements concerning the "book on Russia" may never be made public. Indeed, full documentation probably does not exist. A number of facts, however, argue strongly that there *was* CIA/USIA intermediation on behalf of the book, with or without Kosinski's full knowledge and understanding. One major piece of evidence is the name of the original titleholder on the Doubleday contract: Anthony B. Czartoryski. A further clue was the address to which communications for "Czartoryski" were to be delivered: the Polish Institute of Arts and Sciences in America at 145 East Fifty-third Street.

The clear presumption is that Czartoryski became aware of Kosinski's notes, suggested the possibility of a book to his contacts within the CIA, and then had the manuscript delivered to Doubleday, which already was quite familiar with arrangements of this nature; Gibney served unwittingly to protect the author's identity and the manuscript's origin. A comic sidebar is that Yarmolinsky may well have submitted the book for authentication to people who had approved its content once already.

To understand this process requires that one understand the overlap between Radio Free Europe and the Polish Institute of Arts and Sciences in America, which in turn requires an appreciation of the situation of Polish émigrés in America in the late

1950s; to understand the relationship of both to the Central Intelligence Agency requires an even more subtle grasp of the variety of attitudes, political orientations, and personal value systems within that community. Generally, the Poles who settled in the United States after the war did so because they were unhappy with the way things were going in Poland. Many of them, at least for several decades, hoped and fully intended to return to Poland once things were set right there. They had, therefore, a tendency to band together as a small cohesive community, with not only a common background and a common goal but the determination to keep alive their connection with Polish culture. In the meantime, if there was anything they could do in the direction of *fixing* the situation in Poland, they were more than happy to do it, and if an arm of the U.S. government wanted to pay them for their efforts, all the better. It wasn't, in their view, loyalty to their new country, America, so much as loyalty to their homeland, whose best interests they could serve by ousting its Marxist usurpers. Thus the membership of the Polish Institute, which preserved Polish culture and provided a cafe society away from home for Polish artists and intellectuals, had a natural overlap with the contract employees of Radio Free Europe, which worked to beam the good message back to the homeland.

Upon his arrival in the United States, Kosinski immediately became part of the circle of the Polish Institute, among whose habitués in the 1950s were poets and writers such as Jan Lechon, Kazimierz Wierzynski, Jozef Witlin, and Janta Polczynski. Wierzynski, in particular, offered encouragement to his young compatriot, suggesting that he write up the stories he told about his wartime experiences. Another supporter was Dr. Feliks Gross, a sociologist at CCNY, who employed Kosinski as translator into Polish of a collection of his work. He too heard Kosinski's accounts of his adventures during the German occupation, notably at a dinner party given by Professor Klemens Jedrzejowski. Gross listened somewhat skeptically—he had himself been in Poland before the war and knew the landscape; besides, if the peasants had been as unrelentingly brutal as Kosinski described, how had he managed to survive?—but Gross's wife was greatly impressed, and his fourteen-year-old daughter suitably horrified.

Kosinski's great supporter at the Institute was its president, Stanislaw Strzetelski, who would offer encouragement and come to his defense on many occasions during the first years in America. One of the roles of the Institute was mediation, explaining to persons of rank in mainstream American culture why persons with strange names whom they probably had never heard of— Jozef Chalasinski, for example—were figures of substance and importance on the other side of the world, whose recommendations should carry weight. Another form of mediation involved such tasks as validating a Polish birth certificate for American bureaucracies like the INS (especially helpful when the birth certificate, as in Kosinski's case, was dated in 1950, seventeen years after his birth), and pointing out the reasons that a police check of his juvenile records in Poland was unlikely to produce useful results for an American inquiry. Strzetelski performed this kind of mediation for Kosinski whenever asked, and he did a great deal more.

With Chalasinski now on the far side of the ocean and Lazarsfeld a somewhat austere and judgmental figure, Strzetelski became the central figure of male authority in Kosinski's life. Of the various surrogate fathers to whom Kosinski attached himself, Strzetelski was the one whom, for some reason, he never felt a need to denigrate. He would, in fact, continue to seek Strzetelski's approval even after the publication of *The Painted Bird*, which Strzetelski recused himself from reading on the grounds that the material was too strong for his old-school tastes. When others attacked the book, Kosinski sent Strzetelski an extended explanation and apologia. This enduring quest for Strzetelski's approval may have stemmed from the fact that Strzetelski, uniquely, refrained entirely from negative judgment; he was a man who strove to see the best in people, Kosinski among them, perhaps naively or perhaps in full knowledge that he would sometimes be mistaken.

Most people who got to know Strzetelski felt the same way about him, which was ironic in light of the way he had begun. In Poland, before the war, he had been a nationalist and the owner of a newspaper with anti-Semitic overtones. It seems, however, to have been a case of a young man not yet ready to rise above his immediate surroundings, for in later life Strzetelski appeared genuinely repentant. After a typical story of family flight from the Nazi-Stalinist pincer of 1939, he settled in America and eventually worked at the Polish desk of Radio Free Europe. Unlike its boss, Jan Novak, whom he disliked, he was unwilling to go along with every scheme cooked up to serve the interests of its American sponsors. He finally resigned over the plan proposed by General Lucius Clay to float pamphlets into Poland using balloons. In Strzetelski's view, the plan was simply harebrained to begin with, and if it succeeded in the purely mechanical sense it was likely to have no effect except to get innocent Poles in trouble. The plan went ahead, with an outcome that proved Strzetelski right. After resignation from Radio Free Europe, Strzetelski assumed the presidency of the Polish Institute.

Kosinski met Strzetelski shortly after arriving in the United States, and Strzetelski began bringing this engaging young Pole to the boardinghouse the Strzetelskis kept to supplement their income. There Kosinski found family warmth and uncritical acceptance. Strzetelski saw the best in Kosinski, and as the future would bear out, that best was very fine indeed. Kosinski had a quick mind, able to grasp the essentials of things instantly, and if he had an occasional tendency to jump the gaps and neglect the demands of careful methodology, well, there must be a form of expression suited to his way. Strzetelski encouraged Kosinski to become a writer. At the time, however, Kosinski's recollections of his wartime experiences had not quite congealed into the shape of a novel. What did resemble a book were his research notes on Russia, which were to have been the substance of his doctoral dissertation had he stayed in Poland, and which he was now beginning to try to sell to Lazarsfeld without much success.

The role of Strzetelski in bringing those notes to publication as a book can only be speculation. He may have acted as broker without being aware of it, or he may have suggested the idea or even shown the notes around to friends in publishing, or in Washington. That Radio Free Europe was a CIA vehicle at that time is well established. It is not unlikely that the CIA also contributed financially to the Polish Institute, either by purchasing subscriptions to its publication, *The Polish Review*, or by making direct donations. Dr. Strzetelski must have been aware that the Americans with whom he had contact at the Radio were connected to the American Intelligence community, although this wilfully naive man, who sought the best in people, probably gave the matter little thought.

Put simply, through his close relationship with Strzetelski, Kosinski was ideally positioned to have a CIA-sponsored program of anticommunist books initiate and support his first American publication. Several known facts give plausibility to this scenario. Over the next two years, Kosinski would record a number of Polish-language broadcasts for Radio Free Europe—an invaluable aid to American Cold War policy, but also a valued perk of Polish émigrés in the "right" crowd. In 1958, according to his IRS Form 1099, he received $220 from the Free Europe Committee, the notional private group sponsoring Radio Free Europe, for "information on Polish Radio Audiences." Kosinski's financial problems were well known to Dr. Strzetelski and members of the Polish Institute, and the consulting fee was almost certainly arranged by Strzetelski, or Strzetelski's friends. Finally, Tony Czartoryski, the actual conveyor of the Russia book to Frank Gibney, worked at both Radio Free Europe and the Polish Institute; he was, at both institutions, Strzetelski's creature. The only real alternative to the notion of CIA sponsorship of the book is the notion that its network of support was purely *personal*, beginning with Strzetelski.

Although the work for Radio Free Europe was not clandestine, it was little known because broadcast in the Polish language. Radio Free Europe presented itself as a private endeavor, financed by an ongoing campaign of television commercials asking for contributions. Only a few Poles in New York were aware of Kosinski's work for RFE, and fewer were positioned to put that work together with RFE's CIA sponsorship, let alone to connect it with the later publication of his book. Nevertheless, there were rumblings below the surface. Kosinski was regarded, with some accuracy, as a man whose views in 1958 and 1959 were so strongly anticommunist as to make him virtually a John Bircher; he would have to back away from such views later, of course, even while remaining a relative right-winger within the range of acceptable opinion in New York's higher intellectual salons.

The suggestion that Kosinski had a more extensive connection with the CIA seems to have arisen from the very murkiness of these subterranean rumors. If his book might have received support from the spymasters, might he not have himself been some sort of spook? Kosinski's casting his protagonist Tarden, in *Cockpit*, as a deep-cover operative fanned the flames of such speculation. There is not a single shred of evidence supporting it, and later events would provide powerful evidence to the contrary. Nevertheless, the cloud of secrecy surrounding the publication circumstances of his first nonfiction book would return to haunt him in the controversies of his later life.

As for the book, not only its instant acceptance but its quick production would remain a mystery for many years. How could a graduate student at Columbia—struggling with his course work, engaged in various side projects as a translator, and busy with the details of life in a strange country—how could such a person have turned out copy that could be serialized in the editorially meticulous *Reader's Digest* in less than two years? Above all there was the problem of his unidiomatic English, still frequently lacking in articles and filled with complex hyphenated modifiers clustered before nouns. The answer is simple. He employed a translator, a daytime employee of Radio Free Europe who stayed up late at night turning his Polish text into the English text of *The Future Is Ours, Comrade*. Her name was Ewa Markowska, and she was the daughter of Dr. Stanislaw Strzetelski.

4.

By the fall of 1958, Kosinski had so many irons in the fire that it must have been difficult to keep track of them. In August he had received the contract for the "book on Russia." In September he enrolled to take six courses at Columbia, including Lazarsfeld's demanding seminar "Sociological Theory and Methods" (for which he eventually received a B) and "The Organization of Power in American Society," which gave him, fittingly, his first

A– as an American graduate student. He was, indeed, beginning to get the hang of it. On September 3 he received a reply from Chester I. Barnard, to whom he had written in early August with an appreciation of Barnard's *The Functions of the Executive*. The note to Barnard, the former AT&T executive whose book would be a standard text at business schools for a generation, was an early example of what would become a standard Kosinski approach: go straight to the top. Whatever else he learned about "the organization of power in American society," he was beginning to learn how to approach members of the American elite. His essential insight was that approaching, say, a Cabinet member or the head of AT&T was not necessarily more difficult than approaching a girl on a tram car, and in some ways easier. The girl on the tram might be wary of strangers, but the rich and powerful had a sense of invulnerability that made them, at times, softer targets. Theirs was a small and insular world, a lonely world really, always in need of a new diversion, and it existed behind a protective moat which might serve the privacy of the arriviste quite as well as it served the privacy of the established elite. Nothing in particular came of the approach to Barnard except a polite, belated reply, but Kosinski quietly filed the information for future use.

In November Kosinski changed apartments yet again, moving to 347 West Eighty-seventh Street. Throughout this period Kosinski was busy pulling his notes from Russia into the shape of a book. While Dr. Strzetelski's daughter Ewa worked at the translation into English, Kosinski himself was occupied with translation work in the other direction, and not only of Dr. Gross's manuscript. The status report of the Polish Exchange program of December 1, 1958, noted for the first time that sociology student Jerzy Kosinski was preparing a collection of selected writings by contemporary American sociologists that would comprise a book to be published in Poland around February 1959, a date that proved to be wildly optimistic. It was another of the projects dug up by Dr. Strzetelski to keep Kosinski in funds. Including articles by leading American sociologists—Lazarsfeld was first on the list—the book, which was to be published by the Polish Institute, was to introduce Polish sociologists to a cross-section of the best

American work in the field. In February Kosinski was still engaged in discussions with Jan Wepsiec in Washington, D.C., who was preparing a bibliographical chapter; it would, in the end, be necessary for him to make a number of trips to Washington. The book, entitled *American Sociology 1950–1960*, a textbook designed for students and scholars in Poland, finally made it into print in October 1962, with Kosinski credited as editor and translator.

The following spring, again wrestling with six courses at Columbia (although he eventually dropped "Religion and Value in American Life"), Kosinski resumed his career of explaining the United States to itself as framed by the view of an Eastern European visitor. In March he was a speaker at a Kiwanis Club dinner; his talk must have been well received, for he was invited in August to give a similar speech to the Lions Club. Yet the combination of deadlines and the chronic problem with money continued to bear down on him. In April, as he applied to the Immigration and Naturalization Service for a year's extension of his stay, he also applied for permission to accept employment; the areas he had in mind: market research (in which he had received a B at Columbia), photographic chemistry, fashion photography, and advertising.

In late 1958, not long after he moved into the Eighty-seventh Street apartment, Kosinski noticed some photographs displayed in the window of a neighborhood hardware store. He inquired about the photographer and was told that his name was Joel Charles, and that he was a friend of the store owner's son. An introduction was arranged, and Charles soon became Kosinski's first real American friend. Their relationship in many ways echoed Kosinski's friendship with Jerzy Neugebauer, both in what the two men shared—an interest in photography and women—and in the things they did not share: Kosinski's intellectuality and burning ambition. While they talked photographic technique, however, they did not enter contests together. By this time, it was becoming clear to Kosinski that photography was just a sideline. Joel Charles was a dabbler, too. In the process of training to be an engineer, he was on his way to a career selling steel, but while he studied he was part-time manager of the Kinney parking lot on Eighth Avenue, where Kosinski began to do occasional work on weekends. It was in the area of women, however, that the two men eventually discovered that they were most closely attuned, as their pleasure in pursuit, ecumenical tastes, and lack of inhibitions served to forge a bond. As his career took off, Kosinski would gradually see less of Joel Charles, but he never quite allowed him to drift out of his life. It was as though something in men like Pomorski, Neugebauer, and, now, Joel Charles grounded him, keeping him in touch with the base of the self he shared with ordinary human beings. In the early 1970s, after he had been taken up by New York's intellectuals and glitterati, Kosinski invited Charles to a ski vacation in Switzerland and paid his way, perhaps in an unconscious effort to restore balance to his life and retain connection with the more common ground of being.

Another translation problem also preoccupied Kosinski at that time. Love, supposedly, possesses a universal language, but Kosinski did not find it so. In Poland, his silver tongue had never failed him when it came to seduction, but America presented an altogether new sort of challenge. Not yet eloquent in English, or in the different vocabulary of seduction in America, he found himself at a loss. This experience has an analogue in the episode of the Russian actress in *Blind Date*. When Levanter, the protagonist, wishes to propose lovemaking to an actress he has admired earlier in Moscow, he finds that communicating in Russian frustrates his aims; it lacks the vulgar specifics so readily available in English. As Kosinski would say later, the language for sex is concrete in English, while in Russian there is no vocabulary for the middle range between philosophical description of what happens between the stars and the empty cosmos and the peasant's description of what takes place between animals in the barnyard.

Kosinski incorporated into the story of the Russian actress a story he often told of himself in his early days in America. In the "nonfiction" version, Kosinski and a woman were seated on a sofa—a "Castro convertible"—and he found himself unable to summon the words to request that she stand up so that he could turn the sofa into a bed. Every way he thought of putting it struck him as crude and unsatisfactory. He was trapped in every schoolboy's dilemma, finding a way to put the question that would not alarm the woman and push her away. Thus the plight of Warsaw's master seducer. Like the schoolboy rejected, he could only meditate on the inscrutability of language—the fact, for example, that the word for "Castro convertible" in Polish is *Amerykanka*—literally, "American woman."

That summer he made a number of expeditions to Long Island beaches in the effort to pick up girls. His companion on these forays was Zdzislaw Najder—another I.I.E. fellow whom he had met at one of Mira Michalowska's five o'clock teas for Ford Foundation grantees—who had access to a car. Najder, who eventually became a distinguished political scientist and head of the Polish desk at Radio Free Europe, recalls that Kosinski's English was so doubtful that Najder was compelled to do most of the talking. Kosinski always wore a jacket, but urged Najder to remove his shirt and expose his body. One day that summer Kosinski turned up with a German girl—an attractive blonde named Emma Borward—who also spoke imperfect and heavily accented English. Emma was quite rich, Kosinski told Najder, being a member of the family that was the largest manufacturer of automobile transmissions in Germany. Kosinski never mentioned his writing to Najder, but he frequently discussed two issues that were major themes of his life that summer—his financial distress and his desire to extend his stay in America. He had already spent his grant money, and, often accompanied by Najder, he went around to advertising firms trying to peddle his photographic skills, making one or two small sales. Yet the financial crisis continued unabated, and sometimes when they stopped for a hamburger, Kosinski shuffled his feet and dug slowly in his pockets until Najder, whose circumstances were somewhat better because of a financially comfortable uncle, got the message and paid. Meeting him again many years later, when Kosinski was famous and successful, Najder teased Kosinski by reminding him that he had never repaid a loan of $12.00, which now, Najder said, carried an enormous amount of interest.

As for extending his stay, throughout the early months of 1959, Kosinski was busy wangling for an extension of his Ford Founda-

tion grant, a process begun in December, when he notified the
I.I.E. that he intended to take his orals the following November.
The program specialist, Jane Addams, reminded him that his
grant, and his stay in the United States, were originally planned
to last only until May. By March 11 his application for extension
was essentially complete; Ms. Addams reminded him, however,
that he must state the *exact month* to which he needed it. Kosinski
replied to her satisfaction, and in May an extension was granted
for six months, with the expectation that he would take the oral
exams in October or November of 1959. By now he was showing
evidence that he could apply a universal vocabulary of ingratia-
tion in the American context. He sent Ms. Addams red roses on
one occasion and chocolates on another, thanking her and being
thanked in return.

By October, however, it was clear that the initial six-month extension was not going to suffice. Kosinski was simply not ready
for the grueling ordeal of a doctoral qualifying exam supervised
by Lazarsfeld. He enlisted Dr. Strzetelski to deliver an opening
barrage, softening up the I.I.E. for his request for a second extension. In a two-page letter, which read in part like a "friend of the
court" brief, in part like the judgment of a specialist in the field,
but for the most part like fatherly advocacy, Strzetelski laid out
the importance and the terms of the *American Sociology* project on
which Kosinski was working for the Polish Institute. Strzetelski's
letter stressed the concern at the Institute for Kosinski's financial
situation, mentioning the three unreimbursed trips he had taken
to Washington to do research at the Library of Congress. It further pointed out that Lazarsfeld, Kosinski's advisor, had unex-
pectedly accepted a year's appointment at Harvard, greatly
complicating matters, and added ominously that "Mr. Kosinski's
state of health has worsened considerably during the past few
months." This mention of his health was, so far as the record
shows, the first appearance of an important new theme in
Kosinski's method for dealing with a recalcitrant universe.

Unfortunately, the program specialist who responded was no
longer the pliant and well-softened-up Ms. Addams, but a Ms.
Anita McGrath, who took rather a stiffer tone. She reminded
Kosinski of his early undertakings as to the schedule of his orals

and his dissertation and insisted upon a written request for extension. That request, made four days later, took the form of a legalistic two-page letter with several lengthy citations from the
Columbia University Bulletin explaining how it would have been
technically impossible for him to have completed the degree in the
time and under the terms previously specified. Every graduate
student is a bit of a jailhouse lawyer when it comes to reading
graduate program bulletins, but Kosinski was a jailhouse master
of juridical science. When one put the requirements and Columbia's schedule side by side, his letter demonstrated, the earliest
possible time for him to complete the degree would have been
between November 1959 and February 1960. The letter concluded
with an impassioned statement about the value of *knowing*, as
against merely passing exams, and was copied—interestingly—to
three individuals: Lazarsfeld, Chalasinski, and Strzetelski.

It seemed Kosinski was determined not only to push the system to the limits, but to put his three substitute fathers to the test.
Strzetelski came through with a second letter, recapitulating even
more forcefully his arguments from the first. This time, however,
his letter bore almost entirely the tone of a partisan, concerned,
fatherly supporter. Kosinski had used his time fruitfully, Strzetelski argued, in spite of his impaired health and "the accident
(combustion of his right hand) which made him unable to write
during almost the whole 1959 Spring Session." It was the first
and last mention in the file of the injury to Kosinski's hand,
which had not impaired his ability to produce lengthy correspondence. Chalasinski did not come into play, this crisis making
clear that he was now out of the picture. Lazarsfeld did not reply,
and was not consulted until the decision had been reached.

Ms. McGrath stood firm. She proposed that Kosinski be
awarded the grant but placed under close supervision, meeting
every ten days with a professor in current residence at Columbia,
visiting Lazarsfeld every month to six weeks in Boston, and reporting monthly on his progress. His stipends, paid monthly,
were to be contingent on satisfactory reports. Lazarsfeld agreed to
the meetings and concurred in the overall plan, writing back from
the Harvard Business School that Kosinski "is unusually bright
but needs some strict guidance."

Kosinski wrote Ms. McGrath one more time, another two-page letter essentially protesting the indignity of her proposed terms. This time the letter was copied only to the Polish Institute. There was extensive discussion of the case at the upper levels of the Institute of International Education, but, with acknowledgment that the foundation already had a significant investment in Kosinski, and with some further specifications as to the dates by which he was to complete various academic tasks, Anita McGrath's proposed solution was agreed upon. On February 3, 1960, Kosinski was notified that, contingent upon his meeting these terms, he was awarded a *final* grant to terminate on May 27, 1960.

At the price of a little indignity—what sounded on paper like rude insistence on accountability but was likely to require only the inconvenience of a monthly note or telephone call—Kosinski received a grant rounding out his second full year of Ford Foundation support. And he had reason to hope that by the time it ran out other prospects, long in the works, would be coming to fruition.

5.

While Kosinski squared his situation with the Institute of International Education, he was furiously at work on the "book about Russia." Ewa Markowska, Strzetelski's daughter, was working equally furiously on the translation. It is an interesting aside that in his two letters Strzetelski never mentioned the arrangement to the I.I.E. staff, although he knew very well what was going on—had in fact suggested his daughter as translator. There were several reasons for his silence. It had probably been a tactical mistake to mention the *American Sociology* volume at all; however worthy, this project suggested that Kosinski was not properly focused on the main task at hand. It would, of course, be impolitic in the extreme to let word of this large extracurricular activity reach the authorities at Columbia, particularly since the book contained substantially the same material he was proposing for his dissertation—a study of the role of small groups in the social and political organization of the Soviet Union. It was an amusing breach of protocol, to say the least, that Kosinski was on the brink of publishing a version of his dissertation before submitting it at the university.

Yet there was a larger reason for Kosinski to have Strzetelski withhold information about the Russia book. He had decided to publish it as Joseph Novak—a generically Eastern European surname with an anglicized first name. Years later, he said he had taken the name from actress Kim Novak, then at the height of her popularity. In any case, the fact that Jerzy Kosinski was Joseph Novak would, for years, be known only to a select group of supporters. It was the beginning of a careful compartmentalization. Keeping his different activities from touching, Kosinski ran his life as though he were a one-man intelligence agency—which, of course, sometimes made him seem to be *behaving* like an intelligence agent. This compartmentalization had various purposes at various stages of his life, often having to do with his career goals of the moment. Seen in a large sense, however, they served as part of the general protective coloration in which he sought to hide himself from being known in depth and detail. Like the fur coat which the Greek workers destroyed, the identity as Joseph Novak was one of the layers of "sacred armor" in which he sought always to encase his most cherished, and elusive, self.

For Ewa Markowska, Kosinski's need for subterfuge carried a rather unfortunate consequence. "I can't give you credit for the translation," he told her, then added, "because of my mother and father."

On the face of it, this seemed absurd. But Kosinski could give a plausible, if somewhat tortuous, chain of reasoning. The purpose of the Novak nom de plume was to conceal his identity. The major reason for concealing his identity was to protect his parents back in Poland from the troubles they would have if their son were known as the author of an anticommunist book. If Ewa Markowska were listed as translator, then it would be easy for journalists or Polish agents to trace the book back, through her and her father, to Jerzy Kosinski.

It was the kind of argument that intelligence agencies use for secrecy and that outsiders often regard as outrageous and ludicrous. Yet it had a certain logic. Its problematic assumption was that the world was so focused on the doings of Jerzy Kosinski as to harass his parents. Foreshadowing an element of the future debate on *The Painted Bird*—the fear that certain factual representations would make trouble for his mother—it probably overstated the interest Warsaw authorities would have in seeking retribution through his family.

It is possible, to be sure, that Kosinski sincerely feared for his parents. Yet the major purpose for the Joseph Novak persona, in the short term, was to conceal his authorship from the authorities at Columbia University and the I.I.E. Over the longer term, crediting Ewa Markowska as *translator* might distance the book from American readers and would certainly undercut Kosinski's status as *author*. By not crediting her, he would emerge magically as a published writer in English. Thus his strategy of pretending to have written the book in English served admirably at the moment, although as a policy it would have serious future repercussions.

Ewa Markowska seems to have accepted this condition without ill feeling. Through much of 1959 she lived at the brink of exhaustion, doing her full-time job at Radio Free Europe during the day and translating the latest installment from Kosinski in the evening. For her effort he paid her, all told, eight hundred dollars, reasonable compensation for a translator at that time, although a small amount compared to the royalties the book would eventually earn. The arrangement was strictly between Kosinski and Markowska, without the participation or knowledge of Doubleday.

Kosinski spent many weekends from the fall of 1959 to the summer of 1960 at Markowska's home in Sea Cliff, Long Island, not far from Glen Cove. Markowska's husband, Andrzej Markowski, had taken up arms as a boy of seventeen to join the Warsaw uprising in 1944. Captured almost immediately, he had been spared by a German soldier who saw that he was only a boy. Instead of being shot, he was sent to a concentration camp—giving him a point of connection with Kosinski. Markowski was a lifelong employee of Long Island Lighting, a man clever with his hands who liked to fish. Like Kosinski's boyhood chum Pomorski, he was no intellectual, but he seems to have been a good companion within the fraternal rites of male friendship. They sat together, for instance, watching the Miss America pageant on television, evaluating the women and noting their good points and bad points. Years later Markowska would recall an afternoon when they sat together in virtual silence, a masculine mode incomprehensible to Markowska, sharing a bowl of fruit. At the end of the afternoon the bowl was empty, and the following day the two men kept taking turns in the bathroom.

Kosinski also had a way with the Markowski daughter, Kiki (who was to have an important namesake later in his life), who was constantly entertained by his childlike antics. To Markowska, Kosinski seemed almost a child himself, playful, rascally, a quick-silver mixture of conflicting impulses and contradictory traits of character. Wonderful with Kiki, he was less kind to the Markowskis' dog, splashing it with streams from their garden hose at every opportunity. After a while, whenever it saw Kosinski coming, the dog ran off quickly in another direction. During all these high jinks, Markowska plugged away quietly at her translation.

Kosinski's companion on many of those trips to Long Island was Krystyna Iwaszkiewicz, another Polish émigrée whom he met in the early summer of 1959 at a party hosted by Mira Michalowska. She was the daughter of the former head of the Polish Trade Mission to the United States, now employed at UNICEF, and by a bizarre coincidence she had actually seen Kosinski once before, years ago. After finishing medical school in Poland, she had performed in a grade B movie, for which she traveled to Lodz. There, at the restaurant of the Grand Hotel, she noticed a young man in a trenchcoat at the next table, wearing a camera with a zoom lens looped around his neck. When her party left after the meal, the young man followed and circled them a couple of times before walking off. It was, unmistakably, Kosinski.

Meeting again at Mira's émigré-diplomat salon, they walked and talked for much of the night. They had in common their memories of childhood in Poland and Warsaw life in the middle 1950s. For the year and a half before coming to America, Krystyna had dated Witold Kaczanowski, a sometime painter—who would do work in America under the name Witold-K—and member of the free-floating arts crowd whose path had crossed Kosinski's in Warsaw and would do so again in America. Strangely, Kosinski did not tell her then, or ever, any of his stories about the war. Later others would tell her about his revelations, but he never gave her the standard account of his wanderings, perhaps sensing that, having herself survived the destruction of Warsaw, she might be well enough informed to detect inaccuracies.

As their acquaintance grew into a serious relationship, he urged her to go on a diet. Sometimes her "diet" was conveniently matched to their lack of funds. At one dinner, he ordered the steak sandwich; when she asked for the same, he urged her to have a hamburger instead, in furtherance of her diet. He insisted that no matter what he ate, he could not gain weight, although he ate little, and most often salads, supplementing his meals by drinking Ensure. A good portion of their time together was spent with her posing while Kosinski shot pictures. She should be a model, he said, and some of the photos suggest that this was not an altogether far-fetched suggestion. He urged her to maintain a pouty expression and never, ever, smile. At the time she was a resident in physical medicine at St. Barnabas, and after meeting her supervisor there Kosinski called and asked to "photograph her beauty." The woman agreed and Kosinski went to her home on Long Island and took a large number of photographs. A few days later he sent her a number of elegant prints along with a substantial bill. The woman politely declined to buy them.

Another St. Barnabas friend of Dr. Iwaszkiewicz was Elinor Morrison, who did not much care for her friend's new boyfriend. Kosinski struck her as self-centered, egotistical, and cruel, qualities that presented themselves in stories he told that would eventually work their way into *Steps*. Her husband, Bill, however, liked Kosinski much better, at least at first. Another couple they saw together was Bob Geniesse, whom Kosinski had met at the home of the Ted Estabrooks (who were involved with the I.I.E.), and Geniesse's future wife, Jane Fletcher. The Morrisons, the Geniesses, and the Markowskis thus made up the social circle

Kosinski shared with Krystyna Iwaszkiewicz. They also occasionally got together with Joel Charles. The compartmentalization of
Kosinski's life, even among this group, was extraordinary. He
told the Geniesses and the Markowskis stories from his childhood, though he did not try them on Krystyna; although
Krystyna accompanied him to the Markowski home on Long Island, she was not aware that Ewa Markowska was at that moment working on the translation of *The Future Is Ours, Comrade*.
Krystyna also did not know him as Jewish.

Occasionally, however, he shocked Krystyna with what he did
reveal. He was able to take care of his enemies, he told her, because he had a pact with the Devil. "If I want to neutralize an enemy," he said, "I only have to get in touch with Him."

The Future Is Ours, Comrade is a rather peculiarly shaped book.
It is made up of a number of separate elements and impulses,
and under close examination, the seams show. It is in part a doctoral dissertation in the social sciences, in part a travelogue, in
part a piece of futuristic speculation, in part a rambling ideological statement, and, finally, in an aspect more evident from the
retrospective view, the first statement of a striking vision of the
relationship between an individual and the world. "Conversations with the Russians," though less dramatic than the eventual
title, would have made a satisfactory title from the standpoint of
pure description, as the book consists largely of an account of the
things an Eastern European social scientist is told as he travels
through the Soviet Union. He encounters Soviets at home, on the
public street, in marriage, at work, in the army, in hospitals, in
universities, as policemen and spies, as travelers abroad, and as
consumers. The book concludes with a portrait of a self-serving
careerist apparatchik, a discussion of the treatment of Jews, and a
profile of Russian attitudes toward war and world conflict.

All in all, the book is everything an American propaganda
agency, or the propaganda arm of the CIA, might have hoped for
in its wildest dreams. In broad perspective, it outlines the miserable conditions under which Soviet citizens are compelled to live
their everyday lives. It shows how the spiritual greatness of the
Russian people is undermined and persecuted by Communism. It

describes a material deprivation appalling by 1960s American standards and a lack of privacy and personal freedom calculated to shock American audiences. The Russia of *The Future Is Ours* is clearly a place where no American in his right mind would ever want to live. To an America in the midst of being educated by sociologist David Riesman to question its own "other-directedness," it depicts a society in which any individual, and particularly the successful one, must define himself purely in terms of the collective body. To top it off, "Novak" shows how Party institutions support Russian anti-Semitism. And—best of all from the standpoint of American propaganda—he shows how and why, despite these systematic flaws, the Soviets might confidently expect to win the Cold War within ten or fifteen years.

The impact of such a book would vary with the background a reader brought to it, but it could be expected to serve core American interests with several audiences. In Europe, it would give pause to those considering allying themselves with the Soviets and building a society on the Soviet model. Did they really want to live like dogs, in a world where cynical apparatchiks called the shots? To an American audience, the book might be even more useful. Not only would it reinforce the message that ordinary Russians had a bad life—a message that could never be reinforced enough, given the short attention span of the American public—but it raised a useful alarm about the long-term Soviet threat. It solved, in a way, the basic dilemma of propaganda efforts directed at the Soviets: explaining how the Russians could be irredeemably screwed up and at the same time a very real threat. Readers of *The Future Is Ours* could be expected to be more receptive to hard-line American policy and more accepting of high levels of funding for defense and intelligence spending.

There is, however, a great deal more to *The Future Is Ours* than its usefulness as a piece of American propaganda. It is, to begin with, an extraordinary piece of journalism, as interesting in some of its detailed observations as John Hersey's *Hiroshima*, although far less stylish and, in content, less congenial to the American intellectual elite of the 1960s. It is also significantly less focused on the careful description of physical details; this lack of emphasis on surface description may be attributed in part to the fact that

Kosinski gathered his material not as a journalist but as a social scientist, and in part to the fact that he wrote out of the Russian, and especially Dostoyevskian, tradition, which tends to give less loving detail to physical reality than to underlying social and psychological forces. It is nevertheless filled with marvelous observation, for Novak in the book is not simply a Pole (or "East European") describing Russians for Americans; he seems rather, at times, a true alien, beamed down from Mars to do social research on a randomly selected land mass and compiling his notes on the peculiar patterns of behavior of human subjects for his Martian colleagues.

All of which is to say that, despite its uninflected tone as a travelogue cum research report, *The Future Is Ours* has a *point of view*. The text describes how in Soviet housing, with several families gathered into a single apartment, one doesn't bother locking drawers on the assumption that one's neighbor will eventually have access to those drawers anyway. It goes on to describe the dumping of old people into homes, often by the use of a ruse, because in cramped Soviet housing the presence of an old person, loudly playing the television, is unbearable. There is no overt commentary on these observations, but the author's point of view lurks constantly between the lines. That point of view is sheer unmitigated horror. To be a citizen of the Soviet Union is, in effect, to be in an *army* for life. It is an army from which there are no furloughs and no escapes to private off-duty pursuits. One is always measured against several collective systems, both formal and informal. One must be at once a good citizen, a good Communist, and a good worker, and the book underscores the fact that a man "can never be all right from all angles."

Moreover, in line with Orwell's *1984*, the Soviet system brings out the worst in people in their everyday relations. Not only do they inform on one another, enforcing the collective code in the scramble for competitive advantage, but they are asked to challenge the basic concept of keeping faith with a friend. Apart from the collective view, ethics are unthinkable. The researcher is not so much a partly Americanized Pole shocked at Soviet behavior as that notional sociologist from Mars, deeply shocked by the collective behavior of human beings toward the individual self.

Ironically, the narrator—the Novak persona—unconsciously dem-
onstrates this bankruptcy in personal morals, seducing a young
woman as part of an experiment in order to learn about the workings of the Soviet command economy. Prefiguring chilly and ruthless episodes in *Steps*, yet presented, bizarrely, as a researcher's
device, the seduction suggests that future amoral behaviors may
be traced to the enforced amorality of the Marxist system.

Throughout the book the presence of Novak seems always to
be threatening to break through the surface of objectivity and deliver the account as personal anecdotes with a more strongly centered consciousness. This view raises the possibility that *The
Future Is Ours* is not really so much a travelogue about Russia as
a book about Communized *Poland*, and the specific experiences of
Jerzy Kosinski as a young man in that Poland. Indeed, the description of the problems of privacy in cramped living conditions
recall the circumstances of the Kosinskis at 4 Senatorska Street,
while the Old Home of the book calls to mind the Home on
Wrobliewskiego Street in Lodz, which he photographed with
Neugebauer and would later describe in *Steps*. Perhaps there
were also specific analogues to these descriptions which he encountered during his travels in the Soviet Union, but at the very
least his responses to the Soviet conditions were informed by attitudes and observations already shaped in Poland. The book appears to represent Novak as having a familiarity with the Soviet
Union somewhat exceeding the aggregate amount of time
Kosinski had actually spent as a visitor there. A longer stay, of
course, would have given the book more authority. It is intriguing
to think that, in this light, *The Future Is Ours* may not be far from
a work of fiction.

The book resembles fiction in other aspects as well. It is constructed as a series of self-contained encounters, each of which
stands alone as an anecdote (thus making it highly suitable for
condensation in *Reader's Digest* and excerpting by *The Saturday
Evening Post*). The structure of a series of freestanding anecdotes,
related thematically rather than causally, was to be a major element in Kosinski's work, especially in *Steps* but also, within a
loose plot rubric, in *The Painted Bird*. In effect, Kosinski argues
that life moves forward episodically, not causally or even logi-

cally; its separate events are related only in their having happened to a single central consciousness.

This collection of loosely related anecdotes means that the book as a whole has no narrative focus in the ordinary sense. With a couple of notable exceptions, Kosinski's later novels did not have "plots." The very notion of a plot implies externally imposed coherence, and it was Kosinski's deepest instinct to distrust all externally imposed systems. "Plot is an artificially imposed notion of preordained 'destiny' that usually dismisses the importance of life's each moment," he later told Gail Sheehy for *Psychology Today*. "Yet that moment carries the essence of our life."

In a sense, plots were like large political systems. What had Nazism been if not a large "plot," a fictive plan, imposed upon the real world? And what was Communism if not another "plot," invented by Marx and physically actuated by Lenin and Stalin? Was it not an artificial notion of destiny that dismissed "the importance of life's each moment?" Consider the dual nature of the word *plot*: two meanings (conspiracy and literary device) connected by the intent to impose an artificial structure on reality. In Kosinski's view, all such massive impositions—whether of "plot" proper or ideological system—tended only to distort and falsify reality. The function of the writer, therefore, was to provide a counterpoint to the falseness of plots. The vocation of a writer was to act as a cosmological journalist, rendering little anecdotes that put the reader in touch with the true experiences plot tended to eradicate.

Suddenly, about twenty pages from the end, *The Future Is Ours* takes a turn and attempts to wrap its insights into a summary. The result is one of the more incongruous elements of its structure, useful though it would be to American propaganda purposes. The book suddenly unburdens itself of its "message," a wake-up call from a "Swedish sociologist" saying that Americans had better take this expansionist dystopia *very* seriously. So the wanderings of "Novak" in the Soviet Union had a plot after all. Novak himself suddenly seems to achieve a clearer, more political definition. He accounts for himself to one of his major Russian sources as a scientist who has "forsaken Marxism-Leninism." Useful though this might have been as a summarizing label, it does not begin to do justice to the subtleties of observation and point of view of the book as a whole.

In reality, the sense of *alien*ation underlying *The Future Is Ours* would be not much less evoked by American materialism, and its codes and rituals, than by Marxist collectivity. Somewhere in Kosinski's childhood, at Pasiowa's hut or behind the Warchol fence at Dabrowa, something having to do with the way humans relate to their neighbors had gone very wrong, or, from another point of view, very right. He simply didn't grasp quite how human beings came to function satisfactorily as part of a group. Perhaps the most telling episode in *The Future Is Ours* has to do with the fate of the Soviet citizen overseas who separates himself from his traveling companions; having broken away from his countrymen overseas, he can never return. He is thought of as no longer "one of us."

The traveler's behavior and the group's response suggest the response of the bad child to the four questions in the Jewish celebration of Pesach. "Why are you asking these questions?" the child snaps at the adults.

The emphasis, however, is not on the questions. "Why are *you* asking these questions?" is the way he is heard by the adults. By saying "you" instead of "we" he has set himself apart from the body. By a gesture which is understood as an ill-informed arrogance (but may also be seen as a perverse courage), he has renounced everything to which he might belong.

6.

The spring and summer of 1960 were a heady time in American life. John F. Kennedy was running for President. It was, as Theodore H. White saw it in the first of his *Making of the President* books, a "changing of the guard" in America, but it was also, although few defined it so at the time, a high moment of national psychodrama—of political theater. The Russians might have launched Sputniks and captured the imagination of nationalistic movements in the Third World, but America seemed to be awakening to the challenge with a youthful spirit of renewal. It was an exciting moment to be an American, fraught with peril but full of opportunity as well, and it was an equally exciting moment to be a relatively new arrivee in America, particularly if that arrival included escape from the confines of America's chief geopolitical rival.

The summer of 1960, so eventful for Americans, also marked a clear turning point in the life and career of Jerzy Kosinski. Up to this point, the context in which he operated had been almost entirely Polish. He had been born and survived the war as a Pole, visited Russia as a Pole, and come to America as a Pole, with his life defined, despite his status as a student at Columbia, within the universe of Polish émigré groups. Even his contacts with the larger American enterprise, through Radio Free Europe and the book contract, had been determined by his status as a transplanted Pole. Now, in the spring and summer of 1960, Kosinski would begin to break out into the American mainstream.

The Future Is Ours, Comrade was scheduled for publication on May 20. That same month excerpts began to appear in *The Saturday Evening Post*—the serialization having been arranged by Doubleday. Kosinski, in his transitional guise as Joseph Novak, was suddenly a figure on the American scene. In the course of the month he took a number of actions that suggest the delicate balance between his past, confined within the circle of Polish émigrés, and his future as a fully accredited American. On May 11 he secured the reassignment of rights from Anthony Czartoryski to "Joseph Novak," a nominal and rather halting, but nonetheless significant, step toward being his own man. Having renewed his temporary residency for another year, he also initiated action for a private bill (under the sponsorship of Congressman Dulski) to receive status as a "lawful permanent resident" of the United States. At the same time, Kosinski applied for permanent employment at the United States Information Agency, seeking a position at the level of GS-11. He mentioned to Krystyna Iwaszkiewicz that he was applying for a job that would take care of his chronic financial difficulties, and that he had the inside track to get it; her understanding was that the job had something to do with the UN.

The application to the USIA carries a wealth of implication.

The USIA was the third element of a triad in Kosinski's life which included the Polish Institute and Radio Free Europe. The USIA was, and is, the publicly acknowledged propaganda agency of the United States government, engaged in such activities as sending American scholars and writers on overseas tours. Its subsidiary agency, Voice of America, was the public arm of the U.S. radio propaganda effort, beaming messages into the Soviet Union and Eastern Europe. It was, in effect, the above-the-table propaganda vehicle, while Radio Free Europe, pretending to be run and financed by private citizens, was the clandestine effort.

The questions then arise: How did Kosinski come to apply for a permanent position as an information specialist at the USIA? What made him believe that such a position might be obtainable? And what made him believe that he might be hired at the advanced rank of GS-11, the second-highest grade available to non–U.S. citizens? The answers have to do, in part, with the smallness of the worlds of Polish émigrés and Cold War propagandists, and the significant degree of overlap between the two. Voice of America and Radio Free Europe might exist on opposite sides of a public-private divide, but many people were unaware of the distinction, which is in fact rather blurred. Through his same cluster of Polish exile friends, Kosinski was brought to the attention of Joseph C. Gydinski, who was Chief of Polish Services at Voice of America. Gydinski was his advocate in the application for full-time USIA employment, and while the application was being processed, he managed to find a small task that Kosinski performed for VOA.

But there was a good deal more to it than that. The USIA had, in the 1950s and 1960s, a number of classified programs, and it was through the USIA book development program that the Central Intelligence Agency secretly promoted publications deemed favorable to the American cause. In short, if *The Future Is Ours, Comrade* was aided in publication by American intelligence operatives, it would have been through the USIA. The fact that Kosinski applied for a USIA staff job in May 1960 may have been entirely coincidental; on the other hand, it is consistent with the supposition that he had an "in" at the Agency, giving him reason to believe that his application would be taken seriously. For a young man who still had not received his doctorate and had never held a serious job, the only reasonable qualification for the second-highest civil service rank would be the knowledgeability attested by his book, which was just becoming available at book stores and had not yet been reviewed.

Whether or not Kosinski was aware of any connection between his book and the secret world, his own sense of secrecy gave a peculiar ambiguity to its successful launching. On the one hand, he was now an acclaimed author. On the other, his triumph could not be properly celebrated among the wider circle of his acquaintance because it appeared under another name. If its association with him were disseminated, there would be trouble with the authorities at Columbia and the I.I.E., who would suddenly understand where his best energies had been going for much of 1959. And there may have been genuine concern about the potential impact on his family and friends in Poland. As soon as it hit the newsstand, he rushed out and bought a copy of *The Saturday Evening Post* only to suffer an attack of paranoia as soon as he saw the name Joseph Novak. Could his real identity be found out?

Kosinski often gave as his personal motto *Larvatus prodeo*: I go forth disguised. Now he decided to test his disguise. Ducking into Grand Central Station, he called Doubleday from a pay telephone. He explained that he had just read the excerpt in *The Saturday Evening Post* and wanted to know how he could be put in touch with "Mr. Novak." His call was transferred several times, and he ended up speaking with Adam Yarmolinsky's secretary, who—to his horror—informed him that Joseph Novak was a pen name and promptly provided him with his own name and address.

The reception of *The Future Is Ours, Comrade* was enthusiastic. W. H. Chamberlin, writing in the *Chicago Tribune*, hit the book's thematic points precisely: "the whole picture of Soviet life would certainly not tempt any normal American into investigating the possibilities for migration for permanent residence," he said, but went on to note the Soviet "contempt for 'the degenerate West' and certainty that the future belongs to communism." Richard C. Hottelet, the television journalist and Soviet expert, writing in the *New York Times Book Review*, hailed the book for laying out testimony on which readers could draw conclusions and attested to the seriousness and honesty of "Novak." Emanuel Litvinoff in the *Guardian* corroborated from direct experience what the book had to say about Soviet treatment of Jews. There were quibbles—*Library Journal* found the conversations lively but questioned their authenticity, while *The New Statesman* found "much of it plausible, some of it a little improbable"—but as a whole, the critics agreed that Novak had made an important contribution to understanding of the USSR.

In September, Lord Bertrand Russell—the preeminent philosopher of the age—wrote "Novak" from his home in England an effusive appreciation, saying that the book confirmed and extended his impressions of Russia in the 1920s, and wishing to engage the young author in a continuing dialogue on the Soviet military leaders' disingenuity about the risks of nuclear war. German Chancellor Konrad Adenauer was reported in the press to have read the book and found its contents "alarming." As an intellectual happening, Joseph Novak had clearly arrived. To top it off, the *Reader's Digest* condensed version, published in August, had given the book a second wind; pushed along by good reviews and exceptional "word of mouth," its sales continued at a solid pace long after the two- or three-month period following which all but the biggest bestsellers tend to disappear from the stores. It would continue to sell at a steady, modest pace in hardcover for two full years.

Before becoming fully assimilated into American life, Kosinski was to seize the opportunity for a final backward look at his homeland as personified in Halina Poswiatowska, a young poet whose reputation was already growing toward her present stature as, perhaps, the most important Polish poet of her generation. They met, inevitably, at the Polish Institute. Poswiatowska had arrived in Montreal two years earlier and had undergone open-heart surgery in November of 1958 in Philadelphia, the primary purpose of her trip. Intrigued with America, however, she had lingered—a course of action that would eventually cause difficulties with the Writers' Union, which had conducted a campaign to finance her trip. In the fall of 1959 she had enrolled as a student at Smith College, and during the summer of 1960, the period in which she knew Kosinski, she was taking courses at Columbia and living in a cheap hotel near the Hudson River. Much of what is known of their relationship—an "almost love affair," as she characterized it upon her return to Poland in 1961—is contained in a memoir-story entitled "The Bluebird" ("bluebird" being Polish slang for a shiftless person who lives by his wits without visible means of support), written shortly before her untimely death from the chronic heart ailment in 1966.

Throughout that summer Kosinski and Halina wandered New York's parks and river banks and museums together. Early on in their relationship, they discussed the interplay of language, culture, and loyalty which momentarily joined, but would ultimately separate, them. After kissing her repeatedly in the middle of a park (as she recounts in "The Bluebird"), Kosinski removes a leaf from her hair and offers to walk her home, then adds: "Actually, I have an errand to run, but you can wait, women like to wait, right? Don't frown, it ruins your face and don't try to hide your thoughts, you have a transparent face. There, our native language irritates me sometimes, and you? I forgot about your hot patriotism! I am sure you will stay here and in the long run your patriotism will not run farther than mine. Do you love Poland and everything holy?"

"I love," Halina replies.

"You see. Me too. What I'm saying, I love and adore them, and I never had such a wonderful time as in that funny little country. Here intelligence is measured by the money you have, and there is no way to be seen as smart, to be respected, except to be rich."

"Is it important to you to be rich?" she asks.

"Of course," Kosinski replies. "How about you?"

"As you see," Halina says, a tongue-in-cheek response alluding to her obvious poverty; in less than a year she would return to Poland, where intelligence without money received more respect. Meanwhile they continue the game of mutual almost-seduction on forays into the wilds of the city, often on very hot days. Pleading that he has no means to take her to an exclusive resort, Kosinski suggests that she come home with him and cool off in his bathtub. Halina demurs, but submits to endless picture-taking sessions in picturesque locations—one of them a "fabulous fence" near the port on West Thirtieth Street. There he poses her against posters of Marilyn Monroe, May Britt (twice life size in knit stockings), the Radio City Rockettes in perfectly straight line with their legs hoisted. "Stand here, no a little further, right under her legs," Kosinski commands. "Legs have to be over your head, make one of your faces."

"I don't know what you are talking about," Halina protests.

"Oh, yes, you know it perfectly," he insists. "Do I have to re- mind you? Half close your eyes, your lips, I told you to lick your lips, it's better, no, not like this." He seizes her chin, and when she pleads that it is hot, he accuses her of being stubborn and de- mands that she make the streetwalker's face she made earlier in the park.

In "The Bluebird," Kosinski is a thin, narrow-shouldered man with camera cases always around his neck. He points out the fleshy blondes he prefers and tells her to gain weight. He speaks rapidly, in frenetic, digressive bursts. His own account, many years later in *The Hermit of 69th Street*, is a wistful love story, de- picting an important connection not quite made, as well as a tour de force on the subject of language and translation. His speech is calmer, more measured. As Kosinski in the novel has become Kosky, Halina has become Helena Powska. Sitting on a park bench with Powska, Kosky notes that her armpits are shaved and describes observing as a boy of nine "the hairy armpits of the peasant women." The phrase "hairy armpits," which he translates into French, makes her laugh. Alone together in his room, they engage in conversational foreplay that reads like poetry grounded in the connection between the sacred and the profane. "Touch me," she prompts, leaning against him with her hip. "Touch *cialo poetki*—poet's flesh." She calls herself a poetess "who devoted two-thirds of her poetry to her own falling in love and less than one-third to her failing heart. One who speaks of sex as *milosc*, as love, but also as *zmysly*, the senses. One who writes of sex as a love of procreation, and of creation, sure, but also sex as love, as fucking, as *kochanie sie* but also as—forgive me, sir, for *saying this in your face—pierdolenie*." Thus are united the Polish words, so un- satisfactory in Kosinski's view, for hallowed and profane love.

Rarely have two such literarily gifted lovers recorded their myths of one another. Writing closer to the event, Halina might be presumed to be the more realistic, although Kosinski's version was perhaps equally true as a seasoned heart's reality. Halina's story concluded with a moving portrait of a young man who sees himself damaged in body and spirit, missing a heart, as he puts it, and thus able to pity but not to love. He tells her that he likes but does not love her, admitting that, if she were rich, he would pretend to love her while behaving a hundred times more rudely than he does now. He does not, cannot, love any woman, he tells her, and paraphrases St. Augustine: if the first parents' sexuality were not a sin, sex would be as separate from emotion as any other body function.

And so it is, he tells her, with him. A peasant woman damaged him when he was five or six, took advantage of him sexually, beat him when he did not submit. She and later her granddaughters, age twelve and thirteen, used him, but being a child he found it difficult to satisfy them. Therefore they thrust a stick into his penis, wounding him. Thus his penis grew, and came to conform to his willed control. As for the peasant women, he hated them, the last genuine emotion he had felt for any woman. Halina writes the story with detachment and implicit wonder: the primal myth of a penis wounded and regenerated with magical powers, a penis that had made a round-trip journey to hell. Kosinski relates another response. Women faint with pleasure, he tells her, and a doctor examining this anomaly has told him that he could make his fortune with rich women on the Riviera.

7.

And fortune continued to be very much the issue on Kosinski's mind. Whatever other effects it had on his life, *The Future Is Ours, Comrade* was not the solution to his financial problems. In the first two months it sold more than 3,000 copies, and by mid-August was up to 3,461, a respectable sale by an unknown author but by no means a bestseller. Despite the best efforts of Bill Berger, who had taken over as Kosinski's agent, there was no immediate sale of paperback reprint rights—a further confirmation of the book's limited commercial success. In a 1973 article based on a personal interview, Wayne Warga of the *Los Angeles Times* gave the earnings of *The Future Is Ours* as $150,000, a figure picked up by many subsequent publications, including Norman Lavers' critical-biographical study. The figure is unquestionably greatly overstated. Even including payment for serialization in *The Saturday Evening Post* and *Reader's Digest* and a belated modest paperback reprint, the figure of $150,000 must be inflated by at least ten times the amount earned, with only a fraction of that paid to the author by the summer of 1960.

Money was, when all was said and done, a problem that just wouldn't go away. In Poland, where material goods had been in short supply, it was always possible to scramble around and come up with the necessary means. When push came to shove, one could always find the funds to join a foreign professional organization or finance a trip. In America, however, material possessions were the standard of measure. To be a full participant in America, one had to possess financial wherewithal. As a new immigrant, Kosinski was prey to the standard tragicomic financial mishaps that afflict most newcomers. On one occasion he took a young woman to Passy, then a fashionable restaurant, and made the mistake of ordering from the ladies' menu, which did not list prices. There is an account of the incident in *Blind Date*. When the check arrives, the protagonist, Levanter, first believes it belongs to the table of eight across the room. Then he assumes that, since it is a French restaurant, the bill must be in French francs, and thus divisible by about five to get the amount in dollars.

The scene at Passy (unnamed in the novel) is a classic in the problem of translation between cultures, in which the protagonist gradually is made to understand that the bill is in dollars—a significant portion of his monthly stipend. As he and his date have only thirty dollars between them, he agrees to pay it off in monthly installments. It is a painful lesson in "the relativity of riches in America"—and in cultural difference. The play on exchange rates symbolizes the lesson learned. Thus the application to USIA, and thus the ongoing concern of his friends, who were always striving to dig up projects and sources to keep Kosinski afloat.

One of the friends who took up the cause of Kosinski's finances was Mira Michalowska, who had befriended him from the day after his arrival. Learning that his final Ford grant would run out in May, Michalowska approached Marian Ascoli, a Sears Roebuck heiress who was active in New York charity circles. There was just one hitch. Most of Mrs. Ascoli's charity work was done in Jewish circles, embracing Jewish artists and writers. Was Kosinski Jewish? No, Michalowska informed her, Kosinski was decidedly *not* Jewish. That was unfortunate, Mrs. Ascoli replied, because it would be difficult for her to find a source of support not earmarked for Jewish recipients. She reflected for a moment and came up with a suggestion. Mary Weir, a widow of means within Ascoli's circle of acquaintance, was leaving for Europe shortly and had been looking for someone to catalog her library. Might the young man be interested in doing that?

It could all be arranged. It turned out that Mrs. George Woods, a relative of Mrs. Weir and wife of the head of the World Bank, served on the board of the Institute of International Education. She was perfectly positioned to vouch for him and give an account of his status and predicament. Michalowska put the suggestion to Kosinski, informing him that he would be provided with a stipend and meals. There was a large staff of servants at Mrs. Weir's house, she said, including a cook. Thus the author of *The Future Is Ours, Comrade* accepted a job cataloging a rich woman's library. He asked only one question: Was there a dog?

A decade later, after her death, Kosinski told several different versions of his first meeting with Mary Weir. The various accounts possessed one common denominator: Mary Weir had read excerpts of his book in *The Saturday Evening Post* and sent him a fan letter from the Ritz Hotel in Paris. Ironically, this account may just possibly be true. Kosinski and Mrs. Weir did not meet face to face before he took the cataloging job. Throughout the month of July he worked in her library, which consisted of seven or eight thousand volumes, including a large number of dictionaries and art books, producing a cross-subject catalog. She may well have had a moment of curiosity about the young man, and one of his sponsors may well have called her attention to his book. Or he himself may have sent it to her. If so, she may well have written him a note. When she returned from Paris, they finally met.

There is an account of that first meeting in *Blind Date*. Mary Weir, depicted in the novel as Mary-Jane Kirkland, gives *the use of* her library to Levanter, who sends her flowers and asks her to dinner upon her return from Paris. He has seen pictures of the late Mr. Kirkland, a man in his eighties, and assumes that Mrs. Kirkland is old and frail. When he arrives to pick up Mrs. Kirkland, he is greeted by an attractive middle-aged woman, who he assumes is Mrs. Kirkland's secretary. The "secretary" strings him along, and only later, at a dinner party, does he realize that the secretary is actually Mrs. Kirkland, who was many years younger than her late husband.

This account seems to have been, more or less, the truth. Mary Weir had rather an offbeat sense of humor, and it would not have been beyond her to string a young man along for an evening. Kosinski did a number of improvisations upon that first conversation in the library, all of them hinging upon the fact that he had seen a picture of the late Mr. Weir but not of his wife and that Mary failed to introduce herself immediately. "Oh, you are waiting for Mrs. Weir?" she is said to have asked him; it was to become a standard joke between the two of them. The restaurant he took her to was Passy, where the bewildered maître d' did a double take at the young man who had only recently completed paying off in installments the bill he had run up on his previous visit.

Mary Emma Hayward was born in Indianapolis in 1915. Married in 1938 to Donald Reeve, she was working for National Steel Company in 1941 when she divorced her first husband and married her boss, chairman and CEO Ernest T. Weir, a man more than forty years her senior and one of the last great self-made figures of the American age of industrialization. Although his power, wealth, and position were undeniable inducements, Mary Hayward seems to have been genuinely drawn by Weir's enormous physical vitality and personal magnetism; or perhaps the two areas—position in the world and personal magnetism—are, finally, inseparable. When she divorced her husband, Weir divorced his first wife, and they were married in December of 1941. When his two sons, who were roughly Mary's age, made disparaging remarks about her, he disinherited them and dismissed them from their jobs at his company. In 1944 Mary bore him another son, David. By the time of his death in 1956, he was an elder statesman of American industry, sagely calling for trade with the Eastern Bloc and business alliances with Europe and Latin America and accurately predicting such geopolitical developments as the emergence of a more separate and independent Europe.

When she met Kosinski, four years after her husband's death, Mary Weir still lived in the shadow of ambiguous status and privilege. Never quite accepted by his older friends and business associates, she had functioned dutifully as his hostess, making the arrangements for large elegant dinner parties only to efface herself appropriately while great personages discussed the state of the world. Her own interests lay in the area of art and antiques, which were little valued by the business crowd. She had the servants to supervise and the Park Avenue apartment to oversee, as well as large houses in Weirton (the West Virginia town named after her late husband), Southampton, and Hobe Sound, Florida. And there was travel, but always in a certain style, at a certain level, and as the great man's wife. After her husband's death she had trouble breaking away from the patterns established as his wife and consort. Then, suddenly, Jerzy Kosinski appeared in her life—in her library, to be precise—a young man who was exactly everything her late husband had not been. He was rascally, witty, lighthearted, intellectual, and interested in the arts. He was, above all, *fun*.

The attraction between Kosinski and Mary Weir, as incongruous as it might seem, was virtually predetermined. He was everything she hadn't even known how to seek. She was everything to which the whole course of his life seemed to be directing him. She had never known a man who could free his schedule for a whole day *just to be with her*, who would go with her to a museum (and appreciate the art works) or spend a long lunch at a sidewalk cafe. She had never really walked along the bank of the Hudson River, or realized that one could have lunch or dinner aboard the liner *Queen Elizabeth* when she was docked in New York, or ask for, and receive, a tour of a U.S. Navy submarine, given by its commanding officer. All of these things Kosinski introduced her to, and more. It was like a whirlwind courtship out of a 1930s Hollywood film. She had traveled with Ernest Weir on business, as a dutiful wife, but Kosinski introduced the idea of traveling just for the fun of it, even on the spur of the moment, just for a change of climate or a change of scene, even to places like Las Vegas—which he had visited that summer, using it as his Ford Foundation field trip. It would not have occurred to her that Las Vegas, in its own way, was as much of a phenomenon—a new cultural experience—as Paris or London.

Young Kosinski's imagination and sense of possibility seemed endless, and Mary Weir had equally endless *means* to make daydreams a reality. A typical daydream of Jerzy's was the notion of flying around New York in a helicopter. She had seen the city from the air, of course, while taking off and landing on airplane trips, but the idea of flying around it aimlessly and *at one's will* had never crossed her mind. It was easy enough, however, to rent a helicopter and pilot by the hour. Explored from the air, New York suddenly became a work of art constructed for their delight. As a special touch, the helicopter made a number of turns around the Chrysler Building, the top six floors of which were occupied by Ernest Weir's old company, National Steel. As they hovered, they could see secretaries busy typing—Mary Weir's old job. Later Kosinski would use their helicopter trip as the opening episode of *The Devil Tree*, turning it into a rather less poetic flight with a single passenger, the boyish protagonist Jonathan Whalen.

To Kosinski, Mary Weir was literally the embodiment of the American dream, which had to do with both possibility and means. In Warsaw, one couldn't rent helicopters and fly around the city; it wouldn't have been permitted, and if it had, there would have been no helicopters to rent, nor was there a Chrysler Building to peer into. Mary Weir could make all the possibilities of America become reality for Kosinski, and she could also introduce him into the upper levels of American society, for if she was a classic "poor little rich girl," and something of a loner, she was connected nevertheless with the people who counted in New York and Washington. He was first a guest, then a regular, then her special friend at the dinner parties she gave. She knew how to dress and play the part, and she was prepared to be both teacher and patron. She sent her friend Joe Wade to dress Kosinski in Prince of Wales suits, turning loose in him a lifelong impulse to dandyism which gray student life in Warsaw had partially suppressed. Now in America he could emerge as something of a peacock, even as the world in which he operated suddenly changed from Eastern European gray to American technicolor.

Kosinski was now very much less present in Polish émigré circles. Polish friends were puzzled as they gradually noticed that he didn't come around as often. What had become of Jurek? Then one day Feliks Gross happened to see him having lunch at the Rainbow Room with Mary Weir. He barely recognized the splendid figure a few tables away, who did not seem to notice him at all. *"Something,"* he told himself, "has *changed."*

8.

It is tempting, but reductive, to see Mary Weir as the fulfillment of Kosinski's boast to Stash Pomorski that he would attach himself to a "rich Swedish woman." She was rich and eighteen years his senior, and she could admit him to a world that was otherwise beyond his reach, but as was the case in her own marriage to Ernest T. Weir, the relationship was somewhat more complex. At forty-six, Mary was still an attractive woman, bearing a certain resemblance to the film actress Susan Hayward, whose name she shared. Kosinski later rendered fictive pictures of her in three books, as Elizabeth Eve "EE" Rand in *Being There*, Mrs. Horace Sumner Whalen in *The Devil Tree*, and Mary-Jane Kirkland in *Blind Date*. All three are middle-aged women, widowed by wealthy older men, who become involved with younger lovers. In *The Devil Tree*, after Mrs. Whalen's death her lover writes to her son explaining the very real attraction he felt. Admitting that he might not have found her so attractive had she been "an ordinary office girl," he notes: "Just as an office girl is inseparable from her dreary job, your mother was inseparable from the elegant world through which she moved."

The letter to Mrs. Whalen's son includes the detail that her

lover translated a catalog of her art objects, but refused payment—a fiction that seems to have been very important to
Kosinski. He was sensitive to the notion that he did not meet
Mary Weir on equal grounds. The letter goes on to describe the
physical attraction he felt for her and the things they did on
dates, including plays, museums, lectures, art shows, and drive-in
movies, the last of which she had never before experienced. It further describes the financial stresses of their relationship, incorporating a quip Kosinski frequently made about his relationship
with Mary: that he spent his entire earnings and savings on tips.
It may well be that at some point in their relationship Kosinski
and Mary Weir struck a deal in which he took responsibility for
the tips. He was sensitive to the accusation of being "kept" by a
woman, and a certain exaggeration of her lifestyle, which was undeniably plush, made it plausible that he do his share, and salve
his masculine pride, by taking care of the gratuities.

The more interesting suggestion is that a love relationship does
not exist outside a context—that one's love object often is an entity comprised of many elements, including background and position in the world. In Mary Weir's case, this background
operated at several levels. She was, on the one hand, *America*, and
not only America but the *American upper class*, personified and
present to be mastered, embraced, and enjoyed. At the same time,
she was a woman old enough to be his mother, and her relationship with Kosinski included a good deal of motherly caretaking.
She bought him suits and saw that his routine needs were taken
care of, while providing him the comfortable physical intimacy
offered by an older woman. It should not be surprising that he
preferred to see their relationship beginning in a burst of motherly admiration—the kind of fan letter a woman might send her
bright and accomplished son—rather than in a crass commercial
arrangement.

And there was another, highly revealing, element to this familial psychodrama. Kosinski was drawn not just to Mary Weir's
position in the world, but to the life and achievements of her late
husband, whom he never met. As Horace Sumner Whalen, Ernest
Weir is a dominating figure in *The Devil Tree*, a powerful and remote father who communicates with his son by dictated and un-

signed letters. In what was one of his stranger and less explicable literary productions, Kosinski wrote an article on Ernest Weir entitled "The Lone Wolf," which was published in the Autumn 1972 issue of *The American Scholar*, not long before the publication of *The Devil Tree*. An homage to Weir, and through him to individualistic American capitalism, the article celebrates everything about Weir from his Scottish roots to the business empire he single-handedly created and ruled to the supreme vitality and will which would "give in only to time." Thus in gaining Mary Weir, Kosinski simultaneously gained and lost another father figure, chosen as appropriate to his new country, his new creed, and his new sense of himself as a player in the world.

There is, of course, a powerfully Oedipal undertone to this constellation of affinities, with a kingly father at once chosen and killed off, and it surely played a role in the initial attraction to Mary Weir. That this is not mere conjecture is made clear by a conversation Kosinski had with Tadeusz Krauze, who was by then in New York as a graduate student in sociology. To a shocked Krauze, Kosinski unburdened himself of the revelation that he would like to have sex with his own mother. Before Krauze could respond, he added, "I would like to give her that pleasure."

Near the beginning of *Blind Date*, there is an episode in which the protagonist has sex with his own mother. The elderly father suffers a stroke, and the relationship begins when mother and son both run nude to the telephone to take a call reporting on the father's condition. After the call, mother and son find themselves in an embrace. They remain lovers for years, the relationship bounded only by her refusal to undress specifically for her son or to allow him to kiss her on the mouth. As *Blind Date* is filled with transparently autobiographical material, the episode dares the reader to believe that it is literally true. All things considered, including Kosinski's remark that he *would like to* give his mother that pleasure (thus had not), such a consummated relationship seems unlikely. That Kosinski had an unusually close relationship with his mother was demonstrated in a number of ways, and the incestuous relationship in *Blind Date* is probably best read, out-

---

side its fictional context, as a powerful and obsessive fantasy—a fantasy that he realized, in a sense, through Mary Weir.

At Thanksgiving the relationship with Mary received one more twist when her son David returned home from Wilbraham prep school. The neglected recipient of those letters depicted in *The Devil Tree*—letters instructing him to travel first class and tip the porter one dollar—David Weir had lived the life of the poor little rich boy, kicked out of Milton Academy for insubordination and general underachievement. Now he returned to find his mother involved with a man closer to his own age than to hers. At first, strangely enough, the threesome seemed to work well. The appearance of Kosinski had brought a new openness in the Weir household. There were no longer rules about bedtime and the like, and suddenly there was someone to laugh and horse around with. With David, Kosinski seemed almost a boy himself, albeit a precocious and highly intelligent one. He bought books for David and helped him with his studies. Even David's odd hobby—collecting Nazi paraphernalia—did not seem to bother this new friend. It was a rebellious gesture at bottom, popular at that moment among his social set and designed to outrage Establishment fathers who drew the line at ideological flirtation with Nazism. Kosinski, however, understood it for what it was—a passing teenage phase.

Still, things that Kosinski said, and sometimes did, were planted like delayed-action bombs in David's mind. For one thing, Kosinski had a fascination with cars. He described the game of "book-knock-off," played on city streets, and boasted that he could drive so as to pluck a playing card stuck in a parked car's door. David wasn't so sure he believed that, but before long he got a demonstration of Jurek Kosinski's skill. Charged with driving him back to prep school after one of his vacations, his new friend decided to show him the capabilities of the Continental Mark II which Mary had given him the use of. On the long straightaway crossing the Tappan Zee Bridge, he opened it up to 120, pure exhilaration for a boy who had been told always to do things carefully, legally, and correctly. A little farther along they found themselves stuck on a two-lane road behind a slow driver. As a man who would one day drive Formula One race cars, David was astonished at the fluidity and skill with which Kosinski finally got around the recalcitrant ahead of him—and entertained mightily when Kosinski then slowed to a crawl and used those skills to prevent the car from passing him. He was more than a little shocked, however, when Kosinski persisted with the game in the face of an oncoming truck, causing the other car to run off into a ditch.

Later David would dwell on the peculiar identification between himself and Kosinski. He had wanted an apartment of his own, and Kosinski helped lobby his mother until he got it. Yet once he had it, it was almost as if Kosinski had moved into his life—and moved *him* out. Kosinski retained his own apartment, but he spent more and more time at the Weirs' address—71 East Seventy-first Street, the modestly stated side address for the building at 740 Park Avenue that was the oldest co-op and most desirable residence in New York. His father, in Jurek's imagination, had become Jurek's father, and his mother Jurek's—what? Was Jurek taking over his life?

Meanwhile Kosinski continued to see Krystyna Iwaszkiewicz, often picking her up from work as a resident at St. Barnabas in Mary's Continental Mark II. The extent to which the relationships with Mary and Krystyna overlapped is perhaps remarkable only in being so blatant. His explanation to friends in Krystyna's circle was that he and Mary were only friends, although several of them were puzzled by the sudden upswing in his lifestyle. While moving closer to Mary and accepting her largesse, Kosinski tooled around Manhattan in her Continental Mark II with Krystyna at his side. They often drove up to Westchester to the vicinity of the Tappan Zee Bridge, one of his favorite places, where he took pictures, often of Krystyna and the car. Occasionally he took the Morrisons along as well, terrifying them by driving up to a hundred miles an hour on Manhattan streets. Late that fall he and Krystyna drove to Boston together to visit Jane Fletcher, with the purpose of persuading her that she should marry Bob Geniesse. On the way they were caught speeding and hauled into the station for a fifty-dollar ticket, which was rather severe in those days. Although they couldn't muster the fifty between them, Kosinski managed to make arrangements so that they could continue the trip.

Their attempts apparently worked, as Bob and Jane were married on June 10 of the following year, with Krystyna serving as one of the bridesmaids. In the meantime, Kosinski had made a trip to Boston on his own, with an unstated business agenda, sleeping on Jane's sofa to save money. They stayed up late talking, and Kosinski confided to her that he didn't trust people, because his basic experience of the world was of being betrayed. Then, to her astonishment, he tried to put a move on her, and when she insisted that she was not interested in him in that way, he literally chased her around the living room. In retrospect, it struck her as farcical, Kosinski chasing her around and around her living-room table until he gave up, exhausted, and went to sleep.

That fall Kosinski was busy on the career front as well. There were, after all, the tips to pay. A team of Soviet photographers under a G. Assatiani was going around Harlem shooting a film about poverty and racial prejudice in America. Kosinski proposed to Joseph Gydinski a countermove by USIA, revealing the techniques by which such a one-sided and unfair propaganda vehicle was assembled. On September 28, 1960, the Agency approved one-time use of Kosinski to do a script of seven or eight minutes' duration with a delivery date of that October. The payment was $40. Kosinski tracked the Soviet film crew around Harlem, with which he was quite familiar, and wrote a reportage entitled "The Art of Communist Reporting," which played over Voice of America in several languages in early October.

For his part in counteracting the film, Kosinski would eventually receive a letter of appreciation from Gydinski, which didn't come until more than a year later. At the time, the successful completion of his task seemed to promise Kosinski a far more immediate and tangible reward: his application for a permanent post at USIA had been under consideration for six months, and surely a job offer would now be more likely. Once again he had demonstrated that his unique skill was to stand between cultures, interpreting one to the other, then interpreting one's interpretation of the other, and so on ad infinitum in the eternal regression of double mirrors.

On New Year's Eve, Bill and Elinor Morrison took Kosinski and Krystyna to an open house at the home of the decorator who eventually redid the Rose Room for Jackie Kennedy. Kennedy's inauguration was only a few weeks away, and the sense of electricity in Kosinski's life matched the surge of energy in American politics and culture. A jolt was on the way, however. On February 2, 1961, the chief of the USIA employment division wrote to inform him, regretfully, that he would not be offered a position with the Agency. The letter was somewhat apologetic for the length of time it took to process his application, and it listed in bland and general terms the reasons for saying no, including the comparative qualifications of its many applicants and its own analysis of program needs; Kosinski's qualifications, the letter said, did not meet the Agency's needs as well as the qualifications of other applicants.

What the letter nowhere mentioned was the real reason that Kosinski was not offered a job: that he had failed to receive the necessary security clearance. In response to the Agency's request, on August 22, 1960, the FBI had undertaken a standard investigation, at the "normal" or lowest level of priority, for a security clearance of "Secret," in a hierarchy that graduated from Confidential (really no more than office-level) to Secret to Top Secret and TS Cryptographic. In the papers Kosinski submitted, he included the usual lifetime list of addresses and a careful explanation of Professor Chalasinski's dismissal for "anti-Marxist" attitude and the closing of his institute, which meant that Kosinski no longer had a connection with the Polish Academy in Warsaw. He did not mention the extensive period of travel in the Soviet Union.

On January 23, 1961, the FBI replied that Kosinski was not recommended for clearance. Of the National Agency Checks conducted at CIA, HCIS, and FBI, all were clear except the FBI-Subversive subsection—which is comprised of FBI interviews with neighbors and acquaintances. The chief reason for his rejection seems to have been his acquaintance with two controversial individuals who had extensive security records, one of whom served on the Polish Embassy staff. Buttressing this legalistic barrier, however, were a number of supporting judgments. Although Kosinski stated (accurately) that he was single, several neighbors claimed that he was, in fact, married, and in the process gave a suggestion of irregular lifestyle. One source said that he expressed vociferous anticommunist views, but moderated those views at times in order not to embarrass his friend at the Polish Embassy. And in what may have been a backfiring of his strategy in using the Novak pseudonym, it was noted that a number of interviewees had heard Kosinski express concern about his mother, father, and brother back in Poland. He was, in other words, subject to coercion or blackmail. A postscript by one of the processing officers noted that he appeared to be still a "reserve officer" in the Polish Army.

There are several ways to view the material uncovered in the FBI security check (and revealed incompletely under the rules of the Freedom of Information Act). One is that it is a typically silly FBI document, produced by unsophisticated incompetents, and incorporating misplaced conclusions and hearsay evidence, particularly in the erroneous allegation about his being married. Another way of thinking would have it a scrupulous adherence to procedure, erring on the side of caution to produce a procedural *no* in the Kosinski case. The remaining interpretation is that the FBI, indeed, had a point. The portrait of Kosinski that emerges from the report, whatever the meaning of his personal associations, is of an unreliable man—a man who shapes the perception of his life meticulously, but not with great accuracy. If such behavior disqualifies an individual for a security clearance, then the FBI-Subversive investigation fulfilled its purpose.

On the matter of Kosinski's associations with "controversial" individuals, the FBI itself drew no conclusions. One fact, however, does seem clear: the FBI report makes it *extremely unlikely* that Kosinski ever had any operational relationship with the CIA or any other American intelligence agency. There were no references to previous security investigations, and the content of the report would appear to rule him out for future service as an American operative. As to the suggestion made later among Polish émigrés that he had some sort of connection with Polish intelligence, the report left that door open, but only barely. For wouldn't a Polish internal investigation have reached similar, if not more thorough, conclusions?

The negative reply from USIA more or less firmly concluded the period of Kosinski's life in which he was a Polish exile, with his attention still focused significantly on Poland. Had he been offered and accepted the USIA job, he would have had as his audience his fellow Poles. Cut loose from that possibility, he turned his attention one hundred eighty degrees—to the American audience, which in its modest way had embraced his first book. The day after Kosinski received the USIA rejection, Helen Meyner— wife of Robert Meyner, the governor of New Jersey—wrote him an enthusiastic letter following up their recent meeting at a fundraising dance for the Institute of International Education. He had sent the Meyners a copy of *The Future Is Ours, Comrade*, and they had clearly been charmed by the young Polish author. If he wished seriously to follow up his expressed interest in meeting Ambassador George Kennan—the chief architect of America's Cold War policy of "containment"—Helen Meyner would use her good offices to arrange such a meeting at Princeton.

In the end, nothing came of the effort to meet Kennan, who ducked Mrs. Meyner's request with a convoluted rendition of his complicated travel schedule. For Kosinski, however, it was a step up in the same direction as his fan letter to Chester I. Barnard. He was gradually learning how one approached the *American* rich and powerful, with properly mediated credentials and association with their friends, however improvised that association might be. It was the process that, decades later, would become known as "networking." For the time being, however, Kosinski was stuck with Mary Weir and her New York circle, and without a suitable position.

9.

In the early months of 1961 Kosinski was hard at work on a new literary project. In June of 1960, as the first positive reviews were coming in for *The Future Is Ours, Comrade*, he had signed a contract with Doubleday for a second Novak book on the Soviet Union, tentatively entitled *Charged With Fate*. The advance was a modest $1,750, but with the success of the first book, there was the reasonable expectation of building upon that audience with the second. Since John Kennedy had been elected president in November 1960, the level of Cold War tension had, if anything, intensified, and along with it fascination with the enigmatic adversary—the Russians. In the new book Kosinski set out to show the Russians in far greater depth. He would at once reveal the workings of the Soviet system in their full complexity and present a more personal point of view. In the process he would provide teasing glimpses of the author's persona. He would also employ the research skills he had acquired at Columbia and the Polish Academy, and draw upon the data he had gathered for strictly academic use. As a result, the new book effectively cannibalized his prospective thesis at Columbia.

No Third Path, as the new book was ultimately called, was in some ways even more oddly shaped than *The Future Is Ours*. Beneath its surface one can detect the contours of that unwritten doctoral dissertation. At the same time, it reveals a personal ideological struggle. Lacking the earlier motif of travel and discovery, its central issue is how the narrator finally judges Soviet society: Will he stay and work within it or leave? It is an issue his mentor and sponsor puts to him directly, and upon which he pronounces decisively in the final chapter. It is one thing to experience Russia as a visitor, he says, but once he became sufficiently acclimatized to really understand what Russia was about, to "view himself according to the criteria of that environment," he knew he had to leave. He knew that he would not "succeed in the long run in continuing to accept *this new version of himself which he was to maintain in order to continue to live and coexist with others*." It is a striking piece of self-insight. The Soviet Union was, indeed, not the place for "Joseph Novak." At the same time, it hints at a problem of more generality: Wasn't shaping a version of oneself to "coexist with others" a universal problem?

In some respects *No Third Path* is even more a proto-novel than *The Future Is Ours*. It has the same episodic construction, with a series of small anecdotes instead of overall plot. And it introduces a theme from Kosinski's future life and work—the protagonist as a meddler from outside, dabbling in other people's lives and getting them into trouble. In one instance, his presence calls attention to the "Western" preferences of a young girl who wears her hair in an individualistic ponytail and lowers the front of her blouse. She is expelled from Komsomol, the youth organization, and ordered away to the miserable task of harvesting in a remote area. As he watches her from his departing train, the narrator views her with detachment. This subtly inflected point of view is the stuff of novels, and particularly of philosophical novels, calling to mind the ruthlessly objective voice of Meursault in Camus's *The Stranger*.

In another episode "Novak" tells the story of Demyan V., a wheeler-dealer who is in charge of taking care of honored guests at the Moscow Festival of Youth in 1957. Interestingly, Kosinski later gave friends a clearly fictitious account of his own activities as an organizer at that festival that closely correspond to Demyan's wheeling and dealing. Demyan is presented as an egoist whose heart is more in prospects of travel to interesting places than in the Marxist future. His downfall comes as the result of "some book or article" published in the West, for which Demyan is tracked down as the only possible source. It is tempting, looking back from the perspective of Kosinski's entire oeuvre, to see this as an arch aside, making intertextual allusion to one of his sources for *The Future Is Ours, Comrade*.

The "price of being different" is one of the book's overt themes, examined first in a talented musician who writes dull and predictable music to retain his state position while filing his better and more experimental work in "Drawer IV." Most incisive is the section on *stilyagi*—"zootsuiters" who dress up in fancy foreign clothes, deal in black market currency and goods, and generally function as thugs or criminals. The discussion of the *stilyagi* is an early statement of the close parallel between criminal and creative artist—later an important theme in Kosinski's novels—as the fate of the *stilyagi* echoes the plight of the creative individual. Tolerated by the authorities, and thinking themselves important, they are, however, pushed to the *margins* of the Soviet world, where they can be seized and broken at the will of those in power. Thinking that they negate the system, they in fact affirm it, demonstrating its power to absorb nonconformity and confine it to a harmless niche.

No less provocative than the discussion of *stilyagi* is the examination of Marxist, and anti-Marxist, intellectuals in the West. "Infected by Marxism, even when they oppose it," and envious of the Soviet intellectuals who they think have real influence, these Westerners, Novak argues, actually contribute to the *"psychological* disarmament" of the West. Their motive: resentment of the "half-educated businessmen" who run society; the result: a joyless identification with the gray masses, for whom Western intellectuals actually feel profound distaste.

Along with such ideological probings, there are references to various contemporary Cold War issues. A chapter is devoted to the Chinese, an ethnic group for whom Kosinski had a lifelong personal disaffinity. A current American saying in 1961 was: "The optimists learn Russian; the pessimists learn Chinese." A number of interviews in the text portray the Chinese as *super*-Communists and their students in Moscow as virtual robots of studious application; other speakers deny the notion of a rift between the Soviet Union and China. Another chapter discusses the success of cosmonaut Yuri Gagarin, and the necessity in this case of having a symbolic individual hero. Like *The Future Is Ours*, the book concludes with a more or less tacked-on summary—several pessimistic scenarios for ultimate Soviet victory.

Presiding over the text as a whole, and tying together its various themes, is the rather shadowy figure of Gavrila, a new Marxist incarnation of Dostoyevsky's Grand Inquisitor. Gavrila flinches at neither untruth nor personal indignity in the service of the ultimate triumph. Men are better off having it this way, he argues; the burdens of freedom and possibility are too difficult for ordinary human beings. Only the system can engage life's dangers and possibilities. The system is all-powerful and infallible. It is not even necessary, ultimately, for the authorities to control their citizens, because under the system the citizens control *each other*. As an example, the narrator tells the story of a man who is given a letter to deliver, steams it open only to discover its content includes a foreign language, and finally realizes that he has no choice but to report the letter to the authorities.

And what is set in opposition to the system? At a dinner party, Novak, who has visited the Stalin-Lenin mausoleum, quips that "the icebox goes on humming and *they* just lie there." There is a silence, and he realizes that his joke about the air-conditioning system at the mausoleum has profaned a sacred icon. As a result, he gets to know Varvara, a kindred spirit who shares the view that sacred icons exist only to be profaned. Varvara then tells an exemplary story from her childhood. She and some friends trapped a sparrow and painted it purple, then turned it loose in the expectation that the other sparrows would make it their king. Instead, prefiguring the central metaphor of *The Painted Bird*, they pecked it from the sky, killing it out of "their hate for color and their instinct of belonging to a gray flock."

While *The Future Is Ours* had looked at collective life from the point of view of the individual traveler, *No Third Path* subtly shifted the emphasis toward the plight of the individual within the collective. Joseph Novak, whose invented persona looms behind both books, had edged away from being a notional author, standing outside the text, toward being a fictional *character*, located within. Ironically, *No Third Path* might have been improved if Kosinski had completed this transformation and written it as a dystopian novel. Its message was genuinely frightening, more so than *The Future Is Ours*, and a part of what was scary was that it talked about a *universal* drive to enforce conformity that stood outside any specific system. It had many of the necessary elements—people and ideas and point of view. And the absence of physical description and paucity of dialogue were no more pronounced than in, say, Dostoyevsky's *Notes From Underground*. One can even argue in retrospect that parts of it were invented— Varvara's sparrow, certainly, unless one accepts the improbable coincidence that Kosinski twice in his life encountered bird painters. That sparrow was the key—the theme of the work at which Kosinski, unconsciously in oral trial runs, and now in notes, was already at work.

10.

As Kosinski awaited the publication of *No Third Path*, money problems continued to bear down upon him. His financial situation was something of a paradox. In the early days of his relationship with Mary Weir he had written to both his family and the Krauzes, boasting about his close relationship with the widow of the "King of Steel." He described her as heiress to an enormous fortune, and implied that he had prospects that would change not only his own circumstances but the situation of his family. Among those who were puzzled by Kosinski's ambiguous position was Andy Heinemann, an attorney who had met him through Bob Geniesse. Heinemann was startled when he found that Kosinski tooled around the city in a Continental Mark II. Where did a penniless exchange student come by money for a car like that? This echoed the observation of Feliks Gross, upon seeing a splendidly dressed Kosinski in the Rainbow Room, that "something had changed." When the relationship with Mary began to be general knowledge, there was naturally talk that he had become her "kept man."

And yet despite these touches of high living, there is evidence that neither the success of *The Future Is Ours, Comrade* nor the relationship with Mary had resulted in instant financial salvation. Living with a wealthy woman was a two-way street. If it carried certain perks—stylish clothes and a stylish car—it also involved obligations that produced a strain. There is probably a kernel of truth behind Kosinski's later insistence that, while living with Mary, he spent his literary earnings on tips. There was certainly the matter of masculine pride to be considered. It was necessary to "live up" to her lifestyle, which was both a pleasure and a burden. Interestingly, in *The Devil Tree*, the foreign suitor of modest means does not marry the rich widow. Claiming, as Kosinski did, to have spent his full income on tips, he gives her up rather than give in to an equivocal and unsatisfactory situation. One of the reasons he cites is the need to support his elderly mother, who lives alone in Florida. Kosinski, indeed, helped his parents and later his widowed mother when he could, sending packages of American clothes and other goods more often than money.

At the same time, Kosinski was sending periodic payments to

the Krauzes, gradually whittling down the debt of slightly over a thousand dollars for his plane ticket to the United States. That debt had been a point of contention in the early days after his arrival. As soon as he was situated, with a Ford Foundation grant and a book contract—of which he had informed both his parents and the Krauzes—Alfons Krauze had decided that it was time for Kosinski to begin paying down his debt. When Kosinski, at the safe distance of five thousand miles, dragged his feet, the Krauzes paid a call on the Kosinskis in Lodz, explaining their view of the situation. The parents had not previously met, and the circumstances of this first meeting must have been uncomfortable for both; in any event, payments shortly began to arrive from America, fifty or sixty dollars at a time.

The elder Krauzes would eventually formulate a theory about Kosinski and "the widow of the King of Steel." In their view, he had entered into the relationship with great expectations, but something had gone wrong. Perhaps the vast wealth he expected did not really exist. Or perhaps she withheld the wealth from him or did not entirely control it herself. In any case, the paydown of his debt continued in dribs and drabs, fifty or sixty dollars every few months, with occasional reminders and periodic excuses or promises of another installment in the near future. As a result, Kosinski was in contact with the Krauzes almost as often as with his own family, in the process filling them in on his various troubles and accomplishments, his dire financial straits, and his unhappy love affairs. The correspondence continued, more sporadically, until the late 1960s, when he had finally paid back all but a hundred dollars or so of the debt.

In his correspondence with the Krauzes, Kosinski sometimes touched upon the doings of Tadeusz, who had followed Kosinski in becoming an exchange student at Columbia. The two young men saw each other from time to time, and for a while they made a nostalgic effort to reconstruct the atmosphere of their life in Warsaw at the apartment of the vodka factory worker. The fact that they were both Polish émigrés held them together for a time, and the basis of their bonding was—as always—women. Kosinski had by then managed to transfer his talent for the acquisition of women into the American idiom. Once again Krauze and

Kosinski shared women, and Kosinski introduced Krauze to his great new discovery: *black* women. One night in New York he picked up a black prostitute and in Krauze's presence whispered something into her ear; the prostitute, outraged, pulled a razor from her hair and told him a categorical no. Whatever he had asked for, she was having none of it.

In September Kosinski moved into a new apartment at 440 East Seventy-ninth Street, known as Gregory House, selected by Mary, who agreed to pay the rent. Mary also selected the furniture, using a decorator who purchased objects from Georg Jensen. Really a single room with a kitchen, the apartment had a small room by the entrance which Kosinski converted into a darkroom. As Mary rarely went there, it served Kosinski as a sanctuary and a place to meet with Krystyna, who was still very much a part of his life and who would eventually live there for several months on a sublease after Kosinski married Mary and before her own marriage in 1962.

Kosinski had already begun to travel around the United States with Mary, visiting the Weir home at Hobe Sound, Florida, where he caught a first glimpse of America's rich and powerful at rest and play. On the return from one of those trips, they surprised many of his friends and most of hers with an announcement: They were married. They had taken the step on January 11, 1962, in front of a justice of the peace, in Birmingham, Alabama.

Only a few weeks before the wedding, Kosinski had begun to explain to Krystyna Iwaszkiewicz the nature of his relationship with Mary, and the fact that marriage was a possibility. A month earlier he had met Bill Morrison at a luncheonette and told him about the situation. Mary was putting aside a million dollars for him, he said, and he was going to marry her. "Wouldn't you do this if you were offered this kind of money?" He wanted Morrison to go to Krystyna and explain, to get her to see that his action was reasonable, and that he would eventually come back to her with money. To Morrison, however, Kosinski sounded like a man who knew he was doing something wrong but wanted to be told it was okay. Morrison refused to give the go-ahead, and the conversation marked a turning point as he came around to his wife's view of Kosinski's self-centeredness.

On the day of the departure for Birmingham, Krystyna Iwaszkiewicz received a phone call from Kosinski originating at a snowed-in airport—probably Denver—informing her that he was about to marry Mary. In a passage from *Blind Date* which describes the protagonist's marriage to Mary-Jane Kirkland, Kosinski writes as though it were a spur-of-the-moment decision. They were touring in Mary-Jane's private plane and had the pilot radio to find a convenient stopping point which "permitted marriage without prior application." The information the pilot came up with was that the nearest such place, less than two hours away, was Birmingham, Alabama (an assertion that provoked an irritable response from a Birmingham civil servant, informing the author that even in Birmingham one couldn't just stand up before a justice of the peace; a blood test and valid identification were required). Mary Weir happened not to have a private plane, either. The choice of Birmingham, Alabama, does, however, give an offhanded cast to what both participants must have realized would be perceived as a somewhat unusual union.

The incongruous marriage made Cholly Knickerbocker's newspaper gossip column (actually written by Igor Cassini, brother of designer Oleg Cassini), where the response was a raised eyebrow. Who was the young foreigner of no background who had married an older wealthy woman who was a fully paid-up member of New York's elite? Kosinski later claimed that in retaliation for the column he had reported to U.S. authorities that Cassini illegally received money as an unregistered agent for Dominican dictator Rafael Trujillo, and that as a result of the ensuing investigation Cassini lost his column and was ruined.

The suggestion that he was a fortune hunter would pursue Kosinski for many years, and as with the charge that he was a spy, he could, to a degree, blame his own indiscretion. It was true that the relationship with Mary overlapped other involvements. It was true that she dressed him, paid for his apartment, and provided him with the expensive and high-performance automobiles he loved. In one extreme instance, she flew with him to Los Angeles and arranged an intimate dinner party so that he could meet his idol, Rita Hayworth, an occasion unfortunately marred by Hayworth's preoccupation with the quarrel she was having with her lover, who accompanied her. It was also true that Kosinski boasted of the Weir fortune in letters home to his family and the Krauzes implying that his fortune was thereby made.

Kosinski would address the issue publicly in both *The Devil Tree* and *Blind Date*. In *Blind Date* it is the woman, Mary-Jane Kirkland, who suggests marriage to the protagonist, George Levanter. "Would I stay without the benefit of this setting?" he asks her.

"You'll never know," she replies.

To try to answer the questions posed by Kosinski's marriage to Mary Weir is to assume that human motives in such matters are unambiguously discoverable—that any one statement or posture may deliver the final word on the matter. By marrying Mary, Kosinski would certainly appear to have taken a major step forward in the "life script" laid out in the novel *Nikodem Dyzma*. Yet the very existence of such a highly specific *script* calls into question the notion of motive in the ordinary sense. There is something a little mad about the idea: something not quite real. It's not so much a simple matter of a bright young man who latches on to a rich woman as of a man who actuates an image of himself as "a man who marries a rich woman." Many relationships contain an element of acting out of roles; in Kosinski's case, the role playing was simply more extreme—so extreme as to suggest the existence of a personality disorder.

Mary Weir had a vulnerable quality that made people feel protective of her, and in some of her friends that sense of protectiveness produced a skeptical attitude toward Kosinski. A few of them confronted him directly. One such confrontation is recorded in *Blind Date*, set in the novel in the plush Long Island bomb shelter of a rich friend who states that Mary-Jane is on the list for admission to the shelter while Levanter, despite being her husband, is not. "It's not that you aren't likable," he says. "On the contrary. You are. It's just that one wonders if you haven't made a career out of being so likable."

The man goes on in a speech which Kosinski rendered elsewhere as literal truth, questioning the past of a man who has survived both Hitler and Stalin: "What if there was some deed, some awful price you had to pay to emerge unscathed? How do we know that there wasn't?" He goes on to say that he himself, like every WASP, is completely documented; public records cover every aspect of his life, whereas the foreign interloper is both undocumented and undiscoverable. He concludes by asking: "What does Mary-Jane, your own wife, really know about who you are?"

After they were married, Kosinski introduced Mary to Andy Heinemann, the attorney he had met at the Estabrooks' through his own attorney, Bob Geniesse. Invited to a dinner party, Heinemann was seated next to Mary and found her thoroughly delightful. She took him on a tour of the duplex at 71 East Seventy-first Street, and he was equally impressed with the antique French furniture, a testimony to her knowledge and exceptionally fine taste. The next day he called to thank Kosinski, spoke briefly with a maid, and found himself talking with Mary. She wanted to know what he had thought of everything—the food, the flowers, the furniture—all of which he could sincerely praise. Then she wanted to know what he thought of her friends.

Heinemann hesitated. "May I be honest?" he asked, and when she insisted that he be so, he said, "I think they're the biggest bunch of leeches I've ever met."

"Oh my God, an honest lawyer!" she exclaimed, and hung up abruptly. The next day she showed up at his office with an armload of file folders, her legal papers, and asked him to become her lawyer. Heinemann's statement had tactfully excluded Kosinski, but several years' acquaintance had given him doubts about Mary's new husband. He had listened while Kosinski sat on the floor of the Estabrook apartment telling the story of being hung up by the hands above a leaping dog—in the version Heinemann remembers, the event took place in Cracow, and the dog was a Doberman or Great Dane—and at the same time poking and tormenting the Estabrooks' small dog. Something about Kosinski struck him as not quite right, and his instincts told him that Mary needed to be protected from him. The stories about Kosinski's past were all well and good; as far as he knew, he later said, Kosinski could just as easily have been brought up in Brooklyn.

11.

Only two weeks after his marriage, on January 25, 1962, Kosinski received the news that his father had died in Lodz. His mother telephoned to tell him, and after he hung up Mary was so disturbed by his manner that she called Krystyna Iwaszkiewicz and asked her to come over and calm him. By the time Krystyna arrived, however, Kosinski was sitting at his desk, completely composed; in fact, he appeared irritated that Krystyna had been summoned. The three of them left together within a half hour, Kosinski and Mary to keep a social engagement.

Mieczyslaw Kosinski was buried in the Municipal Cemetery of Doly, on the outskirts of Lodz. There was no question of returning to Poland for the funeral. Yet both the initial expression of shock—whatever it was that alarmed Mary—and the almost instant recovery of composure suggest a good deal about the importance of this complicated relationship, and the extreme difficulty Kosinski had with accepting his own emotions. The public stance Kosinski took on his father over the years was consistent only in its ambiguity. On the one hand, his father was a judgmental and censorious figure, a "formidable SS," as Kosinski called Israel Kosky in *Hermit*; on the other hand, he was a wise counselor who patiently corrected the English in his son's letters and filled his own letters with lovingly detailed English lessons. Kosinski's works are strewn with references to his father's tastes and preferences, such as his particular admiration of Galsworthy, a perfectly respectable but unremarkable bit of literary taste which is significant mainly in attesting to his father's cosmopolitanism and command of languages.

After coming to the United States, Kosinski told interviewers, he had telephone conversations with his father in *Latin*, a device they came up with in order to get around the Polish censors. The story seems, on the face of it, almost certainly apocryphal; what secrets of state would they need to conceal? Perhaps father and son exchanged a few key words in Latin—which had importance as the language of the Catholic Church—but the actual use of Latin for rapid colloquial conversation seems unlikely. As a piece of public relations, however, the story contains several elements useful to the Kosinski myth—an affirmation of personal and familial erudition and emphasis on the severity of the Marxist regime—and it also has a deeper suggestion of affinity between father and son: two deeply alienated men who affirm their connection by communicating over the heads of those around them in a private, esoteric, and archaic tongue.

Yet set against this connection was a powerful denial of his father, not only in attaching himself strongly to other mentors and father figures, but in the modified version of his wartime experience in which he depicted himself as having been *alone*. He was telling these stories more frequently now, to his new American friends as well as his fellow Poles, and his audiences rarely failed to respond with suitable horror and sympathy. But what of his father's role as orchestrator of the family's survival? It was as if, by flying across the ocean, he had somehow removed his parents not only from his present but from his past. To deny his father's role in his own survival, however compelling his motives, was to deny a great deal.

The denial of his father was closely tied to a second denial—of his Jewish heritage. Most people who met him for the first time during his early years in America, Poles as well as Americans, were unaware that he was Jewish. Many assumed that his heritage was Polish Catholic; Kosinski was, after all, a Gentile name. A few friends, influenced by his dark appearance and his stories of the war, thought he might be a Gypsy, an ambiguity he preserved in *The Painted Bird*. Some recall not only the assumption that he was Gentile, but a distinct impression that he was anti-Semitic.

This is, perhaps, not surprising. At a highly impressionable age, he was told—on pain of death—that he was not, and must not ever be, a Jew. Later in life, as he moved to reclaim his Jewish heritage, he would recall a father who spoke very differently: "One day you will know that everything about you—the way you think, dance, try to seduce your high-school girlfriends—has been defined by your tradition. . . . You have your own state within yourself." This was Kosinski speaking to an Israeli audience in Tel Aviv in 1988, a different and later Kosinski describing a different and later father, who acknowledged both Jewishness and his son's "high-school girlfriends."

Beyond the denial of his father and his Jewish heritage was a displacement of feeling itself. Psychoanalytic studies of Holocaust survivors have described the condition of alexithymia, a regression in the form taken by emotions, which makes the affects useless in the processing of information. Psychoanalysts regard this condition as accounting in part for the high level of psychosomatic illness and drug addiction, as well as "numb marriages," among Holocaust survivors. Such individuals have a greatly diminished capacity for love—for romantic or other emotional attachment in the ordinary sense. They have sometimes been described by Freudian analysts as having "as if" personalities; their whole lives, and especially the romantic side of life, consist of going through the motions—*as if* they were actually living their experiences.

There was, certainly, in Kosinski's life an element resembling theater, as though in living day to day he were assembling psychodramas of which he was at once author, producer, director, and leading performer. The creative act was, in a sense, the way he put together his life. The novels he wrote about his experiences—particularly his later works—have almost the quality of "novelizations," those secondary transcriptive works produced to exploit successful films.

Among the first guests invited to dinner with the Weirs were Krystyna Iwaszkiewicz and Joel Charles, alone and as a couple. The four of them sat in Mary's imposing dining room at 740 Park Avenue, with Krystyna, in particular, wondering exactly what the evening was intended to accomplish. Servants arrived with course after course, but Krystyna noticed that Mary ate only a salad and a small filet; as he had done with her, Kosinski had put his new wife on a diet.

In such occasions one can discern the scripting of a set piece, as if Kosinski were trying out, in real life, small elements of a plot. People were like pieces on a chessboard, and he moved them around—sometimes almost randomly, as at the dinner with

Krystyna and Joel Charles—to see what combinations might proved elegant or interesting.

This theater of improvisation contained a note that began to rub old friends the wrong way. Despite the reaffirmation of their bond by the sharing of women, the relationship between Kosinski and Tadeusz Krauze was beginning to show some strains. Unlike Kosinski, Krauze took the discipline of sociology very seriously; he was deeply committed to his studies, and it troubled him that Kosinski was so blithely dismissive of its rigor and of the hurdles required in getting the Ph.D. By then Kosinski was busy looking at alternative ways to get approval of his dissertation. One of them involved Feliks Gross: he proposed a transfer to CCNY, where he would finish his doctorate under Gross's supervision. In Krauze's view, Kosinski had simply run into a buzzsaw in Lazarsfeld, his Columbia supervisor, a man who could not be charmed into dropping the rigor of his requirements. Gross too promptly grasped that Kosinski was trying to get around the question of methodological rigor; he politely demurred and excused himself from being a part of it.

Yet there was another factor in Kosinski's growing estrangement from Krauze. Kosinski was edging into an entirely different world, and on the occasions when his two social sets overlapped, it was unclear whether he was sharing his new life or flaunting it. Ryszard Horowitz, who in the months after his arrival in 1959 had seen Kosinski regularly, described coming to the Park Avenue duplex on Kosinski's invitation. He encountered uniformed valets in the front hall and was shown upstairs, where a housemaid wearing an apron let him into the library. He was left there for a half hour—in his view, it was to give him an opportunity to admire Mary Weir's fine taste in pictures. After a while the housemaid reappeared and led him through corridors to another part of the house, which was dominated by a fountain and a staircase, putting Horowitz in mind of a set from *Gone With the Wind*. And shortly Jurek Kosinski made a grand entrance, slowly descending the stairs in a red tuxedo!

With Krauze, who had known Kosinski in an environment where students shared a night-shift apartment, this new lifestyle did not go down well. Unlike Kosinski, Krauze had taken very seriously the effort of the Marxists to remake Poland as a humane and egalitarian society; whatever the shortcomings of the system that emerged, he felt the goals deserved more than flippant dismissal. Yet now, in capitalist America, flippant dismissal seemed more and more Kosinski's attitude. There were the two Novak books, for instance, which could easily be read as a selling out of his heritage to gain position in American society. And then there was Mary Weir. To Tadeusz Krauze, the whole idea of the relationship with Mary was disturbing. His view was brought to a crisis when he received an invitation to dinner at 71 East Seventy-first. As servants moved in and out of the room, removing one dish and serving another, he defended the socialist ideal, recalling the hopeful atmosphere of Poland in the early 1950s, and commented upon the American problem of unemployment amidst capitalist plenty. "*We* take responsibility for unemployment," Mary responded. "It has good effects."

Something of Mary's attitudes, which were right-wing but by no means exceptional in her set, was expressed in the gifts she bestowed upon Dr. Strzetelski's Polish Institute. To this gathering place for Polish exiles, which struggled to pay its rent and publish its quarterly journal, she gave, undoubtedly at Kosinski's prompting, a Tissot and several British paintings. It was the kind of gift Mary Weir preferred to make—art works expressive of her own exquisite taste. While appreciated, such a gift must have left something of an ambiguous impression upon the Poles. Eventually the Tissot was sold at auction by Parke Bernet, with the proceeds devoted to the more commonplace activities of the Institute.

Krauze was not impressed by Mary Weir's sense of *noblesse oblige*, nor by her cool rationalization of human misery. The last straw was Kosinski's behavior when Krauze's parents came to the United States for a visit. Kosinski owed them a great deal, and even if the loan had turned out to have the usual vaguely unpleasant consequences, they were his good old friends. For a long period he had visited in their home virtually every afternoon. They had written Kosinski as well as their son, hoping to have a warm reunion. The reunion was not to be. The elder Krauze tried repeatedly to get in touch with Kosinski, who finally spoke to him on the telephone. Kosinski was regretful but didn't have time to see him. As with many future episodes, the density of the real was a threat which Kosinski could not allow to intrude into the theatrical world of his own construction.

Another intrusion of the real was not to be escaped, however. Following the death of her husband, Elzbieta Kosinska had decided that it was time to pay her son a visit. She was naturally curious about the astonishing new world into which he had made his way, and now she was able to leave Poland and see it. Kosinski must have awaited her visit with profoundly mixed feelings. It was from his mother, above all, that he had inherited the idea that there was a brighter and more interesting place, and that he could get there. Her flair and her love of brilliance had prevailed, in the shaping of his character, over his father's steady intelligence and stealthy guile. Her fondness for eye makeup and fingernail polish, which had once expressed itself in her son only in brightly colored socks, now was exhibited in Prince of Wales suits and a Continental Mark II. Any son in his position would be proud to show his mother how far he had traveled in so few years.

At the same time, there was a dilemma to be resolved. By that time he had regaled the entire Polish émigré circle and much of Mary Weir's New York society with stories of his catastrophic and *solitary* adventures during the war—the wandering from village to village, the dog that had leaped at his heels, the loss of speech, the reunion at the orphanage where he was identified by his resemblance to his mother and the mark on his rib cage. What if conversation got around to those wartime experiences? What, God forbid, if someone casually asked her where the adult Kosinskis had been during the war? The question had come up, and he had managed to get away with vague answers. Sweden, he sometimes said. It was a big country. Some Poles must have escaped there. Maybe they had gotten there by boat.

The way Kosinski dealt with the situation reveals a great deal about the type of intimacy that existed between mother and son. In the course of her visit to New York, Elzbieta Kosinska met a good number of people—not only Mary and her friends, but the Strzetelskis and members of the Polish émigré circle. They made a day trip to Long Island, where Kosinski, Mary, and his mother spent an afternoon with Ewa Markowska and her family. Instead of shrinking from discussion of his experiences during the war, Kosinski made a point of bringing the subject up. His mother supported his story in every particular, describing the terrible fears she had felt for her son. On that point, everyone who met her in New York agreed.

How did he enlist her support? It is interesting to consider what arguments he must have made, if any were needed. The family had always managed to survive by telling a lie, he might have said. Lies were an essential tool of state; not only Hitler and Stalin, but all political leaders and all governments lied. It might be Camelot in America, but the Kosinskis were Europeans. Americans could buy images like the Kennedy marriage and family (even the myth that Kennedy had produced a Pulitzer Prize-winning book); Americans were innocents, but Europeans— especially worldly Central Europeans like the Kosinskis—knew better. What was a lie anyway, and what was the truth? The minute after an event took place, it meant different things in the memory of each individual who had witnessed or experienced it. What was art but lies—enhanced "truth," nature improved upon, whether visually or in language. Even photographs chose the angle of representation; indeed, photographs, with their implication of objectivity, were the biggest liars of all. Wasn't that the most basic message of the twentieth century? The truth, whether in art or in life, was whatever worked best.

Or perhaps it wasn't necessary to make excuses for himself at all. His mother knew what he had been through in actual fact. She had lived the same history; she was the wife of Moses Lewinkopf, who had survived the Holocaust at whatever cost. She may well have recognized the inner necessity of her son's behavior. She may well have grasped that those half-invented wartime stories had become an important part of his personal capital.

IV

BREAKTHROUGH

1.

No Third Path was scheduled for publication in February of 1962. As late as November 1961, with the first books due for delivery on December 31, Kosinski was still making drastic additions, removals, and corrections to the galleys. This process resulted in exchanges by telegram and letter between "Novak" and his German-language publisher, Alfred Scherz Verlag of Bern, Switzerland, in which Kosinski insisted that they hold up the translation for the corrected galleys, the publisher exhorted him to get on with it, and Kosinski replied adamantly that they should wait for the finished book.

The pattern would persist throughout his career: an obsession with the final surface of texts, resulting in enormous textual changes up to the last possible moment—and sometimes beyond. Kosinski was the kind of author who made publishers' production staffs tear their hair out; one of his novels was republished in a substantially revised version almost a decade after its initial publication (and long after the public had lost interest), while the publication of his final novel was postponed repeatedly for changes that seemed unnecessary to the publisher. This sense of the plasticity of text was also expressed in paperback versions, which were frequently revised and edited drastically.

There is an irony in this obsession. As a writer who lacked perfect command of the language in which he wrote, Kosinski was compelled, as a practical matter, to probe the nature of language itself. Language is one of the elements that bind every individual to his society. People at every level are vested communicants in the linguistic heritage of their tribe, and the most elevated intellectuals are not free of its bond. To no one was this more clear than Kosinski. As he continued to struggle with his doctoral dissertation at Columbia, he was made aware daily of the limitations language imposed upon him as an outsider.

Kosinski did well enough in spoken English, to be sure; his accent and his occasional Slavicisms were charming. But writing was a different matter. He was, quite simply, no Conrad. In written English, the omission of articles or the clustering of modifiers did not strike readers as charming; instead, it made the writer appear ignorant, half-educated, even stupid. Conrad wrote like an angel but could not make himself understood when he opened his mouth; with Kosinski, it was exactly the other way around. Which might not have been such a handicap had not Kosinski been a writer by profession.

From the beginning of his life as a professional writer, Kosinski had to protect a terrible secret: He could not write competently in the language in which he was published. Whenever he wrote a simple business letter, his reputation was at risk. Even a letter he wrote to his British agent, Peter Janson-Smith, required a hasty followup; the solecisms and grammatical errors were explained as the result of failure to proofread.

It was one more in a host of "as if" situations: he had to function at all times "as if" he had perfect command of written English. The fact that he was foreign, ironically, exacerbated the situation. F. Scott Fitzgerald may not have been able to spell, and Thomas Wolfe may have required heavy editing, but their work was clearly their own; no one doubted that they were native English-speakers capable of producing the essential elements of their own books.

The dilemma was straightforward: the ideas and anecdotes of Kosinski's books were his and his alone, but—as becomes clear with the cross-checking of factual analogues and analysis of the "Varvara" anecdote, which he apparently made up—the *actual English words* were not. *No Third Path*, like its predecessor, required a translator. The identity of that translator, at the remove of thirty years, is unknown and likely to remain so. One thing is clear. It was not Ewa Markowska; though still friendly to Kosinski, she had had enough of their previous arrangement.

The need for help, and for secrecy about that help, must have, in any case, been a source of great anxiety to Kosinski; perhaps the worst of its effects was to exacerbate the destructive penchant for secrecy that enfolded his life in general, with the concomitant sense of inauthenticity. In later years, the gradual unraveling of that web of secrets would lead, after extraordinarily convoluted efforts to explain away and cover up, to disastrous consequences.

Another lifelong habit which surfaced with the Novak books was a tendency to become directly involved in the business end of publication. Early on in the process of selling *No Third Path*, while it was still a project known as *Charged With Fate*, Kosinski's agent Bill Berger had exhorted him not to get involved in the contractual discussions with Doubleday. Now, as publication neared, he couldn't resist attempting to micromanage the publishing process, taking the publisher to task for not getting an advance copy to the *Christian Science Monitor* and reminding them to send copies to the Russian departments at Harvard and Princeton. The request shows how far Kosinski had come in understanding the making of a career as an intellectual in America. He had good reason to expect favorable treatment at the *Christian Science Monitor*, as its overseas news editor, Joseph Harrison, had written a glowing introduction. Failing to cash in on this connection would therefore have been a serious oversight.

As for Harvard and Princeton, it was the sort of detail that a publisher might easily forget. Sending complimentary copies there was not likely to stimulate sales, but from the point of view of Kosinski's career it would have a very material impact. Recognition of his work at such intellectual centers would go far toward establishing him as an authority in the field, and it could enhance his academic prospects, perhaps even leading to a job offer. Indeed, Kosinski would eventually spend a year teaching at Princeton, although only after the success of his first two novels.

* * *

Despite these efforts, *No Third Path* bombed. It was, when you got right down to it, more than most people wanted to know about the Russians, or their system. Apart from the indecision of its protagonist, not a great source of suspense as he now resided safely in the United States, it seemed to lack a theme. At least it lacked a *new* theme. It might well have been entitled *The Future Is STILL Ours, Comrade,* or possibly *MORE Future Is Ours, Comrade.* The basic message about the Soviet Union could only be delivered once, the concept of the off-the-boat émigré writer was used goods, and American intellectuals were not likely to be impressed by a book that represented them as marginal stooges, the sort of people Lenin referred to as "useful idiots."

W. H. Chamberlin, who had effused over *The Future Is Ours,* was much more measured about *No Third Path;* again writing for the *Chicago Tribune,* Chamberlin argued that "the book would have gained by a more analytical personal approach on the part of the author," a view that echoed complaints about Kosinski by his professors at Columbia. Chamberlin attempted to lighten this criticism, however, with the observation that "as a collection of undigested raw material of Soviet life and psychology, it is one of the best." *Library Journal* suggested that the author should add a summary and an index, while an otherwise favorable review in the *New York Herald Tribune* observed that some of the interviews appeared to be "composites," and that "one might, in principle, object to a composite interview as involving the author as a *creator*." The *Christian Science Monitor* kicked in with a favorable review, somewhat belatedly, on April 13, which included an interesting error of fact; the author, it said, had "lived for seven years" in the Soviet Union, intensively seeking a place for himself in Soviet society. The reviewers, overall, had taken a more negative view this time of the book's peculiar structure; neither fish nor fowl, it lacked the systematic methodology of an academic study and contained hints and suggestions of fiction without quite breaking through to declare itself a novel. In an oblique way, the critics were onto the central dilemma of Kosinski/Novak's life.

Seen from the perspective of Kosinski's whole career, the Novak books were clearly an apprenticeship. While producing them, he was doing the early working out of the themes that would eventually drive his most successful novels. He was also working out a solution to the problem of producing texts in a language he did not fully command—a solution that would serve him satisfactorily for many years before becoming a deadly weakness in his public position. And there was another aspect in which the Novak works had served as an apprenticeship. A writer's books, he had learned, are only part of the product. The real—the ultimate—product was *himself*, and the books were, among other things, a vehicle for selling that product. The Novak books had provided him with an entrée into American society, served as testimonial of his bona fides with Mary Weir, and provided credentials to support his introduction to the celebrated and accomplished. He would employ this formula, too, throughout his career, again with mixed results. Many writers—Hemingway and Mishima among them, and perhaps even Dickens—have functioned as though the books were only *part* of the personal production, although few writers embraced the concept as wholeheartedly, or as transparently.

By 1962, however, the Novak pseudonym and format had outlived their usefulness. The identity of Novak had begun to leak out, so there was no longer any use in maintaining the pretense that Novak was not Kosinski. His professors were onto it at Columbia, where things were not going well in any case. Besides, the separation of the two identities had begun to confound the larger purposes of his career. Traveling in Mary Weir's elevated circle, he needed to account for himself as something other than a penniless Columbia student who had come to organize her library. To be the author of two critically acclaimed books on the Soviet Union, an expert and a scholar, served that purpose quite nicely. So Kosinski emerged from the closet: Kosinski and Novak became, simply, Jerzy Kosinski.

Following the relative failure of *No Third Path*, Kosinski did what he would often do in the future when New York seemed less hospitable to his charm: he left the country. Along with Mary, he set off on a contemporary version of the European grand tour on April 16, 1962. Their itinerary included England, France, Italy, Greece, Turkey, and Spain. In England he was able to arrive as an author, meeting with his agent and British publisher; he and Mary stayed at the Connaught, where Mary had always stayed with Ernest Weir, and where he enjoyed the best of understated British service.

It was another apprenticeship of sorts, the completion of the education he would have received had he been the son of Ernest Weir rather than Mieczyslaw Kosinski. In Paris they stayed at the Ritz. All the while Kosinski was aware that his new experiences amounted to rich literary capital; sometimes he thought of himself in comparison to Scott Fitzgerald and Stendhal, both obsessed with a wealth they themselves did not have. Having studied human society systematically, he understood that it was a rare privilege to have a glimpse of life at both the top and bottom of the ladder. Before leaving Poland, he had told the Krauzes that he was uniquely privileged by an upbringing that would make him equally comfortable in an English royal palace and a poor tenement. He had proved the one side of his boast by surviving by his wits during his first months in America; now he was making good on the other.

Later he would draw heavily upon the experiences of that trip in works that probed the relationship of money, in its various forms, to larger philosophical and spiritual issues. The opening episode of *Steps*, in which the protagonist seduces a simple peasant girl by displaying the power of his credit cards, was drawn from his travels in Italy. The credit card was a relatively new instrument at the time, and it fascinated Kosinski. Communism might propose doing away with money, but in a sense the capitalists were already doing so. Nothing since man replaced barter transactions with the use of coins had so clearly demonstrated that money was a mere abstraction—an invisible link between one's effort and the material goods and services that effort could command.

This is the essence of the protagonist's childlike explanation in *Steps* that one need only present the credit card to receive any goods one desires. On the one hand, this recalls Marx's "labor theory of value," in which one's only legitimate possession was the value added by one's labor. At the same time, Kosinski's protagonist saw clearly that the credit card was an implement of power—storing up a cumulative measure of his vital force, much like an American Indian's medicine bag. With that implement he could bend others to his will, playing with them as with children, if he so chose. The more of this stored power one could possess, the better. Thus the outsider's interpretation of American capitalism.

On June 25 Kosinski and Mary were in Venice when the *Herald Tribune* revealed that a major panic was taking place on Wall Street. It had been building since the market peaked in January, and it had to do with *steel*. Using his position as a Democratic president, John Kennedy had persuaded the steelworkers' union to accept a moderate, noninflationary wage increase. As soon as the agreement was in place, the major steel companies, led by U.S. Steel, announced an increase in their prices. Kennedy was furious. Feeling betrayed, he employed all the powers of the federal government, including the FBI, to pressure the steel executives for a price rollback, and, with the help of CEO Joseph Block of Inland Steel, he succeeded.

To the financial markets this conflict between the chief executives of a major industry and the chief executive of the nation was a deeply threatening development. The Dow Jones Industrials slid for four months straight, and in June the "Kennedy Slide" became the "Kennedy Panic" or, as some were calling it, the "Kennedy Crash." The newspapers were full of alarm about the possibility of a new Great Depression. When the news reached Mary Weir in Venice, the market had lost almost a quarter of its value, and First National City Bank (now Citicorp), which handled both her money and the Ernest Weir trust, reported to Mary that her portfolio had suffered along with the rest. The market would eventually recover, almost doubling in price by 1966, but the panic of 1962 produced a moment of high anxiety.

Kosinski later used the "Kennedy Panic" for an episode in *The Devil Tree*. The minor character of the novel based on Kosinski is traveling in Venice with Mrs. Horace Sumner Whalen when she receives news that "on the previous day she had lost close to sixty-two million dollars." This news is delivered to the Kosinski character during lunch on a terrace overlooking the Grand Canal. Mrs. Whalen then asks the manager of their hotel for the latest

American newspapers, joking that *Pravda* would probably tell the story more accurately than the *Wall Street Journal*. She is promptly offered *Pravda*, which the hotel manager, admitting that he is a Communist, volunteers to translate. In a revised edition of the book published in 1981, the manager then delivers a monologue about the warmongering decadence of America and cites as its source a speech, published in *Pravda*, by the woman's late husband, Horace Sumner Whalen—the figure in the novel based on Ernest T. Weir.

The amount mentioned in the novel greatly exaggerates Mary Weir's wealth by any method of counting. To have lost "sixty-two million" in the Kennedy Panic of 1962, even if the losses actually took place over several months and not in the three days of panic, and even assuming that her holdings were largely in steel and heavy industries, which were especially hard hit, Mary Weir would have had to have, to begin with, a fortune of several hundred million dollars. This was the estimate of Mary's fortune Kosinski occasionally bandied about—sometimes four hundred million, sometimes five.

It made for a terrific story—the penniless boy from Poland who married the woman with Rockefeller-scale wealth—but it incorporated enhancement on a Kosinskian scale. The assets that provided Mary Weir with the means for her lifestyle were tied up tightly by Ernest Weir's estate, and would pass on at her death to her son, David, for whom they would also be tightly tied up. In any case, the Ernest Weir trust probably did not exceed sixty or seventy million—or roughly the amount "Mrs. Whalen" was described as having lost in a single day: "On paper, of course!" Mary's own net worth, including such properties as the duplex on Park Avenue and a great deal of valuable but illiquid art work and furniture, was probably not more than five or six million dollars.

Other details show that Kosinski was slightly muddled when he came to write the story of that day in Venice. In the earlier, shorter version, Mrs. Whalen is apprised of the situation by her bank; in the revised version, the informant is not her bank but her broker, an odd repository for several hundred million dollars (although not implausible for part of Mary Weir's considerably smaller personal portfolio), while it is not "she" but "her estate" that has lost the "sixty-two million." As the assets of living human beings are not normally spoken of as constituting an *estate*, one may speculate that this unusual usage reflected Kosinski's ultimate discovery that Mary Weir's means were not altogether her own. There was an "estate" involved, all right; it was not Mary's, but Ernest Weir's.

Kosinski and Mary Weir returned from Europe on September 29, 1962, to an America rushing into yet another Cold War crisis. American overflights had discovered offensive Russian missiles in Cuba, and for two weeks in October, Kennedy and Khrushchev engaged in a public game of geopolitical "chicken," culminating in the missiles' removal. It is in such an atmosphere of Cold War tension that Levanter, Kosinski's protagonist in *Blind Date*, is informed that he is not on the select list for admittance to a private bomb shelter.

On October 20 Kosinski informed the Institute of International Education of the publication of *American Sociology 1950–1960* (or, properly, *Socjologia amerykanska 1950–1960*, as it was published in Poland as a textbook), containing a bibliography and translations of articles by leading American sociologists, including Lazarsfeld. It was a fine achievement, but, in the eyes of Columbia and the I.I.E., hardly a substitute for a completed dissertation. The anthology had been a project which rationalized uneven progress in other areas without actually advancing his own work in any material way. In the process, it had involved a side arrangement in which Tad Krauze was brought in to help in translation and editing, ultimately not to the satisfaction of Dr. Strzetelski and the publisher, the Polish Institute. This complication could not have helped the strained feelings between Kosinski and his old friend, who had become a last important link to his Polish past.

Things were ominously quiet on the literary front as well. On September 7, while Kosinski was still in Europe with Mary, Timothy Seldes at Doubleday had sent him a comprehensive list of paperback publishers who had rejected and those who were still considering both of the Novak books. While there was hope, it was a powerful dose of rejection to greet a person upon his return from a four-month trip.

One bit of hopeful equivocation came on September 18 from Pyramid, which had just published John Gunther's *Inside Russia Today* and expressed the desire to see how they did with Gunther's book before making up their minds. Seizing eagerly on this faint hope, Kosinski called and made a lunch date for December 28 with Pyramid's Donald Bensen. Then on December 20 Bensen wrote Kosinski that Pyramid had decided definitely not to do the reprint; as there was no longer any point to their lunch, he was canceling it.

Amidst career disappointments, Kosinski was sustained in part by the joy he took in mischief—particularly sexual mischief. Prostitutes were a favorite diversion, and he particularly favored a group situation, with his staging and spectatorship adding to the pleasure. On one of these occasions, with Mary out for the evening, he included his stepson, David, who was then eighteen. Repairing to the apartment of a friend, the three men disrobed, while Kosinski evaluated the two prostitutes. Kosinski suggested that David try the short, dark, Jewish girl. While such rites of male initiation are by no means unheard of, the situation had a rather contrary impact on David, who had been uncertainly swept along to begin with and had already been sleeping with his girlfriend, so was in no particular need of such initiation. He was rather nonplussed as the girl kept up a running commentary on his performance.

A more serious and rarefied diversion was provided by Lilla van Saher, who lived less than a block east of Kosinski's apartment on Seventy-ninth Street. Van Saher, whose origins were Hungarian, was herself an author and the daughter and sister of well-known Freudian analysts—her father, Ferenc Alexander, having in fact been an early colleague of Freud. She had been married to a financier who managed money for Queen Juliana of the Netherlands, but by the time she met Kosinski she had fallen on leaner times. By the early 1960s, she was hostess to a modish literary salon, which assembled every Thursday at her apartment at 333 East Seventy-ninth. She was an early admirer and great friend of Tennessee Williams, who was a habitué of her Thursday meetings, as was James Leo Herlihy, the author of *Midnight Cowboy*, among other notable figures of the era. The other side of Lilla van Saher's life, of which she made no secret, involved the psychosexual service she provided as a dominatrix. She advertised provocatively in appropriate newspapers, offering to provide sexual "punishment" to men who were in need of it. Many of her "victims" fell in love with her—stricken not only by her beauty but by her wide knowledge of literature and the arts—and the circle of her clients and her literary friends overlapped. Lilla was now well into her fifties, her body thickened somewhat with age although still distinguished by lush and well-shaped breasts, of which she was inordinately proud and which she would bare at the slightest excuse. By the mid-1960s she was doing part-time work for a sex research institute, which eventually got her into difficulty with the postal service. In order to recruit interviewees for a book she was preparing in conjunction with the institute on sadomasochism (which was never finished), she placed ads in American sex magazines using a Canadian mail drop as a screen. When batches of mail were transferred to an American mail drop, Lilla was shortly visited by postal inspectors, who apparently suspected that she was involved in some kind of smuggling.

In Kosinski's relationship with Lilla, there were synergistic advantages which did not immediately meet the eye. His youthfulness and rising star melded perfectly into her coterie of established writer-friends. She was more than willing to serve as his adviser and promoter, and sometimes as his literary hostess. She was happy to give dinner parties introducing him to the likes of Norman Mailer and Gore Vidal, in the process hanging on to her own position and promoting herself. She encouraged him to present his experiences in the form of a novel, and when that novel was ready for publication, she mobilized her coterie to support it. She introduced him to Jim Herlihy, whose blurb would later be used in promoting *The Painted Bird*, and pushed him on Tennessee Williams, whom he sometimes bumped into at Elaine's, then a new restaurant catering especially to writers, to which Williams often repaired upon getting out of bed at three or four o'clock in the afternoon.

Stalking around her apartment in a long, flowing black lace nightdress and high-heeled, high-gloss black shoes, her artful makeup accentuating her sparkling dark eyes, her nails lacquered and her whole body perfumed, she presented the sophisticated eroticism of an Oriental courtesan. Hooked on the wall in the corner of her living room was a life-size plaster cast of her breasts, which on occasion she would ask guests to take down for comparison to the originals. Kosinski enjoyed a more intimate position than the other regulars of her circle; often arriving on short notice, and having the run of her apartment, he would go directly to the kitchen to put on coffee. On equally short notice she prepared for him her specialty—chicken paprika, with large pieces of breast, washed down by a bottle of hock—which he repaid with a witticism, "Ah, Lilla, my dear, spicing your breasts, eager for takers!" Once, accompanied by a friend, Kosinski went through her wardrobe, remarking upon the large array of black underwear with many items trimmed in red or with red roses embroidered on them. "Lilla, have you no shame?" he asked. "These are a parody. Shopgirls wear these things. . . . Why do you buy them? Who can you possibly get?"

To which she came right back: "They are all presents."

And mock though he might, the image of that black underwear would remain in his mind with preternatural clarity, shaping expectation in more than one future relationship. Sexually, despite her age, or perhaps because of it, Lilla approached his ideal. Accustomed to role playing, she was happy to abandon her dominatrix specialty and serve as his "little slave," moving instantly to deliver his heart's desires, however strange. Above all, she had a sense of *play*—of childish enjoyment as well as of staged, artificial drama—a quality he would discover only occasionally throughout the remainder of his life. As a professional practitioner of sexual theater, she was uniquely qualified to accommodate his need to dominate, and she provided for him the perfect vehicle for expressing a side that tended toward psychodrama. She was quite willing to procure young girls for him, often approaching women he pointed out on the street. In interviews and in the novel *Blind Date*, he attributed this procuring, interestingly, to his mother, who supposedly selected his high-school girlfriends, but the fully developed model was clearly van Saher.

Like Mary Weir, another older woman who served him as

mother and lover, van Saher presented a sensibility ideally cali-
brated to appreciate the convolutions of his thought. Yet while
both Mary Weir and his mother were no more than intelligent
women of informed middlebrow taste, Lilla van Saher had an exquisite and subtle grasp of literature, particularly the avant-garde.
They argued violently over matters of literary taste, Lilla putting
forward such favorites of her own as Mailer, Vidal, Williams, and
Truman Capote while he argued their relative insignificance
against the psychological depths of Dostoyevsky or the tremendous breadth of vision of Tolstoy. When he advocated the Russians, Lilla would counter by citing Hungarian writers—Szabo,
Szerb, Déry, Molnár, and Koestler, of whom only Koestler cut any
ice with Kosinski. "But Lilla, my dear Lilla, who could possibly
read that . . . that *Stoff*?" he would say. "It's written by madmen
for madmen." She desperately sought his approval of her own
novel, *Macumba*, a story of cult belief and witchcraft set in Brazil,
but he was dismissive, saying only, "every woman fantasizes
about being a girl running wild in the forest."

Yet Lilla van Saher had indeed run wild. She had once been
raped on the Orient Express by a Hungarian hussar, a story she
told with a relish that undermined its moral moment, and which,
somewhat altered, Kosinski would retell in *Cockpit*. As a young
actress in Berlin, she told him, she had been introduced to
Heinrich Himmler. "Come, Lilla, young? You were never young!"
he remarked, almost killing the story. Begged to resume, she told
of her mandatory post-performance date with the uniformed
Himmler, who had "the face of a dead rabbit, weak, watery eyes,
the handshake of a dying old man, and a limp, peeled shrimp of
a prick that he couldn't get up." Kosinski was titillated by this
connection to one of the century's master bird painters, but
stricken by the pain his flippant response had caused Lilla; he
called her solicitously for days afterward. More than a friend, not
exactly a mistress or lover, she would remain an important figure
in Kosinski's life, whatever his passing romantic attachments, until her death, her rich experience of the world and mature sense
of play and possibility available to him upon demand. In her easy
company his sexual activities rose to a plane of appetite and expectation that would endure the rest of his life, while their ongo-

ing theater of the real was to have, in the year before her death, an extraordinary final twist.

As the beginning of 1963 rolled around, the impasse in Kosinski's career was becoming a fact that could no longer be avoided. The Novak books were, to all intents and purposes, dead, the cancellation of the lunch with Bensen providing a final punctuation mark. The posture as mediating intellectual between East and West had taken him as far as it could for the moment. In the meantime, he was perilously close to burning his bridges at Columbia. While he enjoyed his celebrity as an author and traveled with Mary Weir, he had neglected the necessary preparation for his doctoral qualifying exam, the deadline for which now loomed.

On February 19 Kosinski sat for the examination as required. Midway through, he informed the proctor that he was unable to continue. Eight days later, Mary's personal physician provided a letter under his Park Avenue letterhead testifying that Kosinski had been under his care. It explained that Kosinski was suffering from gastrointestinal complaints, weight loss, fatigue, and general malaise having to do with *the illness of his wife*. His inability to continue with the exam was attributed to a combination of prescription medications—Vistaril, Bonadoxin, and Pro-Banthine with Dartal, along with his usual Dexedrine (which he took so he could function with little sleep).

For the time being, Kosinski's status at Columbia was saved, with a medical excuse once again coming to his rescue. Nor were the problems alluded to in the doctor's letter entirely fabricated. Nevertheless, his flight from the doctoral exam marked a low point in his life in America—his academic career blocked, with no alternative in sight.

2.

On May 26, 1963, the Kosinskis left for a second grand tour, this time including Asia in an expanded itinerary. Their stops included Morocco, Egypt, Turkey, India, Pakistan, Cambodia, Thailand, Indonesia, Hong Kong, and Japan as well as the more standard European stops—Italy, France, Switzerland, West Germany—now augmented by Finland, Norway, and Sweden.

While various distant locales would show up in his future novels, Indonesia seems to have made a particular impression. It became the specific site of a scene in *Cockpit* and the unnamed location of a graphic act of violence in *Steps*. In that scene, the protagonist is witnessing executions in the course of a revolution. In order to avoid becoming a participant, he exchanges his rifle for another man's long knife, only to discover that the next round of killings are to be carried out as beheadings by those holding knives.

The Indonesia that Kosinski visited in 1963 was in the late stages of President Sukarno's rule, just before a several-sided coup led to his gradual ouster by General/President Suharto. Violence was still sporadic in 1963, but in 1965–66, an estimated one million supporters of the Communist Party would be massacred—many by rifle and machine-gun fire, in a manner all too familiar in recent European history, but masses of others by machete. Written up as a distant event by the *New York Times*, the Indonesian purge was one of the least-covered massacres of the twentieth century, but the sketchy reports clearly had an impact on Kosinski, whose travels had given him a concrete point of reference; the text of *Steps* accurately describes the political situation, unusual for the times, in which right-wing students combined with farmers to oppose the left-wing president (Sukarno) and workers.

In Italy, he happened to look into the window of a well-known Florentine tailor shop specializing in formal wear and military dress, and the notion suddenly struck him of ordering a uniform. He went inside and was fitted for two, one khaki and one blue, drawn eclectically from the military dress of several countries and various branches of the service. Both were designed with wide shoulders and lapels, as well as epaulets, compensating for his high waist and narrow shoulders. When they arrived at his hotel, he put the jackets out to bake in the sun, to give them a used and faded look, taking care to cover parts of the chest pockets so that it would appear that they had once had ribbons.

Such disguises, he would write in *Cockpit*, are "never simply a deception or a hoax," but "an attempt to expand the range of another's perception." In what reads like an expansion of his motto—*Larvatus prodeo*—he added that "it is the witness who deceives himself, allowing his eyes to give my new character credibility and authenticity. I do not fool him; he either accepts or rejects my altered truth."

That "altered truth" enabled Kosinski to experience the world as it presents itself to a high-ranking military officer, cutting to the head of queues and receiving the respectful salutes of officers in various services. Parking attendants brought his car immediately, ignoring a line of waiting "civilians," and police in several countries waved him through traffic. All this was quite helpful, he later told interviewers, as Mary's "illness" made waiting in lines uncomfortable and inconvenient.

That "illness" was later described as a "brain tumor" or "brain cancer," which was gradually destroying her, in the process causing bouts of physically induced irrationality and erratic behavior. But Mary's illness, like the military uniform, represented an "altered truth." Since at least 1950, more than a decade before she met Kosinski, she had been subject to severe bouts of depression and heavy drinking, which necessitated occasional visits to an institution in New Haven for drying out.

Mary's alcoholism had not greatly troubled Kosinski in the beginning. In the first flush of a new relationship, she was more controlled, and her occasional bouts may even have served his purposes. Heavy drinking made her tend to be forgetful, and occasionally confused. As a result she had managed not to notice, or pay much attention to, his periodic absences, or to pick up clues to the presence of other women. Now, in the course of an extended trip, the drinking problem that had made her malleable suddenly made her almost unmanageable. Not only did she require massive injections of vitamin B-12, but her behavior was at times uncontrollable without sedation. In Switzerland she had one of her episodes, requiring a doctor's care, and while she recovered Kosinski drove aimlessly around the winding Swiss roads or went rowing on a nearby lake, his solitary thoughts drifting back to his experience in the war.

* * *

There are many paths and sources leading to *The Painted Bird*, and many points from which one might date its genesis. By his own account Kosinski had been making notes even as he worked on *No Third Path*, or as early as 1961. The serious movement from notes to the novel itself, however, apparently began in that summer of 1963. Kosinski would explain the book at times as his effort to present to his American wife the realities of a past which she could not otherwise imagine. There is, no doubt, an element of truth in this assertion—*The Painted Bird* would eventually be dedicated to "my wife Mary Hayward Weir without whom even the past would lose its meaning." Yet the novel must also have been a refuge from Mary, both as a place to turn his attention when she was on one of her rampages and as the promise of deliverance from dependency upon her financial resources. Thus Kosinski's introduction to the 1976 edition, placing the resolve to produce a book from his childhood in Switzerland during the summer of 1963, is probably reasonably accurate.

On September 10 the Kosinskis returned to the United States. The situation at Columbia had gone from bad to worse, and the need to resuscitate his career was approaching crisis proportions. Shortly after his return he received a letter from H. W. Overstreet, the noted anticommunist writer, and his wife Bonaro, announcing themselves as fans of his work and mentioning that they were coming to New York and would like to meet him. Visiting in mid-October, the Overstreets were bowled over by the "Joseph Novak" they met and found to be a charming young man named Jerzy Kosinski. He was the rare author who was as good in person as his books, or even better. They were distressed, however, to learn of the pressures he was under at Columbia and offered the good offices of their friend Sidney Hook, the renowned political scientist whose own intellectual journey away from Communism Kosinski would presumably find congenial. It is not known whether Kosinski actually contacted Hook. By then he was deeply engrossed in the project that was to overtake all other career considerations.

By one way of looking at it, the central creative act in the production of *The Painted Bird* had already taken place back in 1958, when Kosinski began telling Mira Michalowska the expanded version of his experiences during the war. Acknowledging the importance of those Wednesday luncheons at Schrafft's, Kosinski would later salute Michalowska as the person "responsible" for his writing the book. Actually he had begun telling the stories even earlier, to high-school friends like Pomorski, but his emigration to America had given him a new freedom of invention.

Throughout his writing career, Kosinski would feel the need to appropriate an episode first as an autobiographical "fact" before rendering it in the form of fiction. Describing a nascent form of this process, his high-school friend Pomorski would describe three stages in the production of a Kosinski story. First, something happened. Second, something happened and Kosinski was involved in it. Third, Kosinski was the chief character in what happened. The question Pomorski, and others, would ask was whether Kosinski himself needed to believe in that third version in order to tell it as compellingly as he did.

The central invention of *The Painted Bird* consisted in moving the boy from his position as a passive bystander, who survived as a result of the actions of a canny and ruthless father, to central importance as a *solitary* wanderer, surviving by his own wits and good luck. That leap having been made—in Pomorski's scheme, the boy having been transformed into the chief character—it remained to transform the details of his actual experience into a coherent tapestry, working the central incidents in and inventing stories to disguise the seams at the points where the invented text was cobbled onto his own life. It was a task that could be done with freedom in America, as he had gradually realized, because the facts upon which the story was based existed far away in time and place, and on the far side of what seemed increasingly an impenetrable wall. He could be fairly certain that no one within the range of his new American audience was going to interrogate the peasants of Dabrowa Rzeczycka as to whether his version was literally true.

Besides his own experiences, he had numerous other sources and traditions to draw upon. Back in Lodz, Romek Polanski had told stories of his life alone on the run in Cracow, as a Jewish child during the occupation; sometimes listeners to Kosinski's stories got the impression he, too, had been in Cracow. The incident of the dog snapping at his heels had, in the version presented to Andy Heinemann, taken place in Cracow, at the hands of a savage teacher who put the boy on a "cross."

His mother, to whom he had described his project, had sent him a copy of Unuk and Radomska-Strzemecka's *Polish Children Accuse*, a collection of testimony by children who had wandered and suffered during the occupation. It should not be forgotten, however, that the essential imaginative leap had taken place before Kosinski read this book, and that Polanski's experiences, unlike those described in *The Painted Bird*, were predominantly urban.

As his own firsthand view of the peasants was limited by the constrictions on his movement—as well as by the fact that he was a young child—Kosinski turned for detail to Dr. Henryk Biegeleisen's encyclopedic *At the Cradle, In Front of the Altar, Over the Grave*. He was familiar with the work of Biegeleisen, a world-famous Polish anthropologist and sociologist, from his graduate work in Lodz and Warsaw. Now he drew upon Biegeleisen particularly for his accounts of the healing practices and superstitions of the peasants, most particularly superstitions involving teeth and hair, as well as ghosts and vampires. The fact that Biegeleisen's text dealt with a large geographic area going back to the Middle Ages contributed to the novel's feeling of existing outside of specific time and place, while throwing searchers for specific analogues off the track.

For historical context, Kosinski relied upon Gerald Reitlinger's *The House Built on Sand: The Conflicts of German Policy in Russia, 1939–1945*, which laid out the subtleties of the relationships among partisans, marauding bands, and Jews in the occupied territories, and provided an account of the Kalmuk cavalry. *The Painted Bird*, seen in this light, is not only an enhanced personal account but a *researched* "historical" novel, comparable perhaps to Doctorow's *Ragtime*. And along with this historical and anthropological sourcing, Kosinski brought important literary antecedents including Wladyslaw Reymont's *The Peasants* and Henryk Sienkiewicz's *Pan Wolodyjowski*, as well as the international tradition of the picaresque or episodic novel.

Yet the essential core of *The Painted Bird* is an expanded rendering of Kosinski's own experiences in Dabrowa, from which he deletes the presence of his family and to which he adds the element of movement. In real life, only one significant movement took place within the period encompassed by the novel—the family's night flight from Pasiowa's cottage through Radomysl to the semidetached Warchol apartment some twenty-five kilometers away in Dabrowa. In the novel, however, the neighbors in Dabrowa become, each in turn, the source of episodes that take place as the boy moves from village to village.

Some aspects of the text that border upon "magical realism" have their origins in the need to account for that movement. The episode of the giant catfish, for example, was in life a static episode in which, with his friend Andrzej Migdalek, Jurek Kosinski whiled away an hour witnessing a natural marvel. In the text of the novel, his sense of wonder at the giant fish is transformed into the surreal episode in which the boy is thrown onto the fish's inflated bladder and floats downstream to his next calamitous adventure. One may well imagine the ten-year-old Jurek Kosinski standing on the river bank, wishing that he could simply drift downstream like a giant fish; in the novel, that wish is fulfilled.

The portrait of Marta, physically drawn from the goodhearted hunchback Marianna Pasiowa, owes much to Biegeleisen's description of peasant superstitions concerning hair and teeth, while the second old woman with whom the boy stays, Olga, seems to be one of the novel's few creations from whole cloth, serving mainly as a device for incorporating Biegeleisen's description of peasant healing practices. Warchol, the landlord, becomes the farmer Garbos, who strings the boy up by his hands above Judas, the leaping dog, whose name carries a suggestive doubleness: Judas the renegade disciple, the betrayer within the body, and *Jude*, the German word for Jew, the hidden inner essence against which Kosinski had always to be vigilant on pain of death.

That fall, as he labored at the research and writing of the text, Kosinski found himself immersed in an inner drama as well, worked out in a world of primal experience whose images possessed the intensity of dream episodes rendered to a psychoanalyst. The transformations of Lech Tracz, the bird catcher, and Ewka Migdalek, the girl next door, both partake of this primal working out of psychoanalytic issues and processes. It was to Ewka that ten-year-old Jurek Kosinski unburdened his heart, insisting that he was, in fact, Jerzy Lewinkopf, a Jew from Lodz. As punishment for this terrible knowledge, she becomes in the Ewka of the novel a wanton and somewhat older girl who is sodomized by a goat. Her brother Andrzej ("Bumek") becomes the "Quail," with whom she has an incestuous relationship, while her father, the mild-mannered schoolmaster Migdalek, becomes the vicious Makar who gives his daughter to the goat.

The representation of pain and loss eroticized provides a powerful paradigm for understanding the whole of Kosinski's experience. The episode with Ewka is, in a novel of relatively flat action, the emotional climax, moving the boy to renounce God and all principles of goodness and invoke the Evil Ones. It is linked to the more exterior climax, in which he drops a missal while helping serve Mass, is beaten and flung into a pit, and emerges to find that he has lost the power of speech. The story of his loss of speech is an improvisation Kosinski began to tell in his first days in America. In Poland there were individuals at hand still able to set the record straight. Perhaps when Kosinski later wrote that writing in English freed his mind to encounter past experience, he was really describing a liberation from the shackles of historical fact—a liberation that took place first deep within his own psyche. Kosinski stuck to the story of his muteness, with modifications, until his death, and if not true in the literal sense, "muteness" stands as a powerful metaphor for his inability, at first, to give coherent articulation to the horror of his childhood experience.

The articulation of that experience is finally pulled into coherence by a single overarching metaphor—the painted birds of Lech Tracz. Lech Tracz in the novel becomes simply "Lekh": a homonymous spelling not found in the region or in any Eastern European language. Another homonymous association may have asserted subliminal influence. In Hebrew, *lekh* is the imperative of the verb "to go," as to begin an odyssey. It is, in fact, the exact command issued by God to Abraham—*Lekh lekha*—or "Go! Go forth!"—the divine directive to move in a path ordained by God. Interestingly, the episode of Lekh the Birdcatcher is placed near the beginning of the novel, soon after the boy's departure from Marta's burning hut and before his real-life counterpart encountered the actual birdcatcher.

The bird-painting metaphor contains several elements. The alien individual is set apart by beauty. The birds are painted not purple, as in *No Third Path*, but brilliant colors of the rainbow. Yet it is a rarefied beauty that other members of the group misperceive. The painted bird is attacked by its own flock, but the attack is orchestrated by an outside agent—the birdcatcher. The painter of birds is thus an artist of sorts, although an evil artist, weaving the lives of helpless others into his "plots."

Lekh's beloved Ludmila is a pure invention, and an inspired one. While the boy himself is not the bird painter, he becomes the bird painter's helper, setting "traps in places where Lekh himself could not reach." Thus the story moves from "something happened" to "something happened and he was involved in it." And his involvement is greater still. When Lekh carries on his liaison with Ludmila deep in the woods, the boy watches. "Watching" is a central aspect of the "as if" personality, and Lekh and the boy serve as a divided self in which Lekh is the physical side that acts while the boy observes and processes information.

It is the loss of Ludmila, his wild consort, that pushes Lekh to the cruelty of painting birds, and it is the boy—his "watching" self—who witnesses Ludmila's fate. In a scene that closely tracks the punishment of the slut in *Summer*, the fourth volume of Reymont's *The Peasants*, Ludmila is held down by the local crones, symbolically raped with a manure-filled bottle, and beaten to death. As in the metamorphosis of the real-life Ewka Migdalek, the pain of loss and the persecution of beauty are translated into erotic terms, and specifically into the terms of erotically laced violence.

At the end of the boy's journey is a lesson, and a terrible one. Pain and suffering have not, in his case, ennobled. He has discovered, instead, an appetite for the theater of pain, in which he aspires to shuck the role of victim for the role of victimizer. Identification with one's victimizer, sometimes described as "survivor syndrome," has been observed in a range of victims including the hostages of terrorists, survivors of concentration camps, and the historical subjects of slavery. The boy of *The Painted Bird* looks with envy at the snappy uniforms and Aryan appearance of the SS troopers; the creator of *The Painted Bird* appropriates his brother Henryk's miniature Red Army uniform and places it upon the character modeled upon himself, Jerzy, who as an adult would have composite uniforms made to order in Florence.

The boy's imagination is caught between the two most famous wearers of those uniforms—Hitler and Stalin—both of them bird painters on a monumental scale. Both were renamed, self-created men, artists in the larger sense, whose horrific and leaden visions nevertheless dictated the terms of life for a wide swath of humanity. Both walked a line that blurred the distinction between truth and invention, a situation they in turn blurred with elaborate intellectual rationalizations. Such were the unconscious role models presented to the boy as he contemplated casting his lot in life with the "Evil Ones."

In a strange intertextual twist, *The Painted Bird* contains a character, Gavrila, who appears in *No Third Path* under the same name as an "actual" person. Much of *No Third Path* consisted of the debate between "Gavrila" and "Novak" in which Novak conducts a measured retreat from Gavrila's sense of the collective. In *The Painted Bird*, however, Gavrila is set in opposition to an anarchic individualist, Mitka the Cuckoo, whose only principle is that one must respond to mistreatment with a satisfying and well-orchestrated revenge. The boy listens to the patient and humanistic Gavrila, but it is Mitka—the trickster god of egocentric individualism—who wins his soul. In an act of vengeance for a beating, he accompanies a friend called the Silent One who derails a market train—the wrong train, as it turns out. The intended victims were not on the train.

3.

On November 22, 1963, President John F. Kennedy was assassinated in Dallas. There is no record of Kosinski's reaction to what was a watershed event for his generation, but that does not mean that he was unaffected by the Kennedy presidency. Throughout the entire period Kosinski had been in America, Kennedy had been a major presence on the American scene, as undeclared and then declared presidential front-runner, and then as president. While his impact upon a young Polish immigrant can only be surmised, his impact on the larger populace included a fusing of the political elite—"the best and the brightest," as they would be characterized by David Halberstam—with the elite of social glitz, in a highly visible "jet set" of prominent and beautiful people.

There was, in fact, an important point of contact between the Kennedy presidency and the regimes of the great dictators who dominated Kosinski's childhood, notwithstanding enormous differences of substance and values. Kennedy, too, understood that within the world of the second half of the twentieth century, an "image" amounted to a powerful reality. The medium of that image had become, predominantly, television, a subject Kosinski would address in both fiction and nonfiction. And television brought a more subtly nuanced practice of the art of creative representation—or, more bluntly put, of creating a myth and turning that myth into a reality.

November 22, 1963, probably was the high-water mark for this sort of mythification. In its aftermath things began to change. The Camelot myth—of a president who was a devoted husband and family man, of a political leader who (despite being a C student at Harvard) wrote his own books—was gradually picked apart by investigators who had learned to probe beneath the surface of myths.

For someone with Kosinski's predispositions and personal history, the notion of building a life by building a myth must have been unusually seductive. Kennedy's success at manipulating an image, using wit and charm to control public perception at limited moments of contact, updated *Nikodem Dyzma*, Kosinski's fictive blueprint for life; you were what people perceived you to be. The chief task of life was to control that perception. If Kosinski never consciously made such a single calculated decision, he nevertheless proceeded to shape a literary career as if he had, with consequences that were at first dazzling, then troubling, and finally disastrous.

Few texts touch upon as many aspects of contemporary literary theory as *The Painted Bird*. In interviews done within a few years of its publication, Kosinski would explain that its working title had been *The Jungle Book*. The connection of Kosinski's boy to Kipling's wild boy, Mowgli, is perhaps apt, but it has the ring of literary myth, as does his suggestion in the 1976 foreword that the eventual title was suggested by Aristophanes's play *The Birds*. More plausible is the working title he mentioned to a few friends and later admitted to a *New York Times Book Review* writer doing a piece on improbable working titles: *Beneath This Sacred Armor*. Like the eventual title, it places the focus not on the situation but on the boy himself, although it is both more "literary" and more revealing.

Beneath This Sacred Armor has exactly the sort of high-culture writerly pretension one expects to see in serious literary enterprises (consider, for example, titles of major works by Wolfe, Hemingway, and Fitzgerald), and perhaps a little more. Yet it captures, as the ultimate title does not, the boy's sense of existing in layers, pursued by external forces—the Germans, the peasants, the other children—that constantly attempted to get at him beneath his defenses. At the same time, it suggests the problem of the layered existence itself. If there was something beneath the surface that his enemies could not get at, what was it? In what did that true self reside? Thus the working title suggests a rather different reading of the book as a whole; rather than focusing on the persecution of external difference, it shifts the focus to the inner self-examination that persecution inspires.

By the early spring of 1964, Kosinski had generated a substantial amount of text. There was, however, a problem. His command of written English continued to improve, but it was by no means up to the standards required for the polished prose of a novel, particularly a novel of high literary aspiration. The alternatives with which he was presented were limited. Since he had published the two "Novak" books without acknowledgment of a translator, there was no going back. And even if the Novak books had not been a factor, translation posed inherent problems.

Fairly or unfairly, the notion of translation places an additional distance between writer and reader. Works in translation rarely sell as well as works published in the original, and when they do, the success usually follows success in the first language. In the case of *The Painted Bird*, Kosinski had nowhere to go with a text written in Polish. His residence was now in America, he had no access to Polish publication, and publication in Poland was inadvisable in any case, from a number of standpoints. There was only one choice, and that choice was to produce a satisfactory text in English. If Conrad could do it, why couldn't he? Still, it was devilishly hard.

On March 7, 1964, an advertisement for a translator from Polish to English appeared in the *Saturday Review*. It read: "TRANSLATOR WANTED. Polish to English, for full-length fiction to be translated in short time. Must be thoroughly experienced in both. Box F-935."

Among those who answered the ad was Halina Bastianello. She met for three and a half hours with an intense, attractive young man who interviewed her in depth, showed her the manuscript in question, and gave her a synopsis of the plot of *The Painted Bird*. He found her satisfactory in every regard. There was just one hitch: the young man insisted that Ms. Bastianello could not be given credit for the translation. From her point of view, this was a unique and unacceptable stipulation, and she turned down the job.

Others did not. Several editors and translators participated as "consultants" on the English text of *The Painted Bird*. One was George Reavey, who eked out a marginal living and maintained a marginal position in the New York literary scene by doing translations from Polish and Russian. His chief claim to fame was as an early translator of Boris Pasternak. Reavey, whose wife was an avant-garde playwright, also wrote poetry and fiction; like many writers, he had begun with high hopes but had been reduced to taking hackwork to pay the bills. An active member of PEN, he had been forced to borrow money from the PEN account for indigent writers in order to have desperately needed dental work. Now he undertook to work with an intense and driven young man who stressed vehemently that theirs was a private arrangement that must never be disclosed. The pay was $500.

Another translator who answered the *Saturday Review* ad was Steven Kraus. Kosinski telephoned Kraus, who was Polish born, and sent him a chapter of a manuscript just before departing for Europe. Kraus translated the chapter and returned it to Kosinski with the understanding that Kosinski would call and let him know whether he was hired. Kosinski never called, and later, when Kraus saw the English version of *The Painted Bird*, he recognized the material he had worked on as one of the early chapters and concluded that the "trial chapter" must have been a device for getting the manuscript translated cheaply. In any case, he received no payment.

Some years later Kraus met Kosinski in person, at a party, and when they came to know each other slightly, Kosinski proposed that the two of them join together in a prank. Kraus would pick up a girl at MOMA—as he occasionally did—and Kosinski would be waiting in a chauffeur's uniform in the Bentley he was then driving. Kosinski would drive Kraus and the girl to Kraus's modest apartment, where Kraus would dismiss him for the night, leaving the girl to think that Kraus was an eccentric millionaire. Kraus politely declined Kosinski's offer.

Still another of the translator/editors was Aleksander Lutoslawski, a member of the Polish émigré circle and professional translator who also went by the anglified name of Alexander Jordan. Lutoslawski recalls working on the project for several weeks, taking chunks of Polish manuscript from Kosinski and returning them with English translation. Like Ewa Markowska before him, Lutoslawski worked diligently and put in long hours. He also agreed to do the work without receiving formal credit. The money was decent—three or four hundred dollars, as he later recalled—and Lutoslawski didn't see that the translation credit made much difference. He didn't see much merit in the Polish text. In his view, it was a kind of pornography—of sadism rather than pure sex. It was the sort of thing one could translate rapidly, not destined for any great success: really, a project one would be just as happy not to attach one's name to.

As a fellow émigré, Lutoslawski already knew Kosinski slightly. What had impressed him most was Kosinski's ambition—his determination to make his way in America. Some of his projects struck Lutoslawski as ludicrous. One of them, on which he offered to cut Lutoslawski in, had to do with the home manufacture of plastic table mats, or doilies. Kosinski already had a pattern. It was simply a matter of painting the mat and putting it into the oven to bake, a process Kosinski demonstrated. He had seen peasants practicing similar handicraft in Poland, and he was confident that it could make his fortune in America. Reasoning that if the product succeeded someone would make it faster with a machine, Lutoslawski took a pass. Kosinski's other moneymaking idea was to write spy thrillers.

So, at least, went the stories later recounted by Bastianello, Kraus, Reavey, and Lutoslawski. Are they credible witnesses? Given the overall context of Kosinski's career, the assertions seem credible in their broad outline. Bastianello was almost certainly interviewed by Kosinski, Kraus clearly spoke with him on the phone and translated a "sample" chapter, and it seems highly probable that both Reavey and Lutoslawski provided assistance as translators.

The precise nature of that assistance, however, is somewhat more in question. There is, to begin with, the discrepancy posed by the fact that two men put in more or less contradictory claims, with Lutoslawski in particular asserting that the final text was wholly "his." Reavey, too, would later claim that he "wrote *The Painted Bird.*" Such sweeping assertions fall into the area in which memory is likely to prove consciously or unconsciously selective. Kosinski later acknowledged using editors, going so far as to admit that he asked a wide circle of friends to comment on English passages.

"I was not in any way ashamed to expose my manuscript to friends who would read it," Kosinski told Dick Schapp at the time of publication. "I made sixteen, seventeen copies of every draft and showed it to people. I chose some people whose language was not English and some who were Americans. I asked them to mark a little cross next to anything that didn't sound right. If enough people marked a sentence, I knew something was wrong with it."

This was Kosinski's own selective and shaded version. But why show a book in English to readers whose first language was not English? What contribution could they possibly make to the accuracy of English idiom? One way to understand this otherwise strange remark is as a preemptive effort to disarm any rumors or leaks on the question of translation or editorial help. It may also, however, echo an inner rationalization, and help to account for the fact that more than one translator eventually came forth. A single translator would, indeed, be entitled to credit on the title page. If there were several translators, however, they might be viewed as "language consultants," part of a process by which the author tested and refined his use of idiom.

The process suggests a novel produced with Madison Avenue methodology—a product honed by the response of a focus group. Indeed the genius of the novel is a voice so simple and pared down as to be consistent with that of a child, or a foreign-language speaker—or a translator. Whether it is highly stylish or naive is for the reader to decide. It may be dismissed, as it was by Lutoslawski, or hailed for artful elision, like the simple style of Hemingway or Camus. But whether a product of necessity or of intention, the simple style was ideal for Kosinski's narrator and his horrifying story.

Whether that style was Kosinski's, and Kosinski's alone, is another question, and by no means as simple a question as it may appear. It is possible that Kosinski delivered substantial chunks of Polish text to both Reavey and Lutoslawski, using their translations for purposes of comparison. Perhaps he looked to their translations for alternative wordings, or, the other way around, as a working text from which he himself began. There can never be the certainty of examining *the* original working text, which could put to rest all questions. Finally, there is the matter of one additional contributor, Peter Skinner, who entered the process as private editor later, when the manuscript had already been accepted for publication.

There is, ultimately, the larger question of whether it matters exactly how the text was composed. Most readers in English have never read a word in the original by Tolstoy or Dostoyevsky, Camus or Sartre, Gabriel García Márquez or Isaac Bashevis Singer. Yet most such readers would claim that these foreign-language writers have an identifiable personal style in translation; no one would challenge the fundamental authorship of their works, although, conversely, none of these writers attempted to represent their works as having been written in English in the original.

By the complex reasoning of some modern literary theorists, the whole issue of "authorship" is, in a sense, moot; to identify a text in terms of its authorship is to invoke extrinsic criteria. Read the book, this line of argument would go, but accept the indeterminacy of its origin and meaning: focus instead on what you make of it.

The publishing world had its doubts about the manuscript. Even though it was presented as the work of an author with a successful track record (the identity of Joseph Novak now being well known), a number of large New York houses turned it down, among them Farrar Straus, one of the leading publishers of literary works, and Doubleday, which had published the Novak books. Timothy Seldes, Kosinski's editor at Doubleday, wrote delicately of the manuscript's strengths, both as a record of emotional and physical disasters and as a triumph of good writing, but expressed doubts about Doubleday's ability to sell it. His response may have had to do with the relative failure of *No Third Path*. Dutton had finally agreed to do a modest paperback edition of *The Future Is Ours, Comrade,* with publication scheduled for the fall, but *No Third Path* still failed to generate any paperback interest, and hardcover sales had been miserable. Whatever factors were involved in Doubleday's rejection, it was a painful vote of no-confidence for an author who had been an emerging star only four years before.

What seemed to block the book's publication was that there was no ready-made audience for a lugubrious tale of brutality and bestiality—a "pornography of violence," as Lutoslawski called it. Who needed it? This theme would crop up again and again as Kosinski's new agent, James Brown, tried to shop excerpts, and later still, when the more negative reviewers dug in their heels. The manuscript was perilously close to failing to find a publisher when a serendipitous encounter worked in its favor.

Kosinski later told Rocco Landesman, in his *Paris Review* interview, that he had not tried Houghton Mifflin because four friends in New York publishing, all of whom had rejected the book, cited it as the least likely publisher for a manuscript with such "strong" material. One of two major publishing houses located in Boston (the other was Little, Brown), Houghton Mifflin did have something of a reputation for being stodgy, if not downright prudish. The house was sustained by a strong textbook division and was careful to avoid publicity that might undercut its sales to schools; typical authors published by its trade division were such chroniclers of the American upper class as Louis Auchincloss and John P. Marquand and the niche writer of harmless stories for gentle older women who published under the name Miss Read.

In the early summer of 1964, the Kosinskis attended a dinner party in Boston at the home of Harris J. Nelson, a well-known business journalist who had for many years written the "Trader" column for *Barron's.* Harry Nelson's wife, Jerry, was a friend of Mary Weir's from the days when the Weirs regularly vacationed in Hobe Sound, Florida, and the Nelsons had gotten to know the Kosinskis well enough for Harry to serve as a character reference on Kosinski's application for American citizenship.

Among the other guests that evening at the Nelsons' were Giorgio de Santillana, a noted professor of humanities at MIT, and his wife, Dorothy, a widely respected publishing figure who happened to be a senior editor at Houghton Mifflin's trade division. As he often did with new audiences, Kosinski gave the de Santillanas the heavily fictionalized version of his experiences during the German occupation. Dorothy de Santillana found his story "fascinating and very terrible," and Kosinski mentioned that he had a manuscript telling the tale of his disastrous adventures. De Santillana expressed professional interest and followed up with a letter on July 14, requesting that he send along the manuscript accompanied by a list of his previously published work. Thus the manuscript arrived at Houghton Mifflin under the most auspicious possible circumstances.

That summer the Kosinskis had planned another grand tour, including the usual European stops as well as Spain, Portugal, India, and Egypt, but Mary's "illness" compelled a revision in their plans. She had been hospitalized already in May, and by late summer their lives were punctuated by her emotional ups and downs. With an increasingly predictable rhythm, moments of hope gave way to new bouts of heavy drinking and depression, often accompanied by outbursts of physical violence. One such episode was later rendered in *The Devil Tree*, with Mrs. Whalen having to be restrained when she begins throwing expensive jewelry out the portholes of a yacht.

Along with the general inconvenience of such episodes was the problem of social embarrassment. Kosinski's method for dealing with this problem was perfectly in keeping with the tactics used by public figures of the time. There was an official version, and that version said that Mary's social indispositions were temporary and everything was going to be fine. Since alcoholism and emotional problems were regarded as discreditable, however, there had to be an explanation for Mary's abrupt and extended absences; the explanation that carried no discredit, and in fact won sympathy, was physical illness, and the physical illness that seemed most arbitrary (uncorrelated to lifestyle) and won the greatest sympathy was cancer. And if it was cancer Mary had, why not go all the way and make it *brain cancer*, which was the most dramatic, could account for peculiar behavior, and yet had an unpredictable enough course that she could sometimes appear fine.

Thus Kosinski became the immigrant boy from Poland who had arrived with nothing, written several books, and married one of the world's richest women, who, however, had tragically contracted brain cancer and was being seen through it by her stoic young husband. It was a great story, and if it was largely fiction, it was fiction of a high order, grounded in kernels of truth and plausible denial. It took its place in a great fiction-making tradition.

In late summer, at a party filled with Polish émigrés, Kosinski met a young Oxford-educated Englishman named Peter Skinner, who had ironically been steered to the party by Steven Kraus. Skinner happened to have a Polish wife, the indirect reason for his presence at the party. He was living in America because he sensed that an Oxford degree would make better running there for a young man without a substantial family background. He taught English and Russian history at a private school, supplementing his income by use of his wits and erudition, both of which were considerable; at that moment he had a summer job with the National Student Association. Skinner and his wife were leaving the party when Kosinski flagged him down.

"I am Peter Skinner," Skinner introduced himself.

"I am Joseph Novak," Kosinski replied, perhaps wishing to identify himself as an author, perhaps only out of his delight in concealment and obfuscation.

Kosinski seemed to be sizing Skinner up for something; he asked if they could meet later, perhaps for dinner. There followed a series of lunches at Giannini's, two or three of them over a period of four or five weeks. Kosinski seemed to be trying to get at something, although it wasn't clear what. Having met Jim Glendenning, an Oxford friend of Skinner who was present at one of their meetings, Kosinski called Glendenning and made futher inquiries about Skinner. Eventually Kosinski invited him for dinner at Mary Weir's fifth- and sixth-floor duplex at 740 Park Avenue. He showed Skinner his room there, which had matching desks at the foot of matching twin beds.

"A friend of mine has completed a manuscript and would like you to look at it," Kosinski said. He produced a substantial manuscript on heavyweight bond paper, and Skinner began to read. After a dozen or so pages, he gave Kosinski his opinion: The work was potent, but ragged. It needed editing, and if Kosinski wished, he could recommend editors. "I think my friend would prefer *you* to work on this," Kosinski told him.

Thus began Peter Skinner's long and fruitful involvement in Kosinski's creative life. From the beginning he was struck by false notes in the manuscript, unidiomatic usages that suggested to him that the text might have been translated, or generated with the use of dictionaries: for example, the point where a plow turned at the end of a furrow was described as an "epiphany," a word defined in the dictionary as a "turning point," but of a different nature. He pointed out that crows did not flock, as the book claimed; the author must have been referring to rooks. Little by little, the pretense dropped away, and without it ever quite being stated, it became clear between the two men that the manuscript was Kosinski's.

"Did you . . . ?" Skinner would begin a question.

"The boy, the *boy*," Kosinski would correct.

"Did the boy . . . ?" Skinner would rephrase the question.

"I don't remember," Kosinski would reply.

The boy, Kosinski would then explain, was his "fictive self."

From the description of the terrain, Skinner became convinced that the book was set in the Pripet Marshes, but Kosinski remained vague about the setting. When Skinner suggested that they look at a map, Kosinski was evasive.

Kosinski paid periodically and well, and in a manner that did not make Skinner feel like a menial employee. There was no strict accounting of hours, but the pay amounted to a hundred dollars every few weeks—crisp bills placed in a fancy envelope when the amount was less than fifty dollars, a check when it was more, with three singles for cab fare. The cab fare was a bonus, because Skinner invariably took the subway, making up some excuse for needing a half hour or so when Kosinski called.

Working in close proximity, he came to know Kosinski well. The two men occasionally visited Lilla van Saher's salon together, and on other occasions, at the apartment in Gregory House, when Kosinski had a girl coming over, he would have her bring a friend for Skinner. Kosinski also regaled Skinner with various far-fetched schemes for making money, among them the same plan for manufacturing doilies he had presented to Lutoslawski. Another Kosinski idea was a phonograph recording of party noises—glasses clinking, people coming and going, laughter—which lonely people could buy to divert themselves and impress their neighbors; as a supplement to the record, Kosinski had in mind a sort of escort service in which it would be possible to rent a whole group of good-looking people who would rush up to a given address as though going to a party there.

Kosinski's schemes were often based on scams that played

upon people's needs. To Skinner, he was blistering about the bo-
vine nature of Americans; he and Skinner could appreciate this,
he said, as brother Europeans. Even the highest order of American society was not intelligent but merely *cunning*, and had to be
told what to read and eat, what hotels to stay in, and the like. He
was particularly scathing about the charities of the rich. The gifts
of the Rockefellers angered him, he said, because to the Rockefellers they were a drop in the bucket; besides, the Rockefellers
themselves went everywhere in the world for free.

What the American elite needed, he told Skinner, was a resident Eastern European intellectual, and he was prepared to fill
that need. Thus he looked out on an American society that
seemed to him empty, lonely, venal, and inauthentic, even at the
very top—and schemed to infiltrate himself into the middle of it.

While Kosinski began his work on revisions with Peter Skinner, the editorial board at Houghton Mifflin was busy evaluating
Kosinski's manuscript. On September 21 Dorothy de Santillana
wrote to reassure him that the manuscript was "not gathering
dust in our files." As for her own opinion, she was "bowled over"
by his extraordinary telling of the story as much as she had been
in hearing his account firsthand, and she added that in her view
he had been "enormously successful in handling this absolutely
brutal material from a child's point of view so that the peace and
wonder of the natural world are present along with all the horri-
ble documentary of man's inhumanity to man." She did, however, raise one question.

"I notice that one or two of the initial editorial reports refer to
it as a 'novel,' " she wrote. "It is my understanding that, fictional
as the material may sound, it is straight autobiography. You
might let me know which is correct." She closed with her hope
that "your attractive wife is well-recuperated."

Dorothy de Santillana's rather timid question was the first hint
of a controversy that would hang over the book throughout its
history. Because of the manner in which the manuscript came to
Houghton Mifflin—as a result of Kosinski's telling dinner-party
anecdotes that he represented as his personal history—the assumption at Houghton Mifflin was that it was nonfiction. The ar-

gument about fact vs. fiction that originated within the editorial board at Houghton Mifflin would eventually extend into the external literary world, producing broader and broader ripples and eventually pursuing Kosinski even beyond the grave.

Houghton Mifflin in those days employed a committee system for editorial decision-making. Projects of promise were submitted to a number of fairly senior editors, each of whom prepared a written report, and the committee then met to reach a consensus decision. Because of her senior standing and great personal prestige, Dorothy de Santillana exerted great influence, but under the system she did not make decisions alone. Consequently, the Kosinski manuscript was passed around for the usual series of readings and reports. It was in those reports that an interesting discrepancy cropped up.

All readers were enthusiastic and recommended publishing the book. The readers divided, however, as to where the most important merits of the manuscript lay. Philip Rich and Shannon Ravenel (who went on to a distinguished career as permanent editor of the *Best American Short Stories* yearly series and as editorial director at Algonquin Books), stressed the book's literary qualities; it was their reports that injected the word "novel," prompting de Santillana's query to Kosinski. De Santillana had stressed from the beginning the book's documentary importance, as a testament to the quality of life in Poland under German occupation, and de Santillana's superior Paul Brooks, head of the trade division, saw the manuscript the same way.

Despite this subtle division of opinion, Houghton Mifflin accepted the manuscript for publication. The first faint hint of the issues to come took the form of an extended discussion of the liability clause in the contract, which was resolved rather blandly by Houghton Mifflin's reassertion that they would have to accept that there were many cases in which *only the author would know whether a passage was libelous or a violation of another copyright,* which must remain the author's responsibility; there were strict limits on the extent to which they were willing to modify the author's warranty clause.

Kosinski's dawning awareness of the sensitivity of this issue led him to ask at the contract stage for the right of approval of ad copy and news releases; both his agent, Jim Brown, and Paul Brooks at Houghton Mifflin felt that such a right of approval was not an appropriate part of a contract, but Brooks pledged that news releases of a biographical nature would be checked with him beforehand whenever possible. With that matter resolved for the time being, a copy of the contract was sent out on November 18, with a prospective publication date of late summer or early fall of 1965.

The following week Kosinski went to Boston for lunch with Dorothy de Santillana. Chief on his agenda for that lunch was the rather uncomfortable task of beginning to back away from the representation of his manuscript as pure autobiography. The questions that had arisen with respect to the liability clause of the contract had demonstrated that problems concerning the book's supposed facticity would continue to bubble to the surface. One can imagine his discomfort in performing the delicate dance necessary to deny that the book was autobiographical without making the outright admission that he had lied.

Returning to New York, Kosinski wrote de Santillana on November 28, further underscoring and clarifying what he had told her at their lunch. *The Painted Bird* (its title was now in place) was essentially a literary work, not an "autobiographical survey." He used in that letter, for the first time, the argument that the book represented "the slow unfreezing of a mind," a phrase which would recur in both interviews and writing. A formula for dealing with the question of the book's "autobiographical" nature was beginning to take shape. He would deny that the book was literally autobiography, while refusing to say categorically that it was not. The cover for this murky assertion would involve a convoluted discussion of language and the creative process, in which, as he explained to de Santillana, "foregrounds lose in definition, and backgrounds emerge from the shadows." Olga, Lekh, Makar, and Ewka were quite real, he implied, but an anthropologist would have the devil of a time pinning down the facts of their lives.

By the fall of 1964, in several areas of Kosinski's life things had begun to fall into place. On October 28 the first paperback copies of *The Future Is Ours, Comrade* were delivered, a triumph of his determination to keep the Novak books alive. The previous day, the sociology department at Columbia had certified that Kosinski had passed Ph.D. language examinations in French and Russian and had demonstrated the required proficiency in statistics, methodology, and theory. It was, in hindsight, a clear case of too little, too late, but it shows that Kosinski himself had not quite given up the notion of finishing his doctorate. While he now had grander literary prospects, a Columbia doctorate still presented a useful fallback position, and he had managed to narrow the unfulfilled requirements to the main one: his dissertation.

On November 10 writer and critic Virgilia Peterson had written Kosinski a sensitive appreciation of *The Painted Bird*, including lines that could be used in advertising blurbs; another reviewer, Marguerite Young, had already tendered a similarly helpful response. If magazines seemed flatly uninterested in buying excerpts of the forthcoming book (turndowns from *McCall's* and *Redbook* mainly serve to suggest the comic incongruity of sending the material there in the first place), Houghton Mifflin remained enthusiastic. The problems of Mary's "illness" persisted, but even they were overshadowed by the exciting prospects at the turn of the year.

Throughout the fall of 1964, Kosinski's petition for naturalization had been working its way through the necessary stages within the Immigration and Naturalization Service. In one of the last of these, Kosinski submitted a required "supplemental memorandum" concerning his former membership in the Polish Student Organization (ZMP). He explained that he attended monthly meetings but was expelled in 1953 for "refusing to speak on Korean situation unless able to present both sides." He affirmed that he was not an officer, did not believe in the principles of the organization, and did not believe in Communism or the principles of Communism.

His disavowal, while honest enough, had the odd ring of Cold War reasoning which had pervaded the 1950s; in pledging loyalty to the United States, it was regarded as helpful to explain that one had been, at the deepest level, disloyal to one's previous society and its ideas and institutions. The authorities at the INS were satisfied by this standard formulation, which Kosinski presented on January 12. On February 15, 1965, at 9:15 A.M., Kosinski appeared at Room 506 of the United States Court House in Foley Square, the appropriate documents in hand, stepped forward, and was accepted as a citizen of the United States.

4.

On March 13 Kosinski left with Mary for a short European vacation in France and Switzerland. From Paris he sent Houghton Mifflin the end-product of his work with Peter Skinner: a set of heavily corrected galleys—more heavily corrected, in fact, than David Harris, who was in charge of coordinating production and editorial matters, could remember seeing in his experience. He felt compelled to write Kosinski and warn him that the number of changes would probably make it most economic to reset the entire book, with a charge of roughly a thousand dollars against future royalties. He also responded to Kosinski's complaint that there were a large number of printer's errors—possibly an effort by the author to mute criticism of his own substantial changes—by saying that a certain number of printer's errors were to be expected.

What Harris's letters did not mention was that he had written, on March 17, a two-page memo to Paul Brooks, expressing his own serious reservations about *The Painted Bird.* The memo, which followed upon a conversation between the two men at a Boston club, listed passages and episodes that Harris found "distasteful," and numbered no fewer than thirteen pages containing instances of voyeurism, of which Brooks had argued that the book was entirely free. The Harris memo then skillfully detailed the basic division among readers of the book—Shannon Ravenel and Phil Rich seeing it as having literary power, Brooks and Dorothy de Santillana emphasizing its importance as a social document. In the view of David Harris, the book was not satisfactory on either ground. The text itself failed to convince Harris of its historical authenticity, while the episodes seemed to him the product of a mind obsessed with sadomasochistic violence, piling horror upon horror but failing to build to any larger insight. The problem, he added, was not solvable by detailed editing and cutting; it was, in his view, pervasive.

Within Houghton Mifflin, the Harris memo was a bombshell. Aware that he could not, at that stage, stop the publication of the book, Harris expressed embarrassment that Houghton Mifflin was publishing it and suggested a threefold course of action. First, he urged that the book be vetted by Houghton Mifflin's attorneys, who would be required to render an opinion as to whether it was legally obscene and whether they were prepared to defend it. Second, the proofs should be read by members of the company's trade management committee to determine if it might cause loss of textbook sales. Finally, he urged collecting as many favorable advance statements as possible, battening down the hatches for a storm of criticism. If he, as a Houghton Mifflin employee, felt so strongly, Harris argued, it was likely that similar opinions would crop up in the outside world.

With Kosinski still away in Europe, the Harris memo set in motion a flurry of activity by Houghton Mifflin's trade management committee. Paul Brooks contacted Conrad Oberdorfer of Choate, Hall & Stewart, Houghton Mifflin's law firm, and on March 25 Oberdorfer laid out the general question of the legal definition of "obscenity." On April 5, the day before Kosinski's return from Europe, Oberdorfer followed up with a seven-page letter to Brooks comparing *The Painted Bird* to Henry Miller's *Tropic of Cancer*, which had survived an obscenity challenge in Massachusetts Supreme Judicial Court by a four-to-three decision. Rendering his view that *The Painted Bird* was not likely, as a whole, to be judged obscene, Oberdorfer nevertheless set forth a series of needed abridgments, all in the direction of less realism in the representation of sadistic acts; at the same time, he expressed the hope that his suggested cuts would coincide with ordinary editorial considerations, as it was difficult to draw a particular line where the book stepped over the bounds. Among the passages Oberdorfer wished to have toned down were the miller's gouging of eyeballs of his wife's would-be lover, the rape and murder of Stupid Ludmila, the boy's relations with Ewka and her sexual relations with the goat, and the raping and pillaging by the Kalmuk cavalry.

All things considered, Oberdorfer's response showed a reasonable degree of literary sensitivity, if somewhat conservative tastes. He was unable to assess the question of potential libel but suggested the author and his editor consider it.

Kosinski returned from Europe on April 6 and was greeted by the startling request that he make major cuts and changes in the book, for which he had already reviewed the galleys. A telegram from Dorothy de Santillana on April 9 invited him to the de Santillanas' country house, there to work on the galleys and be close enough to question Oberdorfer face to face, if necessary. Kosinski went to Boston the following week, worked over the galleys, and lunched with Paul Brooks.

By April 14 he had made all the changes he was willing to make, and wrote Oberdorfer directly, acknowledging the merit of his literary observations and responding to the requests for abridgments point by point. In general, he excised less in each instance than Oberdorfer had suggested but more than he might have wished. In arguing for leaving in the graphic passages on Stupid Ludmila, he cited passages from Reymont's *The Peasants*, upon which, in fact, the killing of Stupid Ludmila was *very* closely modeled.

Oberdorfer, who was himself leaving for Europe, responded briefly to Kosinski but in more detail to Brooks, specifying the places where he felt further changes were necessary from a legal point of view. Spurred by Oberdorfer's letter, Brooks wrote Kosinski again on April 16, asking for a second round of cuts. Kosinski, by now revealing his thorough exasperation, finally caved in. From that point forward, the tone of his communications with Houghton Mifflin changed. It was his view, he wrote to Brooks on April 17, that *The Painted Bird* was no longer the book it was intended to be; the changes proposed by Oberdorfer and insisted upon by Brooks and the other editors at Houghton Mifflin had destroyed, in his view, a carefully constructed balance between "poetic" and "realistic" elements.

The whole contretemps over possible "obscenity" had been triggered by David Harris's internal memorandum, and subsequent events would show that the legal concern was largely misplaced. Pocket Books would eventually publish a fully restored text without repercussions, and while some critics would object to the novel's "sadism" and local librarians would exercise the occasional predictable censorship, the unexpurgated version ran into no serious legal challenges.

There was in all this, however, a subtext. David Harris had put his finger on something after all, a something that lay, if not in the book itself, in the way people were approaching it. That something had to do precisely with the balance between "poetic" and "realistic" elements. Paul Brooks had walked out of his luncheon with Kosinski still under the impression that the book was *nonfiction*—and in fact wrote a follow-up note reminding Kosinski of the need for a "statement which we are to use in presenting this book as nonfiction." Apparently Dorothy de Santillana had not yet let him in on the substance of her conversation with Kosinski back in November. Or perhaps, with Kosinski's tortuous and roundabout way of putting it, she herself had not fully heard his disclaimer that the book should properly now be regarded as a novel.

In the face of Brooks's restatement of the premise that *The Painted Bird* was to be published as nonfiction, Kosinski brought up for the first time the question of the possible impact of the book upon his mother. Brooks was given to understand that this was an issue that had come up in the course of Kosinski's recent trip to Europe, as a result of conversations with his German-language publishers, Scherz Verlag, in Bern. For his part, Brooks was not having any backing away from the definition of the book at this late stage of the game, and he wrote Jim Brown to that effect. He wanted it *in writing*, he said, so that there would be no misunderstanding in the future, that the book was to be published as nonfiction, not as a novel. He mentioned the statement that Kosinski was working on, "making clear the nature of the book without claiming that it is a straight autobiographical narrative, such as one might write on the basis of a day-by-day journal—which obviously this little boy did not keep."

All of this placed Kosinski in a very awkward position. He had, after all, sold the book to Dorothy de Santillana as an autobiographical account. It did have a broad autobiographical basis, but huge elements of it were purely imaginative, and he knew only too well which elements these were. Among other things, the invented portions encompassed, very significantly, the horrific details that Brooks and Oberdorfer insisted on paring down. They further included, as he knew but Brooks and Oberdorfer could not, fabrications concerning potentially identifiable human beings—the exact sort of fabrications of which libel suits are made—although he could feel fairly confident that the various walls, political and cultural, that separated those individuals from the world of American publishing would serve as an impassable barrier.

All things considered, however, it began to seem prudent to consider the book more formally as a "novel." In fact, Kosinski had been slow and reluctant in using that word. In their response turning down an excerpt, back on December 21, 1964, *McCall's* had referred to the book as a "novel," prompting Jim Brown to note in the margin for his client Kosinski that he had labeled the book clearly as nonfiction. *Redbook* managed to get it right, saying that they couldn't use this kind of material "even if it were fiction," and their response alluded to another element of the text that would eventually contribute to the problem of defining its genre: "the postlude which indicated that the boy escaped to a free country."

That postlude would be the source of a serious problem for Kosinski over the years. De Santillana alluded to the need for discussing the epilogue in her April 9 telegram, urgently summoning Kosinski to make the first round of cuts. By stating that the boy grew up, rejected collective society, and escaped to the West, the epilogue appeared to construct a very direct bridge between the boy inside the book and the author who stood outside it; it was a little like a movie dramatizing the life of a person who wins an Olympic medal or overcomes cancer, in which that person comes on for one minute at the end to give a short inspirational speech. This implication of the epilogue—which was deleted from all but the first printing—was noted over the years by both academic critics like David Richter and reviewers like Andrew Field, whose highly favorable review in the *New York Herald Tribune* would create so much trouble for Kosinski.

Eight years later Kosinski gave an academic interviewer, Jerry Klinkowitz, a version in which the epilogue had been written as a letter to Dorothy de Santillana, who found it so telling that she appended it to the text; it stayed in, he said, because de Santillana cabled him at a Paris hotel, where the cable was misplaced, and used the negative option to leave the material in the published text. No reasonably sensitive reader of that epilogue—which is now in short supply—is likely to accept that its prose is the prose of a personal letter. By the time Kosinski spoke to Klinkowitz, de Santillana was no longer alive, but aside from the overall improbability of this explanation, there is the problem of *Redbook*'s response in February, in which the "postlude" was already incorporated in the manuscript. As Kosinski went over the galleys at least three times between February and the end of April, the story that the epilogue was a last-minute inclusion from a letter doesn't hold up.

By April 28 Houghton Mifflin had in house a blurb from Kosinski, proposed for jacket use, stating that the author "draws deeply upon a childhood spent, by the casual chances of war, in the remotest villages of Eastern Europe." As a legalistic solution to his problems, the line is a small masterpiece. It is entirely true, and at the same time it manages to avoid any specific comment on the precise nature of the book's contents. David Harris wrote Kosinski expressing appreciation for the blurb, but noting that Houghton Mifflin might choose to begin with a statement about the book itself rather than one concerning its writing. It was now Houghton Mifflin's turn to cave; as a resolution to the in-house bickering, it was finally agreed to publish *The Painted Bird* as a novel.

The crisis posed by Harris's questioning of the book's autobiographical nature was over for the moment. Yet Kosinski's sure instincts told him that this problem was likely to recur in other contexts. As a result, he set to work producing a more elaborate statement—a vastly expanded version of the jacket blurb he provided for Houghton Mifflin. Seen outside the context of the dispute over the book's genre, it is one of the odder and less explicable authorial documents of its era.

As long as he was at it, Kosinski apparently decided, he would generate something in the nature of a larger theoretical statement. It would partake of the tradition of Henry James's prefaces, or, more recently, Alain Robbe-Grillet's theoretical essays on the *nouveau roman*, which were designed to introduce his own peculiar novels to the unwashed. A high-toned literary argument, laced with quotes from Jung, Camus, Susanne Langer, Nikolai Chernyshevsky, et al., could provide excellent camouflage for a carefully worded positioning on the subject of *fact* in *The Painted Bird*.

The result was an initial proposal of the theory of "autofiction," a sort of modified autobiography in which much emphasis is placed upon standing outside one's experience and writing about it in an unfamiliar language; its deeper rationale is that all remembered human experience is, in one sense, fiction. This is not quite Faulkner's solution of "lying one's way to the truth." It is, more nearly, an argument that *there is no such thing as truth*—a powerfully nihilistic concept, but a highly interesting one. More political than literary in its genesis, it was perhaps one of the great political inventions of the twentieth century—not telling lies, but telling lies with an elaborate intellectual rationale explaining why the telling of lies is okay.

The final product of Kosinski's theoretical explorations was a document nineteen pages in length, with an epigraph in French from Proust and ten footnotes, citing Proust, Langer, Valéry, Jung and Kerényi (three times), Chernyshevsky, Arthur Miller, and Antonin Artaud (twice). It was entitled *Notes of the Author* and appended to the German-language edition of *The Painted Bird*; Kosinski self-published an American edition as a small booklet, complete with admiring comments on *The Painted Bird*—to establish the copyright, he sometimes explained—and passed the booklets out freely to reviewers, academic critics, and anyone else who expressed an interest in his work.

Interestingly, the first passage of *Notes of the Author* dealing with *The Painted Bird* echoes the language of Kosinski's November 24, 1964, letter to Dorothy de Santillana: "To say that *The Painted Bird* is non-fiction may be convenient for classification, but it is not easily justified." Seven years later, in the *Paris Review* interview, the question is asked thus by Rocco Landesman: "Given the unusual circumstances of your life, many people think of your work—the first two novels, anyway—as non-fiction." Kosinski's reply: "Well, to say that *The Painted Bird* for example is non-fiction, or even autobiographical, may be convenient for classification but it's not easily justified."

The bizarrely incantatory quality of this near-verbatim repetition makes a certain sense if one grasps the psychological pressures attendant to producing it. Like a man destined to undergo a lengthy and wearying interrogation, Kosinski has arrived at a precise formula for representing his actions, and he clings to it with the resolve that arises from fear that the slightest deviation from the script will lead the whole story to unravel. It's called getting the story straight. If he feared that questions concerning *The Painted Bird*'s facticity were going to come up in other and more threatening contexts, he was not mistaken.

5.

In September, as publication approached, Kosinski left for Europe for the second time that year. One of his purposes was to meet again with his European publishers, attending to final details having to do with translation and promotion. Already Kosinski sensed that the book had the potential to do well in Europe. It was a European story, and the moment might well be right for a new, hard look at the experience of the war.

Kosinski landed in Copenhagen on September 14, went to Bern on September 19, where he visited Scherz Verlag and signed off on the German edition containing his "Notes," and went on from there to Paris, where Flammarion was bringing out an edition entitled *L'Oiseau bariole*. After a stop in Germany, he arrived in London on September 29, staying just long enough for coordination with his British publishers. He arrived back in New York on October 1.

This time Mary had been unable to accompany him. For one thing, she was busy moving out of the large Park Avenue duplex to a somewhat more modest apartment at 25 Sutton Place—

ostensibly to scale down a lifestyle that had become burdensome, but actually to distance herself from Kosinski. In the course
of that move, Mary donated some pieces of antique furniture to
the Metropolitan Museum. The way the Met handled her gift
would eventually irritate her sufficiently that she restricted them.
to six pieces in her will, but at the time she found the role of patron highly diverting—so much so that she set out to expand the
role. In later years Kosinski would date the genesis of his third
novel, *Being There*, to an event that took place that summer.

As Kosinski told it, Mary took him along to a townhouse
somewhere between Park Avenue and Lexington, not far from the
homes of the Mellons and Rockefellers, to call on a man in his
eighties who owned a lot of first-rate old American furniture.
Mary's mission was to convince the man, who had been a business friend of Ernest Weir, to will his furniture to the Met. The
old man had been retired since the Depression and did not move
from an upstairs bedroom, with a law firm paying his bills and
even providing a properly screened doctor. Mary went upstairs
to see the old man, while Kosinski explored the downstairs, walking along a hall lined with covered furniture through a back passage to a beautiful and sunny garden set off from the street by a
high wall.

It was a typically precious New York garden, and in it was a
well-dressed middle-aged man. Kosinski asked if he was there to
see the old man, and the man said no, he lived in the house; as
they spoke, he simultaneously watched a TV that he could see
through a large window in one of the downstairs rooms. Later at
a dinner party Kosinski ran into the lawyer who had arranged
Mary's visit with the old man and mentioned the man in the garden. The lawyer was unable to account for him, but mentioned
that there had been a man at the closing of the estate (in the
meantime the old man had died) who insisted that he had lived
in the house all his life but made no claim on the estate.

The unaccounted man was, in Kosinski's version, the germ of
Chance the Gardener (Chauncey Gardiner), and it fits quite plau-
sibly with Mary's activities in the late summer and early fall of
1965, although the anecdote told in later years most likely incorporated another motive, as critics noted the close similarity be-

tween *Being There* and *The Career of Nikodem Dyzma*. It was certainly in Kosinski's interest to point up sources of *Being There* that had nothing to do with the Dolega-Mostowicz novel, and the story about the "gardener" he encountered while accompanying Mary served that purpose admirably.

Overall, the relationship with Mary had been more and more difficult. Mary's loss of control was so severe at times that the possibility of committing her to an institution was discussed with her psychiatrist, Dr. Joseph Hughes. Her son David remembers Dr. Hughes as having advocated the idea. How Kosinski stood on it is unclear. What is clear is that he was caught increasingly often in the uncongenial role of picking up the pieces. Mary had begun to have inconvenient blackouts, sometimes inviting groups of friends to dinner at Twenty One and becoming incoherent by the time the check arrived. Kosinski was thus left to pay enormous amounts, and found himself with the awkward choice of asking her for the money or suffering the drain on his own bank account. So, at least, he would tell the story.

Over the course of the summer, preparations had been continuing at Houghton Mifflin. The quotes from Virgilia Peterson and Marguerite Young were already available for use on the jacket and in advance publicity, and Lilla van Saher had sent the book to her friend Anaïs Nin, asking her to pass it along to Henry Miller. Nin begged off apologetically on behalf of Miller, but sent Kosinski a long note praising the book and offering the right to quote; if the letter didn't contain quotable sections, she added, she would try again. For her part, Dorothy de Santillana acquired one helpful advance blurb—from her husband, Giorgio de Santillana. His reputation at MIT would give his name a vaguely familiar ring for readers and reviewers, some of whom might confuse him with the late philosopher George Santayana, and none of whom was likely to know he was the husband of the book's chief editor.

There had been the usual glitches, compounded by the in-house arguments over the book's character. The advance advertisement in the August 9 *Publishers Weekly* had stated: "In the first weeks of World War II, *the author of this book*, then a boy of six, was separated from his parents in a remote village of Central Europe." Kosinski was understandably furious; slips like the ad, which had its origin in the original understanding of the manuscript at Houghton Mifflin, threatened to undermine the wall he was constructing between the anecdotes he told at parties and the text of the "novel." It was almost a relief that the ad had also gotten his name wrong—spelling it, in large type, "Kosinsky." In a way, it provided cover. If they couldn't even spell his name right, was anything in the ad likely to be accurate?

The Painted Bird was published on Friday, October 15, 1965, with a publication party in the Rizzoli bookstore, at Fifty-sixth and Fifth. As Kosinski's literary acquaintances mingled with Mary Weir's society set, Eugene Prakapas of Pocket Books approached Kosinski to talk business. Pocket wanted to do *The Painted Bird* in paperback; Prakapas would be in personal charge of the project, and he would be more than willing to restore the deleted passages. Prakapas had some ideas, too, about the way to launch the paperback edition. In his view, Houghton Mifflin was blowing it, *priv-ishing* the book, in publishing lingo: printing it but failing to give it support. With a proper cover and publicity campaign, targeted at the right audience, Prakapas was confident the book could be a paperback bestseller—a sort of instant classic.

Kosinski listened with interest. It was all very gratifying, being the center of genuine "literary" attention—a much bigger deal than the publication of the Novak books. The evening was marred only by the absence of Lilla van Saher, who had hoped to be present for her protégé's launching. Kosinski wouldn't learn why until the following day, when publicist Carolyn Amussen of Houghton Mifflin sent him a copy of her telegram conveying best wishes and expressing regret that "ILL HEALTH PREVENTS ME FROM ATTENDING." She was, in fact, already suffering from the beginnings of the cancer that would kill her.

The following morning reviews started to appear, and they were stupendous. Charles Poore, in the daily *New York Times*, said little of the book's style, but treated it as a timeless observation of the worst in human behavior, in which being discriminated against leads one to discriminate against others. Inset in the Poore review, Kosinski's handsome, thoughtful face was presented for the first time in major American media. A day later Andrew Field, writing in the *New York Herald Tribune*, swelled the chorus of praise for what he called "this semi-autobiographical account," adding that "the overall performance is marked by a sureness of emphasis and tone of voice that has high literary merit."

The Field review went on, however, to say that the book was "an unrelentingly harsh portrait of the Poles as willing and even energetic functionaries for the Germans in rounding up and handing over Polish Jews and Gypsies, even though they themselves were the objects of Nazi contempt and marked for extermination." Moreover, Field noted the epilogue, and extracted from it the assertion that "Mr. Kosinski found postwar Communism to be but a logical extension of much that he lived through during the war."

The Field review was Kosinski's worst nightmare. Beside himself with worry, he prepared a letter to the *Herald Tribune* disavowing the line about the Poles having been functionaries for the Germans, and denying that the narrative was set in Poland at all. The promotional staff at Houghton Mifflin was put on the case to be sure that the letter ran, as Kosinski braced himself for the fallout that would certainly follow. The Field comment could hardly have had wider dissemination, as the review was syndicated in the *Washington Post*, the *Chicago Sun-Times*, and the *San Francisco Examiner*, as well as a number of smaller newspapers.

While he waited for the repercussions, favorable notices and letters continued to come in. Geoffrey Wolff in the *Washington Post* and the *Times Herald* praised both the book's historical value and "the richness of [Kosinski's] prose," while Peter Prescott in the *Chicago News* compared it to Anne Frank's diary, "a testament not only to the atrocities of the war, but to the failings of human nature." The comparison to Anne Frank was echoed in a letter from Harry Overstreet, who wrote from Virginia that the book would "stand by the side of Anne Frank's unforgettable 'Diary' "—a quote that was later used in the paperback version. Jim Herlihy also saluted it as "a brilliant testimony to mankind's survival power," another quote used on the paperback. Kosinski's old friend Roger Baldwin checked in, too, praising the book's genuineness and power but expressing mystification about the accompanying pamphlet (*Notes of the Author*), which in his view threatened to detract from the book's testimony as experience.

Most exciting of all, Arthur Miller wrote Kosinski to say that "the Nazi experience is the key one of this century—they merely carried to the final extreme what otherwise lies within so-called normal social existence and normal man. You have made the normality of it all apparent, and this is a very important and difficult thing to have done." This was exactly the impact for which Kosinski had striven, and coupled with the name of Arthur Miller—then at the height of his influence and celebrity—it made for perfect ad copy. Securing Miller's willingness to be quoted, Houghton Mifflin immediately substituted the Miller statement for the copy already prepared for a *New York Times* ad for November 5.

Meanwhile the *New York Times Book Review* had assigned the book to Elie Wiesel, a coup in itself, although Wiesel's initial response was somewhat lukewarm. But Kosinski knew Wiesel slightly, and was able to mention to him that the book was, in essence, autobiographical. The word that *The Painted Bird* was a chronicle of actual human suffering was the cue that Wiesel needed, and on Sunday, October 31, his review entitled "Everybody's Victim" sanctified the book as an authentic Holocaust testament.

"It is as a chronicle that *The Painted Bird*, Jerzy Kosinski's third book (but his first on this subject) achieves its unusual power," Wiesel wrote. "Written with deep sincerity and sensitivity, this poignant first-person account transcends confession and attains in parts the haunting quality and tone of a quasi-surrealistic tale. One cannot read it without fear, shame and sadness."

"Account," "confession," "testament," "document," and "testimony": these were key words in the book's critical reception. While they did little for hardcover sales—Houghton Mifflin had never handled a book quite like this, and perhaps Eugene Prakapas was right about their ineptitude in promoting it—the reviews laid the groundwork for making *The Painted Bird* a classic. Praised and certified as a quasi-historical document, it was positioned for a double life in paperback—as the cornerstone of every course and reading list on the Holocaust, and as a cult book among the young.

Yet Kosinski was soon to discover that he could not have it both ways. The certification of the book's historicity had not gone unnoticed among Poles—and particularly the references to Poland in Andrew Field's review entitled "The Butcher's Helpers." Wieslaw Gornicki, a correspondent at the United Nations for the official Polish Press Agency, read the review in the *Herald Tribune*, and he also noted that in the prologue, the boy was described as being from "a large city in central *Poland*," a reference changed in every subsequent edition to read "Eastern Europe."

Gornicki was outraged. The attack on the honor of Poland angered him both personally and as a representative of the regime. Well connected within the upper levels of the Polish Communist Party, Gornicki would eventually appear in photos on the podium at the elbow of General Jaruzelski, who headed the Communist martial-law regime in the 1980s. Although a Communist and a Polish patriot, Gornicki was no anti-Semite; three years later, back in Poland, he would resign his post in protest against a campaign to drive the remaining Jews out of Poland. The apparent characterization of the mass of Poles as anti-Semites infuriated him.

On November 7 *Ameryka-Echo*, a Polish-language weekly published in Chicago, printed Gornicki's first broadside, a review entitled "It Is Difficult to Be a Pole." Gornicki claimed that Kosinski had depicted Poland as a nation of perverts, and asserted that the only attractive character in the novel was an officer of the SS. A week later *Ameryka-Echo*, apparently having decided that the review was a product of personal animus, printed an apology, along with a highly positive review. It was not the last word to be heard from Gornicki, however. Something in *The Painted Bird* had awakened a durable rage, and upon his return to Warsaw he set out along another course to engage what he saw as the book's slander of the Polish nation. Over the years, he would continue to be Kosinski's nemesis, a sort of detective Javert to Kosinski's Jean Valjean, bent on running down his man and seeing to his proper punishment.

For the time being, however, not even the *Ameryka-Echo* review made much of a dent in the groundswell of praise. Only one critic had the power to dilute Kosinski's triumph, and in a letter dated October 28, that critic checked in from Lodz. Elzbieta Kosinska had read the book in German, the English-language version having not yet arrived from London. She reacted in terms strikingly similar to the postures struck by the mothers of Thomas Wolfe and Ernest Hemingway upon their sons' breakthrough successes; perhaps it was the predictable response of every mother compelled to see her son from this oblique new angle.

Prefacing her remarks with the disclaimer that she was only an "average reader," Kosinski's mother praised the book's form and language and acknowledged that it revealed the dormant "animal instincts" of human beings. She wondered, however, if it really needed the violently sexual scenes with Ewka and Ludmila—scenes that, in her view, outdid Sartre and Zegadlowicz. She was, she explained, old-fashioned. But then, she added, she suffered from the innocence that *he was not with them at that time*. Writing, of course, in Polish, she spaced the letters—Y O U W E R E N O T W I T H U S. The double-spacing might well have had the character of emphasis, but in the context of all that is knowable of the Kosinski family during the occupation, one must conclude that this most remarkable statement was, instead, delivered with a symbolic wink.

As extraordinary as it might appear, the most satisfactory explanation is that Elzbieta Kosinska had agreed with her son to maintain, even in their private correspondence, the fiction that he had been separated from them. So deeply was this myth integrated into the terms of their relationship that she even worked it into her critical response, calling attention to their shared secret by double-spacing. Yet if mother and son had agreed upon a course of conspiratorial deception, it partially served its purpose. Despite the comprehensive accounts of seemingly reliable witnesses, Elzbieta Kosinska's letter to her son will forever leave a slim shadow of doubt.

Having rendered her literary judgment, a qualified yes to her son's book, Elzbieta then went on to commend to him another recent novel, Romain Gary's *La Promesse de l'aube*, a moving story *of mother and son*. She was adamant that her son read it. She then chided him for failing to complete his Ph.D. in timely fashion. Was he delaying the degree to spite her? One could write and earn a Ph.D. too. Literary fame and receptions at PEN clubs would fade, she said prophetically, but Ph.D.'s were solid and permanent; besides, it had been his father's dream. She sent her regards to Mary, along with concern about an injury to Mary's cheek that her son had mentioned in a recent telephone conversation.

One can only imagine a son's reaction to such a letter. Thoughtful and measured, it left little room for rebuttal while carrying in each line the curse of qualified and measured praise from the one whose unqualified approval is most fervently sought. Addressed to her darling son and concluded with the sentiment that the last five minutes of her life would be dominated by thoughts of *him*, it was not even the sort of letter at which one could become angry. It was, in sum, as absolute a message about life as one can receive: that the ultimate success and praise always recede from one's grasp.

Secondary praise, however, was his in abundance. Richard Kim, a star of the moment for his novel *The Martyred*, named *The Painted Bird* in the *Boston Globe* as one of his three favorite novels from that year. The *New York Times* made it one of a year-end list of fourteen works of fiction—among them Mailer's *An American Dream*, Updike's *Of the Farm*, and Flannery O'Connor's story collection *Everything That Rises Must Converge*. The author of the list in the *Times* was daily reviewer Eliot Fremont-Smith, who seventeen years later would be coauthor of the article in the *Village Voice* that brought Kosinski down.

6.

That same fall Kosinski received an invitation to the April in Paris Ball, held on October 28, a fund-raiser for the American Hospital of Paris and at that time the glitziest of New York's charity events. Artur Rubinstein, also a native of Lodz, was going to be there, and Maurice Chevalier would give one of his last public performances, singing "Life Is Just a Bowl of Cherries." Ewa

Pape, Polish-born wife of Walter Pape (of the cottage cheese fortune), was one of the organizers. In putting together a table, she
needed a date for Dr. Roman Czaplicki, a Polish-American chiro-
practor who was coming from Chicago. She arranged for him to
escort Katherina von Fraunhofer, called Kiki, who was the only
female account executive at J. Walter Thompson at the time and
worked on the Cheseborough Ponds account.

The Ball was a great success. Air France flew in two shopping
bags of Parisian perfumes for each guest, topping that year's extensive list of favors, and Chevalier's performance put the whole
assemblage into an exalted mood. In the course of the evening
Kosinski stopped by Pape's table. As a fellow Pole, she had
known him for several years. Once she had even gone to his
apartment on Seventy-ninth Street, but had left in a huff, slam-
ming the door: Kosinski had wanted to photograph her naked
with a rose between her legs. On this particular night, enjoying
the success of his first novel, Kosinski was at his charming best.
Pape presented him to the others at her table, including her
young friend Kiki.

"That's a man I want to meet," Kiki told Ewa Pape. Pape mentioned this to Kosinski a couple of times, but Kosinski had not
paid much attention to the tall, leggy young woman at Pape's table. Anyway, he was busy being one of the season's major new
literary celebrities. Suddenly he was an important figure at the
weekly PEN cocktail parties, which he had been attending more
or less regularly since the publication of *No Third Path*. Now he
had a book in his own name, so that his presence no longer required an explanation, and it was being reviewed and noticed all
over the city, and the country.

One of the writers he met through those PEN parties was Sidney Offit, and on December 1 he came to speak to Offit's writing
class at the New School. The students were charmed and impressed, particularly as many of them had just finished reading
The Painted Bird. Standing in front of them was not only a stylish
writer but a sort of Audie Murphy of the Holocaust, a man who
had been to Hell and returned to write it up.

As the class broke up, Kosinski kibitzed with Offit about the
qualities of various of the young women. One particularly attrac-

tive young woman was about to leave with the young man who sat next to her. Kosinski suggested that if they moved quickly, the young woman would leave with them instead; Offit could have her, if he wanted, but they had to get in fast and cut the young man out. Offit was amused, but took a pass.

They went instead to Trude Heller's, which was rocking with young women in miniskirts dancing to the go-go music of the mid-1960s. Offit enjoyed dancing, and wanted to plunge in, but Kosinski preferred to hang back on the periphery and observe. Offit felt sorry for his new friend and worried that Kosinski was something of a wallflower. It was a little hard to talk above the noise, and Kosinski was primarily a talker. He intellectualized about the women beguilingly. "Now there's a woman ..." he would begin, and would proceed to give an estimate of the woman's sexual preferences and performance, how far she might be expected to go. Was he mainly a watcher and a talker, Offit wondered, or was this kind of talk for real?

The two men left Trude Heller's and began walking through the Village toward an Italian restaurant on Fifth Avenue. Passing the American School of Painting, Kosinski insisted on pausing to look in the windows. He wanted to do that with everything they passed. Kosinski struck Offit as being half the beguiled tourist and half the highly informed tour guide; perhaps it was the perfect metaphor for the position Kosinski had reached in New York. No longer the boy just off the plane from Poland, he knew the city in ways some of its lifelong residents would never know it, while other aspects of American life would remain forever alien to him.

At the restaurant Kosinski asked the owner to send a small portion of every dish on the menu. As the dishes arrived, Kosinski took a bite and passed them along for Offit to finish. He then summoned the owner, complimented him on his kitchen, and made a suggestion. The food was superb, Kosinski said, but he could tell that the business in the evening wasn't enough. He suggested that the owner have a carry-out menu during the day, to serve the lunch crowd from nearby offices; he even made suggestions as to which items the menu should contain.

"I always do this," Kosinski told Offit. In every room he entered, he immediately searched out a place where he could hide;

for every business, he immediately set to work thinking of a way to make it a bigger success. Offit wasn't fully convinced, but the restaurant owner may well have been; a few years later he had put in place a daytime carry-out menu, with great success.

Kosinski had a suggestion for Offit as well. He had read Offit's novels, he said, and thought Offit had a good ear. He couldn't understand, though, why Offit wrote about subjects that were so provincial. He had an idea: write a novel about *masturbation*. It was just one of the endless flow of outrageous and wonderful ideas Kosinski would come up with over the years; Kosinski was *the* great literary idea man, and Philip Roth's *Portnoy's Complaint* would eventually show the possibilities inherent in this one. It wasn't for Offit, however; he told Kosinski he could just imagine going around New York while people pointed at him and said, There goes Offit the Masturbator.

Later that same month Kosinski turned up in Andy Heinemann's office and delivered a bombshell: Mary wanted a divorce. Heinemann was shocked. He knew a bit about Kosinski's inconstancy, but he assumed that Mary knew and accepted it, or that he hid it from her successfully. Why a divorce now? The two men had a long talk about Mary. Kosinski felt that Mary was making a bad mistake. An alcoholic constantly in and out of institutions, she desperately needed someone to provide her life with continuity, to look after her. He suggested that she had suicidal tendencies, and was likely to make a successful attempt if no one was with her. If a divorce was what she wanted, however, he would not stand in the way. Heinemann agreed to help orchestrate the divorce, suggesting another law firm to represent her; he himself felt disqualified because he had met Mary through Kosinski.

Heinemann had never much liked Kosinski, preferring the straightforward and vulnerable Mary. But he had to admit that Kosinski was fair about the divorce. He said he wanted *nothing* for himself, and as the terms were drawn up, that was exactly what he got. Heinemann had heard rumors that Mary had already settled, or spent, $300,000 on him. If so, where was it? There was the Continental Mark II and the Bentley, some nice clothes, and the several grand tours of Europe and Asia. There would be further elaborate travels over the next few years, but there would also be moments of un-Kosinski-like abstemiousness, suggesting that if a trust fund existed, he was for some reason reluctant to use it. The rumor of a secret $300,000 trust fund persisted, however, and surfaced again at the time of Kosinski's death.

The real reasons for the divorce may never be known. Kosinski explained to intimates that the same Dr. Hughes who at one point advocated that Mary voluntarily commit herself had proposed that, in light of Mary's "illness," the interests of both parties would best be served by divorce. An integral element of this version had it that Mary's behavior had to do with a brain tumor, not with a depressive state exacerbated by acute alcoholism. Mary herself told her son that she had caught her husband *in flagrante*, and with a young *man*. This story is not altogether implausible, but it seems unlikely that the limits of discretion could have entirely concealed Kosinski's activities up to that point, in light of his wide-ranging tastes and activities that ran the gamut from affairs to prostitutes to Lilla van Saher.

There were those, especially among his former Polish friends, who felt that Kosinski had become involved with Mary under the assumption that she had far more wealth than she actually had. By this account, the stories he later told, both inside and outside his fiction, of private planes and yachts and casual stock market losses of $62 million were his actual estimate of her wealth. When he learned that her wealth was far more modest, and that most of what there was had been artfully tied up by her late husband, Kosinski dumped her.

Yet this story, too, suffers from the fact that the limits of Mary's wealth must have been apparent to Kosinski long before— probably, in fact, before they were married. Perhaps the Park Avenue duplex, the great dinners, and the ability to travel in princely style *meant* something different in the early days, but it is hard to believe that Kosinski woke up from financial naiveté in late 1965; this version also must contend with the fact that it was Mary who sought and carried through the divorce. Kosinski was blunt about the fact that her wealth and position were a part of Mary's identity, an aspect of whatever attracted him, and the diminution of his ardor, insofar as it was a factor in the divorce, is possibly best seen as part of an overall shifting view of her and her place in his life.

Perhaps divorce was simply, at that moment, the right thing, and for both parties. It was, in any case, amicable. Kosinski continued to be involved in Mary's life, for good or ill, talking to her frequently on the phone, an involvement that made it easy, as the years passed, to neglect to mention that they had ever been divorced at all.

The marriage to Mary Weir had lasted exactly four years, the preceding courtship a little over a year. It was a union of two deeply troubled human beings. Mary had been in and out of institutions, battling acute and chronic alcoholism, since 1950, and while the excitement of a new relationship may have stemmed the tide momentarily, her condition was progressively worsening over her years with Kosinski. She fell into the relationship under conditions in which her potential for good judgment may well have been impaired, after two previous marriages, one brief and unsatisfactory, the other to a man forty years her senior. It is not surprising that she was swept away by the charm of a younger man, especially a man like Kosinski, but it is somewhat more difficult to reconstruct the texture of her feelings over the course of their time together, apart from the fact that much of that time was lived in an alcoholic haze.

What she was to Kosinski is even more difficult to assess. A material provider she clearly was, but the psychological support may have been more important than the actual material possessions. Eighteen years his senior, she certainly embodied some characteristics of a mother, although in all the giving of Prince of Wales suits and Lincoln Continentals and Bentleys, she may have been as unable to give what he sought as the woman upon whom she was modeled. Or possibly it is more accurate to say that Kosinski, conditioned by his childhood, was unable to receive love, or be a participant in intimacy. David Weir's view that Kosinski moved in as lover *and son*, edging him out, may well be accurate.

If so, Mary Weir was for Kosinski an attempt at fulfillment, in form and structure, of his need for a mother's unqualified love. It missed, as it was doomed to miss, the main thing. Like his actual mother, who treasured her brilliant son and was willing to lie for him, but was unable to give him her free and unqualified praise and approval, Mary because of her condition and by her very nature was predestined to withhold it too. Much about her life argues that, like Kosinski, she was unable to love or be loved in the fullest way.

The fact that Kosinski, despite his later reconstructions, initially opposed the divorce, and continued, though with ambiguous intent, to stay in Mary's life, reveals a good deal. If it was money he was after, pure and simple, this behavior makes no sense. For much of their marriage he had lived in her house like the wayward child of a troubled parent, and now it was his task to see that troubled parent to the end of things. Divorce in such a relationship is not a possibility, and although a legal divorce ended their marriage, Kosinski's life *could* not be divorced in the broader sense from Mary Weir's. She would become in future years a cornerstone of the Kosinski myth, the minor detail of the divorce easily forgotten. A mother cannot, after all, divorce her son, nor can a son renounce his mother.

Mary obtained the divorce in Mexico, in January of 1966. That same month the leggy young woman from J. Walter Thompson got a second look. This time it was the Polish Ball, another charity event, put together by and for Polish émigrés such as Witold Sulimirski of First National City Bank. Over the three months since the April in Paris Ball, Kiki had mentioned Kosinski several times to Ewa Pape, who had passed along word of her interest without eliciting much response. But now Kosinski was a free man, a literary celebrity named on the top year-end lists, but a man without a home. This time when he came by Ewa Pape's table to say hello, he paid Kiki closer attention. He seemed bored by the whole ambience of the evening, but she was acutely interested.

At the time of the Polish Ball, Kiki was "engaged" to Timothy Stone, an advertising executive, but her brief encounter with Kosinski brought home to her the limits of her feelings for Stone. The following day she called and broke the engagement. She also called Ewa Pape, who arranged a luncheon for the following Monday at the Drake, where Pape then had an apartment. Pape made the introduction and then left for another engagement, leaving Jerzy and Kiki in the Drake restaurant. As get-acquainted presents, they exchanged books. Kiki gave Jerzy a book of essays by Cyril Connolly. He gave her a copy of *The Painted Bird*, and for good measure his self-published pamphlet, *Notes of the Author*. Unaware that it had been given routinely to every reviewer, she felt singled out as a person of special discernment.

And in a way she had been singled out. No one could listen quite the way Jerzy could, making a woman feel in fifteen minutes that she had known him all her life. Certainly, no one in Kiki's experience had ever talked the way he did. She had been brought up in England, educated at a finishing school amidst British reticence and understatement, where the formal social niceties and the ability to ride horses were given more emphasis than being in contact with one's feelings. This striking, funny, sensual man who was interested in *everything* opened up for her an unexplored side of life.

Kiki was related to an aristocratic Bavarian family—her father had actually been interned in England during the war—and her family had both distinction and eccentricities. Over a century earlier, one of the von Fraunhofers had done pioneering scientific work in optics. More recently, her father had not only been an internee of MI-6 but had married, in sequence, Kiki's grandmother and then her mother. For Kosinski, these must have been quirks of the most delightful and interesting kind, although the fact he seized upon for presentation to the world was the aristocracy of lineage. Though somewhat removed from the family title, Kiki became the "baroness" and was regularly so presented to the world, with only the mildest disclaimer suggesting that in the modern world one bore such titles with a bit of embarrassment.

It was all great fun, more fun, certainly, than having to pretend that Mary Weir's bad spells came from a brain tumor or to explain to his mother why it was necessary to say that he had been separated from her during the war; it was fiction-making of a high order, starting with a base of fact that needed to be improved upon and presenting a story that would stand up to scrutiny by the world. Wasn't this what novelists did? Wasn't it the way of all individuals marked for a larger destiny?

Kosinski left in March for Europe. *The Painted Bird* was being published simultaneously in England and France (the German-language edition having come out at the same time as the American), and his publishers had arranged for interviews and appearances. The book was doing reasonably well in England and France, better certainly than in America, but the German edition was an out-and-out hit. For a Germany struggling to shuck off the collective national guilt for World War II and the Holocaust, its focus on the "Eastern European" peasants may have suggested that sadistic behavior and genocide were not a national trait or the crime of a specific group but part of a universally distributed human depravity; a gentler view is that the book became part of a continuing German examination of the war years. Perhaps both views reflect aspects of the book's success in Germany, where *Der bemalte Vogel* actually made it onto bestseller lists.

With the modest royalty scale on European translations, the success did not make Kosinski's fortune, but it made him instantly an important figure in the world of letters. For a writer who had explained Eastern Europe to Americans and Americans to themselves, through Eastern European eyes, it added yet another wrinkle; a European readership now pointed up to Americans the importance of this "American" author, much as it had with such detective writers as James M. Cain and Raymond Chandler and whole art forms like jazz and blues. Jerzy Kosinski was, and would remain throughout his career, a writer not so much of one country as of the Atlantic community.

Kosinski returned to New York on April 14, and only two weeks later received the best news of all from Europe. On May 2, Flammarion cabled Houghton Mifflin that *L'Oiseau bariole* had been awarded the Prix du Meilleur Livre Étranger—the annual award given in France for the best foreign book of the year. Previous winners included Lawrence Durrell, John Updike, Heinrich Böll, Robert Penn Warren, Oscar Lewis, Angus Wilson, and Nikos Kazantzakis. New York might be the center of publishing, but Paris was still, to many minds, the intellectual center of the universe, and Kosinski had swept the French intellectual world off its feet. Any who had doubted the aesthetic merits of *The Painted Bird* were now shamed into silence. The authority of the "eleven distinguished jurors" was an absolute in New York as in Paris; Kosinski's first novel had swept the board.

Meanwhile he and Kiki had become, in the city's parlance, an item. Various women offered him ever more various enticements, but Kiki offered him something no one else could provide. She could straighten out his files, she told him, and she promptly demonstrated the truth of her boast. It was a talent going back to her early days at J. Walter Thompson. In matters of love, Kosinski was a practical man. One could always find women to serve the more primal urges, but a woman who could provide a central order in one's life was a rare treasure indeed. Moving in together, more or less, while retaining separate apartments in the 1960s way, they became more than an item: within a year, in spite of a few disturbances, they would be a unit against the world.

7.

In June of 1966 *The Painted Bird* was accorded a dubious and highly unusual honor: it was reviewed widely in a nation, and a language, in which it had not yet been published. The first review had actually appeared on March 19, in *Polityka*, the official and nationally circulated cultural weekly of the Communist Party. The reviewer was Wieslaw Gornicki, and in language that closely echoed his earlier piece in the Chicago Polish-language journal *Ameryka-Echo*, he stressed the "naturalistic," almost documentary quality that makes the book feel more like a memoir than a novel. Greatly exaggerating the book's sales and the number of foreign editions in the works at that time, Gornicki renewed the assault on the book as a libel against the Polish nation and regime.

Others quickly joined in. On June 6 *Zycie Partii*, an official organ of the Polish Communist Party with wide syndication in party district newspapers, assaulted Kosinski's "libelous novel" as part of Western propaganda attempting to blacken the socialist countries, splashing filth "not only on socialism but on our nations in general and particularly on the Poles." The review made specific mention of Mrs. Weir, the USIA, Voice of America, and Radio Free Europe, as though they were a cabal behind the book, and noted its enthusiastic reception by "the revanchist press of the German Federal Republic." The Warsaw magazine *Forum* compared Kosinski to Goebbels and Senator McCarthy and emphasized a particular sore point for Poles: the relatively sympathetic treatment of a German soldier. Kosinski, the review argued, put himself on the side of the Hitlerites, who saw their crimes as the work of "pacifiers of a primitive pre-historic jungle." *Glos Nauczycielski*, the weekly publication of the teaching profession, took the same line, accusing *The Painted Bird* of an attempt "to dilute the German guilt for the crime of genocide by including the supposed guilt of all other Europeans and particularly those from Eastern Europe."

Slowo Polskie, a government-owned daily in Wroclaw, called Kosinski a "German-lover" (Wroclaw is the former German city Breslau, to which the citizens of eastern Lvov had been transported en masse, and anything soft on Germans was a particularly sore point there; Jelenia Gora, where Kosinski lived in 1946, is only a few kilometers away); the *Slowo Polskie* piece also explicitly mentioned the reference to Poles in Andrew Field's *Herald Tribune* review as "butcher's helpers," as would the Warsaw daily *Zycie Warszawy* later that year. Newspapers in Gdansk, Lodz, and Cracow took up the same themes. Ironically, *Dziennik Polski i Dziennik Zolnierza*, a Polish émigré newspaper in London, attacked Kosinski for being hard on Poles and praising the *Red Army*, while *Kultura*, the émigré journal in Paris, attacked its sympathetic portrayal of *both Germans and Russians* and its tendentious attack on Poles; it concluded that the book "oscillates between truth and fantasy and that it should be defined as a conscious or unconscious lie."

The one émigré response that mattered to Kosinski, however, was that of Dr. Stanislaw Strzetelski, his old sponsor at the Polish Institute. Strzetelski gently declined to read the book. Pained, Kosinski wrote Strzetelski a careful, multi-page typed explanation of the book, but Strzetelski stuck by his decision. Kosinski's own father had not lived to see the book, and while his mother had sent qualified praise with quibbles, the man who served as a father during the first years in America had now refused, politely, to read it.

Obviously the book had struck a nerve. Was this all the doing of Wieslaw Gornicki? The reviews in Poland strongly suggest an orchestrated campaign. Bearing in mind the fact that the novel was not available in Polish, it is striking that so many of the major Party journals reviewed it in June. It was as though a phantom edition had been published around June 10. Gornicki's March 19 review would have been the equivalent of an advance notice in *Publishers Weekly* or *Kirkus*, a guide and tone-setter for the rest. Whether the reviews were actually *mandated* by the Central Committee is another question, and perhaps is beside the point. Speaking in later years, persons highly enough placed to understand the system argued that an actual mandate was unnecessary. When the government not only has the power of censorship but provides by quota the paper on which journals are printed, a wink and the appearance of a story in a single leading publication are all that it takes to deliver a message to the editor.

On July 19, and again two days later, Kosinski wrote to apprise Paul Brooks at Houghton Mifflin of the Polish attacks. Brooks replied that the rest of the world had recognized the genius of the book, and that the fabrications of the Communist Party in Poland would be transparent to objective observers. This was only to say what Kosinski already knew. Treating the novel as though it were a memoir was simply going to make the Polish reviewers look ridiculous; in the West—France, Britain, and especially Germany, as well as the United States—it would make him a martyr, and provide free publicity. At least the Poles would spell his name right!

But there must have been another worry on his mind. That the book had factual antecedents he knew all too well, and that his imaginative enhancements somewhat changed the role played by various actors he also knew well. Many of them were living people. What if the Polish authorities set out to track those people down? There was the potential of having to fight libel suits, at worst, or face down embarrassing "rebuttals" at the very least. It is difficult to believe that this thought did not cross his mind.

As it turned out, Polish journalists had in fact begun to seek out persons who had known the Kosinskis during the war. Individuals in Sandomierz and Dabrowa remember being interviewed by a man who introduced himself as a journalist as far back as 1966. Official or unofficial fact finders had therefore pieced together at least part of the real story, but had stopped short of attempting a massive exposé. The problem was: Who would believe them? Who were their readers? In Poland, no one had ever heard of Kosinski. In the West, they would be dismissed as ideologues with an ax to grind. Thus Kosinski's initial estimate of the situation had been correct. It was unnecessary to deal with the threat of libel, and there was unlikely to be immediate scholarly or journalistic inquiry into his sources.

As for the negative Polish reviews, they bore out the lessons he had learned in the disputes with the Union of Polish Art Photographers and the Youth Organization: all disputes took place within a political context. The context might work for you or against you, and sometimes it worked most powerfully for you when it appeared to work against you. One thing was clear. His novel would never lack for defenders while it was under attack by the Polish Communists.

Still, the stories he had told in the course of writing and selling the book weighed upon his mind. He was safe for the moment, protected by the ineptitude and distance of his enemies, but there was much to hide. It was this feeling, as much as any fear of a possible return of the Nazis, that made him scan every room for a potential hiding place. The book left him vulnerable, contributing to a state of lethargy and depression which overtook him during the latter part of 1966.

Despite its succès d'estime in four countries, *The Painted Bird* had sold poorly in hardcover in the American market. Kosinski was naturally disappointed, and in his letter to Paul Brooks about the Polish reviews, his disappointment crystallized into a complaint about the amount Houghton Mifflin was billing him for corrections to the galleys. The sum was $972.38—just under the thousand dollars David Harris had estimated and to which he had agreed—but now he seized upon the quantitatively slight corrections requested by the Houghton Mifflin lawyers to blur the picture. In the moral equation, he must have felt justified, notwithstanding the fact that the decision to reset the galleys had been made *before* the request for deletions.

Once again memos flew back and forth at Houghton Mifflin. Kosinski was an author they very much wanted to keep, and their own moral position was the exact reverse of Kosinski's. They had lost their nerve and compelled deletions, minor perhaps but meaningful, to the text of what was clearly a major work of literature; moreover, they had failed in the commercial exploitation of a work that received the most stellar reviews, with bestseller status in Germany to prove that a skillful publisher might have done better. After some debate, they came to a formula: Houghton Mifflin would bear one-third of the cost of the reset, to keep Kosinski happy. Kosinski's royalties, which then stood at $6,147.69, including his half of the Pocket Books paperback advance of $6,250, would be docked only $648.25.

While reviews of *The Painted Bird* came in from France and Britain and, startlingly, from Poland, Kosinski was busy with Eugene Prakapas restoring the passages cut from the hardcover for the Pocket Books edition. In March, Prakapas had written Houghton Mifflin announcing plans to print 300,000 copies and conduct a heavy promotional campaign, and requesting permission to restore the deleted material; Paul Brooks had been disturbed by the implication that Pocket was going for a big sale on the basis of sensationalism, but Houghton Mifflin had no legal basis for denying the request.

In actuality, Prakapas's plan was somewhat grander. He admired Kosinski's book and felt that Houghton Mifflin had simply printed a handful and dumped them down the trash chute, giving Kosinski no support. He now planned, in effect, a second publication. Prakapas had told Kosinski at the Houghton Mifflin publication party back in October that the book reminded him of Hieronymus Bosch. Now he proposed for it a highly eccentric cover—Bosch's *Monster Carrying a Child in a Basket* (detail of *The Last Judgment*). Prakapas had a grand strategy, the core of which was to treat the book as an instant classic. He had a feeling about the potential audience, including young people, which could keep the book in print for a long time. With the narrow margins of the reprint industry, this strategy might not make Kosinski rich. It would, however, make Kosinski.

Through the summer and fall Prakapas worked with Kosinski, not only restoring the text of *The Painted Bird* but also helping spur along the new novel in progress, which he also hoped to publish. Kosinski spent much of his time that summer at the apartment in Gregory House on Seventy-ninth Street, which he had retained after the breakup with Mary Weir. Now his sole living space, it resembled all the other residences of his life: a congested womblike space that seemed overfull even with Kosinski's few possessions, which included mainly cameras, photographic equipment, and books. The rent-stabilized apartment in Hemisphere House at Fifty-seventh and Sixth, where he later lived with Kiki until the end of his life, would have the same utilitarian quality, with combined bedroom and office; even at Mary Weir's magnificent duplex, he had retreated into a single room.

All of Kosinski's chosen residences shared characteristics of the cramped spaces the Kosinskis had occupied during the war, especially the semidetached apartment the Kosinskis had rented from the Warchols in Dabrowa, where living and eating spaces had done double duty; pressured by the postwar Polish housing shortage, he had re-created this ambience in the small flat he shared with Tad Krauze and the vodka-factory worker in Warsaw. To Prakapas and others, he spoke constantly of hiding places—in his own apartments and in every room he entered. Yet the apartments themselves were hiding places of a sort, membranes, customized and cluttered, serving as a second skin to keep the world at bay. Not only did they keep the world out, but in their modest surface they concealed the grandiosity of his ambition and sense of destiny.

That summer, as he told Prakapas, his refuge was under attack. People kept trying to break in—"Poles," he said. Why they persisted wasn't clear. Even less clear was why they failed at a task any reasonably competent burglar could have accomplished in a few minutes. Who *were* these mysterious Poles? Prakapas listened to the stories with interest, never quite sure how much was real and how much was some kind of paranoid fantasy.

The paranoia was not all Kosinski's. Although they were divorced, Mary Weir remained very present in Kosinski's life. He called her several times a week, and she in turn called his friends and business associates, usually when she had been drinking heavily. Among the recipients of these calls were Bob Geniesse— Kosinski's oldest American "friend" and a member of the law firm that now represented him. She asked, as though she did not know, "Where do you suppose Kosinski gets his money? His fancy cars and expensive clothes?" More soulfully, she asked the more troubling question: "Do you suppose that he actually writes his own books?"

Prakapas knew, at least, how Kosinski was writing the present one. In Prakapas's view, Kosinski's command of the English language was, by now, superb. As the work in progress began to take shape, the imaginative part was all Kosinski. The text, however, tended to be repetitive and loose. Prakapas's role was to pin him down, asking: "What is it exactly that you meant here?" As for the strange episodic structure of the new book, that seemed to have a consistency with the philosophy of life that Kosinski expounded to him in off-duty moments. Life is episodic, Kosinski said; it is without coherence, without obvious overall meaning— without *plot.* How else could all of life's weird experiences be accounted for? They didn't fit any scheme. They just *were.*

By the summer of 1966, money had again become not merely a nuisance but an acute problem in Kosinski's life—for the first time since his early days as a student. Quite simply, hardly any of it was coming in. On June 15 Houghton Mifflin had sent him a royalty check for $2,715.53, the last check he could expect to see from them. Mary could not be expected to kick in pocket money, and there was still rent to pay and certain modest amenities of lifestyle to maintain. If there had actually ever been a $300,000 trust fund, there was no evidence of it at this point.

To bridge the period until he could hope to receive an advance on the next novel, Kosinski decided to apply for a Guggenheim. He delivered his application on September 21, for backing "to finish and submit for publication in the United States and abroad a work of fiction presently untitled. In this book the author intends to test several structural and philosophical themes." His references were Boris Pregel, who as chairman of the New York Academy of Sciences had written one of the reference letters in his application to work for the USIA; Peter Berger, a sociology professor at the New School who had admired *The Painted Bird*; Giorgio de Santillana; and Paul Brooks.

The use of de Santillana and Brooks was a masterpiece of timing, and resulted in a little pas de deux of prospects with his former publisher. Houghton Mifflin had become, understandably, concerned about its relationship with Kosinski, realizing that they had in many ways mishandled a major talent. For his part, Kosinski was willing to string them along for a while more. Brooks wrote Jim Brown, opining that he could produce a better reference letter with a look at the new book first. But it was nothing doing; Kosinski already had plans for the next book. Brooks caved in and wrote the supporting letter without access to the manuscript.

Kosinski's statement of plans, edited and polished by Peter Skinner, laid out his aspirations for the untitled work. It was to be a book about a dominant partner in a relationship imposing his past upon the weaker partner, who is, however, more able to be in touch with the present moment. The book would examine man's entrapment by social systems that profess to provide protection, particularly collective ones, but it would also describe the entrapment of the weaker partner by the stronger. There would be no "plot" in the Aristotelian sense, nor any linear chronology, with the contest of the book—as he would later reiterate in his second self-published pamphlet, *The Art of the Self*—taking place in the blank spaces between episodes.

The novel, in other words, was about *power*. The protagonist would maneuver to avoid the power of collective society, but to exert his own, private power over others. The book itself embodied the author's intent to exert *power* over his readers.

Katherina von Fraunhofer—Kiki—was by now a central fact of Kosinski's life. She had gradually assumed the motherly role of Mary Weir, adding such innovations as typing his manuscripts and keeping his files in order. She was marvelous at both. All in all, she typed the entire manuscript of *Steps* a total of twenty-eight times. Money was short, but that didn't worry her. She had a good salary at J. Walter Thompson, and an expense account, and she had faith in Kosinski's future. There were periods when she virtually supported him, finding a way to make it acceptable to his pride. When she mentioned that she needed money for grocery shopping, he would say, "Oh, take it from the drawer." When the drawer where he kept his cash was empty, she paid for the groceries.

The relationship had its delicate moments in other areas as well. Sexually, Kiki was willing but naive. Before she met Jerzy, she had been one of those tall attractive women that many men find intimidating; it was assumed that she had lovers, when what she actually had was a number of male friends and admirers from a distance. Jerzy himself was often insecure about her, interrogating her carefully about her activities when he had been away on a trip—as he was that fall, visiting England, France, and the Frankfurt book fair. She virtually worshiped him, but still he had doubts.

Once after lovemaking she withdrew to the bathroom to put curlers in her hair. "Don't I satisfy you?" he asked, suspecting that she had withdrawn to stimulate herself.

But it was Kosinski whose more adventurous tastes were going unsatisfied. One day he said to Kiki, "Don't you have anything *black*?" Once he explained what he wanted, it seemed a straightforward enough request. Kiki had no trouble procuring black underwear, but she couldn't figure out how to rig the garters and appeared holding them in her hand. Where did they go? "Oh, take them off," Jerzy replied.

These were difficult moments for Kiki, who had gotten herself into a far more complex relationship than she could possibly have imagined. Nevertheless, she stuck with it. Completely taken with Jerzy, she sensed that he needed her desperately. They were bound together by something not quite clear to her but far more important than black garters.

Meanwhile Pocket Books was making good on the promise to make Jerzy Kosinski a household word. A teaser ad in *Publishers Weekly* created a stir, and the Bosch cover proved to be a PR masterstroke. The National Association of Teachers of English put the book on their outside reading list—presumably in part for its value in documenting the experience of World War II in German-occupied Europe. The editors at Houghton Mifflin were stunned by the success of the Pocket campaign—the first printing of 500,000 promptly sold out, and the book eventually went through four additional Pocket printings and subsequently many Bantam printings—and shocked by the book's being made suggested reading for *high-school students*, an endorsement that surprised even Kosinski.

The Polish attacks, meanwhile, seemed actually to advance his career. On December 12 the *New York Times* ran a news story filed in Warsaw, "Poles Are Bitter About Novel Published Abroad," summarizing and quoting the Polish reviews and placing them in the context of Cold War politics and historical Polish anti-Semitism. The article noted that *The Painted Bird* was the most re-quested volume in the United States Embassy in Warsaw, and that Westerners living in Warsaw were often asked by Polish acquaintances whether they have a copy.

A decade later, in his introductory essay to the 1976 reissue of the novel, Kosinski described events of that year in Warsaw. State television had run a series, "In the Footsteps of *The Painted Bird*," he said, interviewing individuals who were said to have been in contact with Kosinski and his family during the war. Crowds of angry townspeople converged on his mother's home in Lodz, compelling her to leave for a few weeks and eventually to move to the capital.

So Kosinski reported in his essay. His mother did eventually move to an apartment in Warsaw, on Belwederska Street, directly across from the Soviet Embassy. She had never been overly fond of Lodz, however, and persons who knew her at the time in Poland—the Urbans, for example, who have no apparent interest in distorting the truth—consider the story of mobs outside her house in Lodz to be gross exaggeration, if not fabrication. That same essay tells the story of a visiting poet who closely resembles Halina Poswiatowska, whom Kosinski knew in America in 1960, but changes the year of her visit to America.

Finally, according to the introductory essay, the Poles who (as he had told friends) had been trying to break into his apartment got in—two of them pushing through the front door when Kosinski answered it expecting a delivery. They pulled out a clipping of the *New York Times* article about Eastern European attacks and threatened to beat him with lengths of steel pipe wrapped in newspaper. He thwarted them by drawing a small revolver he kept behind his two-volume *Dictionary of Americanisms.* He then grabbed a camera and photographed them, threatening to press charges. There is an almost magical quality to Kosinski's weapons—a revolver, a dictionary of idioms in his new language, and a camera—the sort of objects a mythic Joseph Campbell quester/hero might well find himself wielding in the modern world.

Kosinski sometimes disavowed having ever possessed a revolver. He clung tenaciously, however, to the story of the two Poles who were after him. They, or their cousins, would return to track him from time to time in the future. Who were they? Were they flesh-and-blood agents, of who knows what, or figments of his ever fecund imagination? And were they improvements on a story he told, or elements of an inner story working ever richer veins in his psyche? The answer is unobtainable, the question probably wrongly framed. Like figures in Alain Resnais's *Last Year at Marienbad*, they are images, forever pushing in the door of Kosinski's Seventy-ninth Street apartment, threatening and being threatened in turn, entering the room again and again, with each entry incorporating a minor variation.

8.

In the fall of 1966, Rabbi Alex J. Goldman of Temple Beth El in Stamford, Connecticut, read an article about *The Painted Bird* in the *New York Times* and wrote inviting its author to speak at a Friday night service. Kosinski responded positively, sending several copies of the book. Upon reading it, the chairman of the Divine Service Committee recoiled in horror and urged that Kosinski be disinvited. Rabbi Goldman, who was newly arrived in Stamford, was inclined to back down, but Kosinski talked him out of it, assuring the rabbi that his appearance would not cause embarrassment.

On the night of January 6, in frigid weather, Goldman met Kosinski and Kiki at the train station, set them up at the Roger Smith Hotel, and escorted them to dinner with a dozen leading members of the congregation. It was an early tryout of the Jerzy and Kiki road show. Goldman sat Kosinski at the head of the table and suggested that he button up his shirt, which revealed, in Goldman's view, an excess amount of his "manliness." Kosinski hesitated and then agreed. While the others ordered fish or meat, Kosinski asked the kitchen for poached eggs, then left them virtually untouched, explaining that it was the first time he had spoken in a synagogue. In the course of the dinner, Goldman asked him whether he was the boy in the book and whether he was Jewish. Yes, Kosinski said, he was the boy; no, he was *not* Jewish.

The synagogue was filled to capacity, and Kosinski was in good form, speaking well and responding articulately to questions from the audience. Yet Goldman had been pondering Kosinski's answers to his questions at dinner, and he didn't quite believe them. During the social following the talk, he turned to Kiki and mentioned that he had asked whether Kosinski was Jewish, and Kosinski had denied it. She said with a slight, knowing smile, nodding her head, "He's Jewish. He's Jewish."

Yet many people retained the impression that he was not Jewish. Ewa Pape and Feliks Gross, among members of the Polish crowd who knew him well, were given the distinct impression that he was a Polish Catholic with somewhat unusual features; Pape, in fact, remembers him distinctly as an anti-Semite. In the American literary world—the world of the William Styrons, for example, in which he now began to be a regular—he was, simply, a Pole. Others saw him as a Gypsy, a view he promoted by having the boy in the book be seen as "a Gypsy or a Jew"; Elie Wiesel had been apprised of Kosinski's religion, but they got into a quarrel when Kosinski understood Wiesel to say that "the Gypsies weren't important."

Henryk Grynberg, author of *Child of the Shadows*, which described his survival as an "Aryan" in the Polish countryside under conditions similar to those encountered by the Kosinskis, arrived that year as a defector from Poland and was brought around to Kosinski's apartment by journalist David Schneiderman. Grynberg spent an hour with Kosinski during his first days in New York, and recalls his sense of a charming but inauthentic man who spoke with an odd absence of feeling in his voice. Kosinski, he recalls, spoke often of being afraid of Poles. As they left, Grynberg turned to Schneiderman and asked, "Is Kosinski Jewish?" Schneiderman undoubtedly recalled the incident seventeen years later, when as publisher of the *Village Voice* he and Kosinski again crossed paths.

One of Kosinski's new friends in this period was Friedel Ungeheuer, a senior correspondent at *Time,* through whom he met Henry Grunwald, on his way to becoming *Time*'s first Jewish editor-in-chief. Ungeheuer was German, and as a boy had been in the *Pimpfe* and then the Hitler Youth. At one of the publishing events he attended shortly after publication of *The Painted Bird*, a representative of a British publisher was picking at Ungeheuer because of his past. "Shut up, you Brit," Kosinski said. "We are *both* victims."

It was positioning of an exquisitely high order, an absolutely Olympian assumption of lofty moral ground—and easy to criticize with hindsight and out of context. Kosinski did, indisputably, deny that he was Jewish; he also used his status as a victim in whatever manner seemed convenient at the moment. Yet he *was*, undeniably, a victim, and the maneuvering he did within the New York scene is, among other things, symptomatic of his victimization. Of the things stolen from him by the war, the most precious of all may have been a comfortable acceptance of his basic identity.

As he rose in the world, hobnobbing with important writers and intellectuals and then with the very rich, the deprivations became obscured. Yet physically, there remained the series of cramped one- or two-room apartments to which he always retreated. In such cramped quarters, where rooms doubled as kitchen and bedroom, in a childhood perforce shared with Gentiles who could never quite be trusted, he had been told over and

over that he was *not a Jew*. And most people of that world who
were *not Jews*, were, in fact, anti-Semites.

That January the success of the Viet Cong Tet offensive gave le-
gitimacy to those protesting American involvement in Vietnam,
setting the stage for a culture of protest that would sweep up
American youth. David Weir, for one, was already safely out of
the country, and others were beginning to join him in significant
numbers. During February and March, Kosinski traveled around
Europe once again, having found the money somewhere. He returned in March to be notified that he had won a Guggenheim.
From April through December, the Guggenheim Foundation
would pay him six thousand dollars, in three installments.
Deeply appreciative and politically skillful, he set out immediately to have meetings with foundation secretary James Mathias
and president Gordon Ray. By then he understood both that writers were always a welcome addition in the lives of individuals
with material power, and that such men held the means, sometimes without realizing it, to make or break the careers of writers.

Later, in his final report to the foundation, Kosinski would acknowledge that the award came at a time of hesitation and doubt,
while his first novel was under heavy attack in Poland and when
he was at work on an unconventional novel with uncertain prospects. Along with the other uncertainties came a loss of confidence in himself. Perhaps it was the matter of composing, for the
first time, entirely in his new language. Sometimes Kiki put in
emergency calls to Prakapas, bribing him with the offer of a steak
and wine to come over and cheer Kosinski up, put him back on
track. He was threatening suicide, Kiki would say. Would Prakapas come over and do a little work with him, stabilize the situation?

That summer a thoroughly weird episode was unfolding with
Lilla van Saher. One day she had been walking topless on the
beach—a freedom she particularly enjoyed—at the summer house
of Philip van Rensselaer, author of the "Van Rensselaer's World"
column in the Newhouse newspapers and a regular of her early
1960s salon, when she stunned van Rensselaer with an announce-

ment: "I'm carrying Jurek's child, you know?" As van Saher was over sixty, van Rensselaer could not conceal his surprise. "He's been making love with me for years," she went on. "I know you think I'm too old, but women in my country often have children at sixty."

Back at her apartment in the city, she showed van Rensselaer the baby carriage, crib, baby clothes, and other paraphernalia she had assembled. The "pregnancy" became the talk of her circle. And van Saher did begin to have a protuberance in the midsection. In due course van Saher would announce that the baby had arrived, and invite friends over to see it. On each such occasion, however, the child would have been conveniently removed for a walk in the park with a nanny. Among those with whom van Saher shared her folie was Tennessee Williams, who encouraged van Rensselaer to "go along with it." It was, in Williams's view, yet another piece of van Saher's rich psychosexual theater, but one in which she herself had lost touch with the boundaries between reality and fantasy.

Kosinski would eventually use the episode of van Saher's "baby" in *Cockpit*, depicting van Saher as Theodora, an actress of Lebanese descent and the wife of a "Swiss industrialist." Tarden, the protagonist and Kosinski figure of the novel, gives her English lessons, they become lovers, and she recruits him into a secret intelligence service. Some time later, when she is divorced and down on her luck, they meet again; she is supporting herself by "gathering data for a small sex research institute," interviewing "men and women who had responded to personal ads in pornographic tabloids." Although van Saher was, by the end of her life, down on her luck and impoverished, this portrait falls short of doing justice to the lofty position she clung to in the underworld of New York literary society.

Determined to bear a child, Theodora takes hormone shots and makes an agreement to procure young women for Tarden, seducing them and joining in the sexual foreplay on condition that she be allowed to collect his sperm. Then comes the episode of her "pregnancy." At one of her parties, a playwright, whom she has reproached for using her in one of his plays, in turn accuses her of wearing padding to fake the pregnancy. (The real-life van Saher had, in fact, claimed proudly to be Tennessee Williams's model for Princess in *Sweet Bird of Youth*, a character actually drawn more closely after Tallulah Bankhead.) Eventually Theodora sends Tarden a photograph of "their" child, which he is able to identify as a photograph taken years earlier for use in illustrating a medical book.

There, for many writers, the story might have ended. Kosinski, however, provides one more turn of the screw. Theodora has used the false photograph only because the actual baby was born cross-eyed. The child has been given up for adoption. After Theodora dies of cancer, pining for Tarden in a charity ward, Tarden learns of the child's existence but is unable, under the terms of the adoption, to trace it. This version of the story segues into an extratextual twist. In years to come Kosinski told friends, without mentioning van Saher, that he had had a child, which was adopted by a family on Long Island. Interviewed in 1980, on the occasion of the opening of the film of *Being There*, he told Nancy Collins of the *Washington Star* that he had three children, one by a Polish student, one by a chambermaid at a hostel ("but she married someone else") and one living with a family on Long Island.

Lilla van Saher's "child" may stand as the quintessential Kosinski story; like the existence of God, the child is not particularly plausible, but not impossible either, and ultimately neither verifiable nor authoritatively deniable. As with the story of God, it is told by a master storyteller, with a magical premise as stunning as the virgin birth, and it insists on spilling over the edges of the literary text into the real world. The fact that Kosinski involved another, committed coconspirator in the tale poses all sorts of unanswerable questions, many of them analogous to the problem of his mother's letter supporting his assertion that he was separated from his parents during the war. In considering these two episodes, it is perhaps worth noting a practice he later revealed to a lover of misdating book inscriptions and other documents with the admitted intent of confusing future biographers and rendering his life undocumentable. More interesting, perhaps, is the question of whether Kosinski actually came to believe these stories as he told them. And how did van Saher fit? His mother, van

Jerzy Kosinski at ages six and twelve. He often called attention to the difference in the two pictures, especially around the eyes, as evidence of his suffering during the German occupation of Poland.

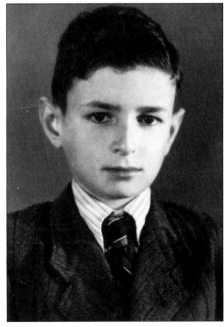

Lp.	Nazwisko i imię	Osoby będące na utrzymaniu głowy rodziny	Wiek	Skąd przybył	Data przybycia.	Zamieszkuje o
96.	Lewinkop Mojżesz kupiec	Elżbieta/żona/ Jerzy/syn/	1891 1899 1933	Łódź,	8.I.40	Zamkowa 8 /Blusztajn/
97.	Landau Lejzor kupiec Tusk	Rojza Sura/c./ Szaja Henoch,s. Chana Ides/c./ Wolf/wnuk/	1883 1910 1906 1914 1938	Łódź,11List.42	29.II 1940	Browarna 10 /Landau/
98.	Makowska Rojza wychowawczyni		1914	Łódź,11 List. 17	22.12 1939	Opatowska 8 /Rubinowicz/
99.	Markus Blima	Fiszel/syn/	1879 1912	Łódź Gdynia,Warsz.	1-I.40	Browarna 5
100.	Markus Salomon kupiec	Mania/żona/ Alfred/syn/	1908 1916 1938	Gdańsk,Feferstat	" "	5
101.	Oliwa Fajga przy mężu	Sara Brucha,c.	1910 1938	Łódź	20.XI 1939	Opatowska 5 /Friedman/
102.	Opolon Chaja szwaczka	Fajwel/syn/	1895 1928	Łódź	31.I.40	Zamkowa 6 /Unger/
103.	Rubinowicz Hinda,Przemysł.	Mira/córka/ Rachela/"/	1905 1927 1936	Łódź,11 List. 17	28.12 1939	Opatowska 8
104.	Rozenberg Nusyn .kupiec	Syma/żona/ Estera/córka/ Dwojra Perla "	1904 1902 1931 1935	Łódź,Podrzecz- na 20	25.12 1939	Opatowska 13 /Tyszler/
105.	Rozenberg Drez- la,bez zajęcia		1873	Dtto	1-I.40	Żydowska 28 /Zylberberg/
106.	Salomonowicz Jerzy,inżynier	Hanna/żona/ Henryk/syn/	1902 1906 1935	Łódź	22.XII 1939	Opatowska 4 /Spiro/
107.	Szterenlicht Aba handlarz	Szajndla/żona/ Mindla/córka/ Liba/"/ Cyrla/"/ Chaja/matka/	1905 1904 1922 1924 1928 1854	Łódź,Żyd.29	15.XII 1939	Mały Rynek 2 /Grynberg/
108.	Trajman Fajga		1875	Łódź	2.I.40	Rynek 5/Trajman/
109.	Tenenblum Moszek kupiec	Rywka/żona/	1867 1870	"	"	Mickiewicza
110.	Tenenblum Nusyn kupiec	Chaja/żona/ Chana/córka/ Majer/syn/	1889 1888 1913 1918	Łódź,Poludn.18	23.12 1939	Zamkowa 1

Portion of the list of Jews drawn up for the German occupational forces, with the family of Mojzesz Lewinkop (*sic*) listed as #96. Jerzy was listed as the only son, and with German thoroughness the neighboring Blusztajn family was cross-referenced. (COURTESY SANDOMIERZ STATE ARCHIVE)

Identity card (front and back) issued by municipal authorities in Sandomierz for Jerzy Nikodem Lewinkopf in March 1941. It was the last document to use the Lewinkopf name. (COURTESY SANDOMIERZ STATE ARCHIVE)

The only surviving photo of the cottage of Marianna Pasiowa, the model for Marta in *The Painted Bird*. The view is from the top of a hill in a straight line between the cottage and the center of Sandomierz. (COURTESY ZENON PAS)

The Lipinski house at 8 Zamkowa near the center of Sandomierz. The house was eventually incorporated into the Sandomierz ghetto and its remaining inhabitants shipped to the camps. (PHOTO BY SALLY RUTH MAY)

The Skobel house on the outskirts of Sandomierz. The Lewinkopfs lived upstairs, under the slanted roof. Skobel hauled them away by horse-drawn cart in the middle of the night. (PHOTO BY SALLY RUTH MAY)

One of the Sandomierz ravines by which the Lewinkopf/Kosinskis moved between the town center and Pasiowa's cottage. The dark, wooded terrain of the ravines must have suggested to young Jurek Lewinkopf the primal forest in which he set the events of *The Painted Bird*. (PHOTO BY SALLY RUTH MAY)

Altar of the church at Wola Rzeczycka. Given Catholic religious training, nine-year-old Jurek Kosinski excelled at his studies and became an altar boy. (PHOTO BY SALLY RUTH MAY)

Alexander "Lech" Tracz, bird trapper and bird painter, fifty years after young Jerzy Kosinski heard tales of him and watched from behind the fence. (PHOTO BY SALLY RUTH MAY)

The small "stable," which is the lone surviving structure among the house and connected "sawmill houses" of Andrzej Warchol, where the Kosinski family lived from the fall of 1942 until after liberation of the region by the Soviet Army. (PHOTO BY SALLY RUTH MAY)

The house on 4 Senatorska Street in Lodz where Jerzy Kosinski spent his adolescence. The apartment suggested the status accorded Kosinski's father as a man with good political credentials and connections. (PHOTO BY SALLY RUTH MAY)

Jerzy Kosinski, about age eighteen, reading braille. Kosinski and his partner Jerzy Neugebauer sometimes used each other as photographic subjects.
(COURTESY JERZY NEUGEBAUER)

The old man Kosinski and Neugebauer recruited as a photographic subject on the streets of Lodz. The old man played a prank on the two young photographers, keeling over as if stricken.
(COURTESY JERZY NEUGEBAUER)

Kosinski on the bank of the Charles River in Cambridge, Massachusetts, 1960, with Krystyna Iwaszkiewicz (*left*) and Jane Fletcher, later Mrs. Robert Geniesse. (COURTESY KRYSTYNA IWASZKIEWICZ RYTEL)

Halina Poswiatowska, one of the most important Polish poets of her generation, who had "an almost love affair" with Kosinski. (COURTESY MARIOLA PRYZWAN)

Krystyna Iwaszkiewicz, Kosinski's first major romantic interest in America, beside the renowned Continental Mark II. (COURTESY KRYSTYNA IWASZKIEWICZ RYTEL)

Elinor Morrison, who with her husband, Bill, spent time with Kosinski during his first years in America. An early version of Kosinski's ubiquitous self-parodying cartoons is on the blackboard behind her. (COURTESY KTYSTYNA IWASZKIEWICZ RYTEL)

More than a conventional editor and yet not quite a co-author, Peter Skinner was also a boon companion. Fellow "Europeans," as Kosinski described them, they shared women, repartee, and a knowledge of literature and culture that was global and eclectic. (COURTESY PETER SKINNER)

Katherina von Fraunhofer (*right*) on the night of the April in Paris Ball, in October 1965, where she first saw Jerzy Kosinski. On the left is Ewa Pape. (COURTESY EWA PAPE)

Jean Kilbourne, photographed
by Kosinski. Her beauty
enslaved his senses like
"opium." No other relationship
in his life came closer to the
ordinary definition of love.
(COURTESY JEAN KILBOURNE)

Kosinski with Sidney Offit (*left*) and Kurt Vonnegut on their
way to the new members' dinner at the Century Club in
November 1974. (COURTESY SIDNEY OFFIT)

Urszula Dudziak, Kosinski's last love, in her apartment. On her right-hand side is a troll—a gift for Kosinski, which he refused. (COURTESY URSZULA DUDZIAK)

Kosinski with his wife, Kiki, and Warren Beatty at the New York Film Critics Awards, 1982. (TOM GATES, PICTORIAL PARADE; COURTESY ARCHIVE PHOTO)

Saher, and, in another way, Kiki all became his collaborators in a reshaping of the public record. What was the inner dynamic of this strange pattern, which borders upon folies à deux? Did they, too, come to believe? But perhaps to ask such questions is only to impose an earthbound and linear definition upon the word *believe*. Indeed, as with the separation from his parents, one cannot entirely dismiss the slim shadow of possibility that van Saher's child actually existed and that somewhere on Long Island a child of most extraordinary genetic origin grew to adulthood.

But it is more likely that the protuberance noted in Lilla van Saher's belly was a manifestation of the stomach tumor she was to die of, attended by the remaining members of her circle, Kosinski among them. Her receding from active life made an immediate dent in Kosinski's social life. In *Cockpit*, Kosinski has Tarden discover that Theodora is being trailed by members of the vice squad. In fact, Lilla van Saher served as his protection from the vice squad. Without her to act as an intermediary in procuring willing young women, he was at constant risk of being nailed by the police himself. It would make a nice story, he told Eugene Prakapas: *Author of Painted Bird Arrested by Vice Squad.*

Although he had edged away from the Polish émigré crowd in New York, Kosinski had retained a connection with a few old school friends in Lodz, among them Wojtek Frykowski, with whom he regularly exchanged letters. Frykowski, a sometimes coarse but witty young man—and a famous raconteur—was possessed of a charismatic personality. He had been married already to Agnieszka Osiecka, an aspiring writer who would make her name in the future as Poland's best-known writer of satirical song lyrics and who, living in Boston, also drifted into Kosinski's circle of Polish friends at this time. Frykowski had also been involved with a young woman named Ewa, whom Kosinski had photographed as a teenager and regarded as the most beautiful woman he had ever seen.

Unlike Kosinski, Frykowski had never quite found the vehicle for bringing his magnetic personality and storytelling skills to bear in a substantive career. He was now living in Paris, and Kosinski's letters urged him to come to America. Finally, with the promise of his friend's guidance in a new career, he took Kosinski up on the offer and arrived in New York. The guidance provided by Kosinski took the shape of an introduction to Abigail "Gibby" Folger, a coffee heiress and recent Radcliffe graduate who lived at the fringe of New York's floating literary-artistic circle.

At about the same time, Kosinski renewed his contact with Roman Polanski, who had made it big in America with his film *Rosemary's Baby.* They met in New York as two homeboys from Lodz, and Polanski remembered distinctly one thing Kosinski had said when they were students. Kosinski had insisted that love was an illusion; it didn't exist.

"Do you still believe love doesn't exist?" Polanski asked.

Kosinski laughed.

A short time later Polanski met with Frykowski, and Kosinski's name came up. Polanski had been in love several times, he explained, and felt it important to share this information. When Frykowski saw Kosinski, he was to "tell Jurek love does exist."

Work on *Steps* occupied much of Kosinski's time for the remainder of that year—so much so that there was no fall tour of Europe. His editor, coproducer, and alter ego was Peter Skinner, whose role was greatly expanded from the text-polishing he had performed for *The Painted Bird.* In many ways, the working relationship between Kosinski and Skinner recalled the earlier collaboration between Kosinski and Jerzy Neugebauer, in which two very different but complementary talents came together to produce a final aesthetic product. As had been the case with Neugebauer, Kosinski provided the ideas while Skinner contributed much of the craft and attention to detail. As had also been the case in photographic projects done with Neugebauer, Skinner did not always grasp, or agree with, Kosinski's intentions.

They met regularly at the Seventy-ninth Street apartment, Skinner coming over after work, around three or four P.M., and leaving by seven or eight. In initial conception, the book began with the "King Arthur" episode. In it soldiers play a game in which strings are attached under the table to their penises, testing their ability to bear pain. It is noteworthy, in psychological terms, that the book began here—focused upon the penis and its ability to endure trauma—even though the episode eventually was placed later and became a relatively minor variation upon the novel's themes.

Kosinski and Skinner always worked to the accompaniment of music, usually, as Skinner recalls, Herb Alpert and his Tijuana Brass. Sometimes Kosinski appeared to ignore the music, as if he had internalized the beat and made it into white sound, but occasionally, as he took notes about discarded drafts, he would bob his head and raise a hand to follow the beat. What struck Skinner as the two men got deeper into the text was a sense that everything in the book was "in the air." Kosinski had a strong attachment to timelessness, which Skinner kept trying to get him to bring down to earth. "Where are we now? When is this? Is this in Manhattan?" Skinner would ask. "It doesn't matter," Kosinski would reply. Or sometimes, as in the passage that would become the book's opening episode, Kosinski would say such things as, "We are driving farther south." All of this troubled Skinner considerably, bumping up against his well-informed sense of what a novel ought to be. "What's the book going to be about?" he asked. Kosinski answered simply, "This is the book."

In some ways the process, as Skinner recalls it, suggests the steps in making a film—particularly the movement from treatment to script to actual filming, with a director in overall control but farming out detail to various supportive craftsmen. While the analogy is inexact, the implication is that a literary text has a series of structures, at different levels of realization. There is the inevitable question as to which level of the text confers authorship. Equally interesting, though, is the model of a text itself. Kosinski frequently suggested among literary friends that a text was an infinitely malleable thing. "There are infinite ways to tell a story," he would say, an assertion at great variance with the notion of some writers that each story had its particular correct form, with words and formal shape coming into being simultaneously. Kosinski's view would seem closer to the view of improvisatory oral storytelling than to the sense of a text associated with the fixed and frozen form of a physical book. There is, certainly, a consistency in his continued reworking of both galleys and published manuscripts, which gives his oeuvre an extraordinary number of variant texts.

As he worked with Skinner, Kosinski paced and dictated, in a halting way. "We are in front of a cafe," he would say, as though the two men together were making a journey into the realm of the imagination, and as Skinner began to write he would provide physical description. Kosinski had certain favorite words—among them *flabby*, *wrinkled*, and *kneaded*. He often paused to consult his extensive library of reference books. Skinner thought he detected other, legitimate influences from Eastern European literature. The peasant girl seduced by credit cards in the opening episode, he thought, owed much to Turgenev's peasant girl who wanted to have "soap like a fine lady." The toilet stalls in which "The Philosopher" sought escape from Marxist collectivity suggested to Skinner the public elegance of the Moscow subways.

"I want to get this thought in," Kosinski would often begin a session, encapsulating his place in the process as the source of *ideas*. The wording was often Skinner's, although sometimes they would argue over a word until Skinner was compelled to go along. Even procedurally it often felt like the daily operation of a movie set, as the novel was not so much written as *produced*. The production included extensive use of Scotch tape and scissors, along with overnight retypings—presumably by Kiki, although she was never present as they worked at Gregory House. Sometimes the retypings contained things Skinner didn't recollect from the previous day's work. As with *The Painted Bird*, the text was tightly controlled. Skinner was not allowed to take work away from the apartment. If for any reason they were interrupted, Kosinski would sweep up the texts and clear the desks.

Sometimes Kosinski would send out for food. Occasionally he would have arranged for girls, often undergraduate groupies from Sarah Lawrence, where Kosinski seemed to have a connection. When they arrived, Kosinski would blow up an air mattress and set it on the floor. The encounters with the Sarah Lawrence girls were brief, as though the girls were carrying through a perfunctory rite or initiation; as soon as they were done, Kosinski ushered them out, once telling Skinner, "Next time we'll swap them." All women were seeking attractive men, he asserted to

Skinner. He was fascinated, Skinner concluded, less by the act itself than by its directorial power. The women themselves were a diversion, which must not be allowed to slow down their work. He had no money from Mary, he explained to Skinner. "We must work hard. We cannot waste time. I have to earn money."

At the very end of the work on *Steps*, an additional hand became involved. Stanley Corngold, a young untenured assistant professor at Princeton, had produced a paper on *The Painted Bird*, in which he saw interesting "comp lit" patterns of theme and influence. Corngold mentioned the book to a friend in Princeton's Slavic department, Joachim Baer, who was at first embarrassed not to be able to identify the author. A few days later Baer returned to Corngold with the explanation that this Kosinski was an *American* author, so of course he wasn't familiar with him, but that if Corngold wished, an introduction could be arranged through a Polish bookseller in New York who knew Kosinski. Thus Corngold found himself having lunch in Manhattan with Kosinski, who informed him that an old Polish friend, Andrzej Wat, always mentioned a Corngold who held a famous Warsaw salon. Himself a would-be novelist, Corngold was flattered by the attention. He agreed to have a look at Kosinski's new book, which he found a little rough. Over several sessions at the Seventy-ninth Street apartment, Corngold suggested a few minor changes, including advice to reorder the ending, which Kosinski ignored.

Yet Kosinski was impressed with Corngold's academic pedigree and told him, with only mild hyperbole, that Corngold was the intellectual friend he had never had in high school. He proposed to Corngold a book to be published together, including Corngold's essay on *The Painted Bird*, his own essay on *Steps*, and an essay on *Steps* to be written by Corngold. The trouble was that Corngold did not admire *Steps* nearly so wholeheartedly as he had admired *The Painted Bird*. He produced an analysis centered around a somewhat arcane intertextual argument having to do with the "decay of insight" of the boy from the end of *The Painted Bird* to the beginning of *Steps*. When Corngold showed him the essay, Kosinski scribbled over it liberally and, to Corngold's disappointment, allowed the project to drop. Instead he employed Corngold to do a final polish on the accompanying essay, *The Art of the Self*, a task Corngold, as literary theorist, found congenial. The manuscript was returned with very few editorial suggestions, and Kosinski complained when Corngold submitted a bill for the agreed-upon fee. In reply Corngold explained that it took time to read and approve sentences as well as to edit them. Corngold would eventually become a tenured professor at Princeton, and a literary theorist and critic of serious reputation. His contribution to *Steps* was by all accounts minimal, but it established a relationship with Kosinski that was to become more important two years later.

Steps is a central text by which to address the place of Kosinski as a writer, examining whether he was a serious, existential writer-thinker or merely a "phenomenon" who managed to put together several "interesting" texts and hoodwink, for a time, the worlds of literature and society. Kosinski's career not only demands evaluation but reverses the process—causing the evaluator to reconsider his own criteria. To begin with, is not a novelist in fact a person who hoodwinks both the literary world and larger society? Does he not persuade them to accept as real, for a time, his private fictions, leaving them more or less wiser for it?

Despite Kosinski's assertion in the Guggenheim application and elsewhere that *Steps* lacks "time terms," it is loosely chronological in structure, telling the story of a young man's seemingly random experiences, first in an Eastern Marxist society, then as an immigrant in the United States. The few departures from the general contours of Kosinski's own life involve episodes such as the opening one—the seduction by the use of credit cards—which are based on experiences that took place after Kosinski came to the West but are placed in Eastern Europe in the book.

The protagonist of *Steps* is nameless, the events are not causally related in a single plot, and there are, indeed, no markers of the passing of linear time. The protagonist is confronted with a series of situations in which he acts or is acted upon; many of the situations are violent or sexual. Often successive episodes serve to comment upon each other. The protagonist takes pitiless advantage of a young peasant woman whom he seduces by describing the material goods that can be obtained with his credit card; in the ensuing episode he is taken advantage of in turn: stranded without money on an island where none of his languages is known, he is compelled to perform sexually to receive food. Laced among the episodes is a continuing dialogue between the protagonist and a woman, sometimes concerning their own relationship and sometimes engaging such topics as the architecture of concentration camps.

The immediate issue posed by *Steps* is whether its episodic structure represents an unhappy pastiche or a bold philosophical statement. As philosophy, this series of encounters is consistent with the "death of God" theology and the attendant philosophy of "situation ethics" popular at the time. The episodes stand apart from social contexts and moral systems; rather than assimilating the protagonist's actions into ready-made frameworks, to be weighed or explained against outside criteria, the reader is compelled to engage pain, lust, anger, and cruelty in absolute terms.

At times the text requires the reader to ask the deepest questions about the self, often a psychosexual self. In one episode, the protagonist arranges for his lover to be touched in a sexual way by a masseur. When he confronts her, she grudgingly admits to the sexual encounter but insists that in the end the masseur's hands were "your hands." Thus the episode interrogates, in effect, the essence of initiative and action. It is as though the masseur is a mere vehicle—a machine—while the "true" self, the entity organizing the sexual encounter, is the mind of the protagonist.

Some of the episodes in *Steps* are more or less demonstrably drawn from Kosinski's personal experience—the visit to the old people's home, for example—while others, like the stoning of the night watchman, which he told in Warsaw to Tad Krauze in 1955, may be based on actual events or wholly invented. The game of "King Arthur," in which soldiers vie to win a gambling game in which their penises are attached to tautened strings (as mentioned earlier), was based on a story that made the rounds in postwar Poland. The key episode of the half-witted woman kept in a cage—and the priest who knew of her abuse by the men of the village and kept silent—is based on an actual incident that took place near Cracow and was reported in the Polish press.

Whatever their source, however, the episodes in *Steps* all deal with *power*. Whether violent or sexual, the protagonist wishes to have an effect on other human beings, and he is acutely sensitive to their ability to have an effect on him. Yet the effect is absorbed by a character, and a voice, that is strangely without *affect*. The book's prototypal episode may be the scene in the sanatorium in which the protagonist makes love with a tubercular inmate without touching her. He touches only with his eyes, while she stimulates herself and touches his *image* in a mirror. He concentrates on the *thought* that it is he within the mirror. The scene resembles the episode with the masseur, but with one important difference: his own image is the surrogate lover.

Few images could better render the individual who is not fully invested in his own actions, who at some level stands back and watches his own life as if it were being played out by an actor. For such a person, fantasy and actual events take place very nearly on the same plane; "reality" is only inner theater to which one has attached one's corporeal being. Seen from this perspective, *Steps* has a plot after all. It is the fragmented story of a man who does not coincide with his own being. Indeed, its very fragmentation is an element in the plot. It is the affliction of a human being who cannot pull his experience of the world, or himself, into coherence.

Steps exists at the point where philosophy and psychology intersect. It is both a statement about a way of coming at events, stripped of context, and a psychological case study of an individual who is unable to be fully present within any context. The stripping away of time, place, or a past extends the deracination of the boy of *The Painted Bird*, who may be either Gypsy or Jew. In *Steps*, Kosinski moves to create a protagonist who denies *all* connection with any group; the book thus parallels a period in Kosinski's life in which he denied his Jewish heritage, seeking consciously to be a man without background. Even when he acts, the protagonist of *Steps* is no one; he is a kibitzer of the human condition, watching someone who is no one at all go through the motions of being a living human being.

Does this dissociative behavior amount to existential engagement of the highest order or borderline madness? Again, the question may be too linear. A similar question was being asked systematically at about that time by R. D. Laing, whose study *The Divided Self* proposed an underlying logic to the behavior of schizophrenics. Kosinski was not, as he had adamantly insisted to Mira Michalowska, psychotic, nor was his protagonist in *Steps*, quite, but in every incident and taken as a whole the book posed a troubling question of point of view: Where was the moral center of the anecdotes? Should one take them from the inside looking out, as profound philosophical judgments, or from the outside looking in, as a case study of a quasi-sociopathic borderline mental state?

Kosinski's application to the Guggenheim Foundation had emphasized his protagonist's resistance to "the collective," and indeed the novel has a subtheme of political and ideological resistance to the socialist collective, epitomized by "The Philosopher" who hides from the world in toilet stalls (where he eventually commits suicide). Yet the "collective" in which the protagonist does not, and cannot, participate is far larger than that. In his final report to the Foundation, Kosinski mentioned that at the time of the book's writing he belonged to no "collectivity." It may be read to mean simply that he had no job or university affiliation, but the choice of words—with their artificial formality and detachment masking profound anguish—suggests a great deal more.

9.

The manuscript of *Steps* was ready for submission in late February. Already the previous September, Kosinski had written Dorothy de Santillana, asking to be released from the option clause Houghton Mifflin held on his next work. On March 15 Kosinski wrote Paul Brooks, announcing that his new novel was finished and mentioning that he was in ill health and considering treatment in Europe; that possible trip to Europe was the major reason given for not sending the manuscript to Houghton Mifflin. Recalling the haste with which *The Painted Bird* had been cut on his return from Europe in 1965, Kosinski was either enjoying a dig at his former editor or rationalizing a business decision—perhaps a little of both. Bob Geniesse, who didn't handle entertainment law, had referred him to Allan Schwartz, who handled the submission. The manuscript had already been delivered to Random House, with Bob Loomis as Kosinski's editor. Although Loomis did extensive editorial work, there would be no question of cuts or changes to satisfy any censorious spirit, and Kosinski felt he could expect good support from a premier publisher.

During the early months of 1968, while Kosinski awaited the publication of *Steps*, the world fell apart. In March, Eugene McCarthy ran a close enough second in the New Hampshire primary that Lyndon Johnson announced that he would not run again for president. Martin Luther King was assassinated in April. In May, French students went on strike and brought France to the brink of civil war. Bobby Kennedy, who had jumped into the presidential race, and emerged as a front-runner, was assassinated in June. In August, Soviet tanks crushed a liberal reformist regime in Prague, and that same month the Democratic Convention in Chicago echoed the images of insurrection from France in May. America seemed to be going through an experience as dissociative as the episodes in *Steps*—breaking up into political and cultural fragments.

Kosinski, for once, was perfectly attuned to the world around him. The whole of American life had seemingly turned into a quasi-sociopathic briar patch. Skirts rose higher and higher, Jim Morrison crooned about wanting to have sex with his mother, and pushing the boundaries of experience became a virtual orthodoxy. Anything went. The world in the streets outside Kosinski's apartment was looking more and more like the world inside his own head.

Things were falling apart in Kosinski's personal realm as well. In July, after three operations, Lilla van Saher died. Kosinski attended her during her final days. He continued to call Mary Weir with regularity, reporting on his conversations with her in calls to Andy Heinemann. "She's going to commit suicide," he warned Heinemann.

Mary had indeed made several halfhearted attempts between 1966 and 1968, but Heinemann didn't know quite how to take Kosinski's warning. From his point of view, Kosinski himself was a large part of Mary's problem. Although they were divorced, he couldn't quite bring himself to let go of her. He kept calling, putting ideas into her head. He would then repeat the wild things she said to Heinemann. When Heinemann expressed doubts, Kosinski produced tapes; he had taken to taping his phone calls, and he played back Mary's wild ramblings and threats. In Heinemann's view, it was Kosinski who drove her into a frenzy.

On the morning of August 1, Kosinski and Mary had one more of their conversations. That same morning she received a hopeful letter from David, who was still out of the country but seemed to be pulling his life together. She spoke to Heinemann twice, both times sounding euphoric over the news from David. But she was drinking steadily, the alcohol coming on top of her prescription barbiturates. Her doctor came by and gave her a shot of vitamin B-12, and she dismissed the servants for the night. She had a seven o'clock dinner date with Hugh Guiler, an investment adviser, but failed to show up; at seven-thirty Guiler called and received no answer. The next morning her cook arrived at Sutton Place and found Mary Weir dead in Kosinski's room, with an empty quart bottle of vodka.

The deaths of Lilla van Saher and Mary Weir, within less than a month, left Kosinski bereft in ways not visible to persons outside his immediate circle. Both women had combined the roles of mother and lover, the model he had hinted at in discussing his own mother with Tad Krauze. Both relationships had provided imperfect, but important, solace for the absence of a mother's perfect love and approval. Without them, the only solution that presented itself was to run harder and faster and climb higher and higher in search of some ultimate validation of the self.

Through Bob Loomis, Kosinski had met William Styron, also a Random House author. Now Styron and his wife Rose became the first link in a long chain by which he would enter the upper levels of American society not as Mary Weir's consort but as an entity in his own right, something akin to the Eastern European intellectual-*cum*-court-jester he had envisioned in conversations with Peter Skinner. He was a delightful dinner guest, at least as long as his repertory of stories lasted. The Styrons embraced him warmly, inviting him again and again to their home in Connecticut as well as their vacation place on Martha's Vineyard.

That Thanksgiving on Martha's Vineyard, as they drove around the western part of the island, Kosinski told Styron of his elegant life with Mary Weir, adding that her business manager gave him cash regularly with which he paid taxis and restaurants. To Rose Styron, shortly after Mary's death, he admitted that Mary had been cross with him for going off with Kiki, and he expressed regret that he had not spent more time with her before she died.

One evening at the Styrons' he was introduced to Sadruddin Aga Khan, the UN Commissioner for Refugees and sponsor of George Plimpton's *Paris Review,* and his wife, Katie. With what struck the Styrons as almost indecent haste, he ingratiated himself with Sadri, who promptly became more central to his social life than the Styrons. One day, when the three couples had planned to have dinner in the city, Rose Styron arrived first and was persuaded to be his accomplice in a prank. Kosinski would hide in his apartment on Seventy-ninth Street, and the others would look for him. They came, looked, failed to find, and began to grow cross; Sadri was ready for dinner, and didn't find the prank so funny. Kosinski finally unfolded himself from behind the cabinets in his darkroom.

Sadri's irritation was not lasting. Kosinski had correctly assessed the world of the vaguely literary social set as a group in need of being entertained, for whom he could be resident entertainer. Immediately after meeting him, Katie had told Marian Javits, wife of the powerful senator Jacob Javits, "I have met a man who is going to be your close friend."

Indeed, Kosinski soon became a frequent guest at the Javitses' dinner parties, as central a position as could be found in New York society. There he sat elbow to elbow with the likes of Henry Kissinger and a string of visiting foreign dignitaries. More important, through Marian Javits he met the all-powerful *New York Times* crowd—the Arthur Gelbs, the Punch Sulzbergers, and the Abe Rosenthals. The association with the Javitses was thus the doorway out of a world where he was one writer among many into a world where he was often the only writer among men and women of the world. Marian Javits, in particular, was charmed by him, and she continued to be his friend even after his stories and eccentricities had become familiar—this despite the fact that one of his eccentricities had to do with her dog. Lying in bed recovering from a leg injury received while riding, she was startled when her dog ran furiously across the room, dripping urine. A moment later Kosinski appeared at her door. Later a friend told her that Kosinski had been observed abusing the dog in a way that would engender such behavior.

At dinner parties in the city, Kosinski could simply go through his repertory of stories from *The Painted Bird* and *Steps*. For weekends in the Hamptons, he had added a prop—an improvised "comet," like the one carried by the boy in *The Painted Bird*. He fashioned it from a perforated tin can attached to several feet of string, filled it with burning or smoldering leaves and bits of wood, and twirled it around in circles to create a bellows action. It was a spectacular performance at night, delighting dinner guests and, especially, their children. Another piece of show-and-tell met with more mixed success. From time to time he insisted on being the chef, cooking steaks in a nest of leaves and pine needles to produce steak a la Polish peasant; sometimes this method succeeded, but it had one notable failure at the home of Arthur Miller, who rolled his eyes sadly at the destruction of expensive prime steaks.

Along with this step up into the literary-social set, one other aspect of Kosinski's life began to show a subtle change. He had met Gil Shiva and his wife Susan Stein, daughter of the major owner of MCA, through Marian Javits. That fall he celebrated Yom Kippur at the Shivas', and the following spring Passover as well, participating in full acknowledgment of his Jewish heritage.

That fall Kosinski accepted a teaching position as a fellow at Wesleyan's Center for Advanced Studies. As he would be teaching for the first time, Kosinski gave a considerable amount of thought to what he was going to present to his students. The appointment took into account his status as a sociologist and scholar as well as a novelist, and his planned seminars reflected that double status. He would present seminars on Literary Analysis, Cooperative Systems, and the English Language.

The subtopics of these seminars reveal the high seriousness with which Kosinski attacked the task of teaching at Wesleyan. His literary analysis seminar included "The Time of Life and the Time of Art: the Poetic Processes" and "The Art of the Self: the Theory of 'Le Moi Poetique' (Binswanger)." The seminar on cooperative systems included several sections on bureaucracy, a consideration of the history of complex organizations, and sections on information storage and analysis and retrieving machines. The topics would have been at home in a graduate school of business administration, and the depth of Kosinski's knowledge in the latter areas is in doubt, especially considering the fact that twenty years later he was still unable to use a basic word processor. However, the very selection of topics helped maintain his position as a social scientist and an intellectual of several portfolios.

The most interesting series of topics, however, came in the seminar on English language. Kosinski proposed to discuss transformational analysis of English sentences, modern English structure (utterances, sentences, words, morphemes), independent functional variables in verb-phrase structure, functions of finite verb phrases, verb substitutes, adverbs, the functions and morphology of adjectives, and the structure of noun phrases. It was a syllabus suitable for a research professor in linguistics, reflecting the broad but by no means systematic knowledge Kosinski had gained as a highly intelligent multicultural individual. Its underlying message, however, was simpler: Jerzy Kosinski was a master of every aspect of English prose. That is, he could speak, read, and especially, *write* it.

The lectures Kosinski delivered at Wesleyan show the extent to which his new fictional skills and techniques were beginning to overtake his role as mediator between cultures and systems. He lectured separately on montage in the novel and on time terms in the novel, both relating largely to *Steps*, and on the "total victim" in modern history and literature and on social prospects for the twentieth century novelist, both of which encompassed *The*

Painted Bird. His multilingual, multicultural background continued to inform such topics as the bilingual vision of language and
reality, English tenses and the Slavic ordering of time, the Marxist
prognosis for the United States, the writer and politics in the
West, and the writer and collectivity in the East.

With all of this, Kosinski cut a great figure on the Wesleyan
campus. Students and colleagues did not miss the range of subject matter he had staked out, and Philip Hallie, the acting director of the Center for Advanced Studies, praised him for having
generously delivered more public lectures than his appointment
required and having conducted enough classes for two faculty
members. An academic Stakhanovite, he found himself an instant
academic star.

The same staking out of intellectual territory stood behind the
production of his second small pamphlet, designed to accompany
the publication of *Steps*. Called *The Art of the Self*, it expanded
upon the statement of plans he presented for the novel to the
Guggenheim Foundation. This time there was no motivation, as
with his *Notes of the Author* on *The Painted Bird*, tc justify the
movement from fact to fiction and Polish to English. *The Art of the
Self* seems rather to be modeled more or less on the essays of
French novelist Alain Robbe-Grillet published in America in 1965
as *For a New Novel*. The book of essays had contributed greatly to
the stature of Robbe-Grillet, presenting his own odd texts as the
cutting edge of a movement and presenting himself as not only a
practitioner but a theoretician of the novel.

With *The Art of the Self*, Kosinski moved to stake out something
of the same place for himself in American letters. In it he expanded upon his rejection of Aristotelian plot and his theory of
an agon, or conflict, between author and reader, taking place in
the blank spaces between episodes. He discussed metamorphosis
as a "leitmotiv," borrowing the Wagnerian term also used by critics of Thomas Mann, and he cited Jung, Sartre, Camus, Genet,
and the Marquis de Sade. He demonstrated his knowledge of
Shakespeare and the *commedia dell'arte*, discussed the psychology
of murder from the standpoint of both murderer and victim, and
analyzed the reversal of roles in Oscar Wilde's *Picture of Dorian*

Gray as a way of reiterating his convoluted rationalization that objective reality is inherently false, anyway.

The Art of the Self also contains a brief but important discussion of suicide, which is seen as an individual's *choice* to die with dignity in one's own time and thus escape both future and past. The argument is reminiscent of Nietzsche and Schopenhauer. Prophetically, the passage notes that suicide imposes on others the necessity for remembering and judging a man, so that even in death his shadow survives; by suicide he creates "the means to outlive himself."

The pamphlet was published under the imprint of Scientia-Factum, with an address given as Gregory House, 440 East 79th Street, New York City, 10021. Scientia-Factum was, of course, Kosinski himself. This arms-lengthening of his self-publication made for more advantageous use of expenses for tax write-offs, but it was also amusing, and entirely in keeping with his proclivity for placing layers of insulation between himself and the world. Scholars, and anyone else, who wrote to Scientia-Factum received replies from Vicki Marshall, a high-powered executive assistant, who passed messages up the hierarchy of this little-known private publishing empire to Mr. Kosinski. Vicki Marshall was, of course, Kiki.

Selections from *The Art of the Self* were published in the *New York Review of Books* on October 20, simultaneously with the publication of *Steps* (as well as later in the *Tin Drum*, the Wesleyan student biweekly). Like *Notes of the Author*, the pamphlet was sent out to reviewers and anyone who expressed an interest in Kosinski, and many academics took the pamphlet very seriously indeed. Kosinski had managed to stake out a position as multiportfolioed intellectual and practitioner-theoretician of the novel.

The reviews for *Steps* were generally favorable. As with *The Painted Bird*, some of the best notices came from persons with areas of expertise somewhat oblique to contemporary fiction. Stanley Kauffmann, whose primary focus was film, praised "this small book" in *The New Republic*, saying that "through all its smoke and fire and pain, a curious pride persists." F. Y. Blumenfeld said in *Newsweek*, "These terse, ghoulish episodes will return to the memory at unexpected moments, stirring up uneasy images, disturbing the reader in the very depths of his own fantasies," while Hugh Kenner, in the *New York Times Book Review,* wrote on October 20: "Low-keyed, efficient, controlled, the prose of *Steps* encompasses the banal, the picturesque, the monstrous, with never a flicker of surprise." Granville Hicks in the *Saturday Review* found *Steps* more frightening than *The Painted Bird* because it described "the complete collapse of human values."

This was also the view of Harry Overstreet, who wrote honestly to admit that he didn't care for the book. And for all the litany of praise, there was a general tone of mystification in the critical response. What was this montage of cruelty, grotesquerie, and ghoulishness up to?

One of the reviews Kosinski liked very much was written by Barry Callaghan for the *Toronto Star.* Kosinski responded with a short, admiring note, with *The Art of the Self* enclosed, then called Callaghan to say, first, that he was coming to Toronto, and, second, that he would like to use the review as the foreword to his French edition. While Kosinski was in Toronto, he accompanied Callaghan for several days of barhopping in the course of which they bumped into Helen Hutchinson, a bright, pretty, independent woman who was the host of a daily national radio show—a Canadian celebrity. Although Callaghan did not know it, Kosinski had already met Hutchinson in New York, where she had interviewed him.

Two weeks later a copy of *Notes of the Author* arrived in Callaghan's mail, and a week later Kosinski himself returned, ostensibly to see Callaghan but actually to attempt a conquest of Helen Hutchinson. For several days he sat around at Hutchinson's house, amusing her children while laying siege to their mother. In the course of this visit Hutchinson took Kosinski to see Callaghan's father, Morley Callaghan, one of the last survivors of the 1920s expatriate circle in Paris, and famous for having once decked Ernest Hemingway. They hit it off, and on a subsequent visit, Barry Callaghan listened as his father and Kosinski discussed writers of the father's generation—the Hemingway and Fitzgerald crowd. The elder Callaghan let it be known that he was not as swept away as his son by *The Painted Bird*, but rather liked *Steps*. After the conversation, Kosinski went off to meet Helen.

Four days later Callaghan saw her, and she told him that Kosinski terrified her. The next week she called him late at night to say the same thing. There is something dangerous about this man, she said. A few weeks later, at 3 A.M., Kosinski called Callaghan, only, he said, to insure that their spiritual bond was still in place. When Callaghan relayed Hutchinson's comment that she was terrified, Kosinski seemed surprised. Within three weeks, as suddenly as it began, the relationship between Hutchinson and Kosinski had cooled.

It was all very much like *Steps*, intense, episodic, self-contained, and without obvious connection to any larger scheme or pattern. Lilla van Saher and Mary Weir were dead. He now lived with Kiki, taught at a great American university, and had love affairs with beautiful women who were celebrities in their world. He had arrived, hadn't he?

Early the following year Kosinski had plans to return to Europe. This time he asked Kiki if she would like to come with him. He made no promises, he told her, no commitments to permanence, and there was certainly no question of marriage, but she was welcome to come if she liked. For Kiki, it was a pivotal moment. While he made clear the limits he intended to place on the relationship, it was a major commitment on her part, turning away permanently from a full-time career in advertising. On the one hand there would be hobnobbing with famous writers and intellectuals at the side of a man she loved and admired. Set against that was the insecurity of her position, and the increasing evidence that this man would never devote himself to a single woman. Kiki decided to take the chance.

Before they left, *Steps* had been nominated for the National Book Award, but the nomination caused Kosinski as much anxiety as joy. Kosinski seriously thought about withdrawing the book from consideration, and discussed it with Bob Loomis. It is perhaps an indicator of the fragility of his ego that the prospective pain of being in contention and losing seemed to outweigh the prospective pleasure of winning. Loomis talked him out of it.

What purpose would be served by withdrawing? Loomis would almost admit that another Random House book, Frederick Exley's *A Fan's Notes,* was a more likely choice, but there was no harm done by being mentioned and not getting the award. It was good publicity in any case.

Kosinski finally bowed to Loomis's judgment. But so much was at stake with a National Book Award nomination that it was painful just to think of it. Winning would bring to fruition all that he had struggled for since beginning to pull together the stories of his childhood into *The Painted Bird.* It would be formal acknowledgment of having reached the top of the heap in American letters. Kosinski cabled Loomis that he could be reached that Monday at his hotel in Switzerland. On March 10, a cable arrived from Bob Loomis with parodistic ten-word eloquence:

YOU WON. YOU WON. YOU WON. YOU WON. COME HOME.

V

BEING THERE

1.

As the train made its way through the Swiss passes, Kosinski lay flat on his back, feverish. At that time, the National Book Award, more than any other literary prize, marked the pinnacle of acceptance into the American pantheon of belles lettres. Never mind that *Steps* was a compromise choice, after two front-runners knocked each other out. Never mind that it was actually a belated, apologetic award to *The Painted Bird*, which had not even been nominated. This was always the way with literary awards, just as it was with the Oscars. Things had a way of evening out. The important writers usually got recognized, eventually, their names certified for the large amorphous audience which had to be told what writing was important. The other 1969 recipients included, for example, John Berryman in poetry, an irreproachable choice that would surely stand the test of time, Norman Mailer in nonfiction for *The Armies of the Night*, and Yale psychiatrist Robert Jay Lifton for his book-length essay *Death in Life*.

The flight across the Atlantic provided to a still-feverish Kosinski a natural occasion to consider the earlier flight that had brought him to America. Twelve years before, he had arrived in a driving rainstorm, with very little but his wits. He had worked the system relentlessly and skillfully, winning useful friends in high places. With help of various kinds, he had published two nonfiction books, and then two novels, one of them an honored international classic, the other now in the process of catapulting him to the acknowledged first rank of American novelists. There had been setbacks, but he was within reach of fulfilling the wildest dreams from his boyhood in Lodz. Starting literally *nowhere*, he had arrived; he was *there*. It marked the momentum peak in the chart of his life—the point of near-vertical ascent; his success might be articulated more fully in the future, reaching a widening audience and bringing ever greater financial reward, but the pure exhilaration of this triumph could never be matched.

Yet at this peak moment of triumph Kosinski must have experienced an undercurrent of unease; thus, perhaps, the fever. It would have been extraordinary if the sense of accomplishment had not been accompanied by a nagging sense of inauthenticity. To the deeply ingrained feelings of hollowness and worthlessness that afflicted so many survivors of the German occupation, there had now been added an array of uncomfortable facts. He knew well that the Novak books had been produced and published in a manner the literary world, if it ever found out, would consider highly irregular. He must also, as he returned in triumph, have considered the significant contributions to the final prose of both *The Painted Bird* and *Steps* of such helpers as George Reavey, Aleksander Lutoslawski, and, particularly, Peter Skinner. It was not that any one action was illegitimate, but taken together, they added up to a cache of secrets that could only become increasingly burdensome. Like many politicians (though far fewer writers), Kosinski now had skeletons in his closet. The importance of those skeletons might be debatable, but the higher he climbed, the more risk he incurred that some enterprising journalist would dig until he turned up the full story. Only then would the extent of his vulnerability be put to the test.

Arriving in New York, he met with Bob Loomis and addressed himself to the problem of the brief speech he was expected to deliver. Instant eloquence of this nature did not come easily to Kosinski, but Loomis was ready to help, as he had been with the novel. The short statement they composed together neatly summarized the moment, the first paragraph acknowledging the openness and freedom he discovered when he first arrived in

America, the second lamenting the current anger and polarization (without taking sides), and the third reconfirming that America was still the place where a writer could express himself spontaneously and without censorship.

The awards dinner was held at Philharmonic Hall before an audience of fourteen hundred writers, critics, editors, and publishers. Kosinski sat at the same table as Berryman, and the two men immediately hit it off. Even in triumph, Berryman bore the mark of the terrific pain and turmoil that would drive him three years later to throw his body off a bridge. In Kosinski, the pain and the ultimate destiny were less visible but no less present. Berryman, however, did not fail to recognize a kindred spirit. He perspired on the outside, Berryman observed, while Kosinski perspired on the inside. Dr. Mason Gross, president of Rutgers and chairman of the book committee, presided over the presentations. Mailer, whose work documenting a 1967 peace march was fashionably anti-Establishment, was the most popular winner, evoking laughter when he retracted a recent statement to a *Times* interviewer that "there's something obscene about a middle-aged man who wins an award." Lifton became the next day's headliner by speaking, again fashionably, about the physical and psychological dangers of nuclear weapons. Yet a jet-lagged Kosinski more than held his own, delivering his two-minute acceptance speech to warm applause. If there had been any doubt about his place in American letters, it had now been removed.

After the ceremony, Kosinski and Kiki lingered only a few days before returning to Switzerland. From there they embarked on a typical Kosinskian grand tour, visiting London, Amsterdam, and Paris before settling in Spetsai, Greece, to spend the second half of July with Clem and Jessie Wood. They had met the Woods in Paris, at the home of James and Gloria Jones. The long chain of introduction had begun with Lilla van Saher, and Kosinski had been passed through Anaïs Nin to Henry Miller, who brought him to meet Jones. The relationship with Jones, who had settled in Paris in part to avoid taxes after the commercial success of *From Here to Eternity* made him a bankable writer, had its ups and downs. Kosinski discovered that Jones could not even read basic traffic signs in French and teased him about his lack of fluency.

Go back to America, Kosinski suggested to Jones, pay your taxes, and simply make more money. Jones, in turn, took to putting visiting Americans onto the sociological sources of *The Painted Bird*, pulling a copy of Biegeleisen down from his bookshelf. How Jones came to know about Kosinski's sources is unclear.

If the relationship with Jones was destined to be uneasy, the relationship with the Woods seemed preordained. Unlike the coarse and common-cloth Jones, Clem—Clement Biddle—Wood was of the same background as the crowd Kosinski met with Mary Weir. He had gone to St. Paul's and Harvard, where he was an editor of the *Lampoon*, Harvard's venerable humor magazine, and his novel *Welcome to the Club*, about racism in the military, had a modest success in 1966. Jessie Wood shared this background, and, better yet, was half French. Her old-world sophistication served her well when she was called upon to intervene in an early crisis between Jerzy and Kiki. Kiki discovered that during their stay in Paris Jerzy was seeing a Frenchwoman. She told Jessie Wood the story over a tearful lunch. She didn't see how she could compete, she said, with the Frenchwoman's beauty and sophistication. Jessie assured Kiki that while these things happened, beauty and sophistication were not necessarily the assets that prevailed over the long term. To console and distract her new friend, she gave Kiki a piece of jewelry.

In July, the Paris affair now behind them, Kosinski and Kiki arrived at the Woods' home in Spetsai, where Kosinski worked his usual magic on the Wood children. The children were especially amused by the way he swam, with his head entirely out of the water like a dog. Their days soon were given over to Jerzy sightings. Delighted, they would race into the house to announce to their parents, "Jerzy is in the water!"

Back in America, protests against Vietnam were beginning to beleaguer Richard Nixon as they had his predecessor, and a new youth culture had begun to form, united by opposition to the war and bonded together by rock music and drugs. That July, when Kosinski was away in Europe, the youth culture held its first assembly, as several hundred thousand young people gathered for the legendary Woodstock rock concert. In late July, Kosinski received a letter from Wojtek Frykowski and Gibby Folger, who were staying at Roman Polanski's home on Cielo Drive in Los Angeles. Kosinski left with Kiki for Paris, from which they were to fly to the United States on August 7. Clem Wood, their host at Spetsai, left for Los Angeles, where he was booked into the Beverly Hills Hotel while working on a film script. It was agreed that the Woods would get together with Kosinski and Kiki in Los Angeles.

What happened next became a small, but enduring, controversy. As Kosinski told it, both as a factual account and as an episode that happened to George Levanter in *Blind Date*, the pivotal factor was the misrouting of part of his luggage in Paris. It was his intention to go directly to Los Angeles without leaving the airport, accompanied by three bags of warm-weather clothes, while three bags of cold-weather clothes were to be held in storage in New York awaiting his return. In the version told in *Blind Date*, the dispute with the French airline clerk has to do with the New York address. She insists that he list a return address in Paris. In irritation at his refusal, the clerk routes all his baggage to New York, which necessitates his stopping over at his New York apartment for the night.

Kosinski clung to this account tenaciously over the years, and it gains in plausibility if one shifts the emphasis slightly to note that he was trying to get the airline to perform an unusual and complicated favor, and that routing all the luggage to New York may have been a simple mistake, with or without French "attitude." In any case, he arrived in New York in the late afternoon of August 8 and found that his luggage had been off-loaded. Deciding to stay in New York, he called Clem Wood at the Beverly Hills Hotel. "I told Sharon you were there," he said, "and she says to come over." As he did not know Sharon Tate, Wood spent the evening with other Hollywood friends.

The following afternoon around 5:00 P.M. Kosinski rang Elzbieta Czyzewska, a Polish émigrée stage and film actress who was married to journalist David Halberstam, and asked if she had been listening to the radio. "Something has happened in Los Angeles," he told her. "Put on the radio."

As the hours went by, the dimensions of what had happened on Cielo Drive became clear. Sharon Tate, who was eight months pregnant, had been murdered, along with her former boyfriend, hairdresser Jay Sebring, Wojtek Frykowski, Gibby Folger, and an unfortunate bystander, Steven Parent. The identities of the victims and the particular viciousness of the murders made it stand out as the crime of the decade. By middle-American standards, the assemblage at Polanski's house was somewhat irregular. Sharon Tate insisted on having her ex-lover Sebring around, and Polanski had responded by incorporating Sebring into his household and making a pal of him. Polanski blew hot and cold about Frykowski, who had helped with his first feature film, *Knife in the Water*, and served as producer of a piece of Polanski apprentice work, the short film *Mammals*. Gibby Folger and Sharon had hit it off, however, and Sebring sometimes used Frykowski as the front man in drug transactions.

The ritualistic writing in blood contributed to the sense of orgiastic chaos, as if whatever happened on Cielo Drive had been some sort of Black Mass. What was this strange gathering? journalists wondered. What had brought together a pregnant starlet and her former lover along with the coffee heiress Gibby Folger and her gigolo boyfriend? Did it, perhaps, have a connection with Polanski films like *Rosemary's Baby* which combined sexuality and violence and often examined dark forces? Had some dark force bound the victims together in death? And if so, was it not in some way a found metaphor for the mad death dance of the 1960s?

In fact, the selection of the house on Cielo Drive by Charles Manson and his "family" eventually turned out to have been entirely random. In the immediate aftermath, Kosinski's major role was in offering, along with Elzbieta Czyzewska, to arrange for Frykowski's burial. In the course of making arrangements, he spoke with Victor Lownes, who had accompanied Polanski home from London, not bothering to mention that he had been planning to visit. At the same time, he mentioned to several reporters that he had been on his way to Cielo Drive when a luggage mix-up at the Paris airport caused him to stay over in New York. By then Frykowski's mother had been reached in Lodz and was on her way to New York with Frykowski's brother to claim the body. Instead of a burial, Elzbieta Czyzewska held a memorial gathering for the Polish émigré circle, at which Kosinski again did not mention that he had been en route to Polanski's house.

The first contretemps occurred when Victor Lownes, Polanski's close friend and operator of the London Playboy Club, happened to read *Steps* on his flight back to London. He was stunned by the violent imagery—a protagonist who tells in neutral tones of feeding glass fragments to children—and he, like many other readers, had trouble distinguishing the narrator from the author whose name appeared on the cover. The story of the mishandled luggage had come to him through the newspapers. His whole experience with Kosinski, he concluded, had been irregular. On August 22, back in London, Lownes sent a letter to the Los Angeles Homicide Division suggesting that they investigate Kosinski. It concluded: "I know that the suggestion is extremely far-fetched, but surely it is worthwhile to check on the mixed-up luggage story, the change in plans on the funeral of Voityck, and Kosinski's whereabouts over that terrible weekend."

Kosinski, in short, struck Lownes as a suitable candidate to have performed the deeds of Charles Manson.

The police, meanwhile, were busy checking out another early, and false, lead provided by Witold Kaczanowski, the Polish émigré painter who signed his works Witold-K, who had knocked around with Kosinski for a time in New York, and who was living in the United States under an expired visa. In fact, Kaczanowski had initially hidden, and been brought forward with the mediation of Elzbieta Czyzewska's husband, David Halberstam. Kaczanowski, who was close to Frykowski in Los Angeles, was apparently the first to argue that Kosinski had not been expected that night and was just seeking publicity. He shared this view with Czyzewska, who recalled that Kosinski had not mentioned any plans to be there, either when he first called to report that "something has happened in Los Angeles" or at the memorial for Frykowski.

Despite the doubts of several individuals, newspaper coverage continued to repeat the story of the luggage mix-up. On December 18, with the Manson gang in custody and obviously the culprits, Kosinski was interviewed by Dick Kleiner, the West Coast correspondent for the Newspaper Enterprise Association. To Kleiner, Kosinski emphasized the way early press accounts had "butchered" the reputations of the victims; while his account whitewashed Frykowski's involvement with Sebring's drug dealing, of which he may have been unaware, it came down firmly on the central point—that the press had treated the crime as though Polanski and his household had somehow brought it upon themselves. The Paris airport incident was mentioned in passing.

The debate about Kosinski's intended presence became public in 1984 when Polanski stated in his biography that Kosinski had *not* been expected that night. Sharon had never cared for Kosinski, the story went, and would never have invited him. As the publication followed close upon a more important crisis of credibility in Kosinski's career, the reviewer for the *Sunday Times* of London singled the statement out for comment. In response, Clem Wood wrote a letter to the editor giving an account that strongly supported Kosinski's version. Yet in Polish émigré circles, the view persisted that Kosinski had seized upon the event to assert a piece of personal melodrama that could not be disproved.

Taking the various witnesses together, there can be little doubt that Kosinski and Kiki had originally planned to be in Los Angeles that night. The core story of a luggage mix-up in Paris is well supported, too, in that Clem Wood heard the story in outline before it would have had any value as part of a fabrication. Whether Jerzy and Kiki would have arrived, specifically, at Polanski's house on Cielo Drive is less certain. In the atmosphere of the household, however, it is quite possible that Frykowski might have invited them, notwithstanding Sharon's dislike of Kosinski. The doubts of Elzbieta Czyzewska and Witold Kaczanowski appear, like the suspicions of Victor Lownes, largely circumstantial. As for Polanski, who had been in London, he was the least likely to have been well informed.

For Kosinski, it was a first wake-up call in the world of celebrity. Although he was only a marginal figure, the event had many elements of controversies to come. The blurring of boundaries between fact and fiction in his novel—a blurring he subtly encouraged—had almost gotten him questioned for murder. His combination of furtiveness and high-flying quest for publicity had provoked antagonism, jealousy, and hostility, and had gotten him into a controversy in which those who knew him would divide sharply between supporters and detractors. Ironically, in the particular event, the story he told seems to have been essentially the truth.

2.

In the aftermath of the Tate/Manson murders, Kosinski began to brood upon his own vulnerabilities as a celebrity. By August 21 this brooding had acquired a particular focus. Peter Skinner had asked, innocently, if he might mention his work for Kosinski on his résumé. In response, Kosinski had Skinner draw up and sign a statement declaring that he had known Kosinski for three years, had performed minor "secretarial services" for him and his late wife, and had entered into no other common "business affiliations." The requirement to sign this "voluntary" statement may well have accelerated a change in the working relationship with Skinner, who now found it inconvenient to follow Kosinski to his academic postings.

That fall Kosinski had accepted a position as Senior Fellow at Princeton's Council for the Humanities. When he came to look for an apartment, the housing representative showed him a semi-detached building at 100 North Stanworth Drive—"a marvelous house for you," the man said, "right next to Khrushchev's daughter!" Kosinski thought for a moment. "You must mean *Stalin's* daughter," he said. It was, indeed, Svetlana Alliluyeva. He had already met Svetlana briefly at the summer place of Allan Schwartz, the entertainment attorney who had now taken over legal matters having to do with his books and who had worked closely with American intelligence in getting Svetlana out of the Soviet Union. Now Kosinski and Lana, as she was called, became friends, a peculiar juxtaposition of past and present which seems to have engendered genuine ontological shock.

More than anything else that had happened to him, it seemed to prove that his destiny was to go everywhere and experience everything—to be a vessel through which the multifoliate forces and manners of his age were brought into confluence. He was a person to whom *everything happened.* Later he made Svetlana a character in *Blind Date*, where the thought of her proximity to Stalin "paralyzed" the protagonist. He said as much in private to his old friend Andrzej Wat in Paris: it was one of the few encounters that awakened in him something akin to awe.

Kosinski and Svetlana conversed only in English, but they soon found that they were bonded by their Eastern European pasts. For Svetlana, Kosinski was a soulmate—someone who felt and described the world with passionate Slavic intensity. She spoke to him of her American husband, William Peters—a kind, good man, but, like so many Americans, a person existing at the surface of life, lacking Slavic depth and subtlety. As Kosinski did with most new acquaintances, he presented her with signed copies of his books. She greatly admired *The Painted Bird*, but found *Steps* devoid of an important subject or theme, a judgment in which she agreed with a growing number of members of Kosinski's inner circle. One may only speculate about the ontological musings on her part when reading of her own father first as a distant, kindly, mythic figure—a father to millions—and then as the creator of a grim blanket of social repression.

Since he had been in America longer than she had, Svetlana relied on Kosinski to explain its workings. Why was it that Mrs. Frank Lloyd Wright, her husband's patroness at Taliesin, expected her to participate in cooking? And wasn't Peters, who held the title of "president," superior to the woman who merely stood behind the organization and funded it? Her ambiguous sense of position spilled over into their relationship as well, as she wandered into his seminars whenever it suited her to have a conversation. When he pointed out that he was conducting a class, she would blithely say, "Dismiss them!"

In the course of the first term at Princeton he also got to know Walter Kaufmann, the distinguished Nietzsche scholar and editor of *Existentialism from Dostoyevsky to Sartre*, a standard work that presented the tradition with the greatest influence upon Kosinski's writing. But despite the diversion offered by Svetlana and the discovery of kindred thinkers like Kaufmann, Kosinski did not find Princeton congenial. He had thoroughly enjoyed Wesleyan, and he would later take great pleasure in teaching at Yale, but he complained of Princeton's clubby atmosphere. Something about it exacerbated his puckish and childlike side. When a professor who lived nearby whistled at birds at night, Kosinski lobbed potatoes over the roof in the man's general direction. His favorite anecdote from Princeton—used as an incident in *Blind Date* immediately following the Svetlana episode—was of a professor of Eastern European origin who ate canned dog food, mistaking it for the popular Smiling Dog brand of beef sold in the Soviet Union.

One convenience of Princeton, however, was the availability of Stanley Corngold, who now stepped into the shoes vacated by Peter Skinner. Corngold was an even more improbable editorial assistant than the Oxford-educated Skinner, possessing already the beginnings of the academic cachet he would eventually attain as senior literary theorist at Princeton. He had compared the boy's recovery of voice in *The Painted Bird* to the ending of Joyce's *A Portrait of the Artist as a Young Man*, and Kosinski knew from his brief efforts with *Steps* and the accompanying pamphlet that Corngold possessed considerable skills as an editor and was willing to work for modest compensation. If he was somewhat overqualified for the task, well, that was Corngold's consideration, not his.

That fall Kosinski delivered to Corngold a manuscript that Corngold remembers as being fully developed in terms of plot, but quite messy. After his experience with *Steps,* he was shocked at the primitive state of some of the prose—this was, after all, the author he had compared to James Joyce—but he went to work on it anyway, at times feeling somewhat exploited. For a complete overhaul of the text, he received a few hundred dollars. He worked throughout the term, sometimes even accompanying Kosinski on trips back to Manhattan, where Kosinski put him up in a hotel room with a single naked light bulb. The compensations included fine meals—he could ask for anything he wanted, while Kosinski, as always, ate next to nothing—but as he wrestled with the prose, and with Kosinski over the matter of payment, his opinion of Kosinski as a writer gradually sank. Nevertheless, for a young untenured assistant professor, it was a kick to work with an author who had just garnered a National Book Award, even if he didn't quite share the judges' high opinion of the work. Kosinski knew everybody, and you never knew who would pop in or where you would end up. Once they even spent a weekend in Connecticut working at Barbara Tuchman's house, which Kosinski had borrowed.

Though desperately reliant upon Corngold's help, Kosinski found ways to keep his new assistant in his place. Once, driving back to Manhattan in Kosinski's Bentley, they stopped at a high-way diner. Always interested in anything having to do with au-tomobiles, Kosinski struck up a conversation with a garage mechanic who was sitting at a nearby table, leaving Corngold with Kiki to do a slow burn. When Kosinski returned to the table, Corngold made his irritation known. "Excuse me," Kosinski apol-ogized, "but I don't yet know the mores of your society. I didn't realize that it might be offensive to converse with someone of an-other class."

Kosinski returned to New York for the Thanksgiving holiday, and on the following day, November 28, he met at the Seventy-ninth Street apartment with a young man named Rocco Landesman for an interview which would eventually be pub-lished in *The Paris Review*'s Writers at Work series. In July Kosinski had received a twenty-three-page fan letter from Landesman, a June graduate of the University of Wisconsin whose extended critical appreciation of *The Painted Bird* and *Steps* had just won the *Harper's* award for an essay by a college senior. Landesman, who would later make his mark as a Broadway pro-ducer, was now a first-year graduate student at Yale Drama School. He arrived at the apartment accompanied by a stunningly beautiful twenty-six-year-old Wellesley graduate named Jean Kilbourne, a friend who admired Kosinski's books and had asked for a chance to meet him. But as soon as the introductions were made, Kiki, over Kosinski's objection, whisked the young woman away to shop, so that the men could focus on the interview.

Back in Cambridge, Jean Kilbourne received a letter from Kosinski, along with a copy of *The Art of the Self*. He had gotten her address from Landesman, he explained, because he had felt an instant connection between them that could not be left unexplored. She wrote back, further exchanges followed, and soon she received a telephone call from Kosinski, who said simply, "I want to see you." With some hesitation, Jean agreed. It took two months to arrange, but on February 19, 1970, Kosinski made the trip to Cambridge. He stayed at the Sheraton Commander, where he hated the feeling of confinement and broke a window in the futile effort to open it. Over the weekend he courted her almost like an undergraduate, taking her to dinner at the Blue Parrot, a popular Harvard Square cafe. On Saturday Jean had a number of friends over for a dinner party, mainly out of fear of being alone with him. Having read his books, she feared that there was something diabolical about him. They discussed her fears, walking and driving around the city together.

"You and I had the same childhood," Kosinski told her. On the face of it, this was a strange, if not altogether disingenuous, remark. Yet Jean had indeed had a difficult childhood. Her mother had died when she was nine, leaving her to the care of an emotionally distant father, a former military officer then working as an executive for the Curtis Publishing Company. Kosinski's remark may therefore not have been purely seductive. In the figure of Colonel Kilbourne, he must have discerned a reflection of the emotionally remote Mieczyslaw Kosinski. He could identify well enough, certainly, with a childhood lived without deep human connection. He talked wonderfully, in a way Jean had never heard anyone talk before, but more important, he listened. And he was patient. The relationship was not consummated during the course of that weekend, but an important bond had been forged.

That same month Kosinski had received word that he was to be honored by the American Academy of Arts and Letters, along with Philip Roth and William Styron, in May. In March he got away for a quick tour of Europe, the highlight of which was sharing a box at the London Symphony with Maestro Leopold Stokowski and the Goddard Liebersons. It marked a dramatic step up, from being a Pole who gathered with bewildered Polish émigrés to being a Pole who enjoyed the company of Poles in exile who had made it to the top of their fields. Sadruddin Aga Khan wrote warmly from Switzerland, thanking him for the photos he had taken there and joking that he in turn had sent Kosinski's photo to the Tuareg Camel Breeders' Association in Timbuktu, an allusion to Kosinski's jokes about the shape of his own nose. Back in America he had an exchange of letters and several phone calls with Polanski, exploring the possibility of doing a film project together. One day he picked up the phone and Polanski asked, "Guess where I'm calling from?" He told Kosinski to go outside and look; he was in a plane directly above Kosinski's house.

Kosinski resumed the pursuit of Jean Kilbourne by mail, arguing against her fears and reservations. She wrote him noting the care he had taken to insure that nothing she received from him could be attributed to him, so that, if he wished, there would be no trace of a connection between them. She reiterated her feeling that he was diabolical. He wrote back that he needed her as he had never needed anyone. He pointed out that he had not touched her in Cambridge. Was this diabolical? Did this imply that there was no trace of connection? His letters to her were soulful, almost schoolboyish. Much of his language reflected student preoccupations of the day. Without her his life seemed a dreadful sacrifice of the natural, he told her, blank and silent, while she awakened in him, in Hesse's words, "promptings of the true self." He insisted that he did not wish to dominate her. Rather he felt that he could be fulfilled by her and through her.

In May, Jean came to New York and stayed at the Seventy-ninth Street apartment, where they became lovers. Although it may have begun as another casual seduction, it was, for Kosinski, the beginning of a long and passionate relationship, in which he revealed himself more openly than in any other. Unlike the other major women in his life to that point, who were often older or otherwise motherly, Jean Kilbourne was ten years younger. She was, upon closer examination, even more stunningly and enduringly beautiful, and she was also highly intelligent. She had worked as a model, but was now a high school teacher (later she taught at Emerson College, including his books in her syllabus). Yet she was also something of a lost soul. Her unhappy childhood traveled with her as Kosinski's did with him, giving her an abiding sense of sadness and vulnerability. Feeling bonded by childhood unhappiness, Kosinski revealed vulnerabilities of his own. He had even been addicted to opium, he told her, when he was in Turkey. The story may have been an embellishment of his experiments with the drug, but it became a metaphor describing an enslavement of the senses aroused in him by Jean Kilbourne. She was his opium. She brought him to the state of euphoria that carries with it surrender.

Jean's beauty was, in reality, the least of it. Their minds worked similarly, and with similar quickness. They shared interests, which verged upon obsession, in the boundaries of human identity—Jean, in fact, had been friendly with R. D. Laing, author of *The Divided Self*, while living in London—and in borderline experiences. Jean grasped instinctively his fascination with the perverse, which in some measure she shared, yet she retained an innocence that made her unlike the hardened sexual companions of his past. From their first meeting there had been a recognition of their common status as outsiders, freaks, aliens—a recognition that Jean described as the "outlaw selves saluting."

More than any other woman, Jean brought out in Kosinski a suppressed sense of romance. On that first weekend in New York they went to see *Women in Love*, the first of many movies they would see together, sometimes more than one a day. Writing to her, talking with her, he sometimes gushed like a young man in his first love. And their relationship maintained a lightness of touch. His nickname for her was "Wigham," which emerged from a newspaper typo turning her home town of Hingham, Massachusetts, into "Higham." In her company he was given to schoolboy pranks, once drinking an entire bottle of brandy to prove that he could control its effect. He made good on his boast, more or less, getting sweetly drunk and then demonstrating his ability to snap out of it and function coherently. He signed copies of his books for her, misdating the signing of *The Painted Bird* to imply that he had known her for years. That would confound future biographers, he told her mischievously. It was, all of it, part of his singular lifelong quest to achieve *control* over all the elements of his life, and then to display that mastery of the world for the unqualified approval of an adoring woman. Jean Kilbourne very nearly filled that role, while at the same time challenging him, increasingly, to break through and become a more authentic self.

The annual luncheon of the American Academy of Arts and Letters rolled around on May 26, with an awards ceremonial to follow in the Academy auditorium. Bennett Cerf then hosted a party at Twenty One in honor of the Random House authors who had been recognized with career awards. Cerf still didn't quite get what was going on with Kosinski. Echoing the view of Peter Skinner, he had thought *Steps* a collection of peculiarly structured short stories. "You wasted so much money," he had told a horrified Kosinski when phoning him in Switzerland after word came on the National Book Award. "Every short story could have been a separate book."

After the party at Twenty One, a group decided to head on to Jilly's to continue their night on the town. Kosinski wasn't familiar with Jilly's, and no one knew the address. Frank Sinatra was the one who had suggested Jilly's, so it was agreed that he would lead the way, with Kosinski and Kiki and Marian Javits following in Kosinski's car. When they got to Jilly's, an attendant in uniform leaped out and greeted Kosinski with a bear hug.

"You know him?" Sinatra asked.

"He parked cars here," the man said.

Sinatra turned to Kosinski. "You SOB, you said you didn't know this place," he said.

Kosinski tried to explain that more than a decade had passed, although the attendant, working at the same job himself, had no sense of time passing. Kosinski had actually parked cars for the Kinney lot around the corner on Eighth Avenue, the lot managed by his friend Joel Charles, but sometimes for big-tipping regulars he would stash a car in front of Jilly's, where he could recover it faster. With Sinatra only partially placated, they moved inside. When the group ordered drinks, Kosinski, who rarely drank, ordered tea.

"You SOB, you shouldn't say that out loud," Sinatra growled. He had heard "tea" as "t," which in his world meant marijuana. Even for Kosinski, certain barriers of language and culture were to prove impassable. A friendship with Sinatra was not ordained by the higher powers.

That May students across the country were in an uproar over Kent State. In late April, Richard Nixon had ordered a military incursion across the Cambodia-Vietnam border with the stated aim of pressuring the North Vietnamese to make peace. This somewhat counterintuitive strategy for peacemaking generated outrage on America's campuses; in the demonstrations that followed, four students at Kent State were shot by nervous National Guard troops. The shootings served to ratchet campus protest up a notch, and even staid citadels of privilege like Princeton became involved.

The year had begun with *Time* magazine designating "everyone under twenty-five" as selectee in its Man of the Year issue. Now, it seemed, everyone under twenty-five was suddenly a statesman, charged with instructing the older generation in the conduct of human affairs. It was a pivotal moment in Kosinski's take on the world, both intellectually and temperamentally. Impish, irreverent, and individualistic as he was, he held no brief for the unearned sense of entitlement he saw in American youth— and especially in Princeton students. He had hustled madly to be on the professor's side of the desk, and now students felt that they were in the front rank, qualified to lecture their professors. What had they ever done? What did they even know of the real world?

It all smacked of earlier movements, in which men wearing brown shirts muscled their way into classes of Europe's great old universities, shouted down distinguished scholars and, ultimately, hauled them off to the camps. American students in 1969 seemed not even to be aware of the history that the tone and texture of their collectivist principles recalled. Whatever he might think on the larger issues of policy, Kosinski suddenly found himself on the side of the naysayers about American youth. They were weak and contemptible, but dangerous. They talked back to their elders because the elders, too, were weak and contemptible, and could be sassed with impunity. One day a student brought Kosinski a rather saccharine and idealistic short story he had written. "I'm sure you won't like it," he said impudently, "because in your work people die."

Kosinski looked at the young man severely. "You know, the very first time I saw you I got the feeling you were going to die young," he said. "In the past twenty years I've had the same feeling about several people and each time I've had it, they died. Of course, I could be wrong this time."

The young man, who was afraid of being drafted and sent to Vietnam, started to cry. Kosinski was both delighted and appalled. What he saw in young people was an escape from individual thought—from the self. Their fondness for loud rock music was a metaphor for the desire to drown out the possibility of individual interchange with others, while the spirit of Woodstock echoed the corporate collectivity of their parents. He found the cause of their fecklessness in affluence and, especially, in television, a medium that reduced everything to the neutrality of a screen on which skyscrapers and doghouses were the same size.

Kosinski was only thirty-seven years old, but he suddenly found himself on the far side of the age divide. His conversations became laced with complaints about students and television. Taking up the arguments of Marshall McLuhan, he began collecting statistics on every aspect of television, including the number of hours it served children as a babysitter. In August, after a conversation in which he presented his views of Princeton students to *Times* op-ed editor Harrison Salisbury, Salisbury invited him to do a piece on students for the op-ed page. The short piece he produced, originally entitled "Denial of Self," was run on October 13, 1970, as "Dead Souls on Campus."

Over the course of that summer Kosinski managed four meetings with Jean Kilbourne, all in New York. During the second, in early July, they had dinner with Steven Aronson, a writer/editor friend of Jean's, and saw the movies *Myra Breckinridge* and *Censorship in Denmark*. At the end of the month, just before Jean left for Turkey, they saw *The Virgin and the Gypsy, Scream and Scream Again,* and *The Dunwich Horror*. Their tastes as a couple were wonderfully eclectic, with almost no film too pedestrian to stimulate the profound entertainment of reaction and discussion; the only taste they did not share was for violence, which moved Jean to sink down in her seat and cover her eyes. She returned from Turkey on August 27, when they had their final rendezvous of the summer.

Also that summer Robert Brustein invited Kosinski to join the faculty of his new program in Drama Criticism at Yale. The two men had met socially, and Brustein found that his empathy for Kosinski was as strong as his admiration for *The Painted Bird*. To Brustein's surprise, his offer, which was put forward casually and on rather short notice, was accepted, with the sole stipulation that Kosinski have an apartment in one of the Yale colleges. To Jean, he explained that the Yale apartment would provide a haven from which Kiki would be excluded—a safe haven (New Haven) on the route between New York and Boston. His title at Yale was to be Professor of Drama and Playwright in Residence—an odd position for a writer who had never written, or even reviewed, a play. On his book jackets Kosinski listed his title as Professor of English Prose, a title that served his purpose admirably but was nowhere to be found in his contract. He was also named Resident Fellow of Davenport College, a position that conferred the on-campus apartment.

Kosinski would later give as one of his reasons for going to Yale the fact that Rocco Landesman was there, and it may well have been so. Landesman had become the special protégé of Brustein, who would appoint him an assistant professor as soon as he received his master's degree. Within a year Landesman, whose own short fiction had been praised by no less a teacher than Isaac Bashevis Singer, would write a dramatic adaptation of *Steps* for production at Yale. He would also be drawn into the circle of Kosinski's editors, eventually being joined by his girlfriend, Barbara Mackay, as Stanley Corngold faded.

In the course of that first fall at Yale, Kosinski managed to see Jean three times, at monthly intervals, but the notion of New Haven as a private apartment in which to escape Kiki proved illusory. Their October meeting was in Boston, where they saw the Jack Nicholson film *Five Easy Pieces* and he took pictures of her on the rocky Laneville beach. They met in November in New York, and only in December did he manage two days alone with her in New Haven.

By that fall a draft of the new novel, thoroughly worked over by Corngold, was nearly finished and ready for submission to Kosinski's new publisher—Harcourt Brace Jovanovich, which had outbid Random House. The novel was short—so short that at times Kosinski was afraid it didn't add up to the necessary length. Trying to reassure himself, he went around to bookstores and libraries, picking up the shortest novel on the shelf and doing the necessary math to count the words. There was precedent, he told himself; Hemingway's *The Old Man and the Sea* was only about 28,000 words, and Dostoyevsky's *Notes from Underground* was roughly the same. You could do a lot in a short narrative, particularly if your subject was a sort of fable. He had called it, in progress, *Blank Page*, and sometimes *Dasein*, taking a term for "being" from Heidegger. As much as Kosinski liked the idea of being identified with Heidegger, though, the term "Dasein" sounded pretentious and incomprehensibly foreign; he settled on its English equivalent—*Being There*.

The protagonist of *Being There* is a middle-aged man who has never left the townhouse where he tends the garden. His meals are prepared by a black cook named Louise, and he spends his free hours watching television. Expelled from the house—and the Garden—at the death of the "old man upstairs," Chance the Gardener is hit by a car belonging to Elizabeth Eve Rand, whose elderly husband is one of the richest men in America and the confidant of presidents. The Rands take him into their home, where they mistake him for a down-on-his-luck financier and mishear his name as Chauncey Gardiner. Asked about his past, he describes the only thing he knows—his work in the garden—which is taken by everyone as a metaphor. As Rand is dying, Chance accompanies EE, as she is called, to a diplomatic reception where his comments about the garden are heard as sage commentary. He is invited to appear on a nationwide television talk show, where his garden metaphor—plants must be pruned, and will grow new branches in their season—reassures the public in a moment of financial crisis. By the end of the book, the president has his aides scurrying without success to dig up information on Gardiner's past, while important power brokers propose him as a candidate for vice president.

One aspect of the novel had given Kosinski trouble. The story called for a romantic involvement between Chauncey and EE, but how was he to write it? What was the sexual nature of this man who knew nothing of the world but what he had seen on TV? For three weeks Kosinski had paused without writing a word. Then the essence of Chauncey Gardiner's sexuality came to him: *he liked to watch*.

Being There may be read as a satire upon the American power elite and a critique of the emptiness of television, both of which it was, but it was a great deal more. It was a novel with a key—several keys in fact, among them keys unavailable even to the well-educated American reader. At one level, the key was Kosinski's own link to Mary Weir and her late husband Ernest T. Weir, steel magnate and adviser to President Eisenhower. If no one noticed this at the time, their ignorance no doubt had to do with the form—an extended fable—which somehow did not suggest real-world analogues. After two novels with protagonists who so greatly resembled the author, Kosinski seemed to have written a book about a man who was unlike himself in every way. Apparently retarded, without intellectual resource or even rudimentary intention in his actions, Chance the Gardener was, on the face of it, as unlike the calculating and cerebral Jerzy Kosinski as it was possible to be.

Yet there were profound underlying correspondences between Kosinski and Chance. Both were men without a traceable past, and both entered the world of the power elite through a relationship with an older woman who had a much older and strategically placed husband. Both men were engaged in something of a high-wire act, walking almost on air and at terrible risk if they happened to glance down. For Chance the Gardener, this high-wire act resides in the metaphor of the garden—the only thing he knows, which must carry him through every situation of his new life. Much of the understated humor of the book lies in the vacuity of an elite unable to discern the emptiness of this performance, a vacuity of which Kosinski was particularly critical at this moment in his life. Much of the book's splendid tension derives from the reader's sense of anxiety for the performer—practically a holding of the breath to see if he can get away with

the trick in yet another situation—a form of projected performance anxiety which Peter Sellers would exploit brilliantly in the
film version. Kosinski's own high-wire act was more subtly articulated, but a man who required his assistants to sign false releases was embarked on the same delicate public performance, at
the same constant risk of exposure and destruction. Many who
were drawn into the larger Kosinski performance—from Park Avenue dinner parties to television appearances—experienced that
sense of projected vulnerability, the feeling that Kosinski might at
any moment look down and make a misstep.

There was also the matter of language. Both the KGB and the
CIA analyze Chauncey Gardiner's vocabulary, syntax, and accent
and find that it is impossible to detect his ethnic background or
origins within the American community. Here, with unwitting
frankness, Kosinski describes a man who is linguistically without
a country—the precise problem of his own writing. (Offered a
lavish book contract, Chauncey Gardiner says simply that he
can't write and is told that it doesn't matter.) Uninflected prose
was the hallmark of *Being There*, as of each of Kosinski's previous
books, the obvious solution to the contribution of many hands.
Like Chauncey Gardiner, he had worked to turn this terrible liability into a writerly asset, promulgating in interviews and his
two pamphlets a theory of language in which translation is the
essence of utterance.

As an idiot savant, a victim of mental retardation, Chauncey
Gardiner bore little resemblance to the quick-witted Kosinski. Yet
upon closer examination, the performance of Chauncey Gardiner
is not so much the product of mental retardation as of an affective
disorder. Even in the world of a fable, a mentally retarded individual could not have held his own quite as Gardiner did in the
company of talk-show hosts, industrialists, and the president. His
problem is not a low IQ, but the fact that he does not coincide
with himself. He is a man whose connection to real life is artificial, or as Kosinski defined Heidegger's concept of *Dasein* for *The
Paris Review* interview, a man who simultaneously "is" and "is
not." The essence of *being there* is *to be seen*; the thing at which
Chance the Gardener finally arrives is not the real world, but the

world he has imagined on the TV screen. To be even provision-
ally alive, one must be seen by others, like an actor in a play.

This key to the book might have been available to readers who
were thoroughly familiar with Kosinski's personal history in
America, but a second key was not. In its protagonist, its structure, its specific events, and its conclusion, the book bore an extraordinarily close resemblance to Dolega-Mostowicz's 1932 novel
The Career of Nikodem Dyzma, which Kosinski had described with
such excitement two decades earlier to his friend Stanislaw
Pomorski. The question of plagiarism is a serious one, and not
susceptible of easy and final answer; ultimately the text of *Being
There* resembles the text of *Nikodem Dyzma* in ways that, had
Dolega-Mostowicz been alive and interested in pressing the matter, might have challenged law courts as to a reasonable definition of plagiarism.

Certain things were clearly original with *Being There,* including
its American setting, the myth of the garden, and the affectless,
non-intentional quality of its hero. Yet one cannot easily dismiss
the issue by saying that *Being There* drew on many traditions and
many writers, from Jonathan Swift to Gogol. It did, certainly, but
the similarity to *Nikodem Dyzma* in plot and anecdote is far closer
than that. In a sense, it was once again the problem of translation,
but turned upside down and inside out; it was not language itself, but a work with plot and social vocabulary from another
culture, that Kosinski had translated into English. Similar transformation is routinely done by screenwriters adapting literary
works, but the original is acknowledged. And Kosinski himself
showed evidence that he was aware of vulnerability on this point.
In the attacks eventually leveled against his work, the charge of
plagiarism was never more than secondary, but he accumulated
large files dealing with charges of plagiarism involving Conrad,
Cagliostro, and others, and a defense against plagiarism was a
central theme in his final novel.

The last, recondite turn of the screw was that Kosinski's best
defense lay in his own personal history. *Being There* resembled *The
Career of Nikodem Dyzma*, yes, but so did his own life. In fact, it
might be most accurately charged that it was his life that drew
unduly upon the Dolega-Mostowicz text. He had taken it as a

manual for climbing to the top by exploiting the lack of acuity of the ruling class. Thus art imitated life which had imitated art; it might have made an elegant legal defense. The element most tellingly contributed by Kosinski was the transformation of the vulgar climber Nikodem Dyzma into the strangely affectless tabula rasa Chauncey Gardiner. The result was a portrait of himself at that moment, by no means a dull and vulgar circumstantial celebrity, but a man profoundly at odds with his own being, for whom "being there" was both achievement of the greatest heights and simultaneous "being" and "not being": a man who felt unable to exist unless he was being seen.

3.

Being There was published on April 21, 1971, to rapturous reviews. On page 7 of the *New York Times Book Review* of April 25, Paul Delany wrote that it was an ironic version of the American success story, and more. R. Z. Shepherd in *Time*, dated the following day, called it a "knuckle ball of a book delivered with perfectly timed satirical hops and metaphysical flutters." John J. McAleer in *Best Sellers* compared Kosinski to Beckett, while Arthur Curley in *Library Journal* felt Kosinski's "economy, precision, and deceptive simplicity" rivaled Jorge Luis Borges.

This was heady company in that heyday of the postmodern, especially for a book that was a short, simple, and highly accessible satirical parable. Better yet, John Aldridge, the distinguished critic who taught at the University of Michigan, did an extended essay-review for the April 24 *Saturday Review* entitled "The Fabrication of a Culture Hero." Aldridge saw *Being There* as a novel that "exists simultaneously on the levels of fiction and fact, fantasy and contemporary history, . . . ingeniously conceived and endowed with some of the magical significance of myth." Only John Updike demurred, noting in a delayed review in the September 25 *New Yorker* that the layout of Kosinski's novels made the author's biography appear to be the final chapter.

The invocation of Beckett and, especially, Borges might seem misplaced for a novel that, however excellent, was quite simple in

language and structure. Yet it had one interesting point of contact
with Borges. In an essayistic short story entitled "Pierre Menard,
Author of *Don Quixote*," Borges had imagined a contemporary
who undertook to re-create Cervantes' *Don Quixote* word for
word. The subtext of the story is a consideration of how the writer's different time and cultural context alter the meaning of an
otherwise *identical* novel, making it wholly new and altogether a
more stunning book. Perhaps no better defense could be assembled against the potential charge of plagiarism. None would be
immediately required in any case. None of the reviewers noticed
that the book's "ingenious conception" bore a resemblance to a
Polish bestseller of 1932.

Flower children loved Chauncey Gardiner, as Kosinski quipped,
because he didn't want anything, but literate adults, who buy the vast
majority of hardcover books, liked him too. For the first time in his
career, a Kosinski novel had respectable hardcover sales. The advance had been $80,000, paid in two installments, a geometric leap
from the $10,000 he received for *Steps*. In the first six months
after publication—its basic hardcover life—*Being There* sold 19,860
copies.

Along with glowing reviews and brisk sales came interviews
that began to treat Kosinski not merely as a writer but as a literary
star. Writing in *Saturday Review* the week before Aldridge's essay,
Cleveland Amory described not Kosinski's literary attributes but
his personal quirks. Amory met Kosinski at his Hemisphere House
apartment, over a brunch prepared by Kiki. Amory queried Kiki's
use of the nickname Jurek, which he wrote as "Yurek."

"It's a nickname for Jerzy," Kiki replied. "You also pronounce
that with a *Y*. Call him anything but Jerry. He hates that."

"The only vanity I have is that *z*," Kozinski said. "I even made
the publisher make the *z* bigger than any of the other letters on the
jacket."

They looked at the book jacket so that Amory could verify the
oversize *z*. The jacket copy provided a segue to Kosinski's biography. *Being There* was not autobiographical, he said, making a joke
about his own future mental retardation. His father was an expert
on ancient Greece and the origin of European languages, but also
had an expertise in the manufacture of felt. His mother was a

concert pianist who never performed. He went on to describe briefly his separation from his parents and experiences during the German occupation. He topped off this rendition of his mythic childhood by giving Amory a demonstration of his ability to hide himself in the confines of a small apartment.

"Once," he told Amory, as he emerged from his hiding place, "I hid for a whole weekend. I came out only for food and work. People were in and out, too, but they never found me."

Such anecdotes mark the emergence of a literary celebrity whose presence is about to become more important than his work. On May 26 he appeared for the first time on Johnny Carson's *Tonight Show* on NBC, then taped in New York. The two men had met socially, and Kosinski had mentioned to Carson that the *Tonight Show* had been one of the sources for his new book. Carson had been taken with Kosinski and scheduled him for April 29, closer to publication date, but at the last minute he was bumped. Now, with the book still selling briskly, he appeared on a guest list that included Mickey Rooney, country singer Mac Davis, and guitarist Chet Atkins. With his exceptionally quick repartee and clipped, accented speech, he was a hit with the studio audience and with Carson himself, who marked him immediately as an intellectual who could function like a show business professional. Carson would eventually have him back for nine more appearances, the last coming in 1980. For several appearances there would be no current novel as hook.

That first night Carson kicked off the discussion with a plug of Kosinski's book, but Kosinski quickly decided—and communicated to Carson—that it was better for an author to come prepared to talk on other subjects. Carson had him back on July 1, when he talked about writing without full command of the language and told anecdotes about consulting telephone operators, and again on September 6, when one of his topics was that it was a mistake for authors to try to sell books on talk shows. His subjects in subsequent appearances included the imaging of women in romance magazines (as wildly animalistic, with forgiving men); the different attitudes toward women of American and European men (with a digression about lower-back pain); romance magazines and true stories; strange letters he received and his manner of writing; decadence (including a hilarious set piece on ads for edible underwear); and the effects of TV on children.

Carson grew to rely on Kosinski's professionalism, and once signaled Kosinski that only eight seconds remained and could he wrap the thought or should Carson? Kosinski did the wrap. A crossover pop-culture star was being born.

This emergence as a figure on the pop culture scene coincided with a major crisis in Kosinski's creative life. He was now the author of five books. Two were nonfiction books drawn from his research and travel in the Soviet Union. His first novel had been based on his childhood experiences during the Nazi occupation, while his second novel, as nonlinear as it might appear, continued to draw upon his life, pulling incidents from his adolescence and young manhood in Poland and his early days in the United States. *Being There*, told as a parable, had reflected the last ten years of his life—the encounter of an outsider with the upper levels of American society. The ending of *Being There*, in which the future of Chauncey Gardiner seems unimaginable, neatly summarizes the creative problem Kosinski now confronted. What could he write next? Where was he to find the material?

A part of the solution seemed to present itself during a tryst with Jean Kilbourne in early April. Jean had kept a detailed journal from adolescence in which she now carefully documented their conversations and recorded details of their meetings. The seeds of a crisis had been planted in March, when she allowed him to read her journals. Moved by what he had learned about himself, he called her from New York, crying on the phone. The journal revealed her deep love for him while capturing him with great clarity. Yet the usual conflicts inherent in a romantic triangle had also begun to impose themselves upon the relationship. In early March she had complained in her journal of his canceling a rendezvous because he considered his stepson David Weir more important. Whatever the reason, he canceled frequently, often after long planning and on short notice. Moreover, from Jean's perspective, the basic story was beginning to show inconsistencies. One minute he would assure her that Kiki knew everything—and indeed, Kiki at times dropped him off directly for assignations at Jean's apartment in Cambridge, once calling to inform Jean that her car lights were on. Next, however, he would complain that Jean had compromised him by leaving her saccharin in his Seventy-ninth Street apartment, adding, "Thanks a lot!"

On April 7 they saw *El Topo* together, and when Jean covered her eyes from the gore, he reassured her energetically that the blood was "only red paint"—a manipulation of aesthetic distance that fit comfortably within the plenary canon of his existence. Together for four full days, they had never experienced greater intimacy. Then, while she was away from the apartment, Kosinski took her journal, along with the letters he had written in the course of their courtship. When she discovered what he had done, Jean was outraged. She felt betrayed and violated, as though her worst fears of his diabolical nature had been confirmed.

From Kosinski's perspective, there was a terrible logic not only in his actions but in the timing. Intimacy was his greatest fear, and if he had slipped into it with Jean as never before in his life, then he had to respond with an equal and opposite reaction. A woman who "enslaved" by loving you was a woman it was *necessary* to betray. How could he better distance Jean than by using their relationship as material for a novel? If he wrote about it, it would become one more "as if" episode—a fiction aspiring to the condition of life. Her journal—itself an imitation of reality—could serve to spur his memory, while the act of stealing it abruptly created aesthetic distance. By taking the letters as well, he could remove every trace of the genuine feelings that had gushed out of him.

With this germ of a novel in place, Kosinski set to work. Once again there was the question of his need for editorial assistants. Despite the clear success of a work done with the help of Rocco Landesman and his girlfriend, Barbara Mackay, the search for editors continued. Lin Harris-Seares answered an ad for editors on the Columbia University bulletin board and reported to her husband that the person seeking help was named "something like Kosinski." "Jerzy Kosinski?" he asked, startled.

Arriving at his Hemisphere House apartment, 60 West Fifty-seventh Street, she was told that her potential employer was looking for help with a manuscript because he had had an accident that hurt his head and caused problems with his eyes. Kiki then administered a test. Harris-Seares was given a text made up of words with big gaps between them. Her task was to fill in the gaps, turning the words into a text—a process strikingly similar to the one Kosinski engaged in with Peter Skinner. She sat and stared at the page, her mind working furiously. What kind of service was she being asked to sell? At last, because she herself liked a crisp prose style, she closed the spaces with minimal additions, leaving the words more or less as they were. A little disoriented, she made her way back to her apartment. She would be notified of the outcome.

No call was forthcoming. She asked herself if there was something unethical in what she had been asked to do, but she didn't mention it to anyone. She felt ashamed of the fact that she hadn't gotten the job. Three years later, when she assisted in the Conversations with Artists series at WBAI (the Pacifica Network), she met Kosinski again a number of times. She wondered if he remembered their interview, but did not bring it up herself, still feeling embarrassed that he had not found her worthy of the job. By then he had published *The Devil Tree*, and parts of it struck her as vaguely familiar—as though it might have incorporated the words she saw on her test.

Another Peter Skinner, clearly, was going to be difficult to find. Besides Rocco Landesman, Kosinski employed another young graduate student at Yale Drama School, Larry Eilenberg, whose official position, conveniently, was designated as graduate assistant. In fact Eilenberg was working on a screen adaptation of *Being There*, which Kosinski, despite many disclaimers, was already determined to turn into a film. His initial effort had involved Gene Gutowski, a Polish emigré who had produced several of Polanski's prize-winning early films. Gutowski put together a package with MGM as the studio and Gore Vidal, whom Kosinski approved, as the screenwriter. With the deal in place, Kosinski phoned Gutowski to insist that the director be Adam Hollander, another Polish-Jewish emigré who had worked as a cameraman (*Midnight Cowboy*) but had no experience as a director. When MGM balked, Kosinski vetoed Vidal, saying that he and Hollander would produce the script, and MGM withdrew from participation. Eilenberg entered the picture as Hollander's replacement, but with MGM no longer interested, a final stab by Gutowski, involving Sidney Lumet as director and Peter Sellers as star, collapsed because Sellers was then deemed unfinanceable.

Like others who worked with Kosinski, Eilenberg was incorporated for a period into Kosinski's daily life, and witnessed parts of Kosinski's theater of the real. Once as they were walking the streets of New Haven, they wandered into a rough neighborhood and were bumped and jostled by a tall and strongly built African-American. Eilenberg wanted to walk quietly away, but Kosinski thrust his hand into the outer pocket of his purselike leather carrying case, which he claimed he had personally designed. To Eilenberg's dismay, he growled, "Hey, you, put your hands up!" and poked his hand into the man's belly as though he had a gun. "I mean it, apologize," he said, backing the man against a nearby building. To Eilenberg's amazement, the man apologized and skulked away. On another occasion, as they were on their way to the beach at West Haven, Kosinski stopped his Buick and had Eilenberg get out and place books on parked cars, much as he had once done with David Weir. Kosinski then gunned the engine and sped down the street, knocking off each book in imitation of the "book-knock-off" game from *Steps*. As always, the lines between art and life were blurred, with each in turn imitating the other.

It was not, finally, Eilenberg but Barbara Mackay, Rocco Landesman's girlfriend and fellow student at Yale Drama School, who stepped into Peter Skinner's shoes as Kosinski's new chief editor and collaborator. Mackay had worked on *Being There* only in the galley stage, but with *The Devil Tree* she was present from the beginning, typing as Kosinski paced, dictated, and threw out ideas and fragments, much as Skinner had done with *Steps*. Unlike Skinner, she was unable to bond with Kosinski as a free-spirited male and fellow European, but she shared Skinner's empathy with Kosinski's human complexity, and she also had sympathy for his reliance upon a complicated compositional process. And like Skinner she was ferociously loyal. Privately she doubted many of his stories, recoiled from some of his actions, and considered him a lazy literary craftsman. But she was not im-

mune to his magnetism, beneath which she could discern a substantial, and wounded, human being. She disapproved of many
elements of his novels, especially what she perceived as misog-
yny, and she felt ambivalent at best about what struck her as a
cavalier and irreverent attitude toward the *words* in his books, but
she did not doubt that he was a compelling storyteller. The irrev-
erence, in fact, was one of the qualities that held her affection; the
private Kosinski she knew delighted in his posture as a secret
send-up of "The Writer," and his decline, in her eyes, took place
as awards and fame caused him to lose his sense of irony about
his place as the Famous Writer. She worked with him as the chief
assistant on *The Devil Tree, Blind Date,* and *Cockpit* (although Peter
Skinner returned to participate on portions of the first draft), and
in the early stages of *Passion Play*. He paid her satisfactorily, adding perks like the gift of one of his old cars, and treated her, as
he had Skinner, as a trusted comrade. That trust would be well
vindicated later, in the crisis over his "authorship" of the novels.
Interviewed by the *Village Voice*, Barbara would take more care
than any other editor in disavowing co-authorship while deline-
ating the unusual sort of editorial services she provided.

At New Haven, Kosinski was coming into his own as a
teacher. From the beginning Yale had provided a more congenial
setting than Princeton. Perhaps it was genuinely less clubby, or
perhaps the mood of Ivy League students had begun a subtle
shift away from the mood of the 1960s. Or perhaps it was
Kosinski himself who had changed, hitting his stride in the classroom. During his first fall at Yale, in 1970, he offered a course in
"Death and the Modern Imagination," which expanded, in a way,
upon his response to the Princeton student. He was shocked
when the students who enrolled overflowed the assigned room.
In order to reduce their numbers, he announced, deadpan, that as
part of the course one of them was going to be required to die.

As part of the class, the Yale undergraduates were required to
write about their own deaths. To stimulate their thinking,
Kosinski brought in members of the Process Church of the Final
Judgement—a group of Satanists who arrived dressed in gray.
They saw themselves as having some sort of tenuous link with

Charles Manson's Helter-Skelter family. Proselytizing in Kosinski's Yale classroom, they urged the students to "accept and embrace *evil* within themselves." This notion was uncomfortably close to Kosinski's own claim to Krystyna Iwaszkiewicz that he could achieve revenge upon his enemies because of a pact with the Devil, and it certainly recalled his actions toward Jean Kilbourne. The classroom episode took an unexpected turn when a young Jewish student went off with the Satanists, prompting an exchange with the student's parents over the pedagogical appropriateness of this classroom activity.

Such provocative pedagogy was characteristic of Kosinski's teaching at Yale, which is remembered fondly by many former students, and by a few as downright brilliant. The choice of subject matter was well suited to his experience. Having lived as a child under the constant threat of death, he now felt himself to be in a culture that pushed death out of sight and out of mind. But there was a more personal side to it. His preoccupation with death went beyond reasonable fears and questions, and seemed to stem from something deeper than a single tangible experience; in psychoanalytic terms, it was not so much concern with death as it was *morbidity*, a feeling of not being alive—a feeling that was, indeed, shared by only a few categories of others, among them survivors of concentration camps. His students no doubt sensed, as did his television audiences, that whatever had happened in his past, he was a man for whom death had a special and very personal reality; it was the one subject on which he was unquestionably in good faith.

His inventiveness in the classroom seemed endless. Once he promised that at the next class he would present two individuals who were "giants in their field," then turned up at the next session with two midgets. For another class, experimenting with student responsiveness to authority of presentation, he announced that they would have the opportunity to interview experts in an area. A couple turned up, announced as professional tap dancers. In actuality they were Joshua Javits, the senator's son and then a Yale student, and his girlfriend. To students arriving at his office, he often remarked that he had noticed that they were not very articulate. He suggested that since his time was limited, they take a pill that would make them more articulate. He then offered a simple aspirin, which they invariably accepted and swallowed. Behind many of these academic performances, and most of his public lectures, was the thinking of the sociologist he had almost become. Like a sociologist, he observed. In particular he observed the beliefs and behaviors of individuals in groups, but his focus was always drawn to the exceptional—the phenomenon or response so peculiar as not to fit within the array of the sociologist's systematic methods.

The same terminology—a sociology of the exceptional—serves broadly as a description of his novels, with an unfortunate progression from extreme experiences deeply felt to peculiar incidents bordering on the trivial. The same spirit was always at play in his life. Arriving for a visit at his Yale apartment, Rose Styron heard a strange tapping sound. When the door opened, she was greeted by Kosinski holding a cane. He was practicing, he said, trying to work out what it would be like when he went blind.

Like death, blindness was a motif in both his life and work. In *The Painted Bird*, the boy had watched a young man's eyeballs plucked out with a spoon, and speculated that perhaps he could now see in another world. Word was gradually circulated that Kosinski, like James Joyce before him, was losing his vision. Numerous friends arrived to be told that he was typing in a dark closet, mastering the technique that would be required when his sight was finally gone. Some, like Geoffrey Wolff, fretted about him, while others, like Rose Styron, assumed that he was looking for an excuse to get away in mid-semester and ski. As he told everyone, the only satisfactory eye clinics for his never precisely named ailment were located in Switzerland. Robert Brustein was finally persuaded to release Kosinski from his teaching obligations for a semester so that his eye problem could be dealt with at the Swiss clinic; shortly afterward Brustein began to receive a series of postcards from Kosinski, who was skiing at Gstaad and then floating down the Nile with Sadri Khan.

Yet, like death, blindness was both a gimmick and a matter about which he was in dead earnest. He did, indeed, *see* the world differently, a product of his inability to see as others. The most commonplace objects, held up to his examination, took on a quality of strangeness, as did familiar gestures, including the simple act of eating. At restaurants he asked for salads with onion and lemon, which he rearranged on his plate but barely touched. Kiki frequently cut up portions on his plate and prodded him to eat, as though eating were an unusual local custom in which the alien Kosinski had to be reminded to participate.

The flip side of Kosinski's abstemiousness about food was his ambivalence about fleshiness. He was drawn to fleshy women, especially women with oversize breasts. He photographed them endlessly and clipped photographs of nudes from magazines, often sending them in batches to Jean Kilbourne. On the other hand, he found obesity almost morally repellent, an attitude captured by the story of the fat man and the cake, which he presented as having happened at a New Haven restaurant during his first year at Yale. As he generally told it, he had watched in horror as an enormously overweight man at a nearby table devoured course after course as part of a birthday celebration. As the last course was about to be cleared, Kosinski summoned a waiter and sent the man a chocolate cake heaped with preposterous extra dollops of whipped cream and Hershey chocolate sauce. The waiter was to explain that the cake had been sent by the thin man at the next table.

With his napkin tucked in in the best French manner, the fat man devoured the cake, blowing kisses in Kosinski's direction as he ate. On the way out of the restaurant, Kosinski paused to receive the man's expressions of gratitude. "Don't thank me," he snapped. "I was hoping that I might have the pleasure of watching you die."

Kosinski's alienation from food calls to mind Kafka's fictional Hunger Artist, who explained on his deathbed after a career of professional fasting that he never found the food he liked. Like his obsession with death and blindness, it was partly a conceit—in fact, before going out he sometimes satisfied his appetite with a meal of Mrs. Paul's fish sticks, the taste for which would in time become a celebrity anecdote in itself. Yet it was not entirely a con, or if it was, Kosinski himself was to be its final, unwitting victim.

Another theme of the Yale years was Kosinski's problematic relationship to his Polish heritage. It was the source of constant jokes and quips. As he fell into the company of the Styrons, the Millers, the Sadruddin Aga Khans, and the Javitses, his estrangement from the circle of Polish émigrés had deepened. The humor by which he contrasted this literary world with his Polish background was embodied in his anecdote of his one meeting with John Hersey, then a Yale housemaster. Hersey, he quipped, had invited him over to help crate up his Mercedes for shipping to Europe because "a Polish person would appreciate the value of an expensive automobile."

In the spring of 1970, he had initiated a request to renounce his Polish citizenship, giving as his reason his fear of being held indefinitely if he should ever be aboard a plane that was forced to set down in an Eastern European nation. To support this, he cited a case in which something of the sort had actually happened. To Jean Kilbourne, who had decided to continue their relationship despite his theft of her journals, he went on endlessly about Lithuanian sailor Simas Kudirka, whom the American authorities had handed back to the Soviets. He was genuinely moved by Kudirka's plight, and genuinely afraid of being himself recaptured by the Polish authorities, however improbable this might be. He did not seem to consider that a government really determined to hold him would not be greatly deterred by his renunciation of Polish citizenship. It is hard to resist the conclusion that the desire to renounce his Polish citizenship stemmed from the need for a *psychological* barrier against a nation, a past, and perhaps a part of himself, all of which posed the threat of reaching out to destroy. The Polish authorities, however, were more than willing to enter into the game; and the exchange of letters grew ever more filled with accusations as the Poles dragged their feet and imposed requirement after requirement, leaving Jerzy Michalowski, husband of Kosinski's old friend Mira Michalowska and now Polish ambassador to the United States, caught impossibly in the middle.

At the same time, among a small group of American friends, he was becoming more noticeably Jewish. Cynthia Ozick, who wrote him an almost gushing letter of appreciation upon the publication of *Being There*, knew him immediately as Jewish, and more—a Jewish survivor and witness to the Holocaust in Poland. In a reshaping of the story that he had once told to Jack Kuper, another survivor who had wandered Eastern Poland as a child— that he was a Jew born to Christian parents—he now told the equally strained variant that, yes, of course, he was Jewish, but his parents had not made this fact known to him until he was twenty-one years old.

4.

By now the academic world, an industry with a voracious appetite for literary raw material, was beginning to discover a rich resource to be mined in Kosinski's work. In particular, two young scholars at the University of Northern Iowa—Dan Cahill, English department chairman and moving force behind *The North American Review*, and Jerome Klinkowitz, whose interest lay in innovative literary forms—discovered that they had a shared determination to bring Kosinski's work within the bounds of legitimate academic study. Their interest prefigured a pattern in which Kosinski's work would excite critical interest in more or less direct proportion to the distance of the university from New York City.

On November 7, 1971—the Sunday after Halloween— Klinkowitz, who had a tentative appointment to interview Kosinski in a few weeks, received a telephone call in Chicago. "This is Jerzy Kosinski in New Haven," said the familiar Bela Lugosi–like voice, "will you please come and see me tonight!" Klinkowitz demurred until the voice added, "I may have to leave the country very suddenly with no advance notice at all. Perhaps I might never return, who knows? I could be dead tomorrow, as the saying goes. So please, we should do the interview very soon while we have the chance."

Klinkowitz took the next flight for New York and had friends drive him up to New Haven, arriving at 9:00 P.M. Kosinski greeted him warmly. As Kiki produced a pair of Heineken Lights, Kosinski asked Klinkowitz about his name. "That's *Klinkiewicz*, Polish, right?" Then Kosinski launched into a discussion of his

306 James Park Sloan

work while two tape recorders turned, Klinkowitz's and his own. At 10:30 the telephone rang, and Kosinski snapped off both tape recorders before speaking, first in English, then French, then Polish. He apologized to Klinkowitz, explaining shortly, "It's my brother in Warsaw."

He went on to explain that he had recently learned that his mother had three—at most six—months to live. Because he could not safely return to Poland, they were to meet in Amsterdam, "a free city." They would meet there on Tuesday.

"Is that what your brother says?" Kiki emerged to interject.

"More," he added. "I was told to look into the matter of disposing of a body in Amsterdam." Kiki gasped. "The flight, the doctors say, will kill Mama."

After the phone call, the interview continued for three hours, as Kosinski went through his stock repertory of stories: his muteness and his separation from his parents during the German occupation; his escape from Poland using forged recommendations from four eminent scholars (the first time this story appeared in an interview); the liberation that came from writing in an alien language; his menial jobs upon arrival in New York; his choice of fiction writing over his first interest, photography. In later years Kosinski would become remarkably adroit at handling academic researchers, sweeping them along with his basic version of his story while skillfully fading to vague generalities when they touched upon potentially troublesome areas. With Klinkowitz, however, he was astonishingly specific in some of his answers. Perhaps it was the real stress of the moment, or perhaps he had not yet grasped the significant distinction between a celebrity interview and an interview by academic critics. Comments made in celebrity interviews were highly perishable and, given the nature of the form, presumed to be inaccurate. Scholars, though they might appear to be slow moving and highly manipulable when compared with the Cleveland Amorys of the world, did not go away. Statements made to academic interviewers became part of the permanent record because they had enduring importance in the interviewer's career.

Klinkowitz published a first, adulatory version of the interview in 1973, in Joe David Bellamy's avant-garde periodical *fic-*

tion international, by which time it contained little that was not already known. Klinkowitz, however, was fascinated with Kosinski and awed by his life and literary accomplishments. He stayed on the case. In 1979, after a visit to Poland led him to a partial revision of these views, he produced a second account of that evening, incorporating the same material but in a context far less supportive of the Kosinski myth. Three years later, in 1982, that second telling would figure importantly in the major crisis of Kosinski's career.

In the meantime, however, one aspect of the evening would prove to be as real as it was melodramatic. Kosinski indeed flew to Amsterdam to meet his mother, who was dying of cancer. Although she survived the trip, it was the last time he would see her. She died on January 21, 1972, ten years almost to the day after the death of her husband, and was buried next to him in Doly cemetery outside Lodz, the Jewish cemetery no longer being in use. Her death effectively severed Kosinski's ties with his brother, who was by then a practicing physician in Lodz. There had been bad feelings between them from the beginning, as Henryk's arrival had disrupted Kosinski's status as cherished only child and must also have been associated with the difficulties of their move deeper into the Polish countryside. And no two brothers could have been more different than the mercurial Jurek and the stolid, plodding Henryk. Returning to Poland near the end of his life, Kosinski behaved generously toward his old nanny, Anna Grzelak, who was allowed to live in and eventually inherited from him his mother's apartment in Warsaw. With Henryk, however, he spent only an hour or two, almost entirely in the company of others.

Kosinski marked his mother's death by throwing himself ever more frantically into his career and his climb upward through the New York social world. *Being There* had been named book of the year by the *Times* of London, and that same day Peter Sellers called Kosinski from London to congratulate him and express his interest in playing the part of Chauncey Gardiner. Gil Shiva, who aspired to a career as a film producer, had bought an option, and the general contours of a film deal began to be visible. Financing proved hard to get, however, and it would be six years before the final package could be put together.

Meanwhile there was his social life in the city. On January 22 Yevgeni Yevtushenko read "Babi Yar" to a rapt audience at Lincoln Center, and that evening Kosinski attended a dinner party at the home of Marian Javits, where Yevtushenko and Henry Kissinger faced each other across the table. Yevtushenko, with his beautiful and sad eyes and next to no English, spent the evening talking with Kissinger, who had no Russian but was determined to have an important human exchange with the dissident poet. It took the shape, finally, of an exchange of watches, as Kissinger examined Yevtushenko's inexpensive Russian watch while Yevtushenko tried on Kissinger's elegant Tissot. At the end of the evening, the Tissot was still on Yevtushenko's wrist.

The next day Kissinger called Marian Javits. "Marian," he moaned, "where is my watch?" The alarmed hostess then called Kosinski and asked him, as a Russian speaker, to remedy the misunderstanding. No Yevtushenko fan, Kosinski amused friends at dinner parties by scribbling commonplace sentiments in verse that he called "instant Yevtushenko." As Kosinski later told the story, it was a scam that Yevtushenko, himself a bit of a con man, had played before. He swapped cheap Russian watches for Rolexes and the like. What he did with the expensive watches back in Moscow, Kosinski couldn't say. Perhaps he sold them on the black market. In any case, Kosinski called Yevtushenko and prevailed upon him to return the secretary of state's watch.

That same winter Kosinski made the acquaintance of Jacques Monod, who had shared the Nobel Prize for Physiology or Medicine with André Lwoff and François Jacob in 1965. Head of the prestigious Institut Pasteur, Monod had written an extended essay-meditation on the philosophical implications of contemporary biology entitled *Chance and Necessity*. Responding to Teilhard de Chardin, the Jesuit paleontologist who argued that evolution revealed the unfolding of something akin to a divine plan, Monod argued compellingly that the evidence of genetics was for a series of random events that were decisive as thresholds in the development of species. Perhaps because the word *Chance* was central in both works, Monod's book and Kosinski's *Being There* were reviewed together in the *San Jose Examiner*. When Monod came to America that winter, a woman from *Le Monde* who had interviewed Kosinski introduced them.

Kosinski was as fascinated by Monod's pedigree as by his work. Monod *père* had come from a distinguished family of intellectual Huguenots, his widow was a Jewish museum curator and archeologist, and Monod himself was a concert-level cellist who had, before becoming a molecular biologist, been offered a job as a symphony conductor—a story oddly reminiscent of the myth Kosinski invented for his own parents, and possibly also mythic to some degree. Are young men in the middle of scientific training often offered symphony conductorships? With his good friend Albert Camus, Monod had also figured prominently in the Communist-backed French resistance. With a family home in Cannes, Monod now lived a life that touched the margins of the world of the international jet set.

With his mother and father now gone, Kosinski saw in Monod the last in a series of surrogate parents, a person to pronounce judgment on his life and work and indicate by his own choices a possible future path. Later this would have a fateful consequence, but now it brought into Kosinski's life a man who combined intellectual engagement with a lighthearted sense of play. One evening in the early days of the friendship, Kosinski took Monod to the World Trade Center, then under construction. Persuading the night watchman that the handsome, distinguished Frenchman was in fact the building's architect, he gained access to the elevator. Together the two men rode to the top and together they surveyed the world's greatest city as only a few workmen had ever seen it.

That spring Kosinski managed to get himself named to the panel of judges for the National Book Award, which gave a nomination to Monod's *Chance and Necessity*. He had only a hazy idea of the larger intellectual dialogue into which Monod's work fit, choosing to emphasize the very partial and qualified principle of randomness, but he did his homework thoroughly, in his capacity as a judge reading 125 books published in English translation—an ironic role that cannot have been lost on him. Kosinski proved a powerful advocate. On April 14, the National Book Award went to *Chance and Necessity*.

Surprisingly, the relationship with Jean had survived the breach of trust, and Kosinski continued to make pilgrimages to Boston to see her. Sometimes Kiki drove him, and was dismissed for a day of shopping while he and Jean conducted a rendezvous. Sometimes they talked of marriage, although Jean could now add a concrete incident to her earlier fears of his "diabolical" nature. As she later saw it, the relationship endured as long as it did partly out of her particular vulnerability. Without quite realizing it, she was a heavy and dependent drinker, and thus prone to blurred judgment. When she changed this part of her life, her relationship with Kosinski would change as well. Yet if the relationship was in some ways exploitative, it also brought her good things. They shared an interest in deconstructing the subtexts of advertising, particularly as directed against women. Above all, the relationship served to build Jean's confidence in herself. Eventually she was able to emerge as a successful public lecturer.

By that spring the book that had begun with Jean's journals was approaching completion. Called *The Devil Tree*, it would be the most mystifying of all Kosinski's novels—a book that made little sense unless read with a key. Two keys, in fact, for there were, essentially, two narrative tracks.

The first, involving the relationship between the protagonist, Jonathan Whalen, and his girlfriend Karen, was largely drawn from the relationship between Kosinski and Jean Kilbourne. Kosinski had made much of the fact that their names had the same initials—JK—and both contained thirteen letters. Now the two protagonists, Jonathan and Karen, combined those two initials and thirteen letters in their names. In a way, the novel, which had almost pulled them apart, now melded them into one.

Many passages incorporate dialogues between Kosinski and Jean, in a manner resembling the disembodied dialogues between the man and woman of *Steps*. Other passages, taken very closely from Jean's journal, render dialogues between Jean and a close woman friend, Connie Lorman, called Susan in the novel, with whom she often discussed her love affair. The push and pull of their relationship—the jealousies that arise between two people who are living other lives, the difficulties of scheduling and last-minute cancellations—become the framework of the Jonathan-Karen narrative.

Sometimes the novel gives quirky or trendy views: Jonathan's arousal by the smell of menstrual blood, Karen's pleasure in the pull of menstruation and preference for natural smells over cosmetics—a topic on which Jean Kilbourne would later lecture. In other instances, the melding of the two characters amounts to an appropriation of Jean's experience; Jonathan's therapy group is, in fact, based on Jean Kilbourne's. Many of the dialogues and interior monologues carry intriguing psychological insights, as in Karen's explanation that seminude pictures of her modeling in European magazines provide a defense against her terror of aging. The exploration of sexuality is almost as interesting as in *Steps*, informed as it is by the sense of a real relationship at stake, but the integration of the sexual and philosophical dialogues is far more problematic.

The reasons have to do with the second track of the novel, whose theme is the American dream realized. It deals specifically with privileged flower children, a category that might in some sense include Jean Kilbourne but principally takes its inspiration from Mary Weir's son, David. For Jonathan Whalen is not a Polish émigré writer but the son of Horace Sumner Whalen, a self-made magnate of heavy industry who closely resembles Ernest T. Weir. Cosmopolitan in many of his views, the elder Whalen is so chauvinistic about America that he fires his loyal and trusted valet for purchasing a superior razor of foreign manufacture. Like Weir, he is depicted as a distant father who communicates with his son by dictated letters. Like David Weir, the lonely boy persuades himself that cigarette butts left in an ashtray contain his father's thoughts. The "devil tree" of the title is the baobab, which to the natives seems to have its roots in the air. The devil destroys the young baobabs, the natives say. Yet this young baobab proves to be a chip off the diabolical old block—suggesting a second reading of the title as a pun: "deviltry." The "David Weir" side of the story chronicles the orphaned Jonathan's struggle to find himself while traveling in Asia as a draft evader, his use of alcohol and drugs, his participation in an encounter group and a secret society, and his fight to gain control of his own inheritance.

Mary Weir is depicted as Jonathan's troubled alcoholic mother. In one scene she is shown on a rampage, throwing expensive jewelry out the window of a cruise ship. Other elements taken directly from life include the French governess who looked after David and Mary's propensity for referring to Pittsburgh as "Shitsburgh." A Kosinski-like character explains to Jonathan how he met Mrs. Whalen as an archeologist and translated a catalogue of her art objects, refusing payment. The Kosinski character does not stay with Mrs. Whalen because of the disparity in their income and lifestyles, citing the old Kosinski theme of inability even to pay the tips.

In essence, Kosinski was splitting his own persona into two parts: an older self only incidental to the novel, and a younger self merged in some sense with Jean Kilbourne and in a deeper sense with David Weir. Such a protagonist presented inherent problems. How could a single individual combine the intellect displayed in the dialogues with Karen and the ditziness imputed to David Weir? How could the David Weir character exercise Kosinskian ruthlessness, murdering his guardians? The real question, however, is what psychological dynamic would impel Kosinski to undertake such a thing.

On the surface it may simply have seemed the solution to his creative impasse—a way to draw upon his knowledge of David Weir, his poor opinion of the affluent flower children, and the rich material of his affair with Jean Kilbourne. Yet with parts that fit together so badly, why did he persevere? Between the failing relationship with Jean Kilbourne and the artistic failure of *The Devil Tree* there is an important linkage. In the one case, a matter of love, Kosinski found himself not quite able to break through to intimate and authentic encounter—to be fully present, coinciding at every point with himself—while in the other, a matter of literary creation, he could not muster the painful honesty of delivering his truest and deepest experience in a character with complexity and depth to match his own. Instead he downloaded and downscaled his emotions into a much more limited protago-

nist based on his perception of David Weir. The crisis of his inner
life and the crisis of his creative life were thus simultaneous. As
for David Weir, he had long suspected Kosinski of trying to usurp
his life. Now in *The Devil Tree* he was doing exactly that. Aside
from being a failed narrative strategy, the book gives a peculiar
display of dissociative personality. It was as though Kosinski genuinely didn't know where he left off and another individual began. Feeling that the borders of the self were weakly defended, he
attempted to shore them up by swallowing David Weir.

The relationship with David Weir is one of the more fascinating, and puzzling, in Kosinski's life. Already he had intervened
actively in Weir's life, bringing him together with his wife much
as he had brought together Gibby Folger and Wojtek Frykowski,
though less openly. In the summer of 1970, while working at an
auto garage he owned in London, Weir was approached by an attractive Polish-born woman named Ewa Fichtner, who seemed to
know a great deal about him already. They saw a bit of each other
at the time, but the relationship did not take in a permanent way.
The next year Weir returned to New York and, having a sudden
yen for Ewa, mentioned it to Kosinski; less than an hour later, he
received a call from Ewa. They began seeing each other and eventually married.

Before meeting Weir, Ewa had been living in Los Angeles as
part of the Polanski circle, trying to get work as an actress. As David's wife, Ewa—formerly a Dior model in Poland, in which role
she was known as "Lolita"—took the heir to the Weir fortune
firmly in hand. Under the terms of Ernest Weir's will, David
could gain full access to his inheritance only by demonstrating
success as a businessman, and Ewa encouraged him to try working at Bache and Company as a stockbroker, an effort that did not
succeed. One day early in the marriage, Ewa received a call from
Kosinski summoning her to New Haven, and to David Weir's astonishment, she left immediately. Piecing together accounts of
their meeting later, he concluded that Kosinski had some sort of
vehicle for blackmailing her. Kosinski's version of the story
would eventually be told in *Cockpit*.

The Devil Tree marked the moment in Kosinski's career when a
critical revision of his work set in. He had received an advance of

$120,000 from Harcourt Brace Jovanovich, a 50-percent increase from *Being There*. The novel was published on February 14, 1973, preceded by negative advance notices. In his prepub review for *Library Journal*, Peter Dollard set the tone: "The characterization is bad, the narrative boring and many parts are simply sopho-moric. . . . All in all, the book reads more like a bad first novel than the work of a mature writer."

On February 11 Robert Alter, an academic critic well versed in contemporary modes, took up the attack in the *New York Times Book Review*. "From beginning to end this is a loose web of stylis-tic and cultural clichés," Alter began a review entitled "Pulp-fiction Style, Pop-Psychology Jargon, and a Genuinely Sadistic Imagination." "Kosinski's prose, with its series of short sentences occasionally embellished by an elaborate simile, runs readily to the characteristic vice of 'simple' styles, which is to fall into the hackneyed formulas of mass journalism and pulp fiction." And Alter did not stop there. *The Devil Tree*, he went on to argue, led him to a rereading of Kosinski's earlier work, exposing the emp-tiness and "sadistic imagination" that lay behind these overin-flated accomplishments.

Kosinski was devastated, both personally and professionally. Describing Alter as a specialist in "Hebrew Israeli poetry," he called upon friends to come to his defense, thus reinvoking the old pattern of recontexting and politicizing criticism. Two sup-porters provided responses, but the Alter review stood, marking a turning point in the way Kosinski novels would be perceived within the informed literary community. Other developments were in the works, however, which would enable him to tran-scend, for a time, this shift in literary fortune.

5.

PEN—the International Association of Poets, Playwrights, Edi-tors, Essayists and Novelists—was founded after World War I by John Galsworthy in order to provide a community for writers and give them a larger voice in world affairs. For years the PEN American Center functioned as a New York social group centered in the circle of two sisters, Marchette and B. J. Chute, each of whom served as president. By the late 1960s a number of writers, led by Charles Bracelen Flood and Thomas Fleming serving successive terms as president, undertook to change the profile of American PEN and increase its clout. In May 1973 they needed a candidate to extend and broaden their work, ideally a writer with a prominent public profile. Flood headed the nominating committee, and his first choice for the presidency was Isaac Bashevis Singer. When Flood telephoned Singer to offer him the post, the response was hysterical laughter.

"Have you ever got a wrong number," Singer said. "If you made me PEN president, I would destroy your organization in three weeks."

Flood and Fleming went back to the drawing board, and settled instead on Jerzy Kosinski. He had not, they realized, been active in the administrative side of PEN affairs, but he had been a regular attendee of the weekly social gatherings since the early 1960s, and as a winner of the National Book Award, he offered the necessary literary stature. As a European, perhaps he could make some inroads in Europe, winning the American branch more respect. Fleming paid a visit to Kosinski's apartment and put the offer to him. Kosinski accepted on the condition that Fleming promise to stay at his side to help with PEN politics, letting him in on "where the bodies are buried." The slate of officers had been drawn up and circulated when Fleming received a telephone call from George Reavey.

Fleming knew Reavey as a poet/translator who regularly attended the weekly PEN cocktail party. During his presidency at PEN, he had arranged for Reavey to receive funds for dental work out of an account maintained for writers who were financially embarrassed. "Tom," Reavey told him, "you can't let that man be president of PEN. He didn't write *The Painted Bird*. I did."

Fleming was appalled. He had heard various rumors about Kosinski. When Kosinski was up for PEN membership, a board member who reviewed for the *Herald Tribune* had put forward a particularly vicious conjecture to the effect that he might have had something to do with the death of Mary Weir. There were also, already, rumors that Kosinski was somehow connected with the CIA, and Fleming himself had heard several versions of Kosinski's escape from Poland. Now he asked Reavey for further details. "Kosinski gave me an illiterate manuscript," Reavey insisted, "part English, part Polish, and part Russian. I put it into prose, added details, and got five hundred dollars." Kosinski, in his view, was both a literary fraud and a cheapskate.

A straightforward man, Fleming went directly to Kosinski and informed him of Reavey's accusation. "Did you give him *The Painted Bird* to work on?" he asked.

Kosinski replied, "I do admit I asked him to help me. I knew him as a translator. Parts were in Russian. I did pay him five hundred dollars. It's all he was worth."

Fleming reflected upon this answer and called Charlie Flood, who also knew Reavey. In the view of both men, Reavey was an embittered man, and not quite stable, a man who felt his own poetry had gone unrecognized, who had somehow ended up far from the glory of which young writers always dream. The two men considered the situation from various angles until Flood finally said, "Let's go with Jerzy. You and I will jointly decide. You talk to George and tell him the decision."

Fleming then called Reavey, who was indebted to Fleming personally and to the PEN organization, and informed him of the decision, adding bluntly: "I hope you don't make this an issue at some PEN meeting." It was the end of Fleming's friendship with Reavey, but Reavey's accusations passed into limbo and Kosinski was elected PEN president.

Although the Reavey flap had been contained without serious damage, it was the first inkling of a problem that would dog Kosinski for the rest of his life and, eight years later, would bring his career and his life to their major crisis. As long as he was an unimportant writer of middling reputation, the Reaveys in his past remained somnolent, but the higher he rose, the greater the incentive for them to make disclosures that could besmirch his reputation. Thus as he cut an ever greater figure, there was a growing buzz of rumor as former acquaintances told their tales within their own limited circles and trackers of this newly established superstar began to encounter contradictions in his story.

As his vulnerability to exposure increased, he must have lived in a constant state of high anxiety. Solidly centered individuals do not fabricate as Kosinski did, so it is a fair presumption that, despite his success, he was acutely aware of the hollowness at the core of his being—a hollowness put into ever starker contrast with his public acclaim. The higher he flew, the more terrible his risk when and if the bubble burst.

In order to fulfill his duties as PEN president, Kosinski gave up active teaching at Yale, although he retained an affiliation with the university, as well as the New Haven getaway at 111 Park Street, until his death. Toward the end, after the *Village Voice* scandal had greatly damaged his position as intellectual-in-residence to the glitterati, he would often speak wistfully of Yale, lamenting his decision to leave.

The doubters about his PEN presidency, however, were in for a surprise. Kosinski took on the job with focus and energy, and demonstrated both political and administrative skills that none of his previous experience had revealed. He had strong and genuine feelings about the persecution of writers and intellectuals—the "freedom to write" issue that put PEN in the same camp as the American Civil Liberties Union and Amnesty International—and he applied libertarian principles uniformly, to regimes of both the Left and the Right, as well as to abuses within systems that were democratic.

If he had any deeply ingrained ideology of his own, it was a sort of paranoid anarchism, with special emphasis on the plight of unusual and gifted individuals within "collectivities." His special geographic interest was, of course, Eastern Europe, but the first specific case in which he became involved was the imprisonment of Iranian writer Reza Baraheni by SAVAK, the Shah's secret police agency. On December 16, together with Joseph Heller and Dwight Macdonald, he made a public plea for Baraheni's release. At the same time he worked behind the scenes with Amnesty International, and through friends like Sadruddin Aga Khan he approached Iranian Prime Minister Hoveyda, calling upon him to honor his best impulses while holding out the threat of continued negative press if the persecution of Baraheni continued. Baraheni was released.

On January 6, 1974, Kosinski joined with Turkish writer Talat Halman, his friend Arthur Miller, and Hannah Arendt, with whom he worked despite cordial dislike, to suggest to U.N. Secretary-General Kurt Waldheim that 1974 be designated World Amnesty Year for 380 writers imprisoned in thirty countries.

Another of his concerns, superficially more mundane, was the question of medical insurance coverage for freelance writers and editors. Because they did not belong to a risk pool, many writers found themselves in George Reavey's position, needing health care they could not afford; PEN was able to provide assistance in individual cases but was unable to solve the larger problem. Now, using PEN's clout, Kosinski prevailed upon Blue Cross to treat freelance writers and editors as a risk pool, enabling individuals to purchase coverage. It was a provisional program for Blue Cross, and it later collapsed. Writers and editors were evidently more unhealthy than many population segments, or at least less profitable to insure. It was, however, an extraordinary tribute to Kosinski's skills at negotiation and persuasion that he got the program off the ground at all. As an observation of gaps in medical coverage, it was visionary.

In February, Alexander Solzhenitsyn was deported to the West, ending a long period of house arrest and harassment in the Soviet Union. Kosinski had often spoken of Solzhenitsyn's plight, lending his public voice to that of International PEN president Günter Grass in demanding that Solzhenitsyn be freed. However, the manner of Solzhenitsyn's departure from his homeland, as a writer tried and criminalized, was less than satisfying. A few days after Solzhenitsyn arrived in West Germany, another Eastern Bloc writer, Mihajl Mihajlov, was denied a passport to attend a California symposium on Forbidden and Discouraged Knowledge. Once again Kosinski spoke out publicly as PEN president, speculating that the denial of Mihajlov's request was linked to Solzhenitsyn's deportation and amounted to a reassertion of the absolute control of the Marxist state.

The year 1974 may have marked the depths of the Cold War from the point of view of the West, and particularly for civil libertarians. American policy in Vietnam had collapsed and the idealism of the 1960s had given way to the self-indulgent "me" generation. The Nixon presidency was rapidly coming unstuck as a result of the Watergate scandal, and later that year, on August 8, Richard Nixon would become the first president compelled to resign under threat of impeachment. The American economy was suffering from the worst recession since the 1930s, the stock and bond markets had collapsed, and a somber and paranoid mood had settled upon American society, with Pink Floyd's *Dark Side of the Moon* and rural gothic films like *The Texas Chainsaw Massacre* emerging as cultural icons. In this atmosphere of suspicion, Senator Frank Church had begun a massive investigation into the historical activities of the CIA, which would eventually turn up material on the CIA/USIA book program and involvement with the Ford Foundation bearing tangentially on Kosinski's early days in the United States and providing fodder for the 1982 *Village Voice* exposé.

At the time, however, amidst this apparent collapse of the West, Kosinski held to a staunch position as a civil libertarian, a position that was not without a price. Informing his attorney Allan Schwartz and other close friends that the KGB was watching him, he renewed his effort to renounce his Polish citizenship, writing the Polish Embassy under a PEN letterhead. The KGB may well have paid passing attention to his activities. Certainly, their chairbound researchers must have clipped mentions of his civil libertarian statements in the American press, noting him as a persistent and annoying adversary.

Yet the PEN job did provide compensating moments. In late April he was elected to a second term as PEN president; on May 5 his presence at the celebration of the twenty-fifth anniversary of the National Book Awards brought pleasant personal memories. Later that month he presided over the annual PEN black-tie dinner held in the Tower Suite of the Time/Life Building, with Carlos Fuentes as guest of honor. Because of Fuentes's prominence in Mexican politics, Secret Servicemen in sunglasses prowled among the guests, whispering into their walkie-talkies. Kosinski was in his glory at this sort of thing. What better indicator of the distance he had traveled from the Warchols' semidetached apartment in Dabrowa than celebrities milling around in the company of Secret Service agents?

Set against the pleasures of the weekly social gatherings and annual black-tie dinners was a chronic problem involving, ironically, the complaints of translators. On June 12 PEN held a translation conference in New York, where the distinguished translator Gregory Rabassa demanded a set rate of pay and credit standards for translators; as its host, Kosinski must have cringed inwardly. More pressing was the complaint of a group of local translators at Columbia University, led by Robert Payne and Frank MacShane, who put together a joint proposal with PEN to the National Endowment for the Arts. At the last minute, the PEN attorney advised the board not to participate, knocking the props from under the Columbia group. Angry, and certain that Kosinski and Fleming had encouraged them and then conspired to pull the plug, they descended upon a board meeting and proceeded to turn it into a shouting match. Fleming shouted right back at them, giving his point of view on the matter, but Kosinski turned deathly white. After things calmed down, he admitted he had been terrified. "I don't like that," he told Fleming. "You Irish, you like fights. I'll be depressed for a day, maybe a week. I won't be able to write."

Escape was provided by Crans-Montana, in the Swiss Alps. Montana and almost-contiguous Crans are situated on a natural balcony high above the Rhone Valley, looking out onto one of the most breathtaking mountain panoramas in the world. The view extends from the Simplon mountains in the east to Mont Blanc in the southwest, taking in the Weisshorn, Zinal Rothorn, Gabelhorn, Matterhorn, and Dent Blanche. The Plaine Morte glacier provides open skiing from almost 11,000 feet, as easy or difficult as the skier chooses to make it—an important point with Kosinski—and with a spectacular view throughout the descent. The climate is unusually sunny and dry, and it is still a center for patients with tuberculosis. Kosinski had discovered the area, in the canton of Valais, when he was traveling with Mary Weir. When the earnings of his European editions, which he held in

Swiss accounts, were sufficient, in 1972, he purchased an efficiency apartment in a modern building, Beaumanière B-4, in Crans.

In its simplicity the apartment was consistent with Kosinski's longtime aesthetic, resembling all his personal dwelling places going back to the semidetached apartment his parents rented from the farmer Warchol. He could take or leave his immediate surroundings, which he regarded as purely functional, and as a refuge from the world. The purpose of one's choice of residence was to gain easy access to something extraordinary—the bright lights of New York, the intellectual sanctuary of New Haven, or the magnificent view and skiing of Plaine Morte. He wrote about Crans-Montana and Plaine Morte in an essay for the *New York Times* Travel section's special skiing edition on November 1, 1981, and incorporated it as a setting in *Blind Date*, the names changed to ValPina and PicSoleil respectively, he said, so that tourists wouldn't rush to go there.

For the most part, Crans served Kosinski as a refuge from the pressures of being Jerzy Kosinski. It was not that his standing as a writer was exactly unknown there, but it was taken as a matter of course. There, he was just another citizen of Crans. Eventually he would invite friends from his literary and social set—Barbara Ungeheuer, who had been on the German Olympic team, skied there, and others of his New York set dropped in—but it was often a place to get together with the less glitzy side of his acquaintance. Soon after buying the apartment he flew Joel Charles over to ski with him, reprising, in a way, their more humble skiing experiences in Connecticut. It was the last time they would be together for any period of time, but suggests a subtle continuity in his life. Even Kosinski couldn't sustain a constant public performance without people and places to which he could retreat.

Situated in the French-speaking part of Switzerland, Crans had a dozen families who traced their roots back to the twelfth century, with all the attendant jealousies and rivalries. It was, in that respect, much like the small universe of Polish intellectuals—or, for that matter, the New York social set—except that here Kosinski could sit back and enjoy the game as a spectator. His closest friends among the local citizens were André Moret, a plastic surgeon, and his wife, Marie Maud; he became especially close to the Morets' son Patrick, an extraordinary stunt skier and daredevil, who, with his brother, took a terrified Kosinski on a glider flight. Exchanging long letters when Kosinski was back in America, Patrick recounted the details of his life, the ordeal of military service, and the like, while Kosinski guided his reading. In turn Patrick pushed upon Kosinski the writings of French philosopher-essayist E. M. Cioran, who also happened to be a favorite writer of Jean Kilbourne and one whose intellectual musings on suicide resembled Kosinski's.

Kosinski first met Moret as the result of a *maladie* not altogether *imaginaire*. New to Crans, he had been feeling ill, with a constriction in his throat, and inquired if there was a local doctor. He was informed that there was a doctor of extraordinary reputation who happened, coincidentally, to be a resident. As he told the story later, the person who sent him to Dr. Moret had taken one look at his nose and assumed that the kind of doctor he needed was a plastic surgeon. In fact, André Moret was able to put his delicate hands to good use with Kosinski, who had small benign polyps in his throat. We'll vaporize them, he told Kosinski, who expressed fear of the invasive procedure. Touch my arm as soon as you feel anything, Moret said. After a few minutes Kosinski asked Moret when he was going to begin and was informed that the procedure was completed.

In the course of that first, emergency, visit, Moret mentioned to his wife that he was looking after a patient named Jerzy Kosinski. There was a writer by that name, she told him, and he happened to have written one of her favorite books, *L'Oiseau bariole*. Introductions were then made afresh, and the Morets invited Kosinski and Kiki to dinner. Afterwards, when locals would ask how he and Dr. Moret happened to meet, Kosinski would point to his nose. "I had this tiny little nose," he would say. "I went to Dr. Moret and asked, 'Would you build a nose for me?'"

Kosinski eventually watched Moret perform a number of operations. In Kosinski's eyes, Moret performed miracles in rebuilding harelips and noses as well as executing skillful cosmetic tucks of faces and figures, yet Moret regarded his work as routine, almost mundane. Kosinski marveled at the skillful cutting, folding, and reshaping—in a way so much like the work of a novelist. Once he saw Moret's hand move inside a patient's skin as if into a pocket. In *Blind Date*, he gave Moret a cameo as an unnamed plastic surgeon driven to defeat blind nature with human rationality.

Kosinski often did first drafts of his novels in Crans, but never final drafts, explaining that he found it difficult to produce satisfactory English prose when the language spoken in his daily life was French. Through much of 1974 he had been working on a new novel, once again, happily, with the help of Peter Skinner. By the end of October he was also reunited with his old publisher, Houghton Mifflin, by a somewhat circuitous route. Both *Being There* and *The Devil Tree* had failed to "earn out" their advances at Harcourt, although the paperback versions of all of Kosinski's novels continued to sell splendidly. As a result, Kosinski became a pathbreaker in a new publishing structure in which paperback rights are sold first, then the hardcover, with escalator clauses built in for hardcover success.

This new trend in publishing acknowledged the growing importance of paperback sales, a pattern that served Kosinski, with his youthful following, particularly well. Bantam was an eager taker, providing Kosinski with an advance that jumped to $225,000, and it was early enough in the game that, when Bantam later backed away from his final novel, he could claim that he had virtually put them into the hardcover business.

The manuscript was then submitted to four hardcover publishers, who were required to bid on it in less than a week. By that time Paul Brooks and Dorothy de Santillana were no longer around. Richard McAdoo and Austin Olney were now the key figures in the decision, and the surviving members of Houghton Mifflin's Trade Management Committee saw the opportunity to remedy their earlier mistake. Their offer of $45,000 was the winning bid.

6.

In May of 1975 Kosinski was due to step down after serving two full terms as PEN president, and the same group who had selected Kosinski now undertook, with Kosinski's help, a search for his successor. They settled on Gay Talese, then known as the author of *The Kingdom and the Power*, about the *New York Times*, and *Honor Thy Father*, about Mafia figure Joe Bonanno. Kosinski knew Talese through David Halberstam and his Polish-born wife, Elzbieta Czyzewska. He approached Talese and informed him that he was the board's choice, and Talese naively accepted. When the slate was announced, all hell broke loose.

This time it was not a matter of subterranean murmurings and a few telephone calls. Donald Barthelme protested, arguing that Talese was only a pop journalist, and Ted Solotaroff joined in, protesting that the organization was being run by a handful of conspirators. The rump group soon enlisted Grace Paley, and, in a crushing blow, managed to get Arthur Miller, then the president of International PEN, to validate the revolt and serve as its spokesman. While various arguments were marshaled against Talese, including the high-handedness of the nominating committee, his lesser status as a journalist, and the subject matter of his work in progress (contemporary American sexual behavior), the real target was, clearly, Kosinski.

Tom Fleming saw himself accused of being high-handed because he had stepped into a vacuum and taken responsibility. In his view, it was just a bunch of New York literary types acting in character. He wanted to make a fight of it, confident that the Talese nomination would prevail with votes from PEN members in the hinterlands. Kosinski and Talese, however, saw discretion as the better part of valor. Kosinski had never liked this sort of power struggle. Talese saw the threat of negative publicity and wrote Fleming to withdraw his name from consideration. The nomination went instead to the rump candidate, Muriel Rukeyser, who reaped the whirlwind, calling Fleming early in her presidency to ask, "Why does everybody hate me? What do I do now?"

Thus Kosinski's PEN presidency concluded on something of a sour note, though not without one more exalting evening. The an-

nual PEN dinner, held on the St. Regis roof on May 29, gave him
the usual salute to an outgoing president and honored President
Léopold Sédar Senghor of Senegal, who also happened to be
Kosinski's translator in that country. Drawing upon that evening,
Kosinski gave Senghor a deliciously naughty cameo in *Blind Date.*
The African leader emerges compromisingly from an inner room
wearing briefs and embraces his redheaded assistant only to re-
emerge a few moments later with the subtle observation that Levanter "might even have forgotten" their first meeting. Unlike
other public figures with cameos in the novel, Senghor is tactfully, if not particularly effectively, disguised as Ronsard-
Thibaudet Samael, President of the African Republic of Lotan.

Once again Kosinski was exalted by the presence of Secret Service
agents, and to turn delight into pure bliss, a prank worthy of his
own design spontaneously unfolded. Just as he was about to begin
the proceedings, one of the Secret Service agents came up to him
and whispered that a ranking French diplomat and his wife had arrived late without their invitations and could not be admitted without Kosinski's verification. "I'll be right back," Kosinski murmured
over the microphone. He then jumped from the dais, zigzagged between the tables, and rushed downstairs, using the emergency express elevator held open as part of security procedures.

"*Mais c'est incroyable!*" the furious diplomat said.

"I'm sorry for the inconvenience, Excellency," Kosinski replied.
"I'm here to escort you, and Madame, to your table. Please follow
me *toute de suite.*"

"It's about time! *Vous savez!*" the diplomat said.

Back up in the ballroom, in front of everyone, Kosinski led the
latecomers to their seats at the table closest to the dais. The diplomat then reached into his pocket, took out a crisp dollar bill,
and presented it discreetly to Kosinski. Accepting the tip gra-
ciously, Kosinski jumped back up on the dais and acknowledged
the tip over the open mike.

"*Mais non!*" the diplomat whispered, loud enough for the
room to break into laughter. "*Ô mon Dieu!*"

Cockpit, as the new novel was called, was scheduled for publication in June. It took the form of a confession framed by two ep-

igraphs, the first from Saint-Exupéry who undertakes to "play my games" from the cockpit of his aircraft during the fall of France, the second from Dostoyevsky's *The Possessed*, where the saintly Tihon comments on the demonic Stavrogin's confession. "Who will understand the true reasons for the confession?" asks Tihon, implying that Stavrogin's motive may be to have an impact on his audience as much as to cleanse his soul.

Kosinski's new novel was indeed confessional to a degree that his earlier works were not, although, as in the case of Stavrogin, not in such a way as to leave him legally culpable. It is the story of Tarden, a retired deep-cover operative of the category known as "hummingbirds," who has a history including games and adventures similar to Kosinski's. In its organization—a series of tight, self-contained, first-person vignettes—*Cockpit* goes back to the form of *Steps*, perhaps revealing the hand of Peter Skinner in the enterprise. Yet *Cockpit* is written closer to Kosinski's personal experience than *Steps.* Places and human beings have moved from the abstractions of *Steps* to become clearly identifiable—his own parents, his roommate Robert (who is so named in the text), Lilla van Saher (who is not); northern Italy and Paris.

The novel also expresses the important themes of his emotional life in more naked form, among them his drive for concealment and control and a need for omnipotence bordering on megalomania. Cast as a confession to a woman, the book begins as Tarden has an encounter with a prostitute at an apartment that is identifiably 440 East Seventy-ninth Street, where he has a cache of photos he has taken of nude women. Feeling short of breath, Tarden speculates on what the authorities would think if he died. His important documents are stored under assumed names in vaults around the city—a practice followed, less elaborately, by Kosinski himself. The novel then moves to an account of Tarden's escape from a collectivist state closely resembling the account of his escape from Poland Kosinski had given to Jerry Klinkowitz, though elaborated with a complexity that struck an amused Peter Skinner as rather excessive.

It is *Cockpit* that recounts the story of the murderous roommate Robert, which he told Mira Michalowska in 1958, and the story of having his own uniform made up, which by then he had already told on the *Tonight Show*, and it gives an account of the prank he may or may not have played by making random phone calls during the period of relocation in Poland after World War II. A subtext of this episode is the powerful suppressed conflict with his father. The State has bullied his father into surrendering property rights, and Tarden responds with phone calls bullying others, sending them scurrying to government offices, an activity that eventually gets his father arrested. Like each of his earlier novels, *Cockpit* plays games at the boundaries of fact and fiction. The story of Lilla van Saher and her false pregnancy is given to a character named Theodora—but with the added twists of an actual child, whom the devious and skillful Tarden cannot track down, and the identification of Theodora as the link between Tarden and the "Service." *Cockpit*'s mixing of such pseudo-confession with factual elements did much to feed the rumors that Kosinski had, indeed, some connection with various intelligence agencies.

Like Kosinski himself, Tarden delights in setting up dramatic scenarios, amusing himself by watching the behavior of human beings in miniplays of his devising. He steps into the life of a critic who has, interestingly, *plagiarized publications in a foreign journal*, and subjects the man to blackmail by the Service. He ferrets out the identity of a thriller writer named Duncan, finds him in a Danish fishing village, and provokes the man's suicide by the threat of disclosure. In his 1988 study entitled *Words in Search of Victims: The Achievement of Jerzy Kosinski*, critic Paul Lilly did what many readers must have done in noting the similarity of the "espionage writer" Duncan to Kosinski himself. Actually Duncan, whose four novels had been progressively less successful, bears a closer resemblance to Trevanian, author of *The Eiger Sanction*, whom Kosinski knew as a Basque living in exile in Toronto and suspected of connections with Basque terrorists. In a sense, however, Lilly was correct: both the plagiarizing critic and the novelist gone underground are psychologically suggestive depictions of a Kosinski who increasingly feared destruction by disclosure.

Tarden, like Kosinski, mesmerizes children, hates "collectivities," dislikes enclosed spaces like elevators (trapped in one, he attempts to dispel panic with an inner discourse on the nature of time); he is fascinated by memories that come to his mind unbidden and by his own blood, which flows without the agency of his will when he picks a scab; he dabbles in sexual improvisation, staging, and voyeurism. *Cockpit* represents, in fact, something of a sexual coming out, as sexual activity with a sadomasochistic undertone is depicted as willed and chosen by a protagonist more closely linked to Kosinski himself; it reveals far more of the inner psychodrama from which his small S-M playlets emerge, giving Tarden far less the character of passive participant or spectator.

Cockpit is, above all, about power. While many of the episodes are more identifiably derived from Kosinski's life than those in his previous work, a large number of them are modified by purely fictional twist endings, in which Tarden/Kosinski asserts his will by wreaking a terrible and ironic revenge. There is a formulaic quality to this new pattern, as though the novel has incorporated power fantasies of omnipotent wish fulfillment. At the same time, however, as if in grudging acknowledgment of the limitations of personal omnipotence, Tarden himself is thwarted and manipulated by game players cast in his own mold. The reader experiences his vulnerability in far greater measure than with the protagonist of *Steps*. Tarden wins some and he loses some. Indeed, Tarden is engaged in constant, artificial struggle with a game-playing world, over dubious prizes, with uneven results.

The ultimate game is played with Veronika, a twice-divorced aspiring actress of Belgian origin, who has been married to a Belgian count three times her age and then to the nephew of a theatrical agent, a nominal marriage keeping her available to be the agent's mistress. Though not classically beautiful, she is a striking woman, and Tarden puts a proposition to her: he will set her up with a thirty-five-year-old businessman whose wealthy parents have died in a plane crash if she, in turn, agrees to make herself sexually available to him on demand. Veronika accepts, marries the businessman, and then begins to renege on her agreement, whereupon Tarden lures her into his apartment, ties and gags her, and photographs her in the course of sex acts—graphically described—with three derelicts he has hired from the street.

The story details Veronika's use of a press agent to establish her as an international celebrity as well as her commissioning a reporter to do stories, and eventually a book, about her life; it mentions her efforts on behalf of her husband, who does not yet have full control of his estate, as well as her struggle to get personal control of his resources and become his chief heir. Tarden suspects that she is about to murder the businessman, and finds an occasion to warn her that he will take action. Promising to return the compromising photographs, Tarden persuades her to attend an air show, where he has bribed a test pilot to turn on the radar while she is standing in front of the cockpit of a new fighter, exposing her to a fatal dose of radiation.

The minidrama of Veronika, Tarden, and the young "businessman" employs many details from the triangular relationship of Ewa Fichtner, Kosinski, and David Weir. The ages are right, as are the physical descriptions, the broad outlines of personal history, the terms of the businessman's inheritance, and the orchestrated article in the Society section of the *Times*. Once again Kosinski was insinuating himself, fictionally, into the life of David Weir. The Veronika episode is not only the book's climactic event but its central "confession." Like the confession of Dostoyevsky's devil-incarnate Stavrogin, it is expressive of a spirit not so much repentant as taunting. While Kosinski's manipulation of David Weir and Ewa Fichtner did not correspond in every particular with the story told in *Cockpit*, it nevertheless would appear to hold a unique place in his life as an example of unmotivated malice. Against the grain of all human sympathy, he seemed to be flirting with the embrace of absolute and primal evil.

By that summer Kosinski's social circle had widened to include the Henry Grunwalds, to whom he had been introduced by Friedel and Barbara Ungeheuer. Grunwald was well along in his rise to editor-in-chief of *Time* magazine; thus Kosinski now had supporters at the top of the two great print-media empires—Grunwald at Time/Life and the Gelb-Rosenthal-Sulzberger group at the *New York Times*. Perhaps no other writer in America held such a strategic position, although its limitations would presently be demonstrated. In July Kosinski paid a visit to the Grunwalds at their home on Martha's Vineyard, finding in their circle of friends a new audience for his repertory of stories and performances.

As always, Kosinski got along famously with the children. The Grunwalds' daughter Lisa, then between her junior and senior years of high school, recorded her first meeting with Kosinski in her journal as one of a list of good things that had happened in her life. That first evening she watched him moving around in his frighteningly skimpy European-style bathing briefs as he undertook preparations to cook the Grunwalds his specialty, steaks à la Kosinski (Polish peasant style). Later he gave demonstrations with his comet, twirling it about skillfully at night on the beach, with sparks flying spectacularly and settling to the sand. An aspiring writer, Lisa remained quite taken with Kosinski, who took an active interest in her poetry. He pronounced her poems *good* and instituted a system he called the Poetry Depot, providing her with stamped envelopes in which to send him her poems wherever he was in the world.

Summer trips to the Grunwald place on Martha's Vineyard became a regular thing for Kosinski and Kiki, and two summers later, just before entering Harvard, Lisa Grunwald published an interview with her guest in the *Vineyard Gazette* in which Kosinski is at his best in talking about freedom and limitation, choice and randomness in life, and suicide as an alternative when one's freedom of action is constricted. Their relationship remained close until her sophomore year at Harvard. By then she had a boyfriend, and Kosinski called her and suggested that a comfortable love relationship would destroy her poetry; what she *really* needed was an obsessive, truly destructive love affair. Finding this response puzzling, and overly familiar, she wrote her father about it. From that point on, the relationship between Kosinski and Lisa Grunwald was more distant.

During the summer of 1975, at about the time he first visited the Grunwalds, Kosinski found himself the victim of a rather Kosinskian hoax. Chuck Ross, an aspiring freelance writer living in Los Angeles, typed up twenty-one pages of *Steps* and submitted them as a sample chapter to four publishers, including Houghton Mifflin, his current publisher; all four publishers turned the manuscript down. Ross wrote up the prank for Harper's *Bookletter*, which published his article just as *Cockpit* was hitting the bookstores. The point Ross was notionally trying to make was that unknown authors have difficulty breaking into print. Yet whether by intention or design, Kosinski emerged along with the publishing houses' readers as the butt of the joke.

Kosinski, perhaps injudiciously, rose to the bait, arguing that Ross should have sent the entire manuscript (advice Ross promptly noted for a second try). Houghton Mifflin, too, felt compelled to comment. Joyce Hartman, their New York editor, wrote to the editor of *Bookletter*, arguing that Ross's breezy cover letter, with the salutation "Hello," was not likely to enhance his chances of a serious reading. After fifteen minutes of tittering in the New York literary world, the matter disappeared. Yet with Kosinski already afflicted with murmurings and mutterings about his stature and methods of composition, the Ross stunt was sure to be filed away in the backs of many minds.

At the same time, a more serious examination of Kosinski's oeuvre was underway in academe. A young scholar by the name of Barbara Tepa had finished a dissertation on Kosinski at St. John's University on April 28, with the title *Inside the Kaleidoscope: Jerzy Kosinski's Polish and American Contexts*. Unlike the other reviewers and critics who had examined Kosinski's work, Tepa was bilingual and bicultural: she spoke Polish and was thoroughly familiar with Polish literature. As a result, Kosinski found himself in unprecedented peril. Tepa represented the greatest challenge to the insulation of his past since the Andrew Field review of *The Painted Bird* had set off Wieslaw Gornicki. One of the tightest compartments in his life seemed about to be compromised; if the bulkhead separating his Polish past from his American present were seriously punctured, Kosinski knew he would list badly, and possibly go down with a whoosh like the *Titanic*.

Ironically, Tepa meant Kosinski no harm. As a Kosinski scholar in the making, it was not in her interest to damage the reputation of her area of specialization. When she asked him for his view of his "Polish contexts," Kosinski assured her that he was unaware of having any. But Tepa already knew better. She had isolated passages in *The Painted Bird* that struck her as being quite close to passages from Sienkiewicz and Reymont, writers with whom non-Polish scholars were unlikely to be familiar, and she could recognize descriptions of peasant behavior that appeared to owe more to Biegeleisen's famous tome than to the author's own experience. Moreover, she was familiar enough with Dolega-Mostowicz's *The Career of Nikodem Dyzma* to remark how significantly it stood behind the plot structure of *Being There*, and she was well enough informed about Polish society in the 1940s and 1950s to know that Kosinski could not have been unfamiliar with it either.

It all added up to a disaster in the making, seven years before the *Village Voice* undertook to disclose and expose, but the disaster somehow did not quite come to pass. For one thing, Tepa read the evidence she had uncovered in the most charitable light. The several cases involving Kosinski texts are, in fact, unimaginably complicated, and Tepa must have been predisposed to give him the benefit of the doubt. It was, after all, the scholar's responsibility to trace down *influences*, and she had certainly done that. She looked at the array of data before her and saw not a scandal in the making but the literary antecedents of a major and prize-winning writer. Indeed, the problem Tepa confronted, but could not quite solve, is the core issue in evaluating Kosinski's work.

Tepa's research was indisputably the most thorough and well informed among the critical studies of his work, and she published several parts of it as articles, including an exceptionally clear and detailed piece on *Being There* and *Nikodem Dyzma* in *The Polish Review*, the journal of Kosinski's old home base, the Polish Institute. The dissertation itself, however, remained unpublished. One can speculate as to the reasons. Tepa was a woman, a Pole, and a wandering scholar whose pedigree and subsequent appointments were of less than Ivy League stature. Perhaps she didn't try hard enough. In 1988 she succeeded in publishing a book-length critical study of Kosinski's oeuvre, but while it contained a solid evaluation of his work, it was less detailed on his "Polish contexts" than her dissertation, and much of what it had to say was by then old news.

Receiving a copy of Tepa's work, Kosinski must have sweat bullets. Yet once again he managed to dodge them. Tepa's work would return to play only a tangential role in the later episode of the *Village Voice*.

7.

The critical reception of *Cockpit* was mixed. The consensus seemed to be that it was better than the disastrously shapeless *Devil Tree* but lacked the freshness and sharp cutting edge of *The Painted Bird* or *Steps*. Christopher Ricks, writing in the *New York Review of Books* on November 27, presented a continuation of a revision of Kosinski begun by Alter's review of *The Devil Tree*. "I cannot see what the retailing of such sick fantasizing can do but minister to wholesale sickness," Ricks wrote, and went on to accuse Kosinski of a "diseased fashionable novelistic imagination ... licensed to commit the cruelest irresponsibilities in the name of administering salutary shocks to the complacent liberal imagination." Peter Prescott, a former supporter, wrote in *Newsweek* that the novel had a half dozen "marvelous and self-contained tales," tales at least as good as anything Kosinski had yet done, but, in an overview which summarized the overall response to *Cockpit*, suggested that new readers try Kosinski's earlier books first. On the strategic third page of the *Times Book Review*, Jonathan Baumbach talked of *Cockpit* "stripping us of our distance" and implicating the reader, terms that had become conventional in discussion of *Steps*, and went on to salute the novel for "brilliantly defying the limitations of its form." In *Time* Stefan Kanfer hailed the book's "terse, unstructured style" and "images of power and authenticity." A rave notice, his review nonetheless brought into the open a word that had been rumbling up toward the surface of the revisionist view of Kosinski: *sadomasochism.*

The reading public liked the book. *Cockpit* made it to the tenth spot on the *Times* bestseller list, an unusual accomplishment for an author associated with high culture, and one of the criteria for triggering Houghton Mifflin's escalator clause for participation in paperback revenues. With *Cockpit*, an interesting phenomenon had arisen in the reception of Kosinski's books. He had become, in a certain measure, as he explained to Marian Javits, reviewer-proof. To the universe of literary critics, a new book might appear flawed and less fresh in what it had to say, but Kosinski had a loyal following, held in part by his media appearances; he had the young people, he told Marian. But there was also a sort of *x*-factor, of which he was only subliminally aware. To new readers, a book like *Cockpit*, whatever its place in Kosinski's oeuvre, was like nothing else they had ever read. The combination of violent and sexual content, accessible language, and the suggestion of profound philosophical depths made it a book that could be read by individuals far removed from the influence of the literary epicenter. His novels turned up, sporadically and unpredictably, in the under-the-counter caches of waitresses and on the dashboards of eighteen-wheelers. They were saying something—a mix of ideas, experience, and human possibility, for better or worse— that ordinary people weren't hearing from anyone else.

Relieved of his responsibilities at PEN, Kosinski was able to explore new forms and new sources of relaxation. After the usual winter respite in Crans, he turned out an extended review of Lina Wertmuller's film *Seven Beauties* for the Arts and Leisure section of the *Times*—the only movie review he ever produced. He didn't much care for the film. Chosen, presumably, for his background as a child under the Nazi occupation, Kosinski went against the grain of current opinion on Wertmuller, finding the film and especially the Giancarlo Giannini character flat, cartoonlike, and fabricated out of cultural clichés. On March 28 he departed for his one and only tour as a lecturer on the "University for Presidents" cruise to Bermuda aboard the *QE2*. An activity of the Young Presidents' Organization, composed of senior executives of American corporations, that year's "faculty" included Angier Biddle Duke, George Romney, the duke and duchess of Bedford, Frank Capra, Arthur Hailey, James Beard, Artie Shaw, Joseph Campbell, Walter Kaufmann, his old friend from Princeton days, and Art Buchwald, who made it a point to attend Kosinski's lectures on, among other things, the contrarieties of young people.

He returned to New York only briefly before leaving for Paris to visit Jacques Monod. Monod had called in December to inform Kosinski that he had been diagnosed with hemolytic anemia. Looking it up in the portable *Materia Medica* he kept close at hand for his own hypochondriacal symptoms, Kosinski had discovered that hemolytic anemia was a serious blood disorder; to survive, it was necessary for the patient to undergo more and more frequent transfusions. Now in Paris Monod announced that he had come to a decision. He would have no more transfusions. A life dependent upon being hooked up to machines was no longer worth it. He concluded the conversation with an unusual request. He would be going to his home in Cannes at the end of May, which happened to coincide exactly with the Film Festival. It was his intention to time his last transfusion so as to die in Cannes. Would Kosinski care to spend a few days with him there? Then came the unusual part. He knew that Kosinski was an expert photographer; would Kosinski care to document his final hours?

With the Festival in full flow, Cannes was a veritable zoo. Polanski was there for the preview of his new film *Le Locataire* (*The Tenant*) and found himself pursued by paparazzi and autograph hunters so ferocious that he would leave before the end of the Festival for out-of-season St. Tropez. Kosinski had previously pronounced on an earlier Polanski film, *Repulsion*, that it was okay, but the scenes with Catherine Deneuve where the camera zoomed in and out were going to be a problem; Polanski had been out of America and didn't realize that this "avant-garde" effect was presented on American TV every day in an Alka-Seltzer commercial. Polanski had apparently been philosophical about his friend's criticism, for he invited Kosinki to attend a private screening of *The Tenant* (which the critics were about to savage). He also asked Kosinski for an introduction to Jacques Monod.

The introduction was made at one of the Festival's continuous stream of parties on the evening of May 27. Monod's pale face was artificially tan, the symptom of his illness camouflaged by the prevalence of tans at Cannes; on the way to the reception his hands at the wheel of his car had shown the symptomatic shaking that characterizes a late stage in the progress of hemolytic anemia. Nevertheless his striking good looks gave him an effortless presence for the starlets. He and Kosinski discussed women—the device for male bonding Kosinski employed with all men, whether of high or low degree—and Monod explained that he loved women with a powerful instinct that was linked to their carrying of life. In Kosinski's photo of the moment, Monod had placed his hand on the knee of the nearest available young woman, who promptly asked how long he was staying in Cannes. Monod replied that he was in Cannes for the remainder of his vacation, perhaps three or four days. At another point, when Monod was introduced as the author of a book entitled *Chance and Necessity*, he and Kosinski enjoyed a delicious moment as a starlet asked if he was in Cannes because of the film based on his book. At length Polanski circulated back into proximity and mentioned that there was something he wanted to discuss with Monod, but it could wait until after the Festival.

"Ask him now," Kosinski said.

Busy talking to a young woman, Polanski drifted away, then drifted back and repeated the message—he had an important question he wanted to put to Monod.

"Ask him now," Kosinski said more firmly.

Once more Polanski and the young woman circled the room and returned, as Kosinski and Monod were preparing to leave.

"Ask him now," Kosinski said a third time.

Polanski's question was never asked. At their last meeting together, Kosinski mugged for Monod between photographs. In one of his routines, he mimed a man about to be shot by a firing squad who still combs his hair. In their last moments, while Kosinski continued to take pictures, Monod smoked a final cigarette and his eyes filled with tears. "Farewell, my dear boy," he told Kosinski, as the sun was setting, and walked inside to lie down. He died at 12:45 A.M.

Kosinski returned to the regular schedule of New York parties and summer high jinks. On weekends he sometimes went with George and Freddie Plimpton and their crowd to Plimpton's mother's place in West Hills, where parlor games were the order of the day. They played hiding games like "murder" and "sardines," in which you must join anyone you find. To Plimpton's surprise, after all his talk about hiding, in his apartment and during the war, Kosinski was not particularly good at the hiding games. "Put the lights back on," he insisted during one game held in a room with lots of furniture and curtains, "I haven't cased the place properly."

On the other hand, he demonstrated his ability to fold himself neatly into a bureau drawer, and when the situation was under his control, he played his usual pranks. Once when the Plimpton group was going in convoy to a party in East Hampton, he was not to be found. He had hidden himself in the back seat of Karen Shaw's Volkswagen. Suddenly he loomed up behind her and put his arms around her neck. Karen, wife of Adam Shaw, son of novelist Irwin Shaw, nearly went off the road. Later Plimpton felt it necessary to remonstrate with Kosinski. "You could have killed her," he said. Nonsense, Kosinski defended himself; he extolled the value of such a shock for producing spectacular orgasms.

The Plimptons and their friends provided a whole new audience for his tricks. Arriving in his huge Buick, the trunk stuffed with his Gypsy's cache, he emerged onto the beach with his peculiar Polish brazier—an upscale comet. Twirling it with his legendary skill, he diverted yet another company with his private fireworks show, sparks burning brightly as they showered to the ground.

In early September, Karol Cardinal Wojtyla visited New York. The future pope was then archbishop of Cracow, an obscure prelate often confused with Polish primate Stefan Cardinal Wyszynski and distinguished most by the fact that he was interested in literature and was himself something of an author. Along with the usual New York sights, the cardinal visited the Polish Institute, touching base with the Polish émigré community. As a ranking Polish-American writer, Kosinski was a natural escort, and he accompanied Wojtyla on his tour, reminiscing about philosophical studies in postwar Poland and skiing at Zakopane, which fell within the Cracow diocese. Kosinski seems to have been drawn to the fatherly presence of the pope-to-be, at least as evidenced by his future response to events involving Wojtyla. Wandering the streets of New York together, they stopped at a newsstand on Fifty-seventh Street, near Kosinski's apartment, to look at a skiing magazine. The cardinal's attention was drawn, however, to the superabundance of girlie magazines. According to critic Alfred Kazin, Kosinski later reported that Wojtyla asked,

"What kind of people sell this stuff?" and Kosinski responded, "Well, Your Eminence, they're usually Jews." Most likely, however, this twist ending reflects Kazin's perspective and his particular outrage; as told to others, the emphasis is placed not on the cardinal's outrage and Kosinski's retort, but on Wojtyla's down-to-earth and earthy curiosity. As in so many instances, Kosinski perhaps told several versions, calculated to maximally entertain or appall, as the particular audience suggested.

Throughout the summer Kosinski was still groping to come to terms with Monod's death, which had had a profound and complicated impact. He felt simultaneous awe and fascination for his experience in Cannes, as if a corner of life's final veil had been momentarily lifted. He had not been present for the deaths of either of his parents, or even for their funerals, and, indeed, both deaths had merely finalized a virtual absence that had begun long before. Later, in his essay "Death in Cannes," he called Monod his "alchemical friend," a friend combining the image of *one's father* and one's best pal. That same essay speaks with ambivalence of the photographs, which he was initially excited about having taken. The compelling features of Monod's death were the fact that, within the constraints of his illness, he had managed to control the terms of his departure from life and how remarkably, expressively alive he remained until almost his final moments. Both themes reverberated for Kosinski, calling to mind the death six years earlier of Japanese novelist Yukio Mishima, who had committed suicide at the age of forty-five at least in part to exert aesthetic control, leaving the world at the moment of greatest spiritual and physical perfection—while in the midst of life.

The philosophical viewpoint Monod derived from science—or rather Kosinski's understanding of that philosophical viewpoint—became the organizing principle of Kosinski's new novel, called in progress *The Small Investor* and eventually published as *Blind Date*. The idea, as Kosinski understood it, was that life consists of a series of unpredictable, yet fully determined encounters—thus the title. Human beings are playthings in the hands of the invisible god of chance. The protagonist is identifiably

Kosinski himself in the person of small investor George Levanter—George being English for Jerzy, Levanter being a seasonal
Mediterranean wind, a person from the Levant (thus Semitic),
and a word in sound and structure not far from his original name
of Lewinkopf. Most of the events of the novel stemmed identifiably from Kosinski's recent life. Many characters appear to come
directly from life, among them Jacques Monod, Charles
Lindbergh, the secretary of state (Kissinger), the Soviet poet
(Yevtushenko), and Manson and his victims. Others have names
that provide a thin layer of fictional cover—as Mary-Jane Kirkland for Mary Weir, President Samael of Lotan for President
Senghor of Senegal, and Madame Ramoz for Imelda Marcos. The
fencer JP is in fact Polish Olympic champion and CIA agent Jerzy
Pawlowski. The cynical Romarkin is his Warsaw friend Andrzej
Wat. Theodora, with her false pregnancy, is Lilla van Saher. Sometimes the changes mimic the conventions of pulp thriller fiction,
as the Persian secret police agency SAVAK becomes PERSAUD,
secret police agency of Indostran. Still other characters, like Serena and Foxy Lady, were drawn from denizens of the sexual
underworld—the other side of Kosinski's life.

Despite its conception as a novel written to a thesis, *Blind Date*
did a remarkable job of documenting Kosinski's life at the time of
his writing. It detailed, for one thing, his increasing involvement
with prominent people—Kissinger, Yevtushenko, Svetlana, Monod, and Léopold Senghor. And by now he had the goods on that
world. Sponsored by Sidney Offit, he was a member of the Century Club. He held court at Elaine's, hopping from table to table
like a prince in the world of intellect. He was a regular at Marian
Javits's dinner parties, the semiofficial prankster of her set. Once
he hid curled up on a window ledge, alarming her husband, the
senator. Another time he concealed himself in a sofa during a reception for Israeli foreign minister Abba Eban, and made his
presence known by poking and kicking Eban from beneath.

Like Hemingway for an earlier generation, Kosinski lived a life
most of his readers could hardly imagine living, and *Blind Date*
was his report to them—the account of a journalist dropped
down from Mars to circulate and report on New York's smart set

in vignettes filed from the existential cutting edge. But the range of his experience went far beyond Hemingway's. If he could send back reports from receptions for heads of states, he also could, and increasingly did, report back from an underworld of prostitutes and S-M practices, and from places in his own imagination far darker than anything Hemingway knowingly allowed into print. Genet might give an account of such scenes and such personal impulses, but not in a form designed to be read by truck drivers and housewives from Kansas City.

From a literary standpoint, *Blind Date* was deeply flawed. The intention of showing the role of chance through slight vignettes gave the book the same feeling of looseness that had afflicted *The Devil Tree*. It felt thin, and lacking in a center. Monod's death, the return of Kissinger's watch, the Manson massacre at Polanski's, an encounter with a woman who had previously been a man: what could link such disparate events aside from the fact that all had been part of the life of Kosinski? Some of the events were almost literal transcriptions; some, like the episodes of anti-authoritarian revenge on behalf of Persian intellectuals (inspired by the Baraheni case he had worked on at PEN) and the imprisoned JP (Pawlowski), had violent Kosinskian retributions tacked on to the actual story; some, like the account of Levanter having sex with his own mother, though teasing the reader with autobiographical hints, seemed contrived mainly to shock and test the reader's limits. Still other elements—a cannon that is fired at a poet's home and wounds a guest—may have a vague thematic connection, but their impact is so trivial as to suggest that Kosinski had begun to think that every quirky event he saw or experienced must have significance.

As for the sexual underworld, there was no denying the book's frankness. From the sexual encounters between Levanter and his mother to the rapes carried out by Levanter and his friend Oscar to the transsexual Foxy Lady to the prostitute Serena, the intensity built progressively. The fascination was precisely that Kosinski was not Genet, nor was Levanter a Genet protagonist; all the unusual sexual tastes of the Kosinski character were presented without inflection, as if they were the absolutely ordinary thing, culminating in a classic S-M scene where Levanter binds

Pauline and thrusts his hand inside her to produce her first orgasm.

Emily Prager, who in the 1960s had played Laurie Ann Karr in the TV soap opera *The Edge of Night*, had first met Kosinski in June 1975, at a dinner party of young socialites on the Upper East Side. A graduate of Brearley and Barnard, she told him she was doing an article for *Viva* on ménages à trois. After the party Kosinski called her, eager to talk further about her subject. As he had with Lisa Grunwald, he encouraged her writing, and they were close for two years. While he was the exact daydream of a Brearley girl of her generation, she managed to keep a perspective about him. She recognized immediately that S-M was the center of his sexuality, which was largely expressed during that period through encounters with prostitutes; the sex act itself seemed to require eighteen million ritual actions in preparation, or such was her observation. At the same time she had genuine feeling for him. She was powerfully drawn by his vulnerability, his loveless existence.

In her story "The Alumni Bulletin," she would make Kosinski a character in his own name; one of three Brearley girls wins a sexual boasting contest with the other two by claiming that she is the Pauline who is tied up and brought to orgasm by Kosinski on page 230 of *Blind Date*. She enriched the detail of the original, naming the designer ties by which the girl is bound. Kosinski himself then knocks on the door and diverts the Brearley girls by his presence and his repartee.

While instructing Prager about writing, Kosinski told her, oddly, "You must never personify actions to yourself." Now the direction he had begun to take with *Blind Date* worried her. Later, when she heard him discussing S-M on talk shows, she called to warn him. He was "personifying." No other celebrity had quite come out and admitted the sort of things that Kosinski was admitting. If he kept it up, she felt, he was asking for a terrible fall.

8.

With an advance of $350,000 to be paid in three installments, *Blind Date* represented another leap in Kosinski's earnings. Once again the proprietary contract was with Bantam, and the hardcover publisher was Houghton Mifflin, which increased its advance slightly beyond the previous one and guaranteed an initial printing of at least 35,000 with a promotional budget to match.

As Kosinski awaited publication, his peripatetic social life branched out once more. He changed his friends every two years, he had told Emily Prager. And now he was in transition again, turning up at the dinner parties of Oscar de la Renta and his wife, Françoise, carrying his court-jester act to yet another New York circle. According to Wendy Luers, whom he met through this new circle, his pattern was not hard to explain. Once he went through his repertory of stories and pranks, it was time to move on. He tended to use up his stories, or perhaps more accurately, to use up his audiences. And what was the truth behind those stories, especially the early ones from his Polish childhood, wondered Luers, wife of Bill Luers, the former ambassador to Czechoslovakia, and herself later director of the Eastern Europe-oriented Foundation for a Civil Society.

Most people didn't ask. If Kosinski had fashioned a persona that was vulnerable, then so were the people among whom he moved. Their vulnerability, as he had grasped instantly with the astute intuition of the emotionally shell-shocked, was their desperate need to be entertained. The American upper class, as he had told Peter Skinner, lived lives of quiet, and sometimes unquiet, desperation. They had to be instructed and entertained like small children, and he, like his own Chauncey Gardiner—like his model Nikodem Dyzma—was quite prepared to entertain them and expose their emptiness in the process. Like a pair of neurotic lovers, Kosinski and America's privileged few lived together in a perfect folie à deux.

Now a new element appeared. Kosinski discovered the Dominican Republic, and he discovered horses. Charles Bluhdorn, CEO of the conglomerate Gulf & Western, had sugar investments in the Dominican Republic, and because the local law restricted the repatriation of profits, he did a very creative thing: at Costazur he decreed a pleasure dome. There was a hotel, the Casa de Campo, fully equipped for such diversions of the affluent as golf, shooting, and polo. The Kissingers went there, and so did the likes of the Sid Basses, the Ahmet Erteguns, Lady Grace Dudley, literary superagent Irving Lazar, the Agnellis of Fiat, and a younger social set that included Mick Jagger and the rock group Foreigner. So did Kosinski's new friend Oscar de la Renta, who was of Dominican origin and put Kosinski onto the Casa de Campo as a wintering spot for the fashionable set.

The standard stay at Costazur was a month, from the middle of December until the middle of January, and by the following year, 1978, Kosinski and Kiki thought of themselves as regulars—so much so that they invited polo friends they had met elsewhere. The crowd even included Polish émigrés, tennis pro Wojtek Fibak and Zbigniew Brzezinski, who just happened to be Jimmy Carter's National Security Adviser. Zbig's arrival, in fact, provided Kosinski with an amusing moment to share. Plagued by drought, the government had restricted the water supply, and the hotel's allotment went for the golf greens, which seemed to them most essential. It was Kiki's task to fetch water to fill the toilet bowl, and in the process she happened to bump into a high official, mentioning in the exchange of pleasantries that Zbig was on his way. The next day the toilets flushed.

A writer's life didn't get better than this. The rich seemed to understand that a writer couldn't afford luxuries, and means were worked out to accommodate Kosinski. He was, after all, splendid entertainment. Even horses could be made available. Kiki's standard pauper's line became, "Brother, can you spare a pony?"

Still another side of Kosinski continued to develop during the fall of 1977, as he awaited official publication of *Blind Date* and the Christmas trip to Costazur. He had gradually become recognized as a Jewish writer, and in August he had lent his name and presence to a National Conference on Soviet Jewry, with Norman Podhoretz and Herbert Gold as sponsors. In October, the city of New Haven became the first American municipality to put up a Holocaust Memorial, and they invited Kosinski as their speaker.

Kosinski, who had denied being Jewish a decade earlier at Temple Beth-El, now spoke openly as a survivor, the culmination of a long public—and private—journey toward acknowledgment of his Jewishness. Even so, he could not resist noting that Elie Wiesel had been considered but rejected because his speaking fee was twice as high. "So," he quipped, "I'm the cut-rate Elie Wiesel."

Published in November, *Blind Date* was a hit. The reviews were mixed. John Leonard in the daily *Times* on November 7 found it a tolerable effort but concluded: "When he learns in his fiction to respect women, he will be a fine novelist." A day earlier, however, writing in the *Times Book Review*, Anatole Broyard seized upon the book as yet another occasion to assault Kosinski's entire oeuvre. The following week Sidney Offit, who was at Kosinski's side, braced himself as they approached Broyard. Broyard had been involved in notable intellectual donnybrooks. Was he about to be caught in the middle of the scene? Kosinski broke the ice. "Thanks for the attention," he said cheerfully.

He had reason to be cheerful. *Blind Date* was his best-selling book in hardcover, with 38,971 sold by the following March, and it hit the *Times* bestseller list. Kosinski felt that he was, indeed, reviewer-proof. And he had projects in the works where the opinions of a bunch of New York intellectuals would be of even less import.

VI

PASSION PLAY

1.

Kosinski spent the late winter of 1978 in Crans with Kiki, starting work there on a new novel. By that time his network of friends and supporters had become so extensive that it was necessary to draft a form letter updating his activities in Europe, signed "Jerzy and Kiki." The recipients included the Henry Grunwalds, the Lewis Schotts, the Joseph Krafts, the Jacob Javitses, the John Johnstons, the Zbigniew Brzezinskis, the Mike Wallaces, the George Plimptons, the Pete Petersons, the Clay Felkers, and the Charlie Bluhdorns. A carefully drafted note mentioned his attendance at human rights gatherings and work with the foreign translators of *Blind Date*. The addresses roughly define the inner circle of Kosinski's life at that time—or at least the public and daylight part of it—as well as a sort of *Who's Who of Movers and Shakers of the Late 1970s.*

He returned to New York in May. By then all the pieces had come together to make a film of *Being There*, with Lorimar as the production company. The key figure was Andrew Braunsberg, whom he had known for years through Polanski and who would be the producer. Hal Ashby would direct, and Peter Sellers would play Chauncey Gardiner. Kosinski himself would turn his novel into a screenplay and receive the screenwriting credit. Kosinski had argued as far back as 1971 that it was a film for an election year, and release was now planned to coincide with the opening of the 1980 presidential primary season.

In interviews given throughout the planning, filming, and promotion, there would be more than the usual Kosinskian mythification about the origins of the film. Most versions involved Peter Sellers as the central figure. As Kosinski liked to tell the story, Sellers had called him in London pretending to be an Englishman actually named Chauncey Gardiner and threatening to sue Kosinski for stealing his life. Sellers sent his car for Kosinski and carried on his charade at a restaurant until another patron identified him and asked for an autograph, whereupon he began his campaign for the part of Gardiner. He pleaded that the part was perfect for him—having been many characters, he was in fact a man without qualities—and that he was perfect for the part. An unknown actor would ham it up to establish his career, while Sellers could do Gardiner's nullity as his real self. After many years of this sort of persuasion, the story goes, Kosinski caved in. An added element in one version is that his final capitulation to corrupting Hollywood came when a studio assigned two Yale students to produce a similar script, thus preempting and stealing his work.

It is wonderful mythification, and it may contain traces of truth here and there. Indeed driven by a sense of his own nullity, Sellers did seek the part. Walter Matthau was another actor who saw in it a vehicle for his particular talents. Yet Kosinski was not at all an innocent ensnared by corrupting Hollywood. As early as 1971 he was busy trying to sell a script written with the help of Larry Eilenberg at Yale Drama School, and he had discussed the possibility with Polanski, who was eventually drawn away to other projects. He then worked for a time in Switzerland with Gil Shiva, his New York friend and aspiring producer, at whose house each year he spent the Jewish holidays. In short, Kosinski had peddled the idea hard for years, through Allan Schwartz, his attorney for creative matters. The Lorimar package was the result of the usual complicated negotiation in which all the necessary principals have to be gotten across a starting line at roughly the same moment, and in the right order. Kosinski's script for

Lorimar was in fact the last of three he had written over a period of six years.

Why, then, did Kosinski persist so strongly in the myth that the film production of *Being There* was forced upon him against his will? By the middle of the long process, after the Klinkowitz interview and other public pronouncements, he apparently felt locked into his protestations. He had represented himself as the Pure Artist refusing to be corrupted by the Mammon of Hollywood, and once having done so, he had to find a way to wiggle out when his book turned into a movie with himself as the screenwriter. But how did he get locked into that position in the first place? The answer seems to lie in the interplay between his wounded psyche and his irrepressible inventiveness as a storyteller. When others mentioned to him the obvious filmability of *Being There*, Kosinski protected himself from the threat of failure by claiming that he did not want his books made into films. To rationalize this defense, he spun an elaborate theory about the relationship of books and films—much as, in *Notes of the Author*, he had spun a theory of language to rationalize the delicate matter of the "autobiographicality" of *The Painted Bird*. A film devotee—he once estimated that he had seen *The Barefoot Contessa* thirty-five times—he talked about the unsatisfactory flatness of movies against the aliveness of novels, which allowed the reader to interact with the text. It was a rather conventional embittered novelist's dismissal of the great art form of the time, delivered with Kosinskian detail and complication; the only difference was that Kosinski was working all the while to make his novel into a high-gloss film. When he succeeded, he once again had to backtrack and rewrite both his theory and his history.

In truth, few novels are as close to a film script in their original state as *Being There*. The narrative passages read, at times, almost like shooting directions, one of the reasons such a highly satirical and fantastic story worked—placing the reader "there," in a visual way. Along with the usual emphasis on dialogue and visual action, the major change sought by Andrew Braunsberg at Lorimar was to set the novel in Washington, D.C., rather than New York. On May 29 Kosinski had written his new/old friend Zbigniew Brzezinski to congratulate him on his success with the

Camp David peace process. On July 5 he wrote the presidential adviser again, informing him of the package put together with Hal Ashby, the director of *Coming Home*, and Lorimar—and identifying *Being There* as a "political" novel. He enclosed a short piece he had done for *Time*, criticizing Solzhenitsyn for taking issue with American culture and effectively biting the hand that fed him. He noted the similarity of his own remarks to those of First Lady Rosalynn Carter, and added that he would be in Washington the week of July 17 and would be happy to see Zbig and his wife Muska, although he recognized that they were busy.

In Washington he worked nonstop with Andy Braunsberg from July 19 to July 26, plugging in details of the new setting. As with everything, the move of the setting from New York to Washington would later have an elaborate theoretical rationale. When he wrote the book, Kosinski would argue, it was pre-Watergate and Washington was a hick town without a past—no fitting place to offset the innocence and blankness of Chauncey Gardiner; thus he chose New York. Now, a decade later and after the Watergate revelations, wicked, wicked Washington served nicely to provide the history and complexity against which Chauncey Gardiner is measured. In reality, at the time he wrote the book, New York was what Kosinski knew. He felt comfortable using it as a setting. As he learned in 1978, one can feel comfortable setting a film in a place one has experienced occasionally, and studied carefully for a week.

There is one psychologically interesting footnote in Kosinski's mythification of the production of *Being There*—the theme of plagiarism, which crops up both in the story of Peter Sellers pretending to be Chauncey Gardiner and in the story of the two writers ordered to generate a knockoff script. Behind the Peter Sellers character who was now to climb to the summit of success in Washington loomed the prototype of Nikodem Dyzma, ever present, and just beneath the surface, as Kosinski worked on the script. Would the airtight compartments sealing off his past—and the Polish pop novel *Nikodem Dyzma*—hold up once his book became a film? Articulated or not, the question projected a small dark spot onto the sun of his success, as he provided two finished copies of the script to Braunsberg by the July 31 deadline.

By that summer the underside of Kosinski's life—his connection with the sexual demimonde—had taken another turn. The indulgent atmosphere of the early 1970s had given rise to a new institution, private sex clubs where individuals could engage freely in any and all sexual activities with consenting partners. The pioneering clubs had been homosexual bathhouses, but they were soon joined by predominantly heterosexual establishments such as Plato's Retreat, which opened in 1969, where the only requirement was that patrons enter as couples. Kosinski had visited the bathhouses on occasion, as an interested spectator, but the couples clubs captured his interest in a more profound way, eventually becoming a virtual obsession.

Kosinski had come to the clubs through a progression that began with casual affairs and overlapping relationships, including Lilla van Saher's procuring and the frequent use of prostitutes, proceeded through the peep-show world of Times Square, and gradually evolved into a relentless search for experimentation and greater intensity. By the summer of 1978, when not working actively on a communal project that required him to accommodate to the hours of ordinary people, he often slept in two shifts, from four until eight in the afternoon and again from four until eight in the morning. This schedule freed his mornings for work, his evenings for often glitzy socializing, and the hours after midnight for night-crawling in the sexual underworld. His particular interest lay in transsexuals, who had clubs and a culture of their own, and his keenest interest was awakened by the intermediate states of transformation.

At dinner parties with New York's elite, he often told stories of that night-crawling, but always in terms that, while calculated to titillate, left just the necessary distance between these two airtight compartments of his life. Fifteen years later, after his death, many of his social set still believed that he made those stories up, or based them on one or two journalistic forays. They were not occasional forays but nightly quests, and they marked a primary area in which Kosinski went beyond such mainstream writers as Hemingway, whose sexual adventures and public frankness seem tame by comparison. It was not difficult for him to come up with women to accompany him. He was, after all, the Jerzy Kosinski who was described by Emily Prager as the ultimate dream of Brearley girls. For an adventurous young woman, a date with Kosinski, with a crowning invitation to four or five hours at a sex club, had the irresistible lure of new and cutting-edge experience. Along with the pickups, he had a series of semiregular companions—a Christine X, a Madeline Y, a Mila Z, who enjoyed the experience and saw advantage in being Kosinski's companion and friend—and eventually he would encounter the perfect companion, who would share the full expression of that element of his life.

Kiki never accompanied Kosinski during his night-crawling, and one might well ask exactly where she stood in all this. His sexual interests were, of course, no secret to her. His capacity for infidelity dated back to their first trip to Europe and his affair with the sophisticated Frenchwoman. But how did she come to accept and tolerate his behavior? In the beginning he had hidden his nightly destinations from her, but over a period of time, with no particular crystallizing incident, she had come to realize where he was going and what he was doing. Perhaps there was never a single moment of decision, at least after her initial decision to accompany him to Europe without marriage and without promises. In Kiki's view, Jerzy was an extraordinary man with extraordinary gifts, needs, and appetites, and that was that. He was enough for her, as she often put it, while nothing was ever enough for him. And wherever he went, whatever he did, he always came back. He evidently found something in their relationship that was not available elsewhere in his travels—the uncritical love and support of a partner who was organized and socially presentable, permissive and self-abnegating, and canny and tough as nails in the promotion of his interests. These qualities, Kiki must have intuitively concluded, were the winners for holding his long-term affection. Girls he could always turn up. What was far harder to find was a new, improved model of his mother.

That summer and fall of 1978, Kosinski did without the usual vacation as he shuttled between New York and L.A. to work on two major projects at once. The new novel was dominated by the three newest elements of Kosinski's life—horses, the Cisneros–de la Renta circle in the Dominican Republic, and his night-crawling experiences at the clubs. At the same time, two new tonal elements appeared. One is the fatigue of his protagonist. Fabian, his polo-player errant, is weighed down by a sense of his aging body and waning powers as no previous Kosinski hero has been. Combining a determination to hold on to his athletic prowess with the decadence of an aging roué, Fabian gives off a whiff of corruption. The freewheeling 1970s were drawing to a close, and in his usual manner Kosinski seems to have been intimately attuned to their final weary excesses through both observation and participation.

The other tonal difference of the new novel was a heavily ornate, occasionally almost purple, prose style, rich in Latinate (as against Anglo-Saxon/Germanic) words. That shift derived in part from conscious intent and in part from the efforts of a new assistant, a sometime theater critic for *Commonweal* by the name of Richard Hayes. Thomas Fleming, Kosinski's old ally from PEN days, bumped into Hayes one day on Third Avenue in the middle of his work with Kosinski. Hayes looked exceptionally glum, and Fleming asked what the problem was. "I'm working for Jerzy Kosinski," Hayes replied, "and it's hell. It's like working in a concentration camp. He searches me before I leave. No papers, no leaks. He makes you do things over and over. The money isn't that good, either."

Hayes needed the money, however, and work on the new novel progressed. In September, Kosinski's work was interrupted by visits from two professors coincidentally named Martin—Richard Martin from Austria and Jay Martin from California—part of the swelling group of academics interested in doing books on his work. Another old acquaintance from Warsaw, Maciej Jachimczyk, who was to have an important role in the distant future, visited from Oxford. Kosinski also undertook the thankless task of dunning his fellow writers for contributions to the ACLU, which was then plagued by dissension and declining membership. Gail Sheehy replied with a contribution, while Philip Booth, Archibald MacLeish, and Kay Boyle politely begged off.

In mid-October Kosinski found the time to coauthor, along with Carl Bernstein, Nora Ephron, Christopher Cerf, and George

Plimpton, a parody called *Not the New York Times*, spoofing the real *Times*, which was going into its third month of a strike. He laughed about the spoof at an exchange of intimate dinners with the Abe Rosenthals, at his apartment and for hamburgers on the Rosenthals' terrace. Rosenthal, feeling under siege at the *Times*, which was not only being struck but was also being sued by women and minorities, wrote warmly in appreciation of the pictures Kosinski had taken of one of the evenings.

On October 21 there was exciting news from the Vatican. Hearing it on television, Kosinski felt the need to share his excitement with someone who could understand. He called Ewa Markowska. "Our boy, Karolek, made it," he said, in a breathless conversation that lasted only thirty seconds or so. Karol Cardinal Wojtyla, the archbishop of Cracow with whom Kosinski had discussed skiing and the sources of pornography, had become the first Polish pope. Kosinski had stood elbow to elbow with Holiness.

Meanwhile the script of *Being There* required a number of last-minute adjustments, with shooting scheduled for early the following year. Several scenes needed to be made more cinematic. Another problem was the ending, which originally had a very flat encounter between Chauncey and EE, while the audience missed the voice-over of the president discussing Chauncey for vice president. Now, ingeniously, Kosinski reached back to page six of the novel, in which Chance "floated into the world, buoyed up by a force he did not see." Out of that brief passage, he invented the stunning final scene in which Chance walks through the woods and out onto the lake, thrusting his umbrella deep into the water but himself being "buoyed up"—walking on water with a multiply suggestive "lightness."

With the script in seemingly good order by December 20, Kosinski left for the now annual Christmas trip to Casa de Campo, returning just in time for the actual shooting, which began on January 16. At the beginning of February he stood outside the Steven-Windsor clothing store in Washington, D.C., on K Street NW, watching Ashby shoot the scene in which Peter Sellers (Chance) is knocked down by Shirley MacLaine's (EE's) limo. The filming was done at night, so as not to tie up daytime traffic, and it was exceptionally cold for Washington, seventeen degrees

Fahrenheit. Speaking of that first night on location, Kosinski told Louise Sweeney of the *Christian Science Monitor* of the sense of awe he felt at the large communal enterprise. "I had a moment when I was truly traumatized by what I saw," he said. "A gigantic section of one of the main streets of Washington, hundreds of extras, dozens and dozens of giant trucks, and I said, 'It's all my fault, in a way. I'm responsible for this.' " He went on to say that he felt the way one feels when one knocks over a glass of water at a table—a $15 million glass of water, in this case.

With such stakes, there were the usual tensions on the set, including speculation as to Peter Sellers's ability to do Chauncey Gardiner without jazzing it up. There was the usual movie-set banter, much of it recorded by the Washington press. Kosinski told over and over the story of Sellers's pursuit of the part—a greatly simplified and dramatized version of the way the package was put together—including such details as Sellers's having stationery made up in Chauncey Gardiner's name. The two men played wonderful comedy scenes against each other, with Sellers often assuming the affectless Gardiner persona. One began with Sellers talking of London hosts who asked him to tell shocking stories, after which British dinner guests tapped the side of the table saying, "Quite good, quite good."

"I've said the most amazing things," Kosinski chimed in of London dinner parties, "and people will say, 'Yes, you're absolutely right.' "

"Yes, you're absolutely right," Sellers intoned as deadpan Chauncey Gardiner.

Another topic was Chuck Ross, who had done a reprise on his trick with East Coast publishers. This time, following Kosinski's earlier suggestion, he had circulated a complete manuscript of *Steps* to fourteen publishers and thirteen literary agents, all of whom failed to recognize the book and turned it down. Ross published the results in *New West* magazine, and this time he succeeded in having the story picked up by *Time*, which ran a piece entitled "Polish Joke" on February 19, with a picture of Kosinski looking pensive. This time Kosinski admitted that it hurt a little when his own former publisher, Random House, rejected the book. "All I know is it makes me feel kind of funny," he said, "just when I'm trying to peddle my new novel."

But there were too many exciting things happening for him to brood long over a small literary embarrassment. In late March the film crew moved to Asheville, where Biltmore, the 250-room mock-French chateau George Vanderbilt had ordered erected against the backdrop of the Blue Ridge Mountains, was to serve as the palatial residence of Benjamin Rand. It was a return trip for Kosinski, who had visited Biltmore earlier during his travels with Mary Weir. Now much of the tension on the set had to do with how Shirley MacLaine would perform the masturbation scene of her character EE, who was based on Mary Weir. Larry Olivier had rejected the role of Rand, MacLaine said, explaining her edginess in terms that would serve to hype the movie, because he "didn't like the idea of being in a film with me masturbating." Melvyn Douglas had taken the Rand part, and now MacLaine's scene was approaching. What would she do at the point where the script said, simply, "MacLaine's improvisation"? She had visited Kosinski in his New York apartment to ask his advice, sitting through a long evening on the small stepladder he used to pull down books from the upper shelves as she agonized over the scene. "What am I supposed to do," she wailed, as Kiki provided warm milk and honey, "use a Coke bottle?"

Now unit publicist Beverly Walker used MacLaine's public squeamishness as the occasion to assert that it was going to be the most talked-about film sequence since the under-the-table sex scene with Warren Beatty and Julie Christie in Ashby's earlier film *Shampoo*. Audiences who witnessed MacLaine's writhing performance a year later would not disagree.

2.

As the filming of *Being There* progressed, the new novel, entitled *Passion Play*, was moving rapidly toward publication. The terms with Bantam were less generous by half than for *Blind Date*—an advance of $175,000 against which Bantam, as before, would pocket the hardcover advance. The reduction was accounted for in part by the fact that *Blind Date* had not earned out for Bantam and in part by the fact that a novel about a polo player was perceived at Bantam as a difficult sell. The hardcover publisher was to be St. Martin's Press. To interviewers on the movie set, Kosinski explained that he had parted amicably with Houghton Mifflin because they were unable to publish the book as promptly as he wished—a plausible answer in light of his desire to have the book out well before release of the film, which was scheduled for early 1980. A second factor driving the move to St. Martin's was that Houghton Mifflin had not met his escalating expectations for hardcover sales. Perhaps most important of all, Charlie Heyward, Kosinski's great advocate at Houghton Mifflin, who was already becoming recognized as an innovator in the marketing of books, had also moved to St. Martin's.

Alice Feder, Tom Fleming's daughter, was named Kosinski's editor at St. Martin's, and when he delivered his manuscript it came accompanied by Kosinski's usual sly flirtatiousness, a tone he reined in upon learning that she was his old friend's daughter. Though assigned the best copy editor at St. Martin's, he promptly embarked on a massive rewrite that soon had everyone in production wringing their hands. At the same time, he insisted on the original tight schedule, pleading fear that something might happen to him—perhaps he would be struck by a car—before the book was published. Quite possibly it was all for effect. He told Feder that while he awaited publication, he had determined to leave his apartment as little as possible, to stay on his block and avoid crossing streets.

Passion Play is the story of Fabian, a modern knight-errant who travels around America and the Caribbean with his VanHome, making his living by teaching, writing, and, especially, playing high-stakes one-on-one polo matches. The VanHome is a mobile version of the ubiquitous Kosinski apartment, a womblike second skin in which he hunkers down against a potentially hostile world. It neatly counterpoints the outgoing Fabian/Kosinski who plays polo and cavorts among the rich and horsey. One of them is Falsalfa, a Caribbean dictator resembling the late Rafael Trujillo of the Dominican Republic, who pays Fabian to make him look good at polo and attempts to involve him in a plot to murder a bothersome journalist. Another is Eugene Stanhope, polo-playing president of Stanhope Industries, loosely based on poloist Michael Butler of Oakbrook, Illinois; Stanhope is first Fabian's friend and then his mortal enemy, thanks to a conflict over Alexandra, who first ignores Fabian, then seduces him, and finally claims that he assaulted her. As his seducer, she insists on sexual dominance, entering him with a dildo as he would enter her.

Although it goes back and forth in time, and moves associatively among unrelated anecdotes, *Passion Play* has an overall plot structure and a general forward movement; the only other book so structured, to that point, had been *Being There.* The central plot involves Fabian's pursuit of Eugene Stanhope's underage niece Vanessa, setting his desire for her against his partially conscientious reluctance to become involved. Kosinskian touches include Fabian's ostracism by other polo players for his overly individual style, as well as his detailed consideration of cruelty, most notably in a technical description of the way Tennessee Walkers are trained to acquire their gait. Biographical details include allusion to his family who died in a "fire," and especially his father, depicted briefly as a gentle teacher who instructed him with folk tales. Old and current issues of Kosinski's life appear: Fabian rejects hosting a television show, choosing the lonely arts of writing and riding, and he turns down Vanessa's offer of a million-dollar gift, which she conceives as allowing him the possibility of choosing her freely. Thus both his current activity as screenwriter and his past relationship with Mary Weir are held up to fictional scrutiny. Reflecting another current Kosinski interest, Fabian plays a prank on a group of visiting Argentine polo players, introducing them to beautiful women who he later reveals are transsexuals. Fabian's published books on horses and horsemanship are a send-up of Kosinski's own, including the second, *Obstacles*, which won the "National Horse Lovers Award." This sort of shallow and parodistic invention is a new note in Kosinski's writing, a teasing quality that feels at odds with the tone of much of the book.

The heart of the book, however, is its depiction of Fabian's sexual interests, and in particular the extended scene in which he brings Vanessa, to whom he refers as his "daughter," to the

Dream Exchange, which is modeled on Plato's Retreat. In the scene a black woman complains that "all my man can do is remember what's long, not how to make it last long." Kosinski used a variant of the line in interviews, with Plato's Retreat serving as the hook for promoting the book. Men who are "inflated" in their view of their sexuality, he quipped, may soon be "deflated." Such quips recall not only his displays of endurance during his youth in Warsaw as Tad Krauze's roommate, but also the speculation of his friend Stash Pomorski that Kosinski cultivated sexual stamina as a compensation for a feeling of inferior endowment.

The novel contains a surpassingly brilliant set piece on the art of sexual seduction—a virtual technical manual, displaying the poetics of Kosinski the sexual seducer, and, by extension, Kosinski the novelist. To persuade a woman to go to the club, Fabian explains, he uses "language and manner divested of palpable sexual intimation." The first step accomplished, he would bring his companion to the locker room, where the patrons in various states of undress would lull her by the "climate of mundane assumption." The "mood of the time and the place" then moved her to acts of intimacy—a covert knowledge shared with Fabian of acts that might never be repeated or revealed outside. Underlying seduction is the partner's participation in the universal drive for knowledge of oneself—a drive that Kosinski understood so well as to make his knowledge a formidable weapon. He expresses this awareness in his desire to allow Vanessa freedom to "experience *herself* in lovemaking with others."

Yet the tone of the Dream Exchange scene is not passionate but strangely weary, as if author and protagonist together are struggling to find a way to rekindle desire. Weariness, weakness, the loss of appetite and power, and the growing awareness of age are, ironically, the strongest subtext throughout a book in which the protagonist is a dynamic man of action, jousting on horseback with his foes. Behind it one glimpses the presence of a profoundly exhausted man, an author for whom the burden of being Jerzy Kosinski has become an almost unbearable weight.

The contract with Bantam was not signed until the end of March, very tight for September publication. Once again Kosinski spent the summer close to home, if not quite as close as he claimed to Alice Feder. In May, he attended a birthday brunch for Jacob Javits, taking rolls of film as usual and receiving the senator's thanks when he provided prints. Still, by his recent standards it was a quiet period, the lull before the storm. Over the course of the summer, as he drove the editors at St. Martin's to distraction with changes, Kosinski was involved in yet another controversy. After Kosinski's own last-minute changes to the script of *Being There*, Hal Ashby had asked Robert Jones, who had worked with him on *Coming Home* and was film editor for the project, to do a final touchup. Now Ashby wanted Jones to receive the screenwriting credit, or at least share it. Kosinski's script had been "dramatically too heavy-handed," Jones argued, and each scene of the actual shooting script was "greatly different" from Kosinski's version. Kosinski, who had known a confrontation was brewing from the day shooting began, was adamant. He had his working scripts to show, and he was determined to make a fight of it.

The real story, as Kosinski saw it, was that Ashby owed Jones a debt for failing to credit him properly in the past. He claimed, in fact, that Ashby had admitted as much in the course of the discussion, asking Kosinski to be helpful and let him reward Jones for past services with a share of the credit. By the time it was over, Peter Sellers got involved. Sellers, who would receive his only Oscar nomination for his portrayal of Chauncey Gardiner, had by then fallen out with Kosinski, reportedly because Kosinski had gone around informing people that Sellers had a face and chin lift. Sellers insisted that Jones was the writer of the final draft, and fumed about Kosinski, who he said had "an ego from here to Mont Blanc." To settle the matter once and for all, Kosinski submitted the matter to the Writers Guild of America for judgment. The WGA arbitrators decided unequivocally in Kosinski's favor, giving him sole screenwriting credit.

In August, he found time amidst jousting with his various foes to play a prank on his fellow members of the all-male Century Club. For years Kosinski had been showing his friends a collection of nude photos he had taken, including dozens of photos of transsexuals at every stage of transformation. Many of them were stunning images of sexual ambiguity, with intermediate stages after hormone therapy juxtaposing impressive penises with hourglass figures and large breasts. The final postsurgery portraits often showed tall, ravishing women. Now Kosinski exhibited three nudes at the Century Club entitled Woman 1, Woman 2, and Woman 3. Only after the members had been left to appreciate the photos for a time did he reveal that they were drawn from his collection of fully transformed transsexuals. "They're perfectly beautiful and feminine," he said, adding puckishly, "The law has never defined sexuality. Why should I?" He told the *New York Post* that he had "one of the largest collections of photographs of transsexuals in the world," an assertion that none came forward to challenge. The *Post* did the story under a picture of Kosinski labeled "Kosinski: transsexual expert."

As with much in his life, Kosinski's preoccupation with transsexualism raises a point-of-view question. Was he, as the Century Club prank implied, a distanced observer, holding up to examination one more piece of the rich human tapestry? In public, he often seemed so. Yet there are clues that his interest in transsexualism stemmed from a powerful inner sexual imago. Rarely did Kosinski include in his books episodes that had no relationship at all with his personal history, and therefore the Alexandra episode in *Passion Play* poses an intriguing question: Is not a woman who insists upon penetrating her male partner equivalent to an incompletely changed transsexual? Kosinski's sexual romps at this time included three-way encounters involving an exceptionally beautiful, partly transformed person called Cheyenne. Is Alexandra an analogue of Cheyenne? Is this a gender transformation more subtle than, but equivalent to, Proust's addition of the feminizing *e* to the names of male lovers? The literal answer seems less important than the revelation of Kosinski's persistence in exploring the boundary between genders—an exploration dating back at least as far as his homosexual advance to Tad Krauze. Here, as much as in any area of philosophical inquiry, his actions would appear to have broken through the limits of ordinary categories.

Earlier that summer Kosinski had entered into a brief relationship that displayed still another side of his eroticism, a side at once poignant and playful, sad and more than a little sinister. While in the waiting room of his doctor's office, on Central Park South, Kosinski noticed a blond woman in her late twenties with a splendid full figure. From the receptionist he was able to find out her name, Joy Weiss, and by calling all the J. Weisses in the Manhattan phone book, he was able to arrange a date with her. Joy Weiss, it turned out, had read his books and was suitably impressed. She worked as an editor at a children's-wear trade magazine, which he told her was appropriate, as she looked like a child.

On their first date Kosinski took Joy Weiss to Arthur's, where she noticed that the waiters and waitresses fixed him with cold stares. "You see these people here?" he told her. "They all have dreams of succeeding. I have contacts in Hollywood." Pointing to a waitress, he told her of his contempt for women who wanted success but not badly enough. "I told them if they slept with me I could introduce them to people. They deserve my contempt because they aren't willing to do everything."

In the course of the dinner he regaled her with an account of a recent dinner with Lee Radziwill—an event that, in fact, would shortly prompt gossip columnist Liz Smith to query him about rumors of a romance. As for Kiki, he described her to Joy Weiss as a woman who took care of him, whom he couldn't do without, who kept his life in order. She dealt with publishers, served as his supersecretary. "I am her whole life," he said. "She has nothing to live for but me. I'm not attracted to her." He then described Kiki cruelly as asexual, explaining that they had been "interested in each other once."

"What did you see in her?" Joy Weiss wanted to know.

"She's *German aristocracy*," he replied instantly, a response that left Weiss, who had grown up Jewish in Atlanta, somewhat perplexed.

Toward the end of the meal he suggested that the two of them go to Chateau Nineteen, an S-M parlor with which he seemed to be quite familiar. She agreed on condition that she not be required to participate or remove her clothes. Once they were there, he moved comfortably among the patrons, chatting as if at a country-club tea. He was particularly friendly with a man who worked in the jewelry district, who was busy masturbating as they spoke. As the man appeared about to ejaculate, Kosinski took Joy by the arm and moved away, explaining that the man was a masochist and would take pleasure in the humiliation of being abandoned.

Kosinski and Joy had three dates in all. During the third, at a less prepossessing restaurant, Kosinski said that he had something important to tell her: He couldn't have sex with her because *he had no penis.* His penis had been damaged during the war, he said, and he went on to deliver gruesome details of an episode of torture left out of *The Painted Bird.* It was his only pleasure, he went on, to perform those sexual acts of which he was still capable, and he hoped that she would permit him that. Curious and moved by his story, Joy consented. Back at her apartment, they touched. She probed for a penis. What would she find? A stump?—and, indeed, there was none. Then, at the climactic moment, he lifted his torso, revealing a fully erect penis, and thrust into her. It was, in her view, very nearly an act of rape.

"Why did you tell me that story?" she asked afterward.

To which he replied in a high-pitched voice: "I like surprises."

They had one further encounter. Five days later he called and explained that he was in her neighborhood, accompanied by a "steady" girl, a law student named Judy. Could the two of them come up? Joy at first said no, explaining that she had bad menstrual cramps, but Kosinski insisted on coming over. The three of them chatted briefly about the neighborhood, and then Kosinski suggested that the two women "get it on." "I thought you two would like each other," he said, "as you are the same age, race, and social status." He then chased Joy around her living room before finally giving up.

While Joy Weiss naturally found her overall experience with Jerzy Kosinski less than edifying, the episode seen as a whole contains elements that, from a more distant perspective, suggest more than simple sexual mischief. There is something vampirish in Kosinski's relentless quest for new sexual companions, but as with the mythic vampire figure, there is a desperation that cuts inward as well as outward. His celebration of his celebrity friend Lee Radziwill, like his exhortation that one should "do everything" for success, suggests the terrible deficit beneath the surface of the striver, while his celebration of "German aristocracy," echoing the boy's admiration of the SS trooper in *The Painted Bird*, suggests the powerful and permanent identification imposed upon the victim by his victimizers. As for his story about his penis, Joy was not the only woman in Kosinski's experience to witness the disappearing-penis stunt, which he also wrote about in *Cockpit*. Yet behind the trickery and near-rape, there was a profound psychological reality. His penis had indeed been damaged in the war—not physiologically, far from that, but in a crushing necessity to hide and protect it that permanently impaired his capacity for ordinary erotic pleasure, driving him toward the playfully sinister world of Chateau Nineteen.

With this side of his life expressed in his writing as never before, Kosinski braced himself for the reviews of *Passion Play*. Reviewers weren't kind. Jerry Klinkowitz, who had been an uncritical Kosinski cheerleader at the time of his 1971 interview, quarreled with the book's sexist tone and antidemocratic fascination with the rich; although Klinkowitz found other things to like in the novel, the tone of fatigue did not go unnoticed. Klinkowitz's review was published in the *Chicago Sun-Times* under the heading "The Aging Kosinski Knight, Questing on the Polo Field." Stefan Kanfer in *Time* set the terms for many reviewers by praising the fine descriptions of polo playing but comparing the prose to popular writer Harold Robbins. Ivan Gold in the *New York Times Book Review* followed in that vein, criticizing a "leaden, arbitrary tone" while praising "virtuoso writing about sex and horsemanship." John Leonard in the daily *Times* found it "lugubrious," a novel in which "a kind of rationalism metastasizes into fascism," while William Kennedy in the *Washington Post* was alone in noting that Kosinski was "much plottier than usual," a development that he felt held out promise for stories less manipulative and richer in spiritual substance.

Despite this decidedly mixed bag of notices, *Passion Play* reached the lower rungs of the bestseller list, in the process becoming the center of a small controversy about the way those lists were composed. The *Times* bestseller list was widely regarded as an important tool in selling books, and St. Martin's provoked the controversy by circulating a memo to the effect that the *Times Book Review,* which Kosinski saw as his enemy, rigged its list. The *Times,* it was argued, circulated its proposed list of bestsellers, giving booksellers only the limited choice of ordering the rankings. *Passion Play* had imposed itself on the *Times,* St. Martin's said, as a write-in too strong to be ignored, and even then the *Times* had asterisked it as a book that was relatively stronger on the West Coast, an assertion the memo also challenged. It was a fine publicity ploy, and one of the payoffs was a piece on Kosinski by Carol Lawson in her "Behind the Best Sellers" column for the *Times Book Review* of October 21.

In the Lawson interview, Kosinski made a point of denying the use of editors, also claiming, in stunning neglect of the facts, that he had never used an agent. The purpose of this latter claim could only have been to emphasize his own skills as a businessman and negotiator, qualities that were increasingly important to him; similarly, he claimed that writing was only an "avocation," another theme increasingly prominent in his self-presentation. Meanwhile he had appeared in *People* magazine on September 10, in a two-page layout with five pictures—one each with former Beatle George Harrison and Polanski, two on horseback, and one at his New York apartment with Warren Beatty and Diane Keaton, there to "urge him to act in their new film, *Reds.*"

Seemingly more and more attuned to the beat of contemporary history, he joined with E. L. Doctorow on October 25 in protesting the prison sentences handed out to six Czech human-rights activists, among them Vaclav Havel, the future president of Czechoslovakia. Earlier that year he had exchanged letters of sadness with Sadruddin Aga Khan over the execution of former Iranian Prime Minister Hoveyda, who had played a constructive role in his campaign to win the release of imprisoned writer Reza Baraheni. Now the Khomeini revolution had overtaken Hoveyda, as it would soon overtake his friends in the Carter White House. On November 4 a group of Iranian "students," expressing the will of a radical faction within that revolution, seized the American embassy, taking fifty-five hostages and beginning the long crisis that would eventually bring down the Carter administration and change the tone of American society.

Kosinski, by contrast, seemed invulnerable. The critics could do their worst, but his books still sold. His movie was due out early the following year, his credit as screenwriter was affirmed, and he was booked onto the Carson *Tonight Show* on January 10, the screenwriter plugging his movie as if he were the star. And the *People* story was true. Warren Beatty—the web of connection here went back through Andy Braunsberg to Polanski—did indeed want him in *Reds*, to play Lenin's henchman Zinoviev, with shooting to take place the next summer in Spain. His secrets, the ones that could really damage him, lay far in the past; witnesses had come forward, their stories had been evaluated by substantial judges, and the worst of the allegations had been dismissed. And anyway, if he could speak openly on talk shows about going to the sex clubs without anyone batting an eye, what could hurt him? His warning to Emily Prager never to "personify actions to yourself," her warnings to him never to go public with his darkest sexual recesses, were the furthest things from his thoughts. And if all of this, the strain of being Jerzy Kosinski, left him a little weary, what should one expect?

In naming his last book, he had focused on two Kosinskian words, *passion* and *play*, which, taken together as "passion play," describe a dark Christian genre dramatizing the sufferings of Christ. It might have profited him to meditate upon it. The "passion" of Jesus, as depicted by St. Mark, prefigures in its story structure a triumphant entry that leads within a short period to public humiliation and death.

3.

Being There was accorded a special premiere showing at the Kennedy Center in Washington on Sunday evening, February 3, 1980. Kosinski had already done a six-minute interview with Gene Shalit for NBC's *Today* on January 25, and *The New Yorker* had kicked in with a rave advance review. Now Washington society turned out for the premiere, with Jack Anderson and Bill Leonard, head of CBS News, adding comments for the next day's stories. Also in attendance were Liz Carpenter, Representative John

Brademas, then the congressional kingpin of arts funding, and Gretchen Posten from the White House, as well as the president and chairman of Lorimar. With the hostage crisis in full flow, Zbigniew Brzezinski was unable to make it, but he was represented by his wife, Muska, and their two sons. Peter Sellers was sick, Shirley MacLaine was making a film in Vermont, and Hal Ashby was off at an unknown location, leaving Kosinski as the evening's major star.

Kosinski rose to the occasion magnificently. Washington was a whole new world for him—and, despite his protestations, a more innocent one than New York—and he set out with all his charm to conquer it. The Monday papers were filled with his beaky profile, talking with this mover and that shaker. The *Star* recycled the old description of Kiki as a "European baroness," as well as her view that Kosinski resembled a camel or a seagull. Sitting patiently while cameras clicked, Kosinski cited the *Journal of the American Medical Association* description of Chauncey Gardiner as "unsane," living at "the line of demarcation between mental health and mental illness," then scored with the Washington insiders by comparing Gardiner to Nixon's behavior and Martha Mitchell's role in Watergate. Titillated by the portrait of themselves—the premiere seemed linked by some weird postmodern bridge to the diplomatic reception in the film—this new audience went for the old Kosinski hook, line, and sinker.

At $35 a ticket for cocktails and movie and $75 for cocktails, movie, and dinner at Desiree, the discotheque at the Four Seasons, the premiere netted $60,000 for the American Film Institute. Those who went for the dinner got to hear Kosinski hold court with the story of his wartime experiences, his escape from Poland, and his marriage to Mary Weir. It contained the usual details, such as arriving with $2.80 in his pocket, and threw in a few tidbits of impromptu invention, such as the fact that 70 percent of his books were purchased by women in the Midwest and Southwest. Asked if he had ever wanted a child, he replied no, he hadn't, but then in a fit of inspiration he confided that he had had *two*, one with a maid in a Polish hostel who married someone else and another with a Polish law student—a child he never saw. Swept along by his own invention, he went on within earshot of the *Washington Star* reporter that he thought there had been a third. Perhaps recalling the Lilla van Saher fantasy, he added that this child had been promptly and legally adopted, and now lived with a family—he knew the name—on Long island.

Had he ever been curious about the child? "No," he told the reporter. "I am curious about grownups, not children."

If socialites hung on every word and reporters transcribed his remarks as received gospel, there was good reason. The audience at the premiere sensed what would soon be made clear: *Being There* was a certified, bankable *hit! The New Yorker* had led the Current Cinema column with its lengthy, thoughtful treatment, giving special attention to the screenplay, which was seen as highly skilled and an improvement upon the novel, and ten major critics eventually put the film on their list of the year's best. The following year the film received a Golden Globe nomination in the comedy/musical category, and Sellers, MacLaine, and Melvyn Douglas all got individual Golden Globe nominations. Caleb Deschanel won the National Society of Film Critics Award as Best Cinematographer. The film was named as an official U.S. entry at Cannes in 1980, and Sellers and Douglas both received Oscar nominations, in the best-actor and best-supporting-actor categories. Although Sellers did not win, he had gotten the previous year on March 3, 1980, the cover story in *Time*. Melvyn Douglas, on the other hand, received the crowning accolade of a long and distinguished film career, winning the Oscar for his portrayal of Benjamin Rand.

And the movie did business. With a budget of $15 million, respectable but far below blockbuster scale, it would stand at one point among the twenty largest-grossing films ever made, a list dominated by high-budget extravaganzas like *Star Wars, The Exorcist,* and *Jaws*. Its appeal was widespread. A little over a year after its release, its foreign earnings alone were $20 million, a tremendous success for the time. The only mild disappointment was that Kosinski himself did not receive an Oscar nomination for the screenplay, a slight that may have been influenced by the Robert Jones flap over the screen credit. Although he and Sellers were at odds over this issue, Kosinski generously cabled Sellers a *bonne chance* from Crans, where he had already retreated with his consolation prize—the best-screenplay award from the Writers Guild of America, which had adjudicated his dispute with Jones.

Although friends commiserated about the Academy's oversight, there was no time to brood about failure to get an Oscar nomination. With his hectic schedule, old friends suddenly found him distant. Michael Wyler, one of his Switzerland crowd, wrote to take him to task for not setting up a meeting so they could have a short time together at the airport in Geneva, and for not acknowledging the effort of a M. Givet, whom Wyler had put forward as French translator of *Passion Play* and who had sent Kosinski a few sample pages. Kosinski replied calmly and charmingly that the Givet oversight had to do with the last-minute publishing arrangements on *Passion Play* and the fact that his French publisher, lately acquired, already had a translator in mind; he explained that he was being interviewed at the Geneva airport and felt it an imposition to have Wyler drive out there, and detailed a business schedule in Crans that made a social call unworkable. It would be less hectic, he hoped, when he came to Paris in May. Mollified, Wyler responded with a letter apologizing for his initial criticism. Such were the burdens of celebrity.

The filming of Kosinski's scenes in *Reds* was set for May and June, 1980, in Spain. By that time, Beatty had already been working on the film for two and a half years, as producer, director, and screenplay writer as well as star, and had invested another three or four years of work before the production was assembled. The film depicted the life of leftist American journalist John Reed, author of *Ten Days That Shook the World*, against the sweep of the Russian Revolution, showing both his violation of middle-class mores back in America and his inner struggle between love and social commitment while working with the Bolsheviks. For Beatty, it was a labor of love, the story of an anti-Establishment Bonnie and Clyde gone international and trendily legit. In a speech to a group of extras, he impressed Kosinski by demonstrating that he had even picked up rudimentary Russian along the way.

Kosinski's role in the film, Lenin's Bolshevik henchman Zinoviev, was to confront Reed with the claims of historical and moral obligation that conflicted with his desire to be with Louise

(Diane Keaton). There was a certain irony in this casting. Zinoviev, until Stalin wearied of him and had him executed, was exactly the kind of mechanical gray collectivist fanatic that Kosinski had spent the better part of his life getting around and railing against. Perhaps, it could be argued, none understood better the mentality out of which the Zinovievs of the world operated. Arriving in Madrid, Kosinski was surprised to discover that Beatty was using actual Russian émigrés as extras. Beatty himself looked tired and puffy with strain, and appeared daily in the baggy woolen trousers of his John Reed costume, engrossed in a Stanislavskian "living" of the story in which Kosinski soon joined him.

Rehearsals of the Reed–Zinoviev scenes, set at the Propaganda Ministry and Zinoviev's office, were held on May 24, with actual shooting scheduled for May 26 at the Palacio Riofrío in Segovia. Transportation from the hotel to the location resembled the maneuver of a medium-sized military unit, dwarfing anything Kosinski had seen in the filming of *Being There*. The relationship between Reed, the sometimes distracted journalist, and the rigidly committed Zinoviev was one of the central elements of the film, second in importance only to the love story, and while the scenes were being shot, Beatty and Kosinski naturally maintained the bonding off-camera, with Beatty as director often coaching Kosinski on his lines. They frequently had meals together, especially breakfasts. One morning Beatty, a notoriously late riser, arrived to be informed by Kiki that Jerzy was upset at having to wait for him and had left.

"Is he really angry with me?" he asked Kiki.

"He never stays angry for long," Kiki reassured. Just at that moment Beatty became aware of something warm in his shoes. "Jerzy, come out from under there," he ordered. Kosinski had concealed himself under the table and was pouring tea into Beatty's shoes. The stunt plagiarized Polanski's stunt, thirty years earlier, of tossing a cup of tea on Kosinski's jacket, although it had the Kosinskian twist of concealment. Later he tried the same stunt in New York with Abe Rosenthal and Punch Sulzberger, who were less wholeheartedly amused than Beatty, perhaps confirming Kosinski's oft-cited maxim that the worst plagiarism is of oneself.

On June 5 the production moved to the Alcázar in Seville for the shooting of the Baku meeting where Zinoviev solicits Islamic support for Bolshevism, and from there it moved on to the small village of Guadix for the shooting of the pivotal train scene as well as the battle scenes. With the town's only hostel commandeered as a storage depot for props, Kosinski and Beatty found themselves sharing a two-bedroom wooden house on the outskirts of the village, with the widow of a Falangist general as their landlady. Without refrigerator or hot water, they made do with a single 40-watt light bulb and a toilet that flushed irregularly; Kiki prepared breakfast on a portable two-ring stove, making toast by propping a slice of bread on a fork over the gas flame. A telephone was installed, and Beatty made a nightly series of calls to America. Thus Kosinski and Beatty replicated the living arrangements of Zinoviev and Reed, who shared a house with very rudimentary facilities, with Reed neglecting his role as revolutionary propagandist to make telephone calls home to America.

To facilitate their last-minute polishing of the critical Reed–Zinoviev exchanges, an electric typewriter was set up on a table in the cramped living room, which displayed photos of the late Falangist general and his staff, and of Franco himself—figures who, in Kosinski's mind, were stand-ins for the czar and his entourage. Under these difficult conditions, Kosinski rewrote his own lines, using the skills acquired in the making of *Being There* and knowledge from his Eastern European past. The showdown comes as Reed seeks transportation out to see the woman he loves and Zinoviev seizes upon the metaphor of a train—the Communists as engineers, the Party providing the track—to persuade Reed to stay. Kosinski reworked his own speech extensively, first writing out Zinoviev's argument in Russian, to test how it would have sounded in the original language, before putting it back into English. The final shooting version, and especially the last-minute addition of the final line, are both credibly Zinoviev and pure Kosinski:

"Thus by going now to Finland, you are abandoning that train.

Remember, Comrade Reed, what matters now is no longer where you're going—it is what you're running away from. It's *your* choice."

Beatty gave Kosinski a place in the credits above Jack Nicholson. Looking back on the experience for a piece he published in *Vogue* in April 1982, Kosinski reveled in the exhilaration of roughing it in Spain while working with Warren Beatty. Swept away by the exaltation of it, he sympathetically quoted a Soviet tourist who compared the courage of Beatty, in presenting Reed in America, to the courage that would have been required in the contemporary Soviet Union to unearth and celebrate the discredited and executed Zinoviev. Thirty years earlier, in the dark hours of the McCarthy era, it might well have been so. By 1980, however, a sentimental and romanticized view of Bolshevik revolutionaries was a conventional Hollywood conceit. That Kosinski, even in his personal enthusiasm for Beatty, could overlook such a fact demonstrated how far removed he had become from his roots in Marxist Poland. It was as if to say that political struggles are really unimportant, that the only important human distinctions are those between the high-flying elite and the rest of humanity. Nothing matters but to fly with that elite, and once a part of it, all politics are personal, beginning with the shared altitude. Kosinski seemed unaware that Icarian wings had borne him upward into dangerously thin air.

Returning from Spain directly to New York without the planned stopover in Paris, Kosinski was at work by early August on a new novel, and he worked hard straight through the fall. On November 4, in an election that had the Iran hostage crisis always in the background, Ronald Reagan was elected president. It signaled a major turn in American culture. Kosinski joined the mood of pessimism that came over the world of the arts, conjuring gloomy and imaginative scenarios for the future that he presented at dinner parties with gallows humor.

With Kiki he made the usual Christmas trip for polo in the Dominican Republic. On January 4 an interview he had done with Maralyn Lois Polak appeared in the Sunday Magazine of the *Philadelphia Inquirer;* oddly, Kosinski talked of his ordinariness, calling himself a "very marginal novelist" and "lesser talent." It

JERZY KOSINSKI 371

suggesting suppressed discomfort about the rarefied heights at
which he was traveling. In February he left for Switzerland,
where he planned to stay until the end of April. Soon, however,
he was pressured by the British Academy of Film and Television
Arts to attend their annual awards ceremony in March. *Being
There* was up for four awards, with Kosinski nominated in the
category of best screenplay, and officials from BAFTA intimated
that it would look like a slight to the Academy if no one connected with the film showed up.

Reluctantly, Kosinski agreed to make the trip. It was, after all,
a grand occasion, with MPs and royals in the audience, black tie,
the works, three full hours of it, and televised throughout the
United Kingdom. Kosinski, with Kiki, was seated with Liberal
Party leader David Steele, journalist Russell Harty, and the Alec
Guinnesses. Kosinski felt certain that he had been dragooned into
attending because an award had gone either to Sellers as best actor or to the picture. He was flabbergasted when his name was
called for best screenplay. The bronze BAFTA statuette—the British "Oscar"—was heavier than it looked, and he almost dropped
it. He stashed the statuette in his room, terrified that it would be
stolen, and went out for drinks and a party where he hobnobbed
with the likes of David Frost and Tony Armstrong-Jones. Could it
get better than this?

4.

While Kosinski's career soared, the elements of a coming crisis
were slowly falling into place. Jerry Klinkowitz had made a trip
to Poland in 1979, where Polish scholars and officials disputed
many of the things Kosinski had told in their 1971 interview. The
problem with these revelations was that Klinkowitz's informants
had an ax to grind. Yet Klinkowitz began to turn up other pieces
of Kosinski mythology that did not scan. Kosinski's claim to a
lifetime of horsemanship was disputed by a man who claimed he
had recently given Kosinski riding lessons in Central Park. This
version would call into question Kosinski's account, published as

fact, of riding horses to death as a boy in Poland, supposedly a story he told Porfirio Rubirosa in the early 1960s. (The notion that he talked horses with Rubirosa, or even met him, while traveling with Mary Weir, was equally suspect.) Klinkowitz also came to have doubts about Kosinski's long-standing protestation that he had resisted the filming of *Being There*. Meeting Klinkowitz at Northern Iowa, Zdzislaw Najder expressed incredulity at Kosinski's extravagant and melodramatic accounts of his departure from Poland, which had him ready to commit suicide if caught. "A cyanide capsule indeed!" Najder told Klinkowitz.

Such revisions were not unusual in the self-presentations of fiction writers. Hemingway and Faulkner, for example, would be caught in fabrications at least as flagrant, with interesting suggestions as to their deepest psychological motives but no great harm to their literary reputations. Klinkowitz wrote up his doubts and discoveries in a piece called "Betrayed by Jerzy Kosinski" and circulated it among major magazines, none of which was interested. Klinkowitz, too, it could be argued, had an ax to grind. As an early cheerleader for Kosinski and his work, he felt taken in. His position must have struck editors as rather narrow and literal-minded, and focused on the marginalia of a writer's life. Unable to publish it, Klinkowitz circulated his piece like a samizdat manuscript among writers and scholars interested in Kosinski, where it became part of the rising chorus of doubt.

Klinkowitz's trip to Poland had been the first event that threatened to breach the tight compartmentalization of Kosinski's Polish and American lives. Friends in his émigré circle, even when feeling abandoned and slighted, had withheld their personal bits of knowledge—some out of personal loyalty, some out of loyalty to a fellow Pole, and some because it simply never occurred to them that anyone might be interested and willing to believe them. The story that Aleksander Lutoslawski had translated all or part of *The Painted Bird* was well known in Polish-American circles, while stories of Kosinski's use of private editors had become a staple of gossip in New York literary circles. While some fudging of biographical facts was to be expected, the proof of wide use of editors and translators held the potential for a full-scale scandal, especially if it was made public knowledge at a moment of vulnerability.

In April *Horizon* did a story about the use of private editors—"heirs to Maxwell Perkins"—which might have served as an early warning of interest in the subject. At the same time it offered a suggestion of mitigating circumstances in its discussion of the deterioration of editing inside publishing houses. Meanwhile, with his early work appearing on reading lists at most major universities, Kosinski was coming under increasing scrutiny by the academic world. Some of the critical studies were harmless enough. Byron Sherwin at Chicago's Spertus College of Judaica had produced a monograph entitled *Jerzy Kosinski: Literary Alarmclock*, which focused on the connection of Kosinski and his work to the Holocaust and Marxist collectivity. Sherwin accepted Kosinski's stories at face value, validating with scholarly authority Kosinski's public account of his childhood, his mastery of English, and his marriage with Mary Weir (no mention of divorce), among other things.

Norman Lavers, a novelist-scholar at the University of Arkansas, embarked on a somewhat more ambitious project, attempting to run down details of Kosinski's life to play against his fiction. Lavers sought Kosinski's active assistance, in the process himself becoming co-opted. It was an awkward position, he soon discovered, to be writing a critical study of an author who line-edited your text. It was also a fine way of getting exactly the public truth and not a bit more. Lavers was sympathetic to Kosinski's view in any case. Nevertheless his book put on public record a more detailed account of Kosinski's life than had yet been assembled, and along with it there was a record of Kosinski's own line-editing, particularly of Lavers's chronology and details of his personal history. This effort to micromanage his public persona would soon come back to haunt him.

Political events were also conspiring to create the conditions for an assault on Kosinski. During the first months of triumphant Reaganism, the community of American writers and intellectuals tilted noticeably to the Left. Despite his paean to Warren Beatty, Kosinski was trapped, both by his background as dissenter to Marxist collectivism and by his close friendship with men on the top floor of the *New York Times,* especially Abe Rosenthal, who, though no Reaganite, was a centrist neoconservative. No aspect of the political culture wars better illustrates Kosinski's vulnerable position than the Jack Abbott affair. In 1973, in his first year as PEN president, Kosinski had instituted a program for prisoners, providing books and magazines, giving writing awards, and facilitating exchange between prisoners who wrote and American writers. One of the participants was Jack Henry Abbott, a convict at Leavenworth, who in 1973 wrote Kosinski a fan letter at PEN, expressing admiration of Stalin along with his view that *The Painted Bird* was supportive of such an attitude. Kosinski wrote back, disabusing Abbott of that notion and providing copies of interviews which made his contempt for Stalin and all his works clear. Abbott then wrote Kosinski a number of critical letters, accusing him of being a capitalist entrepreneur, an enemy of the masses, and a Rockefeller lickspittle. Kosinski finally put an end to the exchange with a letter telling Abbott that his childlike rage and murderous ad hominem attacks were unacceptable. After a silence of many months, Abbott sent Kosinski a letter of apology.

There followed a long crusade in which numerous literary intellectuals, led by Norman Mailer, campaigned for Abbott's parole on the grounds that he was a reformed man and an important literary talent, and Abbott was indeed paroled in time for the release of his book, *In the Belly of the Beast.* Kosinski received an inscribed copy of the book and was one of a half-dozen writers invited to dinner by Abbott because, he said, they were responsible for his literary career. Although he disliked Abbott's book, Kosinski attended the dinner, partly out of curiosity. Swept up in the bonhomie of the occasion, Kosinski embraced and toasted Abbott, actions that would come back to haunt him when, on July 18, 1981, Abbott murdered a waiter and aspiring actor named Richard Adan. Perhaps out of guilt for his peripheral role in the legitimization of Abbott, Kosinski did a quick reversal and provided the *Times Book Review* with quotes and fragments of his correspondence with Abbott for use in the September 20 issue. His view was that the Abbott affair revealed the uncritical attitude of American intellectuals toward violence committed by the

Left; had "Hitlerism" rather than Marxism-Leninism been Abbott's credo, he argued, no one would have been drinking to his success.

Kosinski's part in the Abbott affair both recalled and counter-pointed his overblown praise of Warren Beatty, while the rapid switch in his position contributed to a public image as a chameleon, a quality taken for granted in politicians but less tolerable in intellectual arbiters of public taste and morality. Underneath his various positions was a genuine fear and distrust of collectivities, combined with strong sympathy for the underdog and deep belief in free speech. Yet Kosinski couldn't stop himself from speaking to the immediate audience—in the one instance as acolyte to Warren Beatty, in the other first embracing Abbott, in the close community of New York literati, then backing away in horror when the underside of Abbott was graphically revealed.

On October 9 the first American Writers' Congress met at the Roosevelt Hotel, and under the leadership of Toni Morrison and Victor Navasky laid out an ambitious agenda calling for an end to censorship and endorsing in principle a national writers' union; innocuous in its particulars, the congress was dominated in tone by a leftist critique of Reagan-dominated American politics, and Kosinski was one of very few writers to make a public protest against the aims of the congress. With his personal knowledge of the way national writers' unions actually worked, often serving as the implement for imposing censorship, Kosinski was no doubt sincere in his disagreement with the congress. Taken together with his remarks on Abbott, however, his view on the congress caused him to be marked as a fellow traveler of neoconservatism—a position that would figure strongly in the motivation to bring him down.

There was a certain irony in the fact that, at the very moment when politics—never a matter of personal priority or deep conviction—were laying the groundwork for trouble, Kosinski was beginning to feel the tug of deeper and older, and more permanent, allegiances. The assassination attempt on the pope in May had moved him deeply, as it touched not only personal acquaintance but the part of himself that remained, despite frequent ethnic self-deprecation, Polish. The Solidarity movement was an

expression of that Polishness with which he could wholeheartedly agree, and he pitched in as a visible Polish-American,
meeting with American labor leaders (and later accepting an
award in absentia for Lech Walesa).

His Jewish identity, too, had begun to be more important to
him, and his renewed sense of Jewishness was expressed on a
philosophical plane by an interest in the teachings of Abraham
Joshua Heschel. His mentor in this was Byron Sherwin of Chicago's Spertus College, the rabbi and scholar whose recent critical
study had flattered Kosinski. Of Heschel's writings, Kosinski
found particularly congenial the assertion in *Man Is Not Alone*
that "humanity begins in the individual man, just as history takes
its rise from a singular event." This was close enough to Monod's
philosophy of chance and necessity and his own anarchic individualism to bridge the gap to Jewish theology. To give his theolog-
ical interests a nonsectarian twist, he simultaneously embraced
the Lutheran theology of Paul Tillich.

Tillich, who loved jazz and black women, and who saw no in-
consistency between spiritual life and unfettered sexuality, was a
natural match for Kosinski, and was the psychological model implicit in his theology. "To be a man," Tillich had written in *The
Protestant Era*, "involves this transcending of vital existence, the
freedom from himself, the freedom to say 'Yes' or 'No' to his vital
existence. This freedom, which is an essential part of him and
from which he cannot escape, carries with it the fact that he is
radically threatened." Kosinski was indeed *radically threatened*,
from earliest childhood, and much of his life consisted in the effort to claim his *vital existence*, to say "Yes" to a life in which he
never felt fully present or "real." Upon reading Tillich, Kosinski
was uplifted by the notion that the feeling of unreality with
which he had struggled all his life—the state Freudian clinicians
called alexithymia—was in fact an essential confrontation of the
human condition.

Throughout 1981, Kosinski had been plugging away on his
eighth novel, an extensively researched thriller of sorts, set in the
world of music. The editor assisting on the novel was Maxine
Bartow, whom he had found through Bantam. As had been the
case with Richard Hayes, Kosinski required her to surrender all

drafts and notes when she left the Fifty-Seventh Street apartment, although, ironically in light of the trouble that was soon to come, his compositional process had evolved into a more conventional pattern, as Kosinski presented Maxine with triple-spaced drafts that Maxine reworked, Kiki retyped, and Kosinski reworked in turn. For the first time, a Kosinski novel had two protagonists—Domostroy, an older and written-out classical composer, and Goddard, a young rock star whose concealed identity is the pivot of the plot. Like all of his recent work, *Pinball*, as the novel was called, was filled with teasing allusions to Kosinski's own life. It begins with Domostroy carrying the dead battery of his car, something that Kosinski actually did, and incorporates material from trashy magazines—Candypants (the edible underwear) and advice to middle-aged women to take a lover or redecorate the house—which would appear to have been no more than current, and perishable, Kosinski interests. Domostroy drinks Cuba Libres—rum and Coke. Kosinski, too, after a lifetime of abstemiousness about alcohol, had begun to drink rum and Coke, at the suggestion of his doctor that he calm his nerves with a cocktail containing high sugar content; indeed, as it was an unusual drink in New York circles, he had taken to storing his own bottle of rum at the home of Marian Javits, among others.

Like Kosinski, the young rock star, whose real name is Jimmy Osten, has been involved with an older woman—Leila Salem, whose name suggests Lilla van Saher. The careers of both Domostroy and Goddard/Osten contain parallels to Kosinski's, Domostroy's compositions including *The Bird of Quintain*, *Octaves*, the film score for *Chance*, and a *Baobab Concerto* written at Yale. Jack Abbott is present as a murderous country musician, and PEN is caricatured in Domostroy's presidency of MUSE International. *Pinball* is also replete with tributes—particularly to Goddard Lieberson, and to Boris Pregel, the president of the New York Academy of Sciences, who had taken up Kosinski in his early days in the United States. Both are cited within the text by the young rocker Osten, who has chosen "Goddard" as his public name, and both are cited in the book's dedication, a teasing interplay between text and life. A music award—the Elisabeth Weinreich-Levinkopf

Piano Prize—preserves the name of Kosinski's mother, who was notionally a concert pianist.

Pinball is at one level an artist-novel, examining the creative personality and its methods, and in particular the incorporation of personal history into works of art. Domostroy now performs at the "Kreutzer," a jazz club named after the Beethoven sonata but also for the famous Tolstoy story of the same name, in which the power of music (literary art) is set against sexual passion. Then again Domostroy, his creative juices run dry, seeks to revive himself at sex clubs like Dead Heat, while his youthful alter ego, Osten, fairly bursts with sexual and creative energy but feels driven to conceal his identity. The "thriller" aspect of the plot is driven by the efforts of Andrea Gwynplaine to unmask Goddard, culminating in a shootout where only Osten and Domostroy survive, to offer each other a final salute.

At the deeper level, *Pinball* is a novel about divided personality and disclosure, and as such it is both eerily prophetic and profoundly revealing about Kosinski's mental state. The fatigue that plagued Fabian in *Passion Play* has brought Domostroy's work to a halt. While one may see Osten as the young Kosinski played against Domostroy the old, his status as a rock star also suggests the current side of Kosinski—actor, screenwriter, and celebrity—which has taken flight just as his writing career is being overtaken by self-doubt. The inevitably collaborative nature of art is addressed by both major characters, while Domostroy speaks of music as an art form that does not reveal an accent—an allusion to the inadequate command of English that drove Kosinski to the use of translators and editors. Domostroy is the inner Kosinski, dying from a sense of hollowness and inauthenticity, while Goddard/Osten, soaring through a slightly different creative universe, must avoid disclosure at all costs. Indeed until the midpoint of the book, when Goddard's identity as Osten is disclosed, the reader is tempted to think that the blocked Domostroy and the never-seen Goddard may be one and the same. The inability to pull these two identities together—the increasing gap between high-flying surface and imploding inner being—represents the core problem of Kosinski's life, and even limited disclosure by en-

emies who conspired to entrap him would expose that gap in
such a way as to bring about the final crisis.

5.

Reds was released in December, 1981. It had all the qualities of a
great and important movie—high budget, ideological commitment, sweeping panorama, and a cast of thousands—and critics
tried hard to like it, while the industry accorded it a predictably
large number of Oscar nominations. As a whole, however, their
response was less enthusiastic than it had been to the relatively
unpretentious, and far less costly, *Being There.* Public response
was similarly mixed. Amidst this somewhat subdued reception,
Kosinski more than held his own. Some critics found his acting
on the heavy-handed side, but Vincent Canby, writing in the
Times, felt he was just right as the bloodless apparatchik Zinoviev
and called him one of the great new acting talents of the year.
For Kosinski, it was the beginning of his triumphal entry into
Jerusalem.

Critics were less friendly to *Pinball.* In the daily *Times* Christopher Lehmann-Haupt argued that "Kosinski's long affair with the
English language is not going well," and his criticism of
Kosinski's use of clichés set the tone for other reviewers. In the
Sunday *Book Review*, Benjamin DeMott echoed critiques of *Passion
Play* that had praised the scenes about horsemanship while dis-
missing the book by pinpointing "music talk" as the book's only
redeeming feature. Joshua Gilder in *Saturday Review* dismissed
the book as a "pornographic thriller," while Stefan Kanfer for
Time praised the lampooning of rock lyrics, the description of the
South Bronx, and the informed discussions of classical music before concluding that Kosinski admirers will say, "What a waste!"

In retrospect, the reviews of *Pinball* seem a little severe.
Kosinski received scant credit for his construction of an imaginative and effective plot in an extension of the thriller genre, or for
acute insights into the situation and methods of the artist. A negative critical response was, perhaps, a foregone conclusion;
Kosinski was being measured against his own early work and the

full extent of his literary reputation, which had begun to look somewhat overblown. And the envy factor, with his recent Hollywood successes, should not be overlooked. None of which might have mattered to Kosinski had not *Pinball* been so directly the product of his divided heart. The advance—$300,000—had returned him to the lofty commercial status achieved by *Blind Date*, and early sales figures were promising. Broadway producer Lee Guber saw the potential for a musical in it; he had Tom Ewen, author of *Dreamgirls*, in mind for the book and lyrics. By late spring a meeting would be held at Kosinski's apartment, with an agreement reached in principle and leaked for use in Liz Smith's celebrity column, although the project would be overtaken by subsequent events.

If reviewers did not note the confluence of Kosinski's diverse accomplishments, his multifaceted talents were being celebrated in a larger arena. On February 21, 1982, the Sunday *New York Times Magazine* ran a cover story on Kosinski written by his friend Barbara Gelb, a regular contributor to the magazine who, through her husband Arthur, stood close to the center of power at the *Times*. Breathless in tone, the article repeated the sanctioned version of Kosinski's wartime experiences, a lone boy wandering through the Eastern European countryside, and gave maximum play to his achievements as writer, screenwriter, and actor. It detailed his work for human rights as president of PEN and his early support of Solidarity, his visits to sex clubs, and his presence in the world of social glitz, giving full play to his pranks and quirks. Apart from its wholesale acceptance of the core mythology, the article contained numerous factual errors. It was accompanied by a number of pictures—Kosinski as car parker and riding polo pony, with his parents, Kiki, Polish girlfriends, George Harrison, Roman Polanski, Zbigniew Brzezinski and Diane von Furstenberg, and Douglas Fraser of the UAW. The picture on the cover was of Kosinski in polo gear but stripped to the waist, his narrow shoulders and sunken chest rendered imposing by Annie Leibovitz's camera angle. While the surface of the image suggested polo, the whip and leathers gave it an unmistakable subtext of S-M.

The *Times Magazine* story, and especially the cover photo, were a final straw. Its wanton self-promotion caused it to be filled with traceable errors; David Weir was so troubled by its inaccuracies that he wrote the *Times* and was deterred with great difficulty from undertaking public action—a letter or a suit. Worst of all, it was the ultimate violation of Moses Lewinkopf's admonition to live an obscure life, and of Kosinski's own credo of disguising one's nature. It violated Emily Prager's warning not to go public with the details of his sexual nature, and his own caveat to her that an artist should never make his or her *person* the central issue. It was wretched excess, inviting efforts to expose and bring him down. It is hard, in retrospect, to see his promoting such a piece and posing for such a photo as anything other than a reckless drive to self-destruction. And, indeed, within a month the wheels of that destruction had been set in motion in two separate quarters.

That spring Kosinski proceeded with a number of matters that had been in progress for several months. He served as judge of the Scholastic Writing Awards, as he had agreed to do the preceding December, conscientiously evaluating twenty student stories and turning in his rating sheet ahead of the March 17 deadline. On March 21 he participated in a Holocaust conference at the Waldorf, further affirming his growing interest in Jewish affairs. A second event involving high-school students touched upon the issue of censorship in regard to one of his own books. The previous November thirty female students at Lower Merion High School in Ardmore, Pennsylvania, signed a strongly worded letter to the school principal asking that *Cockpit* be removed from the reading list of the Science and Mystery Fiction class taught by John Osipowicz. Osipowicz had written Kosinski about the incident, and Kosinski phoned him back, suggesting that he meet with the students. On March 24 seventy Lower Merion students arrived by bus at the offices of Bantam Books, to meet with Kosinski and Bantam's publicity director, Stuart Applebaum. Kosinski later told Osipowicz that, not having addressed students since his Yale days, he had donned a disguise and watched their arrival from the drugstore in the lobby. Kosinski gave the group two full hours, speaking for thirty minutes, answering an hour of questions, and lingering for another thirty minutes of one-on-one discussions.

The major ongoing project at this time was a plan to film *Passion Play*, which had been under discussion, off and on, for the better part of a year between Kosinski and Ted Field, a scion of the Marshall Field retailing and communications empire in Chicago, and Field's partner Peter Samuelson. As far back as the previous September, both *New York* magazine and the *Hollywood Reporter* had announced the film as a done deal, with Field's Kinesis Productions as production company and Tony Maylam as director. Kosinski had been working with Maylam on the script, going back and forth from New York to Los Angeles, and by March 18 Maylam was ready with a completely rewritten draft for discussions later that month in Westwood, where Kosinski was to be an Academy Awards presenter.

The selection of Kosinski as presenter was in part compensation for the absence of an Oscar nomination as best screenwriter for *Being There* or as best supporting actor for *Reds* (the nomination having gone to Jack Nicholson, who was better known if one line lower in the credits); it was also part of a search for gimmicks and surprises to boost the show's ratings. Kosinski completed his discussions with Ted Field, reaching a memorandum of agreement on March 26. Two days later a limo that once drove the Marx Brothers picked him up for the Oscar rehearsals. Exiting the limo, he was stunned by the crowd that had assembled for a mere rehearsal.

His final novel, *The Hermit of 69th Street*, gives a hilarious account of his stage fright and difficulties with pronunciation during the rehearsal. Although he always gave the public appearance of complete ease, he had a long history of performance anxiety—often evacuating his stomach and bowels before an important appearance. Earlier that afternoon he had floated in the hotel pool, in an attempt to dispel an attack of nerves. Kosinski was to deliver awards number 21 and 22. The script required that he deliver the line, "The Bible tells us that in the beginning was the word." As detailed in *Hermit*, he struggled with the pronunciation of "word," which came out successively as "world," "ward," "wart," "war," and "worth." Meanwhile he scoped out the giant cue cards located next to the giant TV cameras in the middle of the auditorium, trying to prepare himself for whatever could possibly go wrong.

The following night was stormy, with a driving rain that ruined expensive hairdos and drenched luxurious gowns. Waiting in the wings, Kosinski suffered a sudden attack of stomach cramps and had to be led off by his page to a toilet. Upon returning, he suddenly realized that he was on the wrong side of the stage—the right—while the Oscars he was to present and the cue cards with his speech were on the left. His heart pounding arrhythmically, as it seemed to him, he vomited quietly into a handkerchief as the page led him to the correct side. Arriving with less than a minute to spare, he was introduced by emcee Johnny Carson as the actor in *Reds*, author of the current bestseller *Pinball*, and adapter of his own novel for the film *Being There*. He delivered his line about the "word" flawlessly, his accent providing just the proper note of the exotic, and went on to do a comedy routine about the Ten Commandments being the first script, and then delivered the award for best original screenplay to Colin Welland for *Chariots of Fire*, which was also an upset winner in the best-picture category. Welland humbly thanked Hollywood for giving him a chance. A moment later, with less fanfare but a plug for the screenplay he was "now struggling to write" for *Passion Play*, Kosinski presented the award for best-screenplay-based-on-material-from-another-medium to Ernest Thompson for the adaptation of his own play *On Golden Pond*. Thompson made the next day's newspapers by inviting the audience, in a line from the film, to "suck face."

Six hundred million people around the world had watched Kosinski's flawless performance. It was another supreme moment in the public eye, but it had its price. Worn out by the stress, he was eager to get out of L.A. and over to Crans where he could relax. There was, however, a nagging worry. He had heard rumors that *The Nation* was about to do a story on him. Earlier that month, in San Francisco to promote *Pinball*, he had phoned Victor Navasky, the managing editor, to ask how it was that they were preparing an article without talking to him. The exact content of their conversation is in dispute, but Kosinski hung up without being reassured and placed a second call to Hamilton Fish, *The Nation*'s publisher, whom he knew well. Once again he failed to receive satisfaction. Some kind of story was in the works, but its exact nature was unclear.

The story at *The Nation* had originated with Betsy Pochoda, its literary editor, and it went back a number of years to a letter she had received from Kosinski when she was writing reviews for *Glamour* and *Vogue*. The letter had been riddled with such errors that, in her view, its author could not possibly have been the writer of Kosinski's award-winning novels. Over the years she had picked up literary gossip about Kosinski's supposed "ghost writers" and had decided that such gossip was altogether plausible. In early 1982 she shared her opinion with Navasky, and made him a strange bet. People well enough situated in America, she bet him, could get away with anything, even if their most shameful secrets were revealed. Behind the seemingly flippant wager was a very real question: Could American culture distinguish the real from the fake? Pochoda didn't think so, and as an example she could cite Chuck Ross's stunt of circulating *Steps* in typescript to publishers. Kosinski would thus make a doubly appropriate test case.

Such, at least, is one inside account. The use of the Chuck Ross episode to demonstrate the survival power of "fakery" carries the unmistakable implication that Pochoda had made a negative judgment on Kosinski to start with. The clear suggestion is that without his personal PR campaigns, his work did not stand on its own merit—one of several possible interpretations of the Ross stunt. But the editors of *The Nation* also had personal, and political, reasons to go after Kosinski. The magazine had been the leading organizer of the previous year's American Writers' Congress, with both Navasky and Hamilton Fish on the steering committee. Editors at *The Nation* saw themselves as the last bastion of the retreating intellectual Left, making a courageous final stand against the advance of triumphant Reaganism. Kosinski's friends at the top of the *New York Times* had refused to make a categorical break with the White House—had even embraced certain Reaganite positions—and Kosinski, in turn, had refused to make a clean break from the likes of Arthur Gelb, Abe Rosenthal, and

Punch Sulzberger. From the viewpoint of *The Nation*, Kosinski had broken ranks with the intellectual foot-soldiers and thrown in his lot with the bosses. Thus the decision to do an exposé on Kosinski may reasonably be seen as part of an ongoing culture war over the American soul, and the Barbara Gelb article in the *Times* magazine, written by the wife of one of his cronies and elevating him to superstar status, no doubt provided the crystallizing moment. Kosinski had abandoned his peers and criticized their congress; now it was payback time.

That spring Pochoda had a lunch date with Geoffrey Stokes, a young journalist who often wrote for the *Village Voice* but also did reviews for *The Nation*. Pochoda knew Stokes well—their daughters attended the same school—and now she shared with him her views of Kosinski as well as various rumors about "ghost writers" and his association with the CIA. She asked if he was interested in doing the story. Stokes agreed, but learned almost immediately that Eliot Fremont-Smith, who also wrote for the *Village Voice* and had been a strong supporter of *The Painted Bird* while at the *New York Times*, was already on the case. It was decided that Stokes and Fremont-Smith would collaborate, and that the article would be done for the *Voice*, which also had a leftish political orientation but was less doctrinaire than *The Nation*.

With Stokes as the senior partner, the two journalists set out tracking down editors who had worked on Kosinski's books and examining records at the Ford Foundation and Columbia. Working under the pressure of time, they turned up a very incomplete array of facts, containing a number of inaccuracies. They found a number of editors who had worked on Kosinski's novels—John Hackett, Barbara Mackay, Richard Hayes, and Faith Sale, who had worked on *Blind Date* at the proofreading stage—and they interviewed Halina Bastianello, who had answered the *Saturday Review* ad for a Polish-English translator in 1964 (and who, as it turned out, had written to a *New York Times* reviewer in 1973 about her experience meeting Kosinski). Their exploration of the publishing circumstances of *The Future Is Ours, Comrade* went so far as to associate Frank Gibney with the book (although they got his relationship with the CIA somewhat wrong), and they ran down a first flaw in the cover story, determining that Roger Shaw, the supposed junior editor who acquired the book, was not listed on the rolls of Doubleday employees. They also attacked the details of Kosinski's arrival in the United States as told to Jerry Klinkowitz, citing a *Life* interviewer who said he simply came over on a student visa. Finally, they explored the question of *Nikodem Dyzma*, upon which *Being There*, they implied in their article, was so closely based as to invite the charge of plagiarism.

Throughout the spring Kosinski had once again been involved in an affair, with Dora Militaru, then a twenty-six-year-old film student at NYU, who watched the unfolding of the *Village Voice* affair from her privileged position as a new lover. She met him in January—she had just seen him in *Reds*—at a bar on Fifth Avenue, where she had come with her new French boyfriend. He had been bored and was about to leave, but after talking with her a while, he said, "I am seduced. We'll stay." They chatted for hours, Kosinski entertaining the group with stories about Peter Sellers, and after they left, her new lover, whose name was Benoit, told her simply, "Jerzy is between us." Jerzy telephoned the next morning at nine and for the next ten days wined and dined her, and completely charmed her. Soon she was accompanying him to sex clubs, which she described as "Gestapo cellars," insisting, however, like many of his companions, that she not be required to remove her clothes or participate.

That was fine with Jerzy. What he wanted from her, he repeated, was not some esoteric sexual performance, but her absolute, freely given love. And she did soon discover that she loved him, although, out of an instinct for self-protection, she refused to tell him. It seemed to her very much like an episode out of *Les Liaisons Dangereuses*—love as a potentially deadly game. His life, she soon realized, was filled with games, of varying degrees of deadliness. Sometimes, accompanying her, he wore beards and disguises, complaining about the nuisance of being recognized. Yet it disturbed him when he was *not* recognized. Once, talking to a midwestern couple, he removed his beard and mustache, giving them a severe fright; unable to identify him, they seemed, according to Dora, to suspect him of being a criminal, perhaps a mass murderer. Through all of these performances Dora sensed an edginess. Kosinski struck her as a man who had lost his substance and was looking desperately to regain it by playing with people's heads. A sense of doom seemed to be growing in him, informing his daily actions. He had often given her teasing suggestions of the influence he could wield with producers, and one day he said to her out of context, "Take advantage of me *now*. I don't know what's going to happen to me."

And indeed by late spring Kosinski must have seen clearly what was coming. Beginning in May, Stokes and Fremont-Smith pursued Kosinski in a series of interviews wrestling over the question of editors and the details of his autobiography. Kosinski stuck to his earlier accounts of his arrival in the United States and the terms of publication of the Novak books, and tried to wriggle out of the accusations of editorial assistance. But Stokes and Fremont-Smith had done enough preparation to lay several ambushes. When they cited facts from Norman Lavers's scholarly study, Kosinski denied having knowledge of it, only to be confronted by the statement of Emily McKeigue at Twayne Publishers that Kosinski had personally, and heavily, edited the text. At one point he asked the permission of Stokes and Fremont-Smith to have an observer present during their interview, informing them that he was part of a study conducted by a woman who examined "victims of the Holocaust under situations of stress." When such pleas for sympathy did not put aside their questions, he finally exploded. "Not a single comma, not a single word is not mine—and not the mere presence of the word but the reasons why as well," he told them on May 13. "This goes for manuscript, middle drafts, final draft, and every fucking galley—first page-proofs, second and third, hardcover editions, and paperback editions."

With that quote, the trap laid for Kosinski had been sprung. Whatever errors and gaps their account might contain, Stokes and Fremont-Smith had goaded Kosinski into an outright lie—an understandable lie, certainly, by a man backed into a corner; a lie that could be made to imply more serious fault than it actually proved; but nevertheless a palpable lie. With growing dread, Kosinski began to reestablish contacts with old friends. Barbara Mackay and Maxine Bartow received phone calls with the message that trouble was brewing. Were they with him? They were. Peter Skinner received an invitation to lunch. After a skillful probing of Skinner's state of mind, Kosinski casually mentioned an upcoming article. On June 11, Stanley Corngold received a card from Kosinski, greeting him warmly on his birthday. Around the country, friends and supporters began to get notes from him.

The June 8 edition of the *Village Voice* contained a story entitled "The War for America's Mind: The Conservative Brain Trust Wants You!" The subject of the story was the recently formed Committee for the Free World, a group of intellectuals who sought to place themselves somewhere between radicalism and Reaganism; its charter members included Saul Bellow, Bruno Bettelheim, Norman Podhoretz, and Kosinski. The groundwork for a commando raid in the culture wars was thus in place. On June 11 Kosinski delivered the commencement address at the Dalton School. Two days later he flew to Chicago to receive his first honorary degree, from Spertus College of Judaica. On June 22, 1982, the story broke on the cover of the *Village Voice*, entitled "Jerzy Kosinski's Tainted Words."

6.

Kosinski recognized at once that the *Village Voice* article was the crisis of his life. Almost immediately supporters sprang to his defense, some of them unbidden. Austin Olney, editor in chief of Houghton Mifflin, promptly fired off a letter to the *Voice* saying that while he had often been overwhelmed by Kosinski's flamboyant conceits and artful social manipulations, he had never "had any reason to believe that he has ever needed or used any but the most routine editorial assistance." Houghton Mifflin's New York editor, Joyce Hartmann, spoke out similarly, all in all a generous response from a publishing house with which Kosinski had gone through difficulties. Tom Morgan, a former editor in chief of the *Voice*, also chipped in with a letter criticizing the piece and supporting Kosinski, whom he had met only once or twice at a party. Morgan's support was particularly important because his politics—he was widely known as a liberal—did not bear the contaminating taint of neoconservatism. Morgan urged Kosinski to sue, but Kosinski declined. Publicly he cited his strong support of free speech, although there must also have been concerns about what might emerge during a court case. Bonded by Morgan's courageous support, Kosinski and Morgan became fast friends, and Kosinski would violate a personal policy by providing Morgan's novel with one of the few jacket blurbs he wrote. Five years later Morgan would be best man at Kosinski's wedding, and still later he would accompany Kosinski on his first trip to Israel.

Byron Sherwin at Spertus also checked in with his support, reaffirming an invitation to Kosinski to appear as the Spertus award recipient at their annual fund-raiser in October, before 1,500 guests at Chicago's Hyatt Regency. He mentioned a list of notable predecessors including Arthur Goldberg, Elie Wiesel, Philip Klutznick, Yitzhak Rabin, and Abraham Joshua Heschel himself; the 1978 recipient, Isaac Bashevis Singer, had recently won the Nobel Prize. Kosinski was deeply moved by this support from Sherwin and Spertus, and its direct fallout was a move to make Spertus the ultimate site for his personal papers, with Sherwin serving as coexecutor of his estate. At the same time it accelerated his movement back toward his Jewish roots. In his greatest moment of crisis, the strongest support had come not from his fellow intellectuals, but from those who identified with him as a Jew.

Of the "editors" mentioned in the article, all but Richard Hayes came to Kosinski's defense. Faith Sale acknowledged that her role had been no more than that of proofreader, while Barbara Mackay wrote the *Village Voice* a lengthy letter complaining that she had been misquoted, and that the authors of the piece "thoroughly misrepresented me, Jerzy Kosinski, and Mr. Kosinski's novels." John Hackett was displeased with the article's inaccurate suggestion that he used drugs, and told an interviewer that he was "very disturbed" by the characterization of the nature of his assistance to Kosinski. Only Hayes, who had expressed his sense of exploitation to Tom Fleming, clung to the view that the language of one of Kosinski's books—*Passion Play*—was predominantly his.

There were followup stories in *Publishers Weekly* on July 9 and the *Washington Post* on July 11, but they mainly recapitulated the arguments and counterarguments from the *Village Voice*, adding quotes from several editors. In the meantime, Kosinski himself had responded by leaving town. He and Kiki spent the next several weeks at the California home of Ted Field. There Kosinski entertained the Field children, while back east his literary reputation continued to unravel. There was no longer any talk of making a musical of *Pinball*, and as the *Village Voice* story rippled through the European press, his German publisher—always a strong area for foreign sales—canceled his publicity tour, explaining that it would produce nothing but queries about his involvement with the CIA.

By the end of July, he was back in New York and mustering a more serious defense. His first defender was Jan Herman, who wrote two pieces for the *Chicago Sun-Times*, the first on the origins of the story, the second, on July 25, giving Kosinski an opportunity to deny involvement with the CIA. Dave Smith followed with a piece in the *Los Angeles Times* on August 1, strongly challenging the notion of ghost writers. A number of critics and interviewers had checked in with support, or to clear their names after being quoted out of context, among them Regina Gorzkowska of the University of Alabama, who had done an extensive interview that spring focusing on the Abbott affair, and Dan Cahill, Jerry Klinkowitz's colleague at Northern Iowa, who had made Kosinski his personal specialty.

Back in May, Kosinski had received a long and detailed letter from a young scholar named Paul Bruss, from Eastern Michigan University, who had treated several of Kosinski's novels in a critical study entitled *Victims*, with sections on Nabokov, Barthelme, and Kosinski. In the middle of August, Bruss arrived in New York with his wife, Kath, to interrogate the oracle and be shown around the city. Kosinski found a temporary respite in the visit of the scholar and his wife, taking them first to the Russian Tea Room, a block away from his apartment. Mrs. Bruss in particular was taken by proximity to celebrity—sitting in the very seat where Diane Keaton had sat when she and Warren Beatty were persuading Kosinski to act in *Reds*—and Kosinski decided to take them to Hellfire, the S-M club, along with two of his regular consorts, Madeline and Maud. Bruss was delighted to receive a more sophisticated experience of New York than an excursion to see *Amadeus*, but his wife felt otherwise; a year later, he wrote to tell Kosinski that fault lines in his marriage exposed during that weekend had led the Brusses to divorce.

Meanwhile, matters had come to a crisis in the affair with Dora Militaru. He insisted that she profess her love for him, and when she refused, he hit her repeatedly. Dora broke off the affair. Their relationship soon resumed as a friendship—in January he would grant her his only TV interview, for Italian TV, undertaken within two years of the *Village Voice* episode—but his physical assault ended their relationship as lovers.

Yet nothing could divert Kosinski from his essential problem. As he told Kiki, the *Village Voice* had damaged his credibility irreparably. He would never again be taken seriously as a writer, and his reputation as a writer was the foundation upon which his entire success had been built. Only one means remained for redeeming the whole disaster. When under attack in the past, he had always managed to pull through by enlisting his friends and framing the issue in political terms. It had gotten him through scrapes with the photographers' union in Poland and various academic committees, and he had withstood the challenge to his nomination for the PEN presidency in part because it had raised the hackles of a close-knit group of supporters who had bought into him and saw the revolt in political terms.

Now a defense was being prepared by his friends at the *New York Times*, and Kosinski saw the potential in it for politicizing the whole matter. Initially, Arthur Gelb, the deputy managing editor, assigned the piece to Michiko Kakutani, who was known as one of his protégés. The assignment placed Kakutani in a difficult position. If she looked into the story and found that the charges were valid, the result would be a rather flat piece saying that the *Village Voice* had been right, which under the circumstances, including frequent criticism of the *Times* by the *Village Voice*, Gelb could not possibly want. On the other hand, Kosinski was a man with powerful enemies in the literary world, and there was a consensus that the *Village Voice* assertions about ghost writers and CIA help were accurate in broad outline. One night she complained to John Corry that the story was unwritable because "there's something to it." Eventually Kakutani went to Arthur Gelb and told him she couldn't do the story. The next day Corry himself asked to be assigned to the story.

Corry had met Kosinski at Elaine's back in the 1960s, and liked him. At the time Corry was working at *Harper's* with Willie Morris, who habitually greeted Kosinski's arrival with jokes about the CIA. Now Corry, who was himself a neoconservative, felt he grasped the contours of the attack on Kosinski. It clearly had to do with Kosinski's dissent on Jack Abbott and the American Writers' Congress, and a conspiracy by *The Nation* and the *Village Voice* to lay Kosinski low—a view Kosinski himself did nothing to discourage. It was, to Corry, a simple matter of a put-upon conservative, a phenomenon he knew well enough from personal experience as a lonely conservative in the world of journalism. He read each of Kosinski's novels on consecutive nights and found them not only excellent but uniform in voice, tone, and sentence structure. He called Maurice Friedberg, chairman of the Department of Slavic Languages at the University of Illinois and an old acquaintance of Kosinski's, who assured him that *The Painted Bird* could not have been a work of translation; translation from Slavic, Friedberg said, always leaves visible seams.

Most important, Corry listened as Kosinski provided him with the story of the Polish response to *The Painted Bird*, supported by the array of Polish reviews of his work from 1966. As Kosinski told it, it was a case of long-distance political persecution. At its center was Wieslaw Gornicki, who had written the scurrilous *Ameryka-Echo* review and now stood in full colonel's regalia at the right hand of General Jaruzelski in Poland's martial-law regime. It was Gornicki who had gone around spreading rumors that Kosinski's novels were written by Peter Skinner (whom Stokes and Fremont-Smith had not interviewed), and it was only a small stretch to see the Polish Communists connected with their ideological American brethren at *The Nation* and the *Village Voice*.

On Sunday, November 7, the *Times* published a 6,400-word piece by Corry in the Arts and Leisure section—the longest ever published in that section—under a headline written by Arthur Gelb himself: "A Case History: 17 Years of Ideological Attack on a Cultural Target." The piece laid out the Polish attacks on

Kosinski, the motivation of his detractors, and the rebuttals of his editorial helpers, and it caught Stokes and Fremont-Smith in an embarrassing error. Kosinski had told Barbara Gelb that he became mute when he dropped a missal while serving Mass, and Stokes and Fremont-Smith had made much of a different telling of the same story in a *Penthouse* interview with Barbara Leaming; Corry demonstrated clearly that the two versions were not contradictory (although subsequent research calls both stories into serious question).

Yet despite these clarifications and rebuttals, the *Times* story was a serious mistake. Its primary effect was to confirm to the world that Kosinski was, indeed, a personal and ideological favorite of the top floor at the *Times*. The medium, in effect, was the message. Instead of quelling the accusations against Kosinski, it served to give them new life, and on a wider stage. David Schneiderman, the publisher of the *Village Voice*, responded by accusing the *Times* of Red-baiting in a lengthy point-by-point defense of his reporters. On November 15 Juniette Pinkney in the *Washington Post* questioned the editorial judgment at the *Times* ("New York Times Articles on Kosinski Questioned"), and on November 22 Charles Kaiser, in a piece for the News Media section of *Newsweek* entitled "Friends at the Top of the *Times*," directly questioned the motivation and integrity of Gelb and Rosenthal. Liz Smith made the controversy the subject of her television slot, with focus on the action of Kosinski's friends at the *Times*. In publishing the Corry piece, Kosinski's supporters had hit a tar baby. What started as a minor episode in New York's culture wars had become a national news story.

Kosinski was despondent. It was all now spiraling out of control—his career, his account of his life, and his privileged place in New York society. The whole thing had become an unmitigated disaster. By late fall, he decided to spend as much as a year out of the country. He would, in fact, spend much more than his usual vacations in Switzerland over the next few years, nominally to work in solitude on a new and monumental novel that was to provide his final justification, but largely, as he sometimes admitted, "running from the *Village Voice*."

VII

SACRED ARMOR

1.

If the next several years of Kosinski's life were not entirely given over to running from the *Village Voice*, they were certainly spent living in its shadow. Justly or unjustly, the accusations and insinuations of Stokes and Fremont-Smith had plunged him back into the search for an ultimately defensible inner refuge which had been the unstated theme of much of his life. What refuge could protect one's most vulnerable and deepest self from the world's slings and arrows? Could safety be found in powerful friends? In great accomplishment? In camouflage and hiding places? In association with others of similar background and values?

His first hiding place was California, where his Hollywood friendships provided a layer of insulation. In New York he could not appear in public without facing embarrassed glances and sensing the presence of unasked questions. In L.A. the film people knew him mainly from his recent success with *Reds* and *Being There*. The *Village Voice* affair was an arcane and distant conceit of New York intellectuals, which from a Hollywood perspective had nothing to do with reality. In the late fall Kosinski flew out with Kiki to spend a few weeks as the guests of Ted and Barbara Field. The ambitious filming plans for *Passion Play* had fallen through— Hollywood deals were hard enough to put together without Kosinski's public troubles. As Kiki later put it, Kosinski and Field decided that they preferred being friends to doing business together.

There in the Fields' guest house, he read, tried to write, and struggled to pull himself together. In the mornings Ted often dropped by for coffee, sometimes accompanied by Barbara. It was disruptive to his work process—he tended to be a morning writer—but it was comforting at the same time. In the evenings they had dinner with such West Coast acquaintances as Michael Douglas and his wife, Diandra (known to Kosinski through Michael's father, Kirk, whom Kosinski had met in 1976 at Cannes), who brought along Michael Phillips, producer of *Close Encounters of the Third Kind*. They also had several dinners with John Gregory Dunne and his wife, Joan Didion, whose cool prose style and unflinching observations of human behavior had caused critics to link her with Kosinski.

On several evenings, they went out to movies with the Fields, or over to Warren Beatty's house for private screenings. Kosinski was amused by Beatty's restless habit of replacing a film immediately if it failed to produce instant delight. In this way they saw *Sophie's Choice*, which was pronounced "slow," although Meryl Streep received praise for everything but her atrocious Polish accent. They enjoyed Dustin Hoffman in *Tootsie*, the more so as Kosinski could speak of Hoffman approaching him to doctor the script. He had steered clear of Hoffman's neurotic egocentricity, he explained, and Elaine May had eventually been brought in to fix the script for $350,000. It was all a measure of how little clout the *Village Voice* had in Beverly Hills, and as if to underscore the point, Dino De Laurentiis sent around a copy of the screenplay to Stephen King's *Dead Zone*, inquiring whether Kosinski would care to read for the part of the doctor. It was a typically passing Hollywood thought, but it illustrated how little Hollywood cared for New York's literary gossip.

They lunched with Merv Griffin, who had had Kosinski as a guest on his TV show, and who now told them that as a result of reading *Passion Play* he was on his way to spend Christmas in the Dominican Republic in order to learn to play polo. The mention of Casa de Campo must have produced a tug at the heart, because for the first time in several years, Kosinski had decided not to spend Christmas there. It was the same crowd, really, as his New York dinner-party crowd, with a few international types thrown in, and his standing there depended upon his literary cachet. He would surely face questions and troubled looks until the *Village Voice* thing cooled down. Instead he and Kiki decided to stay through Christmas with the Fields, and deal with the problem of finding perfect token gifts for hosts who had everything and could acquire instantly anything they didn't have.

It was, all in all, a pleasant form of exile, but not a sustainable way of life, and certainly not conducive to work. After Christmas with the Fields, they left for a trip to Hong Kong and Singapore, staying just under a week in each, with a one-day stopover in Manila, returning to New York on January 9. There they packed, paid bills, and made arrangements for an extended absence. In early February they left for Switzerland. Long a retreat from too-present New York society, the apartment in Crans now became the refuge of choice. Kosinski quickly fell into a pattern of working mornings on the new book, then quitting at noon to ski. The past year's stresses and nomadic life had caused him to put on weight for the first time in his life. He would be fifty in June, and the extra pounds had collected in a single place, his midsection, compelling him to leave favorite trousers unfastened and making it impossible to get into some of his ski clothes. Luckily, he and Kiki were about the same size—their standing joke was that he needed the larger bra—and now she was the lucky recipient of a whole wardrobe of hand-me-downs.

Although the writing seemed to be going well, Kosinski soon chafed at the routine, which deprived him of his contact with New York's night life. Never had Kiki's companionship been more important than now, when she provided not only mother-hennish attention to his creature comforts but ferocious public support and uncritical acceptance of whatever posture he assumed under attack. She had long since settled into cheerful acquiescence in his nightly escapades—their understanding was that these adventures had nothing to do with their relationship, which was made of more durable stuff—and now she could even listen to his complaints and offer sympathy. He needed those nights of perverse delight, and whatever Jerzy needed was okay with her.

Early that year they noticed that Crans-Montana had suddenly been discovered by Poles, who were arriving in numbers that amounted to an infestation. Perhaps it was the resemblance to Zakopane, a feature that had appealed to Kosinski as well. Among them were the well-known actors Wojtek Pszoniak and Daniel Olbrychski, architects Danka Mentha and Janusz Lubkowski, industrialist Jan Zylbert, and Ewa Bayard from Cracow, who now lived with her Swiss husband, Jean, a few kilometers away. The presence of so many Poles in one spot stoked Kosinski's paranoia, and noting the ease with which many of them went in and out of Poland, he speculated about their possible connections with Polish intelligence. The Corry piece had seemingly renewed his war with the political powers of Warsaw, and when the Poles began inviting him to a round of dinner parties, he told Kiki, only half joking, that they could easily slip a slow poison into his soup.

Nothing was said about the article, however, and Kosinski gradually let his guard down and participated in what was becoming a lively pocket of the Polish diaspora. The Poles skied together, then gathered on the patio of a local restaurant, Les Violettes, where Kosinski had his own table. There they talked about old times in Poland and complained about the German tourists, who arrived with cars and vans packed with comestibles, to avoid having to buy food, and overran the slopes. One day Kosinski made one of his frequent stops in the middle of a ski run and turned to see another skier struggling in his direction and hailing him by name. It was Daniel Passent, a well-known Polish journalist, who had recognized his face from book jackets. Kosinski immediately invited him for lunch, and they hit it off right away. Kosinski then told Passent that his ski equipment and clothes were unacceptably dowdy. Passent protested, but Kosinski insisted Passent would ski better if better dressed, and offered to spot him a full new outfit. Over Passent's repeated protests, they went to a local ski shop, which shocked Passent by offering to rent them expensive equipment for the day, on personal recognizance. When Passent refused even the offer of rental equipment, Kosinski had the solution. He had just purchased new equipment himself, and Passent would take his old skis and ski clothes. This time Passent's protests were in vain, and he skied for some years wearing Kosinski's natty outfit and struggling with his long skies, which he finally gave away to a tall friend. For Passent, the small bulge in Kosinski's waistline had resulted in quite a windfall.

In early March word came that Charlie Bluhdorn, for years their host at Casa de Campo, had died. He had suffered a heart attack in the Dominican Republic and been misdiagnosed and put on a plane for New York, dying en route. Bluhdorn's death followed closely upon the death of Susan Shiva, at whose home they had spent the Jewish holidays for a decade, and was followed in turn by the death of Horace Taft, the Yale dean involved in bringing him to New Haven. Thus the transitory nature of human existence hung over the late-winter skiing and revelry.

On March 18, 1983, Kosinski went to London to deliver the Scott Dawson Memorial Lecture (Dawson, with Galsworthy, was the co-founder of PEN) at the Royal Festival Hall, following D. M. Thomas, whose *White Hotel* was a current sensation. He and Kiki stayed at the vine-clad Durrants, enjoying English breakfasts of eggs and kippers, and were pleased to find that the *Village Voice* seemed not to have damaged his standing in London. The lecture was well attended—the guests included Harold Pinter and his wife, biographer Lady Antonia Fraser—and D. M. Thomas's ponderous address provided the nimble Kosinski with a highly satisfactory foil. His remarks received a standing ovation. After only a week back in Crans, he was off again to Stockholm to lecture and accept a Freedom Award given jointly by two newspapers, the Swedish *Dagens Nyheter* and the Danish *Politiken*, to Solidarity leader Lech Walesa, who was unable to leave Poland at that time. The selection of Kosinski as Walesa's stand-in showed that the *Village Voice* revelations had had a limited impact in Europe and underscored both his early support of Solidarity and his growing stature as a spokesman for Poles in exile and Polish culture. On the way back from Stockholm he stopped in Paris to visit his old friends Andrzej and Françoise Wat and other Polish friends.

The trips to London and Stockholm lifted Kosinski's spirits but disrupted his work. The task he had set himself with the new novel was staggering—to make his case against the *Village Voice*, in part through intellectual argument and in part by the quality of the novel itself. This kind of pressure, he had begun to discover, was not conducive to creative activity. At the same time he lived with a sense of dread about possible further attacks. He knew all too well the potential for future exposés. The visitors from Poland had informed him of magazines in Poland that had traced down witnesses from the war years and published stories saying his childhood was not as he had depicted it. Among the witnesses, according to the Poles, were some who insisted he had never been separated from his parents.

Along with the Polish stories, there were rumors that the *Village Voice* was gathering material for another broadside. Ever since the previous summer, he had been waiting for the other shoe to drop. It had been reported at the time that the *Voice* had planned a two-part story but had been dissuaded by the fear of legal action and the level of uproar created by the first story. Now, the rumor went, they had broadened their target to include Arthur Gelb and Abe Rosenthal at the *Times*, exposing the way John Corry had been enticed to come to the support of their chum. Among the details circulated was that Corry had been promoted to the coveted position of film critic. In fact Corry had been laterally transferred to the position, which he did not particularly like.

It was Michiko Kakutani who was promoted, winning the job of book reviewer that she had always wanted. In the immediate aftermath of the Corry story, she had received hang-up calls. One Sunday morning Kosinski had spotted her at a book store and tried to avoid being seen in order not to embarrass her. She spotted him at a distance, however, and told Gelb, among others, that Kosinski was stalking her. Shortly afterward, she told Gelb that she was quitting her job to work for *Time*. As Corry later recounted it, Gelb realized that it would appear that Kakutani had been fired for refusing to support Kosinski and met the *Time* offer by promoting her to book critic.

Now Kosinski awaited a new exposé pulling together the juicy tidbits from the top floor at the *Times* with the most scurrilous rumors floating around Warsaw. To calm his fears, he knocked back a heavier and heavier dose of rum and Coke in the evenings. He had never been a drinker, and by the standards of American fiction writers he still had nothing one might call a drinking problem, but the daily dose of rum and Coke did little good for either his work or his waistline.

As winter slipped into spring, no story appeared. On April 23 (St. George's Day, and thus Jerzy's name day) the nearby town of Chermignon, which had already made him an honorary citizen, gave him an engraved pewter tray in gratitude for his many mentions of the area in books and interviews. A week later, with Crans too warm for skiing, he and Kiki made a brief foray to Chamonix to ski the all-season glacier, leaving when they found nothing but bad weather, dangerous runs, tacky gift shops, and North Americans.

The apartment in Crans was even smaller than the one at Hemisphere House, and its exterior, set against the mountain so that the apartment was on the first floor by elevator but the third floor counting up from the parking lot, was ugly—so much so that Daniel Passent's former wife Agnieszka had once wept upon being shown to borrowed rooms there. The attraction, as for most of Kosinski's habitats, lay purely in what it had access to, and with the end of the season it had begun to feel confining. Yet sooner or later this restless marking of time had to end. There had been no new income for a couple of years, and by May, with no skiing and the seasonal visitors gone, Kosinski buckled down in earnest. By now the window boxes were filling with flowers, and black squirrels with batlike ears ran through the fields and trees. For the first time in years Kosinski awoke to the chirping of birds and enjoyed the smell of new-mown grass—none of which was available on Fifty-seventh Street. Yet there was one thing he could get in New York that was unavailable in Switzerland—the sex clubs.

By late June there had still been no new story, and it seemed more and more likely that there was not going to be one. Gradually, Kosinski allowed himself to experience a sense of relief. With a little luck, his career could ride out the storm. It was now mainly work on the new book that was keeping him in Crans, and a natural hesitancy about reentering the New York social world. He had thought about it carefully. Episodes like the *Village Voice* article had a certain half-life, and gradually faded. Yet there was still a bit of facing down to do. It was important, above all, to go about with his head high, for he could be sure his enemies would pounce on any sign of weakness. As for the other side of his life, he would begin cautiously. He was now permanently at risk. He would have to live with the danger of being set up. Any woman he encountered could be a plant, sent by the press. Yet he couldn't live without stimulus. In July, telling himself that he could simply retrieve summer clothes and go immediately back to Crans, he returned to New York.

By late 1983, Kosinski was beginning to resume his established social patterns and travel rhythms. The *Village Voice* had faded as a major topic of conversation in New York literary circles. Enough time had passed for him to sit back and assess the damage, as well as the response among his friends, which had been mixed. When Kosinski returned to New York in July with his head un-bowed, many had not even noticed his absence. His close friends—the Gelbs and Rosenthals, for instance—were fully aware of the pain the episode had caused him, but others were a bit like the doorman at Jilly's when the Polish car parker returned as Jerzy Kosinski in the company of Frank Sinatra. Had Kosinski been away for a while? Had there been some unpleasantness having to do with the *Village Voice*?

Notable among the groups that had shown their loyalty in the crisis were his fellow Polish émigrés. Not one Pole had been quoted by Stokes and Fremont-Smith, and none had come forward in the ensuing furor, although Kosinski was well aware of the contribution some of them might have made to the controversy. Among them were some who had good reason to feel dropped and slighted, and others who held his work in low regard, and still others who knew specific things about his writing or his personal affairs that could have done him harm. All kept their silence. Among themselves they might gossip and complain about him, but he was one of them. He was *theirs*, and with

a spirit akin to proprietorship they forbore from joining his at-
tackers.

For the remainder of his life, loyalty during this crisis would
be an important measure of friendship. In general, his friends
from the worlds of politics and business had been strongly supportive, as had his Hollywood circle. Writers and literary intellectuals had been less so. Perhaps this was only logical. Politicians
lived in a world of routine accusation-and-parry, while businessmen and film celebrities had a shared experience of the vulture-
like press, which was always out to expose their secret failings
and show them in the worst possible light. Whatever their personal causes and ideologies, they were bonded together as an
elite. Among them it was understood that all human beings told
lies under certain circumstances and concealed discreditable facts
about themselves. Most had skeletons in the closet, and viewed
them simply as vulnerabilities to be dealt with by skillful PR.
What mattered, finally, was achievement, and without it, how
could Kosinski—how could anyone—be one of them?

Along with Poles, ironically, Jews had been his staunch defenders, both in his personal circle and in the wider audience for
his books. He was *theirs* too, and perhaps more so. To Jews he
was a rare and precious resource—a Holocaust survivor who had
rendered compelling and important testimony. Who could guess
the impact of his childhood? Certainly not the Jewish community.
After what he had been through, they were prepared to accept a
certain quota of erratic behavior. Loath to join in an attack on one
who had shared in the suffering of the ultimate pogrom, many
were quick to find rationalizations for all the charges against him.
The fact that both Poles and Jews, in different ways, had demonstrated their loyalty provided Kosinski with an interesting contra-
diction. Although the two groups felt toward each other an
enmity long predating the Holocaust, in New York émigré circles
Polish Jews and Polish Gentiles mingled amicably. Moreover, the
ambiguous history of Poles and Jews was embodied in Kosinski
himself—a Jew who bore a Polish Gentile name and had survived
the war disguised as a Gentile. Herein lay the seeds of a strange
inner journey, as Kosinski set out to explore and integrate his Pol-

ish and Jewish roots—and find a way to bridge the distance between them.

The reconciliation of his Polish and Jewish origins became a major theme of the new novel in progress, into which he planned to put more of his life and thought—more of his private self—than in any previous book. He would show not just the surface of dialogue and action but the underlying process and historical sources by which the author constructed them. It would contain tantalizing pieces of fact he had never publicly revealed. It would draw upon hundreds of other writers, in many genres, and two languages, Polish and English, as well as their differing traditions, and also upon a third tradition of Polish Jewish writers in Yiddish. Its audience would include not only his supporters but the recalcitrant group of his fellow writers—his peers—who had fallen short in their support of him during the *Village Voice* crisis. They had accepted the view that he couldn't write. Now he would show them!

In October, back in Crans, he showed what he had written so far to Bantam's publisher, Jack Romanos, who seemed to like what he saw. It was in a sense complete, with fully developed scenes and a beginning, middle, and end, but Kosinski was not ready to let go of it quite yet. He saw the text he showed Romanos as something on the order of an outline, which needed fleshing out. With a commitment from Bantam in hand and the assurance of Romanos's approval in his psychological bank, he set out to enlarge the text and build it into the culminating triumph of his career—a masterpiece. Despite numerous promises that he would be done in a few weeks, this process would drag out for four full years. In the meantime, Kosinski struggled to keep his name before the public eye.

In March of 1984 Kosinski's friends were shocked one morning to see him in a segment of the NBC *Today* show demonstrating his skill of "floating." The May 1 issue of *Life* came out with a story, "How I Learned to Levitate in Water," complete with photos. As Kosinski explained this recently acquired and somewhat jejune skill, floating was a difficult and almost metaphysical art which one should understand in the context of Indian fakirism—walking on hot coals and the like. Thus it stood for a kind of in-

ner peace and harmonious balance between oneself and the
cosmos, as represented in the medium of water. In a personal
sense, clearly, this was an important metaphor. Kosinski had always had a great fear of water—from the icy skating pond in
Dabrowa to the Adriatic, where the Wood children squealed with
delight at the sight of "Jerzy" with his head poking above the
surface—and the ability to survive in water without thrashing
about wildly seemed to him, at least, a great accomplishment.
Buoyancy was, in psychological terms, the great defense against
the depression that increasingly weighed him down; it provided
the happy but ambiguous ending of Chauncey Gardiner's un-
willed ascent to power. It is not surprising, then, that in the new
novel it was the protagonist's ability to float that two reporters
called into question, before drowning him by throwing him off
the end of a dock.

Floating was one of several activities for which Kosinski had a
sudden burst of enthusiasm, and which he shared with the reading public. In 1985 his incidental writing featured a piece in *Polo*
entitled, fittingly, "A Passion for Polo," an expansion of a piece
called "Horses" he had done for *Centaur* in the summer of 1981.
The article marked his return as a guest in good standing to the
annual Christmas activities at Casa de Campo, which he mentioned along with his largely fictitious childhood experience with
horses. The following year he turned his experience at Cannes
during the final days of Jacques Monod into a photo-essay for *Esquire*, which was published in the March 1986 issue with the title
"A Death in Cannes." More interesting but also more flawed than
the pieces on floating and polo, the Monod piece is paradigmatic
of the overall problem of Kosinski's career. In short, Kosinski *told*
the story better than he could *write* it. By coincidence his editor at
Esquire was Lisa Grunwald, the adolescent poet for whom he had
instituted the Poetry Depot now grown up into a writer and editor. Grunwald was stunned by the roughness of his prose and
the difficulty with which he managed revisions. With great reluctance, she found herself beginning to revise the lofty view she
had held of the author of *Steps* and *The Painted Bird*.

Monod's death was a wonderful and moving story when
Kosinski told it orally. Monod's courage, the tears Kosinski saw

rolling down his cheek, and Kosinski's own sense of being present at an almost holy boundary—all of this came across with
great power and authenticity when he spoke. The written version, by contrast, had a hoked-up feeling. It was filled with literary allusions, as if it were necessary to include the intellectual
credentials of both author and subject. Even the description of
Monod's tears ("The drops in Monod's eyes come from Monod,
not from humidity. Call them tears.") had a self-consciously literary feel. It was the pseudosimple style of Hemingway, particularly the late Hemingway, which was in fact quite arch and
mannered. By contrast, *The Painted Bird* had felt genuinely simple,
like the language of Kosinski's oral storytelling. "A Death in
Cannes" was a good story, but in it one could discern the spoiled
remains of what might have been a great story. Its power, which
could not be concealed by excessive stylization, lay in the way
Monod's death brought Kosinski, a man who had spent a lifetime
confronting boundaries, into intimate connection with the ultimate boundary as his like-minded and generous friend invited
him in for a peek beneath the veil. Its enduring poignancy would
be recalled by the single self-conscious expression "Call them
tears," the syntax of which would be echoed five years later in
Kosinski's own suicide note.

2.

The Hermit of 69th Street consumed much of Kosinski's time, and
virtually all of his attention, from the middle of 1983 until its
publication in 1988, and his massive revisions for the paperback
edition would consume him up to the time of his death. Its protagonist is Norbert Kosky—Kosinski, as he told interviewers,
without the sin—a Polish-American writer living a hermetic existence in New York City. The facts of Kosky's life are often, but not
always, Kosinski's, and the use of personal detail gives the novel
the *feel* of being virtual autobiography disguised by playful language. Maxine Bartow, who again served as Kosinski's editorial
assistant, was stunned at the process by which the novel evolved
from a narrative of simple anecdotes, more or less like his earlier

work, into a heavily layered, elusive, evasive, richly footnoted text with a complexity that made it stand as a metaphoric representation of its author.

In fact, *Hermit* includes a continuation of Kosinski's lifelong hiding and mythification with some new and subtle twists. While *The Painted Bird* had told the story of his wartime traumatization as inner theater, in a surreal universe with invented or embellished details, *Hermit* purports to represent this experience as fragments of memory. Kosky's boyhood experiences are placed in the Pripet Marshes, where Kosinski sometimes claimed to have wandered; these are associated through the town name Gliniszcze to the "Marshes of Glynn" in American Georgia, subject of a poem by Confederate laureate Sidney Lanier. Yet Kosinski himself was never anywhere near the Pripet Marshes, nor could his background be characterized as Ruthenian, a conceit carried over from *Blind Date*'s Levanter to *Hermit*'s Kosky.

Strewn throughout the text are brief references to mythic childhood experiences which tantalize without quite yielding insight. There is even a primal scene in which Kosky at the age of eight watches the slightly older "Ewunia and Adam" mutually performing oral sex, as well as a fragment where he is seduced by an older peasant woman and one in which he, at twelve, is accused of molesting a playmate. All offer themselves as clues beckoning both reader and scholar to look at and through the incidents as portholes into the author's true history and deepest being. Yet as in the false dates Kosinski inscribed in books for Jean Kilbourne, there is as much intent to deceive and confuse as to illuminate. Deconstructionist critics have written of the equivocal nature of primal scenes and fragments, whether they occur in novels or in Freudian analysis.

The scenes involving Kosky and his parents also partake of this sense of primal dialogue. Whether from life or as myth (which is to say, Kosinski's received and reconstructed inner reality), Kosky's mother expresses the spontaneous and joyful life force that the father struggles to subdue. The mother uses the boy to tease the father, while the boy is torn between the desire to enjoy the mother's adoration, which has a strongly sexual edge, and the impossible quest to meet his father's standards of behavior and accomplishment. That his father is the lifelong reference point for guilt is strongly postulated by the appearance of a ghost-figure called Pilpul (a Yiddish expression for tedious and overblown argument) who gives the son Polonius-like instruction, criticizing such interests as riding and skiing.

The dialogue between Kosky and his father, which obliquely engages the issues raised by the *Village Voice*, is reminiscent of the Nighttown episode of Joyce's *Ulysses*, in which Bloom's head divides into interrogator and interrogatee, producing insights at a profound and unconscious level. Defending his son, the father alludes to Conrad, saying that "what matters is the spiritual accent of the book, not the writer's own accent." Behind this innocent line, one discerns the struggle to justify editors and even translators in support of a *content* which is all that really matters. In discussing the key episode raised by the *Village Voice*, the father observes that clinically his son is definitely not suffering from "ordinary mutism"—which one may read as the author's indirect acknowledgment that he was never actually mute. As for being beaten and thrown into a latrine, an episode from *The Painted Bird* that Kosinski frequently claimed for himself, the father asks pointedly: "What pond of manure? What pit?" Kosky, whose correction "a pit, really, not a pond" has already suggested the mythic origin of his submersion (as in the story of Joseph), can only reply, "Let's say it was just my latest fairy tale." After this multileveled admission, by Kosky to the ghost of his father and Kosinski to the reader, the scene concludes with the line "The inner theater closes."

Desconstructive criticism, when not merely obscurantist, places sophisticated focus on the reader's approach to apprehending a text. *The Hermit of 69th Street* appears to invite the reader for glimpses of behind-the-text "truth." Yet these truths are at best rabbit gardens, attempting to satiate marauding invaders before they can lay hold of the deeper truth. Kosky himself is compelled to take malic acid for a condition amusingly called *Vorbeireden*—"an occasional need to be vague, or giving an approximate—even phony—answer rather than a yes or no in order to improve one's image of oneself, or one's act, and by so doing forcing the spectators to believe that they are witnessing an act of inspiration, not of simple magic." No definition could better summarize Kosinski's public performance, and in stating it explicitly Kosinski may be seen as giving a sort of backhanded public apologia. The key phrase, however, is "to improve one's image of oneself." All of *Hermit* is inner theater in that Kosinski is struggling, within the tension between his mother's and his father's values, to justify to *himself* his rascally and inconstant, deeply false and wonderfully creative existence.

At the surface level, Kosinski/Kosky's justification is given in a series of metaphoric arguments, in which Kosky compares himself to Conrad, Cagliostro, and James Fenimore Cooper, all of whom were embroiled in literary scandals. Yet while he laid this out for the public—Look! Conrad, Cagliostro, and Cooper were also unfairly maligned!—the model by which he hoped to persuade himself was Balzac, whose biography by Stefan Zweig was among Kosinski's favorite books. Like Kosinski, Balzac employed line editors, as many as six at a time, and drove his publishers to distraction with last-minute corrections. Also, as Kosinski claimed about himself, Balzac functioned as his own agent. And also like Kosinski, Balzac lived on an unusual schedule, sleeping much of the day and working and cavorting through the night. Mention of these parallels is strewn throughout the text of *Hermit*.

Yet there were more fundamental points of similarity in Zweig's portrait of Balzac that Kosinski does not mention but could hardly have missed. Balzac was the great storyteller of his time—possibly of all time—writing volumes that described French society of his day from the poorest to the most elevated, a journey he himself had made by force of his writing. Moreover, Balzac was not a picky stylist, not at least like his successor Flaubert. Rather, the power of his stories leaped from the page. This, together with his voluminous output, more than justified the assistance of line editors. The words, after all, were a mere detail. And Balzac was a congenital, incorrigible *liar*, a trait inextricably connected with his literary genius. Even his *name* was false, upgraded to the noble de Balzac from the unpretentious Balssa. With Balzac, life and art were of a single piece. "When he lied, it was not to deceive," Zweig wrote, "but to indulge his exuberant imagination and his sense of humor. . . . He would tell his friends some tall story and . . . when they didn't believe it make it taller yet." This, in summary, was Kosinski's case for himself, presented to himself; like Balzac, whatever help he might have employed, he was clearly the author of the true and original text—the text of Jerzy Kosinski.

Closely tied to this inner theater of self-interrogation was an examination of the historical relationship between Poles and Jews; partially in the interest of his own divided identity, Kosinski hoped to effect a reconciliation between the two groups. Essayistically, he detailed a history in which Jews were invited to Poland by Kazimierz the Great, who had a Jewish mistress. The extermination camps were located in Poland, his argument would go, because Poland was where the Jews were, and the Jews were in Poland in such numbers because Polish society had been relatively hospitable to them. The argument had a certain logic, but it would make trouble for Kosinski with Jewish audiences for the rest of his life, beginning with his mystification of the audience for a lecture in Los Angeles, at the Streisand Center for Jewish Cultural Arts, in November of 1984; audiences like this one, who came to hear the testimony of a Holocaust survivor, felt toyed with by his evasions and were shocked by his apologia for Polish Gentiles. In *Hermit*, he presented that argument in detail, suggesting that some of the hatred of Poles stemmed from snobbery within the Jewish community itself, in which German Jews saw their Polish brothers as being of a lesser order. He singled out Hannah Arendt as a subtle contributor to this point of view. It was an outrageous and thoroughly heterodox position, certain to divide and perplex his Jewish supporters not least because it contained several germs of truth.

Even more heterodox was his defense of Chaim Rumkowski, the virtual dictator of the Lodz ghetto, who pursued a policy of cooperation, offering up old people and children to appease the Germans. For Kosinski, it was essential to come to grips with Lodz, where he spent his adolescence, where his relatives died or were consigned to death camps, and where he would have certainly perished had his family not gone to Sandomierz and Dabrowa. In the figure of Rumkowski, the question of how to comport oneself under extreme circumstances was brought into high focus. Rumkowski chose one alternative—collaborating to save as many as he could for as long as he could—in keeping with Jewish celebration of the ultimate value of life. Yet he could be criticized for not emulating the Jews of the Warsaw Ghetto who fought to the death under Mordecai Anielewicz, as well as for the possibility of venal self-interest. In *Hermit* Kosinski laid out the case for Rumkowski, as he would in lectures and appearances before Jewish audiences, quoting at length from Rumkowski's speech of September 4, 1942, asking mothers to give up their children.

What lay behind Kosinski's tenacious defense of Rumkowski? Not a fighter himself, despite the rhetoric of his novels, he needed a model of extreme *choice* in the effort to survive. Rumkowski exemplified man caught in a web of *chance*, in a *blind date* with a fate shared by *Poles and Jews*, who looked frankly and realistically at his situation, taking what was, in his terms, the only possible action. In doing so, he reconfirmed the model of behavior in that crisis with which Kosinski was most intimately aware—the actions taken by Moses Lewinkopf.

Throughout this journey into his Polish and Jewish spirit, Kosinski was guided by Byron Sherwin of Spertus College, who had once served as secretary to Abraham Joshua Heschel. Heschel figures only briefly in *Hermit*, but his philosophy stands squarely behind it—an open reverence for life, accompanied by an inclination to celebrate Jewish presence in Eastern Europe over hundreds of years rather than merely to mourn the Holocaust. This attitude would become increasingly important to Kosinski as he worked on *Hermit*, eventually emerging in his public life in the form of a program. While it had inherent merits, it also contained a classic Kosinskian misdirection—an implied instruction to those who wished to examine his life. Look away from the wartime experience (where Kosinski had embarrassing truths to conceal), he was saying in effect, and to the real achievements.

There is another odd feature to the text of *Hermit*. Although Kosinski had a lifelong record of revising work already in galleys, and had reworked and reissued *The Devil Tree* and revised several books significantly for paperback publication, there was a seamlessness to his ongoing revision of *Hermit* that went beyond anything he had done before. Unfolding contemporary events were incorporated in the book—the fall of the Berlin Wall, for instance, and the threat of reunification of Germany—without thought to the book's internal consistency. As a result the final version of *Hermit* has an anomalous chronology, in which the book's present—the point from which the writer tells the story—is both 1982 and 1991. The ages of characters and dating of past events add up only if the years between 1982 and 1991 are seen as a single point. Kosinski could have made a postmodern device of this anomaly, something on the order of García Márquez's *One Hundred Years of Solitude*, but as rendered, the chronology seems almost unconscious. It is as if, for Kosinski, the onward flow of time stopped with the *Village Voice* attack in 1982. The long, rambling, and richly footnoted text of *Hermit* may be read as a prolonged moment of death, in which the author's life, factual and fictional, flashes before his eyes.

3.

Kosinski set Talmud and Tantra side by side in *Hermit*. The interplay of spirituality and sexuality—the sacred and the profane— was very much on his mind, and his footnotes reveal his explorations among such earlier writers on the subject as Mircea Eliade. Years before he had shown David Weir a series of photographs he had taken of a woman revealing the way in which her appearance changed over a period of months as he led her through progressive stages of sexual abandonment and degradation. Now in *Hermit*, Kosinski quoted Eliade who wrote that "the more depraved a woman is [and] the more debauched," the better suited she was to the spiritual side of the Tantric rite. For Tantric rites, he went on, women were "graded" by men, and vice versa, with spiritual and ritual merit correlated to an advanced sexual level. By the same acts that cause some men to burn in hell for a thousand years, he quoted the Tantra, the yogi gains his eternal salvation. In Tantra, Kosinski found a system extending and fulfilling the exploration of self he had begun in *Steps*. The root *tan* in Tantra, he again cited Eliade, meant "to extend oneself beyond one's Self." The vehicle for that extending was an ideal and idealized woman, the essence at once of spirituality and sexuality, called a *dombi*.

The ideal sexual partner of Kosinski's life in that period was Cynthia Cristilli, a waitress and aspiring actress who was twenty-six—half his age—at the time they met. One evening in October of 1984, she recognized him at a bar on Fifth Avenue and offered to buy him a drink. She had read all his books, she told him, and was his biggest fan. She wanted to thank him for the pleasure they had brought her, and then she would leave him alone. Don't be ridiculous, Kosinski replied, and talked with her for hours. From that time on, they saw each other almost nightly whenever Kosinski was in New York. There was something childlike in their relationship as Cristilli remembers it. Sometimes he was like her father, authoritative and even Svengali-ish in choosing her clothing and makeup; sometimes she was like his mother, comforting and amusing him, bringing him out of the dark moods that overtook him now with regularity. Always he had something of the child in him, the irresistible quality of a small lost boy. Adoring him, she took it as her task in life for three years to cheer him up, make him laugh, restore the energy he needed for his work.

Busy writing *Hermit* during much of the time he saw her, Kosinski sometimes called her his *dombi*, to which she snapped back on cue, "Don't call me a *dummy*." The position of ascendancy in the relationship seemed important to him. She didn't challenge him as other women might—as every other aspect of his life did. She accepted. She did not feel degraded by her role as his lover. There was, moreover, something of the Tantric in their nocturnal journeys to Plato's Retreat and other clubs. They were not so much lovers on those occasions as intimate friends on a shared journey of discovery. On a typical evening, Kosinski would pick Cynthia up at the restaurant where she worked—where he soon came to know the owner—and take her for dinner, at which he ate little but talked a great deal. From there they would go to one of the clubs, staying for several hours, then retreat before dawn to another restaurant to discuss and dissect the things they had seen. They came to have names for the regulars—

among them the Prince and Princess, a man with a wonderfully muscular body and a beautiful woman with long black hair. The Prince and Princess always arrived with candles, lit the candles, and made love as an enthusiastic audience gathered to watch. Occasionally a hand emerged from the crowd to touch one of them.

Kosinski, mainly, watched. Ordinary street dress was not allowed beyond the locker area, but for the most part, he and Cynthia wore towels. To a man who had written perceptively of the problems of privacy in Marxist Eastern Europe, the protocol of the sex clubs was fascinating. In cramped Soviet quarters, one did not try to hide private papers or possessions because of the certainty that one's neighbors would get at them anyhow. Plato's Retreat was like those Soviet apartments carried one step further, a place where Kosinski could strip the self to its barest essence in order to inquire into its nature. After hours of waitressing, his companion might be tired and ready to leave quickly, but Kosinski was relentless in his appetite. He roamed and scouted endlessly, as if driven by an insatiable hunger to search for some lost, ultimate scene.

A typical search began with a quick scan of the orgy room, where couples copulated in a sea of pillows. He had an extraordinary intuition for the exceptional. While there were occasional beautiful people like the Prince and the Princess, the majority of customers at Plato's were ordinary people from New Jersey, or perhaps Brooklyn, although the tone was distinctly suburban. Beyond the potbellies and thin legs, however, there were sometimes unusual drives. What interested Kosinski most was the extraordinary hidden within the ordinary. Once he pointed out to Cynthia a physically unprepossessing couple. "Those are the ones," he said. He followed the couple to a room where the man put on garter belt and stocking and the woman dressed in leather and they then removed from their bag an orange ball with which they performed various inventive acts. Like most of the other customers, they were unaware of the identity of the dark man who was watching them. The people who went to Plato's Retreat were not an especially literary crowd. From time to time, however, he would be recognized by a fellow patron. In yet another commentary on the complicated nature of privacy, there was never any effort to "set him up" using the clubs. The owners were careful to protect him against that, and the vast majority of fellow patrons observed the rules. Only once, at Plato's Retreat, was it necessary for the owner to confiscate a photograph.

With increasing public awareness of AIDS, the world of the clubs came under tremendous public pressure. On December 22, 1985, the New York State Public Health Council, by a 14–1 vote, made permanent an emergency regulation requiring the closing of clubs that allowed acts associated with the spread of AIDS. Initially applied only to homosexual bathhouses, the regulation was now applied to Plato's Retreat; that December undercover inspectors visited Plato's and observed a number of acts that fell within the specifications of the regulation. As a result, Plato's was closed "temporarily," first in December of 1985 and again in December of 1986. It was, in fact, the end of the era for Plato's and the sex club world, at least for that era. The closing impacted Kosinski's life in several ways, some of them quite unexpected. Kiki, who professed never to have objected to his visiting the clubs, now saw ominous signs in their demise. They had provided him with needed "release," and their closing would leave a void in his life that could only produce problems. He became far more vulnerable to the stresses of life as a now-compromised celebrity, and by a paradoxical logic, to the approaches of other women.

Suddenly Kosinski was thrown back almost twenty years, to the time before and after his relationship with Lilla van Saher—a time of cruising the streets for prostitutes. With Cynthia Cristilli, his relationship altered as well, as more of their contact now took place uncomfortably close to his daily routine.

Did Kiki understand what she and Jerzy were involved in? Did she know what he regularly did whenever he left their apartment at night? Did Kiki realize that they were lovers? The questions continued to nag at her as the three of them began to spend time together. A clue was provided on a trip to New Haven, in which they walked around Yale together. Back at the apartment, Kiki happened to walk into the room as Jerzy had his arm around Cynthia. It wasn't really even sexual. It was more a simple gesture of affection, but Cynthia immediately detected a mood change, as Kiki left the room. Whatever they did at the sex clubs was one thing, but affection—genuine tenderness—was another, and far more important. It was like an episode from *Steps*. Mere sex was detachable from the most important human affiliations. She began to sense the complexity of the situation with Jerzy, Kiki, and herself.

The dimensions of that complexity became even more clear in February of 1987. While driving to New Haven, just the two of them without Cynthia, Kosinski had turned to Kiki and asked casually, "Should we get married?"

"To whom?" Kiki replied airily.

"To each other," he replied.

"Why?" she wanted to know. "Is something wrong?"

Kiki was not alone in asking the question. Cynthia, for one, was mystified. She had never doubted his devotion to Kiki, but the logic of getting married, at that particular moment, eluded her. There were two questions really. Why get married? And why *now*, after all those years? In an interview given three days before his death to Pearl Sheffy Gefen of the Toronto *Globe and Mail*, Kosinski explained that "a sense of mortality suddenly descended upon me at that time. . . . Kiki, who has been an extraordinary presence in my life, would otherwise have been left with no proof of or access to our past." The explanation calls to mind the language in which he described the lovers in *Steps* in his application for the Guggenheim fellowship and in *The Art of the Self*. The "past" is seen as an almost palpable entity which could be retained or lost, imposed upon another, owned, or placed in the hands of a caretaker.

Kiki's version is somewhat more complicated. The Polish spies, never far removed in his imagination, had returned with a vengeance, perhaps because of his support of Solidarity. Not only was he being watched, but Kosinski felt certain that they had managed to gain access to his apartment. When he returned from a trip, or even a few hours away, it seemed to him that objects had been mysteriously moved around. To put his fears to the test, he and Kiki sometimes left an object in a highly specific and marked location, and sure enough, when they returned the object appeared to have been, ever so slightly, disturbed. Almost five years after the *Village Voice* article, he had a constant sense of being stalked by one entity or another. Enemies were all around him, circling as if he were a wounded stag. A wedding with the cream of New York society in attendance would demonstrate the position he still commanded in the world. It would "show them."

And show them it did. Marian Javits agreed to be the hostess. Tom Morgan and his wife, the former Mary Rockefeller, gave one of the dinners. The rehearsal was set for Valentine's Day, with the wedding itself on February 15. Twenty-eight guests in all—the short list, in effect, of people who mattered in New York—assembled at Marian Javits's apartment on Fifty-seventh and Third Avenue for the ceremony and a dinner upstairs—the location of so many semiofficial assemblages of state. Large black candelabra were brought up from basement storage for the occasion, the furniture was pushed back, and Jerzy and Kiki stood with Rabbi Ted Kupferman for the ceremony in front of the giant circular mirror that dominated Javits's living room. Behind them stood the Sulzbergers, the Grunwalds, the Gelbs, the Rosenthals, the Brzezinskis, the Erteguns, and the Kosners, among others. If that assemblage didn't show the world, what would?

Thus marriage, too, became part of the "sacred armor" beneath which the imperiled self might find refuge. Yet there were powerful ironies in almost every aspect of the wedding. As with his inversion of day and night, Kosinski's decision to marry Kiki inverted the usual sequence in relationships. Most weddings mark a beginning, but this one seemed to seal the end of something. One of those things turned out to be the close relationship with Cynthia Cristilli, and their pattern of nightly forays to the clubs. It was not that she had any expectation of Kosinski. He was old enough to be her father, and while her friends sometimes goaded her when his picture turned up in the papers with Kiki at his side, she had been perfectly content with her role. It hadn't occurred to her that he might leave Kiki for her, and she wasn't at all sure she would have wanted that. Nevertheless, the wedding seemed to contain some sort of statement. In a subtle way she could not quite define, it changed things between them, and the frequency and intensity of their contact now began to fall off. She found herself increasingly interested in a young man who tended bar at a restaurant she and Kosinski frequented, and gradually moved in the direction of establishing another life.

In a further ironic ramification, Cynthia's receding presence created a new vulnerability in the relationship between Jerzy and Kiki. Not only had Kiki and Cynthia become allies, but the relationship with Cynthia had come to protect the relationship with Kiki. Kosinski had always needed an intense outside involvement, and Cynthia had provided a reliable and harmless one. There was stability with her, and even safety, as his sexual activities had become more and more a matter of watching. Now Cynthia was no longer constantly available, and growing awareness of the threat of AIDS had not only closed the clubs; it had raised the stakes of casual liaisons. Increasingly this made for a void in Kosinski's life, which he first attempted to fill by a new kind of institutional involvement.

The research conducted for *The Hermit of 69th Street* into relations between Poles and Jews had brought Kosinski into contact with Antony Polonsky, a Polish émigré teaching at the London School of Economics who had extended his personal scholarship by organizing the Oxford Institute for Polish-Jewish studies. Now Polonsky sought to popularize his work through a similar institute in America that would promote public events and conferences, and through a journal called *Polin* from the Hebrew *poh lin* ("here shalt thou lodge"), which early Jewish settlers had called Poland. The American branch, to be called the American Foundation for Polish-Jewish Studies, was in need of a visible leader and—in a manner reminiscent of the way he had been called to the PEN presidency—Kosinski, with his relatively new but enthusiastic interest in Polish-Jewish matters, was chosen.

Kosinski accepted the presidency of the new organization eagerly, solicited Joseph Brodsky, Czeslaw Milosz, Isaac Bashevis Singer, and Elie Wiesel to appear on the letterhead as special patrons, and began putting together a board comprised of prominent Polish and Polish-Jewish émigrés, American Jews, and personal friends. The rather eclectic group eventually included Zbigniew Brzezinski, the tennis player Wojtek Fibak, Irene Pipes, Mrs. Artur Rubinstein, and Janusz Glowacki as well as such clear Kosinski designees as Tom Morgan, William Styron, Lewis Schott,

Diane von Furstenberg, and Ted Field. The executive director was Michael Kott, son of Polish émigré critic Jan Kott, and the contact with the London organization was another Polish émigré, a businessman with an Oxford Ph.D. by the name of Maciej Jachimczyk.

The foundation immediately began fund-raising and set out on an ambitious series of projects, the first of which was cooperation in the International Conference on the History and Culture of Polish Jews to be held in Jerusalem between January 31 and February 5, 1988, with Hebrew University and the Oxford Institute as cosponsors. Other projects that soon had a concrete life were a celebration of Polish-Jewish writer Bruno Schulz, scheduled for September of 1988, and the establishment of an award to be given annually to a person in Poland who has done the most to preserve the Polish-Jewish heritage.

The presidency of the foundation (a position which Kosinski surrendered to Irene Pipes by the summer of 1988, assuming chairmanship of the board of directors) conformed neatly with his personal exploration of Polish and Jewish roots. He was now more than a writer. He was the representative and spokesman of an entire culture—a Poland now rapidly reopening to the West. At the same time he was a seeker, like thousands of other Polish Jews, separated from his roots and trying to find some basis for reconnection with his own history, with his deepest self. Not merely intellectual and spiritual, this quest would soon take more concrete forms. On May 27, 1987, at the urging of Maciej Jachimczyk, he attended a performance by the Polish jazz singer Urszula Dudziak at New York's Blue Note Club. He was impressed by the performance but even more by Dudziak, who had been married to jazz trumpeter Michael Urbaniak and was now Jachimczyk's girlfriend. Then in December, as one of his duties stemming from the foundation, he spoke at a meeting of the Committee for Medical Aid to Poland, where he was introduced to Jan Byrczek, a jazz performer and impresario who was eager to get involved in the rebuilding of Poland. Both Dudziak and Byrczek would play important roles in Kosinski's return to his Polish roots, along with Jachimczyk and Czeslaw Czaplinski, a photographer who had come to the United States in 1979 and first met Kosinski a year later. First, however, he would visit Israel.

4.

In November of 1987, with his trip to Israel already planned, Kosinski went through a rehearsal of sorts, speaking at a conference on Abraham Joshua Heschel held at Spertus College in Chicago. *Hermit* had just gone to the printer, and Kosinski's remarks were full of the issues that had come to dominate the book. Heschel was the great philosopher of *life*, and what could be more life-preserving than the policies of Rumkowski, who gave up children and old people to the Germans in order to save as many as he could for as long as he could. Kosinski reiterated this position in an interview with a rather surprised Mike Leiderman of WJUF-TV, the network of the Jewish Federation of Metropolitan Chicago. What did he think of the controversy concerning efforts by the Polish government and the Catholic church to "internationalize" the Holocaust, describing it as a crime against humanity rather than a crime against Jews?

"It was both," Kosinski answered. "Civilization turned against the Jews, but it also turned against itself." He went on to give statistics: four and a half million Soviet prisoners of war perished, and two out of every five Poles. "But not for the same reason as the Jews," Leiderman countered. "Perishing is perishing," Kosinski said. Leiderman went on to ask his opinion of Claude Lanzmann's film *Shoah*, which documents anti-Semitic attitudes among the Polish peasantry. It was like interviewing the Swiss about lakes, Kosinski said, asking if they loved lakes, and when they said yes, using that as proof that there were no mountains in Switzerland. Leiderman wanted to know if Kosinski meant to say that *Shoah* was a distortion. "A distortion? I'm saying it's a fantasy trick. Maybe, visually, a great one," Kosinski replied adamantly. His voice shook with the anger of a man who knew his position to be insecure, but was determined to stick with it come what may.

Kosinski arrived in Israel amidst the first major rioting of the intifada, accompanied by Tom Morgan. Morgan's sixteen-year marriage to Mary Rockefeller had just broken up, leaving him, as he put it, "a little down in the dumps," and Kosinski urged him to make the trip to cheer him up. They were booked into the American Hotel, which was in the Arab section. Reporters liked it because it was close to the action, and as an old reporter, so did Morgan. Kosinski was less delighted. Sniffing tear gas, Morgan constantly urged his friend in the direction of the action, while Kosinski just as tenaciously pulled back in the direction of safety. In the course of the trip they went together to the major shrines—the Holocaust museum, the Wailing Wall, and finally Masada. Kosinski, who had always held a Nietzschean view of suicide as an action that could express complex and positive values, was moved by one more instance of suicide as an act of powerful resolve and *will*.

As a speaker, Kosinski was popular among Israeli young people, but much less so among survivors of the camps, and his talks often produced arguments with members of the audience. His basic talk, which he gave in both Jerusalem and Tel Aviv, began with a clever set piece based on a women's magazine article telling how to get a man to propose marriage. Kosinski built laughs as he proceeded through item after item of advice, with the culminating suggestion of cooking a meal for his relatives, whereupon he said abruptly, "I have no relatives." As a lead-in to his Holocaust credentials, it was too much of a shift in tone for survivors of the camps, and it led, inevitably, to argument over *Shoah* and the behavior of the majority of Poles during the war. At one point in Jerusalem when a reporter asked what the Poles had done to save the Jews during the war, Kosinski snapped, "What did the Jews do to save the Poles?"

Although such opinions produced a very mixed response, even the blunt-spoken Israelis showed a modicum of deference to Kosinski as one of the world's most renowned Jewish writers, and the head of a foundation who, after all, had personally raised more than $200,000 to support the conference. The general attitude was puzzlement. Why would a man who had himself suffered so much at the hands of the Poles wish to come to their defense? The reason that offers itself in retrospect, although none of his audiences could have been aware of it, is a highly specific and personal matter of conscience. Many episodes in *The Painted Bird* conformed closely with the image of the Polish peasantry put forward in *Shoah*. In improvising upon his wartime experiences Kosinski had greatly distorted the situation in the Polish countryside as he *personally* witnessed it. For the rest of his life he would insist, as he insisted in Tel Aviv, that he was still alive thanks to the forbearance of the Polish peasants. This sounded absurd to his audience, who added to their own experiences the belief that Kosinski had himself been beaten and flung into a pit of ordure, surviving only by great good luck. Only Kosinski knew that the peasants he had encountered, while certainly no angels, had been nothing like the villains depicted in his novel. His defense of Polish peasants amounted to a convoluted act of conscience. Having stigmatized the particular individuals in the universal statement of his novel, he now undertook to absolve the general body of Poles on the basis of his private and particular experience.

Not surprisingly, this view found a most receptive ear among Poles, inside and outside Poland, particularly as it came with the suggestion of recantation from a writer whose work had been seen as vilifying the nation. Among those who noted the apparent shift in Kosinski's position was his boyhood friend Jerzy Urban, who was now the chief spokesman for General Jaruzelski's martial-law regime. During a trip to New York in 1987, Urban had spoken with Kosinski at a diplomatic reception. Drawing upon his impressions from the New York trip, Urban now explained to General Jaruzelski that Kosinski's attendance at the reception was an evidence of political politeness, and suggested that Kosinski's return to Poland might improve the political climate within the country. Exactly what such an "improved climate" implied was the subject of another bitter controversy, the resolution of which, like the debate over Polish behavior during the German occupation, lay in the eye of the beholder. Many Poles continued to see Jaruzelski as a dictator and the puppet of Soviet masters. Jaruzelski himself, and a significant minority of supporters like Urban, saw him as a hero who had taken the nec-

422 James Park Sloan

essary action to stand between Poland and Soviet invasion, thus preserving the integrity of the nation.

In late February 1988, following his return from Israel, Kosinski spent several days ushering maverick Soviet chess player Gary Kasparov around New York. Chess—his father's game—had always fascinated Kosinski, although he was not a player himself, and he was swept away by the spectacle of Kasparov simultaneously defeating dozens of competent opponents. What better evidence of the power that could be exerted by the human mind? In chess, the intellectual master could dominate all opposition. In the final draft of *Hermit* Kosinski could not resist working in the fiction that an uncle, Max Weinreich, had been a chess master. In the personal statement accompanying his last *Who's Who* entry he asserted that to "help tomorrow's adults become thinking individuals, able to judge and function in a world of pressures, conflicting values, and moral ambiguities," an important aid would be "the much needed introduction of the sport of chess on every scholastic level."

The word, meanwhile, had been passed to him through émigré circles that a visit to Poland would not be unwelcome. After considering the risk that some would feel he had returned too soon, with the martial-law regime still in control, Kosinski made the decision to go. The occasion would be his presentation of the Judaica Award for the Polish Gentile who had done the most to preserve the Polish-Jewish heritage, a program which he himself had created at the American Foundation for Polish-Jewish Studies. In fact, Kosinski had simply decided that it was time to face up to his possible accusers and return to Poland. In April, after a brief flight from Vienna, he arrived in Warsaw.

The homecoming was a triumph beyond his wildest imagining. Not only was he no longer persona non grata, he was a hero. In Poland, no one cared about the *Village Voice*, and the politics of two decades earlier were long forgotten. Kosinski was simply a famous writer—more famous here, by far, than in America, although his books were still not available in Polish. Fans mobbed his public appearances, and strangers stopped him in the street and asked for his autograph. The entire ten days were a continuous ecstasy at the edge of terror. At an author's evening in Cracow, people who could not get in broke down the door, while in Lublin the crowd came through windows, lifted him off his feet, and carried him out.

Events official and quasi-official underscored his importance. A translation of *The Painted Bird* had been commissioned by Czytelnik, a prestigious Polish publisher, and was being prepared by Tomasz Mirkowicz, Poland's finest English-Polish translator. The government chose his appearance at a banquet at the University of Warsaw to deliver an apology for harm done to Polish Jews in 1967 and 1968 and an expression of desire for full normalization of relations with the state of Israel; conveyed through Kosinski's old schoolfriend Professor Janusz Kuczynski, the leak was initially denied, as General Jaruzelski had run into problems getting support within the Politburo, but a week later the substance of Kuczynski's leak was confirmed by Jerzy Urban. Daniel Passent, who with his connections in both camps had provided Kosinski an early conduit to Urban, conducted a ninety-minute interview on Polish television in which Kosinski discussed his working methods, the problems of writing in a foreign language, the origins of *The Painted Bird*, and, somewhat wistfully, his friendship in New York with Halina Poswiatowska, now long dead of the heart defect that had brought her to America. Poswiatowska had instructed him by her sensuousness and instinct for life, he told Passent, and it was because of her that he had later taken to visiting hospitals to read to dying patients. "You can't rent attraction to life," he quoted her, portentously, "and when there are no more stops on that train, it's over." *The Guests of Daniel Passent* was broadcast nationally, and two hundred kilometers away, it was seen by several citizens of Dabrowa Rzeczycka who were astonished to recognize the boy who had spent part of the war years in their village, hanging on the fence outside the Warchols' semidetached apartment. It was the talk of the village for days.

Only a few small incidents marred an otherwise perfect reconciliation. At a restaurant with Urban, a waiter grumbled to Kosinski that he must not know the nature of the man he was with—a reminder that Poland was still a politically divided society. Then at Czytelnik he bumped into Jerzy Pawlowski—the friend from the 1960s upon whom he modeled Olympic fencer JP in *Blind Date*. Pawlowski was doing a book detailing his spying for the CIA. They exchanged pleasantries, and Pawlowski agreed to come to Kosinski's second meeting with students at the University of Warsaw. There a girl sitting with two men in the balcony interrogated Kosinski pointedly about the CIA's financial assistance with his first two books. Later Pawlowski mentioned to Kosinski that he recognized the girl by her voice. Some time earlier he had received a call from the same young woman, asking him to come to the U. S. embassy. Pawlowski called the embassy to confirm, and was told that no call had been placed from there. To Pawlowski it was clear that the girl worked for Polish intelligence. Apparently someone in the middle echelons had not gotten the word that the anti-Kosinski campaign was over. The bulk of the audience, however, had been admiring and enthusiastic, and no harm ever came to Kosinski from the Polish secret police.

The most poignant moments of the trip were reserved for Lodz. There Kosinski was reunited with his adoptive brother, Henryk, now a physician. With Henryk at his side he visited the graves of his parents. At the Museum Sztuki he took part in a press conference opening a photographic exhibition dedicated to the Jewish Cemetery, returning afterwards to the Grandka, the coffee shop of the Grand Hotel, to meet with his old friends from high-school and university days. There he chatted with Jerzy Neugebauer, Stash Pomorski, and Andrzej Kamianski along with others from his class. Catching up after so many years, Neugebauer mentioned that he had been having some troubles with his daughter. "At least you have children," Kosinski told him in a sad voice. From Lodz he went on to visit Cracow, where he spent time photographing the sixteenth-century cemetery outside the Remo Synagogue and visited Auschwitz, less than an hour away. While in Cracow he conceived a new and enormous project—a full-scale restoration of Kazimierz, the quarter named after the king who invited the Jews into Poland, which would stand as a memorial to the Polish-Jewish contribution to European history.

Kosinski returned to America fired with enthusiasm for Poland

and things Polish. The whole country was undergoing a transformation, finding a new life, and he was determined to be a part of it. He was appreciated there. More important, Poland—or *poh lin*, where Jews had thrived for six centuries— was an important part of his soul. The rebuilding of Kazimierz was only one of his ambitious projects. In August, on the way back from a walk with Kiki in Central Park, he bumped into Jan Byrczek again at the Cafe de la Paix. When Byrczek invited him for coffee, he sent Kiki on to the apartment and began serious discussions with Byrczek about founding a business enterprise to advance and capitalize upon the coming Polish evolution.

The first copies of *The Hermit of 69th Street* were delivered shortly after Kosinski's return from Poland. By then the book had a long and troubled prepublication history. Despite the apparent approval of Jack Romanos as far back as October of 1983, Bantam began to hedge as the manuscript tripled in size. Romanos had left Bantam by the time a full draft was submitted in the summer of 1985, and while Kosinski felt that the new readers had also given their approval, he may have been extrapolating from their reluctance to deliver an outright no to one of their major authors. One of the indications that his star was no longer in the ascendant at Bantam came when the publisher ceased reprinting his earlier novels, informing him that the low rate of sales did not justify further reprints. It was a long, agonizing process, but in the end Bantam turned *Hermit* down. Kosinski circulated the book to several other publishers, eventually selling it in 1987 to Jeannette Seaver at Henry Holt for an advance of $100,000, a significant comedown from the $300,000 he had received for *Pinball*. By then the manuscript was twelve hundred pages long, and even Kosinski acknowledged that its length had gotten out of hand. He gave Seaver what seemed to be a free hand in cutting it, and she immersed herself in the manuscript, coming up with a list of suggestions. Again, to Seaver, Kosinski appeared to agree. He left with her suggestions, and then returned with a whole new manuscript that had to be edited from scratch. The book also made demands on its editors and printers that were somewhat unusual in the novel genre, requiring footnotes, text blocks and several kinds of type, and posing legal problems with hundreds of quotations. It was, in short, a difficult book to produce, requiring enormous editorial time. When Kosinski returned with his usual last-minute changes, Richard Seaver, Jeannette's husband and president of Henry Holt, attempted to put his foot down, only to have Kosinski talk him into one more round of revision. When that, too, produced a request for revision, the Seavers insisted on going ahead over Kosinski's vigorous protest.

The critical response was devastating. What praise it received was tepid and dutiful; Edward St. John in *Library Journal* called it "easily the best novel Kosinski has written in years" as if unaware that it was the *only* novel Kosinski had written in years. It received a positive notice in the *Washington Post*, but the *Chicago Tribune* found it unreadable, and Paul Stuewe in *Quill Quire* articulated what others were clearly thinking, writing that "stung by recent accusations concerning his unacknowledged use of nonfictional source material, Kosinski has tacked layers of cranky self-justification onto the bare bones of a fictional framework." The result, Stuewe went on, was "one of the least readable texts I've ever encountered." With reviews like this, it was not surprising that sales were less than mediocre. Worse than poor sales and poor reviews, however, was the terrible silence of publications that had reviewed him regularly in the past.

After his triumph in Poland, with such a reception of a work into which he had poured his heart and at least four years of his life, it is not surprising that Kosinski withdrew still further into the armor of his Polish roots.

5.

In September 1988 the second major project of the American Foundation for Polish-Jewish Studies, a week devoted to the works of Bruno Schulz, was celebrated in New York. Kosinski identified strongly with Schulz, the author of *The Street of Crocodiles*, and although he had moved from president to the more distant position of chairman of the board, he emceed the major evening at Town Hall, presenting the first ten-thousand-dollar literary award to Zbigniew Herbert in the presence of Czeslaw Milosz, Susan Sontag, Elizabeth Hardwick, Michal Komar, Zbigniew Brzezinski, and Wojtek Fibak. Yet despite the success of the Bruno Schulz celebration and the conference in Israel, there was growing tension between Kosinski and the board members who linked the foundation to its Oxford counterpart. The original intent of the Oxford Institute had been scholarly, but now Kosinski seemed to have embarked upon a series of extravagant public undertakings, including his personal decision to commit the foundation to a seven-million-dollar project assembling two exhibit halls at the new Immigration Museum on Ellis Island. To that he had added, since his return from Poland, the plan for a massive reconstruction of Kazimierz on a scale that would exceed the postwar reconstruction of Warsaw's "Old Town."

Kosinski envisioned the construction of several modern hotels and a huge convention center in Kazimierz, turning Cracow into the site of a New Jerusalem drawing Jewish tourists from around the world. There was a certain logic behind his plan. Two-thirds of the world's Jews could trace their roots to Greater Poland, and Cracow—the old royal capital—was unquestionably the epicenter of Polish-Jewish civilization and culture. There was just one problem: there were hardly any Jews there, and most Jews with Polish roots were loath to look back at the country most closely identified with the death camps, preferring to put their hearts—and their financial resources—into Israel. As for the Poles, they were generally uninterested in a project having to do with their once large Jewish population except insofar as it meant an inflow of funds for construction.

To his fellow board members at the foundation, these ambitious plans smacked of grandiosity bordering on megalomania. What drove them over the edge, however, was the idiosyncrasy of his views on the Holocaust in Poland. It was one thing for a private individual to differ with the view presented in *Shoah*, but as the spokesman for a major institution dealing with Polish-Jewish relations his categorical denial of Polish anti-Semitism was deeply troubling. It felt like exactly what it was, the working out of personal issues in the context of a public debate.

As his position with the foundation became more and more

strained, Kosinski hit upon a solution. If the foundation could not accept his views, he would create a foundation of his own, accountable to no one. The name he chose was The Jewish Presence Foundation, and its concept was that Jews should place less emphasis on the Holocaust and look instead to celebrate the thousand years of Jewish accomplishment. Again there is much to be said for the idea in objective terms, but its primary thrust seemed deeply embedded in Kosinski's private psychological needs. It was, in a way, a perfect metaphoric means for stating his own case. Look away from the embarrassing facts of the wartime years, he said in effect, and look instead to the whole record of a lifetime's achievement.

Meanwhile Kosinski's return to his Polish roots had taken a concrete and sexual form in his relationship with Urszula Dudziak. Although he had been impressed when he saw her perform at the Blue Note in May of 1987, early relations between Kosinski and "Ula" had been no more than sociable camaraderie. Often he and Kiki would make a foursome with Ula and Maciej Jachimczyk, as the men always had foundation business to discuss. In private, however, Jachimczyk began to tease Kosinski with his descriptions of Ula's virtues. She could make a man feel as no other woman could, he insisted. It was almost as though he wished to push her upon Kosinski.

By January 1988, before the trip to Israel, the relationship with Ula had become more than friendly, and by the summer, after his return from Poland, it had grown into an obsessive passion that threatened his relationship with Kiki. In her middle forties, Ula Dudziak was well known in Polish jazz circles, and she had been named the most promising vocalist in America in 1975 in the *Down Beat* Critics Poll. Her performances featured an exceptional range of sounds, from moans to screeches, and included imitations of various musical instruments, and she had recorded more than twenty albums. While she had had moderate success in America, appearing at many of the major jazz festivals, her reputation and her roots remained in the smoky world of postwar Polish jazz—the universe of cabaret dissidents that had been so important in Kosinski's youth. If Kosinski's marriage with Mary Weir had in some ways been a marriage with American society, then the affair with Ula was his return for a final passionate embrace of his Polish beginnings.

From Ula's perspective, Jerzy was an answered prayer. Her twenty-year marriage to jazz trumpeter Michael Urbaniak had recently broken up, leaving her alone at the age of forty-four with two daughters, trapped in the relatively impoverished world of jazz performers, and full of doubts about herself as a woman. Maciej Jachimczyk had not been the answer. Now Jerzy arrived in her life, a witty, sexy, energetic man, flawed perhaps but full of life, and, in the universe of Poles, a star. In her view, he literally kept her alive. At their first meeting, at the Blue Note club, she remembered a moment several years before when she had passed him on a New York sidewalk. Recognizing him at a distance, she had worked up the courage to speak to him when, at the last moment, he turned his head, making the greeting impossible. Now he was a part of her life, showering her with the love and romantic attention he delivered so well. The financial assistance he soon began to provide was certainly a factor in her attachment, but it was the emotional shoring up—reviving her sense of herself as a woman—that swept her away.

Yet Ula was not altogether blind to Jerzy's negative side. One night at Marylou's she watched as he heaped lavish praise on the paintings of a Japanese artist that owner Tommy Barado had placed on the walls. The artist himself was brought forth, and Jerzy gave him his card, promising assistance with his career. When the artist made the followup call, of course, it was Kiki who answered, informing him regretfully that Jerzy had left the country for several months. And Ula herself experienced Jerzy's penchant for generous impulses followed by sober afterthoughts. Once, discussing her career, he asked her what a really state-of-the-art home recording studio would cost. She replied that it would come to about ten thousand dollars. He reached instantly for his checkbook, but she told him to wait, she was going away for a couple of weeks and saw no point in leaving ten thousand dollars in her bank account. After she returned, the subject of the recording studio was never again broached. In similar fashion, he proposed adopting her daughters—Kasia, born in 1978, whose adolescent poetry he praised extravagantly, and Mika, who was two years younger. He was wonderful with them, after all, at least in small bursts of attention, and he pushed the idea until she ran it by her irate ex-husband, finally getting a reluctant agreement in principle that it might be in the girls' interest, whereupon Jerzy backtracked quickly, saying that the idea was not fair to Urbaniak after all. As for her career, he told her, contradicting his initial response, that her peculiar wordless style of imitating musical instruments doomed her to insignificance. She should use her wonderful voice in more conventional ways. His favorite song was "All My Trials," and he begged her to sing it for him. When she finally consented, he seemed almost unbearably moved. If she would sing *that* song in *that* way, he told her, all the fame and honors and riches of the world would be hers.

Kiki seems to have grasped almost from the beginning that this relationship was somehow different from all the other women who had drifted through their lives. She struggled as never before to maintain control, accommodating when necessary while trying to nudge her husband in the direction of reason. This time her efforts seemed unavailing. Her rival was not so much an individual as an entire culture, a montage of memory and dream from which she was excluded by language and origin. Ula, in her view, was an opportunist pure and simple, and did not have her husband's best interests at heart. By the end of the summer, the situation had come to the first of a series of crises, with the Kosinskis openly discussing divorce.

On October 5, New York's André Zarre Gallery gave Kosinski an individual show featuring his photographs of Polish and Russian scenes from 1950 to 1957. The following month he and Kiki patched it up, completing a year of frenetic travel by going to Egypt. Ami Shinitsky, the editor of *Polo* magazine, invited Kosinski to join a touring polo team, as honorary member, adding fuel to his fantasies of being an international polo competitor. In Alexandria he remembered seeing the stamp of the port of Alexandria on fine Egyptian cotton that arrived for processing in the textile mills of Lodz. In a piece written for *Polo*, he mentioned the connection between Alexandria and his childhood, citing stories told before the war by his uncle Stanislaw, a classicist, who wrote a book about Hypatia, a fifth-century Alexandrian woman of letters. Suddenly anything and everything provided connection to his early experiences in Poland.

With jazzman Jan Byrczek as his partner he now plunged ahead to form the Polish-American Resource Corporation, known by its acronym, PARC, with plans for a number of ambitious commercial ventures in Poland, using seed capital from America. In typically grand style, he talked of building several million units of housing in Poland, to be paid for by exporting windows back to the United States. Another possibility was buying a large auto plant and establishing a factory to produce light trucks, which would be exported to China. He quoted cost figures for truck production to anyone who would listen and expressed confidence that the big moneymen he had met over the years would be eager to jump in and support these projects.

Although Byrczek had only the limited business experience of a jazz promoter, his close relationship with Ula Dudziak served to give him credibility in Kosinski's eyes. The two of them, Kosinski was convinced, were uniquely positioned by their multicultural backgrounds to grasp the changes in Poland. They were visionaries, and the world would catch up with them sooner or later. Kiki had her doubts about all this. For one thing, it was keeping Jerzy away from the central activity of his life, his writing. She distrusted the whole PARC enterprise, suspecting that it would prove a drain on both his energy and his finances. She could not help observing that it was one more vehicle drawing him deeper into a small group of not entirely savory Poles. In addition to Byrczek and Ula, there was Czeslaw Czaplinski, a photographer from Lodz who was constantly trying to involve Kosinski in his exhibitions and projects. From the perspective of cool reason, he seemed a chronic and useless hanger-on. In the face of Kiki's doubts, Kosinski was adamant. He was going ahead with PARC whether or not she approved. If she didn't like it, she knew the way to the door.

Another Pole who drifted back into Kosinski's life at that time was Agnieszka Osiecka, who also happened to be a close friend of Ula. Kosinski and Osiecka had first met in the fall of 1967, when she came to America on a Ford Foundation grant. They had met again in the late 1970s when Osiecka was living in Boston and taking creative-writing courses. At that time they had discussed writing, and Kosinski shared with her his theory of the liberation in talking and writing about sex afforded by a foreign language. Now he professed to like a story she had written about a man who calls telephone operators to ask whether God exists. He did little to help her publish it, suggesting, when pressed, that she turn it into a play. Osiecka's history included marriages to Wojtek Frykowski and Daniel Passent, both of whose lives were intertwined with Kosinski's. From her failures as a fiction writer, she had gone on to compose satirical song lyrics, becoming Poland's best-known pop lyricist.

From the late 1970s on, whenever Osiecka and Kosinski met, they played a game of story improvisation often based on a current newspaper article. One of the stories took off from a piece in a Polish-language newspaper about a Polish vampire. The novel they co-imagined was called "The Vampire's Wife," and it begins with a vampire on the loose in a small town, perhaps in America, perhaps Silesia. Once a month the man in the story disappears from home and a girl is found dead, and after a while the wife comes to suspect him. She notes that he is edgy for a few days before his nightly absences, and that their lovemaking has a special edge. She begins to follow him, witnesses his acts of rape and murder, and must come to a decision whether or not to tell the police. Eventually she disguises herself as a prostitute and waits for him by the railroad tracks, perhaps as a penance for her complicity, perhaps to share with his victims their heightened experience. As Kosinski and Osiecka walked along the East River improvising, a strong wind scattered garbage and a dirty shred of cloth floated by, as Osiecka thought, like a torn bridal gown.

Without being aware of it, Kosinski had created in the story of "The Vampire's Wife" a perfect metaphor for his twenty-three-year relationship with Kiki. What, indeed, was the vampire's wife to do? Both wife and vampire are trapped by their own natures, and by the history they share. For years Kiki had been dragged away from parties and dropped off at the corner of Fifty-seventh and Sixth as Kosinski left for his nocturnal rituals. He had resisted normal human celebrations such as birthdays and holidays, living instead by the fire of his ambition and the rhythms of the nether world to which he withdrew. Unconsciously, in "The Vampire's Wife," he came as close as he would ever come to empathy with her situation.

Yet whatever stirring of scruple Kosinski may have felt, the relationship with Ula continued to develop and deepen. To Osiecka, who served both of them as confidante, they revealed details of their passion. Kosinski was now spending an increasing amount of time at Ula's apartment on Fifty-eighth Street. Sometimes they would make love through the whole night, withdrawing to dress in costume—he as a rough man in a black sweater, she as an old noblewoman in a granny dress, then later as a streetwalker. Sex could be wonderful theater, Kosinski explained to Osiecka, who wondered how her friends managed this with Ula's two daughters asleep in the next room. She did not note—she could not know—that Ula's face bore a suggestive similarity to his first model of sexuality, Elzbieta Weinreich Kosinska.

In April of 1989, the anniversary of his first trip, Kosinski returned to Poland. It was to be a reprise of his first visit, this time with *The Painted Bird* newly published in a Polish edition. Crowds mobbed the Czytelnik book store, among them Edward Warchol from Dabrowa—who as seventeen-year-old Edek, the landlord's son, had come to ten-year-old Kosinski's rescue when he was beleagured by village toughs on the icy pond. Warchol's brother-in-law, Bronislaw Woloszyn, came too. The crowd waiting to have their books signed was well into the hundreds, some said the thousands, and a line committee was formed, assigning Warchol and Woloszyn numbers 304 and 305. Kosinski arrived in a black consular limousine bearing an American flag. Leaving Woloszyn to hold their place in line, Warchol rushed forward and shouted, "This is Warchol from Dabrowa. Do you recognize me?" Kosinski seemed to nod, but was swept inside.

What happened once Warchol and Woloszyn made their way inside is a matter of dispute. There was a brief conversation in which Warchol greeted Kosinski respectfully as "Mr. Jurek" and introduced himself as "Edward Warchol from Dabrowa Rzeczycka, the son of Andrzej, at whose place you and your parents hid during the occupation." Kosinski, looking frozen, shook his hand mechanically and replied, "My parents are already dead." To this Warchol replied, "And our mom, thank God, is still alive, although she's well over eighty." There was a silence, after which Kosinski said, "Only my brother is still alive." "Brother?" Warchol asked, then realized that Kosinski must be referring to Henryk. "Yes, brother," Kosinski said. "I'm going to Lodz to see him." Then he signed the copy of *The Painted Bird*, and Warchol and Woloszyn began to pass on.

In the course of the conversation, however, they had passed Kosinski a note, which he passed along unread to the Czytelnik rep as he had done with dozens of others. According to Warchol and Woloszyn, the woman who received their note—they assumed she must be his wife—asked if they were indeed the people who had kept him during the war. When he replied yes, there were several rapid conversations in English, and the woman, who was constantly at his side, appeared to be urging him to invite them to the table, only to be cut off by a dismissive gesture. Kiki firmly denies that this latter part of the incident took place, and she would certainly have been unable to read a note written in Polish. Tomasz Mirkowicz, Kosinski's Polish translator who was also nearby, suggests that the note was indeed passed, but to the Czytelnik rep. In any event Warchol and Woloszyn were then moved along with promises that Kosinski would write or contact them.

Regardless of the specific details, the encounter at Czytelnik was the concrete realization of Kosinski's ultimate nightmare. The historical forces that pulled down the Berlin Wall had finally broken through the compartments separating major components of his life. The same commerce between East and West that PARC now sought to advance and exploit had broken down the barrier between his past and his present, exposing his carefully cultivated personal myth to the reality of his personal history. One need only credit Kosinski with a modicum of human feeling for his dilemma to become clear. The event at the Czytelnik book store demonstrated how his need to get in touch with his Polish roots was at odds with his fear of exposure. He may well have *wanted* to have a reunion with Edek Warchol. From a psychological standpoint, he may have *needed* to have a reunion with

Warchol. Such a reunion was the ultimate destination to which all his recent public statements and actions, at some cost, had been pointing. Yet he didn't dare acknowledge Warchol, for fear of the revelations to which such an acknowledgment would lead. To acknowledge Warchol, in short, was to own up to the literal truth about his childhood.

Kosinski still shrank from facing the truth even though his entire life had been taken over by projects conceived in part to make amends for harm he had inflicted by telling lies. There was a hollow space at the center of Kosinski that had resulted from denying his past, and his whole life had become a race to fill in that hollow space before it caused him to implode, collapsing inward upon himself like a burnt-out star. Although he had been unable to reach out to Warchol and Woloszyn, there is a myth among the villagers that he did return to Dabrowa. As their daily lives are still immersed in superstitions and fairy tales, one must view this account with a certain skepticism. The villagers maintain that he came in a large black limousine. As he passed the site of the Warchol apartments, they believe, the limo slowed but did not stop.

Back in America Kosinski threw himself even more strongly into his Polish initiatives, while the relationship with Ula entered a new phase. He was suddenly overcome with a need to have children, and he took Ula to consult with a fertility specialist, although to no avail. Together the two of them took lessons in transcendental meditation. By the summer of 1989 he was spending so much time at her apartment on Fifty-eighth Street that she set aside a space for him to work. In return, he undertook to redo her whole apartment. Vainly Kiki urged her husband to exercise prudence, especially in the matter of redoing Ula's apartment, but when her pleas failed, she wrote the checks—more than three thousand dollars by the time it was finished.

Kosinski was now thinking in millions, not thousands. The schemes for using PARC to build housing and trucks had not come to fruition, but he had come up with an idea requiring less technical expertise and equipment. They would organize a bank, for which the only raw material was money. During the Warsaw portion of his April trip, Kosinski had been accompanied by Jan

Byrczek, and together they had met with officials of Narodowy Bank Polski—the Polish National Bank. At first they were told that to incorporate a bank required a minimum capital of $15 million—more than Kosinski was able to raise—to be deposited along with their letter of intent. Later they were told that the absolute minimum was $6 million. Even that reduced amount was daunting for a group of entrepreneurs whose only asset was a corporate shell, but Kosinski now went to work furiously to raise the money.

The Kosinski-Byrczek group at PARC had already expanded to include Polish-born architect Jerzy Glowczewski and financial expert Zenon Komar. Now he added Witold Sulimirski, a retired executive vice president of Irving Trust, who helped persuade Bankers Trust to join in the venture. The real weight of finding backers fell on Kosinski, who turned to Ted Field. Field kicked in $1.5 million of his own money and enlisted Steve Ross at Time-Warner and William Agee at Morrison Knudsen for similar amounts. A Polish consortium led by Polish Oil and Gas put up the final $1.5 million. In December, with an initial capitalization of $7.5 million, AmerBank—the American Bank in Poland—was issued license number one to form a banking enterprise in Poland, the first foreign bank to be chartered in Poland in half a century. At one point in the proceedings PARC—the organization put together over coffee by a novelist and a jazz musician—controlled one-third of AmerBank's shares.

Thus Kosinski found himself at the center of a network that included a foundation and two overlapping international business enterprises. Yet despite his position as a potential financial magnate, actual cash flow had once again become a concern. In November he wrote Mort Janklow of the Janklow & Nesbit literary agency seeking representation for three possible projects, which Janklow declined. The first, entitled *Dialoghi d'Amore*, was described somewhat vaguely as a writer's search for the lost dialogues of Leone Ebreo, a work of philosophy devoted to passion, desire, and lovemaking. The second was a novel, *Center-State*, about the elected president-for-life of a newly formed republic, which Kosinski saw as a sort of sequel to *Being There*. The third was *Passing By*, a collection of his essays and incidental writing. Kosinski claimed to have done substantial work on each book and projected completion dates of spring, summer, and fall of 1990. Only the third was to see publication, as an edition put together posthumously by his widow.

6.

One is tempted to see in the final two years of Kosinski's life the tragedy of the great man fallen into the company of thugs, rogues, and impostors. T. E. Lawrence comes to mind, in the latter stages of his Arabian campaign, and several of the Roman emperors. Yet Kosinski, if he had something of the great man in his makeup, also had something of the rogue and the impostor. Toward the end of his life, it was as if these traits, hitherto only a part of his psyche, had become personified, assuming the form of individual friends and associates. Once inner voices, they now stood outside his head and whispered schemes into his ears.

In March of 1990 Kosinski and Kiki made the usual spring trip to Switzerland. He intended to work on one of the new novels, but instead worked on a piece about "the second Holocaust," his terminology for the damage done to the history of Jewish accomplishments by excessive emphasis on the Holocaust. While he was in Crans, he experienced a number of physical symptoms that, taken together, seemed to carry a message about his mortality. He had suffered for years from cardiac arrhythmia, and now he began to notice a loss of sensation in the tips of his fingers. He underwent both cardiological and neurological tests, with negative results. His body was beginning to suffer from the common afflictions of late middle age, but the symptoms, which disturbed him so much as to limit his pleasure in skiing, seemed to exist at the border between physical and psychological being.

From the beginning he had written dissociatively of the body, as if it were a piece of arcane machinery, over which it was possible to exert only tenuous and occasional control. In *Steps* the dissociation between body and self had been largely sexual, bounded on the one extreme by a protagonist whose body continued making love as he spoke on the telephone and on the other by the masseur whose hands became the disembodied expression of the protagonist's sexual will. In *Hermit* he had written of Kosky's body as a "constitutional Republic"; now certain elements of that Republic were in rebellion against him.

Though the arrhythmia was real, the acute episodes had many aspects of panic attacks. He suffered one of his attacks during a ski run from the top of Plaine Morte in bad weather, fainting and being dragged to the nearest gondola by Kiki. Strangely, he seemed less troubled by the fainting than by a ruptured tendon in his right thumb, the result of a fall while skiing in Colorado, which was slow to respond to physical therapy. In early summer he collapsed in the rest room of a gas station on the road from Italy to Switzerland. He described to friends the experience of hearing water flushing then finding himself on the floor. He feared, as he told them, that it had been a stroke, although it left him with none of the impairment by which a stroke is normally accompanied. Prompted by the incident, he left Switzerland for the first time without Kiki, leaving her to set things in order before joining him in New York.

For the rest of the summer he worked at the apartment on Fifty-seventh Street, not even venturing to New Haven for a weekend break. Although he had estimated delivery dates in the spring and summer for two works of fiction, he now put them aside to focus on letters soliciting business for PARC and AmerBank. Once again he sought the aid of Peter Skinner, preparing a three-page banking solicitation letter with the care usually reserved for the final draft of a novel. Polished and literary as it was, the letter was unsuccessful in its primary aim of attracting business. Its recipients became bogged down in the wealth of detail and could not figure out what the solicitation was asking them to *do*. To Kiki, it appeared an evasion of Kosinski's central task. On the literary side, he turned out an appreciation of the work of a young sculptor he had met, Rhonda Roland Shearer, and continued redrafting "The Second Holocaust," arguing that contemporary Jews were "Holocaust-bound." In 1988, after the return from his first trip to Poland, the *Times* had given him space on the op-ed page for a piece entitled "Restoring a Polish-Jewish Soul." His views on the Holocaust, however, proved too strong even for his friends, and the *Times* passed on the new piece, as did the *Washington Post*. It was finally published on November 5 by the *Boston Globe*, a forum of distinctly more modest stature.

In September, Kosinski visited Poland for what was to be the last time. AmerBank was scheduled to open the following May. On September 14, he delivered a speech at Cracow's Jagellonian University dedicated to Professor Jozef Gierowski, head of the university's International Institute of History and Culture of Polish Jewry. There he spoke more simply and directly of his family than ever before, describing their origins in Zamosc, Vilnius, and Lodz, and citing his uncle Stanislaw from Lvov as a part of the Polish-Jewish contribution to international scholarship. He went on to give an eloquent and thoroughly researched account of the historic Polish hospitality to Jews and Jewish contribution to Polish culture. Against this backdrop, he discussed the effect of the German occupation, citing thousands of pictures drawn by Polish children to depict their war experiences. In response to such questions as "What happened in your family and among your kin during the war and Nazi Occupation?" almost half could recall only murders and executions. He then cited the work of Stanislaw Baley, who found that over 60 percent of Warsaw teenagers suffered grave psychological disturbances as a result of their wartime experiences.

Few had suffered more profound disturbance than Kosinski himself. One might well ask why, through a lifetime of pain and insecurity, he had never taken the early advice of Mira Michalowska and sought counseling? The answer lay in the myth of omnipotence by which he had managed to survive childhood. To seek counseling would have been to acknowledge the core falsity of the story he told himself about his life. It was the same catch-22 that made him unable to reach out to childhood companions from Dabrowa Rzeczycka. In the Cracow speech, as in his ambitious business programs and cultural foundations, he assumed a tone of Olympian distance in order to speak of the inutterable pain that formed the core emotional experience of his life. Before leaving Poland he made a final trip to Lodz, meeting with his oldest friends and standing once again at his parents' graves as if telling them goodbye.

Back in New York the conflicts with Kiki resumed. He continued to obsess about the affairs of PARC and AmerBank, the only aspects of his life that seemed to be making progress. Reasonable as always, Kiki exhorted him to get letters out with businesslike dispatch and get on with his real work, which for the moment consisted of a massive rewrite for the paperback edition of *Hermit*. The relationship with Ula was on-again, off-again, in the familiar rhythm of more traditional love triangles. Deadlines were set for a decision about divorce, but they always, somehow, passed. Kiki certainly was not interested in a divorce, and she made her views clear. The affair was broken off now by Kosinski, now by Ula, often for as short a period as a few hours. Kosinski found himself essentially in the position of Graham Greene's protagonist in *The Heart of the Matter*, torn between his obligations to his wife and his feelings for his mistress. In the end, there seemed to be no way out except the removal of the object of contention—himself.

Worst of all, as Kosinski confessed to a few close friends, his sexual powers—which had astonished his friends and served him so well as an affirmation of life—had begun to fail him. Age and illness had taken their toll, and perhaps a divided conscience as well. The clubs, which had so powerfully stoked his drives, were gone. In the 1987 interview with Mike Leiderman for the Jewish Federation Network he had responded angrily to Leiderman's suggestion that there was an excess of sex in his books. "Not enough," he had snapped, talking over Leiderman's final word. "Why not?" Leiderman wanted to know. "Because it's a force of life," Kosinski replied. "I don't know of any other." Beyond sex, an overall fatigue and ennui had set in. Being Jerzy Kosinski was an endless and strenuous task. Alone at a restaurant with Ula, he suddenly slumped down in his chair, saying, "I'm tired of *me*."

Toward the end of that year a strange meeting was arranged. Kosinski had occasionally mentioned that he would be interested in meeting Geoffrey Stokes, the senior coauthor of the *Village Voice* attack. Marylou's, located on West Ninth Street, was one of Kosinski's favorite restaurants. He was a close friend of the owner, Tommy Barado, and had once played a prank on Norman Mailer there, posing as a hyperactive waiter. One December evening as he sat in Marylou's, Stokes walked in accompanied by two friends, Michael Caruso, a former *Voice* editor, and Chris Calhoun, then advertising manager at *The Nation*. A mutual friend had found Stokes having a drink at the Lion's Head bar and suggested that it might be an occasion for talking with Kosinski. Caruso and Calhoun were enlisted to lend support. Once Kosinski had joked to the French newspaper *Libération* that he ought to kill Stokes. In print the quip had come across deadpan as a threat. Stokes was taking no chances.

Now the two men had a long talk. "You ruined my career," Kosinski said at the beginning. Stokes apologized for the inaccuracy in the piece having to do with a sequence of events in *The Painted Bird*. Kosinski then acknowledged that he had made extensive use of editors, but argued that their help did not compromise the fact that the books were his alone. "Why didn't you say that *then*?" Stokes asked, adding that it could have been the beginning of an interesting debate. Kosinski gave Stokes his theory of the overall affair, including the bet between Pochoda and Navasky and the conspiracy to trap and destroy him. As to his reasons for not entering into a debate, he told Stokes, "You don't understand. All my life I've been hiding." Leaving Marylou's they hugged in a gesture of reconciliation.

Kosinski had finally finished revisions for the paperback version of *Hermit*, to be published by Zebra Books. A full 40 percent of the text was changed from the hardcover edition, including the revisions the Seavers wouldn't allow him to make at the last minute, although none of the changes made the book appreciably more accessible for readers. Now Kiki urged that they go to Los Angeles to visit Ted Field and his new wife, Susie, accompanying the Fields to Aspen for Christmas if things should work out that way. She had various reasons for pushing this plan, including the relative ease of the travel, but it was also true that an extended visit with the Fields would put her husband out of reach of Ula. The plan was to fly directly from Aspen to Florida, in order to enjoy the warm climate and play polo at the Palm Beach Polo Club.

Instead, Kosinski insisted on returning from Aspen to New York for New Year's, putting aside Kiki's objections with the argument that the altitude in Aspen would be bad for his heart. In

New York there was, of course, Ula. While he was there he worked with Czeslaw Czaplinski on a rather bizarre project—a book to be published in Poland with the title *Kosinski's Passions*, combining text with Czaplinski photographs of Kosinski. Among the photographs were a series showing Kosinski in disguise, wearing a mustache, a wig, a mask, and a polo helmet. By the end of January they were making final corrections to the text. Late that month he called Ewa Markowska, touching base for the first time in years. She began to tell him that her husband Andrzej, with whom he had companionably watched the Miss America contest in 1959, was dying of cancer. Before she could finish the sentence he cut her off, saying, "Don't tell me anything bad."

Nor was his own heart problem a pure fabrication. His pulse ranged from 40 to 200, and the medication he took to slow it down made him sluggish. While nothing showed up on heart monitors but arrhythmia, his doctor wired him up to a sophisticated electronic system so that he could call instantly for instructions if he was overtaken by one of his spells. Thus reassured, he drove down to Florida with Kiki in February and stayed in an apartment he rented from Ami Shinitsky. He showed Shinitsky the heart-monitoring machine with a certain pride. Always fond of gadgets, he took a perverse delight in the fact that his vital signs could be broadcast to his doctor back in New York. Riding did not go well, however. Never a masterful equestrian, he now had trouble with the jarring from the horse's motion and found himself unable to take more than a half-hour of riding.

By early April he was back in New York and again involved in a host of projects. On April 10 Czeslaw Czaplinski visited him to discuss an essay called "New York: The Literary Autofocus" that Czaplinski had talked him into providing for an exhibit of Czaplinski's photographs scheduled for August in Warsaw. Czaplinski remarked on the fact that Kosinski was still wearing pajamas in the afternoon. "I must confess that my health is deteriorating," Kosinski said. His heart medication made him groggy until early afternoon, and it seemed to be affecting his memory. He told Czaplinski he was afraid he had the beginnings of Alzheimer's. He confessed that he had forgotten his way home while in Florida, and that the day before he had been joined in a restaurant by a number of people he could not recognize, but who seemed to know him well. With Ula Dudziak, he had been unable to recall what restaurant she was talking about when she proposed going to their "favorite place."

Friends who saw Kosinski socially in April were left with a mixed impression. Lisa Grunwald had found him world-weary at an *Esquire* party the previous winter. "Look at this same old stuff," he had told her amidst the literary chatter. Now at the party given by her father to celebrate the publication of her novel *The Theory of Everything*, she found him very depressed, but admired his ability to muster courage for a social occasion. In mid-April Abe Rosenthal, too, was concerned about the evidence of illness and depression when they met for a friend's birthday party at the Russian Tea Room, and again a week later at a small dinner party at Brio, a restaurant on Madison, given by Gay Talese. At the same party some of his good friends were completely deceived by his social composure. Talese, who saw him mainly across the table talking with Mike Wallace and John Chancellor, thought he looked fine.

He had often spoken of suicide, but most of his friends discounted his oblique threats. To Gil Shiva, his talk of suicide had always had a detached quality, as if he were describing theoretical means which might be employed by an abstract "someone." Shiva was more aware than most of Kosinski's battle with physical aging. Now he noted that Kosinski's tan extended to the palms of his hands. Kosinski admitted that he was consuming heavy quantities of carrot extract to maintain a tanned and youthful appearance. Yet the last week in April, when Shiva hosted a Shakespeare Dinner at which Kosinski was unusually quiet, Shiva's first thought was that he had not given his friend a good enough seat. Cynthia Cristilli had often been shown his cache of pills, but a telephone call that week did nothing to trigger a sense of alarm. Other friends, in retrospect, had the distinct impression that he had told them goodbye. In late April he attended his last PEN black-tie dinner, touching base with the literary crowd. The Styrons were there, and HarperCollins editor Ed Burlingame, who had not seen Kosinski in years. To Burlingame, Kosinski ap-

peared haunted, ravaged. They had a long and affectionate conversation, mainly about the 1960s when they had hung out together at publishing events, and Kosinski introduced Burlingame to everyone in earshot as one of his oldest friends.

Kiki, too, would remember incidents that might have served as
clues. One morning in late April Kosinski staggered around the
apartment as if drunk. She thought he was mugging until finally
she said, "Come on, Jerz, cut it out." When he continued to stag-
ger, she realized that he was really buzzed, and chalked it up to
the medication. Later she wondered if he had been testing the
strength of his sleeping pills. His dejection also made its way to
the surface in random comments. Critic Welch Everman had been
preparing a major critical study of Kosinski's work, and when the
book did not arrive, Kosinski worried that Everman had dropped
the project, telling Kiki, "Even Welch Everman has given up on
me." The bulletin board on the wall of his bedroom-study had
evolved into a portrait of his life as seen from late April 1991. It
contained, among other odds and ends, pictures of him playing
polo, floating, cartooned as *Don Quixote*, and posed by his car in
a trick photo with a road sign for "Switzerland"; a beribboned
Polish eagle and an article on trade with Poland; pictures with
Ted and Susie Field and the Field children, as well as a sunset
from the Field boat; an article on Jan Lechon, the Polish poet who
committed suicide in New York; poems on being a Jew in the
twentieth century by Muriel Rukeyser and on "How Can You Become a Poet?" by Eve Merriam; and a copy of the PEN charter,
with the section underlined that pledged members to "oppose
such evils of a free press as mendacious publication, deliberate
falsehood, and distortion of facts for political and personal ends."

On Tuesday, April 30, Kosinski gave his final interview to
Pearl Sheffy Gefen of the *Toronto Globe and Mail*. In it he went
over basic themes of his life and work, reaffirming such aspects
of his personal myth as his muteness and his separation from his
parents during the war. He threw in unmistakable intimations of
mortality. "There are days when I see myself as a profoundly he-
roic figure," he told Gefen, "and there are days when I see myself
as a decrepit figure about to die." He mentioned that he was
scheduled to fly to Warsaw on Sunday, May 5, for the grand

opening of AmerBank on May 17. He would return on May 20, he told her, adding, "But first, let's see if I go." That same day he met with Jan Byrczek to discuss the opening of the bank and made a date for the following week to make pictures with Byrczek's daughter Aleksandra. At noon on Thursday, May 2, he met again with Byrczek, who was flying ahead to Warsaw on a 6:00 P.M. flight. He was still expressing doubt that he would make the trip, but Kiki observed that he always expressed doubts about travel; she was confident that he would go.

In the late afternoon there was the book party at the apartment of the Taleses to launch Senator Cohen's novel, *One-Eyed Kings*. Kosinski circulated easily, a star in a firmament of stars. He presented his copy of the novel for Cohen's signature, chatted briefly with Gay Talese, and traded family news with Wendy Luers, his friend from Christmases in the Dominican Republic. The Kosinskis left the party early, around 7:30. Responding to Ula's phone message, Kosinski spent the next five hours with her, eating dinner at Wolff's, watching the Greenaway film, and having a cup of tea at the Parker Meridien. Suddenly he said to her, "I can't see any way out. There is only one solution." They had been discussing a move to Florida—Jerzy, Ula, the two children. Kiki, of course, objected. Now Ula, caught up in the discussion about Florida, understood him to be saying that he would act with or without Kiki's consent. On this note, they parted for the night. When he later phoned her from his bedroom study, she asked what his plans were for the following day. He told her that he had an event in the evening, but was free during the day. "Great," she said, "I'll kidnap you and we'll go to Central Park." "OK," he said. "When I get up tomorrow I will call you."

They were the last words anyone heard him speak. Then, if he had not already done so, he inscribed copies of his books to Kiki and Ted Field. Kiki would later believe that his inscription in *The Painted Bird* amounted to a rededication of the book to her. He also wrote out a note to Kiki. "I am going to put myself to sleep now for a bit longer than usual," it read, then added, in a self-consciously literary echo of his Jacques Monod piece, "Call the time Eternity." Explaining the action he was about to take, the note said that he did not wish to be a burden in his increasing "decrepitude," of which Kiki was the "prime victim." He added that only she had mattered to him "as did my life from day to day," and urged her to "embrace our friends." Then to the alcohol which was already in his system he now added a large dose of sleeping pills. Removing his clothes, he lowered himself into the bathtub of the small bathroom behind his study. He twisted a plastic shopping bag around his head, completing the method recommended by the Hemlock Society and described in *Hermit*, assuring that he would not survive in a brain-damaged condition. There sometime after 1:00 A.M. he availed himself of the only perfect refuge known to humankind, wrapping himself in the sacred armor of death.

7.

Shortly after nine the following morning Kiki saw that his bed was made up and thought, that's terrific, the bed is made and he's already up and about. Soft music was coming from the bathroom, and she walked in and discovered the body. She immediately called Ula, asking her whether they had had some sort of argument. Ten minutes later she called again and invited Ula to come over to say farewell. His body bore what looked to her like scratches, explained by the doctor as a symptom of the body's struggle against death. When the paramedics and police arrived, Ula left. There would be no funeral or memorial, in accordance with Kosinski's instructions. An autopsy was performed, as in all cases of sudden death, and the New York medical examiner concluded that it was the synergistic combination of the drugs—ethanol (alcohol), glutamates (sleeping pills), barbiturates, and opiates—not asphyxiation, that had caused his death. The sleeping pills were the substance present in the highest concentration in his blood. After the autopsy, his body was cremated. The urn bearing his ashes was placed in the closet of his bedroom-study, beneath the famous uniforms and disguises. There it remains—a last dissociated element of self—as though emblematic of the difficulty in assigning Kosinski his final place.

An extraordinary number of people have a clear recollection of what they were doing when they heard of Kosinski's death. Those who had attended the party the evening before were shocked, with the exception of Abe Rosenthal, who had been more aware than most of Kosinski's precarious state in recent weeks. Ted Field in Denver heard Kiki's voice on the phone saying, "He finally did it." Jan Byrczek received phone calls from both Kiki and Ula as soon as he got off the plane in Warsaw. Ahmet Ertegun, in Boston to give the commencement address at the Berklee School of Music, was pricing an antique desk with friends when the news came over the radio; the salesman had just told them the desk was $14,000, and when a tear rolled down Ertegun's cheek, the salesman quickly said, "Don't get upset, we can do a better price for you." Gil Shiva got an early call from Kiki and tried to keep the news from his son, whose twenty-first birthday party was the "event" to which Kosinski was committed on May 3; he succeeded until the party began, but one of his son's friends innocently blurted the news. Krystyna Iwaszkiewicz Rytel heard the news with her husband, whose comment was that Kosinski was fortunate; deeply depressed himself, he would soon follow the same course Kosinski had chosen.

In Boston Jean Kilbourne, now married, received a telephone call from a friend. In Lodz, Jerzy Neugebauer, in bed with a woman, heard the news on the radio and wept. "What's the matter with you?" the woman asked. "Did you expect something of him?"

Some deaths have the effect of pulling people together, while others leave a world that, in the absence of the departed, is destined to fly apart. Kosinski's death had both effects, though with the greater emphasis on the latter. While many of his friends rallied to Kiki's side, the Fields in particular, the terms of his business relationships bore the seeds of conflict. On May 17 Kiki flew to Poland and cut the ribbon for the opening of AmerBank. Already differences among the partners were becoming apparent. The Jewish Presence Foundation began to fade quietly into oblivion, while Kiki and Jan Byrczek entered into a struggle for control of PARC, and thus of AmerBank. Disputes over title to shares led inexorably to legal action, with Kiki eventually becoming the bank's board chairman. In March of 1991 Kosinski had updated his will, although still leaving his papers and the bulk of his estate to Spertus. A tug-of-war over control of the estate soon erupted between Kiki and officials at Spertus. These disputes were only surface exhibitions of the larger struggle over Kosinski's legacy. With Kosinski there was a complex question not only of *who* and *what* he was, but of *whose* he was. Each of the many groups touched by his life naturally saw him in light of his relationship with them. Poles and Jews could argue over his essential identity, and whether he had been a hero or a villain.

No aspect of the legacy is more difficult than a final assessment of his work. Few creative figures have left a more problematic oeuvre, and almost any categorical statement about it is subject to challenge. As a thinker/doer Kosinski belongs to the tradition in which the margins of culture inform the center. His explorations of identity and sexuality delivered to his audience a series of disquieting truths about themselves. As a writer, he was clearly not the stylist he was initially credited as being—the surfaces of his books owed too much to others—but neither was he the pure fraud that facile and incompletely informed criticism made him out to be. He was, if nothing else, a great storyteller, whose stories at their best seemed to have mythic resonances. In the age of oral storytelling he would have been recognized as indisputably great. Forced to compose in a foreign language, however, he had difficulty putting his stories into final form. Books—the frozen Gutenberg artifacts—were not ideally suited to his talent. Even here his life and work existed at a boundary, testing the more expansive postmodern conceptions of a literary text.

Quite apart from his enduring value as a writer, his life serves to illumine the cultures in which he lived, beginning with the conditions in Poland under German occupation. He is a virtual case study of the power of human oppression to exert permanent influence on a human personality. His wartime experiences drove many actions throughout his life, up to, and perhaps including, his suicide. One is left with a tantalizing but unaswerable question: Would he have been different without that childhood, and if so, how? The books he wrote of his experiences within the Polish and Soviet socialist regimes in the late 1940s and 1950s now seem prophetic in describing a way of life that was miserable for those who were caught up in it, but formidable in its posture toward external adversaries. He had a clearer vision of collectivist regimes than most writers of the time. He knew, and his life demonstrated, how oppressive conditions cripple both the state and the soul. Terrible pain does not necessarily ennoble, nor are the wounded always made strong at the broken places. Yet he also understood and demonstrated how human beings learn to recapture a necessary minimum of pleasure under terrible conditions. Though deeply pessimistic for most of his life, he thus foreshadowed the revolt that would open the East to a new and more expansive sense of life.

American society embraced Kosinski from the beginning. In the process it displayed both a receptivity to strangeness and novelty and an absence of critical judgment that seems at times to spring from an abiding New World naiveté and at times to expose the deepest emptiness and need. Kosinski, in turn, played the American power elite masterfully. He patterned his life on the game plan contained in *The Career of Nikodem Dyzma*, a second-rate Polish bestseller about a con artist. Yet there was truth in his early assessment that New York society needed a resident European intellectual, and he filled that role compellingly. He was in a way exemplary of an age in which art no longer looked like art, the boundaries between high culture and kitsch were dissolved, and writers were no longer confined within the mold of visionary, if alcoholic, gravitas. Essentially without a political view, he managed to politicize attacks on his career and his character. When in difficulty, he had a genius for persuading powerful supporters that their interests and their honor lay in defending him. Like all great charlatans, he laid bare the flaws and conceits of those he defrauded, but he also gave good value. In the end no one was so badly damaged by the con as himself.

Yet he was not always false. The questions he posed about identity and sexuality were quite real, however unwelcome the insights they sometimes brought. The New York literary world tired of his books and his shenanigans, but among new readers in the hinterlands, his novels never lost the power to shock. His peculiar dissociative sense of the self may have derived from the psychopathology of his own life—in particular from his experience during the German occupation—but its pathological origins do not nullify the power of his insight. His mixture of incongruous qualities was matched perfectly with the time in which he lived, particularly the 1970s, when he became an important cultural icon.

He lived in an age of incongruities, in which both books and human beings spilled over the boundaries of their genres. Hopping from table to table at Elaine's, holding court as celebrated writer and head of the world's most important writers' organization, writing a film and acting in one, and telling lies both inside and outside the storyteller's frame, Kosinski was, both symbolically and physically, never far from the center of that age. It seems only fitting that a man who gained recognition as one of the most important American writers of that literary epoch was not, by origin, American, and that even his status as a writer was called into question. Actor, celebrity, and trickster, he was both less than a writer and more.

But he was a writer, too. *Steps*, which won him the National Book Award, will likely remain a troublesome text, but it warrants consideration in its use of the novel to present ideas, and its formal innovation cannot be disregarded. Nor can the appeal of *Being There*, as novel and film, be lightly dismissed. Notwithstanding the controversies attendant to its construction, it struck a very American nerve, and will remain one of the texts that document the attitudes and political culture of the 1970s. At least one of his works, *The Painted Bird*, seems likely to stand. Odd in every respect—its expansion of experience into a surreal inner theater, its construction with help from editors and translators, its lack of dialogue, and its existence at the shadowy border between fiction and personal statement—it remains a major aesthetic response to the Holocaust and a provocative documentation of the complex and reverberative consequences of violence and evil. For this alone, Kosinski is likely to have an enduring niche in the annals of human self-examination that make up literary history.

Notes

AS   Kosinski, *The Art of the Self*

BD   Kosinski, *Blind Date*

BT   Kosinski, *Being There*

C   Kosinski, *Cockpit*

CP   Siedlecka, *Czarny ptasior* (Black Bird) (trans. by Agnieszka Kmin)

CWJK   Teicholz, *Conversations with Jerzy Kosinski*

FF   Czaplinski, *Jerzy Kosinski: Face to Face*

NOA   Kosinski, *Notes of the Author (on The Painted Bird)*

H   Kosinski, *The Hermit of 69th Street*

NTP   Novak (Kosinski), *No Third Path*

PB   Kosinski, *Passing By*

PI   Kosinski, *Pinball*

PP   Kosinski, *Passion Play*

PW   Lazowski, *Prywatra wojna* (Private War, trans. by Alexandra Gerrard)

S   Kosinski, *Steps*

TBP   Kosinski, *The Painted Bird*

TDT   Kosinski, *The Devil Tree*

TFIOC   Novak (Kosinski), *The Future Is Ours, Comrade*

ZS   Czaplinski, *Zycie po smierci Jerzego Kosinskiego* (The Life After Death of Jerzy Kosinski) (trans. by Alexandra Gerrard)

Prologue: May 2, 1991

page 2   "Hell is other people": AS, 34; PB, 239.
page 3   "You looked lovely tonight, Ulenka": ZS, 23.

I. Moses' Son

1. page 7   In the first weeks of World War II: TPB, 1.

2. For the picture of pre–World War II Lodz, I am indebted to Dr. Arnold Mostowicz, who has written widely on Jewish Lodz and knew the Lewinkopfs slightly. Dr. Mostowicz also called my attention to I. J. Singer's novel *The Brothers Ashkenazy*, which is highly evocative of a somewhat earlier Lodz.

page 8   "Live your life unnoticed": HH, 116.
           "born in Russia": Cleveland Amory, *Saturday Review*, Ap 17, 71 (in CWJK, 7).
page 14   "a piano player too bosomy to play a piano": H, 65.
           "Don't I look like a Gypsy?": H, 66.
           "Breast Symphony is what your father likes": H, 119.
           "suitor": H, 66.
           "the famous chess player born in Lodz": H, 65.
page 15   "Don't ever let the waves of the mundane": H, 393.
page 16   "Your life is more important": H, 121.

3. Iwo Cyprian Pogonowski's *Jews in Poland* contains a detailed chronology of the military collapse and unfolding of the Holocaust in Poland. Joanna Siedlecka's *Czarny Ptasior*, while tendentious in tone, accurately traces the movements of the Lewinkopf/Kosinski family during the German occupation. Sandomierz residents who recall the Lewinkopf/Kosinskis include Roman Izykowski and his wife Zofia, Maria (Justynska) Medrzak, Maria Wiktorowska, and Zofia Rogowska. Zenon Pas contributed stories passed down in his family.

page 20   "a dirty Jew": CP, 21.
4. page 25   "She was old and always bent over": TPB, 3.
           "glutinous threads . . . bubbly saliva dripping from her lips": TPB, 3.

5. Edward Warchol, Bronislaw and Stefania Woloszyn, Jan Pamula, Stanislaw Madej, Celina Skazowska, and Andrzej Migdalek were particularly helpful in fleshing out details of the Kosinskis' life in Dabrowa Rzeczycka.

page 28   "The priest took me away in a borrowed cart": TPB, 121.
           "became subdued . . . into the hut": TPB, 122.
page 29   "How can we ever repay you?": CP, 60.
           "Let us all survive": CP, 60.
6. page 32   "Zydi, Zydki": CP, 24.
page 33   "Jude, 'raus": CP, 24.
           "a powerful-looking, monstrous fish": TPB, 24.
page 34   "Zydek, Zydziok": CP, 47.
           "Mame, Mame": CP, 48.

7. Aleksandr ("Lech") Tracz still lives in a small cottage festooned with bird traps and cages. It was possible to infer much from the details of his appearance and the way in which he is received in the small community of Dabrowa, but he could not, in any ordinary sense, be interviewed.

page 37   "I *have* my body but I also *am* my body": H, 492.

8. For general background and an account of the execution of Martin Fuldner, I owe much to *Private War*, the memoirs of Dr. Eugene Lazowski, published in Polish and privately translated by his daughter, Alexandra Gerrard; Mrs. Gerrard assisted me by translating Polish documents and texts. Dr. Lazowski, who courageously saved many Jews and other Poles from deportation to the camps by persuading the Germans of the existence of a typhus epidemic, spent the war within a few kilometers of the Kosinskis.

page 43   "Jude, Jude" and following dialogue: CP, 78–79.
page 44   "Don't worry, Martin": PW, 187.
page 45   "You are wrong": PW, 190.
9. page 47   "born in Russia . . . who had escaped the Bolshevik Revolution": Amory, op. cit.
10. page 51   "a kind face": TPB, 198.
           "very black, bushy hair": TPB, 199.

II. Aspirant

1. Jerzy Urban provided details of the Kosinskis' life in Jelenia Gora along with a helpful overview of political, economic, and social life in postwar Poland. Henryk Kosinski provided one important piece of information.

page 56   "When I was twelve": C, 111.
page 60   "I gave my father the message": C, 112
page 61   "own hands of Bumek and Ewa": Andrzej Migdalek, Sep 29, 94.

2. Stanislaw Pomorski provided valuable insights into Kosinski's high-school career.

page 62   "in the presence of fifty-seven members": FF, 18.
           "an imperialist American lifestyle": FF, 25.
           "was hostile towards the socialist reality": FF, 26.
page 65   "one of the best books ever written": Stanislaw Pomorski, Jun 7, 94.

3. Jerzy Neugebauer confirmed and expanded upon published interviews concerning his relationship with Kosinski.

page 67   "Honoratka ... Nothing clever was ever said": JK at Beit Hatsufot, Israel, Feb 2, 88.
page 68   "Thank God it isn't raining" and ff.: PP, 231.
           "All my father saw": PP, 231.
           "There is nothing wrong with cafes," and ff.: JK at Beit Hatsufot, Israel, Feb 2, 88.
page 69   "Why did you do that?" and ff.: Kiernan, *The Roman Polanski Story*, 27.
page 71   "You aren't a navvy": FF, 31.
           "I was surrounded, pushed, pulled": S, 48.
           "Some of the patients I selected": S, 48.
page 72   "the realization that one day I would become": S, 50.
page 74   "You don't believe me": Jerzy Neugebauer, Jun 6, 94.

4. Compelling inside accounts of the role of Jozef Chalasinski in the "thaw" of 1956 are presented in Allan A. Michie's *Voices Through the Iron Curtain: the Radio Free Europe Story* and Robert T. Holt's *Radio Free Europe*.

page 78   "scholarly incompetence ... bourgeois learning": Holt, *Radio Free Europe*, 166.
           "I regret if I have been unable to convince you": ibid.
page 82   "university-educated ski instructor ... indoctrinate the local ski teachers": BD, 23.
           "What, according to Comrade Stalin": BD, 24.
page 83   "We still have two hours": Janusz Kuczynski, Jun 2, 94.

5. Tadeusz Krauze provided information on Kosinski's life as a student in Warsaw.

> page 85   "the para-military student defense corps": S, 37.
>
> "You think I'm an alcoholic numskull" and ff.: BD, 49.
>
> page 86   "between tram stops . . . a nice ass": Tadeusz Krauze, Jun 3, 94.
>
> "I'm going to fuck her": ibid.
>
> "I would like to make your portraits": ibid.
>
> page 87   "I found Anna": ibid.
>
> page 88   "I'm Jerzy Kosinski, and I'm calling from *Trybuna Ludu*": ibid.

6. The real story of Kosinski's departure from Poland is pieced together from a number of sources, but the broad contours become clear when material from the Ford Foundation archives is laid alongside files procured under the Freedom of Information Act from the U.S. Immigration and Naturalization Service. As to the "Russian alternative," few episodes in Kosinski's life have given rise to more speculation regarding possible conspiracies, particularly among his fellow Poles. After forty years, the record available in official Russian archives is scant. The Foreign Intelligence Service and the Ministry of Internal Affairs, though willing in principle to search for and render files (particularly under the rubric of the commission for rehabilitation of "repressed individuals"), report no surviving records under any Cyrillic variant of his name. The Federal Security Service—the primary successor organization to the KGB—deflects substantive inquiries politely in language that closely approximates the formulaic responses of the CIA to inquiries under the Freedom of Information Act, declining to acknowledge either the existence or the nonexistence of a file. Nominally willing to provide dates of entry into and departure from the Soviet Union, the FSS presents researchers with the same foot-dragging and inefficiency that afflicts FOIA requests to the FBI, as well as with the high probability of lost or improperly catalogued files. At Lomonosov University, which is now more commonly known as Moscow State, or by its initials, M.G.U., there are no administrative traces of Kosinski's presence in either the history or philosophy departments; sociology, a discipline discredited by its origin as the child of anti-Marxist Max Weber, did not exist as a separate department at M.G.U. until the middle 1980s. Assistant Dean Artour L. Demtchouk conducted a thorough review of philosophy department files of the period, finding no record of residency, registration, or enrollment in any Cyrillic variant of the name Kosinski. In the history department, Assistant Dean

Lera Leonova, who has been a member of the department since 1953, and who knew all graduate and foreign students, feels sure that she would have recalled Kosinski had he been a regularly enrolled student, and cannot recall his ever having been present. In summary, the weight of the evidence is that Kosinski's status in the Soviet Union carried at most a casual relationship to Moscow State University and was for the most part a free-lance tour deriving primarily from his status as Jozef Chalasinski's student and his father's son.

page 89 "three priorities on my list": George Plimpton and Rocco Landesman, "The Art of Fiction: Jerzy Kosinski," *Paris Review*, no. 54 (Summer 1972) (in CWJK, 26).

"Get out the first chance you get" and ff.: H, 423.

page 91 "the fence that crosses it": BD, 55

"You are here, on one of the coldest days": BD, 56.

page 92 "To leave the country legally": C, 18.

page 95 "Professor Chalasinski with whom I spoke yesterday": JK to Jiri Kolaja, Sep 25, 57.

page 96 "Take whatever you can from others": FF, 104.

page 97 a "monograph on the plight": C, 36.

III. Getting There

1. Kosinski's arrival in America is outlined in files of the Immigration and Naturalization Service. Further details were provided by Peter Skinner, with whom Kosinski discussed his coming to America while working on *Steps*.

page 98 has "done nothing ... timeless, unmeasured": S, 108.

page 100 "Polish perspectives on American family life": JK to Shepard Stone, Jan 11, 58.

"feels that it might be preferable": Shepard Stone to I.I.E., Mar 21, 58.

page 102 "oncle," "mai," "scientific worker": INS file on JK.

page 103 "broke the color barrier in Harlem": biographical piece "On Kosinski" appended to Bantam paperback version of several of his novels.

"drive it at high speed": S, 123.

2. Among those who contributed to the account of Kosinski's first years in America are Mira Michalowska, Krystyna (Iwaszkiewicz) Rytel, Bob and Jane Geniesse, Bill and Elinor Morrison, and Andy Heinemann, as well as Tadeusz Krauze. Documentary material included files of the Ford Foundation, Columbia University, the Immigration and Naturalization Service, and the United States Information Agency (received under the Freedom of Information Act).

> page 105 "Have you children?" and ff.: Mira Michalowska, Jun 4, 94.
> "Come to the party": ibid.
> page 106 "I had a terrible night": ibid.
> page 107 "terrible experiences during the Occupation": ibid.
> page 108 "Now, listen!": ibid.
> "Mira ... I really know very well the difference": ibid.
> "In that case ... *write a book*.": ibid.

3. The CIA/USIA "book development" program is described in the Final Report of the [U.S. Senate] Select Committee to Study Governmental Operations with Respect to Intelligence Activities, published in April 1976. Ewa (Strzetelska) Markowska, whose name first came up in a discussion of another subject with Krystyna Baron of the Polish Institute in New York, became a primary source, as did Frank Gibney, who consented to be identified and interviewed after the author spoke with Adam Yarmolinsky. Cross-referencing of names suggested the probable course of events for which a solid paper trail may not exist; the name of Anthony B. Czartoryski, for example, appeared on Kosinski's first contract, in a followup article by the *Village Voice*, and in association with both Radio Free Europe and the Polish Institute before it came up, incidentally but tellingly, in conversation with Frank Gibney. The Freedom of Information/Privacy Office of the CIA stonewalled all queries and appeals, citing exemption clauses (b)(1) national defense and foreign policy and (b)(3) protection of sources and methods. The CIA response to both an initial request and an appeal stated, in the somewhat baroque language of the intelligence community, that by this action they were "neither confirming nor denying the existence or nonexistence of such records." Barring a change in CIA FOIA policy, absolute certainty on Kosinski's relationship with the CIA cannot be obtained. The weight of the evidence suggests that Kosinski's two Novak books were advanced and supported by the CIA through the USIA book development program, but that Kosinski had no other relationship with American intelligence agencies beyond, perhaps, the routine debriefing accorded many foreign arrivees from Communist countries.

> page 111 "no reason to think that the author was Kosinski": Adam
> Yarmolinsky, Dec 19, 94.

4. Zdzislaw Najder provided information supporting the narrative of this chapter.

> page 122 "Mr. Kosinski's state of health has worsened": Stanislaw Strzetelski to I.I.E., Oct 24, 59.
>
> page 123 "the accident . . . 1959 Spring Session": ibid.
> "is unusually bright but needs some strict guidance": Paul Lazarsfeld to I.I.E., Dec 15, 59.
>
> **5.** page 125 "I can't give you credit for the translation": Ewa Markowska, Jul 19, 94.
>
> page 128 "photograph her beauty": Krystyna Rytel, Jan 14, 95.
>
> page 129 "If I want to neutralize an enemy": ibid.
>
> page 131 "can never be all right from all angles": TFIOC, 75.
>
> page 133 "Plot is an artificially imposed notion": Gail Sheehy, "The Psychological Novelist as Portable Man," *Psychology Today* (Dec 1977) (in CWJK, 122).

6. Along with his INS file, USIA files received under the Freedom of Information Act, and incorporating FBI background checks, provided a factual framework for Kosinski's life during his first half-dozen years in America as well as a means for cross-checking information from other sources.

> page 137 "the whole picture of Soviet life": *Chicago Tribune*, May 29, 60.
>
> page 138 "much of it plausible": *The New Statesman*, Oct 22, 60.
>
> page 139 "almost love affair": Ryszard Matuszewski, Jun 3, 94.
> "Actually I have an errand . . . As you see": translated by Alexandra Gerrard from Halina Poswiatowska's "The Bluebird" in Mariola Pryzwan's *O Halinie Poswiatowskiej (About Halina Poswiatowska)*, pp. 358–359.
>
> page 140 a "fabulous fence . . . not like this": ibid., 370.
> "the hairy armpits of the peasant women": H, 157.
> "Touch me. . . *pierdolnie*": H, 170–171
>
> **7.** page 142 "the relativity of riches in America": BD, 213.
>
> page 147 "*Something* . . . has *changed*": Feliks Gross, May 19, 94.
>
> **8.** page 147 "a rich Swedish woman": Stanislaw Pomorski, Jun 7, 94.
> "an ordinary office girl" and ff.: TDT, 127.
>
> page 149 "I would like to give her that pleasure": Tadeusz Krauze, Jun 3, 94.
>
> **9.** page 156 "view himself according to the criteria of that environment": NTP, 375.
> "succeed in the long run": NTP, 357.

page 158   *"psychological* disarmament": NTP, 335.
page 159   "the icebox goes on humming": NTP, 105.
            "their hate for color": NTP, 107.

10. David Weir provided important details of his mother's marriage to Kosinski. The Kosinski–Mary Weir relationship depicted here also incorporates the recollections of Bill and Elinor Morrison, Bob and Jane Geniesse, Andy Heinemann, Krystyna Rytel, and several others who knew the Kosinskis more briefly and distantly.

page 162   "Wouldn't you do this": Bill Morrison, Dec 21, 94.
page 163   "permitted marriage without prior application": BD, 221.
page 164   "Would I stay without the benefit": BD, 220.
            "You'll never know": ibid.
            "It's not that you aren't likable": BD, 222.
            "What if there was some deed": BD, 223.
page 165   "What does Mary-Jane, your own wife, really know": BD, 223.
            "May I be honest?": Andy Heinemann, Nov 15, 94.
            "Oh my God, an honest lawyer!": ibid.; also David Weir, Nov 1, 94.

11. Dr. Henry Krystal, a Freudian analyst who had interviewed Kosinski and is himself a survivor of the camps, brought to my attention personally and through his writing the condition of alexithymia and the general anhedonia that often afflicts survivors.

page 166   "formidable SS": H, 41.
page 167   "One day you will know that everything about you": Kosinski at Beit Hatsufot, Israel, Feb 2, 88.
page 170   *"We* take responsibility for unemployment": Tadeusz Krauze, Jun 3, 94.

IV. Breakthrough

1. Philip van Rensselaer and Peter Skinner provided information supporting the account of Kosinski's relationship with Lilla van Saher. In addition to submitting to several interviews, Skinner provided a lengthy written reminiscence dealing with van Saher and other aspects of this period of Kosinski's life. Both his memory of conversations and his descriptions of van Saher and her apartment were exceptionally vivid, and at places this narrative incorporates his actual language, which paraphrase could only have diminished.

page 176   "the book would have gained . . . undigested raw material": *Chicago Tribune*, Feb 25, 62.

"composites . . . one might, in principle": *New York Herald Tribune*, Mar 4, 62.

"lived for seven years": *Christian Science Monitor*, Apr 13, 62.

page 179   "on the previous day she had lost": TDT (first edition), 108.

page 180   "On paper, of course!": TDT (first edition), 108.

page 181   *The Future Is Ours, Comrade* had been rejected by Pocket, Bantam, Popular Library, NAL, Avon (twice), Dell, Meridian, Fawcett, Grove, and Dolphin, but was still under consideration at Ace, Berkley, Macfadden, Norton, Viking, and, most hopefully, Pyramid. *No Third Path* had been refused by Pocket, Bantam, Avon, Dell, Fawcett, Meridian, Grove, and Anchor, and was still out with Ace, Macfadden, Berkley, Popular Library, Norton, and Viking.

page 184   "Ah, Lilla, my dear . . . takers": Peter Skinner, Apr 15, 95.

"Lilla, have you no shame . . . They are all presents": ibid.

"little slave": Philip van Rensselaer, Oct 5, 94.

page 185   "But Lilla . . . by madmen for madmen": ibid.

"every woman . . . wild in the forest": ibid.

"Come Lilla, . . . you were never young": Peter Skinner, Apr 15, 95.

"the face of a dead rabbit . . . get up": ibid.

2. page 188   "never simply a deception or a hoax . . . an attempt": C, 130.

"it is the witness who deceives himself": ibid.

page 189   "my wife Mary Hayward Weir without whom": TPB dedication.

page 194   "traps in places where Lekh himself": TPB, 41.

"something happened . . . he was involved": Stanislaw Pomorski, Jun 7, 94.

3. The argument about translators for *The Painted Bird* is hinged upon the unimpeachably reliable account of Thomas Fleming, whose information, however, was at one remove. Steven Kraus and Aleksandr Lutoslawski (Jordan) provided accounts of their own participation, while Peter Skinner, from the vantage point of his own editorial assistance at a later stage and as an acquaintance of Kraus, was helpful in framing the question and assigning proper weight to the various versions. The revealing Kosinski–

Dorothy de Santillana correspondence, along with internal Houghton Mifflin memoranda, is housed in the Houghton Mifflin authors collection at Harvard's Houghton Library.

page 198 "TRANSLATOR WANTED": *Saturday Review*, Mar 7, 64.

page 200 "wrote *The Painted Bird*": Thomas Fleming, May 21, 94.

"I was not in any way ashamed": Dick Schapp, "Stepmother Tongue," *Book Week* 14 (Nov 65) (in CWJK, 5).

page 202 "pornography of violence": Aleksandr Lutoslawski (Alexander Jordan), Oct 26, 94.

page 203 "fascinating and very terrible": Dorothy de Santillana to JK, Jul 14, 64.

page 205 "I am Peter Skinner . . . I am Joseph Novak": Peter Skinner, Dec 26, 94.

"A friend of mine has completed a manuscript": ibid.

"I think my friend would prefer *you*": ibid.

page 206 "Did you . . . ? . . . I don't remember": ibid.

page 207 "not gathering dust in our files": Dorothy de Santillana to JK, Sep 21, 64.

"enormously successful in handling": ibid.

"I notice that one or two": ibid.

"your attractive wife": ibid.

page 209 "autobiographical survey": ibid.

"the slow unfreezing of a mind": JK to DDS, Nov 28, 64.

"foregrounds lose in definition": ibid.

page 210 "refusing to speak on Korean situation": Supplemental Memorandum, JK files at Immigration and Naturalization Service.

4. page 211 "distasteful": David Harris to Paul Brooks, Mar 17, 65.

page 214 "statement which we are to use": Paul Brooks to Jim Brown, Apr 15, 65.

"making clear the nature": ibid.

page 215 "even if it were fiction": Lilian Kastendike to Jim Brown, Feb 1, 65.

"the postlude which indicated": ibid.

page 217 "To say that *The Painted Bird* is non-fiction": NOA, 11; PB, 203

page 218 "Well, to say that *The Painted Bird* . . . is non-fiction": George Plimpton and Rocco Landesman, op. cit. (in CWJK, 24).

5. The story of the old man in the garden is consistent with Mary Weir's charitable activities and interest in antique furniture, but lacking in independent confirmation; it should perhaps be viewed as part of the Kosinski apocrypha.

page 220 "In the first weeks of World War II": *Publishers Weekly*, Aug 9, 65.

page 221 "ILL HEALTH PREVENTS": Lilla van Saher to JK, Oct 15, 65.

page 222 "this semi-autobiographical account": *NY Herald Tribune*, Oct 17, 65

"the overall performance": ibid.

"an unrelentingly harsh portrait of the Poles": ibid.

"Mr. Kosinski found postwar Communism": ibid.

"the richness of [Kosinski's] prose": *Washington Post*, Nov 4, 65.

"a testament not only to the atrocities": *Chicago News*, Nov 6, 65.

"stand by the side of Anne Frank's unforgettable 'Diary' ": Harry Overstreet to JK, as quoted in TPB.

"a brilliant testimony": James Leo Herlihy to JK, as quoted in TPB.

page 223 "the Nazi experience is the key one": Arthur Miller to JK, as quoted in TPB.

"It is as a chronicle": *New York Times*, Oct 17, 65.

page 224 "a large city in central *Poland*": TPB (first edition), 1.

page 225 The letter of Elzbieta Kosinska to her son, dated Oct 28, was translated separately by several individuals, among them Irina Serafin and Alexandra Gerrard.

6. The meeting and early relationship with Katherina von Fraunhofer draws upon accounts by Ewa Pape, Dr. Roman Czaplicki, and others, as well as Mrs. Kosinski herself. There are various public versions, from interviews and articles, all of which must be viewed with some skepticism. Sidney Offit and Andy Heinemann also contributed to the portrait of Kosinski's life at this time.

page 227 "That's a man I want to meet": Ewa Pape, Oct 31, 94.

page 228 "Now there's a woman": Sidney Offit, May 21, 94.

"I always do this": ibid.

7. page 235 "libelous novel": *Zycie Partii*, Jun 6, 66.

"not only on socialism": ibid.

page 236 "the revanchist press": ibid.

"pacifiers of a primitive pre-historic jungle": *Forum*, Jun 6, 66.

"to dilute the German guilt": *Glos Nauczycielski*, Jun 19, 66.

"German lover": *Slowo Polskie*, Jun 20, 66.

"oscillates between truth and fantasy": *Kultura*, Jul–Aug, 66.

page 241 "Where do you suppose, Kosinski gets his money? . . . Do you suppose he writes his own books?": Bob Geniesse, Dec 15, 94.

"What is it exactly that you meant here?": Eugene Prakapas, Dec 11, 94.

"to finish and submit for publication": Application for Guggenheim Fellowship submitted Sep 21, 66.

page 243 "Oh, take it from the drawer": Katherina von Fraunhofer Kosinski, Sep 22, 94.

"Don't I satisfy you?": ibid.

"Don't you have anything *black*?": ibid. Kosinski himself told this story to, among others, several women with whom he had liaisons.

"Oh, take them off": ibid.

8. Rabbi Alex J. Goldman, Philip van Rensselaer, Dr. Stanley Corngold, Henryk Greenberg, William and Rose Styron, Ewa Pape, Dr. Feliks Gross, Roman Polanski, and Peter Skinner all contributed information supporting the narrative of this chapter.

page 246 "manliness": Rabbi Alex J. Goldman to JPS, Jul 12, 94.

"He's Jewish. He's Jewish": ibid.

"a Gypsy or a Jew": TPB, 2.

"the Gypsies weren't important": Katherina von Fraunhofer Kosinski, Oct 5, 94.

page 247 "Is Kosinski Jewish?": Henryk Greenberg, Dec 8, 94.

"Shut up, you Brit . . . We are *both* victims": Katherina von Fraunhofer Kosinski, Oct 5, 94.

page 249 "I'm carrying Jurek's child": Philip van Rensselaer, Oct 5, 94.

"He's been making love with me for years": ibid.

"I know you think I'm too old": ibid.

"go along with it": ibid.

"Swiss industrialist": C, 51.

"gathering data for a small sex research institute": C, 58.

"men and women who had responded to personal ads": ibid.

page 250 "but she married someone else": *Washington Star*, Feb 4, 80.

page 252 "Do you still believe love doesn't exist?": Roman Polanski, Jul 12, 94.

"tell Jurek love does exist": ibid.

page 253 "Where are we now?": Peter Skinner, Dec 26, 94.

"It doesn't matter": ibid.

"We are driving farther south": ibid.

"What's the book going to be about": ibid.

"This is the book": ibid.

"There are infinite ways to tell a story": JK to JPS, 1977.

page 254 "We are in front of a cafe": Peter Skinner, Dec 26, 94.

"I want to get this thought in": ibid.

"Next time we'll swap them": ibid.

page 255 "We must work hard": ibid.

page 257 "your hands": S, 42.

9. Marian Javits, Bob Loomis, Gil Shiva, Barry Callaghan, and Helen Hutchinson supplemented information provided by sources cited for previous chapters.

page 260 "She's going to commit suicide": Andy Heinemann, Nov 15, 94.

page 262 "I have met a man": Marian Javits, Dec 24, 94.

page 266 "the means to outlive himself": AS, 23; PB, 231.

"this small book . . . through all": *The New Republic*, Oct 26, 68.

page 267 "These terse, ghoulish episodes": *Newsweek*, Oct 21, 68.

"Low-keyed, efficient, controlled": *NYTBR*, Oct 20, 68.

"the complete collapse of human values": *Saturday Review*, Oct 19, 68.

page 269 YOU WON: Bob Loomis to JK, Mar 10, 69.

V. Being There

1. Interviews with Jessie (Mrs. Clement) Wood and Elzbieta Czyzewska provided support to the narrative of this chapter.

page 273 "Jerzy is in the water": Mrs. Clement Wood, Jan 27, 95.

page 274 "I told Sharon you were there": ibid.

"Something has happened in Los Angeles": Elzbieta Czyzewska, Oct 24, 94.

page 276 "I know that the suggestion is extremely far-fetched": Barbara Leaming, *Polanski: a Biography*, 109.

2. Rocco Landesman, Jean Kilbourne, and Katherina von Fraunhofer Kosinski each provided accounts of the *Paris Review* interview, to which George Plimpton added his perspective. Jean Kilbourne generously provided access to her private papers and journal.

page 278 "a marvelous house for you": Katherina von Fraunhofer Kosinski, Sep 21, 94; also, BD, 77.
"You must mean *Stalin's* daughter": ibid.
page 279 "Dismiss them": ibid.
page 281 "Excuse me . . . but I don't yet know the mores": Stanley Corngold, Jan 30, 95.
page 282 "I want to see you": Jean Kilbourne, Jan 28, 95.
"You and I had the same childhood": ibid.
page 283 "Guess where I'm calling from": K. von F. Kosinski, Sep 21, 94.
"promptings of the true self": JK to Jean Kilbourne, letter reconstructed by Jean Kilbourne.
page 284 "outlaw selves saluting": JK to Jean Kilbourne.
page 285 "You wasted so much money": K. von F. Kosinski, Oct 5, 94.
"You know him?": K. von F. Kosinski, Jul 11, 94.
"He parked cars here": ibid.
"You SOB, you said you didn't know this place": ibid.
"You SOB, you shouldn't say that out loud": ibid.
page 287 "I'm sure you won't like it": Kosinski, "Dead Souls on Campus," *NY Times* op-ed, Oct 13, 70; PB, 145.
"You know the first time I saw you": ibid.
"In the past twenty years": draft of op-ed piece.
page 289 "old man upstairs": BT.

3. Jean Kilbourne provided the story of Kosinski's use of her journals in the composition of *The Devil Tree*, detailed in this and the following chapter, and opened her papers and journals, as well as her personally annotated copy of the novel. She also shared her reconstructions of correspondence that Kosinski destroyed. In the recovered journals she had restored names and dates which he had blacked out with felt-tip pen.

page 293 "knuckle ball of a book": *Time*, Apr 26, 71.
"economy, precision, and deceptive": *Library Journal*, Apr 1, 71.

"exists simultaneously": *Saturday Review*, Apr 24, 71.

page 294 "It's a nickname for Jerzy" and ff.: Cleveland Amory, op. cit. (in CWJK, 6).

page 295 "Once ... I hid for a whole weekend": ibid.

page 297 "Thanks a lot!" Jean Kilbourne journals.
"only red paint": Jean Kilbourne, Apr 14, 95.
"something like Kosinski" and ff.: Lin Harris-Seares, Jun 17, 94.

page 298 "Have you been ill?": K. von F. Kosinski, Jul 12, 94.

page 299 "Hey, you, put your hands up!": Larry Eilenberg, Oct 27, 94.
"I mean it, apologize": ibid.

page 301 "giants in their field": John Taylor, "The Haunted Bird," *New York*, Jul 15, 91, p. 31.

page 303 "Don't thank me ... I was thinking": JK to JPS, 1971.

page 304 "a Polish person would appreciate": JK to JPS, 1978.

4. Jerome Klinkowitz added specific information to an ongoing dialogue with the author that goes back twenty years.

page 305 "This is Jerzy Kosinski in New Haven": Jerome Klinkowitz, "Betrayed by Jerzy Kosinski," *Literary Subversions: New American Fiction and the Practice of Criticism*, 136.
"That's *Klinkiewicz*, Polish, right?": ibid, 137.

page 306 "Is that what your brother says?" and ff.: ibid, 138–139.

page 308 "Marian ... where is my watch?": Marian Javits, Dec 24, 94.

page 314 "The characterization is bad": *Library Journal*, Dec 15, 72.
"From beginning to end": *NYTBR*, Feb 11, 73.
"Hebrew Israeli poetry": JK in letter to JPS, Feb 14, 73.
Kosinski first wrote, then called, asking the author of this book to write a response to the Alter review. It was a difficult task, as I had my own reservations about *The Devil Tree*, but I wrote a response to what seemed to me then an illegitimate backward projection by Alter, bashing Kosinski's earlier work by reading it through the prism of the current novel. The response was published as an article in *Third Press Review*. Kosinski also prevailed upon Cynthia Ozick to respond, directly to the *Times*.

5. Thomas Fleming provided an account of Kosinski's involvement in PEN and PEN politics.

page 315   "Have you ever got a wrong number": Thomas Fleming, May 21, 94.

                "Tom ... you can't let that man be president": ibid.

page 316   "Kosinski gave me an illiterate manuscript" and ff.: ibid.

page 320   "I don't like that": ibid.

page 322   "I had this tiny little nose": K. von F. Kosinski, Jul 7, 94.

6. page 324   "Why does everybody hate me?": Thomas Fleming, May 21, 94.

page 325   "might even have forgotten": BD, 130.

                "I'll be right back," and ff.: "Exegetics: Jerzy Kosinski," *The Paris Review* 97, Feb 85, pp. 96–97.

page 326   "play my games": C, Epigraph.

7. Emily Prager contributed information supporting the narrative of this chapter.

page 333   "I cannot see what the retailing": *New York Review of Books*, Nov 27, 75.

                "marvelous and self-contained tales": *Newsweek*, Aug 11, 75.

                "stripping us ... of its form": *NYTBR*, Aug 2, 75.

                "terse, unstructured style": *Time*, Aug 4, 75.

page 336   "Ask him now" (repeated three times): JK to JPS, 1977.

                "Put the lights back on ... properly": George Plimpton, Sep 22, 94.

page 337   "You could have killed her": ibid.

page 338   "What kind of people ... usually Jews": Alfred Kazin, "Jews," *The New Yorker*, Mar 7, 94, p. 65.

                "alchemical friend": PB, 15.

page 341   "You must never personify actions to yourself": Emily Prager, Dec 29, 94.

8. Ahmet Ertegun and Wendy Luers expanded upon Katherina von Fraunhofer Kosinski's account of the horsey life in the Dominican Republic.

page 343   "Brother, can you spare a pony?": K. von F. Kosinski, Jul 11, 94.

page 344   "So ... I'm the cut-rate Elie Wiesel": JK to JPS, 1977.

                "When he learns in his fiction to respect women": *NY Times*, Aug 2, 75.

                "Thanks for the attention": JK to JPS, 1975.

VI. Passion Play

1. Larry Eilenberg and Allan Schwartz provided information lending support to the narrative of this chapter.

> page 351   "I'm working for Jerzy Kosinski ... either": Thomas Fleming, May 21, 94.
>
> page 352   "Our boy, Karolek, made it": Ewa Markowska, Jul 9, 94.
>
> page 353   "I had a moment ... responsible for this": *Christian Science Monitor*, Mar 1, 79.
>
>   "Quite good, quite good" and ff.: *Washington Post*, Style, Feb 2, 79.
>
> page 354   "All I know is it makes": ibid.
>
>   "didn't like the idea": *Washington Star*, Feb 9, 79.
>
>   "What am I supposed to do ... Coke bottle?": K. von F. Kosinski, Jul 11, 94.

2. Joy Weiss provided information lending support to the narrative of this chapter.

> page 357   "all my man can do": PP, 247.
>
>   "language and manner ... mundane assumption": PP, 236.
>
>   "mood of the time and the place": PP, 237.
>
> page 358   "dramatically too heavy handed": *New West*, Apr 21, 80.
>
>   "greatly different from Kosinski's version": ibid.
>
>   "an ego from here to Mont Blanc": *Entertainment News*, Mar 4, 80.
>
> page 359   "They're perfectly beautiful ... Why should I?": *NY Post*, Aug 15, 79.
>
> page 360   "You see these people here? ... everything": Joy Weiss, Mar 14, 95.
>
>   "I am her whole life ... She's *German aristocracy*": ibid.
>
> page 361   "Why did you tell me ... I like surprises": ibid.
>
> page 362   "leaden arbitrary tone ... horsemanship": NYTBR, Sep 30, 79.
>
>   "lugubrious ... into fascism": *NY Times*, Sep 13, 79.
>
>   "much plottier than usual": *Washington Post*, Sept. 16, 79.
>
> page 363   "avocation": Behind the Best Sellers, NYTBR, Oct 21, 79.

3.   page 365   "European baroness": *Washington Star*, Feb 4, 80.

> page 366   "No ... I am curious about grownups, not children": ibid.

page 368   "Is he really angry with me?" and ff.: K. von F. Kosinski, Sep 22, 94.

page 369   "Thus by going now to Finland": *Reds* shooting script.

page 370   "a very marginal novelist ... lesser talent": Maralyn Lois Polak, *The Writer as Celebrity: Intimate Interviews*, p. 39.

4. Kosinski gave a detailed account of his role in the Jack Abbott affair in an interview with Regina Gorzkowska published in the *Society for the Fine Arts Review* at the University of Alabama, Spring 1982.

page 372   "A cyanide capsule indeed!": Klinkowitz, "Betrayed by Jerzy Kosinski."

page 376   "To be a man" and ff.: Paul Tillich, *The Protestant Era*.

5. Dora Militaru provided information supporting the narrative of this chapter. John Osipowicz provided the story about the Lower Merion censorship incident. Henry Dasko, a Polish–Canadian businessman and literary journalist who knew Kosinski during his last years, provided a framework for the story of the "bet" behind the *Village Voice* story.

page 379   "Kosinski's long affair": *NY Times*, Feb 25, 82.
           "pornographic thriller": *Saturday Review*, Mar 82.
           "What a waste!": *Time*, Mar 22, 82.

page 382   "The Bible tells us": script for Oscars, Mar. 28, 82.

page 383   "suck face": *NY Times*, Mar 29, 82.

page 386   "I am seduced. We'll stay": Dora Militaru, May 19, 95.
           "Jerzy is between us": ibid.

page 387   "Take advantage of me *now*... happen to me": ibid.
           "victims of the Holocaust": Geoffrey Stokes and Eliot Fremont-Smith, "Jerzy Kosinski's Tainted Words," *Village Voice*, Jun 22, 82, p. 41.
           "Not a single comma ... paperback editions": ibid, p. 1.

6. page 388   "had any reason to believe": *Village Voice*, Jul 6, 82.

page 389   "thoroughly misrepresented me": ibid.
           "very disturbed": Dave Smith, "Kosinski Whodunit: Who Ghost There If Not Jerzy?" *Los Angeles Times*, Aug 8, 82, p 5.

page 392   "there's something to it": John Corry, *NY Times: Adventures in the News Trade*, p. 203.

page 393   "running from the *Village Voice*": K. von F. Kosinski, Jul 7, 94.

VII. Sacred Armor

1. Information supporting the narrative of this chapter was contributed by Katherina von Fraunhofer Kosinski and Daniel Passent.

    page 405   "The drops in Monod's eyes ... tears": PB, 27.
                    "Call them tears": ibid.
2. page 406   "Marshes of Glynn": H, 116.
                    "Ewunia and Adam": H, 26.
    page 407   "what matters is the spiritual accent": H, 424.
                    "ordinary mutism": ibid.
                    "What pond of manure? ... inner theater closes": H, 428.
                    "an occasional need to be vague": H, 124.
    page 408   "to improve one's image of oneself": ibid.
                    "When he lied": Stefan Zweig, *Balzac*, p. 113.

3. Cynthia Cristilli, Marian Javits, and Kiki von Fraunhofer Kosinski provided information supporting the narrative of this chapter.

    page 411   "the more depraved a woman is": H, 332.
                    "graded": ibid.
                    "to extend oneself": H, 547.
    page 412   "Don't call me a *dummy*": Cynthia Cristilli, Aug 2, 94.
    page 413   "those are the ones": ibid.
    page 415   "Should we get married?" and ff.: K. von F. Kosinski, Jul 11, 94, and in various interviews and articles.
                    "a sense of mortality": Pearl Sheffy Gefen, "Jerzy Kosinski, the Last Interview," *Lifestyles* (Winter 91) (in CWJK, 229).
    page 416   "show them": K. von F. Kosinski, Jul 7, 94.

4. Tom Morgan, Daniel Passent, Jerzy Urban, and Janusz Kuczynski contributed information supporting the narrative.

    page 419   "it was both": Interview with Mike Leiderman, WJUF-TV, Nov 87.
                    "A distortion. .... a great one": ibid.
    page 420   "a little down in the dumps": Tom Morgan, Jul 15, 94.
                    "I have no relatives": JK at Beit Hatsufot, Israel, Feb 2, 88.
                    "What did the Jews do to save the Poles?": ibid.
    page 422   "the much needed introduction of the sport of chess": *Who's Who in America*, 1990–1991

page 423 "You can't rent attraction to life": Interview with Daniel
Passent, *The Guests of Daniel Passent*, Polish National TV.
page 424 "At least you have children": Jerzy Neugebauer, Jun 6, 94.
page 426 "easily the best novel": *Library Journal*, Jun 1, 88.
"stung by ... ever encountered": *Quill Quire*, Oct 88.

5. Elzbieta Czyzewska, Michael Kott, Ami Shinitsky, Agnieszka Osiecka,
and Urszula Dudziak contributed information supporting the narrative of
this chapter. Joanna Siedlecka's *Czarny Ptasior* contains an account of the
meeting at Czytelnik book store. Substantially different versions of the occasion are remembered by Katherina von Fraunhofer Kosinski and the citizens
of Dabrowa Rzeczycka, Bronislaw Woloszyn, and Edward Warchol.

page 433 "Mr. Jurek ... I'm going to Lodz to see him": CP, 133.

6. Geoffrey Stokes contributed information supplementing published accounts of his meeting with Kosinski; Lisa Adler, Gay Talese, Gil Shiva,
Wendy Luers, Ed Burlingame, Bill Styron, Rose Styron, Urszula Dudziak,
and Katherina von Fraunhofer Kosinski all helped flesh out the picture of
Kosinski's final months.

page 437 "the second Holocaust": PB, 166.
page 438 "constitutional republic": H, 92.
"Holocaust-bound": PB, 166.
page 439 "What happened in your family": draft of "Hosanna to
What?" (initially "The Second Holocaust").
page 440 "not enough ... Why not? ... Because it's a force of life ...
I don't know of any other": Interview with Mike Leiderman,
WJUF-TV, Nov 87.
"I'm tired of *me*": Urszula Dudziak, May 19, 95
page 441 "You ruined my career": Russ W. Baker, "Painted Words,"
Village Voice, Mar 15, 94, p. 59.
"Why didn't you say that *then*?": ibid.
"You don't understand. All my life I've been hiding.": Taylor, op cit, p. 34. The account of the conversation drawn
from an interview with Geoffrey Stokes and presented in
Russ Baker's article of Mar 15, 94, in the *Village Voice* renders
this line with a meaningful difference of nuance. In the *VV*
version, Kosinski replies, "You don't understand, you don't
understand. There are *things I have to hide* (italics added)."
page 442 "Don't tell me anything bad.": Ewa Markowska, Jul 9, 94.

"I must confess that my health is deteriorating.": "Kosinski's Masque," by Anthony Haden-Guest, *Vanity Fair*, Oct 91, p. 208.

page 443   "favorite place": ibid.

"Look at this same old stuff": Lisa (Grunwald) Adler, Jul 7, 94.

page 444   "Come on, Jerz": K. von F. Kosinski, Sep 21, 94.

"Even Welch Everman has given up on me": ibid.

"How Can You Become a Poet?": Eve Merriam.

"oppose such evils": PEN Charter.

"There are days ... Let's see if I go": Pearl Sheffy Gefen, "Jerzy Kosinski, the Last Interview" (In CWJK, 230, 237).

page 445   "I can't see any way out. There is only one solution": Urszula Dudziak, May 19, 95.

"Great ... tomorrow I will call you": ZS, 20.

"I am going to put myself to sleep ... embrace our friends": Kosinski's suicide note as shown by K. von F. Kosinki. A copy is filed with the New York Medical Examiner, and the note was presented in its entirety in the BBC film "Sex, Lies, and Jerzy Kosinski," produced by Agnieszka Piotrowska and aired Apr 27, 95.

7. Numerous friends and acquaintances shared with me their unusually intense responses upon learning of Kosinski's death. Katherina von Fraunhofer Kosinski and others who prefer not to be named described the outlines of the legal contest over Kosinski's legacy.

page 447   "He finally did it": K. von F. Kosinski, May 9, 1995.

"Don't get upset, we can do a better price for you": Ahmet Ertegun, Nov 11, 94.

"What's the matter ... expect something of him?": Jerzy Neugebauer, Jun 6, 94.

BIBLIOGRAPHY

I. Novels by Jerzy Kosinski

(Kosinski often revised substantially between the hardcover and paperback editions. In this book, citations are from the first paperback edition except, as noted, in the case of *The Devil Tree*, which was presented in a revised hardcover edition.)

The Painted Bird. Boston: Houghton Mifflin, 1965.
    New York: Pocket Books, 1966 (paperback; author's original text restored).
    New York: Bantam, 1972 (paperback).
    Boston: Houghton Mifflin, 1976 (revised with new introduction).
Steps. New York: Random House, 1968.
    New York: Bantam, 1969 (paperback).
Being There. New York: Harcourt Brace Jovanovich, 1971.
    New York: Bantam, 1972 (paperback).
The Devil Tree. New York: Harcourt Brace Jovanovich, 1973.
    New York: Bantam, 1974 (paperback).
    New York: St. Martin's, 1981 (revised and expanded edition). The St. Martin's edition is the version utilized in this book.
Cockpit. Boston: Houghton Mifflin, 1975.
    New York: Bantam, 1976 (paperback).
Blind Date. Boston: Houghton Mifflin, 1977.
    New York: Bantam, 1978 (paperback).
Passion Play. New York: St. Martin's 1979.
    New York: Bantam, 1980 (paperback).

Pinball. New York: Bantam, 1982.
  New York: Bantam, 1983 (paperback).
The Hermit of 69th Street. New York: Seaver, 1988.
  New York: Zebra, 1991 (paperback).

II. *Nonfiction books and pamphlets by Jerzy Kosinski*

Documents Concerning the Struggle of Man: Reminiscences of the Members of the Proletariat (published in Polish). Lodz, Poland: Scientific Society of Lodz, 1955. Also, in *The Review of Social and Historical Sciences* (1954) 4:411–32.
The Program of the People's Revolution of Jakob Jaworski (published in Polish). Lodz, Poland: Scientific Society of Lodz, 1955. Also in *The Review of Social and Historical Sciences* (1954) 5:207–36.
American Sociology: Selected Works (published in Polish, edited by Jerzy Kosinski). New York: Polish Institute of Arts and Letters, 1963.
The Future Is Ours, Comrade (under the pseudonym Joseph Novak). Garden City, N.Y.: Doubleday, 1960.
No Third Path (under the pseudonym Joseph Novak). Garden City, N.Y.: Doubleday, 1962.
Notes of the Author on "The Painted Bird." New York: Scientia-Factum, 1965.
The Art of the Self: Essays à propos "Steps." New York: Scientia-Factum, 1968.
Passing By: Selected Essays, 1962–1991. New York: Random House, 1992.

III. *Other works by Jerzy Kosinski*

"Dead Souls on Campus." *New York Times,* October 12, 1970, p. 45.
"The Reality Behind Words." *New York Times,* October 3, 1971, p. 3.
"The Lone Wolf." *American Scholar* 41 (Fall 1972): 513–19.
"Packaged Passion." *American Scholar* 42 (Spring 1973): 193–204.
"To Hold a Pen." *American Scholar* 42 (Fall 1973): 56–66.
"Against Book Censorship." *Media and Methods* 12 (January 1976): 20–24.
"*Seven Beauties*—a Cartoon Trying to Be a Tragedy." (review of Lina Wertmuller film *Seven Beauties*) *New York Times,* March 7, 1976, pp. 1, 15.
" 'The Banned Book,' as Psychological Drug—a Parody." *Media and Methods* 13 (January 1977): 18–19.
"Is Solzhenitsyn Right?" *Time,* June 26, 1978, p. 22.
"Our 'Predigested, Prepackaged Popular Culture.' " *U.S. News and World Report,* January 8, 1979, pp. 52–53.
"Time to Spare." *New York Times,* May 21, 1979, op-ed page (p. A19).
"Telling Ourselves to Make It Through the Night." Review of *The White Album,* by Joan Didion. *Los Angeles Times Book Review,* May 27, 1979, p. 29.

"Combining Objective Data with Subjective Attitudes." *Bulletin of the American Society of Newspaper Editors* 43 (July/August 1981): 19.

"A Brave Man, This Beatty. Brave as John Reed." *Vogue*, April 1982, pp. 316, 318, 319.

"How I Learned to Levitate in Water." *Life*, Vol. 7, No. 4 (April 1984): 129–132.

"A Passion for Polo." *Polo*: Official Publication of the United States Polo Association, May 1985, pp. 115–18.

"Exegetics." *Paris Review* 97 (Fall 1985): 92–95.

"Death in Cannes." *Esquire*, March 1986, pp. 82–89.

"Restoring a Polish-Jewish Soul." *New York Times*, October 22, 1988, p. I, 27.

"The Second Holocaust." Boston *Sunday Globe*, Focus, November 4, 1990, p. A17.

IV. Interviews with Jerzy Kosinski

Abrams, Garry. "Jerzy Kosinski Leaves 'Em Amused, Bemused, and Confused." *Los Angeles Times*, November 14, 1984, View section, pp. 1, 12.

Amory, Cleveland. "Trade Winds." *Saturday Review*, April 17, 1971, pp. 16–17.

Cahill, Daniel J. *"The Devil Tree*: An Interview with Jerzy Kosinski." *North American Review* 258 (Spring 1973): 56–66.

———. "An Interview with Jerzy Kosinski on *Blind Date*." *Contemporary Literature* 19 (Spring 1978): 133–42.

———. "Life at a Gallop: Interview with Jerzy Kosinski." *Washington Post Book World*, September 16, 1979, p. 10.

Christian, George. "A Passion for Polo." *Houston Chronicle*, October 7, 1979, pp. 18, 22.

Collins, Nancy. "Jerzy Kosinski Is the Zbig of Books." *Washington Star*, February 10, 1980, pp. F1, F8.

Gefen, Pearl Sheffy. "Jerzy Kosinski, the Last Interview." *Lifestyles*, Winter 1991, pp. 18–24.

Gorzkowska, Regina. "Jerzy Kosinski: An Interview—*Pinball*: Aspects of Visibility." *Society for the Fine Arts Review* 4, No. 2 (Summer 1982): 3, 4.

Griffin, Patricia. "Conversation with Jerzy Kosinski." *Texas Arts Journal* (1977): 5, 11.

Grunwald, Lisa. "Jerzy Kosinski: Tapping into His Vision of Truth." *Vineyard Gazette*, July 29, 1977, pp. A1–2.

Klinkowitz, Jerome. "Jerzy Kosinski: An Interview." *Fiction International* 1 (Fall 1971): 30–48.

Leaming, Barbara. "*Penthouse* Interview: Jerzy Kosinski." *Penthouse*, July 1982, pp. 128–30, 167–71.

Movius, Geoffrey. "A Conversation with Jerzy Kosinski." *New Boston Review* 1 (Winter 1975): 3–7.

Nowicki, R. E. "Interview with Jerzy Kosinski." *San Francisco Review of Books*, March 1978, pp. 10–13.

Plimpton, George, and Rocco Landesman. "The Art of Fiction." *Paris Review* 54 (Summer 1972): 183–207.

Schapp, Dick. "Stepmother Tongue." *Book Week* 14 (November 1965): 6.

Sheehy, Gail. "The Psychological Novelist as Portable Man." *Psychology Today* 11 (December 1977): 52–56, 126, 128, 130.

Silverman, Art, L. Lee, and D. Bordette. "The Renegade Novelist Whose Life Is Stranger Than Fiction." *Berkeley Barb* 641 (November 25–December 1, 1977): 8, 9.

Sohn, David. "A Nation of Videots." *Media and Methods* 11 (April 1975): 24–26, 28, 30–31, 52, 54, 56–57.

Szonyi, David M. "Profile: Jerzy Kosinski on the Writer and the Holocaust." *Jewish Times*, April 9, 1982, pp. 69, 79.

Tartikoff, Brandon. "Jerzy Kosinski." *Metropolitan Review*, October 8, 1971, p. 104.

Teicholz, Tom. "My Books Are Weapons, a Blind Date with Jerzy Kosinski." *East Side Express* 2 (February 1978): 11, 16–17.

———. "Being There and Staying There: Jerzy Kosinski." *Interview*, February 1980, pp. 34–35.

Warga, Wayne. "Jerzy Kosinski Reaches Down into Life and Writes." *Los Angeles Times Calendar*, April 22, 1973, pp. 1, 54.

Zito, Tom. "Sellers and Kosinski: Alliance for the Absurd." *Washington Post*, February 2, 1979, pp. D1, D5.

V. Books and articles about Jerzy Kosinski

Aldridge, John W. "The Fabrication of a Culture Hero." *Saturday Review* 54 (April 24, 1971): 25–27.

———. *The American Novel and the Way We Live Now*. New York: Oxford University Press, 1983.

Anderson, Don. "The End of Humanism: A Study of Kosinski." *Quadrant* 113 (1976): 73–77.

Baker, Russ W. "Painted Words." *Village Voice*, March 15, 1994, pp. 58–59.

Bolling, Douglass. "The Precarious Self in Jerzy Kosinski's *Being There*." *Greyfriar* 16 (1975): 41–46.

Boyers, Robert. "Language and Reality in Kosinski's *Steps*." *Centennial Review* 16 (Winter 1972): 41–61.

Brown, Earl B., Jr. "Kosinski's Modern Proposal: The Problem of Satire in the Mid-Twentieth Century." *Critique: Studies in Modern Fiction* 22 (1980): 83–87.

Bruss, Paul. *Victims: Textual Strategies in Recent American Fiction.* Lewisburg, Pa.: Bucknell University Press, 1981.

Cahill, Daniel J. "Jerzy Kosinski: Retreat from Violence." *Twentieth Century Literature* 18 (1972): 121–132.

———. "Jerzy Kosinski: A Play on Passion." *Chicago Review* 32 (1980): 18–34.

Carter, Nancy Corson. "1970 Images of the Machine and the Garden: Kosinski, Crews, and Pirsig." *Soundings* 61 (1978): 105–22.

Coale, Samuel. "The Quest for the Elusive Self: The Fiction of Jerzy Kosinski." *Critique: Studies in Modern Fiction* 14 (1973): 25–37.

———. "The Cinematic Self of Jerzy Kosinski." *Modern Fiction Studies* 20 (Autumn 1974): 359–70.

Corngold, Stanley. "Jerzy Kosinski's *The Painted Bird*: Language Lost and Regained." *Mosaic* 4 (Summer 1973): 153–68.

Corry, John. "A Case History: Seventeen Years of Ideological Attack on a Cultural Target." *New York Times*, November 7, 1982, Arts and Leisure section, pp. 1, 28–29.

———. "The Most Considerate of Men." *The American Spectator*, July 1991, pp. 17, 18.

———. *My Times: Adventures in the News Trade.* New York: Putnam, 1993.

Cunningham, Lawrence S. "The Moral Universe of Jerzy Kosinski." *America* 139 (November 11, 1978): pp. 327–29.

Czaplinski, Czeslaw. *Jerzy Kosinski: Twarza w twarz.* (: Face to Face). Warsaw: Reprint Publishers, 1991.

———. *Zycie po smiercie Jerzego Kosinskiego.* (The Life After Death of Jerzy Kosinski). Lodz: Atena, 1993.

Daler, John Kent von. "An Introduction to Jerzy Kosinski's *Steps*." *Language and Literature* 1 (January 1971): 43–49.

Dasko, Henryk. "Jerzy Kosinski—ostatni rozdzial." (—the Final Chapter). Supplement to *Zycic Warszawy* (Warsaw Life): *Ex Libris* (special number), December 1992.

———. "Trucizna." (Poison). Supplement to *Zycic Warszawy* (Warsaw Life): *Ex Libris* 48 (March 1994): 12, 13.

Everman, Welch D. *Jerzy Kosinski: The Literature of Violation.* The Milford Series, Popular Writers of Today, Volume 47. San Bernardino, Cal.: Borgo Press, 1991.

Gelb, Barbara. "Being Jerzy Kosinski." *New York Times Magazine*, February 21, 1982, pp. 42–46, 49, 52–54, 58.

Gogal, John M. "Kosinski's Chance: McLuhan Age Narcissus." *Notes on Contemporary Literature* 4 (January 1971): 8–10.

Gordon, Andrew. "Fiction as Revenge: The Novels of Jerzy Kosinski." In *Third Force: Psychology and the Study of Literature*, ed. by Bernard J. Paris. Cranbury, N.J.: Associated University Press, 1985, pp. 280–90.

Haden-Guest, Anthony. "Kosinski's Masque." *Vanity Fair*, October 1991, pp. 202–08.

Harpham, Geoffrey Galt. "Survival in and of *The Painted Bird*." *Georgia Review* 35 (1981): 142–57.

Hazlett, Bill. "Writer Nearly Shared Fate." *Los Angeles Times*, August 12, 1969, pp. 3, 18.

Herman, Jan. "Did He or Didn't He: *Village Voice* See Ghosts and CIA Spooks—but Kosinski Says They're Imagining Things." *Chicago Sun–Times*, July 25, 1982, Show/Book/Week section, p. 25.

Hicks, Jack. *In the Singer's Temple: Prose Fictions of Barthelme, Gaines, Brautigan, Piercy, Kesey, and Kosinski*. Chapel Hill: University of North Carolina Press, 1981.

Hirschberg, Stuart. "Becoming an Object: The Function of Mirrors and Photographs in Kosinski's *The Devil Tree*." *Notes on Contemporary Literature* 4 (1973): 14, 15.

Howe, Irving. "From the Other Side of the Moon." *Harper's* 238 (March 1969): 102–05.

Hutchinson, James D. "Authentic Existence and the Puritan Ethic." *Denver Quarterly* 7 (Winter 1973): 106–14.

Johns, Sally. "Jerzy Kosinski." In *Dictionary of Literary Biography Yearbook*: 1982, edited by Richard Ziegfeld. Detroit: Gale Research, 1983, pp. 169–74.

Kaiser, Charles. "Friends at the Top of the *Times*." *Newsweek*, November 22, 1982, pp. 125–26.

Karl, Frederick R. *American Fictions 1940–1980: A Comprehensive History and Critical Evaluation*. New York: Harper and Row, 1983.

Kazin, Alfred. "Jews." *The New Yorker*, March 7, 1994, pp. 62–73.

Kennedy, William. "Who Here Doesn't Know How Good Kosinski Is?" *Look* 35 (April 20, 1971): 12.

Klinkowitz, Jerome. "Insatiable Art and the Great American Quotidian." *Chicago Review* 25 (Summer 1973): 172–77.

———. "Two Bibliographical Questions in Kosinski's *The Painted Bird*." *Contemporary Literature* 16 (1975): 126–28.

———. *Literary Disruptions: The Making of a Post-Contemporary American Fiction*. Urbana: University of Illinois Press, 1975. Revised, 1980.

———. "Betrayed by Jerzy Kosinski." *The Missouri Review* 6 (Summer 1983): 157–71.

Kuper, Jack. "Who Was Jerzy Kosinski?" *Toronto Life*, June 1993, pp. 56, 58–61.

Lale, Meta, and John Williams. "The Narrator of *The Painted Bird*: A Case Study." *Renascence* 24 (Summer 1972): 198–206.

Langer, Lawrence L. *The Holocaust and the Literary Imagination*. New Haven, Conn.: Yale University Press, 1976.

Lavers, Norman. *Jerzy Kosinski*. Boston: Twayne, 1982.

———. "Jerzy Kosinski." *Critical Survey of Long Fiction*. New York: Salem Press, 1983, pp. 1556–66.

Lilly, Paul R., Jr. "Comic Strategies in the Fiction of Barthelme and Kosinski." *Publications of the Missouri Philological Association*, April 1979, pp. 25–32.

———. "Jerzy Kosinski: Words in Search of Victims." *Critique: Studies in Modern Fiction* 22 (1980): 69–82.

———. "Vision and Violence in the Fiction of Jerzy Kosinski." *The Literary Review* 25 (Spring 1982): 389–400.

———. *Words in Search of Victims: The Achievement of Jerzy Kosinski*. Kent, Ohio, and London, England: Kent State University Press, 1988.

Lupack, Barbara Tepa (*see also* Tepa, Barbara Jane). "New Tree, Old Roots." *Polish Review* 29 (1984): 147–53.

———. "Hit or Myth: Jerzy Kosinski's *Being There*." *New Orleans Review* 13 (Summer 1986): 58–68.

———. *Plays of Passion, Games of Chance*. Bristol, Ind.: Wyndham Hall, 1988.

Madden, Isabel Bau. "A Key to Jerzy Kosinski's Suicide Lies With His Widow, Friends Say." *New York Observer*, July 27–August 3, 1992, pp. 1, 21.

Mortimer, Gail L. " 'Fear Death by Water': The Boundaries of Self in Jerzy Kosinski's *The Painted Bird*." *Psychoanalytic Review* 63 (1976–77): 511–28.

Northouse, Cameron. "Jerzy Kosinski." In *Dictionary of Literary Biography*, ed. by Jeffrey Helterman and Richard Layman, 1:266–75. Detroit: Gale Research, 1978.

Packman, David. "The Kosinski Controversy." *Crosscurrents* 3 (1984): 265–67.

Petrakis, Byron. "Jerzy Kosinski's *Steps* and the Cinematic Novel." *Comparatist*, February 1978, pp. 16–22.

Polak, Maralyn Lois. *The Writer as Celebrity: Intimate Interviews*. New York: Evans, 1986.

"Polish Joke." *Time* 113 (February 19, 1979): 94, 96.

Prendowska, Krystyna. "Jerzy Kosinski: A Literature of Contortions." *Journal of Narrative Technique* 8 (1978): 11–25.

Richey, Clarence W. "*Being There* and *Dasein*." *Notes on Contemporary Literature* 2 (September 1982): 3–15.

Richter, David H. "The Three Denouements of Jerzy Kosinski's *The Painted Bird.*" *Contemporary Literature* 15 (Summer 1974): 370–85.

Rider, Philip R. "The Three States of Jerzy Kosinski's *The Painted Bird.*" *Papers of the Bibliographical Society of America* 72 (1978): 361–84.

Rosen, Richard. "Heirs to Maxwell Perkins." *Horizon* 24 (April 1981): 50–53.

Ross, Chuck. "Rejected." *New West* 4 (February 12, 1979): 39–42.

Sanders, Ivan. "The Gifts of Strangeness: Alienation and Creation in Kosinski's Fiction." *Polish Review* 19 (1974): 171–89.

Schiff, Stephen. "The Kosinski Conundrum." *Vanity Fair*, June 1988, pp. 114–19, 166–70.

Schneiderman, David. "Kosinski's Friends See Red." *Village Voice*, November 16, 1982, p. 16.

Sherwin, Byron L. *Jerzy Kosinski: Literary Alarmclock.* Chicago: Cabala Press, 1981.

Shinitzky, Ami. "Life Is a Drama: Jerzy Kosinski: The Man and His Work." *Polo* 5, 3 (September 1979): 21–23, 44.

Siedlecka, Joanna. *Czarny ptasior.* (Black Bird). Gdansk, Warsaw: Marabut/ CIS, 1993.

Sloan, James Park. "On Kosinski." *University Review* 18 (Summer 1971): 1.

———. "Literary Debunking, or How to Roast Your 'Favorite' Author." *Third Press Review* 1 (September/October 1975): 10–11.

———. "The Man from Elsewhere." *The Reader*, June 26, 1991, pp. 10, 32–33.

———. "Kosinski's War." *The New Yorker*, October 10, 1994, pp. 46–53.

Slung, Michele. "The Wounding of Jerzy Kosinski." *Washington Post Book World*, July 11, 1982, p. 15.

Smith, Dave. "Kosinski Whodunit: Who Ghost There If Not Jerzy?" *Los Angeles Times*, August 1, 1982, pp. 3–5.

Spendal, R. J. "The Structure of *The Painted Bird.*" *Journal of Narrative Technique* 6 (1976): 132–36.

Stokes, Geoffrey and Eliot Fremont-Smith. "Jerzy Kosinski's Tainted Words." *Village Voice*, June 22, 1982, pp. 1, 41–43.

Straus, Dorothea. *Virgins and Other Endangered Species.* Wakefield, R.I., and London: Moyer Bell, 1993. [The chapter on Kosinski, entitled "Demons and Other Supernatural Presences" (pp. 161–70) was also published in altered form in *Partisan Review* and, in part, in *Small Press*.]

Taylor, John. "The Haunted Bird." *New York*, July 15, 1991, pp. 24–37.

Tepa, Barbara Jane (*see also* Lupack, Barbara Tepa). *Inside the Kaleidoscope: Jerzy Kosinski's Polish and American Contexts.* [An unpublished doctoral dissertation in the Department of Philosophy, St. John's University, New York.]

———. "Jerzy Kosinski's Polish Contexts: A Study of *Being There*." *Polish Review* 22 (1977): 52–61.

———. "Jerzy Kosinski Takes Another Chance." *Polish Review* 23 (1978): 104–108.

Tiefenthaler, Sepp L. *Jerzy Kosinski*. Bonn, West Germany: Bouvier Publishers, 1980.

VI. Other books and articles

Abbott, Jack Henry. *In the Belly of the Beast: Letters from Prison*. With an introduction by Norman Mailer. New York: Vintage, 1982.

Adelson, Alan and Robert Lapides. *Lodz Ghetto: Inside a Community Under Siege*. New York: Viking, 1989.

Bair, Deirdre. *Anaïs Nin: A Biography*. New York: Putnam, 1995.

Bettelheim, Bruno. *The Uses of Enchantment: The Meaning and Importance of Fairy Tales*. Middlesex: Penguin, 1985.

Biegeleisen, Henryk. *U kolebki, przed oltarzem, nad mogila*. (At the Cradle, In Front of the Altar, over the Grave). Lvov: Instytut Stauropigjanski, 1929.

Brustein, Robert. *Making Scenes: A Personal History of the Turbulent Years at Yale, 1966–1979*. New York: Random House, 1981.

Dobroszycki, Lucjan. *The Chronicle of the Lodz Ghetto 1941–1944*. New Haven and London: Yale University Press, 1984.

Dolega-Mostowicz, Tadeusz. *Kariera Nikodema Dyzmy*. (The Career of Nikodem Dyzma). New York: Roy, 1950.

Eliade, Mircea. *The Sacred and the Profane: The Nature of Religion*. Trans. by Willard R. Trask. New York: Harper and Row, 1961.

Fuks, Marian, Zygmunt Hoffman, Maurycy Horn, and Jerzy Tomaszewski. *Polish Jewry: History and Culture*. Warsaw: Interpress Publishers, 1982.

Greenberg, Henry. *Child of the Shadows*. Trans. Celina Wieniewska. London: Vallentine, Mitchell, 1969.

Heschel, Abraham Joshua. *The Earth Is the Lord's: The Inner World of the Jew in Eastern Europe*. New York: Farrar Straus Giroux, 1949.

Hilberg, Raul. *The Destruction of the European Jews*. New York: New Viewpoints, 1973.

Hlasko, Marek. *Killing the Second Dog*. New York: Cane Hill, 1990.

Holt, Robert T. *Radio Free Europe*. Minneapolis: University of Minnesota Press, 1958.

Kiernan, Thomas. *The Roman Polanski Story*. New York: Delilah/Grove, 1980.

Korbonski, Stefan. *The Jews and the Poles in World War II*. New York: Hippocrene, 1989.

Kridl, Manfred. *A Survey of Polish Literature and Culture*. New York: Columbia Slavic Studies, 1956.

Krystal, Henry, ed. *Massive Psychic Trauma*. New York: International Universities Press, 1969.

Krylov, Ivan Andreevich. *Kriloff's Fables*. Trans. by C. Fillingham Coxwell. New York: Dutton, 1970.

Kuper, Jack. *Child of the Holocaust*. Garden City, N.Y.: Doubleday, 1968.

Kuprin, Aleksandr Ivanovich. *The Duel*. Trans. and with an afterword by Andrew R. MacAndrew. New York: New American Library, 1961.

Laing, R. D. *The Divided Self*. New York: Pantheon Books, 1969.

Lazowski, Eugeniusz Slawomir. *Prywatna wojna*. (Tr. by Alexandra Gerrard as *Private War*). Warsaw: Cieslak and Szajcer, 1993.

Leaming, Barbara. *Polanski: A Biography—the Filmmaker as Voyeur*. New York: Simon and Schuster, 1981.

Lenkowski, Stanislaw. *Z zycia i kultury antyku*. (From the Life and Culture of Antiquity). Lvov: Filomata Editions, 1934.

Lermontov, Mikhail. *A Hero of Our Time*. Tr. by Vladimir Nabokov in collaboration with Dmitri Nabokov. Garden City, N.Y.: Doubleday, 1958.

Michie, Allan A. *Voices Through the Iron Curtain: The Radio Free Europe Story*. New York: Dodd, Mead, 1963.

Monod, Jacques. *Chance and Necessity*. Tr. by A. Wainhouse. New York: Knopf, 1971.

Orzeszkowa, Eliza. *Dziurdziowie*. (Holes Pecked [by a bird]). Warsaw: Ksiazka i Wiedza, 1952.

Owen, David. "Betting on Broadway." *The New Yorker*, June 13, 1994, pp. 60–73.

Pawlowski, Jerzy. *Najdluzszy pojedynek*. (The Longest Duel). Warsaw: Da Capo/Zebra, 1994.

Pinkus, Oscar. *The House of Ashes*. Schenectady, N.Y.: Union College Press, 1990.

Pogonowski, Iwo Cyprian. *Jews in Poland*. New York: Hippocrene Books, 1993.

Polanski, Roman. *Roman*. New York: William Morrow, 1984.

Prager, Emily. *A Visit from the Footbinder, and Other Stories*. New York: Simon and Schuster, 1982.

Pryzwan, Mariola, ed. *O Halinie Poswiatowskiej: Wspomnienia, listy, wiersze*. (About Halina Poswiatowska: Memories, letters, poems—title as translated by Tomasz Mircowicz). Warsaw: "EM-KA," 1994.

Rawson, Philip. *The Art of Tantra*. New York: Oxford University Press, 1978.

Reitlinger, Gerald. *The House Built on Sand: The Conflicts of German Policy in Russia 1939–1945*. London: Weidenfeld and Nicolson, 1960.

Reymont, Wladyslaw. *The Peasants*. Tr. by M. H. Dziewicki. New York: Knopf, 1942.

Ringelblum, Emmanuel. *Notes from the Warsaw Ghetto.* New York: Schocken, 1974.

Robbe-Grillet, Alain. *For a New Novel.* New York: Grove, 1965.

Schulz, Bruno. *Sanatorium Under the Sign of the Hourglass.* Tr. by Celina Wieniewska. New York: Walker, 1978.

————. *The Street of Crocodiles.* Tr. by Celina Wieniewska. New York: Penguin, 1977.

Seneca, Lucius Annaeus. *The Stoic Philosophy of Seneca: Essays and Letters of Seneca.* Trans. with an introduction by Moses Hadas. Gloucester, Mass.: P. Smith, 1965.

Sherwin, Byron and Susan G. Ament. *Encountering the Holocaust.* Chicago: Impact, 1979.

Shoah, an Oral History of the Holocaust, the complete text of the film by Claude Lanzmann, preface by Simone de Beauvoir. New York: Pantheon, 1985.

Sienkiewicz, Henryk. *Pan Wolodyjowski.* (Mr. Wolodyjowski). Warsaw: Panstwowy Instytut Wydasniczy, 1955.

Singer, Israel Joshua. *The Brothers Ashkenazi.* Tr. by Maurice Samuel. New York: Knopf, 1936.

Tillich, Paul. *The Protestant Era.* Tr. and with a concluding essay by James Luther Adams. Chicago: University of Chicago Press, 1948.

Tyrmand, Leopold. *Zly.* (The Evil One). Warsaw: Czytelnik, 1966.

Unuk, Jozef, and Helena Radomska-Strzemecka. *Dzieci polskie oskarzaja.* (Polish Children Accuse). Warsaw: Pax, 1961.

Witkiewicz, Stanislaw Ignacy. *Insatiability.* Tr. by Louis Iribarne. London, Melbourne, New York: Quartet, 1977.

Zeromski, Stefan. *Przedwiosnie.* (Before Spring). Warsaw: Czytelnik, 1946.

Zweig, Stefan. *Balzac.* Tr. by William and Dorothy Rose. London: Cassell, 1970.

ACKNOWLEDGMENTS

Many individuals made contributions without which this project could not have been undertaken or completed. Two stand out for assistance at the very beginning. Gene Ruoff, from his position as head of the Institute for the Humanities at the University of Illinois at Chicago (UIC), provided a grant without which an indispensable research trip would have been extremely difficult, and, as an old friend, he contributed his conviction that I could succeed in this new genre. Dominick Abel, far more than an extraordinary literary agent, encouraged me to undertake the project, provided many suggestions from the outset, and sustained me along the way with the support that can come only with long friendship.

In addition to the grant from the Institute for the Humanities, UIC provided released time from teaching and several grants funding overseas travel. A fellowship from the National Endowment for the Humanities insured that I would be able to complete the book.

Katherina von Fraunhofer Kosinski (Kiki) generously provided access to files and manuscripts and introductions to members of the Kosinski circle, as well as sitting for many hours of conversation about her late husband. Her leads were of great importance in launching my research, and she was an important source for many accounts in the text.

It was my great good fortune to have exceptional help with the multicultural aspects of the project, in particular Agnieszka Kmin, then a graduate student at the Institute of English Studies at the University of Lodz, Poland. Not only was she a translator of extraordinary skill, for both written documents and often rapid and heavily inflected spoken testimony, but her savvy and sensitivity to nuance made her an exceptional research assistant. I also owe a debt of gratitude to Ewa Bednarowicz, through whom I found Agnieszka. Julita and Tomek Mirkowicz, distinguished translators who came to Kosinski through putting his works into Polish, opened their home to me and kindly took me in hand during several trips to Poland. In America, I was equally fortunate to have the help of Alexandra Gerrard, who not only provided translations of written documents, often under great time pressure, but helped me to understand Polish culture and the experience of the German occupation. Serendipitously, she made me aware of the very helpful memoir *Private War*, published in Polish by her father, Eugene Lazowski. Jonathan Brent, Robert Porter, and Mary Habeck, who offered particularly helpful suggestions deriving from her work at the Yale Russian Archive Project, all assisted in preparations for my research trip to Russia; in Moscow I benefited greatly from the guiding hand of Anastasia Takhnenko, and from the splendid research assistant/interpreter Anastasia secured, Guzel Bilialova.

Among archivists and keepers of records, the list of those to whom I owe thanks includes Faith Coleman and Ann Newhalle of the Ford Foundation; Yevgenii Maksimovich Primakov, Archive of the Foreign Intelligence Service of Russia; Thomas Tanselle of the Guggenheim Foundation; Mary Ronan of the National Archives; Betty Falsey of Harvard's Houghton Library; Bret Werb of the United States Holocaust Memorial Museum; Lt. Col. Oleg Aslangerjevich Hotiagov, Central Archive of the Ministry of Defense of the Russian Federation, Podol'sk; Konstantin Sergeevich Nikishkin, Head of Center, Central Archive of the Ministry of Internal Affairs of the Russian Federation; Ellen Borakove of the Public Affairs Office of the New York Medical Examiner; Krystyna Baron, Librarian of the Polish Institute of Arts and Sciences in America; Don Skemer, Department of Rare Books and Special Collections, the Princeton University Library; Mal Theoharous of Radio Free Europe; Norma Spungen of Spertus Institute; and Susan Rubio, Assistant Producer of Carson Productions. I am grateful for the assistance of Lola Secora, Freedom of Information/Privacy Act Officer at the United States Information Agency; Mikhail Yevgenievich Kirilin, Public Relations Officer, Federal Security Service of Russia; and Sarah Jones, FOIA/PA Officer for the New York District of the Immigration and Naturalization Service, U.S. Department of Justice. I am indebted to Grace Contro for skillfully arranging often very complicated travel, sometimes on short notice, and to Linda Vavra and Frankie Warfield for their patience and competence in the administration of travel grants.

At Dutton Signet, Arnold Dolin took the project over in midcourse and earned my profound gratitude for his support and his many helpful suggestions. I am also grateful to Ann Marlowe for copyediting of exceptional substance and detail.

Only a minority of biographers are privileged to know their subjects personally. I knew Jerzy Kosinski for twenty years, not as an intimate friend but as something more than an acquaintance, in a relationship defined by his occasional trips to Chicago and my occasional trips to New York. While direct observations or words spoken to this author figure sparsely in the text, the pleasure of knowing this enigmatic man informs every page. Few men have lived lives more challenging or engaging for a biographer, so full of paradox, so open to various interpretive modes, or so fitting as illustration or commentary bearing upon the great artistic, cultural, and political issues of the time.

Many of Kosinski's friends gave generously of their time and permitted exceptionally intimate glimpses of their own lives. A few made efforts that require singling out for mention. Peter Skinner not only submitted to numerous interviews, but ransacked his records for various forms of documentation and provided extensive written narratives of observations about his long relationship with Kosinski; in a few instances, his language was so precise and compelling as to discourage paraphrase, and in several instances I have shamelessly appropriated his wording into this text. Jean Kilbourne not only submitted to an extended series of interviews but generously provided access to her private papers, which show a side of Kosinski that would not otherwise have come to light. Elzbieta Czyzewska took the time on many occasions to orient me about the Polish community in North America, often providing the introductions that are indispensable within that community particularly.

The biography of a writer less than five years dead is in significant measure an oral history, and this was very much the case with Jerzy Kosinski. A large number of individuals who knew Kosinski—and others who possessed valuable information bearing upon the context of his life—took the time to share their information with me, some of them on several occasions and over many hours. For some of them, the recollection and sharing of experience was painful, for others cathartic, while for many others, I suspect, it provided an opportunity to reexperience cherished moments. I am grateful to all who spoke with me, including the following: Lisa (Grunwald) Adler, Jerome Agel, Krystyna Baron, Maxine Bartow, Piotr Bikont, Fran and Jonathan Brent, Robert Brustein, Edward Burlingame, Jan Byrczek, Barry Callaghan, Joel Charles, Stanley Corngold, John Corry, Cynthia Cristilli, Dr. Roman Czaplicki, Elzbieta Czyzewska, Henry Dasko, Artour Demtchouk, Urszula Dudziak, Larry Eilenberg, Ahmet Ertegun, Welch Everman, Alice Feder, Thomas Fleming, Greg Gatenby, Jane and Robert Geniesse, Frank

Gibney, Jim Glendenning, Rabbi Alex J. Goldman, Henryk Greenberg, Feliks Gross, Henry Grunwald, Lin Harris-Seares, Andy Heinemann, Ryszard Horowitz, Patty and Jerry Hotchkiss, Helen Hutchinson, Zofia and Roman Izykowski, Mark Jaffe, Marian Javits, Elaine Kaufman, Alfred Kazin, Karen Kennerly, Andrzej Kern, Jean Kilbourne, Jerome Klinkowitz, Michael Kott, Joanna Kranc, Steven Kraus, Kasimierza Krauze, Tadeusz Krauze, Zygmunt Krauze, Jill Krementz, Dr. Henry Krystal, Janusz Kuczynski, Jack Kuper, Rocco Landesman, Adam Latawiec, Eugene Lazowski, Lera Leonova, Bob Loomis, Connie Lorman, Wendy Luers, Aleksandr (Jordan) Lutoslawski, Barbara Mackay, Stanislaw Madej, Michael Mahon, Norman Mailer, Andrzej Makowiecki, Marek Malicki, Ewa Markowska, Ryszard Matuszewski, Maria Medrzak, Mira Michalowska, Andrzej Migdalek, Dora Militaru, Arthur Miller, Julita and Tomasz Mirkowicz, Hugh Morehead, Patrick Moret, Tom Morgan, Elinor and Bill Morrison, Arnold Mostowicz, Don Muir, Zdzislaw Najder, Jerzy Neugebauer, Ron Nowicki, Sidney Offit, Agnieszka Osiecka, Cynthia Ozick, Jan Pamula, Ewa Pape, Zenon Pas, Daniel Passent, Jerzy Pawlowski, Peter Pelts, Oscar Pinkus, Agnieszka Piotrowska, George Plimpton, Roman Polanski, Stanislaw Pomorski, Emily Prager, Eugene Prakapas, Gordon Rogoff, Zofia Rogowska, Krystyna Rytel, Allan Schwartz, Jonathan Schwartz, Lore Segal, Timothy Seldes, Ami Shinitzky, Gil Shiva, Peter Skinner, Geoffrey Stokes, Rose and William Styron, Maciek Swierkocki, Gay Talese, Tom Teicholz, Malgorzata Terentiew, Barbara Ungeheuer, Jerzy Urban, Sam Vaughan, Edward Warchol, Rosa Weinrib, David Weir, Joy Weiss, Bel Weissman, Maria Wiktorowska, Stefania and Bronislaw Woloszyn, Jessie Wood, Adam Yarmolinsky, Suzanne Zavrian, and Anna Zukowska.

Finally, a few personal notes. I profited greatly from consultations with my adult children, Gene and Anna, both of whom work in areas involving research and writing, and in whom I am fortunate to have consiglieri of the highest order. Good friends and colleagues Michael Anania and Mike Lieb each provided encouragement and an extremely helpful and timely insight, while Don Marshall was supportive both personally and in the tangible area of rearranging faculty assignments to facilitate my research. A special debt is owed to Ellen and Norman Galinsky, who welcomed me into their household on my numerous trips to New York with an expansive hospitality undaunted by my not-always-convenient comings and goings. From Sally Ruth May I received advice, criticism, encouragement, acceptance, and the kind of sustaining support without which this book could never have been undertaken.

INDEX

Being There (novel, 1971):
autobiography in, 147; and *Nikodem
Dyzma*, 66–67, 220, 292–93, 331–32,
348; film deal, 307–8; genesis of,
219–20; and plagiarism, 6, 292, 294,
386; published, 289–96, 307–9;
sales, 294; value of, 450; written,
289–93, 356
Bellamy, Joe David, 307
Bellow, Saul, 388
Bemalte Vogel, Der (German version of
The Painted Bird), 234
Bensen, Donald, 182, 186
Berger, Bill, 141, 175
Berger, Peter, 242
Bernstein, Carl, 351
Berryman, John, 4, 270, 272
Best Sellers, 293
"Betrayed by Jerzy Kosinski"
(Klinkowitz), 372
Bettelheim, Bruno, 388
Biegeleisen, Dr. Henryk, 191, 192, 273,
331–32
Blind Date (novel, 1977), 424;
autobiography in, 12, 57, 82, 85–86,
91, 120, 142–44, 147, 149, 163–65,
181, 184, 274, 279, 280, 321, 323, 325;
editor/collaborator, 300, 385;
published, 338–42, 344, 354;
written, 338–41
Block, Joseph, 179
"Bluebird, The" (Poswiatowska), 139
Bluhdorn, Charles, 342, 345, 398
Blumenfeld, F. Y., 266–67
Blusztajn, Rebeka, 20
Bogucki, Rysiek, 55
Bolshevik Revolution, 11
Bonanno, Joe, 324
Bookletter, 330–31
Booth, Philip, 351
Borges, Jorge Luis, 293–94
Borowski, Tadeusz, 4, 6
Borward, Emma, 121
Bosch, Hieronymus, 239, 244
Boston Globe, 226, 439
Boyle, Kay, 351

Braunsberg, Andrew, 345, 347–48, 364
British Academy of Film and
Television Arts, 371
Brodsky, Joseph, 417
Brooks, Paul, 208, 209, 211–15, 237,
239, 242, 259–60, 323
Brothers Ashkenazy, The (Singer), 9
Brown, James, 202–3, 209, 214, 215,
242
Broyard, Anatole, 344
Bruss, Kath, 390–91
Bruss, Paul, 390–91
Brustein, Robert, 288, 302
Brzezinski, Muska, 348, 365
Brzezinski, Zbigniew, 343, 345,
347–48, 365, 380, 416, 417, 427
Buchwald, Art, 334
Burlingame, Ed, 443–44
Butler, Michael, 356
Byrczek, Aleksandra, 445
Byrczek, Jan, 418, 425, 431, 435–36,
445, 447

Cagliostro, 292, 408
Cahill, Dan, 305, 390
Calhoun, Chris, 441
Callaghan, Barry, 267–68
Callaghan, Morley, 267–68
Camus, Albert, 6, 72, 157, 201, 202,
217, 265, 309
Canby, Vincent, 379
Capote, Truman, 185
Career of Nikodem Dyzma, The (Dolega-
Mostowicz), 65–67, 100, 164,
196–97, 220, 292–93, 332, 348, 386,
449
Carson, Johnny, 295–96, 364, 383
Carter, Jimmy, 363
Carter, Rosalynn, 348
Caruso, Michael, 441
Cassini, Igor, 163
Centaur magazine, 404
Central Intelligence Agency (CIA),
100–1, 111–13, 115–17, 129, 136, 153,
154, 316, 319, 385, 390, 391, 424